Globalizations and Social Movements

Globalizations and Social Movements

Culture, Power, and the Transnational Public Sphere

Edited by
John A. Guidry,
Michael D. Kennedy,
and Mayer N. Zald

Ann Arbor

THE UNIVERSITY OF MICHIGAN PRESS

Published in the United States of America by
The University of Michigan Press
Manufactured in the United States of America
♾ Printed on acid-free paper

2003 2002 2001 2000 4 3 2 1

A CIP catalog record for this book is available from the British Library.

Library of Congress Cataloging-in-Publication Data

Globalizations and social movements : culture, power, and the transnational public sphere / edited by John A. Guidry, Michael D. Kennedy, and Mayer N. Zald.

p. cm.

Includes bibliographical references and index.

ISBN 0-472-09721-0 (cloth : alk. paper) — ISBN 0-472-06721-4 (pbk. : alk. paper)

1. Social movements—History—20th century. I. Guidry, John A. II. Kennedy, Michael D. III. Zald, Mayer N.

HN16 .G57 2000
303.48′4′09041—dc21 00-033805

Contents

Preface and Acknowledgments

Few would dispute that we live in a period of increased global exchange, transnational interaction, and cultural interdependence. Flows of human migration, lowered transportation costs, the spread of global capitalism, and the growth of electronic media and television spanning most nations have had profound effects on our everyday lives and on politics. This transformation has inevitably raised questions about how scholars think about the world. Until the emergence of the post–cold war order in the 1990s, the nation-state and the cultural or geographic region was the envelope, or container, providing boundaries for research in many disciplines of the social sciences and humanities. Processes of globalization do not make the nation-state or the region irrelevant, but globalization does change our perspectives on nations, states, and cultures. "Flows" of all sorts of things, material and not, across boundaries of nations and regions become more important; local practices and policies are embedded in transnational processes and ideologies.

In 1994 the Mellon Foundation, concerned that area studies might have become too isolated from recent intellectual and analytical advances in the humanities and social sciences, asked several universities to submit proposals for seminars and programs that would promote interdisciplinary and cross-regional/cross-national approaches to various intellectual issues. At the University of Michigan, in response to the Mellon Foundation request, the International Institute solicited proposals from the faculty for seminars and workshops. Michael Kennedy, a sociologist specializing in Eastern Europe and a student of the Solidarity movement, and Mayer Zald, a sociologist working on organizational theory and social movements, submitted a proposal for a year-long seminar to focus on globalization, social change, and social movements. We argued that much of contemporary social movement theory in political science and sociology had developed in the United States and, more recently, Western Europe. We did not know how well it traveled, how useful it would be when applied to the kinds of movements that had emerged in the developing world, the former Soviet Union, and other regions around the globe. Moreover, social movement theory had not come to grips with the cultural component of movement action and was not integrated with the growing literatures on resistance.

In the fall of 1994, the foundation generously funded several seminars and workshops that had been proposed at Michigan. Combined with substantial supplementary funds from the International Institute, a year-long seminar was organized for 1995–96. Eminent scholars from around the world visited for periods ranging from one week to two months. Two postdoctoral and four predoctoral Sawyer Fellows participated, as well as visiting dissertation students from other universities and doctoral students at Michigan.

Toward the end of the year, we decided to organize a graduate student conference on the topic of the seminar. John Guidry, at that time a Sawyer predoctoral fellow in political science at Michigan, took the lead in organizing the conference. The conference included papers by students in the seminar as well as other doctoral students at Michigan. It was a rousing success. The coherence of the conference and the quality of the individual papers led us to believe that by bringing together some of the papers from the conference and some of the contributions of visiting scholars to the year-long seminar, we could make a substantial contribution to an important intellectual issue. John Guidry not only organized the conference, but he has taken the major responsibility in bringing the volume to fruition. Although all three of us have had a hand in shaping the volume and writing the introduction, John deserves the major credit (though we all share any blame!).

We are deeply indebted to David William Cohen, the director of the International Institute, and the Mellon Foundation for making the seminar and conference possible. Rebecca Armstrong, the institute's liaison and administrator for the seminar, made the task of running the seminar and the conference seem easy. John McCarthy, Jackie Smith, Paul Wapner, and Sidney Tarrow provided excellent comments on the first rendition of the volume, which led to extensive revisions. Charles Myers, our editor at the University of Michigan Press, has shown great faith in this project and given us the time and feedback we needed to develop the volume. Thanks also to Jane Tiedge at Augustana College for clerical assistance and to V. Ravishankar at the University of Michigan for indexing.

Finally, the editors would like to acknowledge our gratitude to the contributors to this volume. Their hard work and commitment to the project has been crucial at every stage, first in response to our initial call to them in the summer of 1996 as we began to develop the themes and overall vision of the volume, and second in response to the reviewers' comments on the volume as a whole and its individual chapters. And a special note of thanks goes to Gay Seidman, who participated in the 1995–96 Sawyer Seminar and graciously accepted the task of reading the entire volume, including the introduction, in order to write a concluding chapter that would not simply repeat the introduction or summarize the volume's content but would challenge and extend the themes that emerge in this book.

CHAPTER 1

Globalizations and Social Movements

John A. Guidry, Michael D. Kennedy, and Mayer N. Zald

Globalization describes what a number of people perceive as a fundamental change in the conditions of human life. Just what has changed and how it has changed, however, are matters of great contention. Nonetheless, current writing on globalization focuses on some specific trends that appear to have pushed the sources and implications of social action beyond state borders. Recent transformations in transportation and communications technologies have altered our sense of distance, radically compressing time and space (Harvey 1989; Giddens 1990, 1994). Territorial states have apparently lost some of their capacities to establish order or mediate change within their borders (Sassen 1996). The number and power of intergovernmental institutions and multinational corporations have grown remarkably (Smith et al. 1997; Keck and Sikkink 1998; Risse-Kappen 1995). The communications media are increasingly global in both their reference and their reach, and the media also help provide resources in the building of transnational epistemic communities of immigrants or like-minded activists (Appadurai 1996).

Social movements ride the waves of these global processes and formations; in turn, they begin to define new ways of understanding how the world is being transformed. From the vantage point of social movements, globalization offers contradictory possibilities. On the one hand, to the extent that globalization appears to reduce the ability of states to act within their own territories, social movements are dislocated from their usual position of petitioning states to redress grievances. The supposed weakness of states vis-à-vis globalization means that social movements must direct resources toward international linkages and partnerships that can diminish movement autonomy in the home country. On the other hand, globalization has provided social movements with new, possibly significant opportunities and resources for influencing both state and nonstate actors. Keck and Sikkink (1998) illustrate this potential with their discussion of the "boomerang effect," in which national human rights (or other) movements can bypass their own target state and rely on international pressure from other states and the transnational human rights movement to help accomplish goals at home.

Conceiving globalization as a new opportunity structure for social movements allows us to examine movements within important frameworks that are already highly developed in social movement theory. A "political opportunity structure" is the way that present allocations of resources and power privilege some alternatives for collective action while raising the costs of others.The political opportunity model allows us to contextualize both social movements within globalization and visa versa, since we can problematize the latter either as an independent or dependent variable in movement analysis (McAdam 1996, 29–37)—that is, movements can both be affected by and transform political opportunity structures. The flexibility afforded by such a perspective opens up the possibility for analysis of the discursive, mutually transforming relations between states and societies (Migdal et al. 1994).

But political opportunity structures are only one part of the larger theoretical apparatus that social movement research has at its disposal. Along with opportunity structures, McAdam, McCarthy, and Zald (1996) identify mobilizing structures and cultural framing as important analytical perspectives that help us understand how movements emerge, develop, and accomplish—or fail to accomplish—their goals. Globalization brings important new resources to the mobilizational efforts of movements. For example, the transnational human rights movement, ideologically grounded in the United Nations' International Declaration of Human Rights and mobilizationally organized around such transnational movement organizations as Amnesty International, provides national human rights movements with ideological and material resources that help sustain claims against individual states.[1]

Globalization also modifies, and in many cases amplifies, the ability of national movement organizations to frame their claims in terms that resonate beyond territorial borders, thereby allowing national organizations to obtain resources from abroad. For instance, international agreements and treaties on human rights have helped local groups to frame their grievances in ways that allow these groups to disrupt and affect national politics without necessarily challenging local cultural practices and values. Indeed, sometimes framings borrowed from abroad can bring local cultural politics into higher relief in a way that helps to fend off some of the homogenizing effects of globalization.

But globalization is highly contested in both conceptual and empirical terms. Both theory and empirical evidence allow us to pose several questions about any essential nature of globalization. Is globalization primarily economic? With the expansion of free trade and common markets, capital can structure production processes with less regard for state borders or the local consequences of action, resulting in a kind of unassailable "economic citizenship" for multinational corporations (Sassen 1996). Is globalization a process of cultural change that is producing a "world society" in which social and political relationships the world over are increasingly rationalized in Western, liberal, and bureaucratized systems

(Meyer et al. 1997)? Is it a process by which the media and migration alter the nificance of state borders in producing "national" identities that themselves come, ironically, increasingly transnational (Appadurai 1996)? Or is it a process by which social movements can help structure a transnational public sphere of contention that would serve as our best defense against the tyranny of individual states or powerful nonstate organizations such as multinational corporations, as Keane's (1996) writing on civil society and democracy suggests?

Giddens (1994, 4) attempts to cut through this complexity by defining *globalization* as "action at a distance," that is, the ability of actors in one place to influence events in other places through economic, political, or media processes. Giddens's definition provides an accurate analytical description of globalization, but it is less helpful for understanding the complexities of globalization in the everyday worlds of people and states. In particular, "action at a distance" seems to emphasize the transnational at the expense of understanding localized participation in, and reaction to, the global. In this volume, we bring together cases from diverse perspectives—analytical, empirical, and disciplinary—that illuminate both the general, theoretical properties of globalization and the diverse ways in which it is experienced around the world.

Globalization has in fact brought social movements together across borders in a "transnational public sphere," a real as well as conceptual space in which movement organizations interact, contest each other and their objects, and learn from each other. "Action at a distance" does not really occur from a distance. This action originates some*where,* proceeds through *specific* channels, does some*thing,* and has concrete *effects* in *particular* places. That action is, however, mediated by discursive relationships that are forged in a transnational public sphere. Tracing the origins, mediations, and effects—global or local—of such action is the subject of this volume. To the extent that the following chapters examine the diverse ways in which globalization manifests itself in movements and localities, we are invited not to speak of a singular globalization but rather to recognize its plurality with a variety of *globalizations.*

We rely upon a substantial amount of research in the fields of social movements and globalization. For example, McAdam, McCarthy, and Zald (1996), along with other scholars (Tarrow 1994; Morris and Mueller 1992), synthesize work on social movements and point us clearly toward the continuing relevance of political opportunity structures, mobilizational structures, and cultural framing as conceptual tools for understanding movements. Smith, Chatfield, and Pagnucco (1997) work within these traditional forms of social movement analysis to examine the kinds of movement organizations that involve themselves with—and indeed thrive upon—transnational linkages and opportunities. Keck and Sikkink (1998) provide a comparative examination of human rights, women's, and environmental movements that explores the ways in which transnational spaces for discourse and action are transforming the nature of collective action. In these studies, the role of culture as either the object or the lens of inquiry is secondary, but in other work on globalization, such as that of Robertson (1992), culture is a central feature of analysis.

Among those studying globalization, Meyer et al. explore the emergence of a rational-bureaucratic "world society" and the contributions made by social movements to the building of it (1997, 165). The world society school has given us a compelling picture of the proliferation of rational-legal structures that Max Weber identified as crucial to modernity. This imagery suggests a disproportionate transformation across the world, however, where *globalization* or *world society* refers primarily to the "modernization" of the non-Western world. Robertson (1992) and Appadurai (1996) also discuss the positive contributions that social movements bring to the development of globalized society, though these authors see a more discursive and varied process than Meyer and his colleagues find in their research. All these writers integrate the relationship of social change—even at the most globalized levels—to transnational as well as highly localized cultures, but in general their focus is *globalization.* An analytical focus on the transnational can distract us from the significance of the local in transforming globalization itself. At the same time, thinking about localities, we can approach globalization from a marked place, from a particular grounding, and as such the local helps to clarify and balance the analytical effort.

The studies collected in this volume are written from a diversity of disciplinary locations—sociology, political science, anthropology, and history. Many of the chapters reflect interdisciplinary concerns, such as religious or women's studies, as well as contextual expertise in very different parts of the world, including Russia, Uzbekistan, Ukraine, Poland, Germany, Palestine, Nicaragua, Brazil, the Caribbean, South Africa, Kenya, India, Taiwan, and Japan. The methods used by the contributors are diverse as well, including quantitative data analysis, documentary analysis in archives, and ethnography. Consequently, each author has different theoretical traditions, conceptual anchors, and domain assumptions guiding his or her work. Nevertheless, within this diversity, the authors share a common concern for understanding how social movements and globalizations intersect, and the dialogue they offer among disciplines and places is important. Indeed, we take some inspiration from the literature on globalization for the ways in which we have been able to bring these essays together.

The sum intention of this collection is more than a call to understand particular movements in distant or globalized spaces better. It is also an invitation to think through our frames of social movement theory so as to attend properly to the challenges an expanded notion of globalization invites. In particular, we believe that theorizing the relationship of social movements to public spheres, modalities of power and resistance, identity formation, and the normative penumbra of movements and movement theory not only enables us to grasp more fully the consequences of studying the intersection of globalizations and social movements. It also invites fresh perspectives on those movements already well researched. In the balance of this introductory essay, we shall address each of these issues in turn, by considering how some of the literature, and especially this volume, suggests a rethinking of these categories of inquiry in the study of social movements and globalizations.

The Transnational Public Sphere and Globalizations

Meyer et al. (1997) describe the development of "world society" as an isomorphic process[2] through which rational-legal institutions are increasingly embedded in sociopolitical structures and practices around the world. In other words, the nature of states, political institutions, contentious practices, and juridical norms around the world are coming more and more to operate by way of the rational, bureaucratic norms that may be found in the industrialized democracies. This rationalization is comprehensive (167), regardless of the diversity apparent in world culture. Of course, there are deviations from the norms of world society such as human rights violations or the cronyism of politics in many developing countries. For the authors, however, these deviations do not challenge their overall thesis. They analyze deviations through the notion of "decoupling," in which a state or a set of particular institutions diverges from the development of world society, much like a boxcar might be decoupled from the train that has been pulling it. Decoupling is apparently a temporary situation that will be pulled into line by the continuing growth of world society norms and practices. For Meyer and his colleagues, the international notability of such decouplings—for example, human rights abuses in many states or the nepotism/cronyism of the Suharto regime in Indonesia—instead confirms the weight of world society on political discourse within and among states.

Meyer and his colleagues bring social movements into their work, placing movements as active agents in the deepening of world society and its norms. They write,

> Many of the international nongovernmental organizations have a "social movement" character. Active champions of central elements of world culture, they promote models of human rights, consumer rights, environmental regulation, social and economic development, and human equality and justice. They often cast themselves as oppositional grassroots movements, decrying gaps or failures in the implementation of world-cultural principles in particular locales and demanding corrective action by states and other actors. Agents of social problems, they generate further structuration of rationalized systems. (Meyer et al. 1997, 165)

Such directionality in globalization is also apparent in those works more focused on social movements themselves. In her introduction to the Smith, Chatfield, and Pagnucco volume, *Transnational Social Movements and Global Politics: Solidarity Beyond the State* (1997), Elise Boulding writes that "The social movement perspective, with its focus on *the passion for human betterment for the planet as a whole,* gives a sense of the powerful dynamics at work in a phenomenon that has cried out for more adequate documentation . . ." (ix, emphasis added). The phenomenon she refers to is "the great flowering of international nongovernmental organizations (INGOs) in this century" (ibid.). This characterization of a "social movement perspective" is by no means unique. It is rather common, implicitly or explicitly, in the social movement literature and carries with it assumptions that movements push societies in particular directions, toward democratization, emancipation, or self-determination (see, e.g., Giddens 1990, 158–63). While the emancipatory characterization of a social movement perspective is not inaccurate, it reflects only one part of the larger social movement experience within globalization—the *kinds* of "transnational social movement organizations" collected in the Smith et al. volume, examples of which are also discussed in the chapters by Ball, Rucht, and Seidman in this volume.

Liberal and emancipatory visions of the globalization of social movements presuppose that the principles governing social action in the liberal democracies of advanced capitalism can be extended into societies and cultures the world over. Movement analysts and activists can recognize those rationalizations associated with democratization or market capitalism. They depend more directly, however, upon a transnational version of the public sphere, where movements can act and the implications of those actions can be carried forth into a discussion of the rights of subjects and the imperatives of states and organizations.[3]

Jurgen Habermas's ([1962] 1989) account of the bourgeois public sphere was meant to identify a new kind of space in which rational critical discussion by citizens, rather than sheer economic logic or the instrumentalities of state power, could assist in the formation of state policies and civil, political, and social rights. Thirty years later, he still finds the public sphere exemplary, noting that the bourgeois public sphere carried its own potentials for self-transformation (1992). He recognizes its transnational potential, too, invoking the 1989 demonstrations that brought down communism. As in his other discussions of the public sphere, however, he is careful to note the real limitations of these spheres. The demonstrations achieved their objectives only by being broadcast on global television networks that are themselves guided by principles other than those defining the democratic potentials of the public sphere (456). Regardless of its correspondence with the communicative rationality with which Habermas is concerned, this notion of a potentially transnational public sphere has nonetheless become a critical element in the constitution of globalization and the role of social movements in it.

We understand the "transnational public sphere" to be a space in which both residents of distinct places (states or localities) and members of transnational entities (organizations or firms) elaborate discourses and practices whose consumption moves beyond national boundaries. The consequence of this transnational public sphere is not simply its own development. Like globalization, it involves "action at a distance" that must be understood in terms of its consequences for real actors, all of whom occupy specific places and communities. That is, the transnational public sphere is realized in various localized applications, potentially quite distant from the original production of the discourse or practice in question.

The communication networks that compose the transnational public sphere are uneven in terms of authorship and consumption and thus move ever further away from the egalitarian presumptions of democratic public spheres.[4] Nonetheless, this transnational public sphere offers an alternative site not only to places that lack or have heavily censored public spheres but also to places that have relied on more local or national spaces for the elaboration and contest of principles and practices. The demonstrations of 1989 in Eastern Europe clearly relied on the transnational public sphere to augment the consequence of their protest by emboldening their compatriots in other countries with examples of successful protest and by putting any repressive tactics under global scrutiny (Oberschall 1996). The repression of Tiananmen shows, of course, that to globalize social movements hardly guarantees the liberalization of authorities. It does, however, suggest just how important the global-local encounter is for mobilizing movements. CNN and the protesters relied on one another for information and legitimacy in the framing of the students' collective protest (Calhoun 1989, 1994a; Keane 1996, 174–75).

This transnational public sphere offers a place where forms of organization and tactics for collective action can be transmitted across the globe. It is the medium through which various forms of collective action and social movement repertoires become "modular" and transferable to distant locations and causes (Tarrow 1994, 6). It also provides the space where material resources can be developed and distributed across national boundaries in ways that limit the nation-state's capacity to sanctify and demonize practices with cries of patriotic and alien influences. For example, the Helsinki Accords of 1975 provided a global reference for opposition movements within the Soviet bloc. Poland's Committee for Workers' Defense in particular used the fact of its government's endorsement of this document on human rights to publicize the government's denial of human rights to protesting workers in the late 1970s in the transnational public sphere (Lipski 1985). More generally, the spread of human rights ideologies and movements exemplifies the power and consequence of this public sphere's global reach (see Ball, chap. 3).

Although one might view the transnational public sphere as heuristically distinct, one should not analyze it apart from national and more localized public spheres. The principles and practices that emerge in globalized space evoke local responses that transform and contest global practices in their applications. Some originally local responses may become part of globalized discourses and thus seek to diminish the distinction between the transnational and the localized public sphere. Other movements may seek to contest globalized discourses and preserve some aspect of their locality that they maintain is distinct from, and perhaps opposed to, globalization. The interactions between transnational and local public spheres, movement actors, their antagonists, and different actors within the state can be quite complex, as Guidry (chap. 7) shows, challenging our understanding of the roles movement actors might play in politics, the sovereignty of national states in light of international conventions, and even the nature of the boundary between the state and the public sphere.

The transnational public sphere appears to be expanding its reach. Two processes contribute to this. The movement of people around the globe, creating various diasporic or epistemic communities, generates various communication networks that help to constitute this public sphere (Appadurai 1996). At an organizational level, the multiplication of firms, social movement organizations, and nongovernmental organizations (NGOs) that cross state boundaries appears to generate the associational base for a "nascent"[5] transnational civil society, itself the social infrastructure of the public sphere. These organizations often represent the interests of dispersed communities, but they can represent apparently global ideas such as human rights, free markets, labor rights, or democracy.

The expanding reach of the transnational public sphere means that local movements are always potentially global. They might involve actors that are geographically removed from the site of contention. Also, there are any number of actors in the transnational public sphere—organizations, governments, and the mass media—that will thrust such movements under global scrutiny. These actors observe and record events in distant localities; they bring to light actions that may, from the point of view of protagonists, appear to be local concerns. This globalization of social movements can work in a variety of ways. In the first instance, movements in a distant place might be used to clarify conditions at home. For example, the broadcast of the Los Angeles riots/rebellion of 1992 (sparked by the verdict in the Rodney King trial) was also viewed in Brazil, whereupon Brazilian racial practices could be contrasted favorably with North American racial hypocrisy. In the second instance, the transnational public sphere can be used to challenge the hegemony of a nation-state in defining the jurisdiction of a conflict. The Russian military intervention against Chechnya and the Mexican government's repression of the Chiapas revolt were clearly matters of national interest to the governments in question and to realists in international affairs. They were, however, powerfully challenged by the presence of international nongovernmental organizations on the ground and solidarity movements abroad, which used various spaces in the transnational public sphere, from the United Nations to global media, to challenge these states' legitimacy in deploying violence. When the Nigerian government arrested writer Ken Saro Wiwa, transnational human rights organizations turned what the Nigerian authorities wished to be an exclusively national question into a global one.

The transnational public sphere is thus an opportunity structure that is recognized most clearly in the core countries of the industrialized West, but it is appreciated even in relatively marginalized sites in the non-Western world as well. Through the transnational public sphere, resources such as organization structures, movement tactics, funds, and personnel flow across borders. Local actors use these resources in their struggles, contributing to the diffusion of increasingly uniform methods of contention even over highly local issues.

To a considerable extent, this image of a transnational public sphere overlaps with the vision of progressive social movements and world society discussed at the beginning of this section. In this picture, social change moves in a direction that looks much like the replication on a global level of forms of political contest as we know them in the democracies of the industrialized world. This may very well be accurate, but it bespeaks of both a selection bias in our recognition of globalized social movements and a view of public spheres that looks suspiciously Western, uninflected by the critiques of the universalizing vision of the public sphere itself. In what follows, we suggest several cautions that might attend this particularly progressive vision of a transnational public sphere.

First, *to the extent that globalization reflects not some underlying master mechanism of rationalization but rather an unleashing of communicative capacities invited by the development of global media and a transnational public sphere, globalization becomes a process that is embedded more in historical contingency than driven by a specific teleology.* In no small measure, the shape globalization takes depends on the character of communication, the identity of participants in that exchange, and the issues they bring to the table, and as such globalization does not necessarily imply any particular direction beyond, perhaps, the speed with which communications and other exchanges are elaborated. As Keck and Sikkink (1998, 213) observe:

> The globalization process we observe is not an inevitable steamroller but a set of interactions among purposeful individuals. Although in the aggregate these interactions may seem earthshaking, they can also be dissected and mapped in a way that reveals great indeterminacy at most points of the process. There is nothing inevitable about this story: it is the composite of thousands of decisions which could have been decided otherwise.

Public spheres, whether transnational or national, are thus characterized by a measure of contest and contingency that is difficult to recognize, or at least emphasize, under a rubric of rationalization. They are volatile and do not preclude the possibility of violence or, as Keane (1996) notes, "uncivil society." Local and globalized actors push differing agendas and visions of civilization. At the same time, the tactics, the discourses, and even the values of some groups may be assimilated by others to generate outcomes that evolutionary portraits might be at pains to recognize. Thus, the McDonald's Corporation becomes "environmentalist," the Indian Bharatiya Janata Party (BJP) a defender of democratic diversity, and the Afro-Brazilian movement Olodum the distributor of its own MasterCard. Public spheres even offer the possibility of rendering globalization in the vernacular and the plural. As Arjun Appadurai writes (1996, 10),

> The megarhetoric of developmental modernization (economic growth, high technology, agribusiness, schooling, militarization) in many countries is still with us. But it is often punctuated, interrogated, and domesticated by the micronarratives of film, television, music and other expressive forms, which allow modernity to be rewritten more as vernacular globalization.

Appadurai's critique of the globalization thesis thus resonates with Keck and Sikkink's (1998) interpretation. They both invite us to view globalization as the outcome not only of a process of contingencies but of necessary diversity based on the heterogeneities of globalization, from the vernaculars of globalization to the differentiation of global flows themselves. Our second emphasis, therefore, is that *globalization is not a singular process but should be understood in the plural: globalizations.*

To the extent that we attune ourselves to the variety of globalizations, we reinforce the conceptual value of the "transnational advocacy networks" that Keck and Sikkink (1998, 32–34) study. They focus on the transnational flows of information, resources, and tactics that approximate some of the qualities of the public sphere in more national spaces. Benedict Anderson (1998, 58–77) has used similar concepts to elaborate upon his original vision of imagined communities with "fax nationalism." This is also akin to what Appadurai (1996) identifies in those diasporic public spheres that recognize the significance of global flows of a nation's population (i.e., migration) and their communications for the structuring of national public spheres. In general, then, the transnational public sphere is composed of many more networks, or publics, than the notion of a single public sphere suggests. This refinement works well with the reconstruction of public sphere theories for nation-state democracies.

Public spheres have always been based on systematic exclusions. There are always people who have standing in the public sphere and others who do not. Habermas's bourgeois public sphere was not only constituted by class-based but also gender-based and other exclusions. Even when formally opened to the excluded, the extent to which the identities of participants must conform to constitutive models—for example, the extent to which women must assume masculine roles—is evident. As Calhoun (1995, 242) writes, "all attempts to render a single public discourse authoritative privilege certain topics, certain forms of speech, and certain speakers." Calhoun thus finds some virtue for democracies in the proliferation of multiple publics united in a common sphere.

The coherence of a common public sphere that invites multiple publics to participate is, however, a difficult concept to grasp. Without the unity afforded by the nation it appears nearly impossible. The symbol of the nation and the ideology of national self-interest enables a common public sphere within nation-states to be imaginable. A postmodern sensibility emphasizing difference undermines the ease with which the commonality of that national public sphere can be imagined. It is even more difficult to imagine a *transnational* public sphere that has no global imaginary uniting the variety of publics constituting it.

Nevertheless, this transnational public sphere is crucial for social movement action. It is also crucial to the recognition of the potential for reconstructing not only issues appropriate for global discussion but the identities that are attached to them. If our imagination of that globalized space—the transnational public sphere—is constrained by preexisting networks defined by particular diasporas or single issues, the potential for refiguring the role of social movements and the contingencies of history are limited. *Our third principal caution, then, is that we need to retain that very tension between the proliferation of diversity, through multiple publics, and the homogenization and globalization suggested by a single transnational public sphere in order to recognize the ways that social movements can generate contingencies, transformations, and reconfigurations of both identities and power.* In order to recognize and elevate this tension, therefore, we need to be able to recognize and elevate the conditions that enable and expand access to the transnational public sphere.

In broad strokes, one could paint the following picture of the transformation of the transnational public sphere. A European public sphere existed even prior to the Enlightenment (Calhoun 1995, 264–65). It became more broadly accessible to the popular classes as mass print culture helped to generate broader reading publics. Those imagined communities made of print (Anderson 1983) helped to generate national identities that would eventually coalesce to become the leading, legitimate identity granting persons access to a transnational public sphere organized around courts of international diplomacy. With the advent of "globalization," however, that nation centeredness has shifted in interesting ways. As Ball demonstrates in chapter 3, human rights discourses have spread across the global system, limiting national claims to sovereignty and domination in the definition of *globalization.* As Rucht illustrates in chapter 4, social movements in the core of the world system have especially extended their reach, intervening on behalf of constituencies far beyond their life worlds.

But while the nation has apparently diminished in significance for these globalizing movements, national imaginaries remain powerful in shaping social movements outside the core—and, one might argue, even within it if the importance of disaporic and immigrant communities is considered. Contests over national sovereignty and rights of return for the Crimean Tatars hardly suggest the eclipse of the nation in framing globalizing social movements, as Uehling demonstrates in chapter 11. At the same time, one cannot assume that the nation, ethnicity, or any other assumed or imposed identity suffices to explain collective action, as so many are wont to do in an era in which civilizations are said to collide (Huntington 1996). Derluguian's analysis in chapter 12 of the networks and power relations that guide the Cossacks suggests a very different picture of their identity and role in social change than invocations of Russian national character or Cossack legacies imply. Van der Veer's study of the Sikhs in chapter 13 shows just how much we miss by attempting to explain their character with imputations of fundamentalism.

As one discusses the character of movements that enter the transnational public sphere, one must also attend to the ways in which they enter that space. Some movements exist primarily in that space, as the human rights movement has. Some enter to obtain resources or acquire strategies, as the Brazilian children's rights movement has (chap. 7). Other movements, such as those of the Crimean Tatars and the Cossacks, tend to remain within a geographically limited (in this case a post-Soviet) space and are brought into a more transnational public sphere by the actions of their interpreters. Indeed, to analyze the "address" of movements in transnational space, one should attend not only to their activists but to their analysts.

Movement analysts—all of those involved in this volume as well as the broader community of movement scholars, journalists, and applied researchers—are part of this transnational public sphere. This is especially apparent, for example, in the case of movements involving indigenous peoples when terms are applied to indigenous practices in order to make them recognizable to those from other groups or areas (see Rogers 1996). This book and each of its chapters thus contributes to a globalization experienced as the emergence and growth of this transnational public sphere. The authors are North American, Caribbean, European, Russian, and Taiwanese not always living in their countries of origin. The studies have taken them around the globe to Brazil, Poland, Russia, Nicaragua, Taiwan, India, South Africa, Lebanon, Palestine, Israel, and elsewhere, and the transnational relationships that have helped create these studies are themselves examples of the generative forces that exist in the transnational public sphere. This book is thus not only a comment upon or analysis of globalization, but a contribution to it as well.

Our fourth caution, therefore, is that *one should attend to the variety of ways in which social movements enter the transnational public space, are potentially transformed by the encounter, and perhaps even influence globalizations themselves.* That is to say, the transnational public sphere renders the global and local mutually transformative. Social movements as a whole—their objects, participants, leaders, *and analysts*—are all part of this process.

There are many ways in which social movements might be transformed or can effect some kind of change in the process and formation of any particular globalization. Because globalization disperses resources throughout the world system, and as nation-states cease to be the obvious fulcrum on which the claims of social movements might be realized, the efficacy of social movements cannot always be found in the redistribution of resources or the formulation of policies. Instead, one might attend to the transformations in identity of movements and their constituencies as well as to the articulation of alternative civilizational or moral concerns.

Our fifth and final point, then, is that *the analysis of social movements and the transnational public sphere should attend in particular to the transformation of normative issues and identities in various globalizing discourses.* In this volume, we attend less to the emergence of world society than we do to the transformations it inspires at local and global levels. We not only ask how human rights concerns are spread and how they become an instrument of state policy. We also attend to how the quest for a Palestinian or Taiwanese state enters the public sphere not only in that world region or its colonial or neocolonial network but beyond as well. One should also look to the ways that social movements combine elements from local and transnational imaginaries in the articulation of their needs and demands, as Bayard de Volo demonstrates with the Mothers of Matagalpa in chapter 6 and Gay Seidman suggests in chapter 14's discussion of the anti-apartheid movement. New "syntheses" of poorly articulated or even competing norms may be the real consequence of the encounter between globalizations and social movements.

We believe that it is safe to presume that the rationalizing impulses identified by Meyer et al. and the emancipatory goals identified by Boulding will both be important features of globalized social movements; they may even wind up as the dominant logics seen in social movements around the world. That is the conclusion suggested by Ball in chapter 3, and the chapters in part II demonstrate that the civilizational concerns associated with liberal democracy, legal-rational processes, and the emancipation of oppressed groups are being incorporated into movement frames in diverse places. In this sense, the transnational public sphere is realizing part of its promise. But given the contingencies, contests, and communicative uncertainties associated with this transnational public sphere, a focus on the multiplicity, historicity, systematic tensions, and normative transformations involved in making that global space ought to be at the center of our attention. Consequently, the modalities of power and resistance, along with the attendant processes of identity formation and the normative penumbrae of movements and movement theories, ought to be a direct focus of research on social movements and globalizations.

The Global/Local Nexus: Power, Culture, and the Normative Penumbrae of Social Movements

Both globalization and social movement research provide us with important ways to examine global change and the role of social movements in them, but their concern with the global side of the problem underplays the identities, activities, and effects of social movements in specific *localities*. As Appadurai (1996, 11) puts it, globalization means "locality is no longer what it used to be," but far from emphasizing the disappearance of locality that is implied in much writing on globalization Appadurai also wants us to understand that globalization helps create locality. The production of the local can be jarring and can even produce violent efforts to link specific places with globalized discourses and practices. As a singular process with many levels of interpretation and experience, the meeting of the global and local is a disruptive process that challenges both sides; yet this process is increasingly the main context for the development of collective action outside the dominant global circuits of transnational social movements.

The fluidity of the globalizing context forces us to consider social movements not as ends in themselves but as actors involved in larger contexts of social transformation. As contentious actors, social movements in globalization bring to the fore disparities in power not only between different actors but between different states as well. The notion of a global/local contest or relationship itself seems shot through with power relations. The world society perspective attempts to show that the local gives way to the global, while those closer to Appadurai's position emphasize how globalizations bring localities the ability to resist and challenge any notion of a world society. At a transnational level, issues of culture and the normative connotations of collective action are also brought into higher relief. But social movement theory has begun to come to terms with the challenges of thinking through power and culture in global terms only recently. The studies collected in this volume help us to push movement theory beyond its disciplinary and historical boundaries. At stake is not only how to theorize movements within discursive globalizations but the globalization of social movement theory itself (McCarthy 1997).

Before 1975, the majority of academic social movement theory was being developed in the United States.[6] The movement analysis agenda was dominated by an implicit metatheory of movements as a variation on the voluntary organization sector, and the mobilization of resources was the key to success or failure in movement activity.[7] Movements were not theorized as antisystemic, as Marxists might view labor, at least potentially. Instead, they were viewed as an alternative means of expressing a democratic pluralism or, as in the case of civil rights movements, helping to realize democratic pluralism. But the pluralist supposition underlying movement theory at that time was rarely made explicit, and it did not need to be. Movement theory was operating in a disciplinary space, sociology, that was relatively ahistorical, taking for granted the conditions of its activity.[8]

In the late 1970s and 1980s, however, movement research outside North America began to change this situation. European studies found, especially in the work of Charles Tilly and his students, a ground for linking social movement theory and a historical sociology focused on both state making and economic cycles and for integrating studies of revolution and social movements (Tilly 1978, 1979;

Tilly, Tilly, and Tilly 1975). Context—historical, social, and economic—became central, for movements were only a means by which to tell a larger story, not an end in themselves, as in the earlier North American school with its pluralist supposition. In Russian and East European studies, the major social movement, Solidarity, was approached more within a framework of systemic transformation than as a movement to be compared with other movements.[9] When moved to a developing world context, social movement theory combined revolutionary studies with some of the concerns of democratic pluralism, seeking the incorporation of marginalized and dispossessed groups (see Eckstein 1989; Escobar and Alvarez 1992). Labor and community movements (Seidman 1994), women's movements (Alvarez 1990; Jaquette 1989), urban social movements (Stokes 1995), and religious movements (Levine 1986) and their connections to other movements (Mainwaring 1989) expanded the scope of social movement literature concerning the grievances of marginalized groups.

After the events of May 1968 in Europe, "new" social movements based on the mobilization of emergent, rather than marginalized, identities became important objects of inquiry (Pichardo 1997). Inspired by theorists such as Melucci (1980, 1981, 1989) and Touraine (1971, 1977, 1981, 1988), theories of new social movements focused on forms of social action that were not animated by Marxist concerns of material resources and the redistribution of the social product. Instead, struggles over quality of life issues shifted movement goals toward the rearticulation of identities and the elaboration of alternatives denied by systemic constraints. The struggle for historicity by all subjects, rather than simply the marginalized, reflected this new post-Fordist moment (Steinmetz 1992).

Although the distinctions among these regional traditions have begun to fade with the globalization of social movement inquiry,[10] one may nevertheless identify three regionally inflected metatheories of power underlying the study of these movements. In the first instance, power is broadly dispersed and available to those who mobilize resources to obtain it. Pluralism underlies this model. In the second, power is concentrated and the mobilization of movement resources is undertaken in order to contest those who have power by those who do not. A more binary conception of power underlies this model. Finally, in the third instance the new social movement theorists treat power less directly, more in terms of the struggle to escape from it or realize agency within it than to use or capture it.

When we turn to globalizations and social movements, transnational movement theorists such as Keck and Sikkink (1998) or Smith et al. (1997) tend to view power in terms of the voluntary sector model, somewhat along the lines of the North American school that dominated movement studies until the late 1970s. These writers focus more on the mechanics of social movements and mobilization than on the nature of power that is either contested or sustained by movements. But for theorists who seek to engage movements at the nexus of the global and local a more complex approach to power relations is helpful.

The nature and stakes of the global/local contest are eloquently expressed in Patrick Chamoiseau's novel *Texaco* (1998), which tells the story of a historical conflict between an urban invasion neighborhood, called "Texaco" after the property's original owner, and the "City" of Fort-de-France, Martinique. Texaco is populated mainly by descendants of slaves and marroons. The City has changed from the outpost of colonial France to the local Creole metropole, bringing modernization to the island by way of its own elite. The story bridges several historical globalizations—colonialism, the African slave trade, the emergence of the world capitalist system, decolonization, modernization, and development—by tracking the struggle of those victimized and marginalized by these dislocations to capture the City rather than being swallowed by it. After some years of accommodation between the City and Texaco, a road is extended from the town to the edge of the invasion. A young urban planner working for a bureau of the city council arrives in Texaco to begin surveying it and is hit by a stone. The planner is referred to ironically and mockingly as "the Christ," the one sent by higher powers to save them, the one representing the ideas and beliefs of the modernizing, missionary metropole (10):

> But, if they stared at us, we certainly stared back. It was a battle of eyes between us and City, another battle in a very ancient war. And in that war a cease-fire had just been broken, for the construction of that road could only bring a police crackdown to make us clear off; and we waited for that assault every minute of every day, and amid this nervousness the Christ made his appearance. . . . Looking at him, one thought of one of those agents from the modernizing city council which destroyed poor quarters to civilize them into stacks of [housing] projects, or one of those bailiffs from the old dirt-poor days who would enjoin us to disappear. That's probably why he was hit by the stone and lost that bit of blood which slid along his cheek.

Such a context, if not absent, is at least relatively neglected in most studies of globalization and social movements. Appadurai (1996) focuses on the nature of this process and its conflicts at the most discursive levels, and his use of Indian examples to illustrate his concerns begins to elevate the local. Nonetheless his concentration on media and migration ultimately directs the gaze toward the transnational and away from the mechanics of movements or movement organizations at the global/local nexus. A growing number of individual studies have begun to examine these issues in such a nexus (see, e.g., Berner and Korff 1995; Rogers 1996; and Hernández Castillo and Nigh 1998). This volume, especially part III, brings social movement studies explicitly into this terrain of the global/local encounter. The scene written by Chamoiseau enables us to appreciate the terrific importance of context, and in particular that nexus of global and local, but it remains to work out the consequences of this particular notion of context for social movement theory.

Rather than begin with protest or the formal mobilization of resources to frame protest or take advantage of political opportunities, Chamoiseau's scene directs our gaze to those hidden scripts, those local sources of resistance around which movements might form. *An approach to power relations that begins with the ubiquity and contradictoriness of power and resistance, rather than an approach based on transparent and fundamental antagonisms typically characterizing the approach of both movement actors and their analysts, is critical to the study of the encounter between movements and globalizations.*

Social movement theory tends, however, to work with the theory of power relations that movements themselves deploy. Scholars such as Touraine (1981) and Morris (1984), for example, seek to elevate the struggle waged by the social movement itself, clarifying its conditions of action. In such an approach, the authors clearly sympathize with the movement in question, and they accept its theory of power relations as the starting point for their own refinement. In apparent opposition to such an approach, a long tradition of Marxist scholarship and its kin have charged social and especially labor movements with a kind of "false consciousness," a mistaken understanding by movement activists themselves of the power relations underscoring the movement. For example, Jadwiga Staniszkis (1991) argued that Solidarity's 1980–81 form of rebellion was in fact a means of reproducing the rule of Soviet-type society because it challenged only those who would redistribute the social product rather than the mechanism on which that redistribution was based. In all of these cases, however, the authors can work with a relatively coherent definition of *the system* (i.e. the context of power relations) and the logic of the struggle the movement wages or ought to wage. Globalizations, however, make the definition of the system's character more difficult and subject to many more interaction effects.

In this situation, "resistance" becomes an especially helpful concept. Resistance is especially important when the practices of social movements and public protest are either more dangerous or less traditional or when they are more individuated and difficult to recognize. But the conceptual/disciplinary home of resistance is in cultural studies, and it is often treated by social movement theorists as a kind of preliminary to the more effective form of resistance associated with social movements. One task of globalizing social movement theory thus rests in examining the ways in which understanding resistance can help us problematize power as it is involved in both movement activity and movement theory.

Cultural studies tends to treat far more problematically just what the object of social contest is and where resistance might be found. For instance, Henry Louis Gates Jr. (1994) challenges the practice of some African American academics who call theory the white man's game. He argues, in contrast, that such a form of resistance helps to reproduce white domination. At the other extreme, cultural studies can involve whole societies in resistance. For instance, Marshall Sahlins (1994) has shown how entire peoples can reassert existing cultural forms in order to subordinate European goods to the fulfillment of traditional ends. In neither case would these be taken as social movements or public protest, but they are central examples of resistance.

Rather than being subordinated to the more efficacious movement, in cultural studies resistance is subordinated conceptually to a notion of "practice." To study practice is to study the ways in which culturally and historically constituted subjects become agents in the active sense—how their actions and modes of being in the world sustain and sometimes transform the structures that made them. Resistance is thus a form of practice, and movements are not qualitatively different forms of engagement but subject formation and resistance on a different scale. Rather than theorizing resistance as extraordinary and momentous, as movements and especially public protest are usually imagined, resistance is a part of everyday life, to be found in even the most mundane of circumstances. Hence, routinization, while spelling the transformation and perhaps the end of movements, is nonsensical in thinking of resistance. But resistance also means rethinking the basic theory of power operating within social movement theory.

Theories of resistance in cultural studies thus tend to operate with a more complex theory of power relations than social movement theories do. While the latter organize their conception of power on a few basic axes, cultural studies conceives power in multiple and potentially contradictory formations. Using the concepts of cultural studies to think about movements, the relationship between movements and resistance is not only a matter of intensity but concerns the ways in which power is conceived among actors. As Dirks, Eley, and Ortner (1994, 5) suggest,

> movements often themselves become removed from everyday experience, their members coming to see popular behavior as something to be educated, improved, disciplined. At the same time, the people on whose behalf such movements claim to speak often find the language and mechanics of these movements remote and alienating. The complex and problematic relations between social movements and disorderly popular culture, involving distinctions of class and gender, ethnicity and race, roughness and respectability, are becoming central to the contemporary problematic.

A few examples are illustrative. South Asian historiography has long been cast in a nationalist framework in which the struggle for liberation from the British organized the analysis of movements, but since the early 1980s this historiography has been challenged forcefully by the subaltern studies school and other scholars (see Guha 1982, 1983, 1984). Partha Chatterjee (1993a, 1993b) in particular argues that while Indian nationalists may have claimed to represent the wishes of the Indian people at large this assertion is problematic. The nationalist movement was based upon modular expressions of statehood and sociopolitical organization that were themselves products of the imperialist rule from which South Asians sought to escape. Likewise, in the study of Poland's Solidarity movement the emphasis on conflicts between state and society, between Soviet power and the Polish nation, or between dictatorship and democracy led analysts to overlook the ways in which class and gender privileges shaped the movement.[11]

From the perspective of resistance and cultural studies, movements become quite different from what we are accustomed to in movement theory. At once, movements imply both the priority and clarity of some forms of social action but at the same time the potential if not necessary repression of other actors or forms of action. With this critical disposition toward movements, resistance may not simply be a less powerful response to situations of oppression. Analyzing resistance might enable us to understand better the contradictory qualities of oppression that movements can highlight but also can hide.

These concerns invite partisan responses, to be sure, but they also invite reflection on how to research relationships among resistance, movements, and power relations. As social movement theorists develop more deeply cultural approaches in their analyses (e.g., Snow et al. 1986; Snow and Benford 1988; Tarrow 1992; Johnston and Klandermans 1995; Carroll and Ratner 1996), resistance and its attending conceptions of power relations (see Ortner 1995) become more important. Without considering resistance in ways suggested by cultural studies, it becomes much more difficult to theorize the relationship between movements and power, especially at the nexus of the global and the local where the transformations of identities, movement problematics, and power relations are most labile.

Much as we have sought to retain the tension between multiple networks and a single transnational public sphere, our attention to the multiplicity of resistance should not distract us from the analytical questions surrounding the mobilization of more significant resources in movements. For example, Nick Dirks (1994, 5) has argued that ritual, a prototypical site of cultural reproduction, is "brimming" with resistance and produces moments in which hierarchies of all sorts might be overturned. But not all forms of resistance produce social movements that might issue more sustained challenges to hierarchies. Which forms of resistance do become articulated in—or even transformed into—movements? And which kinds of resistance are subordinated in a movement's mobilization? With this volume, *we suggest that one of the principal challenges before social movement theory is to consider the articulation between resistance and various transnational movement practices, a question whose answer requires a cultural approach that attends to vernacular and context.*

While culture, power, and context might be important to the study of all social movements, they are more demonstrably so where movements are simultaneously engaging global and local sets of power relations and cultural formations. Sometimes the movements are obviously transnational, but as the globalizing space becomes ever more pervasive we propose that social movements be studied in their global articulation. And one of the most important sites in this articulation rests in the glow of the "normative penumbrae" of social movements—all the connotations, civilizational concerns, and moral impulses, explicit and implicit, surrounding movements and movement theory.

By "normative penumbrae" and "civilizational concerns" we mean more than just ideological commitments and cultural impulses that might tend toward ethnocentrism. Civilizational concerns articulate different visions of the "good society," the normatively desirable condition of a society toward which social action, and social movements, are directed. To understand the civilizational concerns of movement actors is to understand something important about the reasons a particular movement exists and why actors are able to overcome sometimes damning odds. But the possibility of a single transnational public sphere does not translate into the universalization of these normative concerns; the globalization of social movements and our theories of them force us to confront the diversity of civilizational concerns at stake.

The differing civilizational concerns of movement theorists and actors help to explain why the emerging transnational civil society and public sphere that is pictured in much current scholarship does not, of necessity, tend toward a more peaceful, democratic world. As the British political theorist John Keane (1996, 114) notes, civil societies and the public spheres that nurture them, whether local or transnational, are continually plagued by the possibility of violence due to the "openness that is characteristic of all civil societies—their nurturing of a plurality of forms of life that are themselves experienced as contingent." Civil societies are "self-questioning, self-destabilizing" (125). This is not to say that civil society necessarily promotes violence either. For Keane and others, the public spheres nurtured by a vibrant civil society are a great resource in the struggle to find peaceful means of resolving disagreements and, as the human rights movement exemplifies, monitoring the violent or abusive actions of public authorities.

"Universal principles," such as the freedom of expression in a public sphere, self-determination, or human rights more generally represent the kinds of rationalizing impulses that Meyer and his colleagues examine, but in the transnational public sphere they become problematic. The quest for self-determination, so vividly displayed in the diffusion of nationalist projects in our world today, exemplifies the diversity contained within such a universal principle. Self-determination might, as many but not all Poles argue today, involve the subordination of the national project to European integration, an apparent contradiction. In another example, more directly conflictual, the self-determination of the Baltic nations and Russian national interests highlight the potential for conflict among competing nationalist projects. That is not surprising, of course, since within the universalizing commitment to the right of all nations to self-determination lie competing claims by particular nations over their rights and responsibilities before other nations. Even the claims associated with liberal citizenship and human rights can get caught on the shoals of these competing national claims. In the Russian government's critique of Baltic citizenship policies, for example, Estonia and Latvia can be criticized for exclusive citizenship practices. This limitation on human and civil rights, however, must be interpreted not only within a national framework but within the international security concern that attends Baltic-Russian relations (Kennedy and Stukuls 1998).

Human rights, while therefore universalizing in intention and grounded in the globalizing power of the United Nations–sponsored Universal Declaration of Human Rights (1948) and other conventions, is received, understood, and articulated very differently with various locales depending on that particular project's relationship to locally defined normative projects. The "normative penumbrae" of social movements are therefore not only to be found in the intentions of those who articulate movement visions but in their reconstitution in various locales across the globe. The diversity of localities and the fluidity of the transnational public sphere render the meeting of global and local a highly volatile and charged context; the modular movement practices learned from labor or women's movements can provide movement organizations with very different visions of civilization elsewhere. Whether it is desirable or not to develop a movement theory resonant with the movements themselves, such a task is very difficult and at least risks analytical purchase.

Thus, the relationship of theory to the world is not unproblematic, and the normative penumbrae of theory are at least as important as those of movements. Appadurai (1996, 18) writes that "any book about globalization is a mild exercise in megalomania, especially when it is produced in the relatively privileged circumstances of the American research university." He cautions us to be conscious of the ways in which disciplinary positions and the concerns resonant in sites of theoretical production may influence the pictures of either globalization or local phenomena that become part of public, transnational discourse. Analysts frequently study the kinds of movements that resonate with and demonstrate current theories, but when actors and analysts from across the world share the normative penumbrae of globalization it is unlikely that the particularities of those values and practices will be problematized. For instance, most Poles are unlikely to mark the Western bias of Meyer et al.'s world society because of their wish to join that West and leave the dystopian world of Soviet-type socialism behind. Communist rule, they might say, certainly decoupled them from world society. The normative penumbrae surrounding their vision of globalization are likely to be markedly different, therefore, from those in countries such as Uganda, Kenya, or India, whose principal imperial center has rested in the heart of Western liberal democracy.

When we take movement theory to places outside the familiar terrain of Western democracy, we must attend to the ways in which the normative penumbrae of movement theory articulate the locality or local struggle in question. Sometimes these normative frames impede our understanding of the movements in question, as van der Veer (chapter 13) suggests for "fundamentalist" accounts of Indian religious movements. Sometimes, however, we might need to attend more directly to the normative penumbrae of the movements themselves to find inspiration, as Seidman (chap. 14) suggests in her analysis of the anti-apartheid movement.

Social movement theory or practice neither should nor can be devoid of normative penumbrae; movements and movement theory exist in no small part because of these moral commitments. As such, the analysis of movements can proceed with greater clarity and purchase on human events if these normative penumbrae are more explicit in the analysis of globalizations and social movements. This not only contributes to a greater awareness of the conditions producing theory; it also enables a more direct incorporation of these normative penumbrae into the critical reconstruction of social movement theory. To recognize the civilizational concerns surrounding movements is especially important for the mutual formation of social movements and globalizations, especially when we understand that movement theory itself plays a great role in contributing to the resources that are communicated in the transnational public sphere. Consequently, the analysis of globalizations and social movements must not only attend explicitly to the resources, opportunities, identities, and frames associated with the movements. It must directly attend to the normative penumbrae of movements and their study. We suggest, however, that this is particularly challenging for a variety of reasons.

First, collective action at the nexus of globalizations and social movements problematizes the identities and interests of social movements and their constituencies. While movements demand the strategic prioritization of interests and identity, that strategic invocation becomes more difficult when frameworks for struggle appear to be produced at a distance. Especially in a context in which national identities have a somewhat hegemonic status (at least in the "formal" political arena), a local movement receiving aid from a globalizing network, whether communist or liberal, environmentalist or corporate, is subject to the charge that its identity is inauthentic and its interests alien. To deny the legitimacy of such a charge might be correct strategically or morally, but it fails to treat with sufficient respect the potentially contradictory quality of power relations and the complexity of the global/local encounter. One familiar normative approach to social movements—to accept the framework of the movement itself—is therefore likely to be more problematic within this particular nexus of global and local forces.

Second, within this globalizing space it becomes more difficult to leave aside the quality of the field of power relations in which movements operate. Binary oppositions are today more difficult, as the world system is no longer organized in the binary logics that underscored the cold war. Nationalist oppositions might enable the reproduction of binary logics, but that kind of theory of power relations is unlikely to serve much analytical use for anyone other than those who project only one side of the struggle. Also unsatisfactory is the approach to power favored by the "new social movements," in which the autonomy of the movement in its search for historicity is much more central than an analysis of the field of power relations itself. This position is unlikely to provide the analytical and normative purchase it could in Western Europe, where relative wealth enabled questions of quality of life to take precedence over matters of the possibility of life (Inglehart 1977), the latter a greater priority in a number of globalized contexts.

As we suggested in the first half of this essay, the existing transnational public sphere is much more fractured, potentially exclusive, and power laden than our projects of liberal hope—within social movement theory or elsewhere—might wish. To the extent that our analysis of social movements uncritically presupposes that sphere's value and accessibility, we are reproducing the normative grounding underlying resource mobilization theories at their inception. Equally, if not more importantly from an analytical perspective, we stand to lose some of our ability to understand movement dynamics through the lenses of cultural frames and political opportunities.

To what extent is problematizing the normative penumbrae of social movements important? They are obviously important if movement analysts are influencing the conditions of action for the movements themselves, an explicit goal of many analysts. Even for those who invoke a scientific distance, these normative frameworks induce a selection bias into the literature as they influence the choice of movements to be studied and the conceptual tools brought to the table. It is perhaps not surprising, for instance, that the heretofore dominant vision of globalizing social movements has rested primarily on those movements that reflect the values liberals hope to see extended into world society in the future. It is also not a surprise to see those movements take advantage of the relatively open public spheres characteristic of the globalizations that are most optimal. But there are other movements that might be studied, with much more ambivalent relationships to the globalizations such a liberal vision promises.

We are not in a position to articulate a normative framework that might substitute for the liberal hope; nor are we implying a desire to do so. We do, however, present this volume in an attempt to problematize these assumptions of globalizing social movements and their analysts by bringing to the table a diverse set of cases. Part I's chapters consider the kind of movements that reach out across and move about in transnational space in the pursuit of a world society in which rationality and emancipation figure as beacons of hope and even destiny. Parts II and III take the task several steps further, by attending to those movements whose locations, characters, and struggles present much more complicated stories of power and justice than a single vision of emancipation might recognize.

The story of the urban planner in Chamoiseau's *Texaco* is instructive. As he recuperates from his injury with Marie-Sophie, the quarter's founder, he finds himself listening to her tell her story, and he is given "new eyes" (165) with which to understand the encounter of modernity and its "others." The urban planner's new vision enables him to see in Marie-Sophie's story the cultural vernacular of blacks (rural agrarian workers, formerly slaves and free persons) and coolies (East Indian, Chinese, and others brought to Martinique by the French) in their struggle with the Creole mulatto city and its modern French pretensions.

> Urbanity is a violence. The town spreads with one violence after another. Its equilibrium is violence. In the Creole city, the violence hits harder than elsewhere. First, because around her, murder (slavery, colonialism, racism) prevails, but especially because this city, without the factories, without the industries with which to absorb the new influx, is empty. It attracts without proposing anything besides its resistance—like Fort-de-France did after Saint-Pierre was wiped out [by a volcano's explosion]. The Quarter of Texaco is born of violence. So why be astonished at its scars, its warpaint? The Creole urban planner must rise above the insalubrious, become a medium. (148)

The planner's revelation offers some inspiration to the social movement theory we hope to cultivate. One of the principal challenges before social movement theory is to explain the ways in which discursive globalizations and the normative penumbrae of social movements are themselves mutually implicated in accounts of movement practices and outcomes. This is not to suggest that social movement theory should abandon the normative impulses that have drawn so many to engagement with movements. Rather, we suggest that it could be driven to engage the resonant and dissonant motifs in the civilizational concerns of movements across the world. Indeed, if the emancipatory hope of the transnational public sphere is to become real, it must not only incorporate more actors but listen more carefully to those who have been excluded. In the process, we both refigure and reaffirm the inclusive logic on which the hope of the transnational public sphere is based.

Overview

In part I of this volume, "Movements in Globalized Space," Keck and Sikkink (chap. 2), Ball (chap. 3), and Rucht (chap. 4) examine movements in the transnational public sphere that resemble the kinds of social movements usually seen in literature on movements and globalization. These chapters shed light on the importance of an emerging transnational public sphere and how movements may participate in discursive globalizations of the kinds that represent the development of world society. As Keck and Sikkink examine historical precursors to the kinds of transnational movements analyzed by Ball and Rucht, they show us how both social movements *and* globalizations have a historical depth that is usually ignored in writing on both phenomena. Ball examines what is in many ways the quintessential transnational social movement—human rights—and demonstrates that the movement's success lies not only in the way it can mobilize resources or frame issues. Rather, the human rights movement finds a great resource in the *encoding* of human rights language and principles into the governing documents of states. In this sense, a movement's relationship with the state is more complex than simply making claims against the state; in the case of human rights, the movement grows as it can use the state against itself.

Chapters 2 and 3 show how organized groups of people come together in a transnational public sphere that allows ideas to both motivate people and set the norms for their discourse. As these norms become shared across borders and debated in transnational spaces (colonial cities, international conferences, and so on), the public sphere becomes strengthened and more of a resource for collective action. Rucht's case of "distant action" demonstrates this quite clearly, showing a transnational public sphere at work in full color. Publics in one place make common cause with publics elsewhere; their work takes place in and helps define the transnational public sphere.

Yet the transnational public sphere that movements participate in also focuses our attention on the cultural and power-laden dynamics at the nexus of the global and local. Not all movements have a rationalizing logic like that of the Universal Declaration of Human Rights—a charter document that sets out the movement's goals in transparent language and urges states to sign on to the program. In many movements, the meeting of global and local is a much less certain affair and the question is much more open as to who has a legitimate claim to the moral high ground and who does not. Self-determination may be an emancipatory principle, but, as we have discussed, it may also be exclusionary and may even—in the case of the former Yugoslavia—contain a rationalization for "ethnic cleansing." It is in this space and at this level of global/local interaction that our task takes on the greatest urgency, in both analytical and normative terms, and thus the lion's share of this volume examines the complexities and contradictions that emerge in the global/local nexus.

In part II, "Globalizations and Movements in Nation-States," the challenge of articulating the local and transnational becomes even more apparent. These chapters also treat culture as something used by movements to develop political purposes, agendas, and mobilizational-communicative frames for their organizations. Kubik (chap. 5), Bayard de Volo (chap. 6), and Guidry (chap. 7) explore the meeting of local cultures and ideas that are all in some way globalized, transportable, or modular. Rather than treat the movement itself as globalized, the discursive frames that the movements deploy are themselves assessed in relation to that transnational public sphere.

Kubik emphasizes the domestic resonance of most Polish protest, but his essay is developed within a larger narrative of a "return" to Europe, itself a particular kind of globalization. In many parts of Poland, as in other parts of the postcommunist world (Stukuls 1997, 1998), this globalization is understood as a kind of normalization, and as such globalization does not become the object of protest. Instead, while everyday life might become ever more global, social movements and protest need not articulate globalization as a problem at all. Furthermore, movements may be less likely to appeal to extranational audiences when their focus of hope, or protest, is channeled through a space whose sense of national sovereignty has only recently been won. The global enters Polish protest, therefore, only implicitly, as part of the normative penumbrae shaping not only political protest but the development of the nation and civil society itself. The other chapters in this section emphasize, rather, the pervasiveness of globalizations in movement activities.

Motherhood in Bayard de Volo's Nicaraguan case is an explicit cross-cultural identity marker (see also Navarro 1989). The identity is itself mobilized in the context of other global references, including *revolutionary struggle* and *civil war* during the *cold war.* Guidry examines the framing of *citizenship* as a children's rights movement struggles in the context of several overlapping globalizations—*neoliberal economics* and the *global city, democratization,* and the use of *legislative strategies* to both limit and empower the *state* to advance claims of citizenship.

Kubik, Bayard de Volo, and Guidry all attend to specific processes of framing and cultural negotiation, but the latter two emphasize movement organization, action, and collective experience. Alongside the first three chapters of this collection, they especially emphasize the importance of social movements as a category of inquiry.[12] While social movements may have diffuse characteristics, at an organizational level they share some important dynamics, particularly with respect to the ways that they channel and direct culture and forms of resistance into public spheres at both the national and transnational levels. The role of the social movement *within* national borders is thus every bit as important as the transnational movements themselves (Keck and Sikkink 1998; Smith et al. 1997). Part II's chapters also emphasize the continuing importance of the state to social movement theory and our considerations of globalizations—in each case, the national state is important, not only as a target of action but as another actor that can push the movements' agenda forward. In Guidry's Brazilian case, movement actors must reexamine their own roles, which increasingly lead them into positions of cooperation with, rather than contention against, the state.

The seeming pervasiveness of the transnational public sphere is evident in both the diffuse and specific senses that culture plays in social movement development. Beyond the explicitly transnational movements examined in chapters 2 through 4, perhaps only the cases of mothers in Nicaragua and the movement for the rights of children and adolescents in Brazil demonstrate the kinds of "globalizing" connections that might place those movements alongside those examined in, for example, Smith et al.'s 1997 collection.

Whatever the networks, these movements show the international "modular-ity" of collective action repertoires (Tarrow 1994, 6). Suggestive of globalization's pervasiveness, these movements have not consciously adopted globalized strategies. They do what movements do elsewhere, and these practices come to them through the complex and often diffuse workings of the transnational public sphere. Local activists might learn strategies by reading newspapers that detail movement activities elsewhere in the world. Limited contact with representatives of an NGO or an arm of some national progressive organization helps to globalize the local; for example, the pastoral activities of the Catholic Church in Latin America brings globalized processes to specific places and groups without intentionally working to globalize those organizations.

As we turn to issues of power at the global/local nexus, processes of identity formation, history, and social memory become ever more important for social movement theory. Part III, "Movements, Identities, Cultural Transformations," takes up these issues. The movements examined by Peteet (chap. 8), Lo (chap. 9), Perales (chap. 10), Uehling (chap. 11), Derluguian (chap. 12), and van der Veer (chap. 13) elaborate processes of identity formation tied to specific contexts. They are less inclined to look at culture through the lens of a "toolbox" (Swidler 1986), as so many movement theorists do when they explain the cultural frames that movements choose in order to take advantage of or even create political opportunities. Instead, culture shapes, as much as it provides resources for, movement action. Instead of movements mobilizing preexisting identities, they become the expressions of the contradictory conditions and cultural practices experienced by those who protest. From this perspective, oppression is not taken as a given, something naturalized; it is something that must be recognized and named through cultural processes—in the same way that, from the other side of the table, oppression must be created and sustained through some cultural process. A more instrumentalist approach to culture tends to become useful when movements are already formed and strategies are more important than identities.

In Peteet's discussion of Palestinian refugee camps, we see how the movement became a feature of identities embedded in a problematic history and the physical spaces they have occupied. To no small extent, the movement itself expresses the life world in near totality. Peteet offers a powerfully grounded analysis of identity formation, its importance for movement actors, and the discursive dynamic that emerges between movement action and actor identities.

Lo's chapter brings to the consideration of identity the tools of social movement theory: her explanation of their movement, and its downfall, rests very powerfully on a theory of political opportunity structure and resource mobilization. Taiwanese physicians, trained by the Japanese to be tools of the imperialist project, play a discursive and important role in shaping Taiwanese national identity. The physicians wind up in contradictory positions, "in-between" different evolving and in some ways competing identities, but the case shows, like Perales's discussion of sport in the Caribbean, how local actors can turn the cultural products of the imperial/globalizing power to their own uses.

Turning to the Caribbean, Perales continues this story of how local action in the periphery can subvert and reproduce globalizing discourses from the center and in so doing create identities and repertoires of action that provide a generative basis for social movement organization. The crucial point raised by the piece is that before movements can acquire collective action repertoires they need to *imagine* what they want and *experience* it *collectively*—and this is what sport is and provides. Sport in the cases outlined in the chapter generates counterhegemonies via experience and imagination—think of sports as generative performance. In this case, movements might depend on the prior establishment of practices that enable actors to recognize their commonality and discrimination in an existing system.

Uehling's global space is a particular post-Soviet one. The breakup of the USSR left Crimean Tatars in a new transnational space, no longer a single state, imagining a return to what had become a foreign land. Nevertheless, relying on the familiarity bred by Soviet times, Crimean Tatars can return, invoke memories of a place never seen, and contest images held by Russians and Ukrainians of a people desperate to return to their home. Post-Soviet space is, however, relatively self-contained, as actors rely upon networks and images that are familiar to those leaving communism, if not to others who may only recognize communist rule in their applause for its exit from the world stage. In this case, memory inspires a movement that survives the most challenging of conditions.

Derluguian's space is even more peculiarly post-Soviet, for the global networks that the Cossacks travel and draw upon are even more circumscribed than those of the Crimean Tatars. The Cossack is an identity with deep historical resonance in the lands of the former Russian empire. It has entered the transnational public sphere more recently, however, as an example of the traditional and fundamentalist proclivities of those spaces outside an upwardly ascendant core, as examples of ressentiment. To identify such phenomena as a movement in this globalizing volume serves two purposes. First, it invites us to view other kinds of collective action based less on the model of a voluntary organization and more on the basis of nonstate military organization. Second, it also draws attention to the potential for movements resting beyond the progressive imagination, beyond that normally envisioned transnational public sphere resting on an extension of liberal principles.

Van der Veer's essay clarifies the second point. An important part of social movement globalization occurs not only when movements acquire resources and symbols available in the transnational public sphere but also when they are placed in that sphere as exemplary of a particular discursive globalization that transnational actors deploy. Fundamentalism, as the antipathy of the principles of the Enlightenment's global extension, becomes simultaneously the global threat and the clarifying other that allows a post–cold war world to discover its organizing antagonistic principles. Van der Veer suggests, however, that such a label may have less to do with the movement in question and more to do with the principles of globalization itself, which seek to name that movement at a distance.

The chapters of part III enable us to see the critical purchase to be gained by understanding the vernaculars of social movements and their cultural contexts. We see how everyday actors develop grievances and larger cultural-political concerns through collective identities and action—even if that action is as presumably innocuous as playing baseball or meeting with physicians in professional settings. At the same time, these essays are also crucial to the task confronting us when we speak of social movements.[13] These authors suggest that movements based on formal organization, and even based on the imagery of the social movement itself, may not suffice to help us recognize those important processes of collective action that shape social transformation beyond the rountinized formal structures of institutionalized politics.

Gay Seidman's concluding chapter extends the reflections in this introduction. She examines the preceding chapters against another case of classic transnational movement action—the anti-apartheid movement. She draws our attention to the significance of how we envision both the global and the movement and whether we might not elevate the significance of their interaction by refocusing our analytical lens. In particular, she questions whether analysts have not missed some of the insights that activists have long brought to bear on the globalization of social movements, at least in terms of the movement's reference categories. Internationalism, she suggests, is far more present than we might notice through a more parochial local, or even national, academic focus. Her rendering of the anti-apartheid struggle shows how normative accounts of movement identities, and their implications, travel well beyond territorial borders. In the end, she invites us into the fray of uncertainties this nexus of global and local produces.

Conclusion

In assembling this collection, we have sought to walk a fine line between the utter diversity of movement activity in the world and the need for a set of orienting concepts that can travel back and forth across time, space, culture, and identities. The twelve original studies and Gay Seidman's concluding discussion of the anti-apartheid movement have taken us around the world, from more familiar kinds of movements—human rights, anti-apartheid, women's suffrage, environment, children's rights, Polish protest—to very different experiences of movement development and identity—Palestinian refugee camps, neo-Cossacks, Indian fundamentalists, Nicaraguan mothers, Cuban baseball players, a remembered homeland in the Crimea, Taiwanese physicians—which challenge our theoretical task.

This is an old problem that lies at the heart of social inquiry—how to tell a common story out of different, distinct versions of similar processes. The diversity of globalizations and responses to them does not need to be a fetter on movement or globalization theory; indeed, the world society on the horizon seems to be one in which a mutually transforming relationship among global and local processes gives rise to plurality as a driving context for everyday life and political relationships. In seeking the thread or threads that can help us tie together this collection—which we believe reflects very well the variety of movement processes at work in the world today—we suggest that movement theory needs to gain greater purchase on some apparently consistent features of movements in globalizing contexts. Specifically, we point to the relationship of movements with public spheres, modalities of power and resistance, identity formation, and their normative penumbrae; these are critical to understanding social movements and collective action.

For some, globalization means a proliferation of localities that communicate through transnational media and defend themselves against both each other and states. For others, globalization means a consistent homogenizing of sociocultural processes through which transparent, rational norms provide boundaries to human behavior the world over. Neither perspective does justice to the complexity, and interactive quality, of globalizations. An overemphasis on the significance of the local and localities in globalization risks missing the importance of those transnational modular forms that organize our recognition of particular places. Privileging the global, on the other hand, leads us to recognize the deviant only as aberrant or temporary rather than as a moment in which the global could potentially be refigured locally. As these local actions become communicated through the transnational public sphere, the nature of "globality" is at stake. While we cannot ignore the more powerful forces shaping the global—for example, neoliberal economics, the dominance of North American cultural products, and the weight of international human rights commitments—we must recognize that none of these more dominant globalizations can be taken for granted.

This collection provides us with examples that touch various points on the continuum between global and local, between generality and diversity. Our conceptual emphases on public spheres, identity, and the global/local nexus centers our attention on the complexity of encounters between global and local. Allowing room for complexity in our understanding of concepts such as the transnational public sphere or the normative penumbrae of movements is not a way to avoid concrete definitions, hypotheses, or conclusions. Rather, admitting the complexity of the transnational public sphere is simply to recognize it for what it is—a messy process of cross-cultural and transnational communication by means of which communities seek to establish claims over action in the world—whether at home or at large. Collective action in this setting will be contentious, potentially and actually contradictory, sometimes violent, sometimes successful, sometimes an utter failure. But to see social movements at work here is to see collective action in terms that we can understand and debate. In so doing, we globalize social movement theory itself and contribute to the very processes that we try to understand.

NOTES

1. Waltz 1995 provides a compelling comparative study of how international resources aided human rights movements in Algeria, Tunisia, and Morocco in the 1980s; see also Keck and Sikkink 1998.

2. Of course, this must be accompanied by the loss of isomorphism at the local level, where "configurations of people, place and heritage lose all semblance of isomorphism" (Appadurai 1996, 46) and where the processes of globalization themselves—"of people, machinery, money, images and ideas following increasingly non-isomorphic paths" (37)—lose that character.

3. This is the explicit concern of Keane (1996), who finds democracy and civility in public discourse dependent upon a vibrant civil society/public sphere. This concern is implied, even where it is not explicitly developed, in both Keck and Sikkink 1998 and Sassen 1996.

4. Note in particular how Sassen (1996) discusses the dangers of a new "economic citizenship" that privileges multinational firms and corporations in transnational economic discourse.

5. *Nascent* is used here in the sense of accepting Keck and Sikkink's (1998, 32–34) critique of this concept.

6. McAdam, McCarthy, and Zald (1996) review social movement theory and provide a collection of studies that gives a definitive overview of how developing movement theory is being applied. Morris and Mueller (1992) offer a similarly important collection, and Tarrow's *Power in Movement* (1994) is emerging as a classic text that attempts to synthesize social movement theory and the movement phenomenon in the late twentieth century. Johnson's (1996) volume offers a complete consideration of the importance and uses of cultural framing in social movement analysis.

7. For a major collection articulating this vision of social movements, see Zald and McCarthy 1987.

8. This is not to say that sociology was completely ahistorical. Historical sociology and history, however, were intellectual spaces relatively separate from the sociology of movements. Work such as Moore's (1966) and Skocpol's (1979) structural analyses of revolutions in a variety of regions, including the United States prior to the twentieth century, are some of the best examples of this school. But even here, while history became more salient to the story, the cultural dimensions of these structural sociologies were of limited relevance.

9. While these studies all drew upon a more global theoretical vision to interpret Solidarity, they did focus on the relationship between the movement and the system it was to transform. Touraine et al. (1983) emphasized its evolution as a total movement, Kennedy (1991) its class alliance, Ost (1990) the movement's antipolitics, Laba (1992) its workerist roots, Staniszkis (1986) its self-limitation and moral politics, and Kubik (1994) its cultural construction of society versus the authorities.

10. The examination and analysis of these kinds of internal mechanics and dynamics of social movements are the main contributions that one finds in the recent work (see McAdam, McCarthy, and Zald 1996; Klandermans, Kriesi, and Tarrow 1988; Morris and Mueller 1992; and Johnston and Klandermans 1995).

11. Kennedy 1991 provides a partial exception to this pattern.

12. To this extent, volumes such as McAdam, McCarthy, and Zald 1996 demonstrate very clearly the patterned and somewhat consistent nature of social movement organization across societies in a way that gives much purchase to the notion that movements remain a relevant category for understanding social change. The task of globalizing social movement analysis that we undertake in this volume only strengthens and extends what has been accomplished in movement theory.

13. A number of writers question whether the category "social movement" continues to retain any real analytical or descriptive utility. These writers would rather concentrate on "protest," claiming that this is a real example of what the collective accomplishes, a measurable phenomenon more tangible and appropriate to our attention. See Kreisi et al. 1995, chap. 5; Kubik 1998; and Ekiert and Kubik 1999.

PART I

Movements in Globalized Space

CHAPTER 2

Historical Precursors to Modern Transnational Social Movements and Networks

Margaret Keck and Kathryn Sikkink

When we suggest that transnational social movements and transnational advocacy networks have become politically significant forces in international relations over the last several decades, we immediately face a series of challenges.[1] Many people question the novelty of these phenomena. After all, internationalism in various forms has been around for a long time. Others ask about significance—have these campaigns ever produced important social, political, or cultural changes? On what basis do we attribute such changes to network activists' work rather than to deeper structural causes?

A look at history can give us some insights into these questions. In this chapter, we examine two historical campaigns that cast light on the work of modern social movements and transnational advocacy networks. They include the 1833–65 Anglo-American campaign to end slavery in the United States and the efforts of the international suffrage movement to secure the vote for women between 1888 and 1928.

We selected campaigns in which foreign linkages or actors were central to the organizing effort, although the degree and nature of international involvement varies.[2] Both campaigns were lengthy and difficult, but both contributed to major political change. The international women's suffrage movement took over a half a century to secure the vote for women in most of the countries of the world, and the Anglo-American antislavery campaign succeeded only after sixty years of effort and a hugely destructive civil war.

These campaigns began with an idea that was almost unimaginable even by its early proponents. That they could abolish slavery or gain the vote for women seemed impossible. One of the main tasks that social movements undertake, however, is to make possible the previously unimaginable by framing problems in such a way that their solution comes to appear inevitable. But such changes are neither obvious nor linear. They are the contingent result of contestations over meaning and resources waged by specific actors in a specific historical context.

International Pressures for the Abolition of Slavery in the United States: 1833–65

The antislavery movement, which began by demanding the abolition of the slave trade and then promoted the emancipation of slaves, spanned many countries over an entire century.[3] In its scope, methods, and sensibilities, it is the most obvious forerunner of the movements discussed in this book. We examine only one piece of this global campaign, the Anglo-American network in the period 1833–65, which focused primarily on the emancipation of slaves in the United States.

British abolitionist sentiment in the late 1700s and early 1800s focused first on the abolition of the slave trade, in which British merchants and capital were heavily involved. After it was formally abolished in the United States and Britain in 1807, abolitionists sought a legal prohibition on slavery in the territories controlled by the British, which was secured in 1833. After these "closer to home" issues were resolved, the British abolitionists turned their attention to what they considered the most glaring instance of modern slavery, its practice in the United States. The Irish MP and antislavery leader Daniel O'Connell encouraged the movement to "enable us to begin the work with the vile and sanguinary slaveholders of Republican America. I want to be directly at them. No more side-wind attacks; firing directly at the hull, as the seaman says, is my plan."[4] One British antislavery publication urged Americans to "wipe out the shame which renders [you] a scorn among the nations of the world," while an address of the Irish Unitarian Christian Society to its brethren in America called slavery a "plague-spot in America, a cancer which must be boldly cut away," and a "compilation of the greatest crimes against God and men" (Stange 1984, 59, 61).

So, as the British antislavery movement expanded from a domestic pressure group concerned with changing British policy to beginning to become part of a transnational network, it chose America as its first target and initiated a transatlantic campaign in coordination with U.S. antislavery groups. The campaign culminated in the emancipation of slaves in 1865, with the end of the Civil War, and the passage of the Thirteenth Amendment.

Like their counterparts in the target states of modern networks, many U.S. policymakers and citizens resented this British "intervention" in their affairs. One clergyman said, "we do not like the tone of English criticism upon us"; another complained of the British Anti-Slavery League meddling in American affairs and asked why there was not a league to oppose serfdom in Russia or polygamy in Turkey. A common complaint was that the British did not understand America's domestic institutions and thus should stay out of its affairs (Stange 1984, 63, 73, 84). Pro-slavery forces in the United States argued also that the condition of the lower classes in England was "far inferior" to that of American slaves. A congressman from South Carolina denounced the British "exclamations and denunciations" of American slavery that filled "every public journal in Great Britain," despite poverty in Scotland and "enslaved subjects" in Ireland (Fladeland 1972, 160).

Historians and political scientists have argued at great length over whether the end of slavery was the result of economic or moral pressures.[5] The most current and careful historical research argues that economics simply cannot explain the demise of slavery and finds that the impetus behind abolition was primarily religious and humanitarian. Robert William Fogel (1989) concludes that a quarter century of research on the economics of slavery shows that it was "profitable, efficient, and economically viable in both the U.S. and the West Indies when it was destroyed. . . . Its death was an act of 'econocide,' a political execution of an immoral system at its peak of economic success, incited by men ablaze with moral fervor" (410).

Some historians, instead of seeing economics and morality as dichotomous explanations, consider how the rise of capitalism and changes in the market contributed to changing perceptions, conventions about moral responsibility, and the techniques of action that underlay the wave of humanitarianism in the period 1750–1850 (Haskell 1985). This approach fits nicely with Tarrow's (1994) argument that social movements emerged in the eighteenth century from "structural changes that were associated with capitalism" such as "new forms of association, regular communication linking center and periphery, and the spread of print and literacy" (48).

Technological and institutional change can alter the "moral universe" in which action takes place by changing how people think about responsibility and guilt and by supplying them with new ways to act (Haskell 1985, 356). For Thomas Haskell, humanitarianism requires not only the "ethical maxims that make helping strangers the right thing to do" but "a technique or recipe for intervening—a specific sequence of steps that we know we can take to alter the ordinary course of events"; this "recipe" must be sufficiently routine to use easily (358). Here we have Tilly's "repertoires of contention," leading to Tarrow's "modular" repertoires. Haskell shows how technological change and the market facilitated the appearance of recipes that humanitarian groups, especially the antislavery movement, later embraced. Tarrow reminds us that collective action repertoires like boycotts, mass petitioning, and barricades were pioneered within particular struggles and then were diffused to or emulated by other social movements (1994, 40–45). Foner captures this effect in the United States: "If anti-slavery promoted the hegemony of middle class values, it also provided a language of politics, a training in organization, for critics of the emerging order. The anti-slavery crusade was a central terminus, from which tracks ran leading to every significant attempt to reform American society after the Civil War" (1980, 76).

The transnational antislavery campaign provided a "language of politics" and organizational and tactical recipes for other transnational campaigns as well. The women's suffrage campaign initially drew many of its activists and tactics from the antislavery movement. The movement against foot binding in China set up anti-foot-binding societies similar to the antislavery societies in Britain and the United States. The "society" itself was a prominent recipe. The modern versions of these societies are nongovernmental organizatons (NGOs), and they have become even more specialized and diverse, offering a wider selection of organizational and strategic recipes.

In Britain and the United States, activists set up local, regional, and national antislavery organizations that frequently exchanged letters, publications, and visits. In Britain, approximately 400,000 persons signed petitions against the slave trade in 1791–92 (1 out of every 11 adults); in 1814, abolitionists gathered 750,000 names (1 out of every 8 adults); by 1833, 1 of every 7 adults, or twice the number of voters in the most recent elections, signed petitions in favor of the emancipation of slaves (Fogel 1989, 212, 217, 227). This was clearly a mass movement, not a small group of elites. In the United States, the movement matched or may have exceeded that of Britain at its peak. In 1838, authors estimate that there were 1,350 local antislavery societies in the United States, with between 120,000 and 250,000 members (Aptheker 1989, 56). The movement's petitions overwhelmed the congressional machinery, and were so divisive to the political and regional compromises inherent in each party that the House voted first to table them and later not even to receive them.[6]

The backbone of the movement in both countries was made up of Quakers and the "dissenting denominations"—Methodists, Presbyterians, and Unitarians, who brought a deeply religious, evangelical, and philanthropic spirit to the movement in both countries (Abel and Klingberg 1927, 2). They also drew on a tradition of transatlantic networking and information exchange that had flourished among them during the last decades before American independence (Olson 1992). Some members of the antislavery movement, especially in the United States, were more influenced by Enlightenment ideas of equality and liberty than by Christianity (Foner 1980, 66). The British religious denominations were more unified in their antislavery sentiment than the American denominations and tried to encourage their American religious counterparts to take more forceful positions against slavery. British Unitarians, for example, were horrified to learn that the American Unitarian Association had named a slaveholder to their honorary board of vice presidents and agitated against it until the association abolished the board (Stange 1984, 96).

Antislavery groups in the United States and Britain borrowed tactics, organizational forms, research, and language from each other. They used the tactics of the petition and boycotts of slave-produced goods and hired itinerant speakers very successfully on both sides of the Atlantic. Many of these tactics originated in Britain, and the transnational network served as a vehicle for diffusing tactical recipes and collective action repertoires from one domestic social movement to another. In some cases, the antislavery network did more than transfer repertoires, becoming a place for transnational political communication that mutually altered the tactics used on both sides of the Atlantic. Despite internal divisions, British and American groups often arrived at common positions such as opposition to the colonization schemes proposed on both sides of the Atlantic by the 1830s. The British abolitionist campaign for immediate emancipation of West Indian slaves led the American movement to switch its main demand from gradual to immediate emancipation. As to mutual influence, the U.S. antislavery movement eventually may have encouraged the British movement to include women on a more equal footing. The British movement, on the other hand, particularly encouraged U.S. church establishments to take a strong stand against slavery (Aptheker 1989, 91, 150).

One of the most important tactics the abolitionists used was what we call information politics and human rights activists a century and a half later would call the human rights methodology: "promoting change by reporting facts" (Thomas 1993, 83). The most influential example was the volume *American Slavery as It Is: Testimony of a Thousand Witnesses.* Abolitionist activists Theodore Weld and Angelina and Sarah Grimke compiled the book from testimonials of individuals and extensive clippings from southern newspapers. *American Slavery as It Is* became the handbook of the antislavery cause, selling more than a hundred thousand copies in its first year and continuing to sell year after year (Miller 1996, 332–33). William Lee Miller's description of the book shows how it foreshadowed many of the modern publications of transnational movements and networks, both in its scrupulous attention to reporting facts and in its use of dramatic personal testimony to give those facts human meaning and to motivate action.

> Although this book was loaded with, and shaped by, a quite explicit moral outlook and conclusion—no book was ever more so—its essence was something else: a careful assembling of attested facts, to make its point. . . . The author or compilers did not simply tell you the facts and let the facts speak for themselves; they told you repeatedly what to think of these facts. Nevertheless . . . it tried to persuade you by assembling overwhelming piles of undeniable specifics. (325)

The diffusion of tactics through transnational networks could never have led in itself to the emergence of a full-fledged antislavery movement in the United States. As Fogel points out, "Although England provided the spark for a new American crusade, the fire would neither have been lit nor sustained without kindling and a large reserve of fuel." Both the kindling and the fuel were domestic: there were militant leaders to spread the idea and "a public ready to receive it" (1989, 267, 269).

Fogel's fire metaphor serves well for describing the types of interactions we see in these two historical cases: foreign influence or transnational linkages often provide the spark, but that spark only catches and sustains fire with domestic kindling and fuel. There must be an idea, advocates to spread it, and a public ready to receive it. But how do we know when a public is ready to receive an idea? Why do some ideas resonate while others do not? In the case of the antislavery movement, the "vast supply of religious zeal" created by the Protestant revival movements of the early nineteenth century heightened the receptiveness of religious communities in Britain and the northeastern United States to antislavery ideas (Fogel 1989, 267–69). Revival theology emphasized each individual's capacity and responsibility for salvation through his or her good works and efforts to root out individual and social sin. In this worldview, not only was slavery an example of social sin, but the slave was being denied the individuality essential for personal salvation. Temperance movements also appealed to this sensibility, because alcohol was seen as a major example of personal sin that led to social sin, and many antislavery activists also participated in the temperance movement. Yet some apparently congruent concerns such as "wage slavery"—that is, low wages and poor working conditions among the working classes in the North—did not resonate with the Protestant sensibility. Workers, however poor, were free to strive both for salvation and to improve their lot in life; slaves were not.

The world antislavery conferences held in London in 1840 and 1843 solidified Anglo-American cooperation. But the 1840 conference also sharpened internal divisions within the Anglo-American antislavery movement when the English majority refused to seat several black and white women elected as American delegates. They seated the women in the balcony as spectators, where part of the U.S. male delegation, including the fiery abolitionist William Lloyd Garrison, joined them. This led to a split in the movement, and the Garrisonians were not invited to the 1843 conference.

The antislavery campaign resembled modern transnational social movements and the advocacy network definition in terms of the dense exchanges of information among its members. The communications technology of the time of course imposed a different pace on the transatlantic movement. British abolitionists argued in the mid-1800s that "America was no longer a distant land: it was only two weeks away" (Stange 1984, 96). Despite the distance, British and American antislavery groups exchanged letters, publications, and speakers and were honorary members of each other's societies. (American antislavery speakers in Britain attracted large audiences; some early British speakers in the United States barely escaped lynching.)

After having been serialized in an antislavery newspaper, Harriet Beecher Stowe's novel *Uncle Tom's Cabin* sold three hundred thousand copies in the United States in the first year (about one copy for every eight families in the North) and more than a million copies in Great Britain in eight months in 1852 (Fogel 1989, 342; Stange 1984, 140). In writing her novel, Stowe relied on the abolitionist compendium of facts and testimony *American Slavery as It Is,* even, she said, sleeping with it under her pillow. "In 1853, she published a 'key' to Uncle Tom's cabin—a defense of its authenticity, an answer to those who said such things do not happen, or are rare—which drew heavily and explicitly on the testimony in *American Slavery as It Is*" (Miller 1996, 334). Stowe made a triumphant speaking tour of Britain in 1853 from which she returned with more than twenty thousand pounds sterling for the cause. Even Queen Victoria probably would have received her had the American minister not objected that this would appear to be a British government endorsement of the abolitionist movement (Fladeland 1972, 354–56).

As in many modern issue networks, the line between government and movement was fuzzy in Britain. Many leading antislavery crusaders in the early 1800s, such as William Wilberforce, were members of Parliament, and they could often count on the abolitionist sentiments of members of the government (Fladeland 1972, 52). In the United States during this period, the abolition movement had few sympathizers in government (although in the late 1830s it gained champions such as John Quincy Adams in Congress).

The transnational dimension was most influential and decisive when government links with civil society were impaired. In antebellum U.S. politics, southern dominance in political institutions and northern fear of breaking up the Union kept abolitionist sentiment out of these institutions.[7] Ironically, it was the constitutional provision allowing a slave to count as three-fifths of a person in determining congressional districts and electoral votes that gave the South this control of political institutions (Fogel 1989, 339). The South used its dominant position to silence debate over the issue of slavery, first tabling and then refusing to receive antislavery petitions, even those raising issues clearly within the congressional purview such as slavery in the District of Columbia.

These gag rules, prohibiting members from introducing antislavery petitions or resolutions, made transnational linkage politics an attractive strategy for American abolitionists; by joining with British activists and at times leveraging the power of the British government on behalf of the antislavery cause, they could amplify their own voices.

For years, John Quincy Adams and a handful of antislavery representatives were virtually alone in defending the right to petition against slavery. Throughout his long battle against the gag rules, Adams's strategy was to frame slavery as an issue of civil liberty. When Congress tried twice to censure him for introducing petitions against it, Adams conducted a brilliant defense, accusing supporters of gag rules of suppressing the constitutional right of petition and interfering with the most basic of civil liberties, the right of legislators to speak their minds freely in Congress.

By 1841–42, Adams had more support, especially from Joshua Giddings of Ohio and a number of other antislavery advocates in Congress. The abolitionist activists set up what Giddings dubbed a "select committee on Slavery," to plan a congressional strategy on abolition, do research and writing for congressional speeches on slavery, and print and circulate the speeches around the country since officially printed documents "would be far more valuable than abolitionist tracts and pamphlets" (Miller 1996, 405). In those days a congressman had no staff, so the members of the select committee made the unprecedented decision to use their own funds to rent rooms and hire a research assistant to do fact-finding for their speeches. They hired Theodore Weld, one of the most prominent abolitionist "agents" and speakers. Weld was also the leading researcher of the antislavery movement and had helped compile *American Slavery as It Is.* As an itinerant abolitionist speaker, Weld had helped convert three of the congressional members of the select committee to the cause, so he was a logical choice for staff. He agreed to do the work because "these men are in a position to do for the Anti-slavery cause by a single speech more than our best lecturers can do in a year" (405–6). The select committee was a strange hybrid somewhere between the NGOs that lobby Congress today and the modern committee or congressional staff. It was a forerunner of the modern network where activists and policymakers collaborated on a joint project motivated by principled ideas.

With the rise of new antislavery leadership in Congress, British abolitionist influence in the United States waned (Fladeland 1972, 342). Paradoxically, it was a transnational factor, immigration, that robbed the South of its historical dominance of political institutions. The "huge influx of foreigners into the North after 1820" affected the distribution of House seats and electoral votes, giving the North the possibility of gaining control of the Federal government (Fogel 1989, 319).

The task that fell to the new political antislavery leadership was one that only domestic leaders could carry out—a reinterpretation of the meaning of the Constitution. Before 1842, politicians and abolitionists alike believed that the Constitution prohibited the federal government from interfering with the issue of slavery. It was this "federal consensus" that had to be undermined for the antislavery campaign to proceed (Fogel 1989, 282). This interpretive task fell to the new political leadership in the House. With Weld's help, and following in the footsteps of Adams, they claimed for themselves the role of defenders of the Constitution. In a 1937 pamphlet, Weld first developed the theory that freedom was national and slavery local, so whenever an individual left a slave state's jurisdiction, in the territories, in the District of Columbia, or on the high seas, "freedom instantly broke out." In 1842, Congressman Giddings used such a theory to turn the classic arguments of southern slaveholders against them. In an argument that grew out of the work of the select committee, he claimed that "if the Federal Government had no constitutional right to interfere with slavery in any way" then it followed that the federal government "had no constitutional right to support it."[8] This line of argument then allowed the antislavery members to challenge the fugitive slave laws and the legalization of slavery in Washington, D.C. With the population shift to the North and savvy coalition building by some of the antislavery forces, this reframing helped the new Republican Party put together a fragile but winning coalition in the 1860 elections that brought Lincoln to power (205).

The outbreak of the Civil War did not immediately unify the Anglo-American antislavery alliance around a strong common purpose. Many leaders in the antislavery campaign were pacifists and found it hard to support any war. The carnage and destruction on the battlefield appalled British humanitarians, some of whom were sympathetic to the South's claim that it was fighting for independence against an imperial North. Particularly troubling was the fact that the leaders of both the South and the North denied that slavery was a cause of the war. Although "the most explosive confrontations between North and South throughout the antebellum period related to slavery," political constraints prevented both northern and southern leaders from identifying slavery as the source of the conflict (H. Jones 1992, 16). Lincoln understood that many northerners were unwilling to fight to free blacks and that an antislavery campaign could even drive the border states out of the Union. Yet his refusal to make emancipation a war aim left an increasingly moribund abolitionist movement in Britain in disarray and allowed the British government to focus on its commercial interests rather than moral issues (16).

Southern leaders believed that the British textile mills' dependence on southern cotton would force the British government to recognize and support the Confederacy. "Nobody but crazyheaded abolitionists ever supposed for a moment that England would not recognize the Southern Confederacy" the *Richmond Whig* declared in early 1861 (Jenkins 1974, 1:5). Still, Confederate leaders understood that vocal support of slavery would not help their cause to gain British support.

The southern leaders were not just engaging in wishful thinking. By mid-1862, the three most powerful men in the British government, Prime Minister Palmerston, Foreign Minister Lord John Russell, and Chancellor William Gladstone, were all leaning toward offering to mediate the Civil War jointly with France. This would have favored the South and most likely would have provoked a northern refusal followed by British recognition of the Confederacy. Spurred by Confederate military victories, which made southern separation appear irrevocable, by economic distress in the British textile industry, where almost a third of the mills were closed, and by popular distress at the war's carnage, British leaders felt that public opinion would support the peacemaker (H. Jones 1992, 151, 165).

By early 1863, well before the decisive military victories at Gettysburg and Vicksburg that turned the tide of the war in the Union's favor, the British leaders had changed their minds and instead maintained a policy of "wait and see" neutrality. What led to this shift in British policy?

One factor was Lincoln's September 1862 Emancipation Proclamation, which reinvigorated the antislavery movement and clarified the moral dimension of the conflict (Owen 1994, 111). Initially the British press and public pointed to the hypocrisy of freeing slaves in territories over which Lincoln had no control and perceived the proclamation as an incitement to slave revolt in the South (Jenkins 1974, 2:176; H. Jones 1992, 225). In the aftermath of the Indian Mutiny, British fear of "servile insurrection" played a role "in shaping and distorting" the initial response (Jenkins 1974, 2:158).

Yet the proclamation also reinvigorated the antislavery movement, which organized a series of large meetings and rallies in support of the Union in December 1862 and January 1863. When the feared slave revolt in the South failed to materialize, British leaders began to understand the long-range implications of Lincoln's proclamation. It paved the way for the end of slavery, and it clarified the war aims of the North so that any British offer to mediate the conflict put the country in the position of condoning slavery.[9]

In the end, antislavery sentiment in Britain was "one of a combination of influences" that helped keep the British from recognizing the Confederacy and extending aid to it, an act that most agree could have altered the outcome of the Civil War (Fladeland 1972, 386). Considering how close the British came to recognizing the South, each factor weighing against intervention was important. William Seward, Lincoln's secretary of state, convinced the British that his government would perceive any intervention as a hostile move, with all the complications that entailed for the unprotected border with Canada. Neutrality in the Civil War also kept Britain's hands free to handle difficult diplomatic situations in Europe. But there was also a moral dimension to the debate. The Emancipation Society's campaign helped mobilize British public opinion in favor of the North, convincing leaders that any policy that appeared to favor the slave states would be divisive and unpopular (Jenkins 1974, 2:269; Owen 1994, 114).

In the case of abolition, a nascent transnational advocacy network, mobilized around a moral issue and using some tactics similar to those of modern social movements networks, succeeded first in helping create abolition as a pressing political issue in the United States and then, when the issue ultimately contributed to war, became a crucial factor in preventing British recognition of the South.

The International Movement for Women's Suffrage

Historians and international relations scholars have paid remarkably little attention to the international dimensions of movements for women's suffrage. Recent historical research, however, stresses the mutual influence and international cooperation among suffrage movements around the world (Dubois 1994, 254). Nancy Cott argues that "anyone investigating feminism at the turn of the twentieth century cannot fail to recognize that she or he is looking at an international movement, one in which ideas and tactics migrated from place to place as individuals in different countries traveled, looked for helpful models, and set up networks of reform" (1994, 234).

The international movement for women's suffrage began with women's involvement in antislavery organizations in Britain and the United States. Their experience at the World Anti-Slavery Conference in 1940, when the English majority refused to seat women, spurred Lucretia Mott and Elizabeth Cady Stanton to press forward with an organized movement for women's rights that led to the historic meeting of 1848 at Seneca Falls, New York. Likewise, an early split in the suffrage movement in the United States came when suffragists' Republican allies supported the ballot for freed male slaves but not for women. Parallel to the contribution that the civil rights movement and "freedom summer" made to the women's movement in the 1960s and 1970s, these early connections and evolutions remind us that besides diffusing repertoires movements in their shortcomings sow the seeds of future movements (McAdam 1988).

When Elizabeth Cady Stanton first suggested a suffrage resolution at the Seneca Falls meeting in 1848, even her most resolute supporters were afraid that it might make the movement look ridiculous and compromise their other goals (Griffith 1984, 54). Voting was considered the quintessential male domain of action. Other issues, such as equality before the law in matters of property, divorce, and children, better pay for working women, equal access to jobs and education, and application of the same moral codes to the behavior of men and women, were much less controversial than the proposal that women should vote. Resolutions regarding these issues passed unanimously, while the suffrage resolution was carried by a small majority and only after eloquent speeches by Cady Stanton and abolitionist Frederick Douglass (Buhle and Buhle 1978, 96–98).

We might consider these other initially "less controversial" issues present in 1848 at Seneca Falls the "noncases" with which to compare women's suffrage. Why did suffrage, originally perceived as more radical, become the goal of a successful global campaign while some of the other issues were still unresolved? We argue that suffrage, like slavery, was a clear example of denial of the most basic legal equality of opportunity. The causal chain was short: the law (and the state behind the law) denied women the right to vote. The solution, a change in the law, was simple. The issue lent itself to framing and action that appealed to the most basic values of the liberal state—equality, liberty, and democracy.

Like the abolitionists, most early women's rights advocates were motivated by the religious revival movements. The slogan of Susan B. Anthony, for example, was "resistance to tyranny is obedience to God." Other early suffragists, instead of asserting that women are entitled to equal rights and citizenship by virtue of being human (the liberal human rights idea), framed their arguments in terms of women's difference from men and the unique qualities, such as morality or nurturing, that they could bring to the public realm (Berkovitch 1995, 21). Opponents of women's suffrage also believed that women were different, claiming that if given the vote women would be too conservative, too tied to the church, or too supportive of banning alcoholic beverages. Nineteenth-century campaigns against prostitution and trafficking in women ("white slavery") or for special protective legislation for women workers were thus premised on the idea that women's vulnerability and fragile nature required special protection (23–46).

Although many domestic suffrage organizations were active in the nineteenth century, it was not until 1904, when women's rights advocates founded the International Woman Suffrage Association (IWSA), that an international campaign for suffrage based on an Enlightenment frame of equal rights was launched (Berkovich 1995, 46–50). In fact, there were three or four overlapping campaigns with different degrees of coordination. Suffrage groups were often divided by political and personal differences and disagreed over the same kinds of choices that modern movements and networks face: single issue focus versus broader demands, lobbying and political tactics versus grassroots organizing, and radical civil disobedience versus legal forms of opposition.

Unlike the antislavery movement, the women's suffrage movement relied more on symbolic and pressure politics than information politics. The problem women faced was more about entrenched social attitudes and practices than lack of information or understanding. Nowhere did women find more powerful organizations, such as other governments, willing to use their leverage or devote resources to promote women's suffrage beyond their borders. The British government initiated an active global antislavery campaign after 1834, but it never made votes for women a foreign policy demand. Nor were suffrage organizations able to use accountability politics, for no government would accept international obligations about suffrage to which it could later be held accountable. As a result, women used symbolic politics more than any other tactic, and when their peaceful tactics produced meager results they sometimes turned to civil disobedience and provocation. Many activists were prepared to break the law to gain attention for their cause and to go to jail to defend their beliefs.

The first and often overlooked international organization promoting women's suffrage was the World's Women's Christian Temperance Union (WCTU). Because it believed that the vote would allow women to secure prohibition and physical security for themselves and their children, the WCTU changed from a conventional Protestant women's group to a politically aggressive organization fighting for a wide range of issues, including suffrage (DuBois 1994, 256). One WCTU activist traveled all over the world, "leaving in her wake some 86 women's organizations dedicated to achieving woman's suffrage" (Nolan and Daley 1994, 13). Everywhere that women gained the vote between 1890 and 1902—Australia, New Zealand, and the states of Wyoming, Utah, Colorado, and Idaho—the "members of the WCTU were by far the most numerous among the suffragists" (Grimshaw 1994, 34). The WCTU was especially important for the early enfranchisement of women in New Zealand and Australia; suffragists from those countries later traveled to Europe and the United States to spread the story of how they had won the vote and what it meant to them.

The second strand of the international women's suffrage movement came from the women's groups associated with the Second Socialist International. In 1900, the Socialist International passed the first pro-woman suffrage resolution, but suffrage only became a fundamental demand of socialist parties in 1907 (DuBois 1994, 262). Socialist women around the world were not supposed to cooperate with "bourgeois suffragists," but in practice socialist and nonsocialist advocates for woman suffrage cooperated extensively.

The third strand of the international movement was the independent, militant suffragettes (so-called to distinguish them from the more moderate suffragists). The suffragettes advocated public agitation, civil disobedience, and eventually even violent tactics to further their demand for the vote. By confronting speakers at meetings, chaining themselves to fences in front of government buildings, throwing stones through windows, and participating in street demonstrations that often ended in clashes with police and hostile male spectators, the suffragettes invited imprisonment, and once jailed they engaged in hunger strikes and were fed by force. The best-known suffragette organization was the Women's Social and Political Union (WSPU) in Great Britain, under the leadership of the Pankhurst family, whose tactics had tremendous international influence. Although it did not endorse the more militant tactics of the suffragettes, the International Woman Suffrage Association "provided a conduit for their influence" (DuBois 1994, 267). In their regular international meetings, suffragette militancy spread among IWSA members, who brought it back to their home countries. American suffragists who participated with the WSPU in Great Britain later took its militant approach and tactics back to the United States to lead the more militant wing of the women's movement there (Holton 1996, 109, 155).

A fourth strand of the international suffrage movement included women gathered in the International Council of Women (ICW), founded in 1888. Although after 1904 it adopted a strong women's suffrage stand, the ICW was not prepared to give the issue priority over the other issues on its agenda, which included demands for equal pay for equal work, access to professions, maternity benefits, suppression of traffic in women and children, peace and arbitration, the protection of female and male workers, and "development of modern household machinery to relieve women from household drudgery" (*Women in a Changing World* 1966, 23, 27). Although not at the forefront of the movement, the ICW contributed by promoting communication among women's organizations in diverse countries. Furthermore, it worked actively with intergovernmental organizations and conferences, including the International Peace Conferences at the Hague and the League of Nations. In 1907, it was one of only two international nongovernmental organizations whose delegations the president of the Second Peace Conference at the Hague consented to receive (141). This may be the earliest example of the now established practice of granting NGOs a special role in international conferences.

The focused and militant IWSA expanded more rapidly than the ICW did in the early twentieth century: eleven countries were represented at the IWSA's founding conference in 1904, while forty-two were there at its tenth congress in 1926.[10] International congresses took place approximately every two years, and between them suffrage leaders and activists kept in touch with each other through letters, exchanges of books and pamphlets, visits, and speaking tours.[11] Despite their different national backgrounds, these women developed a common way of thinking. The correspondence of two leaders from the Netherlands and Hungary in the early 1900s, for example, reveals that despite totally different social and political situations "these two were able to describe all kinds of events in similar terms. The common language encouraged a feeling of solidarity" (Bosch and Kloosterman 1990, 15).

Suffrage activists testified that their international connections provided support, inspiration, and ideas for tactics and strategies. As with the antislavery movement, ideas and tactics spread through the travel of key activists, family connections, and exchanges of letters, pamphlets, and newspapers. Some of the main tactics used symbolic politics to highlight the conflict between the discourse of equality and democracy and the actual situation of women. When Elizabeth Cady Stanton and her colleagues composed the Seneca Falls "Declaration of Sentiments" of 1848, they used the language of the Declaration of Independence to frame the demands for women's rights. According to one of her biographers, "Cady Stanton's appropriation of the Declaration of Independence was a brilliant propagandistic stroke. She thereby connected her cause to a powerful American symbol of liberty" (Banner 1980, 40). Similarly when a small handful of women's rights activists in the United States began tax protests, refusing to pay taxes on their property until they were permitted to vote, one activist explicitly drew on the Revolutionary War slogan of "no taxation without representation" and requested that the local authorities choose the Fourth of July to auction her property in payment (Sterling 1991, 367–72). Although the tactic did not catch on in New England, it was adopted in England by radical suffragists in the early twentieth century (Holton 1996, 107, 11–12, 155, 163, 167, 174). American suffragists also took symbolic advantage of the 1876 centennial anniversary of the American Revolution to press their demands for women's rights.

Transnational linkages between U.S. and British suffragists played an important role in a crucial principled and tactical debate among British suffragists over how inclusive the demand for women's suffrage should be. Voting in Britain was still linked to property, and married women could not own it. Many suffragists believed that demanding the vote for married women was too extreme and thus advocated a more limited suffrage for spinsters with property. British radical suffragists believed that activists must demand the vote for all women and linked their demand to the need to further democratize British society and extend the vote to all men as well. Suffrage activists in the United States supported the position of advocating the vote for both married and single women. Elizabeth Cady Stanton, who visited England frequently, attempted to "strengthen the resolve" of her British allies on this issue. Her diary records that she tried to impress upon her colleagues that "to get the suffrage for spinsters is all very well, but their work is to elevate the position of women at all points. . . . That the married women of this movement in England consent to the assumption that they are through marriage, practically represented and protected, supported and sheltered from all the adverse winds of life, is the strongest evidence of their own need for emancipation."[12] Radical suffragists were more active in international networks than the more moderate British leaders, perhaps because of "their more marginal standing in their own country," and the international connection served "as a valued endorsement of their own distinct identity" (Holton 1996, 65). Cady Stanton contributed to the formation of the first suffrage organization in Britain to "formulate its demand in terms which expressly included married women" and drew upon "the transnational network" formed by her and her friends and colleagues for its early support (76). Although the radicals were a minority in the British suffragist movement, their inclusive position eventually became the dominant one within the British women's movement and around the globe. So resounding was the success of this position that we usually forget that British suffragists initially failed to advocate the vote for married women.

Speaking tours were an especially effective way of spreading the suffrage movement internationally. In 1913, two leaders of IWSA traveled to Asia and the Middle East. Upon their return, one reported "the tangible results of our trip are that we are connected with correspondents representing the most advanced development of the woman's movement in Egypt, Palestine, India, Burma, China, Japan, Sumatra, Java, and the Philippine and Hawaiian Islands, and also in Turkey and Persia, which we did not visit" (Whittack 1979, 52). National suffrage societies from four of the countries they visited became members of the IWSA over the next ten years. The formation of a women's suffrage organization did not always lead to winning the franchise. Women in Switzerland, for example, first demanded suffrage in 1868 but did not receive it until 1971. Yet most states granted suffrage after decades of focused organization by women's groups. Founding dates of national suffrage organizations are often twenty to thirty years earlier than the dates on which suffrage was granted.

Sometimes international congresses headlined the issue effectively enough to promote national debates. In the Netherlands, host to the 1908 International Congress of the IWSA, the press provided a great deal of generally favorable coverage. Membership in the national suffrage organization grew from about 2,500 to 6,000, and men founded a Men's League for Woman Suffrage. Dutch women won the franchise in 1919, and the 1908 conference was viewed as "a decisive breakthrough to the Dutch public which until then had stood somewhat aloof" (Bosch and Kloosterman 1990, 46).

The United States, Canada, and many European countries granted women the right to vote in the years during and immediately following World War I. Many woman suffragists joined in the patriotic war effort, but others used the war aims as yet another symbolic vehicle to press for women's suffrage. Militant activists in both the United States and Britain pointed to the hypocrisy of fighting a war to make the world safe for democracy while at the same time denying it to half of their own populations. Subsequently, international suffragism focused on Latin America, the Middle East, and Asia, in part through the activities of some of the same international organizations (e.g., the IWSA, renamed the International Alliance for Women) and in part through larger working-class movements and revolutionary nationalism (DuBois 1994, 270–71).

The international campaign for women's suffrage led to surprisingly rapid results. Suffrage was almost unimaginable even for visionary advocates of women's rights in 1848. It took until 1904 to found the first international organization dedicated primarily to the promotion of women's suffrage, the IWSA. Yet less than fifty years after the founding of the IWSA, almost all countries in the world had granted women the vote. As new countries formed in the wake of decolonization, they enfranchised women because of women's contribution to the independence struggle but also because suffrage was now one of the accepted attributes of a modern state. The international campaign for women's suffrage is a key part of the explanation of how votes for women moved from unimaginable to imaginable and then to standard state behavior.

Conclusions

The two historical campaigns examined in this chapter suggest some insights for the study of modern transnational movements and advocacy networks. They clearly indicate that transnational social movements and networks are not an entirely new phenomenon. Both the antislavery and women's suffrage movements involved fully activated networks whose dynamics were very similar to modern networks and social movements. They differed mainly in the speed of communications and the kinds of actors involved.[13] The antislavery societies' connections to and pressures on actors in the state foreshadow the work of modern NGOs and networks, as does their emphasis on gathering facts and testimony. Intergovernmental organizations and private foundations that play a central role in modern networks were absent; their place was taken by private philanthropy.

Nevertheless, the number, size, professionalism, density, and complexity of international linkages among modern transnational social movements and networks have grown so dramatically in the last three decades that the modern transnational social movement sector differs substantially from its historical precursors. As Hugh Heclo remarked about domestic issue networks, "if the current situation is a mere outgrowth of old tendencies, it is so in the same sense that a 16-lane spaghetti interchange is the mere elaboration of a country crossroads" (1978, 97).

A second insight from these historical precursors has to do with the time span over which one can evaluate the success of movements. Both movements were eventually very successful, but the time span over which success is measured was one of decades and even centuries. Historians suggest that such change was relatively rapid: "It is remarkable how rapidly, by historical standards, the institution of slavery gave way before the abolitionist onslaught, once the ideological campaign gained momentum. . . . [W]ithin the span of little more than a century, a system that had stood above criticism for 3,000 years was outlawed everywhere in the Western world" (Fogel 1989, 204–5). These campaigns also suggest that, although early change comes very slowly and with great difficulty, with time change may develop a momentum of its own. For women's suffrage, it took more than eighty years, from the Seneca Falls conference in 1848 until 1930, for twenty states to adopt women's suffrage. In the next twenty years, from 1930 to 1950, some 48 countries adopted women's suffrage laws (Ramirez et al. 1997).

While there is still inadequate information to make a conclusive argument, it also seems likely that the speed of normative change has accelerated substantially in the later part of the twentieth century as compared to these earlier movements. This is not surprising given the new speed of communication and transportation, but the cases of suffrage and abolition may still be useful in reminding activists and scholars that change often happens very slowly.

These movements suggest that the international or transnational dimension of movements was essential for the success of the campaigns but also that transnational influences may have more impact at some stages of campaigns than at others. In the antislavery campaign, transnational influences were especially important at the early stages in the United States, when gag rules blocked consideration of slavery in the U.S. Congress, and then later, when the antislavery movement helped discourage the British government from intervening in the Civil War on behalf of the South.

A quantitative analysis of the cross-national acquisition of suffrage rights reveals a different dynamic at work for early and late adopters of women's suffrage (Ramierz et al. 1997). Prior to a threshold point of 1930, no country adopted women's suffrage without strong pressure from domestic suffrage organizations. At this point, both a strong domestic movement and international linkages were important for achieving suffrage. Between 1890 and 1930, Western countries with strong national women's movements were most likely to grant female suffrage. After 1930, however, international and transnational influences became particularly important for norm adoption, and some countries adopted women's suffrage even though they faced no strong domestic pressure to do so.

But strong and dense linkages between domestic and foreign actors does not in and of itself guarantee success for a transnational movement. Advocacy campaigns take place in organizational contexts; not only must their ideas resonate and find them allies, but their organizations must overcome the opposition their opponents array against them. In the language of social movement theory, we must consider them as parts of "multiorganizational fields" (Klandermans 1992). The antislavery campaign was a very strong transatlantic network that confronted powerful, entrenched, economic interests with a well-developed ideology, strong political representation, and institutional and legal support in the state's rights provisions of the U.S. Constitution. The early abolition movement in Britain faced a weaker and smaller opposition—mainly from the British West Indies planter class. The British women's suffrage groups were the best organized among the national members of international suffrage organizations, but suffrage was granted in New Zealand, Australia, Finland, Denmark, Norway, and the USSR, as well as in a number of U.S. states, before women received the vote in Britain.

Finally, what about the argument that moral campaigns are thinly disguised efforts to further other interests? Abolitionists in Britain often combined antislavery principles with support for British imperialism. They believed that imperialism would spread Christianity, westernization, and the benefits of trade and ingenuously saw no contradiction among these principles (Craton 1974, 293; Fogel 1989, 388). Suffragists sometimes argued that educated and cultured women had a better claim to the vote than uneducated, immigrant men or former slaves.

Activists sometimes saw the victim as an unproblematic "other" who needed their assistance, and the reformers rarely recognized their own paternalism. Nevertheless, the British antislavery activists did not reserve their criticism for the foreign or distant other but displayed equal if not greater paternalism and vehemence when talking about the United States. Activists portrayed southern slaveholders as vile and evil. Although some freed blacks like Frederick Douglass played prominent roles in the transatlantic campaign, for the most part the "victims" of slavery were absent from the movement. The frequent inability of reformers to transcend their historical setting, however, does not undermine the significant challenges they made to dominant social and political orders or their contributions to political transformation.

NOTES

1. This chapter draws on material from chapter 2 of our book *Activists beyond Borders: Advocacy Networks in International Politics* (1998). We thank Cornell University Press for granting permission to use it here. Although much of what we say here is relevant to the study of transnational social movements, we prefer to use the term *transnational advocacy networks.* A transnational advocacy network *includes those relevant actors working internationally on an issue who are bound together by shared values, a common discourse, and dense exchanges of information and services.*

2. Sidney Tarrow, for example, in his historical survey of social movements, focuses mainly on national movements, although he discusses the transnational diffusion of repertoires of collective action and concludes with a section on the increasing transnationalization of modern social movements (1994, 193–98). In a recent essay, Tarrow (1995b) expresses some skepticism that the world is now entering an "unheralded age of global movements" and encourages "comparatively bold historical studies" of transnational movements.

3. Protests against slavery began much earlier; Quakers in Pennsylvania, for example, first protested it in the 1680s. But the real movement spans the time from 1787, when British abolitionists launched a public campaign against the slave trade, to the emancipation of slaves in Brazil in the 1880s (see Fogel 1989, 205). Surveys of the antislavery movement by political scientists are provided in Tarrow 1994, Ray 1989, and Nadelmann 1990.

4. Quoted in Fladeland 1972, 260.

5. For an overview of the debate among historians, see Davis 1987, Ashworth 1987, and Haskell 1987. For political scientists, see Ray 1989 and Nadelmann 1990.

6. This debate is the subject of William Lee Miller's fascinating book, *Arguing about Slavery: The Great Battle in the United States Congress* (1996).

7. Southerners had held the presidency for forty out of fifty-two years, the speakership of the House for twenty-eight of thirty-five years, a majority on the Supreme Court and in the Cabinet, and "every Senate President pro-tem since the ratification of the Constitution" (Fogel 1989, 339).

8. This is the line of argument that Giddens took in the Creole case (Miller 1996, 454; Fogel 1989, 336).

9. See Owen 1994, 113–14; Jenkins 1974, 2:153–55, 398; and H. Jones 1992, 171–93.

10. See Whittick 1979, 32, 92. Delegates from eight countries were present at the founding meeting of the ICW in 1888, and by the seventh meeting, in 1925, approximately twenty-eight countries were represented (*Women in a Changing World* 1966, 53, 203, 350).

11. See Griffith 1984, 181, 193, 214; and Bosch and Kloosterman 1990.

12. Quoted in Stanton and Blatch 1922, as quoted in Holton 1996, 63.

13. Tarrow has challenged transnational social movement researchers to identify whether "the new technology of global communications and cheap internal travel are changing the dynamics of movement diffusion or only the speed of its transmission" (1995b, 22).

CHAPTER 3

State Terror, Constitutional Traditions, and National Human Rights Movements: A Cross-National Quantitative Comparison

Patrick Ball

Introduction

According to one data source, there were 69 domestically focused, human rights nongovernmental organizations (HRNGOs) in the world in 1970; by 1992, there were more than 659.[1] Not all countries experienced this increase equally. Among relatively repressive countries in 1992[2], Ethiopia, Indonesia, and the Democratic People's Republic of Korea (DPR-Korea) had 4 or fewer human rights groups, while Peru, the Philippines, and South Africa each had 40 or more. Why are these countries so different? What explains the relative importance of this kind of social movement to people in different countries?

Human rights groups are founded by activists who find human rights to be a convincing and compelling language with which to criticize state violence. Activists who find human rights to be relatively more compelling are more likely to found human rights organizations than are activists who find such arguments less relevant. And activists in countries with indigenous rights traditions, based primarily in liberal consitutions, are more likely to find the language of international human rights to be compelling relative to activists in countries without such traditions—at least during the early years of domestic human rights organizations' formation, 1977–83.

Sometime in the middle of the 1980s, the language of human rights became sufficiently general throughout the world that the local origins of human rights activism became less relevant to potential HRNGO founders. Instead, the international public sphere of the human rights debate grew large enough for individuals in countries without indigenous liberal traditions to become aware of the international interest in claims made in terms of rights. This explanation is therefore explicitly limited to the "early adopters," the first countries in which human rights groups emerged.

The explanation proposed in this chapter examines nongovernmental, domestically focused, human rights organizations. These groups should be distinguished from international human rights organizations, including nongovernmental organizations like Amnesty International and intergovernment groups such as the United Nations (UN) Verification Mission in Guatemala (MINUGUA). Government groups, such as Dr. Leo Valladares's National Human Rights Commission in Honduras and quasi-governmental organizations such as the recently concluded Truth and Reconciliation Commission of South Africa, are also outside the scope of this study. Groups that fall within the explanation proposed here include the Legal Resource Centre of South Africa (LRC), the nongovernmental Human Rights Commission of El Salvador (CDHES), and the Prague Helsinki Committee. Previous studies of HRNGOs, including Scoble and Wiseberg 1981; Welch 1995; Waltz 1995; Crystal 1994; Brysk 1993, 1994; and Lowden 1996, have described HRNGOs in various countries, sometimes in comparative perspective. But none of the studies has proposed a more general theory about why these groups emerged in the countries that they did. This chapter will propose such an explanation.

The Emergence of International Human Rights Norms

Based on the victorious Allied powers' World War II war aims, the Universal Declaration of Human Rights (UDHR) established a liberal international "regime" (Donnelly 1989, 205ff.) without specifying an explicit philosophical basis for those claims (Burgers 1992; Sohn 1995; Hencken 1995; Nickel 1987). The hypothetical "liberal" regime mandated by the UDHR inter alia requires that states treat citizens with equality before the law, provide due process, and refrain from torture (Howard and Donnelly 1986; Donnelly 1987; Dworkin 1977). By agreeing to the UDHR, almost every state in the world accepted these norms.[3]

However, accepting the norms at an international level was not always followed by their implementation in domestic law. The wide range of constitutions in play after World War II (Murphy 1993, 7–9) guaranteed that the aspirations defined in the UDHR would be unevenly available to the world's people (Safran 1981; Früling 1993). But in countries where strong constitutional guarantees of individual rights echoed the international standards, and where those rights were routinely or massively violated by the state itself, the state acted hypocritically.

Hypocrisy by the powerful is an important theme in the analysis of social movements. Violations of the rules of the moral economy have been documented as among the most powerful motivations for moral outrage and consequent social movements (Thompson 1971; Scott 1976; Katznelson 1986; Moore 1978). Violations of human rights are even more powerful than most hypocritical acts because the norms being violated are universally accepted. Henkin (1990a) notes that when states violate human rights they are forced to conceal or deny their violations, or at least justify them. The hypocritical maneuvering opens opportunities for social movement activists to criticize state violence: if states deny responsibility for the violations, HRNGO activists can present evidence linking the state to the acts; if states try to claim that such actions are necessary, activists can challenge the claims in international forums, such as the Inter-American Human Rights Commission. The promises that governments make to citizens, in the forms of constitutional guarantees and international agreements, provide a structure for political opportunities. Actual violations of rights create concrete opportunities for activists to make uniquely powerful arguments in favor of social change. These arguments are uniquely powerful because rather than calling for a radical restructuring of society along new lines they are based in the claims to legitimacy the state has already made.

The language of universal human rights is a foundation of international and transnational discourse about state action, that is, the public sphere. The social movement organizations analyzed in this chapter—HRNGOs—are explicitly *not* transnational groups. They are locally based groups that focus on abuses by local officials. However, the power of such groups' arguments derives in part from the vocabulary of human rights defined in the international public sphere.

During the early 1980s, the Salvadoran CDHES made strong claims about actions taken by the government of El Salvador. By framing the state's actions as unjust according to the norms of the Universal Declaration of Human Rights, the CDHES was able to attract international attention, including funding from Europe, congressional and civil society delegations from the United States, and international campaigns on its behalf by Amnesty International. Only a few years earlier, other groups had made claims about similar actions by the government that had been framed as class oppression or un-Christian, and they had elicited noticeably less support. Obviously other factors contributed to the rise in international attention paid to El Salvador, but activists' use of an internationally understood vocabulary of injustice made their arguments more comprehensible and more compelling to the international audience.

The importance of the international audience should not be overstated. The emergence of the international human rights movement changed the political opportunity structure for activists resisting local state terror. In the mid-1970s, the UN's International Covenants came into effect, regional intergovernmental groups in the Americas became more powerful and effective, and a number of international nongovernmental organizations (NGOs) emerged to hear and amplify criticisms made at the local level. All of these developments made local groups more powerful and effective than they would have been on their own, but none was the proximate cause of local groups' formation. Nor do the international developments illuminate why activists in some countries adopted human rights language and others did not.

Hypotheses and Theory

Given state violence, more liberalism means more HRNGOs, and less liberalism means fewer HRNGOs. Three hypotheses combine my contentions about state violence with one operational definition of liberalism, as a constitutional tradition, in a testable form.

> I. Among countries at a similar level of state terror, those with stronger domestic and international legal commitments to rights will have more human rights groups.
>
> II. Among countries with similar formal commitments to human rights (including domestic guarantees and international treaties), those with more state terror will have more human rights groups.
>
> III. Although there may be macrolevel international differences between countries (e.g., population, national wealth, level of economic inequality, global region) that explain some of the differences in numbers of human rights organizations among countries, these differences will not exclude the effects suggested in the first and second hypotheses.

The hypotheses make predictions about the number of human rights groups in a given country. For this purpose, "human rights groups" are defined as groups that fit the following three criteria: (1) they are private groups, that is, neither governmental nor intergovernmental; (2) they address one or more issues of civil and political rights; and (3) they focus attention on their own countries. For the remainder of this chapter, these groups will be referred to as human rights nongovernmental organizations or HRNGOs. Also note that the first three hypotheses refer to differences among countries. At no point do I predict when in a given county's history human rights groups will emerge. Rather, the prediction is about which countries at any time would have more groups.

The first hypothesis suggests that more rights guarantees mean more HRNGOs, while holding state terror constant. If a country's educated activists have been extensively exposed to ideas about constitutional limits on just action by the state, and if the country has a long tradition of making guarantees to its citizens about the bounds of just state action, then activists will be more likely to respond to state terror by forming HRNGOs than activists in countries with weaker or more recent rights guarantees.

The second hypothesis suggests that countries experiencing state terror will have more HRNGOs relative to countries not experiencing state terror, controlling for state commitments to rights guarantees. The definition of HRNGOs suggested earlier includes only those organizations that focus on their own country. Activists in countries without state terror are unlikely to found organizations to combat it in their own countries. Activists in very violent countries without constitutional traditions are unlikely to found many HRNGOs because rights language and tactics would be less available to them relative to activists in countries with longer constitutional traditions. That is, it would be easier to cross the bridge from constitutional to human rights than from no rights to human rights.

The combination of the first and second hypotheses implies that countries with little state terror and a weak tradition of domestic or international guarantees will have few HRNGOs, while countries with much state terror and strong guarantees will have more HRNGOs. The combination of high state violence with strong guarantees leading to many HRNGOs is the hypocrisy hypothesis. States that violate promises they have made to their citizens are more likely to have more HRNGOs.

The third hypothesis suggests a set of control variables that should not exclude the effects of the first two. If HRNGOs tend to serve approximately the same constituency size, then countries with more people should have more HRNGOs. If HRNGOs are formed by middle-class professionals, then wealthier countries should have more HRNGOs. Finally, if one region of the world (e.g., Latin America; see Scoble and Wiseberg 1981, 9–10) tends to have relatively more HRNGOs, and its countries also have longer constitutional traditions and severe state terror, then the larger number of HRNGOs might simply be a coincidence of regional variation. The economic and population controls will be tested as additional independent variables in the regression runs. The regional difference will be tested by performing separate parallel regressions on countries in Latin America and countries not in Latin America.

Data and Measures

The hypotheses propose two independent and one dependent variable; these are the substantively important variables. The independent variables are (1) state terror and (2) domestic and international commitments to rights; the dependent variable is the number of HRNGOs in each country. In addition, there are three control variables: national wealth, national population size, and the region to which a country belongs. Measures are proposed for each of these six variables. Each measure of a particular variable may be calculated or transformed in various ways according to particular theoretical specifications or in order to conform to necessary statistical assumptions. For each measure, this section describes (1) the source and characteristics of the data and (2) any transformations appropriate for this measure. Note that the unit of analysis below is *country*[4] and that the analysis considers groups of countries at fixed points in time.

Measures of the Number of HRNGOs

Since 1976, Human Rights Internet (HRI) has built a data base on human rights organizations and other governmental and nongovernmental organizations. By means of periodic surveys, HRI develops directories of organizations so that organizations in the West and North can make contact with organizations in the South and East. Their objective is to collect information on all human rights organizations of any kind. In other work, I have found no systematic biases in HRI's data relative to those of other directories of human rights organizations (see Ball 1998, chap. 4).

HRI's data are structured by organization, with each classified according to its founding date, date disbanded (if appropriate), geographic location, type of organization, issues with which it concerns itself, and geographic area of attention. I chose only organizations that were not governmental, intergovernmental (i.e., UN), or regional (i.e., the Organization of American States, the Organization of African Unity); that had geographic foci that included their own countries; and that included at least one human-rights related theme. The information for some organizations that fulfilled these criteria is incomplete. For example, in 1989 the world average was 3.9 HRNGOs with complete information in the data set per country; these countries also had (on average) an additional 3.1 HRNGOs for which the year of founding is missing. Across all countries, the number of HRNGOs with and without founding information correlate at $r = 0.69$; thus, countries with more HRNGOs with complete data tend also to have more HRNGOs with missing founding dates. The analyses that follow are based on organizations for which the complete date data (founding and disbanding, where appropriate) are available. Even if the data on organizations in some countries are systematically less complete than in others, the analysis based on HRNGOs with available founding date information would be closely related to the entire population of HRNGOs, given the strength of the correlation. Figure 3.1 shows the distribution of numbers of HRNGOs in 1986.

The number of HRNGOs is very strongly skewed to the left of the distribution: zero is the modal category. Furthermore, three countries have relatively many HRNGOs, for example, thirty-seven or more in 1986.[5] The difference between zero and one (or between one and two) HRNGOs seems to me more important than the difference between thirty-five and forty such groups. In 1986, 90 percent of all countries for which data on all substantive and control variables are available (a subset of the countries in fig. 3.1) had nine or fewer HRNGOs. The predictions should be more meaningful among countries at the low end of the scale, that is, the 90 percent with nine or fewer HRNGOs. To reduce the variance, the square root of the number of HRNGOs found in the HRI data set will be used as the dependent variable. In situations in which a variable is highly skewed, such as the distribution shown here, using the square root tends to "civilize" the count, that is, bring it closer to normality (Tukey 1977, 83–84).[6] Given that this variable will be predicted in the regressions, it is helpful that it be closer to normally distributed.

Domestic and International Legal Commitments

The central idea in this chapter is that by making commitments to respect human rights state leaders enable political organizing based on those commitments. There are two kinds of commitments that governments make with respect to human

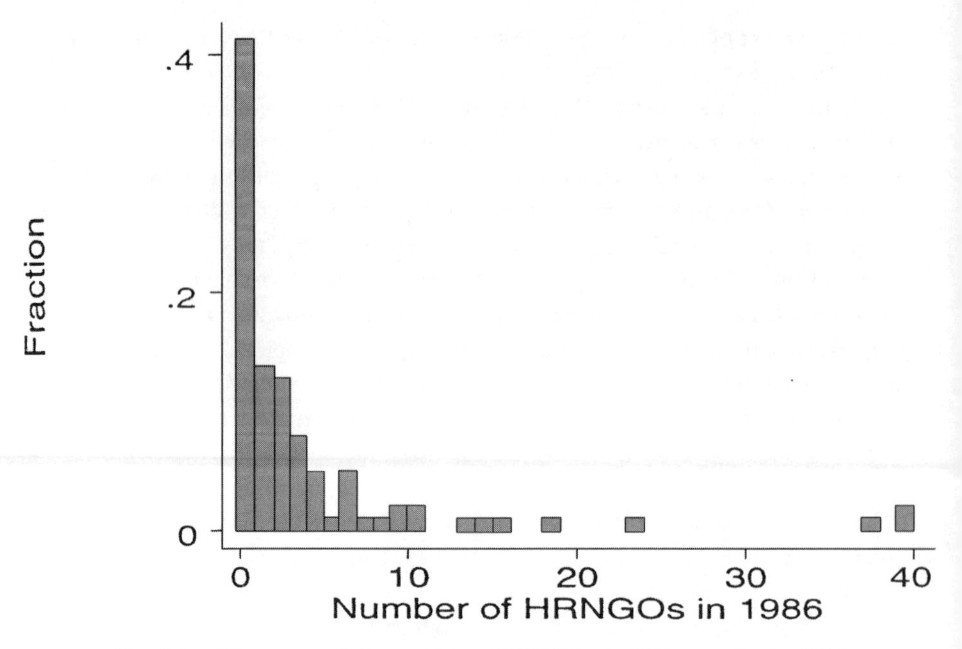

Fig. 3.1. Histogram of the number of HRNGOs in 109 countries in 1986. (Data from Human Rights Internet Masterlist, 1995.)

rights: constitutional guarantees to citizens and international agreements with other states. This section proposes measures for both concepts.

Measures of Constitutional Guarantees

Domestic legal commitments are constitutional guarantees. John Boli collected data on the constitutions of 153 countries at six points in time: 1870, 1890, 1910, 1930, 1950, and 1970 (see Boli-Bennett and Meyer 1978; and Boli-Bennett 1981). Not all countries existed in each of the six points at which the constitutions were coded, and of countries that existed not all had constitutions at all points. Since each coding point notes the year that the coded constitution took effect, the data are not limited to being cross sections at the coded years. The data are longitudinal and continuous.

Boli analyzed the constitution in effect during the focus year for the presence (in some cases coded for strength) or absence of approximately sixty rights and responsibilities. For this study, the nine civil and political rights most often violated by repressive regimes and invoked by HRNGOs were selected. These are the rights to: freedom of association, due process, equality before the law, sanctity of the home, inviolability of the person, freedom from cruel and inhuman punishment, petition for redress, free speech, and refusal to testify against oneself. The data set was reshaped so that each record represents one country in a specific year; these data were then merged with the HRNGO data. The measure for each of the nine rights in each year is the difference between this year and the year in which the right was first established in the country, that is, the age in this year of this right. The measure used in the analysis is the average age of the nine rights.

The average age of rights was chosen as the basis for this measure for several reasons. The constitutional tradition of a given country is composed by the entirety of the rights usually encompassed by a constitution. Although some rights are more important than others, they do not act individually to encourage HRNGO formation. Furthermore, I argue that it is not the existence of the rights but their tenure that provides a basis for activists. The tradition of rights gives activists the vocabulary and judicial precedent that provide HRNGOs with their intellectual basis. The current existence of particular rights is important, but recently emergent rights are less important than rights of long standing. People need to learn about rights, and the idea that government is limited in particular ways needs to be generalized throughout the society before state actions violating guarantees can be seen as hypocritical.

Because the measure of constitutionalism depends on the age of the tradition, variation in older constitutions is more important than variation among younger traditions. I argue that the difference between the effects of two versus three years of a given right is not the same as the difference between eighty-four versus eighty-five years. Instead, differences between later years are more important than differences between earlier years. The hypothesized effect of constitutional guarantees is the result of the development of a culture and vocabulary of rights as responses to perceived state injustices. For example, with each successive generation of university-trained lawyers who are versed in rights, an increasing number of ordinary citizens will be exposed as clients to the lawyers' suggestions about rights-based claims they can make against the state. Over time, a state limited by rights guarantees may accrue a longer judicial tradition that becomes increasingly difficult for state leaders to sweep aside while maintaining their legitimacy. Traditions about how and when guarantees can be suspended develop and are written into constitutions, which leaves state terrorists in the uncomfortable position of having to write elaborate justifications in order to evade outright hypocrisy and illegitimacy: the elaborate justifications for rights suspensions can themselves be the basis for human rights organizing (see Ball 1998, chap. 6). But all of these effects require time: time for the legal language of rights to enter the vocabulary of elite activists, time for judicial precedent and training to accumulate, and time for citizens to learn to associate state adherence with rights guarantees with legitimacy. The quantitative reflection of the time needed to develop a tradition will be the use of the squared average age of rights. In reverse of the measure of HRNGOs, in which the square root of the count will be used, the squared average age of the nine rights will be the measure of constitutional tradition.

International Rights Agreements

Following the logic of the previous section, international agreements are hypothesized to promote the formation of HRNGOs because each agreement gives domestic activists grounds on which to argue that certain state actions are illegitimate. Seven international agreements relevant to this idea are presented in table 3.1.

A country's adoption of the international norms begins the year it ratifies the treaty, thereby becoming a state party to the agreement. Thus, following the measure of constitutional guarantees, the measure of a given country's commitment to international legal norms in a given year is the average time to which the state has been a party to all the treaties listed in table 3.1. The values for this measure were calculated from the United Nations' listing of the dates on which countries became parties to the treaties listed.

Measure of State Terror

Michael Stohl and others read and coded the annual reports of Amnesty International (AI) and the country reports of the U.S. Department of State (DoS) for the period 1977–91 (see, e.g., Carleton and Stohl 1985, 1987; and Poe and Tate 1994). The coding was done using a scale produced by Raymond Gastil and others at Freedom House. Although the substance of the Freedom House ratings has come under substantial and well-founded criticism (e.g., Scoble and Wiseberg 1981b; Brockett 1992), Carleton and Stohl (1985) argue that the scale as such is a reasonable comparative device with which to measure states' repressiveness.[7] In general, a higher score reasonably reflects a higher level of violence noted by the par-

TABLE 3.1. International Human Rights Treaties with Dates Open for Signature

Treaty Name	Adopted by the UN General Assembly and Open for Signature
Convention on the Prevention and Punishment of the Crime of Genocide	1948
International Convention on the Elimination of All Forms of Racial Discrimination	1966
International Covenant on Civil and Political Rights	1966
International Covenant on Economic, Social, and Cultural Rights	1966
Optional Protocol to the International Covenant on Civil and Political Rights	1966
Convention on the Elimination of All Forms of Discrimination against Women	1979
Convention against Torture and Other Cruel, Inhuman, or Degrading Treatment or Punishment	1984

Source: United Nations web site http://www.un.org/Depts/Treaty/toc.html, October 1995.

ticular source. The most important part of the coding scheme is reproduced from Carleton and Stohl 1985, 212–13.

1 = "Countries . . . under a secure rule of law, people are not imprisoned for their views, and torture is rare or exceptional. . . . Political murders are extremely rare."

2 = "There is a limited amount of imprisonment for nonviolent political activity. However, few persons are affected, torture and beating are exceptional. Political murder is rare."

3 = "There is extensive political imprisonment, or a recent history of such imprisonment. Execution or other political murders and brutality may be common. Unlimited detention, with or without trial, for political views is accepted . . ."

4 = "The practices of level 3 are expanded to larger numbers. Murders, disappearances, and torture are a common part of life. In spite of its generality, on this level terror affects primarily those who interest themselves in politics or ideas."

5 = "The terrors of level 4 have been extended to the whole population. . . . The leaders of these societies place no limits on the means or thoroughness with which they pursue personal or ideological goals."

Stohl and his collaborators coded two sources, so that for each country there is one measure according to the U.S. Department of State reports and a second measure according to the Amnesty International annual reports. After examining both, I chose the AI measure because it is more likely to represent consistently the perceptions of the opposition intellectuals most likely to found human rights groups. The DoS reports may be systematically biased according to U.S. geopolitical interests. In regimes not then in favor with the United States, the DoS would be likely to overstate violations, whereas we might expect that the department would underreport violations in U.S.–backed regimes. In contrast, the AI report would be more likely to be free of this bias.[8]

The state terror measure is lagged one year relative to the measure of the number of HRNGOs. That is, the AI report for 1981 covers events and conditions in 1980. The code for year t corresponds to state terror experienced in year $t - 1$. Using this measure implies that the effect of state terror occurs quickly. Activists do not procrastinate in their response: once state terror begins, activists must respond by forming HRNGOs.

The measure is treated as continuous, although it is defined as merely ordinal. Ordinal measures may be used as if they were ratio variables (in which 2 is twice as great as 1) because in practice the difference is usually unimportant (Blalock [1960] 1979, 444). Using five dummy variables to represent the five levels on the state violence measures uses four more degrees of freedom in the model compared to using the measure as a single continuous variable. Given the very minor formal difference between using the measure as ordinal or continuous, a single continuous parameter will be used.

Control Measures

In the hypotheses, I suggest three other macrolevel factors that may influence the number of HRNGOs in a given country: overall wealth, population size, and global region. Measures for these variables are described below.

To measure the general national wealth, I chose its annual gross domestic product per capita. Although GDP excludes capital investment, human capital, and unexploited mineral wealth, the level of production in a country indicates the general level at which a given country is economically active. If national wealth influences the formation of HRNGOs, there should be a positive relationship between GDP and the number of existing HRNGOs in a given year. The GDP data are calculated in constant (1987) dollars; the data are from the Penn World Tables, version 5.6 (Summers and Heston 1991). Some country-years are missing from the tables; missing periods were linearly imputed using existing years in the data.

Countries with many people may have more HRNGOs than countries with fewer people. If HRNGOs have a normal constituency size, then ceteris paribus more people would mean more HRNGOs. The population data come from the World Bank's measure of population size in its Social Indicators of Development series (World Bank 1994).

Methods and Findings

The hypotheses proposed in the first section will be tested by several analytic measures. First, the distribution of the number of HRNGOs in countries is considered by region in figure 3.2 as the first test of the suggestion in hypothesis III that Latin American countries have many more HRNGOs than countries in other regions. Next, a visual test of the relationship between the age of a country's constitutional tradition, the level of state terror experienced by that country, and the number of HRNGOs in that country is presented in figure 3.3. Three sets of regression models (two models in each set) complete the analysis. In the first set, all countries for which there are complete data on the dependent and independent variables are compared. Based on the finding in figure 3.2, Latin America is considered separately. The second and third sets present regression analyses of identical models run against Latin American and non–Latin American countries.

Some regions of the world have many more HRNGOs than others; Scoble and Wiseberg (1981a) suggested that Latin America was particularly rich in HRNGOs in part because of its much longer history of state institutions relative to the postcolonial nations of Asia and Africa. A boxplot in figure 3.2 presents

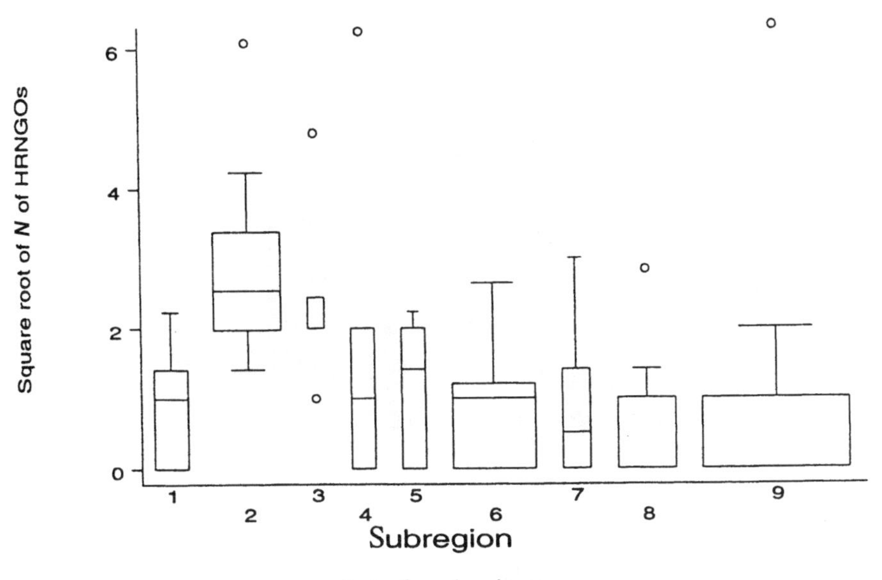

Codes for subregions:

1 = English- and French-heritage Americas
2 = Latin America (Spanish and Portuguese colonial heritage)
3 = South Asia
4 = Southeast Asia
5 = East Asia
6 = Catholic and Protestant Europe
7 = Orthodox Europe
8 = North Africa and the Middle East
9 = sub-Saharan Africa

Fig. 3.2. Boxplot of the number of HRNGOs (1986) by region

an overview of the distribution of the square roots of numbers of HRNGOs in each country by region. The regions include the English- and French-heritage Americas, Latin America (as defined previously), South Asia, Southeast Asia, East Asia, Catholic and Protestant Europe, Europe under the Orthodox churches, North Africa and the Middle East, and sub-Saharan Africa. Countries are grouped by common cultural and colonial heritages rather than strictly by geography. None of the Pacific nations are included because none has complete data for HRNGOs.

The width of each box is proportional to the number of countries included in that region: there are many countries in sub-Saharan Africa and relatively few in South Asia, and so box 9 is wide and box 3 is narrow. Several interregional variations should be noted. First, as Scoble and Wiseberg (1981a) observed, there are more HRNGOs in Latin America (Spanish, Portugese, and Dutch Heritage Americas) than in other regions, although South Asia is close. South Asia, however, has relatively few countries, and its relatively high regional average is skewed by India (with twenty-six HRNGOs in 1986). The finding for Latin America is more robust because of the much larger population represented by the distribution shown

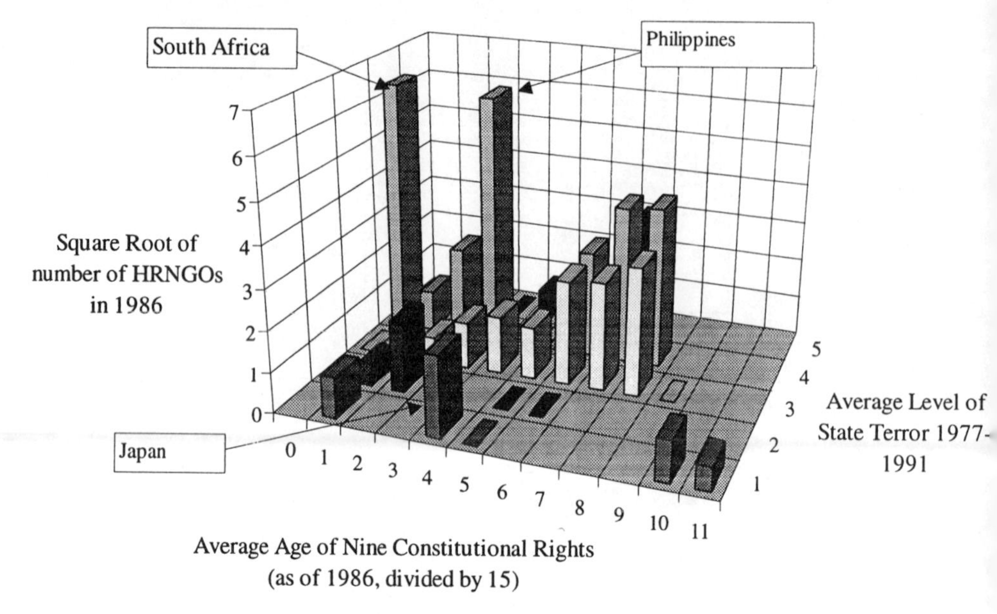

Fig. 3.3. Square root of the number of HRNGOs by average age of nine rights and average level of state terror

in the boxplot. Second, in Spanish and Portuguese America, Southeast Asia, and sub-Saharan Africa there are extreme outliers, three countries with many more HRNGOs than any others; the outliers in categories 2, 4, and 9 are represented by small dots far above the boxes. The outliers are Peru, South Africa, and the Philippines. The tremendous difference between Latin America and the other regions suggests that it should be treated differently in the analysis. Thus, in the regressions the regional difference will be considered in parallel regression models run separately for countries in and out of Latin America.

Figure 3.2 provides a visual test of the two substantive hypotheses. The height of the bars represents the average of the square root of the number of HRNGOs in countries that fall into each cell of the matrix. The matrix is organized by levels of the average age of nine rights (as of 1986) and by the average level of state terror experienced by that country during 1977–91. In order to spread the countries evenly, the ages of rights are divided into eleven categories.[9] Some combinations of age of rights and average level of state terror include more than one country; in these cases, the height of the bar indicates the average of the square roots of the number of HRNGOs in these countries.

Within a level of state terror, reading left to right in figure 3.2, the bars generally increase in height. This observation supports hypothesis I, that within a level of state terror countries with longer constitutional traditions have more HRNGOs.

Within a level of average age of constitutional rights, reading front to back, again the bars generally seem to increase in height, although there is less consistency and a major complication. This observation supports hypothesis II, that at a certain level of rights guarantees more state terror means more HRNGOs. There is one substantial inconsistency. Countries that on average experienced state terror level 5 have on average many fewer HRNGOs than countries that on average experienced state terror level 4, suggesting that as state terror increases to a level at which it is generalized throughout a society activists are no longer able to organize HRNGOs. The effect of extreme and generalized state terror may need to be understood in its local context since some countries at level 5 do have many human rights groups (see Ball 1998, chap. 5).

Several bars are much larger than predicted by the hypotheses. Three are noted on the graph: Japan, South Africa, and the Philippines. South Africa is the most poorly predicted case, and it is particularly interesting. It is coded by Boli as having no constitutional tradition because the South African constitution guaranteed no rights. Instead, rights were defined in the common law tradition in which rights were protected (when they were) by judicial processes, especially habeas corpus. Judicial remedies were available only to a very small proportion of the population. Even so, the tradition of legal process was so ingrained that the principal leader of the opposition to apartheid, Nelson Mandela, gained prominence as a lawyer and expressed throughout his life a profound commitment to the rule of law (Mandela 1994). The relative autonomy and extraordinary strength of the South African judiciary led to wide use of legal forms, including human rights, in opposition to apartheid (Abel 1995). Thus, without a constitutional tradition, strictly defined, South Africa had a relatively autonomous judicial sphere that provided HRNGO activists with the potential for action against state abuses. South Africa is worth an analysis of its own, but it is so extremely different from other countries that it will be dropped from the quantitative analysis. Despite the measurement problem with South Africa, this graph provides a rough beginning to confirmation of hypotheses I and II.

Although vivid, the test in figure 3.2 cannot incorporate the control variables or the measure of international human rights commitments. Nor does the figure provide a way to determine which effect (state terror or constitutional tradition) is stronger relative to the other. Further analytic tests of the hypotheses are presented in a series of regressions predicting the square root of the number of HRNGOs in a given country in each of two years. Regression models that include data on all countries in all years simultaneously are beset with problems of autocorrelation and heteroscedasticity. The hypotheses address only the differences among countries and do not consider when in each country's specific history activists might choose to found HRNGOs. Instead the prediction is that countries with older rights commitments will have more HRNGOs earlier than other countries. Cross-sectional analysis at particular time points adequately tests this question.

The test years 1983 and 1989 were chosen because they occur near the beginning and end of the development of national human rights movements. Before 1983, there were so few movements that no analysis is possible. In 1989, the democratization of the Soviet bloc fundamentally altered the international political opportunity structure. These two years are as far apart as possible without entering periods in which the data are either very sparse or mean something different. The first model presents a regression of the independent variables against the square root of the number of HRNGOs in a given country, including all the countries available for each year. The results are presented for 1983 and 1989 in table 3.2.

For this and the two tables that follow, a relatively loose significance test ($p < 0.10$) was chosen because there are very few cases. In both 1983 and 1989, all the coefficients for the three substantive independent variables are significant and in the predicted direction for both 1983 and 1989. Both models fit the data reasonably closely, with R^2 of approximately 0.32: the models explain approximately one-third of the variance on the dependent variable. Note that the beta coefficients for the three substantive variables are greater than 0.20, whereas the betas for the two control variables are less than 0.18. Thus, the control variables are weak and, with one exception, insignificant. Population has a very small effect in 1983, which disappears in 1989. This model provides strong evidence that both of the substantive hypotheses (I and II) are correct (see "Discussion"). The economic control can be excluded from further testing. The population control will be retained in order to consider the effect of population size in the analysis that controls for the effect of region. This model will be recalculated for the countries in Latin America (see table 3.3) and for the countries outside it (table 3.4). Note that there are a small number of countries for which the data on GDP were missing. Therefore, there are a few more countries in table 3.3 and table 3.4 together than in table 3.2.

TABLE 3.2. Unstandardized and Beta Regression Coefficients against the Square Root of the Number of HRNGOs, 1983 and 1989, for All Countries

	Year of Data			
	1983		1989	
Independent Variable	Unstandardized Coefficient	Beta	Unstandardized Coefficient	Beta
State terror	0.541***	0.450	0.460***	0.315
Average age of rights (squared)	4.24 E − 5**	0.246	4.31 E − 5*	0.208
Average age of treaties	0.069*	0.218	0.092***	0.336
GDP (per capita, constant $, 1987)	−8.30 E − 6	−0.024	−6.85 E − 5	−0.177
Population (millions)	1.47 E − 3*	0.169	3.75 E − 4	0.038
Constant	−1.185**		−0.387	
Number of observations	80		84	
Probability > F	0.000		0.000	
Adjusted R^2	0.329		0.325	

*$p < 0.10$. **$p < 0.05$. ***$p < 0.01$.

In Latin America, state terror does not have a significant effect in 1983, but it does positively influence the formation of HRNGOs in 1989. Relative to the effect of rights, however, the effect is weak. The standardized contributions of each independent variable can be compared by the beta coefficients. The beta coefficient of state terror in 1983 is less than one-third of the corresponding coefficient for the squared age of rights. Rights are still a stronger effect than state terror in 1989, although the difference is not as great as in 1983. Nonetheless, constitutional rights have a strong and consistent effect. Although the effect for each unit change is very small in 1983 (0.000209), the average of the squared rights variable is large (9,470). The net effect of the age of rights can be great. For example, the differ-

TABLE 3.3. Unstandardized and Beta Regression Coefficients against the Square Root of the Number of HRNGOs, 1983 and 1989, for Countries in Latin America

	Year of Data			
	1983		1989	
Independent Variable	Unstandardized Coefficient	Beta	Unstandardized Coefficient	Beta
State terror	0.280	0.210	0.451*	0.369
Age of rights (squared)	2.09 E − 4***	0.657	1.08 E − 4*	0.463
Age of treaties	−0.026	−0.052	0.011	0.038
Population (millions)	0.003	0.081	0.001	0.041
Constant	−0.719		0.437	
Number of observations	17		19	
Probability > F	0.029		0.031	
R^2	0.567		0.510	

*$p < 0.10$. **$p < 0.05$. ***$p < 0.01$.

TABLE 3.4. Unstandardized and Beta Regression Coefficients against the Square Root of the Number of HRNGOs, 1983 and 1989, for Countries not in Latin America

	Year of Data			
	1983		1989	
Independent Variable	Unstandardized Coefficient	Beta	Unstandardized Coefficient	Beta
State terror	0.255**	0.255	0.041	0.034
Age of rights (squared)	−7.22 E − 6	−0.050	−3.75 E − 5	−0.209
Age of treaties	0.070**	0.274	0.068**	0.300
Population (millions)	1.59 E − 3**	0.244	1.50 E − 3*	0.192
Constant	−0.445		0.536	
Number of observations	69		78	
Probability > F	0.015		0.053	
R^2	0.173		0.119	

*$p < 0.10$. **$p < 0.05$. *** = $p < 0.01$.

ence between the predicted number of HRNGOs for Guatemala and El Salvador in 1983, considering only the effect of their relative ages of constitutional rights, is 3.8.[10] Neither international human rights treaties nor population size meaningfully affects the predicted number of HRNGOs in Latin American countries. The models explain over half the variance on the dependent variable (0.56 and 0.51, respectively). Given the strength of the coefficients and the high proportion of variance explained, constitutional rights do have a significant and substantial effect on the formation of HRNGOs in Latin America.

The quantitative picture outside of Latin America is very different. The models from table 3.3 are reproduced for the countries outside of Latin America in table 3.4.

Although state violence is strong and significant in 1983, it disappears in 1989. In 1983, the difference between a relatively respectful country (level = 2) and a relatively repressive country (level = 4) accounts for a 0.5 difference in the predicted square root of the number of HRNGOs. The most important finding is that the age of rights is not significant, nor is it even close to significant in either year. In contrast to Latin America, the age of rights in the constitution has no relationship with the dependent variable. The age of treaties has the largest beta coefficient of any of the independent variables in both years. Furthermore, it is consistently significant, although it adds only a small bit of explanation to the model. In 1989, the difference in the predicted square root of the number of HRNGOs' international rights commitments in Canada (high international commitments) versus Cameroon (low international commitments) is 0.69, significant but not large. Population is also significant, and it explains a very small amount of variance. The increase from a country of five million people to a country of one hundred million adds about one-sixth to the square root of the predicted number of HRNGOs in both years. Relative to the model in Latin America, none of the independent variables explains much variation in numbers of HRNGOs, given that the R^2s are 0.17 in 1983 and 0.12 in 1989, respectively.

Discussion

In the whole-world model in table 3.2, all three substantive variables are significant and in the predicted direction. The level of state terror, constitutional rights, and the age of treaties all positively affect the predicted number of HRNGOs in a given country in both 1983 and 1989. In both years, the models predict about one-third of the variance in the number of HRNGOs among countries. These facts together give very substantial support to hypotheses I and II. In countries at the same level of state terror, the ones with longer constitutional traditions will tend to have more HRNGOs, and among countries with the same constitutional tradition the countries experiencing state terror will have more HRNGOs.

However, when the data are decomposed by region, the story is much more complicated. The conditions under which human rights organizations are formed in Latin America are different from those of the rest of the world. This may be in part because the decolonialization of Latin America occurred 150 years before the liberation of the colonial nations of Africa and Asia. The common experience of Latin American countries with high state terror, long domestic rights guarantees, and many HRNGOs relative to African and Asian countries, which are lower on each of the variables, determines the finding in table 3.2. The statistical relationships among Latin American countries' levels of constitutional tradition, state violence, and the number of HRNGOs confirm the hypotheses. As Scoble and Wiseberg (1981a) observed, the very different colonial history of Latin America has given its countries much longer to develop constitutions, courts, and civil society more generally. Since these are the conditions predicted to facilitate HRNGO formation, this finding seems especially important.

The finding that countries with relatively longer constitutional histories have more HRNGOs within Latin America bears further investigation. In table 3.5, the seventeen countries for which there are complete data in 1983 are shown according to the average age of nine constitutional rights and their levels of state violence.

As the regressions presented in table 3.3 would suggest, even within Latin America longer constitutional traditions mean more HRNGOs. The countries with

TABLE 3.5. Latin American Countries in 1983, by their Average Age of Rights and Level of State Violence

Age of Rights	Level of State Violence 1	2	3	4	5
62.3			*Cuba*		
64					*Guatemala*
76.1				Bolivia	
89.4			Haiti		
93		*Nicaragua*			
93.7		*Costa Rica*			
95.8				*Uruguay*	
100.5				Paraguay	
102.1			Venezuela		
103				Honduras	
105.1			**Mexico**		
106.5				**Colombia**	
109				**Peru**	
115.8					**El Salvador**
123			**Argentina**		
123.7				**Brazil**	
128.4				**Chile**	

Note: The five countries that have only one HRNGO are in italics and circled; the seven countries with more than five HRNGOs are in bold and boxed. The remaining countries have more than one but five or fewer HRNGOs.

more HRNGOs are concentrated toward the bottom of table 3.5, indicating that their constitutional traditions are longer than those of the countries in the rows nearer the top. Similarly, the countries with fewer HRNGOs are concentrated nearer the top of the table in rows indicating shorter constitutional traditions.

Although the countries with more HRNGOs are also found toward the right of the table, indicating that they are relatively repressive, the countries with fewer HRNGOs are spread evenly across the table. In Latin America, the effect of state terror is not as direct as the effect of the constitutional tradition. However, it is useful to note that the countries with many HRNGOs are those experiencing state violence. The explanatory problem is that some countries experiencing severe violence do not have many HRNGOs. The repressive countries with few HRNGOs are those with younger constitutional traditions (e.g., Guatemala relative to El Salvador[11] and Bolivia relative to Chile). State terror does not seem to have much influence in the absence of a constitutional tradition.[12] Despite limitations, the model predicts more than half the variance in the dependent variable, which gives very substantial support to the hypocrisy hypothesis.

The countries outside of Latin America present greater explanatory difficulties. Constitutional tradition explains none of the meager variance explained on the dependent variable (see table 3.4). State terror is an important influence in 1983, but not in 1989, which was the reverse of the effect in Latin America. The instability of the effect of state terror suggests that its effect may be related to influences not captured in this model. In particular, hypocritical terror may have the predicted effect while terror in states with few or no rights guarantees may not provide a basis for human rights claims (see Ball 1998, chap. 5).

Those countries outside of Latin America that tended to become states parties to international instruments earlier are consistently more likely to have more HRNGOs. This is another analysis of the hypocrisy hypothesis, generalized from hypotheses I and II: countries that violate promises they have made to respect rights will thereby open political space for human rights organizing. The promises a country makes are not limited to constitutional guarantees. For some countries, especially those of Eastern Europe following the Helsinki Accords, international agreements may have been more important than domestic guarantees (Korey 1993). This finding raises an additional question: how do international commitments affect HRNGO organizing? International commitments could give activists another mechanism for recognizing state hypocrisy. States with liberal origins, even those without constitutional traditions arising from those origins, might be more likely than states without liberal origins to become states parties to the international instruments. States that are vulnerable to pressure from more powerful countries might be more likely to join international agreements, and thus, repressive regimes that enter into international human rights agreements may be weaker or more dependent than repressive regimes that do not enter into international agreements. Human rights activists in weak states may benefit from the attention of the public in the weak states' patron countries. These questions deserve considerably more attention in future work. The absence of an effect of constitutional tenure on the predicted number of HRNGOs in countries outside of Latin America should also get attention. What other differences in national legal and judicial structures might HRNGO activists use as a basis for bridging to international human rights ideas and tactics?

Conclusions

Five conclusions can be drawn from this analysis. First, as Scoble and Wiseberg (1981a) predicted, the process by which activists found HRNGOs in Latin America is very different from the process in Asia or Africa. The difference is almost certainly related to the much greater length of time that the Latin American states have been independent relative to the postcolonial Asian and African states. There are two possible effects the greater age of rights might have; the first effect, constitutional tradition, has been explored here. However, the prevailing anticolonial ideology of the early nineteenth century, when the Latin American states became independent, was liberalism. By the middle of the twentieth century, when the Asian and African states gained independence, liberalism had declined as the anticolonial ideology in favor of Marxist nationalism. Thus, a lower age of rights may also correlate with less rights-friendly state founding ideologies. But even as liberalism declined as the ideology of choice for anticolonial revolutionaries the UDHR gained general international acceptance and was given the force of law by international covenants. Thus, in countries outside of Latin America the international agreements predicted HRNGO formation.

Given the difference between Latin America and the rest of the world, it is clear that constitutions have a huge effect in Latin America. The effect is consistent across time, and it is intuitively attractive when the countries are examined more qualitatively (see table 3.5).

Third, state terror plays an important role in HRNGO formation, but its effect is complicated by factors excluded from the model here. Extreme state terror has a much weaker effect than slightly less extreme state terror, as is shown in figure 3.2. The regression coefficient for state violence is not significant in Latin America in 1983 nor outside Latin America in 1989, but it is significant in Latin America in 1989 ($t = 0.075$) and outside Latin America in 1983 ($t = 0.035$). Given the relatively small number of cases in both regressions, these are substantial t-values. In addition to the curved, nonlinear effect of state terror between levels 4 and 5, it is very likely that some unmeasured influence on state violence is varying collinearly with it. Such an effect would explain the erratic significance of the parameter.

Fourth, international legal agreements are important in the absence of constitutional guarantees. The coefficients estimated for the effect of the tenure of international human rights guarantees had the strongest and most consistent effect of all the coefficients in the regressions run for countries outside Latin America. The absence of the effect of international guarantees in Latin America may be the result of domestic activists first using constitutional guarantees as their basis for human rights activism. Where such guarantees are absent, activists then turn to the international commitments their state leaders have made.

Fifth, a constitutional guarantee may not be the only indicator of a liberal tradition. As the brief reference to South Africa suggested, countries in the common law tradition may have rights guarantees, or at least legal recourse, outside the constitutional definitions. This avenue of organization for human rights activists should be considered in greater detail (see, e.g., Ball 1998, chap. 7).

This chapter has provided strong evidence for the hypocrisy hypothesis. During the period of early HRNGO formation, state hypocrisy led to the formation of HRNGOs. Activists exploited the weakness of the hypocritical position required by the international public sphere in order to stregthen claims for justice. In this use of hypocrisy lies an insight: although noble international agreements made by brutal state leaders may seem cynical or meaningless, in the context of a globalizing regime of international human rights, activsts have learned how to hold states accountable for these promises. The leaders of the apartheid regime and the rulers of the military dictatorships of Central America were each, in the end, dragged from power by social movements built on the norms and values of international human rights.

NOTES

1. This and other measures of nongovernmental human rights organizations come from the Human Rights Internet Masterlist, a data base compiled in 1995 providing information about organizations concerned with human rights and social justice worldwide.

2. "Relatively repressive" means countries with average Stohl codes of 4 or higher. DPR-Korea is missing this code for this year.

3. There continues to be debate about whether human rights norms are universal. For reviews, see Nickel 1987, Donnelly 1989, Freeman 1994, and Afshari 1993.

4. I recognize the possible problems with national tradition and country as units of analysis (e.g., McMichael 1990). For a historical-contextual interpretation of these ideas, see Ball 1998, chaps. 4–6.

5. The outlying countries are South Africa (forty), Peru (thirty-seven), and the Philippines (thirty-nine). The country with the next highest number of HRNGOs is India with twenty-six.

6. It is worth noting that the number of human rights groups in a country is very strongly correlated with the number that existed there in the previous year ($r = 0.99$). This makes intuitive sense: during the period being studied, funding for and international attention to human rights were increasing rapidly, and so human rights groups disband far less frequently than they are founded. Therefore, the number of groups in a country in a particular year is usually those that existed the previous year plus new ones founded since. However, in part this is also an artifact of the data. Groups that disband tend not to return sur-

veys, and so once a group enters a data base, it is difficult to determine whether it has simply stopped responding or is no longer active. Other groups, however, can and do report on groups in their country that no longer operate. Since there is occasionally information that a group has disbanded, even though we rarely know exactly when it ceased to function, it can be determined that relatively few groups in the sample became defunct.

7. There are a variety of other unidimensional measures of national human rights performance. As with Stohl and his collaborators (see, e.g., Carleton and Stohl 1985), however, the measures are all based on codes of qualitative analyses of the national situations in a given year. For a highly critical review, see Barsh 1993. For a methodologically sophisticated exemplar, see Gupta et al. 1993 (note that even after very sophisticated analysis the measure proposed by Gupta et al. correlates closely with the other measures). Carleton and Stohl 1985 is used here because it is methodologically transparent: the codes are based on clear categories, without any statistical manipulation that might add confusion without adding explanatory power.

8. Poe and Tate (1994) offer a similar argument about the DoS codings. In their empirical work using the Carleton and Stohl data base, they find that a dummy variable for "leftist regime" predicted a higher DoS score but had a weakly negative (but not significant) result predicting the AI score. From the Poe and Tate finding, and my general sense that Amnesty International is less biased than the U.S. Department of State, I will use the AI measure.

9. Each category is the integer part of the average age of nine rights divided by fifteen. This calculation (chosen by trial and error) is used in order to make the graph as visually comprehensible as possible.

10. The average age of the nine rights in 1983 was 64 years in Guatemala and 115.8 in El Salvador. By squaring each and multiplying by the coefficient, the effect on the predicted square root of the number of HRNGOs is calculated. The squared difference between the two countries' values yields the predicted difference in the number of HRNGOs.

11. Only a few years earlier Guatemala had more HRNGOs, but extreme repression had forced them to disband. The root question is therefore why the Salvadoran HRNGOs were more robust in the face of extreme repression than their Guatemalan counterparts. See Ball, Kobrak, and Spirer 1999.

12. Given the paucity of cases in Latin America (seventeen and nineteen, depending on the year), there are too few to perform an effective test of an interaction effect between constitutional tenure and state violence.

CHAPTER 4

Distant Issue Movements in Germany: Empirical Description and Theoretical Reflections

Dieter Rucht

Globalization is by no means a new trend, but it has clearly accelerated in recent decades. Capital, commodities, people, ideas, and knowledge not only transcend national borders but connect very distant parts of the globe that in previous times had few, if any, relations. Social movements take part in this process. They both mirror and to some extent mold processes of globalization. They serve as watchdogs that highlight problems, form networks and alliances across national borders, and engage in political struggles to alleviate and ultimately solve what they perceive to be intolerable aspects of globalization and other trends.

Social movement research has begun to take these developments into account (Smith et al. 1997; Keck and Sikkink 1988; della Porta et al. 1999), though the state of knowledge about the globalization of social movements is still far from satisfactory. First, the concept of transnational or global social movements is unclear or at least underspecified. Does an essentially local mobilization that includes groups from both sides of a national border in a struggle against the construction of a chemical plant belong in the same category as worldwide organizations such as Greenpeace International and Amnesty International? Second, we know little about the volume and characteristics of transnational movements' mobilization in comparison with national and subnational mobilization.[1] Are we overestimating the scope and significance of social movements "going global" simply because this is a fashionable topic? Does knowledge about some major international movement organizations and fairly limited case studies on particular issue areas and conflicts provide adequate grounds for determining the specificities, if indeed there are any, of transnational movements? Third, it is unclear to what extent the theoretical tools developed with regard mainly to national and subnational movements are applicable to the field of transnational social movements. For example, can we simply add to the category of "national opportunity structure" another layer dubbed "international opportunity structure" to explain transnational mobilization?

In accepting Appadurai's (1996, 18) caveat that the study of globalization phenomena is a "mild exercise in megalomania," it seems wise to focus on aspects of the globalization of movements in a particular context before we move to broader studies that may eventually lead to solidly grounded generalizations. Thus, the aim of this chapter remains relatively modest. It focuses on one particular aspect of the globalization of social movements, namely, movements that while not necessarily acting transnationally put forward issues that are distant and/or international, if not global, in their character.[2] Moreover, the analysis is restricted to such movements in a particular place and time, namely, (West) Germany since 1950. Nevertheless, as will be shown, the analysis of this case has implications and lessons that extend far beyond this thematic and regional focus. In particular, the focus on nationally or subnationally bounded mobilization on distant issues provides a theoretical challenge insofar as it can hardly be conceived within the terms of a "strong" version of rational choice theory.

In this chapter, I will start with some brief conceptual and theoretical reflections on the subject of distant issue movements. Then I will present the empirical case of distant issue movements in Germany, relying mostly on a unique and large quantitative data set of protest events. Finally, the topic under research will be related to two broader questions: first, the theoretical puzzle of how to explain distant issue mobilization, which apparently is based on altruistic motives rather than seeking personal or structural improvements in the activists' own situation; second, I will briefly refer to the conditions that facilitate or restrict mobilization on distant issues.

1. Distant Issue Movements: Solidarity beyond Borders

According to the well-known typology embodied in Parsons's systems theory and other theoretical traditions, modern societies are based on a mix of three elementary coordination mechanisms and related societal spheres: (1) hierarchy, ultimately relying on coercion, is the mechanism that typically dominates the realm of the state; (2) contract is the mechanism that prevails in economic transactions that for the most part are based on money; and (3) solidarity is the social "glue" that emotionally binds people together based on various principles ranging from kinship or other forms of commonality through pity and compassion to universalistic values. Let us take a closer look at solidarity, which is of particular interest here.

The term *solidarity* bears at least two different meanings, which, from an analytical viewpoint, should be disentangled. In its broadest and most common sense, solidarity implies the expectation and practice of mutual support. Because solidarity may be based mainly on experiences or expectancies of exchange (Douglas 1989), though not necessarily on equal terms, the concept is not inherently bound to altruism. The slogan "workers unite" may be driven by a tactical consideration, for example, since the chances of success are higher when efforts are joined. Or the driving force behind common practice may be the hope of personal gain. In this case of solidarity within the group, we cannot rule out selfish motives as the key factor (Hechter 1988, 1990). The second meaning of *solidar-*

ity is the truly altruistic action, that is, lending a helping hand to others who need it or advocating the interests of others who have no strong voice or arm. The point here is that these actions, driven by pity, compassion, empathy, or a respect for human dignity and rights, are undertaken without the expectation of personal benefit. In practice, both types of action are often intrinsically bound together, so that the convenient generic heading of solidarity is easy at hand. Moreover, because of the high moral value and recognition of altruistic behavior, actors tend to cast their fight for the benefit of their own group, and probably the underlying motive of personal gain, in terms of altruistic frames so that the cause gains greater legitimacy.

But besides the situation in which personal and collective gains go hand in hand, there are types of action in which the altruistic component is more subtly cast in doubt. We may first think about providing help and support for those in our immediate or close environment, for example, relatives, neighbors, or homeless people in the town where we live. A skeptic may argue that some kind of expected personal benefit may well be involved in such activities: the chance that we may depend on the reciprocal help of relatives or neighbors in the future or the assumption that a rising number of homeless people will create social conflicts or damage the reputation of our beloved hometown and thus be detrimental to business and property values.

To rule out such somewhat doubtful cases, we could go a step further and focus on engagement in issues that are geographically distant from the actors. However, precisely because of growing international or even global interdependencies, some issues may be far away but still have repercussions in the place where the activists have raised the problem. The nuclear accident in Chernobyl is just one among many examples. Opposition to nuclear plants in distant places may well be driven by concerns about someone's own health and safety. In a similar vein, supporting the struggle for fair wages in Asian textile industries may be a reasonable strategy for textile workers in Central Europe because they know that low wages elsewhere may affect their own wage levels and ultimately jeopardize their jobs.

Finally, we can consider mobilization on issues that are not only geographically distant but are so distinct in their nature that the group of advocacy actors cannot expect any direct benefit from the action. (We may, however, assume that some sort of nonmaterial benefit may be included, for otherwise the action would appear to be completely random, "irrational," or senseless.) Even when we acknowledge that not many people are ready to sacrifice—or pretend to sacrifice—their time and energy for the sake of a public good without seeking personal gain, we can hardly deny the existence of such altruistic political mobilization. The history of totalitarian regimes provides striking examples of people risking their lives to save those of others (Oliner and Oliner 1988). But under less dramatic circumstances we also find examples of people making great investments in order to improve the situation of others, notabably of underprivileged groups with few means to defend their own interests (Berry 1977).

Certainly most individuals in the Western hemisphere who are engaged in Third World issues fall into this category. They mobilize for issues that are not, or are only very indirectly, related to the situation in their home countries. They try to reduce hunger and poverty, provide medical and social services for those who cannot afford them, protect the lives and cultures of indigenous people, attempt to free political prisoners, fight torture, and defend the natural environment in countries thousands of miles away where conditions are often known only through secondhand information. Usually individuals and groups with these concerns, as long as they are embedded in a broader network of mobilization for social change, are referred to as Third World or solidarity movements. Because both categories have disadvantages,[3] I refer to these groups as *distant issue movements*. These are defined as movements that mobilize for issues that are not related, or are only very indirectly related, to the situation of the mobilizing groups in their home countries.[4] In most cases, these movements cannot expect an improvement in their own material situations as a result of their activities. It is important to note that DIMs do not necessarily mobilize transnationally. Nevertheless, they can be attributed to the category of transnational movements insofar as the issues they raise refer to foreign countries and quite often have a transnational dimension.

Regarding collective activities of social movements from this angle, we can then classify them according to the criteria of (1) who benefits and (2) the geographical distance between the actors and the beneficiaries. If for reasons of parsimony we simply provide binary values for each of the two dimensions, this leads us to a fourfold table (see table 4.1). An example of category A in the table would be a strike for higher wages in a specific industrial plant. Those who strike do so hoping for a personal benefit, though in formal terms they are striving for a collective good. Thus, "free riders" working in the same plant may profit from the strike as well. Caring about neighbors and homeless people in one's immediate environment would fall into category B and opposition to a distant nuclear power plant category C. Finally, mobilization on distant issues for the exclusive benefit of other individuals or groups falls into category D. It is this kind of mobilization that, along with category C, has hardly been empirically studied beyond single cases. And it is this category that also poses a challenge for rational choice theory.

To my knowledge, there exists no coherent body of theory that allows us to

TABLE 4.1. Types of Solidarity Mobilization

	Personal Benefit through Group Action	Other Groups' Benefit
Close issue	A	B
Distant issue	C	D
	Self-interested distant issue mobilization	Altruistic distant issue mobilization

explain the existence and the particular features of distant issue mobilization. Based on our daily experience, we may assume that most collective action that takes place can be attributed to category A. First and foremost, people have to care for their own survival and quality of life. They do so quite often in collective action based on preexisting bonds and solidarity networks. These are both reaffirmed and strengthened by collective action while at the same time success is made more likely. Actions in category B are supposedly much less frequent. But still they have a long and respectable tradition, ranging from the historical abolition movement to the anti-apartheid movement to countless activities on behalf of deprived groups in our own local or domestic environment. To some extent, geographical distance from other groups can be "emotionally" bridged as long as these are perceived to be part of the same large community, for example, a nation-state or an ethnic group that may be dispersed across various countries. With the growing interdependencies resulting from globalization processes, we can hypothesize a considerable increase of this type of self-interested distance issue mobilization (category C). As some writers have pointed out, we live in a society in which human-induced risks flourish and become ubiquitous. Many incidents have demonstrated that what happens in distant countries may directly affect our personal lives. No wonder that people aware of these causalities also care, and may then mobilize, around distant issues that affect their domestic and even local conditions of life. Clearly, the availability and abundance of information about distant issues impinging upon our personal lives contribute to the growth of concerns that are geographically distant.

As for the category of *altruistic* distant issue mobilization (category D), however, we have few reasons to assume that this also should be a growth sector. The existence of hunger, misery, torture, political repression, genocide, and countless other evils in many and distant parts of the world is not a new phenomenon, and neither is knowledge about their existence. Even if we were to assume that these problems have increased, we cannot be sure that there is a direct correlation between the size and number of problems on the one hand and mobilization targeting them on the other. What probably does make a difference are the visual images of these evils provided by modern means of communication, most notably television. But television was introduced decades ago. Moreover, with the growing flood of information about all the misery, there may be a deadening rather than a mobilizing effect. So we would not expect a significant increase of mobilization focusing on such problems. Unfortunately, this assumption is difficult to investigate empirically because self-interested and altruistic distant issue mobilizations are often inextricably linked. Hence, the empirical part of this chapter will essentially deal with the broader category of distant issue mobilization, whereas parts of the theoretical discussion focus only on the altruistic variant.

When asking which parts of the population are most likely to participate in DIMs, we can hypothesize that the well-educated and better-off groups are overrepresented. The reason for this is not that these groups have a greater sense of compassion or are generally more inclined toward altruistic behavior. Rather, we may assume that mobilization around distant issues is facilitated by other factors. First, such mobilization requires information about distant issues and probably also about their causation.[5] This, in turn, is strongly correlated to the level of education. Second, these groups tend to be in a better economic and cognitive position to adhere to postmaterialist and universalist values, which presumably are an important factor for an engagement in DIMs. Thus, we can assume that DIMs rely heavily on distinct "conscience constituents," defined as direct supporters of a social movement organization "who do not stand to benefit directly from its success in goal accomplishment" (McCarthy and Zald 1977, 1222). These constituents demand and support social movement action based upon claims in or about faraway lands and places, thus building bridges between groups that will probably never meet. Finally, the better-educated and economically privileged also tend to travel more and have more contacts with foreigners, both in their home countries and abroad.

2. Distant Issue Movements in Germany: An Overview

This section is an attempt to empirically map the volume and structural patterns of the protest actions of DIMs in West Germany. Before making a close examination of these actions based on a large data set, it may be useful to first provide a brief overview of the origins and development of these movements.

Although several charity and human rights organizations in Germany were created much earlier,[6] most DIM groups, in particular Third World groups, emerged only with the student movement of the 1960s. The latter movement strongly criticized the capitalist order and its negative consequences, particularly for countries that were poor and economically dependent on the First and Second Worlds. In fact, several significant protest incidents of the emerging student movement were linked to official visits to Germany of officials from Central Africa and Persia. The common denominator of the DIMs that developed out of the student movement was the call for "wordwide equality and justice." Particularly during the decline of the student movement in the early 1970s, its more radical strands identified themselves with the so-called liberation movements in Third World countries—movements that for the most part were influenced by Marxist and socialist ideas. These strands of the DIMs considered themselves the natural allies of liberation movements in the Third World, although few direct contacts were established.

When it became clear that the Marxist liberation movements in Third World countries either failed or, once in power, were more concerned with increasing their own power than empowering underprivileged groups, the DIMs in Germany largely abandoned their revolutionary rhetoric. Rather than expecting social progress as an automatic consequence of a revolutionary breakthrough, the movements focused on concrete problems such as poverty, exploitation, repression, and torture. Nevertheless, the movements continued to pursue a radical course, which was conceived as an alternative to the established forms of foreign aid and developmental policy. Strongly influenced by other social movements that arose during the 1970s, the DIMs broadened their thematic scope, often trying to link issues of human rights with those of ecology, peace, women, and labor.

During the course of the 1980s, the sharp boundary between the previously autonomous DIMs and the established development agencies blurred to some extent. On the one hand, the ongoing critique of the autonomous groups was partially accepted by the established institutions on both the national and international levels. On the other hand, the DIMs recognized that most of the problems they were addressing could only be solved by incremental steps that for the most part required a joint effort of established institutions and autonomous groups. Overall, the DIMs became more pragmatic and professional. In part, they were even embraced as an important complement by public agencies and received financial support.

For various reasons, the DIMs in East Germany took a different course. First, in the German Democratic Republic there existed no student movement that could provide momentum to the rise of DIMs. Second, the Marxist ideology, including the critique of capitalist exploitation of Third World countries, was expressed by the state itself and thus could not be used by autonomous groups as a tool against the state. Finally, the Communist state closely watched the independent groups and, once they became too independent from official institutions and/or deviated from the prescribed ideological course, did not hesitate to repress them. Nevertheless, since the early 1970s a small number of such DIM groups, mostly hosted and supported by the Protestant Church, did emerge (Letz 1994). The groups became stronger when opposition against the regime increased immediately before and during the so-called *Wende* in 1989–90. But when political changes took a different course than the oppositional groups would have wished (Rucht 1996) most groups underwent a crisis and only gradually seem to have been able to redefine their role in the new political and institutional setting of a unified Germany.

The Quantitative Significance and Evolution of the West German DIMs

In Germany, as elsewhere, DIMs are still a largely unexplored phenomenon. It is hard to assess their numbers, though we have some indications on the total number of groups that are engaged in the policy domains in which DIMs are also active. Estimates of the number of human rights organizations in the world range from roughly 1,000 (Shelly 1989, 45) to several thousands (Young 1991, 922). These figures appear to underestimate the actual number of groups. Consider that the UN World Conference on Human Rights in Vienna in 1993 was attended by two thousand representatives from more than 1,500 groups (Shriver 1993, 525). Certainly many groups, particularly those that are small and located in Third World countries, did not have a chance to participate in this conference. Another indicator is the number of groups involved in outstanding conflicts. For instance, the struggle against the Narmada Dam in India is currently supported by 700 nongovernmental groups of which many are not are based in India. Another example is the anti-apartheid movement in the United States. According to a nationwide survey of nearly 1,000 organizations conducted by the Washington Office on Africa, "379 organizations listed apartheid as their primary focus, while nearly 600 others devoted considerable efforts to problems in the region." (Culverson 1996, 148). Finally, various handbooks, directories, monographs, and articles indicate a large and growing number of groups, many of which are DIMs, in different parts of the world (Bergensen and Parmann 1994; Ekins 1992; Fisher 1993; Walls 1993; Wiseberg 1992; Chatterjee and Finger 1994; Princen and Finger 1994; Wapner 1996; Keck and Sikkink 1998; Rucht 1999).

A hint about the distribution of DIM organizations at the international level is provided by a survey on transnational social movement organizations. According to an analysis based on several issues of the *Yearbook of International Organizations,* the number of groups that to a large extent dealt with distant issues increased from 110 in 1953 to 631 in 1993 (Smith et al. 1995). Out of seven thematic areas, the human rights issue was by far the most important as measured in terms of numbers of existing organizations, with a slowly increasing share of 23 percent in 1983 and 26 percent in 1993, followed by the (significantly faster growing) area of the environment, which reached 15 percent in 1993.[7] Again we can assume that the underlying data base is selective in that it represents mainly the larger and more formal organizations.

Unfortunately, we lack quantitative studies of DIMs in various countries. However, based on a comparative analysis of protest events initiated by new social movements in four Western European countries (1975–89) we can at least get a clear idea of the level of these movements' activities (Kriesi et al. 1995, 20). In terms of the distribution of unconventional events drawn from a systematic sample of newspaper reports, the "solidary movement"—which covers a major part of all DIMs[8]—accounted for 6.3 percent of all unconventional events in West Germany. Thus, it places only seventh out of nine different new social movements (after the peace movement with 18.7 percent, the anti-nuclear power movement with 12.8, the ecology movement with 11.3, antiracism with 8.7, and the squatters' and other countercultural movements with 6.7 each).[9] Hence, in relative terms, the solidarity movement's protests in West Germany are less important than those in Switzerland (where it ranks first with 15.2 percent) and the Netherlands (second rank with 13.2 percent) but more prominent than those in France (4.4 percent).

Probably a more telling indicator of the protest activity of solidarity movements is the number of people they mobilize in unconventional protest events per million inhabitants. Measured in this way, the German movement again turns out to be relatively weak (six thousand participants, sixth rank out of ten movements), particularly when compared to Switzerland (nineteen thousand participants, third rank) and the Netherlands (fifteen thousand participants, second rank—together with nuclear energy) (Koopmans 1995, 53). From a comparative perspective, then, we can conclude that the mobilization of the West German solidarity movement is modest compared to both the same kind of movement in other countries and other movements within Germany.

Nevertheless, the solidarity movement is not marginal when judged by the frequency of or participation in unconventional events. For instance, in all four countries it clearly outnumbers the women's movement, which usually is counted among the principal new social movements.

Drawing on a large data set collected in the Prodat project[10] on protest events in West Germany from 1950 to 1994 (and East Germany from 1989 to 1994), we can provide more comprehensive and detailed information about the quantitative relevance and structural patterns of distant issues. The sources of information were two national-circulation tabloid newspapers, the *Süddeutsche Zeitung* and the *Frankfurter Rundschau*. For pragmatic reasons, a sample was chosen that covers all Monday issues plus the Tuesday to Saturday issues of each fourth week. The current data base entails detailed information, as far as it was provided by the newspapers, on more than thirteen thousand protest events.

For the analysis presented here, distant issues were operationalized in a more inclusive way so that they were not restricted to solidarity movements as defined by Kriesi et al. (1995). Based on a selection procedure that essentially referred to a combination of the geographical location or scope of the problem addressed and a considerable number of thematic issue areas,[11] the data show that distant issues are far from insignificant. Out of the total of 12,180 protest events in West Germany, 824 (6.8 percent) referred to distant issues.[12] In terms of participants, these issues represented 12.9 percent, a considerably higher proportion than that of the events.

Table 4.2 shows that the two measures of the volume of distant issue protests exhibit a discontinuous course over time. In terms of protest events, there was a low but increasing number until the mid-1960s, then a sharp increase in the second half of that decade, followed by a gradual decline, which did not, however, descend to the low levels of the first period. Participation in these events shows a strikingly different picture. About four-fifths of the participation in the forty-five years investigated is concentrated in the first half of the 1980s. This reflects mainly the mass mobilization against Reagan's Strategic Defense Initiative (SDI) and, to a greater extent, plans to deploy new nuclear missiles in various countries (Cooper 1995). To be sure, this was not a genuine distant issue, so these numbers have to be interpreted with great caution. The second highest participation was reached in the first half of the 1990s (5.2 percent). Then follows participation in the second half of the 1960s—years that were outstanding in terms of the number of events. The average amount of protest per period varies greatly. Overall, however, distant issues attract significantly more people per protest (17,849) when compared to all issues (9,392). In terms of both events and participants, the distant issue protests do not follow the trends of all protests combined but approximate much more closely the trend of new social movements, whose patterns are outlined elsewhere (Rucht 1998).

The Carriers of Distant Issue Mobilization

Drawing again on the Prodat data base, there are several ways to get an idea of the kind of groups that are the main carriers of DIMs. A first indication is the geographical location of their protests. If distant issue mobilization is strongly influenced by the level of education and factual knowledge, then we should expect a concentration of these issues in the big cities. Table 4.3 displays the proportion of distant issue mobilization in nine major cities as opposed to the rest of the country. In line with our expectation, the figures demonstrate that indeed distant issue mobilization is strongly concentrated in these nine cities, which are also those attracting the most protest on all issues. Whereas the population of these cities represents only 14.5 percent of the overall population,[13] they attracted more than half of the overall protest events and 71 percent of distant issue protests.[14] Certainly, this high figure also reflects strategic considerations insofar as state and, more importantly, national governments can be seen as crucial actors in bringing about changes in foreign affairs. This proabably also explains why Bonn, though not the

TABLE 4.2. Distant Issue Protests and All Protests, Distribution and Size, West Germany, 1950–94

	Distant Issues			All Issues		
Period	Protests (%)	Participants (%)	Participants per Protest	Protests (%)	Participants (%)	Participants per Protest
1950–54	1.0	0.1	1,552	4.9	9.9	21,370
1955–59	3.4	1.7	15,881	4.5	9.8	24,786
1960–64	4.7	0.1	331	5.8	7.8	15,918
1965–69	23.4	4.7	3,512	15.2	9.9	6,854
1970–74	18.2	2.5	2,203	10.9	5.3	4,872
1975–79	15.3	2.6	4,846	13.8	5.7	4,020
1980–84	16.6	81.7	69,484	15.5	23.5	12,025
1985–89	9.6	1.3	2,277	14.1	8.9	5,673
1990–94	7.8	5.2	16,511	15.3	19.2	10,555
Total	100	100	17,849	100	100	9,392
N	824	7,318,073		12,180	56,606,767	

leading city with respect to all protests, is on top with regard to distant issue mobilization (16.7 percent).

When looking at some social or other characteristics of the groups involved in distant issue mobilization, to the extent that the protesters did represent a relatively coherent group, we find a significant overrepresentation, compared to all protests, of young people, religious groups, representatives of interest groups and parties, and intellectuals (table 4.4). Amazingly, students are only slightly overrepresented, whereas the strong underrepresentation of workers does not come as a surprise (protests by workers usually focus on issues of domestic employment, wages, working hours, safety, and so on). We cannot assume that most protesters are individuals who just follow a call for action and then disperse until the next protest takes place. With very few exceptions, protest is based on an infrastructure of preexisting groups that exist and meet in the penumbra if not in the full shadow of public attention. These groups form the backbone of the movement, and their members form the majority of the participants in the more frequent and smaller events. Only occasionally do protests attract masses of people who are not part of a regular movement constituency. What do such networks of mobilization look like?

The German DIMs can best be described as a set of loosely coupled networks of a wide variety of groups. Regarding their concerns, one can distinguish (1) groups dealing with a multitude of issues in particular countries or regions, (2) groups focusing on particular topics or projects (e.g., prisoners of conscience, fair trade, medical service, and education), and (3) groups that are mainly part of the infrastructure of the movement. The latter, for example, produce newletters or specialize in networking.

TABLE 4.3. Local Distribution of Protests in West Germany, 1950–94 (percentages)

	Distant Issues	All Issues	Inhabitants in 1970
Bonn	16.7	8.5	0.49
Frankfurt	16.0	9.7	1.07
Berlin	13.6	11.8	3.47
Munich	7.0	6.6	2.16
Hamburg	7.2	5.3	2.95
Stuttgart	4.0	3.2	1.02
Hannover	2.7	3.1	0.84
Cologne	2.1	2.7	1.41
Düsseldorf	1.7	2.4	1.11
Total of nine cities	71.0	53.3	14.5
Other locations	29.0	46.7	85.5
Total	100	100	100
N	824	12,180	61,508,000

Source: Prodat and Statistisches Jahrbuch, 1971.

In terms of organizational structure, one can identify, first, relatively large, formal, and centralized organizations. A typical example is Amnesty International. The 550 local groups of the German section included a total of 10,400 members in 1995. Another 5,000 are individual members (a status that was created only recently), and still another 17,000 make financial contributions without being members of the organization (Buchsteiner 1995, 3). These figures have remained fairly constant until the most recent period. A second example of a nationwide organization, though much smaller and less formal, is the Society of Endangered Peoples (Gesellschaft für bedrohte Völker), which was created in 1970 as an outgrowth of the Committee to Help Biafra. In the early 1990s, the society had 5,500 individual members and an annual budget of 1.7 milllion deutsche marks, of which 1 million came from donations and the rest from membership fees and sales of brochures and other items. On the other side of the organizational spectrum, we find a plethora of small, informal, and mostly local groups. For the most part, they involve only 10 to 20 members.

A third type of group consists of a small core of organizers who, often relying on a professional public relations strategy, are financially supported by people who are not otherwise active in the movement. An example of such a group is Cap Anamur, an organization that initially was created to rescue Vietnamese refugees ("boat people") but later widened its thematic scope. Among other things, the organization has targeted the production and export of land mines that for the most part hurt or kill members of the civilian population even years after a war has ended. Cap Anamur is run mainly by Rupert Neudeck, a medical doctor and political entrepreneur who has specialized in human rights issues.

While the larger organizations mainly act independently, a considerable number of the smaller and more politically oriented groups are part of a nationwide

TABLE 4.4. Social Characteristics of Protesters, West Germany, 1950–94 (percentages)

	Distant Issues	All Issues[a]
Youth	19.5	13.6
Students	13.5	12.9
Religious groups	12.6	5.2
Officials of interest groups/parties	12.5	8.4
Intellectuals	8.4	4.4
Workers	6.4	29.0
Women	3.0	2.6
Other	24.1	23.9
Total	100	100
N	824	8,131

[a]Immigrants/ethnic minorities (539 cases) are also excluded from the "all issues" category.

network, the so-called BUKO, or Bundeskongress entwicklungspolitischer Aktionsgruppen (Federal Congress of Action Groups for Development). This network was formed in 1977 to coordinate activities along thematically oriented campaigns focusing on Third World issues. In the 1990s, it had about 300 groups that could be considered members. By the late 1990s, this number has shrunk to 200. Altogether, however, it has contacts with 2,100 groups (Bräuer 1994, 47). The themes and strategies of the BUKO are discussed during its annual meetings, which are usually attended by three hundred to five hundred people. Although the BUKO is said to have been in crisis for many years, somehow it has been able to continue its activities.

While the BUKO mainly represents the radical branch of the movement, including its anticapitalist and anti-imperialist tendencies, other groups, for instance, those that are inspired by Christian thought or moral rather than political humanism, tend to form their own networks without, however, considering themselves antagonists of the BUKO network.

When we look at the types of organizational carriers, leaving aside the mixed cases, we find that in a majority (55.2 percent) of distant issue protests formal interest groups and/or church groups are involved (see fig. 4.1). This proportion, however, is lower compared to all protests on all issues. Informal groups and networks represent 28.3 percent of the cases and are overrepresented in comparison with all protests. Also, political parties, representing the remaining 17 percent, are overrepresented. Overall, the informal and networklike structure is less salient than we would have expected on the basis of the available literature. The aggregate of DIMs is an analytical unit of analysis. At a closer look, it is composed of more distinct movements that, from the viewpoint of their adherents, form a more natural social and political category. Nevertheless, the fact that time and again members of these more specific movements form broader alliances and join for protest indicates that DIMs are more than just a statistical conglomerate (fig. 4.2).

At the center of these movements, one could probably place the groups that are part of the solidarity or Third World movement.[15] According to an insider's estimate, 3,000 to 5,000 autonomous Third World movement groups currently exist in Germany (Bräuer 1994, 32). There are indications that the number of these groups has not changed considerably during the last fifteen years.[16] Only some of these groups are components of a nationwide or even a worldwide organization such as the International League for Human Rights, Amnesty International, Oxfam, Terre des Hommes, the International Fellowship of Reconciliation, and Doctors without Borders. In Germany, the largest organization, with about 555 local groups in 1998, is the national section of Amnesty International.[17] Probably the second largest organizational component, though more like a loose network than a regular association, are the so-called Third World Shops (or One World Shops), which sell products from Third World countries in the spirit of fair trade ("Trans-

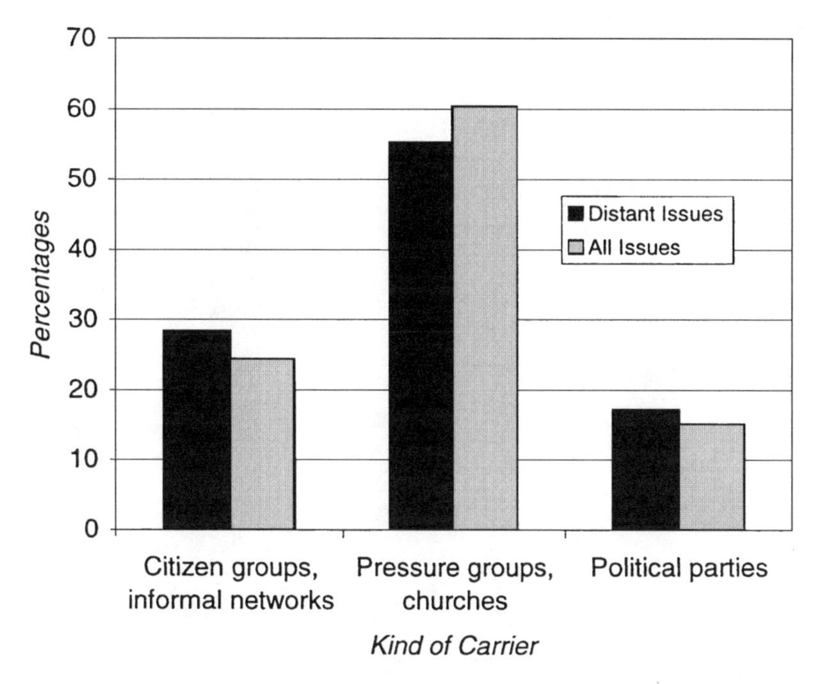

Fig. 4.1. Organizational carriers of protest, 1950–94

Fair"). By the early 1990s, there were 550 of these shops in West Germany (*Die Tageszeitung,* August 17, 1992, 3).

The backbone of the Third World movement, and thus the DIMs, however, consists of independent grassroots groups that often focus on particular problems and/or geographic areas. Based on more documentation of the plethora of leftist and alternative groups in Berlin (Stattbuch 1995), we can get an idea of the distribution of these groups, though their actual number may be higher due to the selective bias of the source. The edition of 1995 lists 51 Third World groups, which can be divided according to geographical and thematic areas.[18] These figures underreport the actual number of groups. Olejniczak, in her detailed survey of Third World groups in West and East Germany, identified 123 in Berlin and 128 in Hamburg. The nine cities that attracted the most DIM protests (see table 4.3) were also among the first ten cities—besides Münster—that had the largest number of Third World groups (1997, 371). Overall, the author estimates that the Third World groups in West and East Germany include six hundred full-time staff and about twenty-five thousand volunteers who can be regarded as core activists (423).

Obviously, protest mobilization is just one among several indicators of the relevance of a social movement. While, for example, the antinuclear movement's rationale, as its label indicates, is basically rooted in protest, other movements, including the women's movement and the DIMs, are also strongly engaged in con-

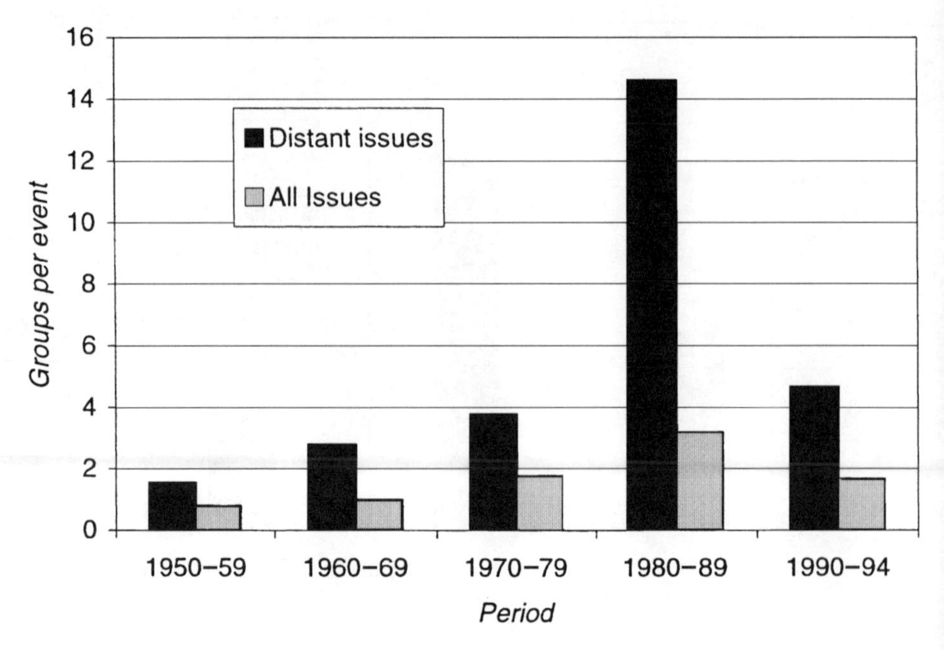

Fig. 4.2. Average number of groups per event

structive activities such as running houses for battered women and providing financial support for local communities in Third World countries. Although no quantitative data on these kinds of activities are available, the number of existing groups can serve as a rough indicator. In this regard, I would speculate that the DIMs in both Germany and other Western countries are among the strongest new social movements.

Areas and Targets of Mobilization

It is already obvious that DIMs engage in a wide range of thematic areas. To a different degree, they are present in nearly all the main areas that have been categorized for the protest data set. Table 4.5 informs about the relative weight of these thematic areas for distant issue protests and all protest issues. A comparison between all protests and distant issue protests shows that the latter have a very special profile. About half are protests related to matters of peace and disarmament. With the probable exception of the first half of the 1980s, when the NATO double track decision was at the center of mobilization, it cannot be assumed that peace protests, among them those against the Vietnam and the Gulf wars, are essentially dealing with close issues. Another great proportion of distant issue protests falls into the domain of democracy and human and civic rights (34.1 percent). Compared to all protests, these two areas have a much higher weight. All the other thematic areas within the distant issue protests are marginal if not nonexistent. In some respects, for example, labor, farmer, and infrastructure, this is what one would have expected. In other respects, for example, women, education, and leftist ideology (as a generic and broad category such as protest against imperialism), the numbers are astonishingly low.

In terms of the geographical dimension or location of the distant issues, the broad category of international and/or global issues represents 59.3 percent of all distant issue protests. This category was coded when issues relating to more than one continent were involved. Unfortunately this code also implies cases in which one or several European countries, together with countries from another continent, were involved. These latter cases, strictly speaking, cannot be counted among distant issue protests. The remaining protests refer to Asia (17.8 percent), Africa (7.4 percent), the United States (5.9 percent), Latin America (5.9 percent), and the former Soviet Union (3.5 percent). No protests on issues in Australasia were registered. The proportion of protests concerning the United States appears to be low, given this country's role in world and developmental politics in particular. But this number may be an artifact of that role precisely because the United States is often included in the category of international/global issues.

Targets of distant issue protests can be located in both First and Third World countries but can also be international agencies (fig. 4.3). According to the protest event data, the overwhelming majority of those protests for which a specific target could be identified were state authorities (85.4 percent). This proportion is much higher than for all protests. By contrast, private companies, a natural target of many labor protests, play only a minor role in distant issue mobilization (5.9 percent).

TABLE 4.5. Thematic Areas of Distant Issue Protests and All Protests, West Germany, 1950–94 (percentages)

Thematic Area	Distant Issues	All Issues
Labor/worker claims	1.5	19.5
Nuclear energy	1.3	5.3
Immigrants/ethnic minorities	4.6	7.2
Farmers	0.0	0.7
Women	1.5	1.9
Peace	50.7	15.2
General ideology	2.5	5.6
Infrastructure	0.1	4.7
Democracy/human rights/participation	34.1	25.18
Environment	1.9	3.3
Education	0.7	6.7
Social welfare/deprivileged groups	1.1	4.7
Total	100	100
N	824	10,784

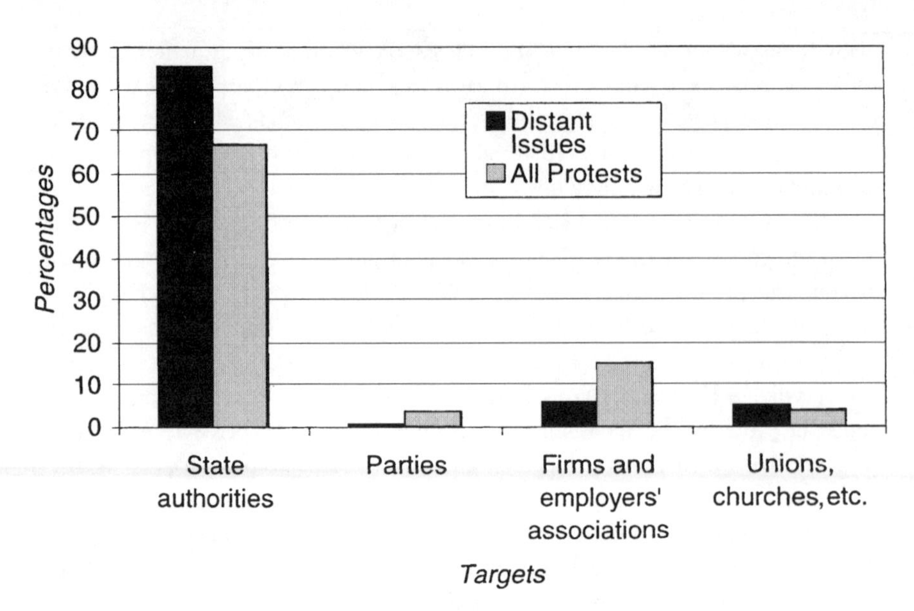

Fig. 4.3. Targets of protests

Strategies and Actions

As indicated, the dominant strategies of the DIMs have changed over the last twenty-five years. The hopes of overcoming the capitalist regime by means of a joint revolutionary act of both Third World and domestic "liberation movements" have largely faded away. Overall, the DIMs are still critical toward governments in general and established foreign aid policies in particular, but the movements tend to pursue a rather reformist and pragmatic course that does not necessarily preclude collaboration with state authorities. The movements have become aware of the multicausality of many problems for which not only capitalism can be blamed, of the limits of seemingly "easy solutions" for very different and highly complex problems, and, above all, of their own limitations in changing structural conditions that are deeply rooted historically and worldwide in scope. Nevertheless, this disillusion about potential breakthroughs has not resulted in widespread demobilization and apathy but rather in more modest though tenacious activities. These can be sorted into three categories, namely, distributing information, organizing protest, and providing practical aid.

First, probably the most important and time-consuming activity of DIMs is to collect and distribute information, as the sheer number of their journals and newspapers indicates.[19] Because the ordinary citizenry is usually poorly informed about the situation in distant and—notably—poor countries, due to both a lack of interest and, according to the perception of the movements, widespread misinformation by mass media and governments, the DIMs somehow attempt to educate the public about these countries' problems and their underlying causes. Given the range and depth of these problems, this would be an endless task. Therefore, the movements' information policy focuses on the more structural aspects of distant issues and/or illustrative cases that could highlight the nature of the problems. Of course, the problems selected are not only derived from a perceived hierarchy of needs but also according to perceived opportunities to mobilize, such as changing global power relations or contingent events that could provide a "hook" for bringing particular issues onto the public agenda. Usually, such attempts to inform and educate both their own adherents and the wider public are condensed into particular campaigns. Outstanding campaigns of the BUKO network, for example, have concentrated on the policies of the domestic pharmaceutical industry regarding Third World countries, the export of weapons, the economic and social situation of women, and the financial policies of domestic and international actors regarding Third World countries (Bräuer 1994, 34–45).

Second, in many instances, information campaigns are combined with various sorts of protest activities, ranging from peaceful demonstrations and protest letters to acts of civil disobedience to violence.

The protest event data on West Germany show that confrontational and violent actions play only a minor role in distant issues (table 4.6). In terms of protest numbers, appeals (collection of signatures, open letters, distribution of flyers, petitions) are the most important category for distant issue mobilization (47.2 percent) but not for all protests. The virtual lack of institutional procedures available to citizens in order to intervene in international and global issues explains why "procedural" protest is nearly absent. By contrast, heavy violence (6.5 percent) is relatively more frequent in distant issue mobilization compared to all protests (5 percent). When it comes to the number of participants, almost all mobilization concentrates on the category of appeals and demonstrative protests, with 81.5 and 18.2 percent, respectively.

TABLE 4.6. Types of Action, West Germany, 1950–94 (percentages)

	Distant Issues		All Issues	
	Protests	Participants	Protests	Participants
Appeal	47.2	81.5	28.2	37.87
Procedural	0.2	0.0	4.3	0.43
Demonstrative	36.7	18.2	48.9	60.26
Confrontational	7.7	0.2	11.1	1.29
Light violence	1.6	0.1	2.5	0.11
Heavy violence	6.6	0.0	5.0	0.04
Total	100	100	100	100
N	813	7,315,700	12,001	56,448,352

It may be interesting to see which social groups tend to favor which types of action. Table 4.7 cross-tabulates some selected groups with a simplified type of action composed of three categories (moderate/confrontational/violent). Almost all the actions in which the protesters withheld their identities ("clandestine") were violent (96.4 percent). Besides this, only in the category of youth did violent protest have a sizable though minor share (5 percent). Confrontational protests were relatively significant only in the categories of women and to a lesser extent youth, students, and, probably surprisingly, representatives of interest groups and parties.

Protests are particularly massive when any official event takes place, for example, the visit of a statesman who is susceptible to bearing responsibility for some Third World problems or a large international conference that provides an opportunity to organize counterevents that are likely to be reported by the mass media. As a matter of fact, the largest protest campaign devoted to problems of Third World countries was launched when Berlin hosted a congress of the International Monetary Fund and the World Bank in 1987. Besides numerous minor protests before and during this congress, a large demonstration supported by more than 130 groups was organized and eventually attracted some eighty thousand people (Gerhards and Rucht 1992; Gerhards 1993).

A third major activity of the DIMs is various forms of practical aid. Again, these include a wide variety of measures. For the most part, any sort of material aid requires raising money, which then can be spent to provide food, medical care, training, technical facilities, and so on. An outstanding and highly disputed case of financial support was provided by the campaign Weapons for El Salvador due to the initiative of the leftist-libertarian journal *die tageszeitung* in the 1980s. The collection of money particularly devoted to buying weapons for a "politically correct" purpose was not only criticized by outsiders but also by some of the DIMs. In particular, groups that strictly endorsed the idea of nonviolence and/or were engaged in the peace movement felt uneasy about this campaign, while parts of the

TABLE 4.7. Dominant Social Characteristics of Distant Issue Protests by Action Type, West Germany, 1950–94 (percentages)

	Action Type			
	Moderate	Confrontational	Violent	Total
Youth (N = 161)	82.0	13.0	5.0	100
Students (N = 110)	89.1	10.9	0.0	100
Religious groups (N = 102)	94.1	5.9	0.0	100
Officials of interests groups/parties (N = 101)	91.1	8.9	0.0	100
Intellectuals (N = 69)	97.1	2.9	0.0	100
Workers (N = 52)	96.2	3.8	0.0	100
Women (N = 25)	80.0	20.0	0.0	100
Clandestine (N = 56)	3.6	0.0	96.4	100

radical Left supported it without hesitation. Another variant of practical help by individuals and groups was working for several weeks or months on local projects in Third World countries such as the construction of a school in a rural area or the creation of an irrigation system in a dry zone. In the 1980s, Nicaragua was a preferred location for members of a number of leftist groups, who went there to support the Sandinista movement and get a flavor of a "true" leftist revolution. However, when the revolutionary fever cooled and they were subjected to a daily routine, some sins of the leftist governments became more obvious (e.g., repression against Miskito Indians), and when the conservative forces won national elections in 1990 this kind of practical support faded.

Of course, the three major forms of activity I have described can also be combined. One example that links the attempt to inform the public with the zeal to protest are the so-called tribunals. These represent a quasi-judicial investigation of a supposed violation of human rights, eventually ending with the sentence of a jury that is composed of outstanding personalities. The best known of these investigations are the Russell Tribunals, which, on a few occasions, were held in Germany.

In surveying the findings presented here, it becomes clear that distant issue mobilization differs in various and partly significant ways from the patterns of all protests. To a greater degree than the latter, distant issue mobilization is concentrated in the large cities, focused on a few dominant areas (peace and democratization/human rights), relying on young people and religious groups, targeting the state, and including a slightly greater proportion of violent events. Further and more detailed research, including a more sophisticated analysis of the Prodat data set alongside the available qualitative information on individual protests, will provide more insights. Instead of engaging in this endeavor, however, an attempt will be made to move toward the interpretation and explanation of distant issue mobilization from a more general perspective.

3. Mobilizing for Distant Issues in a Theoretical and Practical Perspective

Distant Issue Engagement and Rational Choice Theory

Politics in modern societies is predominantly perceived as a competitive and contentious game in which rational actors pursue nothing other than their own interests. The assumption is that these actors can only be mobilized when the perceived costs and benefits lead them to expect more advantages than disadvantages from participating in this game.

The expected gains resulting from political participation materialize in the successful defense or acquisition of goods. From the perspectives of rational choice theory and the underlying paradigm of methodological individualism (Becker 1970; Riker and Ordeshook 1973), the kind of good at stake—be it individual or collective, material or immaterial—does not in principle matter for the explanatory task. The same basic assumptions are made regardless of whether a political actor fights to get more money, change electoral rules, or abolish torture. By the same token, a similar assumption holds regardless of whether the action is individual or collective or undertaken by small informal groups or large and formal organizations.

According to the paradigm of methodological individualism and the version of rational choice theory presented by Mancur Olson (1965), people usually join a political group or organization only in exchange for selective material benefits or when they are forced to join. In this perspective, which according to Taylor (1988, 63–97) is based on a "thin" rationality, a collective good provided by the group or organization is just a by-product of members' concerns that in fact are essentially nonpolitical and self-centered. If this assumption is correct, participation in political elections[20] or, even more so, in an advocacy group is highly unlikely because by definition these groups neither provide material incentives nor force people to join them. In the case of DIMs, such participation should be still more unlikely because for the most part it is an activity for the sake of strangers who belong to other cultures, live far from the advocacy groups, and are seldom in direct contact with these groups. No wonder that, compared to other activities in, say, unions, political parties, or sports clubs, participation in DIMs is relatively rare and therefore confirms the assumptions of rational choice theory.

On the other hand, we have to acknowledge the fact that in the German case tens of thousands of people do adhere to DIMs, and that a sizable proportion of all protest mobilization is devoted to distant issues. Moreover, many of the activists are deeply involved and committed. They sacrifice considerable amounts of time and resources in putting distant issues on the agenda, protesting, and providing material and nonmaterial support for underprivileged groups far away. How can rational choice theory account for this fact?

In response to its critics,[21] rational choice theory has dealt with the objection that not all purposive action is driven by the expectation of material benefits that outweigh the perceived costs. A first answer provided by rational choice theorists is that people often hide their true egoistic motives in order to make their actions appear more legitimate. For instance, it has been argued that political entrepreneurs who fight for a common cause do so primarily because they expect personal gains related to or resulting from their particular job (Salisbury 1969; Frohlich and Oppenheimer 1974; Moe 1980). However, this argument was made with regard to groups rather different from DIMs, and in general it hardly applies to the rank and file of political organizations. Therefore, rational choice theorists tended to expand their concept by introducing "expressive benefits" in voters' calculations (Brennan and Lomasky 1993) and "soft incentives" (Opp 1986, 1989; Collard 1978; Margolis 1982) when it comes to explaining participation in protest activities. According to Sabatier, who takes a critical stance toward this expansion of the concept, two other types of incentives have been suggested to explain participation in voluntary organizations:

- Solidarity—social rewards that derive from associating in group activities
- Purposive—rewards associated with ideological or issue-oriented goals that offer no significant tangible benefits to members (Sabatier 1992, 102).

The solidarity argument may provide one among several answers to the free-rider problem raised by Olson.[22] Indeed, many people avoid participation because they will profit from the good provided anyway or because their contribution would be quantitatively insignificant for the outcome of the collective enterprise. However, people dodging participation will also be cut off from a potentially rewarding experience that may motivate other people to participate even knowing that their contribution will not make a significant difference in producing the collective good. What encourages these people to participate is the expected experience of community, solidarity, and mutual support (Wilson 1973; Schlozman et al. 1995). This is more likely to be found in citizen initiatives, voluntary associations, and social movements than in highly competitive groups or organizations with obligatory membership. The search for the experience of solidarity may be a sufficient reason for participation in a collective enterprise even if its explicit goal is unlikely to be achieved in the short or medium term. Melucci, in paraphrasing McLuhan, has stressed the following: "The medium, the movement itself is a new medium, is the message" (Melucci 1984, 830).

However, just because so many groups promise the experience of solidarity, some even in combination with selective incentives, we can hardly assume that the search for group solidarity is a key factor for explaining adherence to DIMs in particular. Moreover, as the case of many donors who are nonmembers or nonactivists in these movements demonstrates, the search for group solidarity may even be irrelevant for providing support. Thus, a more powerful explanation for adherence to DIMs lies in purposive rewards.[23]

Supported by strong empirical evidence (e.g., Passy 1998), we can expect that members and supporters of DIMs will be strongly committed to universalistic values of human rights in general and justice, equality, and solidarity in particular. It is doubtful that respect for these values can be reduced to the search for some kind of "narcissistic" satisfaction, as Olson (1965) seems to believe. Although there are no reasons to assume that constituents of DIMs are morally superior to those participating in various other movements, including advocacy groups in domestic issues, it seems that DIM activists tend to emphasize above all the universal validity of these values, thus being concerned about their violation in principle, and consequently they worry even about issues far from their home. Moreover, we can assume DIM activists to be well informed about the structural and, in particular, political causes of the problems they are addressing. Therefore, probably in contrast to typical supporters of charity organizations, DIM activists also tend to promote political diagnosis and develop a political strategy regarding distant issues. In line with this is the fact that DIM activists, like most followers of new social movements, primarily recruit from the well-educated and politicized segments of the middle class (for Switzerland, e.g., see Passy 1998, 88).

Rational choice theory has been developed in studying the behavior of individuals in relatively standardized situations with a clear cost-benefit relation, for instance, in explaining the behavior of consumers in markets or choices in competitive situations in which clear rules of the game are at hand (e.g., coalition building between political parties). This is the area where the theory has proven to be most powerful. Also, when it attempts to explain the decision to join or not join a conventional membership group that offers some sort of material benefit, rational choice theory still seems to have considerable explanatory power because for the most part this is a single and well thought out decision that usually also implies some sort of regular financial contribution to the group. However, the economically oriented version of rational choice theory turns out to be of little value in explaining participation in voluntary associations, citizens groups, social movements, countercultures, and the like (Hirsch 1990). Without denying the rational and instrumental component inherent in many social movement activities, some scholars have emphasized the fact that expressive behavior and spontaneous action may also play an important role (Killian 1984). These aspects, they argue, cannot be adequately grasped by a rational choice approach. Although this may be true, it does not provide a good argument in the case of DIMs, as it necessitates the assumption that these movements are overwhelmingly based on sponteneous action—an assumption that would be hard to defend. However, it appears that involvement in such groups differs in several other ways from the standard situation that rational choice theory has in mind.

First, such an involvement is hardly the result of a single key decision[24] but rather the consequence of an ongoing process of gathering information and forming an opinion about the issues at stake, becoming acquainted with the movement's means and goals, identifying with the movement, and helping to define its opponents.

Second, unlike a situation in which somebody buys a car or joins a political party and in that moment develops a relatively clear idea about costs, adherence to a movement does not imply the perception of a fixed amount of costs. In the case of social movements, it is typically not the organization but the individual who decides when and under what conditions participation takes place. The individual chooses the kind, degree, and timing of involvement. To be sure, in some social movement groups there may be social sanctions when a person remains inactive or provides no financial support, but hardly any formal consequences exist for those people. Also, the threshold for the exit option as a potential source of anticipated costs tends to be low. Exit requires no formal declaration and thus facilitates entry and reentry into the movement.

Third, expectations about the gains to be achieved by social movements tend to be rather diffuse.[25] Particularly in the case of distant issues, achievements may be relatively hard to assess in terms of causal attribution and side effects. Thus, activists may be more driven by vague hopes for political change, strong feelings of moral obligation (which are not necessarily goal oriented), or an internalized altruistic desire to lend a helping hand to those who suffer most. The same argument also applies to activities that may benefit future generations but do not promise a reward other than a moral one to those who presently participate in them.[26]

Fourth, social movement groups tend to be flexible and open to participants who want to mold the groups' structures and strategies. Movements usually provide opportunities for very different talents to find a niche according to their specific abilities and needs without being "captured" in a formal or quasi-formal contract—as in the case of buying a good or signing a membership form. Thus, movements are not only mechanisms to achieve explicit political goals but also terrains of creative social action and self-realization beyond predefined duties and rights.

In short, the model of "homo economicus" has its limits and should not be stretched to cover all instances of human behavior that, in the wide sense of the word, can be called rational. Why should we assume that individuals follow the same logic when buying a tangible good, raising a child, adhering to an advocacy group, or sacrificing their lives for a political idea? In each of these situations, the individual probably acts as he or she does simply because acting differently would make him or her feel less satisfied. This trivial assumption, however, is not to be mistaken for a universal concept of *economic* rationality. If people buy items on credit without being able to afford them and therefore completely ruin themselves, they also feel good when buying, though we could not qualify this behavior as economically rational.[27] Coming back to our case, Sabatier is correct in stating: "Expanding self-interest to include the personal satisfaction from altruistic acts renders the entire enterprise non-falsifiable. *Any* behavior becomes 'self-interested,' and *any* benefit can be reclassified as 'selective,' that is, accruing only to the individual who participated" (1992, 105). Therefore, instead of sticking to a concept by introducing more and more supplementary conditions in order to cover what are perceived as "special cases," we should take into account that different forms and goals of behavior may require different kinds of explanation (Greven and Willems 1994).

The persistance of mobilization for distant issues, the wide variety of advocacy groups historically and in the present, and the increasing number of nonprofit organizations (McFarland 1992, 66) can hardly be conceived in terms of an economic cost-benefit calculus. Rather, we should acknowledge that advocacy participation, though sometimes only pretended, really exists. If this is true, it is a form of behavior in its own right, which therefore, from an analytical perspective, should be separated from a collective enterprise that basically serves to provide mutual benefits (Young 1992, 924). If a reliance on moral explanation could make rational choice theory "untestable" because it "it is not possible definitely to say whether a given individual acted for moral reasons or for other reasons" (Olson 1965, 61), then rational choice theorists simply have to surrender when faced with complex situations of decision making or, as Opp (1989) tries to do, find ways to measure all relevant motives for participation in protest activity. Exploring whether or not this is feasible in standardized surveys whose questions about protest participation are decontextualized would require a separate discussion.

Difficulties and Prospects of Distant Issue Mobilization

Given the abundance of political issues and interest groups, most collective actors tend to complain that they do not get enough attention and support relative to how they perceive the importance of their concerns. Thus, we should not be surprised to find the same kind of complaints among DIMs as well. The question, however, is whether these movements face more or different kinds of difficulties in mobilizing than movements dealing with domestic issues that for the most part affect the average citizen more directly.

Taking the number of groups, protest events, and mobilized people as indicators, one can hardly argue in principle that DIMs are confronted with many more obstacles than other social movements. As shown, in at least two out of four European countries the solidarity movements were surprisingly strong in terms of their protest activities. Also, the persistence of groups and their activities over time is an indicator that mobilization for distant issues may be cumbersome but proves to be possible. Although the empirical figures suggest that getting and keeping distant issues on the agenda is more difficult than for issues such as nuclear power or AIDS, it is not so clear whether mobilization for distant issues is harder than advocacy protest for close issues such as homelessness in the domestic countries. Theoretical considerations would suggest so, but protest data do not support this assumption. Nevertheless, we should not underestimate the difficulties of DIMs. If we take another reference point, for instance, the amount of money and time the average citizen spends on various kinds of sports, distant issues are relatively marginal.

Comparing DIMs with other new social movements, one may assume that widespread ignorance about the issues and their background is the major difficulty DIMs are confronted with when it comes to mobilizing the broader public. Given the lack of systematic research, however, it is hard to say whether this particular difficulty is at least partially compensated for by an extraordinarily strong and steady participation of the core activists in these movements. It seems that DIMs exhibit less membership fluctuation than most other new social movements. Because the task of many DIM groups is so huge and the effect of their activities is often so minor and/or indirect, it is likely that this kind of participation requires an outstanding motivation and firm convictions. Although this pattern resembles that of a religious belief, we cannot assume that the majority of the activists are driven by religious motives.[28]

Despite the fact that most citizens lack direct experience with distant issues and usually are not well informed about them, it appears that the seriousness and scope of many distant problems is so obvious that at least a small part of the citizenry is affected and provides some sort of support for DIMs. Moreover, groups such as Greenpeace have demonstrated that putting distant issues on the agenda depends not just on the "objective" scope of the problem but may be largely dependent on the way it is presented. In terms of relevance as perceived by scientific experts, the killing of baby seals in Alaska or the disposing of facilities for oil drilling on the bottom of the ocean are "minor" problems, but they have been successfully problematized. People experienced in media work have shown that human rights issues may also reach a large audience. For example, rock concerts were organized to raise money against apartheid in South Africa. More recently, even the classic human rights organization Amnesty International has become acquainted with such forms of public relations.

Whether these "modernized" forms of event-oriented media work could and should replace the mostly silent but steady traditional activities in DIMs may be disputed among the activists. But why shouldn't both forms complement each other? If we differentiate our measures of success, both kinds of mobilization have their value. A single rock concert for a distant cause may, at least superficially, inform tens of millions of mostly young people. It may also result in millions of dollars in support for the cause (and, of course, for the communications industry). On the other hand, we should not forget that the nonspectacular work of thousands of activists is not always in vain. Although from the perspective of the individual group the task of getting attention and support for a particular distant cause is often discouraging because so many relevant issues compete with each other, the combined effect of these groups sometimes helps to bring about change, as the more recent development of rights policies in Argentina, Guatemala, Peru, and other countries demonstrates (e.g., Brysk 1993, 1994; Forsythe 1991; Pagnucco 1997).

4. Conclusion

As in many other countries, highly decentralized and heterogenous distant issue movements have developed in West Germany in recent decades. The empirical findings show that these movements clearly differ from the patterns of the aggregation of all protest. However, if we compare DIMs with other new social movements, we find a great deal of structural resemblence.[29]

From a theoretical perspective, the very existence and persistence of DIMs represent a challenge. While for good reasons we assume that people can best be mobilized when their own interests are at stake, the DIMs are an outstanding and clear-cut case that hardly fits the conventional rational choice model. To be sure, DIMs are much weaker than, say, trade unions. It remains true that most people participate only for their immediate substantial benefits. However, DIMs represent a major segment of new social movements, though—in relative terms—their protest activity seems to be less prominent in Germany compared to the Netherlands and Switzerland. Several thousand DIM groups exist in Germany. Many of their members devote much energy to coming closer to achieving their ends. In terms of rational choice theory, the movements' size, and in particular the high level of involvement of their adherents, remain a puzzle. Why do so many people spend so much of their resources for the sake of strangers who belong to other cultures and live far away from those who take an advocacy role? Should we call this participation irrational because it does not provide a direct and tangible benefit to the activists? Is this just a hidden form of seeking personal advantage?

The answer is no. Instead, we have to acknowledge the importance of reasons other than material incentives as a driving force behind participation, namely, the search for solidarity and, particularly in the case of distant issues, adherence to political and moral convictions that provide standards of how to act and what to achieve even when, in economic terms, the costs seem to be prohibitive.

NOTES

An early and very preliminary version of this chapter was presented at the annual meeting of the American Sociological Association, Washington, D.C., August 19–23, 1995. I am grateful to John D. McCarthy, the editors of this volume, and two anonymous reviewers for their comments on previous drafts and to Richard Steer for his editorial assistance. I also wish to thank the numerous people at the Wissenschaftszentrum Berlin für Sozialforschung who have contributed in the past few years to creating the data used for the analysis.

1. John McCarthy (1997, 259) reminds us what ought to be done: "But if the study of transnational movements is to fully join the mainstream of social movement analysis, it must also be based upon newly generated, or aggregated, systematic evidence about the shape and extent of transnational movements over time and across space."

2. Hence, transnational movements, defined by Tarrow (1997, 184) as "sustained contentious interactions with opponents—national or nonnational—by connected networks of challengers organized across national boundaries," overlap but are not identical to distant issue movements (DIMs) as conceived in this chapter.

3. First, the reference to the Third World has become problematic because of both the progress some countries in this "world" have made and the recent breakdown of the Second World. Moreover, my reference point is not the distinction between different worlds but the aspect of distant issues, which could, for example, concern the violation of civil rights in a relatively distant First World country. Second, the term *solidarity movement* is

too broad for my analytical purposes because it also includes groups that engage in domestic issues, for example, groups fighting for the rights of asylum seekers in the activists' home countries.

4. No impact of the issue's outcome on the domestic situation can be expected when advocacy groups engage, for example, for political prisoners in China or for an endangered indigenous group in New Zealand or Guatemala. In many other issues, however, some sort of substantive feedback on the activists' situation can be expected. This is true, for example, when one engages to save the rain forests of South America, whose existence may not only affect the regional but the world climate. In such a case, it is difficult to assess the weight of the altruistic component of action.

5. When deprivation and degradation in distant areas are mainly perceived as fate or even as the fault of those who suffer, then distant issue mobilization will remain low. When, however, structural factors, including (neo)colonialism and unfair terms of trade, are perceived as the main causes, there is a greater chance that people in the capitalist core countries will engage in acts of solidarity.

6. For a brief overview of domestically oriented human rights groups in West Germany, see Narr 1995.

7. In 1993, these two areas were followed by women's rights (9 percent), peace (9 percent), world order/multiissue (8 percent), development (6 percent), and self-determination/ethnic (5 percent).

8. However, we should not forget that DIM groups also exist within movements that are identified under a different label. For instance, protests attributed to the women's or ecology movements may also involve distant issues.

9. When considering only new social movements, the share of the solidarity movement is 8.6 percent.

10. For details on the design and method of this project, see Rucht and Ohlemacher 1992; Rucht, Hocke, and Oremus 1995; and Rucht and Neidhardt 1998.

11. The operational definition of *distant issue movements* was based on the following selection criteria. First, only protests in *West* Germany were selected. Second, based on a code for the geographical reference or scope of the underlying problem that induced protest, the areas Latin America, the Soviet Union, the United States, Asia, Africa, Australasia and the Pacific Islands, and "international" were selected. The latter category was only used when more inclusive categories such as Europe or Africa did not apply. Third, immigrants and ethnic minorities as social carriers of protest were excluded because these groups may have close links to groups in distant areas and therefore may act, at least in part, self-interestedly. Fourth, twelve broad thematic areas (see table 4.6), which cover almost all the coded issues, were selected. At that point, this combined selection procedure led to 897 distant issue protests, including also those that were against the rights of women, refugees, and so on. Finally, only those protests were selected in the twelve areas that promoted the interests of the disadvantaged and deprived groups, that is, pro-women, pro-refugees, and so on. This led to the final number of 824 protests that are the basis for all the following calculations on distant issue protests in West Germany. The figures presented here differ from those in an earlier version of this essay (see notes) because at that point the data set was still incomplete and another selection procedure had been applied.

12. In East Germany, for which we have data from 1989 to 1994, the picture is strikingly different. Leaving aside 1989, which was a very special year, only five distant issue protests were registered in the period from 1990 to 1994 (out of a total of 823 protest events) compared to sixty-four distant issue protests in West Germany (out of total of 1,866 protest events).

13. The year 1970 was chosen because it falls roughly in the middle of the whole observation period.

14. For the number of participants, the proportion of activity in these nine cities out of all distant issue mobilizations was considerably lower (21.1 percent).

15. Olejniczak (1997) has conducted an excellent, still unpublished study of the Third World movement in Germany, including a survey of 40 umbrella organizations and 238 individual groups based on 2,221 identified groups.

16. In the mid-1980s, Balsen and Rössel (1986, 503) estimated that there were a total of three to four thousand groups in West Germany. On a local basis, one can trace the development of these groups according to the so-called *Stattbücher* that exist in various cities in Germany. The *Stattbücher* are collections of brief self-portraits of all kinds of leftist and alternative groups dealing with issues of peace, women, ecology, urban restructuring, and so on. For Berlin and Cologne, several issues of these directories have appeared since 1978 and the mid-1990s, respectively. If we exclude the first issues, which tended to be highly selective in documenting local groups, we find that the number of groups categorized under the label Third World has remained fairly constant in Berlin but has decreased (from twenty-six to ten) in Cologne.

17. In 1993, Amnesty International had sections in 51 countries, of which about half were in the Third World. The total membership was 1.1 million (*Der Spiegel,* July 12, 1993, 126). According to more recent sources, Amnesty has around 1 million members in 162 countries. Much bigger, though less political, however, are the Red Cross and Red Crescent, which claim to be supported by 250 million people.

18. The counts for the various categories are as follows: global/universal orientation, twelve; Asia and the Middle East, seven; Latin America, five; Africa, four; Pacific, two; human rights, general, five; refugees in the Third World, one; women in the Third World, two; friendship associations, six; Third World Shops, seven.

19. Altogether, the German groups concerned with Third World issues produce about eighty journals and newsletters, chief among them *Peripherie, Blätter des iz3w, FORUM entwicklungspolitischer Arbeitsgruppen,* and *ila—Zeitschrift der Informationsstelle Lateinamerika.* Based on her detailed survey, Olejniczak (1997, 425) estimates that 1,400 Third World groups, through their newsletters and journals, reach about one hundred thousand people.

20. Under the heading the "paradox of participation," the relatively high voter turnout in elections has been widely discussed (e.g., Strom 1975). But it seems to be only a paradox in light of the hard core version of rational choice theory.

21. See Etzioni 1988 and Green and Shapiro 1994 for a critique of the application of rational choice theory beyond the economic sphere.

22. Olson himself (1982) has acknowledged the existence of social incentives, but he assumed that these are only relevant in small groups.

23. For a more general discussion of purposive rewards of voluntary and other organizations, see Hirschman 1982 and Margolis 1982.

24. Several theorists expanding or criticizing the rational choice concept have argued that such single decisions are the exception rather than the rule (Taylor 1988; Hardin 1982).

25. To be sure, rational choice theorists agree that in many situations decisions are made with incomplete information and hence in uncertainty about the benefits (and costs). For an early reflection on this, see Simon 1957, 198. For a discussion of "bounded rationality," see March 1978.

26. Rational choice theorists may, and in part do, argue that moral satisfaction can be a selective incentive. If, however, the concept of rationality is stretched so far, one wonders

whether there is any human action that cannot be called rational. In this case, the concept would lose its discriminatory value and become tautological (Fireman and Gamson 1979).

27. Esser (1991, 60) therefore concluded that rational choice theory is always "subjective" because it has to be conceived from the criteria and perspective of the actor and not the observer.

28. Olejniczak (1997, 385) found in her systematic sample of 238 Third World groups that 32 percent were religious groups.

29. Olejniczak's research (1997) provides strong empirical evidence that Third World groups are an integral part of the broader family of new social movements.

PART II

Globalizations and Movements in Nation-States

CHAPTER 5

The Irrelevance of Nationalism (the Relevance of Globalism)? Cultural Frames of Collective Protest in Postcommunist Poland, 1989–93

Jan Kubik

One of the primary contentions of this volume is that there is no single globalization but rather a set of globalizations occurring at various levels, through various means, and at various speeds.[1] Some forms of globalization, such as the "Westernization" of the global economy, may indeed have triggered powerful resistance, often assuming a form of cultural "antiglobalism" (Escobar 1995). This chapter's primary goal is to determine whether Poles reacted to the "globalizing" postcommunist economic reforms with resistance or protest couched in terms of antiglobalizing, for example, nationalistic, frames.[2]

This focus on frames, and thus on the culture of protest, is warranted in the Polish case for three reasons. First, in Eastern Europe culture has always been intricately interwoven with politics (Szporluk 1990; Bibo 1991; Kennedy 1994). For example, Polish struggles against the partitioning powers during the nineteenth century were waged with guns and swords as often as with poems, paintings, and folk songs.

Second, in Poland the 1989 revolution was as much a *cultural* as a *political* revolution.[3] During the 1970s and early 1980s, a substantial number of people engaged in the formulation, development, and defense of a counterhegemonic vision, which served to delegitimize the state socialist system and simultaneously allowed these people to constitute themselves as an "appositional" *cultural class* of Solidarity. I interpret Solidarity, then, not as a trade union or a movement but as a cultural class in statu nascendi, never fully consolidated, subjected to the tremendous internal centrifugal tensions that operated *together* with the centripetal forces of symbolic unification. By 1991, centrifugal political (both programmatic and personal) tensions destroyed Solidarity (as a specific cultural class), but throughout the 1980s a substantial portion of the Polish populace "belonged" to it, either actively, by engaging in various clandestine activities, or passively, by giving it their moral support. The cultural frame that held this class together was built as a polar vision of us/the people/Solidarity versus them/authorities/communists. One suspects that such a dramatic polarization should have some impact on the post-1989 political culture.

Third, as Ekiert and I determined (1998a, 1998b, 1999), popular protest has played a crucial role in Polish postcommunist politics; it has become a more important channel of communication between the state and society than in other Central European states. As a result, discourses spawned by protest organizers have become pivotal components of the postcommunist political culture in that country.

What can we gain, though, from couching an analysis of postcommunism in terms of the debate on globalization(s)? The principal gain from such an approach is that it puts into sharp relief the contrast between Central Europe and the rest of the postcommunist world. Such crucial aspects of postcommunist transformations in Central Europe as economic and political restructuring are instances of rapid globalizations par excellance. Whereas the governments of Central European states opted for an unprecedented opening to the West and a wholesale and almost unconditional importation of Western political and economic models, most other governments that emerged in the postcommunist world proceeded with much more caution if not outright hostility toward "European" institutional models.[4] On the other hand, it is clear that, whereas postcommunism has often become synonymous with political instability, economic chaos, and increasing misery, Central Europe has embarked on a path of solid democratization and economic growth. In brief, embracing Western European economic models and practices seems to have become a significant precondition or component of economic growth and political stability. By contrast, incomplete and inconsistent "economic Westernization" has become associated with economic malaise and political chaos.

At the same time, the process of Europeanization has been multifaceted and has not run smoothly in every postcommunist state. Some groups and organizations rejected, for example, the viability of "Western" neoliberal economic prescriptions. Others expressed serious doubts as to whether Western political models and practices are suitable for their part of the continent. Nowhere, however, was the opposition to Western imports more ferocious than in the domain of culture. Invoking such foundations of domestic or regional specificity as a deeper or truer religiosity, a separate political history, or the inimitable complexity and profundity of their national identification, some groups and political entrepreneurs challenged the wisdom and desirability of full or even partial Europeanization.

There can be no doubt that the cost of Europeanization, which in its economic dimension is founded on the neoliberal economic blueprint, has been high. Moreover, some analysts predicted the unfolding of the following pessimistic scenario: rapid economic reforms would result in high social costs and intense dissatisfaction among the populace. This dissatisfaction was expected to be especially intense during the early stages of the reforms' implementation, when their results were either insignificant or outright negative. The heightened level of dissatisfaction would then lead to the magnification of social protest, which in turn was expected to help topple reforming governments and remove the neoliberal elites from power. In particular, it was expected that the economic aspect of Europeanization (acceptance and implementation of neoliberal reforms) was going to produce a specific backlash: the eruption of anti-European narratives designed to demonize Europe and its institutions, the (re)assertion of local identities, and the rejection or reformulation of Europeanization.

In the Latin American, Asian, and African contexts, globalization has developed into a complex, contradictory, and hotly contested process. The diffusion or imposition of the economic practices of the West (Europe, the First World, and so on)—usually seen in the West as merely disseminating proper and truly sound economic know-how—has led to the intensification of various forms of cultural and/or political resistance. The essence of this resistance has been the rejection of the West's claims to intellectual, organizational, or cultural superiority.[5] Not infrequently, grassroots resistance evolved into or was complemented by violent riots (Greskovits 1998; Walton 1991; Walton and Ragin 1990; Walton and Seddon 1994) or took the form of massive movements that framed their opposition to globalization in terms of populism and/or nationalism. As a result of such cultural resistance culminating in direct political action, economic and political globalization has often been derailed or slowed. Has a similar scenario developed in Central Europe?

Given the abruptness, depth, and breadth of the economic transformations in Poland (dubbed "shock therapy"), one could expect high levels of cultural resistance, rioting, and organized opposition led by movements or trade unions. After all, the Poles' claim to fame has been their ability to organize themselves in a movement-cum-trade union—Solidarity. Furthermore, one might expect that a substantial part of such a protest wave would be framed in terms of anti-Western rhetoric. Have expectations of an anti-Western (or anti-European) backlash been fulfilled? Did such a backlash occur at the beginning of the restructuring when the social costs of reforms were very high and their benefits dubious?

To answer these questions, I will analyze relevant aspects of the elite political culture and the cultural frames of protest politics. Elite political culture[6] will be reconstructed through the analysis of political rhetoric and symbolic displays by leading politicians. The same method will be used to reconstruct collective action frames: I will analyze dominant demands, slogans, visual symbols, songs, and rhetoric employed by the protestors.

The Dualism of the Polish Elite Political Culture

During periods of rapid social change, culture becomes fragmented and *decentered* (Tarkowska 1993; Jawłowska 1994), yet at the same time the link between culture (discourses, symbols, rhetoric, and so on) and politics intensifies. There seem to be two basic mechanisms that propel this process. First, as Swidler observes:

> Culture has independent causal influence in unsettled cultural periods because it makes possible new strategies of action—constructing entities that

> can act (selves, families, corporations), shaping the styles and skills with which they act, and modeling forms of authority and cooperation." (1986, 280)

Second, many people during such unstable periods tend to retreat into their private or parochial worlds. It is well established that "the pattern of retreat into parochial institutions . . . is a characteristic response for many people when faced with a larger society that is culturally unfamiliar" (Wilson 1991, 213). If escapism is a frequent reaction to unfamiliarity resulting from instability and rapid change, then the public space is left to elites and political entrepreneurs (Bourdieu's professionals). As a result, they have a unique opportunity to "model the forms of authority and cooperation" in political space without a challenge they would have to encounter had the situation been more stable and civil and political societies more active.[7] In brief, during the periods following the downfall of the "ancient regime" social control over political entrepreneurs is relaxed and consequently they face a unique opportunity to engage in defining the shape of the emerging political and social order. Consequently, under such circumstances collective protest is not simply a symbolic struggle to *challenge* or *support* the hegemonic frame legitimating the incumbent regime's power; it is a struggle to *establish* a new hegemony for the whole of society and its political order.[8]

This is exactly what has been happening in Poland since 1989. Polish elites have engaged in a bitter struggle to find suitable and acceptable cultural capital and construct out of it a viable hegemony, that is, a durable set of cultural frames that can produce enough consensus around their programs of postcommunist consolidation. During my 1990–91 fieldwork in Poland and in subsequent studies, I came to the conclusion that the political cleavages routinely specified by Polish sociologists are not sufficient to construct a complete picture of Polish politics.[9] What I felt was urgently needed was an articulation of a "hidden cleavage" of Polish politics, whose presence I sensed and observed in myriad political actions, particularly in 1991–92.

There were many indications that during the early consolidation phase (1989–93) Polish elite political culture was polarized.[10] This bipolar cleavage existed "above" or "beyond" the multiplicity of other cleavages and can best be construed as an opposition between *the logic of the rule of law* and *revolutionary logic*. The former is based on an axiom that holds that social (political) life during the transition should be regulated as much as possible by the existing (though obviously evolving) system of laws. Otherwise, it is argued, the peaceful and gradual revolution will inevitably degenerate into Jacobian terror and will "devour its children." The latter is founded on the belief that it is impossible to carry out meaningful reforms without a prior cleansing of the political realm of all vestiges of the previous system (e.g., former communists still occupying positions of influence).

Politics based on the rule of law (above other principles) tends to correlate with (1) a conviction that post-1989 Poland is *discontinuous* with the Polish People's Republic and (2) an emphasis on (democratic) *procedures* over (any) political *substance.* Politics based on revolutionary logic tends to go together with (1) a belief that a decisive break with the Polish People's Republic has not yet occurred and (2) defining politics more in terms of cultural/political substance than procedures. Thus, often at its heart lie questions of identity: who is the majority and who is not a legitimate participant in the political community? In contrast to the logic of the rule of law, which is usually *inclusive* and *formalistic* in its definition of *citizens,* revolutionary logic tends to be *exclusive* and *substantive* in its definition of *true members.* In Poland, there is a tendency to define *true members* as Polish Catholics, thereby excluding members of religious and ethnic minorities who are concerned that they may become second-class citizens.[11] When *Polishness* is defined as a specific cultural (rather then political or civic) identity, the task of linking this identity to more inclusive constructs, such as "Europe," is more difficult than in the case of the formal and more inclusive "Polish citizenship" preferred by the reformists.

The dichotomy I am proposing here resembles and partially overlaps with other dichotomous conceptualizations of post-1989 politics in the former Soviet bloc. Jowitt writes about "civics" and "ethnics" (1990, 195), J. F. Brown about "moderates" (those seeking conciliation) and "radicals" (those seeking confrontation) (1993, 71), and Michnik about "the ethnocentric versus the democratic temptation" (Tismaneanu 1992, 3). Wnuk-Lipiński (1994) offers a different yet also bipolar conceptualization, defining "two responses to a radical social change" as fundamentalism and pragmatism. Ziółkowski (1993) develops a contrast between the "universalistic-market-achievement-modernization-individualistic-anti-

TABLE 5.1. Revolutionaries versus Reformists

	"Revolutionary" Option	"Reformist" Option
(1) Diagnosed relation of the post-1989 political order to state socialism	Continuity (at least partial)	Discontinuity (considerable)
(2) Postulated regulation of transition	Revolutionary logic	Rule of law
(3) Postulated logic of transition	Clean cut ("ruptura")	Gradual ("reforma")
(4) Postulated regime's basic principle	Substantivist (rule of majority)	Formalist (rule of law)
(5) Principal cause of economic problems	Post-1989 policies	Pre-1989 policies
(6) Principal political objective	Completion of the deconstruction of state socialism	Acceleration of the consolidation of the new order
(7) Attitude toward tighter incorporation within "Europe"	Reserved, sometimes hostile	Friendly, often enthusiastic

egalitarian" and "particularistic-protective-claiming-traditional-communitarian-egalitarian" constellations. Particularly relevant here is a pair proposed by Skotnicka-Illasiewicz and Wesołowski, who in their study of Polish parliamentarians distinguish two extreme tendencies: "The first group perceives Europe as a configuration of civil societies with high cooperative potential; the second perceives it as a configuration of ethnic communities with high dominance potential" (1995, 210).

Differences between both styles of politics, which I will call revolutionary and reformist, are summarized in table 5.1. It is important to remember that many "revolutionaries" (e.g., Olszewski or Kaczyński) did not transgress the rules of the democratic political game in practice; their revolutionary inclinations, however, were clear in their rhetoric.

Frames of the Elite Political Culture

The public discourse developed by Polish political elites during the 1989–93 period provides many examples of the dualistic (bipolar) conceptualization of the country's political field and culture. The reformists often saw themselves as enlightened Europeans and their opponents as narrow-minded provincials and hateful revangists. Revolutionaries in turn defined themselves as true anticommunists and protectors of the nation who faced a cosmopolitan alliance of the Reds and the Pinks. In extreme conceptualizations, the revolutionaries' enemies were portrayed as alien manipulators such as foreign capitalists, Masons, and Jews. Master frames of the elite political culture contain several elaborate versions of these basic distinctions. What follows is a collection of statements illustrating this phenomenon.

A. *Reformists Conceptualizing Revolutionaries*

Reformist frame 1. Revolutionaries are extreme. Example: Jan Lityński (an influential politician of the Democratic Union) when asked whether accusing Wałęsa for secretly collaborating with the communist security forces was a political game or a folly, answered:

> Game comes in later, initially you have revolutionary vigilance, as in the case of Nechayev, Dzerzhinsky, or leftist and rightist terrorists: the rejection of what exists or existed in the name of the total elimination of evil. This must lead to folly, to the disavowal of values in whose name one is acting. (*Gazeta Wyborcza,* July 22, 1992)

Reformist frame 2. Revolutionaries are populist, for they prevent or delay the consolidation of the "normal" parliamentary system. Example: Alexander Hall (the most prominent leader of the "reformist Right") described the main dilemma of Polish politics in the following fashion:

> I believe, that the time has come to consolidate the forces of all [political] groups which want to stabilize parliamentary democracy in Poland. And this calls for a cooperation of people representing Christian-democratic, conservative, and moderately social-democratic (in the western sense of the world) views. In my interpretation the program of the party or coalition that is being formed around Jan Olszewski, and to which Antoni Macierewicz belongs, is based on a conviction that the system we now have in Poland must be replaced through early elections and these elections—it seems both parliamentary and presidential—[they] want to win by rousing people's anger directed against elites. . . ."[12]

Reformist frame 3. Revolutionaries are unsophisticated. This frame was rarely used in the official public discourse, yet it emerged in many private conversations we had with various reformists during the 1989–93 period. It has been reported, for example, that a prominent politician of the "reformist" Democratic Union referred to the "revolutionary" politicians as "stinking men with wet palms."

Reformist frame 4. Revolutionaries are evil (demonizing). Example: Antoni Macierewicz was sometimes accused of having "evil eyes." It is important to note that, according to Garrison and Arensberg, in the Mediterranean, where the phenomenon of the evil eye is particularly widespread, it is associated with clientelism (i.e., weak formal institutionalization). Certain forms of the evil eye phenomenon correlate with "a system of plural, stratified, societies organized in unstable states with redistributive economies" (Galt 1982, 666).

Reformist frame 5. (Some) revolutionaries tend to espouse exclusive "ethnic" nationalism, which may isolate Poland in Europe and lead to negative social and economic consequences. Balcerowicz observes:

> The word "alien" generates strong negative emotions. That is why those who want to discourage us from using *foreign experiences and money*—important factors in accelerating development—play with the expression "alien capital." Their renunciation of outside models seems to be genuine and often results—I surmise—from their lack of knowledge about the world." (1995, 460–61; emphasis added)

B. *Revolutionaries Conceptualizing Reformists*

Revolutionary frame 1. Reformists are crypto-communists, for they collaborate with or at least protect the interests of the former communists. Macierewicz (one of the most prominent politicians of the revolutionary Right) observed: "Today's Poland needs the unification of the Right. In order to shatter *the vicious circle of the post–roundtable drama,* which is being played out in front of our eyes. . . . We need to liberate Poland from the Left's rule, which is based on lies, enslaves our nation, and attempts to subdue it to the power from the East" (emphasis added).[13]

Revolutionary frame 2. The break between the Polish People's Republic and the post-1989 system has not yet occurred or has not been decisive enough. In Macierewicz's words: "First of all, the communist system continues. . . . It is a personal, economic, and political but also legal continuity since the Stalinist constitution still holds. Only the labels have changed. In Russia, the system's continuity is even more pronounced than it is in Poland."[14]

Revolutionary frame 3. Solidarity politicians who participated in the roundtable negotiations and later formed the Ruch Obywatelski—Akcja Demokratyczna (ROAD: Civic Movement—Democratic Action) and the Democratic Union are associated with the Reds—former communists from the Polish United Workers' Party. This association is so close that they merit the name Pinks. The Pinks' frame was very influential in the elite political culture of the early 1990s.

Revolutionary frame 4. Reformist economic policies ruined the Polish economy. Macierewicz observed:

> We are talking—first of all—not about building a revindicative wave. This wave exists. This wave of social discontent exists. It is a drama that parties that call themselves "the Right"—like yours—do not want to notice this wave, or perhaps they believe that they can ignore it. But this wave results from the mistakes that are being committed [now].

Revolutionary frame 5. Reformists are "impure" Poles who do not protect the interests of the nation. Jackowski writes:

> Ineffectual mirages of a united Europe are being replaced by a concept of Euroregions, advocated by doctrinaires who [also] espouse the loss of identity by Poland and who do not need a homeland, for "they have their capital in Brussels." (1993, 187)

For revolutionaries, the most negative features of their political opponents were synthesized in the Pinks' frame. The framing strategy employed here can be reduced to a simple three-step precept: (1) convince people that there is only one Left, an alliance of Pinks and Reds; (2) persuade them that this more or less explicit alliance between some segments of the opposition and former communists has its beginnings in the roundtable negotiations of 1989; and (3) label your political enemy as a member of this Left. The conclusion, explicitly stated or merely suggested, is unavoidable: if a party, person, or movement, was identified or identified itself as leftist or Pink it had to be classified as a successor to "existing socialism" (totalitarian communism), which had left the country in shambles.

In particular, the Pinks were often portrayed as a-national or antinational cosmopolitans, either indifferent or hostile to the best interests of the Polish nation. The Pinks, who according to Jackowski included members of the (nonexistent) Polish United Workers' Party, the Democratic Union, and the Liberal-Democratic Congress, were "united by a common cult of demoliberalism" and strove to implement in the former Soviet bloc a model of economic development that was "a new version of socialism 'with a human face': social-democratization of Eastern Europe" (1993, 181).[15]

Although I was unable to assess its popularity and influence with great precision, I believe that the Reds-Pinks versus others conceptualization of the post-communist political field came to dominate elite political culture during the 1989–91 period. This conceptualization set the terms of political discourse in Poland for years to come; it was successfully employed prior to the 1998 parliamentary elections, which produced strongly polarized results (Jasiewicz 1998; Markowski 1998).

One more important phenomenon should be noted here. Wasilewski observed that by 1993 the Polish political elite was less polarized than before and more fragmented along several cleavage lines. Moreover, he determined that amid this fragmentation new, multipolar, political divisions were slowly emerging. As he put it: "The new structure reflects political and ideological differences in a more distinct and coherent way than the old bipolar structure" (1995, 129).

Wasilewski's conclusion can be slightly modified: although the (structural) bipolarization of the political elite was diminishing, the bipolarization of the political discourse was cultivated with an indefatigable zeal by many political entrepreneurs. Most importantly for this study of globalization/Europeanization, the elites' attitudes toward European integration did not show signs of depolarization. Actually, as Skotnicka-Illasiewicz and Wesołowski observed: "The attitudes towards integration reflected in the programs of different political parties, and those of members of parliament, are much more polarized today than at the beginning, in 1989–91" (1993, 210).

In the next section, I will analyze the symbolism and rhetoric of protest in order to determine to what degree protest organizers framed their actions in the bipolar terms I detected in the elite political culture.

Europeanization and Nationalism in Protest Frames

Having identified the main frames of the elite political culture, I set out to determine whether these or similar frames were employed by organizers and participants of collective actions. In particular, I wanted to see whether and with what frequency protest actions were framed in terms of globalizing (pro-Western) or nationalistic (anti-Western) discourses. I knew from journalistic accounts that nationalistic frames were used; the task was to determine with what frequency they were employed relative to other protest frames.

Our research protocol contained three items designed to record both the slogans displayed or recited by protestors and the comments they offered to journalists. Unfortunately, the press accounts did not always contain this kind of information. In 1989, out of 314 recorded protest events, accounts of only 32 (10 percent) provided information concerning the political rhetoric of slogans and participator comments. Information for the following three years is, however, more comprehensive. For 1990, out of 306 event descriptions, 67 (22 percent) contained relevant information; for 1991, out of 292 case descriptions, 100 (34 percent) contained information pertaining to rhetoric. For 1992, the ratio is 117 out of 314 (37 percent); for 1993, it is 83 out of 250 (33 percent).

Slogans and participator comments from 399 protest events were grouped into five basic types of frames.[16] While constructing this typology, our primary consideration was to determine how often the polarizing frames developed within the elite political culture were employed by the protestors. In other words, we wanted to determine the strength of the alignment between the most radical frames of the elite political culture and the framing (conceptualization and symbolization) of protest. The five types, the subtypes, their examples, and relevant comments follow.

1. Anti-communist and anti-Soviet frames. These frames were particularly suitable for challenging the legitimacy of the pre-1989 political order and those of its institutions that continued to exist afterward. They should therefore be used frequently in 1989 and 1990, when the institutions of communism were gradually phased out, and afterward their usage should decline. Examples of such frames include "Down with communism," "Down with the commune," "Soviets go home," "Down with the Soviets," and "communists, consider your own Nuremberg."

2. Polarizing frames (nationalistic and anti-Semitic). We identified three subtypes of polarizing frames.

2.1. Polarizing frames rejecting the post-1989 political order as illegitimate. Employment of such frames could mean only one thing: a total (even if only symbolic) rejection of the post-1989 political order. We were particularly interested in finding out whether protestors were inclined to employ the Pinks master frame and/or its derivatives. The dominant frames of this group were "the commune" (*komuna*)—in reference to Solidarity governments and institutions—the "crypto-commune," and the "Judeo-commune" (*Żydokomuna*). We decided, however, to classify the latter with other anti-Semitic frames. Many frames in this category were used in slogans beginning with "Down with," as in "Down with the commune" or "Down with the Judeo-commune." They served to delegitimize the post-1989 political order by defining it as a continuation of communism. Other examples of frames belonging to this group include "Communists to

Cuba," "Magdalenka = Targowica,"[17] "Crypto-commune, stay away from our property," "Enough of the crypto-commune's rule," "Solidarity is selling the interests of the working people and nomenclature," and "Okapizm + Walesism = Komunism."[18]

2.2. Nationalistic polarizing frames (purity frames). These seem to have served to delegitimize the post-1989 political order by defining it as ethnically/nationally *impure* and calling for its purification. The most frequent examples were "Poland for Poles," "Long live the Great Poland," and "We won't allow Polish soil to be taken away."

2.3. Anti-Semitic polarizing frames. These served to reject the post-1989 political and social order by defining it as controlled by or associated with Jews. There appear to have been two basic subtypes of such frames: (1) those associating Jews with communism, as in "Down with the Judeo-commune" (Precz z Żydokomuna) and (2) clear-cut anti-Semitic slogans, including "The only good Jew is a dead Jew." Any issue, it seems, could be incorporated into an anti-Semitic frame, which then served to turn a political opponent into an alien, as in "Walesa, the Jew." For example, social policies of the Mazowiecki government, personified by Labor Minister Jacek Kuroń, were attacked in the slogan "Shame! We do not want soups. Let Kuroń himself eat them!"[19] But on another occasion the following quasi syllogisms were displayed: "Jews to the oven," "Kuroń to the oven," and "Make soup out of Kuroń."

3. Reformist political frames. Slogans employing these frames did not call for the rejection or abolition of the regime; neither did they seek to delegitimize it by indicating its national impurity or "Jewish connections." They simply criticized policies or politicians. For example, on March 7, 1990, a demonstration organized by citizens' committees displayed a placard that declared, "The government is not enough—(local) self-government is needed." On May 1, 1992, during a rally organized by the Social-Democracy of the Polish Republic, a journalist noted the following slogans: "Enough corruption!," "Stelmachowski to a parish office" and "Lech Wałęsa must go—no replacement."

4. Frames criticizing specific economic policies. "Economic" slogans and self-comments expressed a wide range of concerns. They were often moderate, as exemplified by the quotation "The aim of the strike is not to force pay raises but to defend the enterprise against bankruptcy." Other examples are "We protest against the drastic salary reductions in light industry" and "Amnesia can be cured. Kaszpirowki—heal our ministers."[20]

Slogans criticizing the government's economic policies were sometimes personalized. Then their most frequent target was Leszek Balcerowicz, deputy prime minister and finance minister in the Mazowiecki and Bielecki governments. For example, on May 24, 1990, demonstrators displayed the slogan "The Balcerowicz program—to be corrected." On one occasion the slogan "Replace Balcerowicz" was accompanied by another pronouncing "We apologize for the [road] blockade" and the comment "We do not want to block Poland, but we want to unblock thinking about agriculture."

5. *Frames concerning specific issues (ecological, feminist, AIDS-related) and local problems.* According to our analysis, this type had four subtypes.

5.1. *Ecological slogans.* Examples: "Life in Zabrze = a death sentence," "The Czorsztyn Dam = the death of nature," and "Nuclear energy—stop."

5.2. *Slogans and statements expressing feminist issues as well as pro-choice or pro-life concerns.* The slogan "Spring is yours—ass is ours" (meaning the choice of abortion is a woman's right) was yet another take on the theme "Something is yours, something else is ours," which was initiated with "The Winter is yours, the Spring is ours," often heard after the imposition of martial law on December 13, 1980. It was also used by Michnik in the summer of 1989 in his famous proposal "Your President, our Prime Minister."

5.3. *Slogans related to AIDS.* Examples: "We do not want Kotański and his protégés"[21] and "Fags—get out."

5.4. *Slogans or statements expressing concrete, specific (often local) concerns and demands.* Examples: "The Holocaust will never happen again," "The PZPR buildings for the university," "The press, radio, and television lie," "Remove the sex shop," and "Poles demand the recognition of Lithuania's independence."

The frequency distribution of the five types of frames is presented in figure 5.1. Due to the methodology of data gathering, our data base may be incomplete. Thus, the following conclusions must be taken with a grain of salt and should be read only as an attempt to identify general trends. These trends are clear, however.

First, throughout the whole period the protest rhetoric was predominantly nonpolitical: economic and various specific frames were used in 50 to 70 percent of protests, regardless of which government was in power. Second, the usage of political frames was on the rise throughout the analyzed period. Third, radical polarizing frames explicitly indicating the symbolic rejection of the post-1989 political and social order were used infrequently during Mazowiecki's and Bielecki's terms in office. However, the use of such frames was intensifying systematically. In the pre-Mazowiecki period of 1989, they constituted 4 percent of all slogans and self-comments; during the Mazowiecki reign, 8 percent; and in 1991, under Bielecki, 9 percent. Their usage increased dramatically under Olszewski (27 percent) and under Suchocka (27 percent).

Fourth, anticommunist and anti-Soviet rhetoric, so prominent in the 1989–90 protests, was gradually disappearing during subsequent years. It must be noted, however, that its basic frame, "Down with the commune," was transferred from one set of circumstances to another: first it was used against the communists and then, with increasing frequency, against the post-1989 regimes. "Down with the commune" and "Down with the Judeo-commune" were the two most popular polarizing frames used to delegitimize the post-1989 political regimes.

Fifth, anti-Semitic and nationalistic (antiglobalist, anti-Western) protest

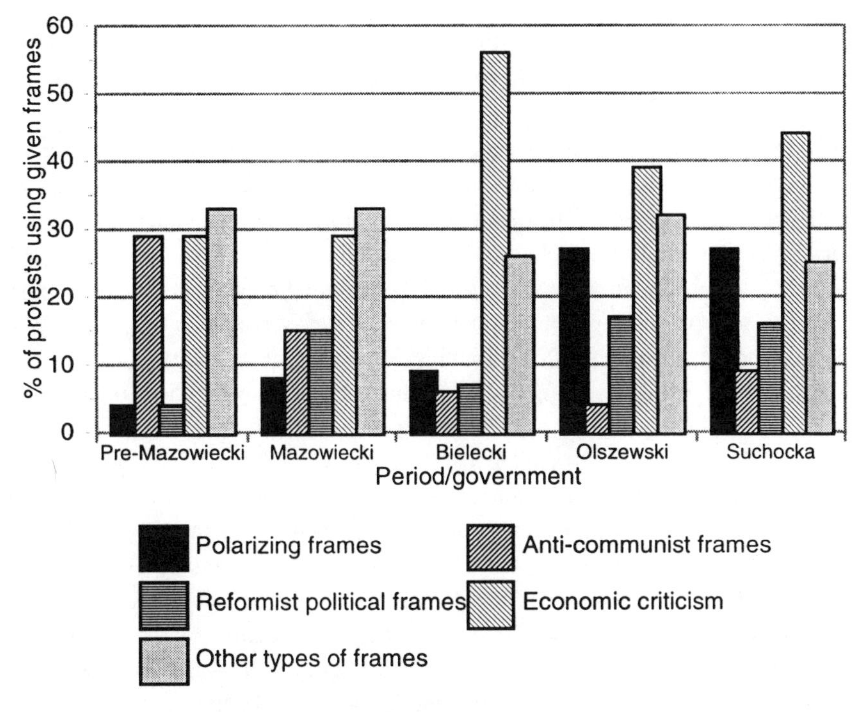

Fig. 5.1. Protest frames, 1989–93

rhetoric *intensified* in 1992. Our researchers did not detect such rhetoric prior to April 5, 1989 (the conclusion of the roundtable negotiations), at all; during Mazowiecki's term in office, anti-Semitic and nationalistic frames constituted 2 percent of all frames. During Bielecki's tenure (mostly in 1991) it was 1 percent. But during the premierships of Olszewski and Suchocka (1992–93) usage went up to 18 and 16 percent, respectively.[22]

The period from 1989 to 1993 can be divided into two subperiods. During the first 2 to 3 years of postcommunist transformation (1989–91), the radical polarizing political frames (including nationalistic ones) were scarcely used. But during the Olszewski/Suchocka period (1992–93) their usage escalated.[23]

I can only hypothesize why these polarizing frames were used during the 1992–93 period more often than before: during this period their *narrative fidelity* increased.[24] Kolarska-Bobińska observed that within the popular political culture the "we-society versus them-the authorities" frame became much more popular in 1992–94 than it was in 1990:

> The "us" (society) versus "them" (government) division perceived in the 1980s disappeared entirely in the [early] 1990s, giving way to conflicts in the various structures of state authority, as well as within the various groups within Solidarity. Two years later *in 1992, the "us"-"them" dichotomy came*

> *back to life in full vigor* (in 1992—23 percent of these who perceived conflict mentioned such a division, in 1994—21 percent). (1994, 154; emphasis added)

There exists, therefore, an intriguing correlation: during the 1992–93 period the tendency to portray the political field in terms of a bipolar cleavage reemerged both within the popular political culture and in protest rhetoric. I am unable to determine which caused which. Was it radical protest rhetoric that influenced people's vision of reality or was it people's increased radicalism that forced the protest leaders to employ more radical frames to stay in tune with the populace? I do not know. Yet the radicalized framing of sociopolitical reality is clearly detectable; what is truly puzzling is the fact that it occurred while the economic situation in the country (at least as measured by the main macroeconomic indicators) was sharply improving. If we agree that this radicalized rhetoric contributed to the increased magnitude of protest during the 1992–93 period,[25] then we would also confirm Lipset's observation that people's political behavior is shaped by their *perceptions* of the economy (and polity) and is not simply determined by a configuration of "objective" economic (or political) factors (1993, 7).

According to Wasilewski (1995), during the same period polarization within the political elite began to dull and several crosscutting cleavage lines emerged. This means that while a certain congruence between the popular political culture and the protest rhetoric (the revival of symbolic polarization) arose the elite's own political culture was showing signs of depolarization and moved in an opposite direction. There was, however, a significant exception to this trend: the question of European integration and the wider problematic of the relationship between "Polishness" and "Europeanness" polarized the parliamentary elite more visibly at the end of the period than at its beginning (Skotnicka-Illasiewicz and Wesołowski 1995, 210).

Conclusions

During the 1989–93 period, when radical economic reforms were implemented, Polish society was not as passive as some studies on electoral behavior indicate (Markowski 1992). Protest activities were widespread, and they indicate the existence of a specific, "rebellious," civil society that was more dynamic and vibrant than the Polish political society (Ekiert and Kubik 1999).

Contentious collective action became a major mode of participation in this rapidly growing civil society. Uncomfortable with routine parliamentary democracy and dissatisfied with certain aspects and results of the neoliberal economic program, many people chose organized protest as their preferred mode of public participation. Some of them turned to militant populism,[26] finding in its polarizing master frames a guide for their actions, but most engaged in protest (strikes and demonstrations) to put forth demands related to their everyday (mostly economic) concerns. For them, it seems, collective protest was a mode of civic action based on the acceptance of the existing order; while protesting, people wanted to correct governmental—mostly economic—policies, not to abolish the emerging regime. "The economy, stupid" was the principal concern of social protest during the first four years of the postcommunist transition. The most popular political program (or philosophy) that can be reconstructed from the analysis of protest frames would combine decisive, though specific, economic demands with a moderate political agenda ("do not topple the whole system but force the government to change some of its policies").[27]

It is thus clear that the conflict between globalization (Europeanization) and nationalism did not dominate the rhetoric and symbolism of protest, whose main focus remained economic and pragmatic. A scrutiny of the Polish postcommunist political culture through the prism of my analysis of protest framing and through various studies of Polish sociologists leads to the conclusion that the themes of globalization and/or antiglobalization were marginal. They did not play a central role in the way people framed their problems nor did they dominate Poles' imagining of their location in the world. Moreover, quite paradoxically, the usage of nationalistic and anti-Western slogans intensified not during the early, most painful stages of economic and political restructuring but later, when the economic results and peoples' assessment of them were improving.

The increasing magnitude of protest and the intensifying usage of radical protest frames during the 1989–93 period reflected institutional chaos, particularly the lack of well-defined and routinely accepted channels of interest articulation and mediation. Through protest, people were expressing their disappointment with the inaccessibility of the state and the ineffectiveness of political parties. But protest actions were not an expression of growing disenchantment with democracy and economic reforms, as happened in Latin America and Africa; protest continued to intensify while the legitimacy of the whole system was systematically increasing and people's assessment of their situation leveled off (Ekiert and Kubik 1999).

Additionally, the high institutionalization of protest activities meant that they became a routine mode of political participation, and rather than undermining democratic consolidation they enhanced it. A threat to consolidation comes from spontaneous, poorly institutionalized outbursts of collective rage, often accompanied by violence, or from organized actions framed in terms of (antiglobalist) nationalism or populism (see Greskovits 1998; Walton 1991; Walton and Ragin 1990; and Walton and Seddon 1994). Such protest actions were marginal in Poland.

At the same time, however, the question of European integration (as a form of globalization) and the symbolic location of Poland within Europe was posed with increasing frequency on all three levels of political culture identified in this chapter (elite, popular, and protest). First, the issue of European integration, over which the symbolic battle between globalists and antiglobalists was fought, polarized the parliamentary elites more decisively during the 1992–93 period than earlier. Second, the increased use of nationalistic frames and frames calling for the rejection of the post-1989 sociopolitical order (which was built on an idea of gradual integration with Europe) may be construed as an indication that the vigor and visibility of the antiglobalist option within protest politics intensified. Third, the popularity of the antiglobalist option among the populace at large seems to have intensified, too, as the polar vision of the social world regained some of its popularity. Nonetheless, it continued to be a minority choice; the support for closer links with Europe remained strong.

The main conclusion of this study is that, in stark contrast to Latin America, the implementation of the neoliberal economic program (Balcerowicz's "shock therapy") did not result in widespread cultural and/or political resistance and/or protest. Most people have accepted the necessity of a major restructuring of the political and economic systems along the lines congruent with Western models and experiences. For them, it seems, "the return to Europe" was not an unwanted and externally imposed form of globalization but rather an expected and deserved "re-globalization" of Poland. There emerged some grassroots resistance against Europeanization and the anti-European rhetoric intensified somewhat in the discourse of both the political elites and protest organizers. But this opposition did not evolve into outbreaks of violence nor did it take the form of more massive movements that would frame their opposition to globalization in terms of populism and/or nationalism. There is no room here to attempt an explanation of this phenomenon (see Greskovits 1998), but I would hypothesize that the most important reason why so many Poles acquiesced to radical globalization-cum-economic reform would have something to do with their conviction that they were "returning to Europe." And no matter how high the cost, this re-Europanization was highly desirable and culturally satisfying. In contrast, neither Africans nor Latin Americans can invoke a narrative of returning to the West in their attempts to come to terms with various globalizations.[28]

NOTES

1. For indispensable words of critique and encouragement, my gratitude goes to my dear Martha, Mike Aronoff, Grzegorz Ekiert, the participants of the Michigan seminar, anonymous reviewers, and, most prominently, to the editors of this volume. The data come from a research project Ekiert and I have conducted over the last several years. For its detailed results and necessary credits, see Ekiert and Kubik 1999.

2. Explicitly antiglobal frames need to be analyzed if we are to understand the complex relationship between the global and the national/regional/local.

3. Kubik 1994a, 1994b. For similar arguments emphasizing the significance of cultural factors in the fall of state socialism, see Goldfarb 1989. Barbara and Bronisław Misztal write: "The birth of Solidarity, an outcome of this *new political culture* gave rise to

hopes that a social struggle would be capable of transforming the Eastern European social system" (1988, 98; emphasis added).

4. As the authors of chapter 1 point out, there are many potential centers of globalization, but so far Eastern Europeans experience globalization mostly as Europeanization or Westernization.

5. As Escobar put it: "The grassroots movements that emerged in opposition to development throughout the 1980s belong to the novel forms of collective action and social mobilization that characterized that decade. . . . Resistance to development was one of the ways in which Third World groups attempted to construct new identities. . . . [T]hese struggles were fundamentally cultural" (1995, 216).

6. For a useful discussion of this concept, see Putnam 1971.

7. As Tarrow observed (following Wildavsky), it takes "entrepreneurs making deliberate culture *choices* to turn mentalities into collective action" (1992, 55).

8. On the concept of a symbolic struggle over the regime's legitimacy, see Gamson 1988, 219. See also Harding, who conceptualizes his work in the following way: "How are shared understandings reconstructed in the course of the collective actions that compose a movement?" and "This essay proposes that social movements are one mode through which hegemonic worldviews are challenged and, to the extent a movement is successful, shifted. In this context, a movement is a prolonged series of conflictual interactions between individuals and groups challenging and those defending a hegemonic worldview" (1984, 379–80).

9. Two cleavages seem to have been most prominent in various analyses: political and economic liberalism versus populism, and secularism versus religiosity.

10. The impact of this bipolarization has been felt in Polish politics well beyond 1993. For example, it strongly influenced the results of the 1997 parliamentary elections (Jasiewicz 1998).

11. Assessments of the size of various minority groups vary. According to *The Warsaw Voice* (September 15, 1991), in Poland there were about 350,000 Germans, 350,000 Ukrainians, 200,000 to 250,000 Byelorussians, 30,000 Slovaks and Czechs, 25,000 Lithuanians, 25,000 Romany, and 15,000 Jews. All the minorities totaled about 1 million, which was about 2.5 percent of Poland's population. According to minority associations, there were 250,000 Byelorussians, 250,000 to 300,000 Ukrainians, 700,000 Germans, 25,000 to 30,000 Slovaks, 15,000 to 20,000 Lithuanians, and about 10,000 Romany (see Klosinska 1992).

12. See the transcript of an exchange that took place on Polish television between two representatives of the "Right," Alexander Hall and Antoni Macierewicz (RFE/RL Research Institute, *Polish Monitoring,* October 2–4, 1992, no. 438, 27–31).

13. *Polityka,* May 12, 1992.

14. *Ilustrowany Kurier Polski,* September 18–20, 1992.

15. Another quote from Jackowski: "Among the followers of socialist-demoliberalism [*soc-demoliberalizm*], for it is a specific religion of the end of the 20th century, there are many people who bounced from wall to wall. After being militant Marxists they became ostentatious (religious) believers and finally joined the ranks of 'enlightened Europeans,' who must do the thinking for the society unprepared for democracy and lead it toward a bright future" (1993, 87).

16. The resulting typology produced mutually exclusive categories that covered almost completely all the reported cases; it therefore comes quite close to the ideal of proper classification. It must be remembered, however, that our data base, because it is derived from journalistic accounts, is incomplete and all the conclusions must remain somewhat tentative.

17. Magdalenka is a location were unofficial talks took place during the roundtable negotiations of 1989. For some people, it came to symbolize the beginning of the alliance between some segments of the opposition (the Pinks) and the communist authorities (the Reds). Targowica, a place were a pro-Russian confederacy was announced in 1792, functions in the Polish collective memory as the ultimate symbol of treason.

18. *Okapizm* refers to the Citizens' Parliamentary Club (OKP), which represented Solidarity in the Parliament and was dominated by the people who later formed the Democratic Union. *Walesizm* means an ideology, a way of thinking characteristic of Walesa and his supporters. Since the politicians related to both the OKP and Walesa in 1990 decisively dominated the political scene, the slogan equates the whole of Polish politics with communism.

19. This demonstration was organized by the Konfederacja Polski Niepodległej (KPN; Confederation for an Independent Poland) and Polska Partia Socjalistyczna—Rewolucja Demokratyczna (PPS—RD; Polish Socialist Party—Democratic Revolution) on January 22, 1990. Kuroń helped to set up a system of soup kitchens for the poor, which became known as "Kuroń's soups."

20. Kaszpirowki was a Russian faith healer who often worked in Poland, where he was extremely popular.

21. Kotański was the main organizer of social service and aid organizations for drug users and people infected with AIDS.

22. It is worth repeating that due to the limitations of our data base our numbers should not be taken to represent the intensity of any given type of rhetoric in a given year. We interpret them only as indicating trends. In this case, the trend is the significant growth of nationalistic and anti-Semitic rhetoric in 1992–93.

23. Radical frames were employed systematically by only four organizations or types of organizations: (1) Tejkowski's Polska Wspólnota Narodowa–Polskie Stronnictwo Narodowe (Polish National Union–Polish National Party), the Narodowy Front Polski (Polish National Front), and other extreme nationalistic movements; (2) the KPN; (3) radical trade unions such as the Chrzescijański Zwiazek Zawodowy "Solidarnosć" imienia J. Popiełuszko (Christian Trade Union "Solidarity" under the name of J. Popieluszko) and the Federacja Związków Zawodowych Gorników (Federation of Miners' Trade Unions) led by Rajmond Moric; and (4) Samoobrona (Self-Defense).

24. The framing has narrative fidelity when it "strikes a responsive chord in that it rings true with existing cultural narrations" (Snow and Benford 1988, 208–10).

25. Given the type of data at my disposal I cannot test this proposition. It is, however, plausible.

26. Following Conovan, *populism* is defined here in the most general sense: "All forms of populism without exception involve some kind of exaltation of and appeal to 'the people,' and all are in one sense or another antielitist" (1981, 294).

27. Kolarska-Bobińska reports that "Almost a half of all Poles evaluate the development of democracy in our country very negatively. Yet the lack of acceptance of parties and the rulers in a democratic system leads to the replacement of elites, not to the rejection of the whole system. Delegitimation of democracy may lead to its replacement with authoritarian rule, but the latter system of governance is accepted only by 20 to 25 percent of Poles" (1992, 11).

28. I am indebted to Grzegorz Ekiert for pointing out to me the significance of the distinction between discourses of globalization and reglobalization.

CHAPTER 6

Global and Local Framing of Maternal Identity: Obligation and the Mothers of Matagalpa, Nicaragua

Lorraine Bayard de Volo

Introduction

During the Nicaraguan Contra war, the Mothers of Heroes and Martyrs of Matagalpa choreographed a dance invoking the loss of their children in the revolutionary struggle. As the song's chorus implores "Where is the guerrilla's grave?" onstage a mother dressed in black frantically searches among marching soldiers for her missing son. At last, his lifeless body is laid before her. In a scene reminiscent of Michelangelo's *Pieta,* she cradles his body, weeps, and searches the heavens for consolation. The song continues, and the lyrics lend meaning to the death of her son—this fallen guerrilla lives on, embodied in all the poor and oppressed of Nicaragua. With new conviction, the mother stands, dons her son's cap, takes up his rifle, and marches offstage to join the revolution.

This dance was performed regularly before a variety of audiences, including international observers. Audiences of these *internacionalistas,* or *Sandalistas* (a Nicaraguan play on words referring to both Sandinista sympathies and Birkenstocks), were fertile fields for imagery steeped in maternal grief. Spalding Gray, in one of his witty monologues, spoke of his encounter with these Mothers of Matagalpa:

> They were like a combination of an AA meeting and a very perverse performance art piece. You have to realize these mothers have been testifying to every fact-finding group that's come through over the years. . . . They look like they've come from a foreign planet, like the planet Grief. They have such grief and sorrow emanating from them. I've not seen anything like it. I felt like I didn't have to hear them speak. We could meditate on their aura for ten minutes and get the message. But they *do* talk, and they tell their stories. (1992, 33:55–34:26)

Such maternal imagery or an "aura" that evokes emotions across cultures is a powerful instance of discursive globalization. That I would compare the Mothers' dance to Michelangelo's *Pieta,* a piece of art replicated and identifiable around the world, points to the global potential of such maternal discourse. That Spalding Gray was "exposed to" the Mothers, who implored his delegation, "Please, please, go tell your President Reagan to stop these horrors," further indicates the globalization of protest (Gray 1992, 35:05–35:10). Maternal mobilizing in Nicaragua entailed both an inward-looking process of identity and solidarity formation and an outward-looking process aimed at shaping dominant discourse and gaining external support. Both processes, in the case presented here and for collective action more generally, are increasingly global in terms of both perspective and implication.

In this chapter, I focus on the discourse and political consciousness that supported the mobilization of Nicaraguan mothers of the fallen, particularly to the extent that these can be said to have a global character. Of course, people are not compelled to mobilize solely in response to discursive constructs or a common political consciousness. Other factors, particularly domestic and international economic and political structures, also lend themselves to the whys and hows of collective action. In the case of these Nicaraguan Mothers, the political and economic contexts of dictatorship, revolution, war, structural adjustment, and the feminization of poverty all fundamentally shaped their collective action. Here, however, I examine collective action frames that in the U.S. context have been shown to inspire and legitimate social movement activities (Snow and Benford 1992; Gamson 1992).

The importance of injustice, agency, and identity frames of action are well supported in the literature (Snow and Benford 1992; Gamson 1992). To these, in the context of a Nicaraguan mothers' collectivity and beyond, I have added an obligation frame, which I argue was key in the promotion of maternal collective action and international solidarity. I also introduce the concept of "mobilizing identity"—an idealized identity promoted by the state or contending parties to create a collectivity out of previously unorganized individuals and through this collectivity shape and channel their actions. The two concepts, mobilizing identity and obligation, in this case are of particular interest to feminist political inquiry to the extent that they rely on essentialist arguments, which limit the demands and possibilities for change of mobilized mothers even as they propel members and their international supporters into the streets to protest.

Frames, Layers of Identity, and Obligation

Social movement research increasingly recognizes the meanings actors give to their actions as analytically important and focuses on political consciousness and collective action frames. The latter are sets of beliefs and meanings that promote social movement activism. William Gamson delineates three components of collective action frames: injustice, agency, and identity (1992). The injustice frame involves a sense of moral indignation that necessitates a collective response. The agency frame refers to the belief that an unjust situation is alterable. And, finally, the identity frame is the process of defining a "we" in opposition to some "they," the target of collective action.

Gamson also distinguishes between layers of collective identities. The organizational layer includes identities built around organizations—for example, the Sandinista Party. The "solidary" group identity is constructed around people's social location—such as poor mothers (1992, 85).[1] Gamson points out that an adversarial "we" versus "they" identity frame often goes hand in hand with a recognition of an injustice frame and is a necessary component of collective action frames (85, 114). Collective identity is treated in this chapter as the recognition of an adversarial framework in relation to the organizational identity of the Mothers' group.

But in the tradition of Alberto Melucci I stress that collective identity involves the recognition of oneself in others and the collective development of emotional investments in each other (Melucci 1989, 35). For the Mothers of Matagalpa, the solidary group level of identity lends itself less to an adversarial "we" versus "they" and more simply to the development and appreciation of "we." As such, I make an analytical distinction between identity as a shared bond and adversarial identity based upon these two levels of identity.

In moving from political consciousness to action, I distinguish two frames relevant to this case: agency and obligation. Agency is the notion that "we" *could* successfully respond to an injustice. Obligation is the notion that "we" *should* respond to an injustice. Obligation is an extra push from recognition of injustice, identity, and agency to action, and it played a key part in mobilizing the mothers of the fallen. It also was instrumental as the Mothers directed their discourse beyond the boundaries of their own group—for example, Spalding Gray's fact-finding delegation. Through the expression of maternal grief, the Mothers directed the obligation frame outward with the aim of mobilizing international opposition to U.S. foreign policy.

Work by Nancy Hirschmann supports the centrality of obligation frames in women's organizations. She has argued compellingly for a feminist rethinking of obligation, one that recognizes the importance of nonconsensual obligation in women's lives (1992).[2] Obligation, she argues, should be taken as a starting point for women, a standard against which other issues are measured. Her work is useful in underlining obligation as an epistemological force in women's lives.

Mobilizing Identity: Sandinista Framing of Women as Mothers

Collective action is, in part, constructed through discourse. The ways in which identities are framed structure the socially sanctioned subjectivities available to actors and in turn the manner in which they mobilize themselves politically (Weedon 1987, 21). In the case of the Mothers of Heroes and Martyrs, a political organization controlled by the Sandinista National Liberation Front (FSLN), it is vital to look not only at the specific directives and aid given by the FSLN but also to examine the more subtle ways in which the FSLN mobilized women by framing maternal identity.

Research on Nicaraguan women has shown that the FSLN focused on mothers of combatants and their practical gender interests arising out of traditional gender roles as opposed to more feminist concerns (Molyneux 1985; Randall 1994). However, we still know very little about how, in the language and imagery found in popular Sandinista texts, women were appealed to and represented. What sort of political claims and social identities were sustained by these gendered discourses? How did these identities change over time?

To address these questions, I examined the pro-Sandinista newspaper *Barricada* from 1979 through 1993 along with numerous other popular texts. From its inception in 1979, *Barricada,* termed the "Official Organ of the Sandinista Front," took on a mobilizing role to disseminate the FSLN's ideological line (Jones 1992, 62–63; Valdivia 1991, 357). Throughout the Contra war in the 1980s, this newspaper was a key weapon on the ideological front, supported by popular slogans, political advertisements, artwork, songs, poems, graffiti, plays, and speeches.

In mobilizing a nation to war, ideas, symbols, and goals are reined in by the state, as individual voices must appear to speak as one. Since a nation's way of life is to be protected, voices outside the mainstream appear as a threat, and so the most traditional representations of masculinity and femininity are to be found during wartime (Cooke and Woollacott 1993, ix; Elshtain 1987). Indeed, I found that maternal symbolism was standard fare in Sandinista discourse in shaping subjectivities that would mobilize men and women into defense work, encourage them to protest Contra violence, and organize, or at least placate, the mothers of drafted or fallen combatants.

A series of gendered images—"mobilizing identities"—dominated Sandinista discourse. Maternal mobilizing identities were idealized images projected by the state upon certain groups of women in order to create a collectivity out of previously unorganized individuals and through this collectivity control their actions. The mobilizing identity is framed in order to align with the individual interests, values, and beliefs of the targeted sector (Snow et al. 1986). In the Sandinista state's drive to mobilize women against the counterrevolutionary threat, safe, familiar, and traditional images were adopted and tinkered with to promote the revolutionary agenda.

Most important for my purposes here was the mobilizing identity of *Las Continuadoras* (the continuers)—mothers who carried on the struggle where their fallen children had left off. Sandinista discourse supported the notion that just as the martyred Christ lives on in all Christians martyred Sandinistas lived on in all free Nicaraguans. Dead combatants lived on particularly through their mothers in the struggle. Mothers of the Heroes and Martyrs were given primary responsibility, as *Las Continuadoras,* for keeping alive the memory and the ideals of the fallen.

Sandinista framing of *Las Continuadoras* posed mothers who were resentful of their children's deaths, particularly those who blamed the FSLN, as acting against the wishes of their children, sullying the memory of their children, and even contributing to the destruction of that which their children gave their lives to protect. The implicit argument was that working to build and defend the revolution lessened the chance that these precious lives were given in vain.

Las Continuadoras: *Local Needs and Global Desires*

The Mothers of Heroes and Martyrs were the women who organized in this image of *Las Continuadoras.* In addition to archival research and one year of participant observation, I conducted fifty-five open-ended interviews with the most active members of the Mothers of Matagalpa. What interested me most in the interviews was to understand the meaning members themselves gave to their collectivity and their construction of identity.

The majority of these Mothers of Matagalpa were very poor women over the age of fifty, which in Nicaragua placed them toward the end of their lives. Although every Mother lived with at least one child, more than 70 percent were single or widowed. All had lost a son or daughter in the revolution or war, and more than 30 percent had lost more than one member of the immediate family. Members' small government pensions (in 1992, an average of about twenty dollars per month per fallen combatant) supplemented a meager household income. Most of the organized Mothers (67 percent) had no paid work. Those who did earn money usually worked in the informal economy, for example, making tortillas, selling food on the street, or working as a maid.

The Committee of Mothers of Heroes and Martyrs of Matagalpa began as a small group of primarily poor women organized by the FSLN in 1979. Its purpose involved what one member termed "decorative representation."

> *Interviewer:* Why did the Frente want to organize the Mothers?
> *Doña Juana:* Because you know that in a revolution, mothers are spearhead, a force. A force that has a morality to it with which to confront whatever situation comes about. . . . And respect is felt for mothers.

As with the U.S. Gold Star Mothers and the Soviet Heroic Mothers of World War II, the Mothers of Heroes and Martyrs contributed to the war effort by symbolically representing their fallen children in order to channel their grief, raise troop morale, and soften opposition to the draft. Thus, such mothers' organizations operate at multiple levels. They are directed inward to the members themselves in helping women manage their grief. They also project outward to the nation as a propaganda force (Bayard de Volo 1998). Yet, unlike many earlier versions of such mothers groups, a significant aspect of the Mothers of Heroes and Martyrs' propaganda effort was aimed at an international audience. This is not surprising given the role played by the U.S. Reagan and Bush administrations in perpetuating the Contra war and the international solidarity movements that arose in opposition to U.S. involvement.

Unlike other Sandinista mass organizations, in 1984 the Mothers of Matagalpa set out on its own to more effectively confront both the economic and political crises arising from the Contra war and its members' emotional and financial needs. The Mothers were outspoken opponents of amnesty for imprisoned Contras, and after the FSLN lost the 1990 elections they were prominent figures in the strikes, marches, and sit-ins protesting neoliberal economic policies. After 1990, although the war was officially over and death rates dramatically decreased, the Mothers of Matagalpa grew rapidly. The group gained support from international nongovernmental organizations (INGOs) as the new Chamorro administration implemented structural adjustment programs that drastically reduced poor people's access to education, health care, and welfare. Poor mothers of fallen Sandinistas who formerly had not been attracted to the Mothers' Committee by its Sandinista ideology or its maternal community were now attracted to its small economic safety net. By 1994, the Mothers of Matagalpa had over two thousand members. They had developed housing and income-generating projects, supplied an environment for members to gain both empowerment and new skills, and provided an avenue for middle-aged and older women to mobilize politically.

Mothers of fallen Contras also began approaching their former enemies in the Mothers' Committee for support. By 1992, the Mothers of Matagalpa accepted all mothers of the fallen, regardless of political affiliation. The decision to include Contra mothers was a contentious issue within the Mothers' organization. Yet the acceptance of Contra mothers would play very well to the international solidarity groups on which the mothers were increasingly reliant for funding in the post-Sandinista era. "Maternal love overcomes political enmity" was a story that international observers seemed anxious to hear. But it was a story many Sandinista Mothers were not ready to tell, so the decision to include Contra mothers was made by the Mothers' leaders at the urging of several international solidarity organizations. Ironically, international fact-finding delegations were enthusiastically told what many Mothers themselves did not know—that Contra mothers had indeed joined the group. In the neoliberal context, the need for international economic support outweighed the priority placed on democratic decision making. Thus, the limited autonomy from the FSLN the Mothers had established in 1984 was largely forfeited in the early 1990s, offered up to a distant yet intensely well-meaning leftist international public.

Conveying Identity and Mobilizing Mothers

The mobilizing identity of *Las Continuadoras* was projected onto mothers of the fallen and the national and international public conscience through many sources: the Sandinista mass media, speeches, forums, assemblies, mass organizations (primarily Association of Nicaraguan Women, Luisa Amanda Espinosa [AMNLAE], neighborhood committees, popular churches, and the army), and countless other ways. But the actual mobilization of the mother upon the death of a soldier was not automatic. So questions arise: How did members come to see themselves as "the Mothers"? How did individuals recognize their common situation and develop a more or less stable "we"? There is nothing essential about a group of social actors' sense of "we"; rather, collective identity is a negotiated process influenced by dominant discourse and held together with emotional bonds.

In the following pages, I analyze the process through which individual mothers of war dead developed a political consciousness based upon experiences, emotions, and perceived differences from others. This consciousness drew from the *Las Continuadoras* mobilizing identity and closely mirrored action frames of injustice, agency, and obligation. I begin with members' testimonials of loss and suffering—narratives that were central to the Mothers' identity and solidarity. As this was generally the topic of the first conversations members had with each other, it is an effective way to introduce the dominant themes and defining experiences of the Mothers.

Next, I turn to the issue of difference, of specificity, which is central to the construction of an identity. My question: what was the perceived difference between women and men that led mothers to mobilize collectively and separately from fathers? Because the flip side of a shared sense of "we" is a group's difference from others and the specificity of their situation, it is important to examine the Mothers' perceived nonadversarial difference from others as well as the adversarial "they" that is linked to an injustice frame.

One defining task assigned the Mothers was the delivery of the news of a soldier's death to the family. Consoling and consciousness raising with the soldier's mother was a primary concern of the visiting Mothers. They demonstrated to her how to be a Mother of the Heroes and Martyrs, framing it according to the *Las Continuadoras* mobilizing identity. An injustice frame was intricately linked with an identity frame, for these Mother/messengers directed maternal resentment away from the Sandinista state and pointed the finger of blame at "them," the enemy, the Contra. Agency and emotional investments were also conveyed during these visits. As an addition to literature on cultural framing, I present the case of obligation as a relevant frame of collective action.

Mothers' Testimonials of Personal Loss

The Mothers knew the details of the deaths of many sons and daughters. They knew the story behind each others' physical and mental scars, behind the homelessness of some, behind the orphaned grandchildren of others. Their testimonies of suffering, tinged always with dignity and sometimes with triumph, generated the first and most basic current running between the Mothers. The sharing of these testimonials with each other and visiting delegations sparked the notion that indeed they shared a common identity. The following is one member's testimonial—singular yet tragically all too typical.

Doña Elsa's daughter Martina was a university student and Sandinista combatant who died just a few months before the FSLN victory in the city of Leon. She secretly removed her daughter's body from the hospital morgue under the nose of Somoza's National Guard, which was looking to arrest whomever claimed the body. In her narrative, she, the mother, is reborn through the ideals, examples, and lessons of life (and death) of her daughter.

> My daughter fell right before the triumph. I went to recover her body in Leon. I washed her skin, closed her eyes. I didn't cry one bit. I said, "I'm not going to cry, daughter. I have to be brave like you were. You were brave. I am brave because you came from me. I'm not going to shed a tear, and I'm not going to let anyone see that I am your mother." Clearly you feel it, and you cry when no one can see you. But what would have happened if I had gone sobbing to take my daughter out of the hospital where the Guard was waiting and waiting? I took my daughter out like God made the world. That's how I got her out—secretly.
>
> Three bullets had entered her. Her body was torn apart. Nonetheless, she died happy. She had a happiness about her as if she were laughing. As if she were saying, "I triumphed!" That's how it was the day she fell. She was a woman who, when she entered into something, she entered into it completely. And I knew what she was doing and why she did it. And so this courage stays with you.

Stating more than once that "our children were prophets," Doña Elsa, like so many members, saw her child's death as a sacrifice that would compel more people to organize and build the revolution. As such, Doña Elsa framed her identity in the image of *Las Continuadoras.* Her political consciousness was fundamentally altered through the example set by her martyred daughter, and she felt an obligation to carry on where her daughter had left off.

Specificity in Maternal Collective Identity: "A Mother Feels More Pain"

To explore the Mothers' notions of their specificity in relation to their solidary group identity, I asked, "Why were there no Fathers of the Heroes and Martyrs?" After all, fathers had also lost sons and daughters. This question caught many

Mothers off guard. The differences between mothers and fathers and the implausibility of having a committee of fathers seemed so obvious to them.[3] Integral to the Mothers' collective identity was the notion that maternal experience uniquely shaped women's interpretation of the value of human life. The maternal experience fed the emotional bond between members, and at the same time it nurtured a language of maternal specificity. The identity differences, although they drew from biological differences (in this case, women's ability to bear children), were socially constructed. But the specificity of mothers from fathers, "we" from "they," was not adversarial in relation to their collective action as much as it was a source of community and empowerment.

Most often, their explanations centered on the question of who suffers more at the loss of a son or daughter—the mother or the father. No one responded that men suffer more, and only a very few argued that fathers and mothers suffer equally at the loss of a child. Doña Bibiana, who lost one son and three grandchildren in the Contra war, explained: "A father is the same as a mother; they suffer. My son has three fallen children, and he cries when he remembers them. It afflicts him completely. . . . He is like a mother, I say, because he has suffered." Yet, as her response reveals, the term *father* does not evoke images of suffering and grief quite like the term *mother,* and so this motherlike father is more the exception than the rule.

Several other Mothers stressed that the father's suffering depended upon his relationship with the rest of the family. A father's involvement in and dedication to the home and family life will lead him to grieve the death of a child. However, in the common case of an absent or detached father the death of a child will have a much greater impact on the mother. The Mothers of Matagalpa sometimes explained that while fathers suffered when their children died they hid it because of a male identity based upon a machismo that forbids men from crying. A mother's response to loss—open grieving—was considered to be more legitimate, honest, and healthy. Doña Chepita told me that her husband suffered so at the death of his son that he drank himself to death:

> To say that the mother suffers most is untrue. It's like I said—the father always hides [his feelings]. They don't connect with others; they don't feel comfortable showing their feelings, unlike us. Men never want to lower themselves. They never want someone else to say, "He's not a man because he cries." And this is not true! I tell you, the man who cries from pain is the better man. [Men] deal with their pain in a different way. They drink in order to forget. And perhaps this is worse. We women come together, perhaps we have some activity. We feel in the middle of everything. We trust each other. . . . And men don't.[4]

Among those I interviewed, however, the clearly dominant view was that mothers suffer more than fathers at the loss of a child. Doña Josefina, normally shy and soft-spoken, was adamant on this point. She used specific examples to make her case that the mother-child bond and sense of responsibility was stronger than between father and child, leading mothers to suffer more upon losing a child. She recalled trips she took into the war zones to see her son, zones where ambush was always a threat and where in 1985 a group of mothers and family members (all female) traveling to see men in the army were attacked. This tragic incident touched Nicaraguans deeply, and several Mothers referred to it as an example of mothers' devotion to their children:

> The father isn't going to suffer like us mothers. . . . During the war, we didn't sleep, thinking about what could have happened to one of our children. I went to San Jose de Bocay, to Cua, to see my son when the war was in full swing. They told me not to come [because] something could happen to me, but I didn't pay any attention and always went to see him under any condition. I went with other mothers. There were no buses. It was prohibited because [the Contras] could lay down mines. I refused to be held back. I always went, and the father didn't. He didn't worry. Only mothers went. Nobody is going to tell you that fathers died going to see their children. Only mothers died.

The Mothers also supported a narrative that privileged mothers' labor (both birthing labor and the labor of raising a child) as an exclusive source of knowledge concerning the costs of war. In explaining why they believed that mothers suffered more at the death of a child, and in turn why they joined an organization to confront this singular pain, the Mothers often stressed the importance of pregnancy, birth, and raising a child in creating an emotional and physical bond between mother and child, melded through physical dependence, pain, and regular contact. Doña Geronima explained to me that the death of a child "is more painful [for the mother] because the father creates the child then goes off to work. He isn't seeing the children all day. But the mother lives her life giving them food. She lives cleaning them."

The Mothers' responses often dealt explicitly with the body, their gendered, female bodies, and their socially constructed emotional responses to embodied experiences. Many, like Doña Carmen, spoke of the fetus's dependence on the womb and the painful birth: "For the mother, the child was in her womb; she felt the pain of giving birth to the child. And so perhaps [the death of a child] is harder for the mother." As this quote suggests, the members of the Mothers of Matagalpa viewed the experience of pregnancy and the pain of labor as giving them access to privileged knowledge about the cost of bringing a child into the world (Ruddick 1989, 156–57).[5] In this maternal discourse, individuality gave way to a self/other bond created through blood shared in pregnancy and blood shed in birth—a bond that was only strengthened in the raising of a child. In the mutilation of this fused self/other—to destroy fruit of my womb is to destroy me—the mother was destroyed but goes on living.

The importance of the link these mothers made between pain at the birth of a child and suffering at the death of that child, and in turn the link formed between mothers of the fallen by their shared experience, was uniquely illustrated by Doña Juana. She suggested that mothers who gave birth through cesarean sections might not suffer as much at the loss of their children:

> I believe that the pain [of a mother upon the death of a child] has to be the same pain, independent of the position of each mother because I believe that to give birth to a child—well, perhaps those that have a cesarean don't feel this pain of natural childbirth, I don't know—but I say that if they are born by natural childbirth, one feels the same pain. Perhaps these mothers who had their children by operations don't feel the same pain.

In other words, if the pain of natural childbirth is the same for all mothers, the pain of losing a child must be the same, regardless of each mother's individual situation. As a rule, the Mothers stressed their sameness, their equality in this respect.

In sum, because fathers had not physically experienced pregnancy and the birth of their children and, if present at all, were less involved in the daily domestic life, most of the Mothers interviewed said that fathers felt the death of a child less intensely. According to some, men's incapacity or unwillingness to express emotions about the loss of a child also inhibited their ability or likelihood to organize over it. Perhaps most importantly, as the Mothers' responses imply, "fathers" did not represent a strong solidary group identity for men of their class background in Nicaragua. In the construction of maternal uniqueness in relation to the loss of a child, the Mothers both formed the basis for emotional bonding and empowered themselves, as difference was presented as giving the group special access to knowledge.

Injustice and Adversarial Identity: "It Was the Contra That Killed Them"

The Mothers' Committee was not a spontaneous collective maternal reaction to the death of sons and daughters. Although the Sandinista media tended to present the Mothers of Heroes and Martyrs as a group that arose "organically" among the members themselves, it was created by the FSLN, particularly through the Sandinista women's association AMNLAE.[6] Indeed, the Mothers' Committee of Matagalpa did not even have its own coordinator until 1983. Before then, its meetings were presided over by an AMNLAE representative. The FSLN had three primary goals in organizing the mothers of the fallen. First, it sought to draw a group of grieving and potentially resentful mothers into the Sandinista fold. Second, like all FSLN mass organizations, the Mothers was to provide a communications link between this sector of women and the party. Third, the Mothers was seen as an effective vehicle through which to mobilize the imagery of motherhood in the FSLN's local and international propaganda efforts.

As an auxiliary to AMNLAE, the Mothers of Matagalpa could be depended upon to support the demands of pro-FSLN organizations, to stage demonstrations against Contra atrocities, and to recount the tales of the deaths of their loved ones to foreign delegations and the media. As Doña Juana explained: "When (international) solidarity brigades came, we had to be there giving testimonies so that the brigades knew the truth that we had suffered and so that they knew what a revolution was—what had been fought for and why we were organized, in order to continue the struggle of our children." The focus of the committee during the 1980s was on consoling mothers and eventually mobilizing them as Sandinista combatants on the propaganda frontline, which extended internationally. As the Contra war intensified, the FSLN, through the media and its mass organizations, saw to it that the Mothers' resentment was redirected, their protests were planned for them, and their image was appropriated, all for the larger purpose of winning the war.[7]

In recalling their work during the Contra war, the Mothers stressed the healing effects of their committee and spoke of how they urged other women to join them—to leave the house and begin to discuss their losses with mothers who shared their pain. The importance of this contact with the Mothers' Committee was not lost upon the Sandinista army. In the early years of the war, the FSLN recruited Mothers of Heroes and Martyrs to deliver the news of war deaths and to comfort the grieving family, hoping to lessen resentment and check counterrevolutionary propaganda. According to Doña Nacha, the Mothers had the moral authority to both give sympathy and conduct consciousness raising with the family:

> We delivered so many dead. . . . And do you know why we did this? Because . . . we knew how [the mother's] heart would stop as we told her, "The one that we bring is your child." We were sent ahead of the rest to prepare her, to cry with her. . . . We went first to accompany her as other mothers. And also to talk with her. We cried as much as she did! The death hit her like it hit us because to deliver the dead child was like the delivery of our own dead child. And so we tried to make things easier on her. . . . When you lose your child it seems to you that you're the only one that this has happened to. And you ask "Why? Why?" You stop eating because of your nerves, and so you become depressed. But later you begin to reflect and see that they had to die so that many things are gained.

Here we find injustice and agency frames combined in the theme of losing in order to gain, which was key to the *Las Continuadoras* identity and the construction of the meaning of death in war. The injustice frame, in this case, did not so much involve the notion of whether a wrong had been committed. Mothers generally did not need to be convinced that the killing of a child was a tragedy. Rather, the FSLN, through the media it controlled and its mass organizations, shifted the blame to the counterrevolution, placed a positive spin on the death, and suggested a mode of action: "Martyrs had to die so that others might live to carry on the revolution—it was the only way when contras were attacking innocent people."

During the visit, the Mothers, as representatives of the FSLN, helped the family make wake and burial arrangements and informed the mother about government benefits and pensions. If the mother of the dead soldier showed resentment toward the Frente (FSLN)—and many did—the visiting Mothers tried to refocus her anger on the Contras. In the words of Doña Leonor:

> It was very hard to go to a house and tell a mama, "Your son fell." . . . Many mamas blame the Frente, but the Frente never was to blame because the Frente never said "Kill them." It was the Contra that killed them. . . . [The mothers] would start to cry, and they would ask how could it be that their children died. Some reacted badly. They would say, "This isn't my son." And "It's the Frente's fault that my son fell." In this work, we would say to them that it wasn't the Frente that was killing them. It was the Contra. If the Contra wasn't in the mountains, they wouldn't have died.

The fusion of injustice and adversarial identity frames is clear in this quote. In assigning blame for death, the Mothers stressed identity on an organizational level—they were not just mothers, but Sandinista mothers, enemies of Contras.

The Mothers' task was also to impart an adversarial identity frame to visiting *internacionalistas* through the retelling of their children's deaths at the hands of the Contras. Reagan and the Contras were intended to be seen as the clear adversaries of those who sympathized with the Mothers' grief. However, this task did not necessarily complement the Mothers' Committee's goal of improving its members' lives. Speaking with another Mother about their son or daughter's death was often therapeutic. Yet telling foreign audiences over and over again about the lurid details of that death—"When they delivered his body, it was so destroyed I couldn't recognize his face"—though it strengthened international solidarity, undermined the Mothers' own emotional healing.

Identity and Emotional Investments: "Knowing That You Lost as I Lost"

Through counseling so many grieving mothers, this group of Mothers as messengers of death developed a stronger sense of what it meant to be a Mother of the Heroes and Martyrs. In their visits to deliver the news of death, they acted out the identity of Mother of Heroes and Martyrs, thus both constructing and solidifying their own sense of a maternal collective identity. In acting out an identity, putting image into practice, individual members had to clarify for themselves what the identity involved. They were forced to fill in the blanks and bridge the gaps left by inevitably incomplete and contradictory discourses. The Mothers infused their message of death with revolutionary-style sacrifice for a higher cause. And in this act, Mothers/messengers became the prototypes for future *Continuadoras*.

This first contact between the mothers of newly fallen and the Mothers/messengers was a key event in the framing of identity and the development of emotional investments in the collectivity. They emphasized, or rather demonstrated, the new identity the grieving mother now shared. As Doña Elsa explained, "[W]e just hugged her and transmitted to her the strength, the love, the courage. It was necessary to demonstrate at those moments the pain that we have had and how to bear the pain upon seeing our children destroyed." They encouraged the mother to participate in the Mothers' Committee, stressing that contact with other Mothers with whom they could share their feelings was vital to emotional health. Mothers spoke fondly of their first contact with the committee, describing members as affectionate, attentive, loving, and "people who care." Doña Nacha remembered it this way:

> Doña Berta came to me. I was grieving, very sad. She told me to meet with [other Mothers] and talk in order to understand my pain and the pain of others—to know that you lost as I lost; that your pain is the same as mine. . . . This way you can be consoled. If you stay inside your house, you are suffering. You are remembering things and thinking that you are all alone.

Here, Doña Nacha directly addresses a key component in the development of her sense of identity with the Mothers' Committee—"to know that you lost as I lost"—and the emotional benefits to be gained from it. Many mothers did not find the comfort and understanding they needed within their own homes. It was important for them to connect with others who "have the same pain"—to connect with a maternal solidary group. The notion of shared pain as the bond that united the Mothers was a consistent theme throughout the interviews and was fundamental to the emotional investments individuals made in the collectivity.

Over time, these emotional investments deepened and became another reason, a goal in and of itself, for membership in the collectivity. One woman explained her almost daily participation in the committee's work this way: "I felt a friendship with all of them. That was another thing I gained from the committee—to have a friendship with each one; to make intimate friends. I felt happy. I felt peaceful. I felt trusted because I love them, all of them. That's how it is."

Agency: "Alone You Can't Do Anything, Organized You Can"

Another important factor in the framing of collective action was that of collective agency (Gamson 1992). Sandinista discourse within its mass organizations consistently stressed solidarity and organization in order to challenge those in power or receive recognition and material support from the state or international agencies. One Mother, Doña Ana Maria, spoke of how members accompanied each other to overcome crises: "United, one has greater strength. If we have economic problems, or some other problem, we solve them together. For this reason, we live united, always."

Repeatedly, Mothers explained in the interviews that, "Alone you can't do anything, organized you can." Working together, the Mothers had a sense of political efficacy that they felt would not exist if they worked alone. As Doña Ventura put it: "[W]e have to unite because all united we will accomplish something. Alone you aren't going to do anything. But among everyone, and with each one doing a bit, all together we will get something done."

The agency frame was important in the mobilization of these mothers. While the obligation and injustice framing convinced them that action was necessary, the agency frame convinced them that by working together change was possible. Spread primarily through mass organizations and the experiences of their children, the Mothers were firm believers in the idea that "united, you can get something done."

Obligation: "So That Blood Is Not Shed in Vain"

As mentioned earlier, the obligation frame can be useful in understanding how a collectivity moves from agency to action—not only *could* they do something in response to this injustice but they *should* do it. Hirschmann argues that women's obligations, particularly as they relate to the private sphere, have been required more than consented to, as liberal consent theory would have it (1992, 13). She suggests that this is often accomplished through essentialist discourse—women are "naturally" more suited to mother, care, and nurture (14).

One way of examining how the Mothers of Matagalpa themselves viewed politics, obligation, and their own activism is through a Sandinista twist on a distinction made by Carol Gilligan between two concepts of morality: a morality of rights involving abstract laws, autonomous individuals, and universal principles, which she argues is more typically expressed by men; and a morality of responsibility and care involving connection with others and situatedness more often expressed by women (1982; see also Hirschmann 1992). Gilligan has been rightly criticized for presenting this culturally and historically bound "womanly ethos" as a universal and even innate female trait, "thereby [alienating] the experiences of many poor, working class, and Third World women" (Scheper-Hughes 1992, 401). Furthermore, in Sandinista Nicaragua, men as well as women were appealed to through an obligation frame stressing the responsibility to "maintain eternal gratitude to and veneration of our homeland's martyrs and . . . continue the shining example of heroism and selflessness they have bequeathed to us" (FSLN 1986, 181).

Still, it is important to recognize that even though this "morality of responsibility" is a social construction that varies significantly across time and space, many women (and men), including members of the Mothers of Matagalpa, are invested in their own version of it and understand their identities and actions in terms of it. As such, it can be a key frame for collective action.

The Mothers of Heroes and Martyrs of Matagalpa confronted the crisis of the Contra war using a language of responsibility more than liberal notions of individual rights. They appealed to emotions and emphasized emotional and physical trials of the family, community, and nation. When they did discuss rights, they emphasized the right to peace, the right to survival. Most strikingly, when circumstances compromised the right to survival, they spoke of their own acts of caring and their right to be cared for. Thus, the language was one of interconnection and reciprocity in which obligations flowed two ways—to care and be cared for, to have responsibility toward others and to have others be responsible for them.

Their language in the interviews relied heavily on two words: *deber* (duty, debt, owe, must, should) and *compromiso* (obligation, commitment). The force of duty and obligation ran strong in the Mothers' Nicaragua, in which individual rights were eclipsed by responsibilities to others. The Sandinista state used this moral force effectively. Sandinista rhetoric mobilized many women as *Las Continuadoras* by emphasizing what was owed in the memory of "our heroes and martyrs." The logic went as follows: so that blood was not shed in vain, the best way we can pay homage to our fallen children is through participating in the revolutionary process. The mothers owed at least that much to their children's memory, so the discourse went.

Statements made by members reflected the deep sense of connection and responsibility they felt toward their dead family members and how this influenced their political ideals, goals, and alliances. Obligation and commitment to the fallen were mentioned again and again as they explained why they took up the struggle through the Mothers' Committee: "This struggle of one's children was also an obligation . . . signed with pain and blood. And so this struggle, I believe, is unbreakable, and it is a struggle that we won't betray, not even for a minute." The survival of the revolution symbolically meant the survival of those they had lost—martyrs only really die if the revolution dies. Doña Maria related how the fallen Sandinistas lived on through the revolution and their loved ones' participation in it.

> As long as we participate . . . [in] our revolution, our children haven't died. Our children continue to live because they fought so that we would know our culture, so that the poor would have land, so that the poor would have a house. . . . And so we can't stop struggling for land for the *campesino,* for housing, for health because for all this our children died. . . . The important

> thing is to keep alive the memory of the heroes who loved us. . . . It's that as long as we struggle, they haven't died—nor are they going to die.

An obligation frame was interwoven with injustice and adversarial identity frames. Not only were young men obligated to make the ultimate sacrifice on behalf of the revolution's heroes and martyrs, but their mothers were obligated to carry on the struggle against their children's enemies.

Martyred sacrifice was framed in such a way as to obligate others, including international observers. Spalding Gray's encounter with these same mothers was no coincidence. A steady flow of fact-finding delegations arrived in Nicaragua during the Contra war, a flow that dwindled but survived in the 1990s. Such delegations generally met with political officials to learn revolutionary history and recent legislation, with teachers to learn about the Sandinista educational system, with medical personnel to learn about Sandinista health care, and so on. Yet in "finding facts" about the destruction wrought by U.S.-funded Contras, they were less likely to meet with military officials than with the Mothers of Heroes and Martyrs.

The Mothers generally sat in a large circle with the delegation. One by one they told of how their loved ones had died, how they received the bodies, and perhaps some details on the condition of the remains. They often ended with a plea, "Please go tell your President Reagan . . . " Obligation, I believe, was the key frame employed by the Mothers in an attempt to stimulate the action of others, these *internacionalistas.* Linked to an injustice and adversarial identity frame—the death of these mothers' beautiful children at the hands of a foreign-financed army was clearly assumed to be wrong—the obligation frame was constructed around the terrible nature of the deaths, the Mothers' profound grief, and for U.S. visitors their own indirect complicity in those deaths. Gray perceptively likened the Mothers to an Alcoholics Anonymous meeting—the Mothers' testimonials had a confessional air in that they "shared" with strangers the most painful moments of their lives. But these confessionals were not meant as therapy to ease the Mothers' burden of grief. Rather, they were in a sense "performed" to burden others with the obligation of carrying their message back home. Although my research cannot testify as to the specific influence these encounters had on the future actions of the *internacionalistas,* I do argue that the Mothers intended to impart a sense of obligation and solidarity beyond the borders of Nicaragua. As the meeting broke up amid tearful maternal hugs and promises, the *internacionalistas* would depart resolved and certainly obliged (in the Mothers' eyes) to "do something."

Conclusions

In the process of maternal collective identity, collective action frames are continually internalized, reframed, and projected outward. In posing collective action frames this way, one has the sense of constant motion, a process that seeps into individual subjectivities and percolates across national borders. The Mothers' collective identity must be seen as in part externally created by a Sandinista state. Yet the Mothers did not passively adopt the collective action frames. Rather, they worked with the inevitably rough outlines of these frames to make them personally relevant as well as effective for their changing goals and needs. Moreover, they set out to shape the collective action of visiting solidarity brigades, particularly through an emotion-laden obligation frame.

The salience of the maternal obligation frame in this case demonstrates the importance of looking to discursive resources as they are both externally projected onto a collectivity (in this case from the Sandinista state) and as they are internally mobilized to generate international solidarity. The Mothers' own framing of maternal identity depended upon a link between obligation and maternal experiential knowledge. They constructed maternal knowledge through giving birth, feeding, clothing, and nurturing their children, and these involved the maternal obligation to protect their children and, by relation, their children's ideals and memory. In placing the Mothers of Heroes and Martyrs of Matagalpa on solidarity brigades' itineraries, *internacionalistas* recognized the power of maternal grief in globalizing the Sandinista struggle. Interestingly, despite their growing self-help projects, the Mothers stressed grief and even helplessness in their testimonials to international delegations. In the Mothers' experience, this played well in gaining international support—better than maternal rage and often better than stories of empowerment, personal growth, and self-help.

On a cautionary note informed by feminist thought, idealized images of women can be both enabling and constraining, being used by the state, international solidarity groups, and grassroots women's organizations to legitimate their political agendas but with an added effect of reinforcing a system of representations that constrict the political avenues culturally available to women. Through new applications and reinterpretations of traditional maternal images, Nicaraguan mothers were expected to take on new, politicized responsibilities, to take an active part in the construction of a new society, and to enter traditionally male political activities. Women could now be political actors, enter the political arena, and try to effect Sandinista-sanctioned change. Yet women should still be predominantly mothers, sacrifice their own interests, and make demands on behalf of others, be it their own families or the "Nicaraguan family."

Examination of the pervasive mobilizing identities of women provides new insight into the FSLN's failures on the road to women's emancipation. Previous studies on women in Sandinista Nicaragua have emphasized the economic and political constraints of war (*Envio* 10, 34). Yet attention must also be paid to the manner in which the FSLN fought the war on a symbolic level, revealing its active role in the reinforcement of traditional gender roles through maternal images. The FSLN appealed to middle-aged and older women through an identity most Nicaraguan women were comfortable with, the mother. However, in this male-dominated society the most respected traits, those which conferred status and power, were those typically associated with men and the glorification of stereotypical feminine traits actually worked to keep women in their separate and not equal places.

The prominence of obligation frames in the case of Mothers of Matagalpa—directed inward within the group and outward to international solidarity groups—suggests that future work on collective action frames, particularly in terms of women's organizations, should pay special attention to discourse on obligation. We must also reflect upon the implications of using traditional maternal imagery in international forums to bolster a political cause. More recently, the wars in Chechnya and Bosnia were symbolically fought in the international arena through the use of maternal imagery—recall the news photos and video clips of wailing mothers. As a general rule, these mothers do not have voices, only tears. Such images are effective tools in establishing international obligation and injustice frames. Yet they can be unidimensional to the point of damaging women's own attempts to move beyond immobilizing grief to try to effect change.

NOTES

1. Gamson also points to a third layer of collective identity—movement identity—which would include, for example, peace activists.

2. Hirschmann presents a critique of liberal theory through the use of feminist standpoint theory, the object relations theory of Nancy Chodorow, and the moral psychology theory of Carol Gilligan.

3. Patricia Chuchryk received similar responses from Chilean women (1989, 140–41).

4. This is similar to the statements made by the mothers of the disappeared of Argentina, Chile, and El Salvador, who described the difference between mothers and fathers in terms of their ability to deal with strong emotions. Although men grieved alone, women gained strength by openly expressing and sharing their grief, and they united on that basis. See Chuchryk 1989 and Fisher 1989.

5. Ruddick presents an analysis of women's thinking as it develops out of the work that mothers do—feeding, clothing, nurturing, protecting, and training their children. She writes, "Their knowledge derives from the work of mothering, which though it can be shared equally with men, has been historically female. It also derives, at least in part, from an experience or appreciation of female birthing labor on which all subsequent mothering depends" (1989, 186). Ruddick argues that maternal thinking is constructed; however, her work is often interpreted and applied in more essentialist terms. The Mothers of Matagalpa themselves made arguments for "women's difference" using both explanations: women's experiences as mothers and women's nature. I argue that this women's difference is constructed, yet it is regularly explained in dominant discourse (as well as certain feminist analyses) as natural.

6. This is not to deny the very active role certain well-known mothers of the fallen took in the creation of the Mothers of Heroes and Martyrs.

7. There are similar cases throughout Latin America. As Sonia Alvarez attests, "In

contemporary Latin America, political regimes, parties, and organized sectors of civil society have reacted to today's women's movements . . . by harnessing women's political activity into 'auxiliary' women's organizations, co-opting women's movement organizations and/or appropriating their political discourses, acquiescing to limited demands through public policy making, or suppressing women's movement demands altogether" (1990, 20).

CHAPTER 7

The Useful State? Social Movements and the Citizenship of Children in Brazil

John A. Guidry

> It's not enough to write the law. It's important to know the law and struggle for its application. . . . There are people who think that "now that boys and girls know about the statute [of the child and adolescent], they're becoming rebellious and demanding." When people erroneously appeal to the law as a guarantee of impunity, this misunderstanding must be corrected. But to appeal to the law to demand one's rights is the exercise of citizenship, and for this no one can be criticized, even a child.
>
> Fr. Bruno Sechi[1]

> What is most responsible for these kids' level of delinquency are the laws authorized by the government, in favor of these minors. They give minors a lot of advantages and take authority away from parents. Today, a parent can't punish a child the way he would want to. I think it's something generational, a generation of rebellious kids. . . . And the government is here taking away parental authority, giving everything to minors without knowing if all these kids really deserve it.
>
> Lorena—thirty-eight, housewife and small *comerciante*[2]

Fr. Bruno Sechi is a Catholic priest living in Belém, Brazil, the large port city that serves as the "gateway to the Amazon." He has worked on the behalf of street children in Brazil for more than twenty years and is a major figure in the Brazilian human rights movement. Lorena lives in a squatter invasion on the outskirts of Belém. She is raising three young boys on her own, making a living as a *comerciante,* a small-time merchant. From her house and a small stall at the community preschool, she sells bread, soda pop, ice, and candy; her monthly income fluctuates with sales but rarely climbs over one hundred dollars. At stake in the contrast between Father Bruno's and Lorena's statements is the fate of Brazil's movement for children's rights and the movement's crowning achievement, the Statute of the Child and Adolescent (SCA), which was signed into law on July 13, 1990.

The story of the SCA, however, demonstrates some important ways in which state-movement relations have shifted under the impact of economic globalization and the transnationalization of discourses concerning democratization and citizenship rights. With the passage of the SCA, the movement for children's citizenship rights has begun in some important ways to move beyond the realm of contentious action against the state and into the state itself. As movement activists take up official and quasi-official positions implementing the statute, the public sphere and the state begin to intersect, providing opportunities for the movement to affect the popular values concerning young people, especially youth offenders and marginalized, poor children. The state has become "useful" to the movement in ways that have forced movement actors to reevaluate their roles in social discourse, political action, and the public sphere.

The Brazilian movement for children's human and citizenship rights counts on its side (1) a national network of social movement organizations (SMOs) fighting for the rights of children, (2) support by potent social institutions such as the Catholic Church and the Brazilian Bar Association, (3) international linkages to the worldwide human rights movement and the growing movement for street children, and (4) the institutionalization of the movement's goals in a comprehensive national law, the Statute of the Child and Adolescent. The SCA lays out not only the rights of children but also the obligations of parents and the state toward children; further, it establishes the legislative basis for localized government agencies, including a juvenile justice system and neighborhood advisory councils (*conselhos tutelares*) that will oversee the law's implementation at the local level.[3]

In both the movement's success and the challenges that face it, one sees the impact of several aspects of local/global contests as they are played out in everyday situations and as they involve notions of citizenship in democracies. During the 1980s, the number of street children and children at risk in Latin America and elsewhere—including the industrialized world—grew dramatically, and this problem lies at the intersection of several trends in the global political economy. The debt crisis of the early 1980s, continuing flows of internal migrants into Third World cities, the rise of informal economies in the cities, and the short-term effects—unemployment, shrinking wages, and high prices for basic foodstuffs—of structural adjustment programs created to deal with the debt crisis have created an urban crisis in most developing countries.[4] The present context of widespread poverty, crime, slum growth, and abandoned children goes well beyond the crisis addressed in the urbanization literature of the 1970s (see Nelson 1970 and Perlman 1976); with the deepening of globalization, the crisis of poverty in cities and the effects on children have worsened.

Berner and Korff (1995) write about slums as part of a globalized city, and children at risk constitute a majority of the population in this impoverished quarter of the global city. Slums and their inhabitants are the opposite side of a global city that is usually discussed in terms of the financial centers, high rises, and urban professional classes of Hong Kong, Bangkok, London, and São Paulo. The latter are the beneficiaries of a new kind of economic and cultural citizenship from which poorer residents of the global city are excluded (see Sassen 1996; Stevenson 1997; and Clarke and Gaile 1997). As with all discursive globalizations, the growth of the less glamorous, poorer side of the globalized city has provoked local responses. Berner and Korff concentrate on responses to economic and cultural marginalization by examining slum movements in Manila and Bangkok. Slum movements contrast with the upper-class end of the globalized city because slum movements are not interconnected in the same way that the new financial centers and their populations are through fiber optics and other new technologies of communication. Slum movements have modular characteristics (Tarrow 1994) of mobilization and organization that render them similar across cities, but their inspirations, aims, and actions are highly localized.

The movement for the SCA is decidedly rooted in the struggle against the worsening conditions for poor children in Brazilian cities and the countryside, but it differs from the localized slum movements Berner and Korff examine. This movement in Brazil represents an attempt by activists of varying classes to use a global discourse of citizenship grounded in the international wave of democratization that swept across Latin America in the 1980s and theorized by writers such as T. H. Marshall ([1950]1992), applying this discourse to a class of future citizens, children, in order to counter some of the changes in urban poverty that have emerged over recent decades. Though organizations dedicated to the problem of child abandonment and street children are key actors under consideration here, the larger movement for the SCA exemplifies a cross-class movement typical of a globalized, urban, civil society that began to emerge in the 1970s and 1980s. By crossing class boundaries, this movement brings the upper and lower ends of the globalized city together, providing an opportunity to break the isolation of impoverished communities. The movement uses the Brazilian state to address the problems of children, bringing the state into a clash of globalizations—an exclusionary social citizenship related to the rise of the neoliberal state as opposed to a universal notion of human rights—in a way that supports and perhaps even enhances the sovereignty of the state by making it the filter through which globalizations must pass, affirming Sassen's (1996) contention that the withering of state sovereignty is too simple a way of thinking about globalization.[5]

In the end, the contest over the SCA and its implementation highlight the ways in which the public sphere, at the local and transnational levels, is evolving. The international aspects of the movement demonstrate the importance of a transnational public sphere in making things like the citizenship of children an important national issue in a particular country, but the main arena of conflict is in the Brazilian public sphere. As members of the movement find themselves in official positions in organs such as the *conselhos tutelares,* which attend to individual cases of the violation of youth rights, the practical separation of the public sphere and the state is blurred. When does the movement activist stop being an activist and become part of the state? How does this affect the way we conceive of a social movement, which is mainly understood as contentious collective action challenging the state? Can a movement take advantage of the state without becoming co-opted by political forces? Finally, how does the transition from a movement seeking to change values in society into an organized effort to implement national legislation impact our understanding of the state and its sovereignty in a globalizing world?

Global Contexts and the Movement for the Statute of the Child and Adolescent

The social movement that promoted the passage of the SCA is a broad-based coalition of individual social movement organizations (SMOs), institutional actors, activists, politicians and ordinary people. In structural and organizational terms, the movement for children's rights fits rather closely to an ideal-typical case of successful social activism as we might draw it up using the familiar tools of social movement theory. In ideological terms, the development of a universal discourse of children's rights can be traced in a number of international accords going back to the Universal Declaration of the Rights of Children in 1959, and continued through a number of conferences and conventions in the 1980s and 90s.[6] Figure 1 provides a general outline of the movement's structure and the lines of influence that were necessary to pass the SCA in 1990. At the base are a variety of grassroots and social movement organizations that together began to promote causes related to human rights (broadly conceived) during the 1970s, the years in which Brazil's military dictatorship (1964–85) began to lessen control and repression in political life. The figure presents a tidy model of the SCA's passage, but the lines of influence work in all directions. The constitutional assembly of 1986–88 had tremendous effects on the movement as an opportunity structure that opened up the potential for movement development. As the ability to influence politics developed in the transition from authoritarian rule, movement organizations themselves became stronger. The growth of civil society and the public sphere in Brazil gave organizations the opportunity to grow; this happened not only in the movement for the SCA but across all social movements in Brazil, including labor (Seidman 1994), human rights, and the women's movement (Alvarez 1990). What follows is a brief sketch of the actors involved and the political, economic, and cultural contexts in which they act.[7]

Globalizations 1: Democratization and the Reawakening of Civil Society

By 1975, the Brazilian military government had significantly lessened controls over associational life and attempted to rein in the repression of opposition activity. In 1979, with the ascension of General João Figuerido to the presidency, the regime officially began a policy of *abertura,* or "opening," through which it sought gradually to ease the military out of power through contested elections. There is no clear agreement as to the military's real objectives in the *abertura,* and it is widely debated whether the policy was truly pro-democratic or simply an attempt to construct a delegated democracy that could maintain military autonomy and prevent the Left from obtaining real political power.[8] But the goals and intentions behind the *abertura* are not at issue here; the fact is that after 1979 Brazilian political and associational life—civil society—emerged from years of clandestine or highly constrained activity. It is in this context of a renewed and invigorated public sphere that the movement for the SCA was able to make its claims and ultimately pass the statute.

With the *abertura,* the country's political opportunity structure changed, and previously excluded groups opposed to the military regime began to define more specific objectives apart from the general goals of human rights and opposition to authoritarian rule. This and the already established concerns of SMOs and opposition parties with human and civil rights created a political context in which groups pressing for the rights of children could carve out some space and define their mission and strategies. This is not to say that children's rights were not an issue before 1979; they were, and a large number of mainly Catholic Church–related groups were heavily involved in creating schools and programs for street children and youths in poor neighborhoods. The next major change in the political opportunity structure came between 1985 and 1987, the period following the inauguration of civilian president José Sarney and leading up to the constitutional assembly (*constituinte*) of 1986–88. The congressional elections of 1986 placed the opposition Brazilian Democratic Movement Party (PMDB) in a commanding position over national government, and that congress also served as the constitutional assembly that was to write the basic governing document of what was then called the Nova República, the New Republic.[9] The congress sought to make the constitutional process accessible and open to large numbers of citizens by allowing ordinary people to place issues on the constitutional assembly's agenda via petition. As few (or many, depending on one's point of view) as thirty thousand signatures could force the congress to debate whether and how the constitution would address agrarian reform, labor matters, the civil rights of minors, and other issues.[10] Although many movements failed to secure their sought-for language in the country's new governing document, the movement for children's rights counts articles 227 and 228 of the Brazilian constitution as one of the movement's "most impressive victories."[11] These articles are the constitutional basis for the SCA.

> *Article 227:* It is the obligation of the family, society and the State, with absolute priority, to secure for children and adolescents the right to life, nourishment, education, leisure, professional training, culture, dignity, respect,

Estatuto da Criança e Adolescente
Statute of the Child and Adolescent, signed July 13, 1990

Fernando Collor, president of Brazil, 1990–92

Congress

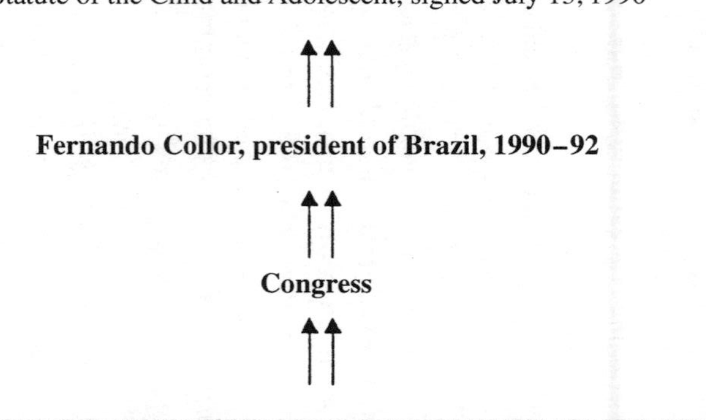

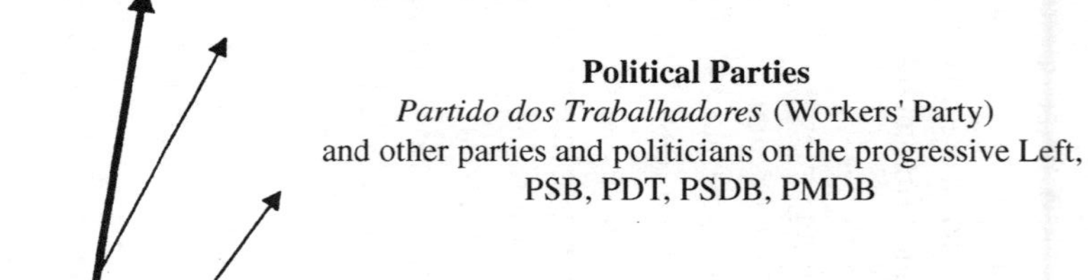

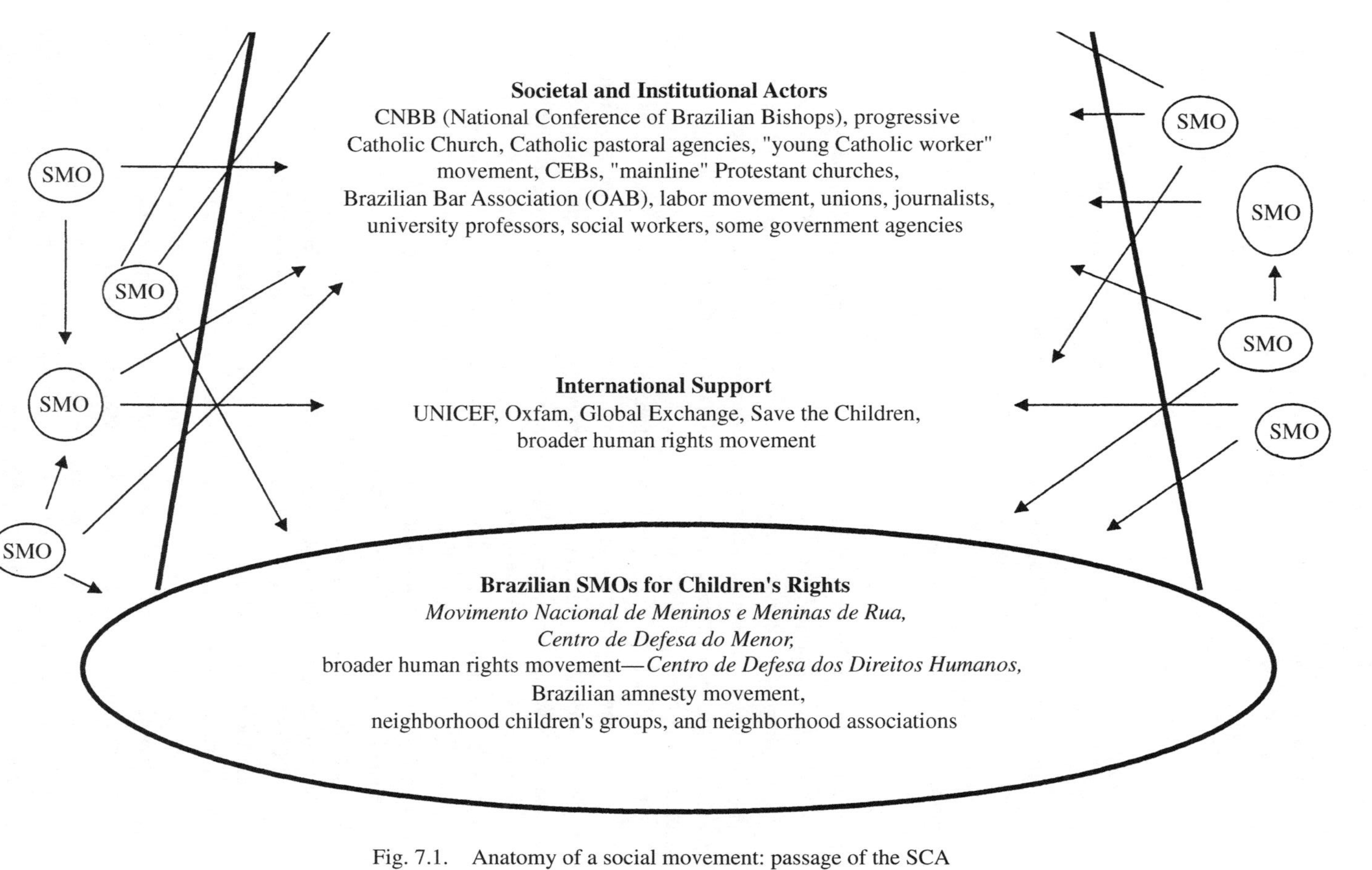

Fig. 7.1. Anatomy of a social movement: passage of the SCA

> freedom, and family and community life as well as to place them safely away from all forms of negligence, discrimination, exploitation, violence, cruelty, and oppression.
> *Article 228:* Minors under eighteen years of age are penally not responsible subject to the norms of special legislation.

The process of *constituinte* both opened up opportunities for movement activity and forced the movement to organize extensively in order to attract the public support and signatures necessary to influence the congress. For this, the movement relied on a broad array of support from sympathetic organizations and institutions both within Brazil and internationally. Inter- and nongovernmental organizations (IGOs and NGOs) such as the United Nations, UNICEF, and a host of children's rights organizations around the world were crucial in lending material and ideological support to the movement. International NGOs dedicated to children's causes and the eradication of poverty and hunger placed Brazil's new constitution in the light of global scrutiny.[12] Finally, and perhaps most importantly, the support of the Catholic Church, via the National Conference of Brazilian Bishops (CNBB), numerous diocesan pastoral agencies, and longtime leaders such as Father Bruno, lent important institutional validity and weight to the claims of organizations involved in the movement. As such, an emerging transnational public sphere was crucial to the development of the movement for the SCA.

The new opportunity structure provided by Brazilian democratization, the reemergence of civil society, and the renewal of the public sphere can be problematized against the wave of democratization sweeping the world at the time, beginning in Southern Europe in the 1970s and moving across Latin America, Africa, and Asia with varying degrees of intensity. Early analysis of what Huntington (1991) calls the "third wave" of democratization stressed institutional change and the trade-offs involved in having authoritarians leave power (see O'Donnell et al. 1986 and Diamond et al. 1989). Theorists and students of democracy debated differing positions and created a new, high-profile journal, *The Journal of Democracy,* to air their concerns. These debates stressed the normative and practical benefits of liberal democracy, heralding a new era of hope in world politics.

By the 1990s, scholars began examining the limitations of contemporary "democratization" as it developed against the backdrop of the end of the cold war and the ascension of neoliberal economics as an unquestioned framework for the global political economy. O'Donnell (1993) writes of the "low-intensity citizenship" that results from the failure of democracy to address the economic (and hence political) marginalization of poor citizens in spite of the egalitarian discourse of democracy, an issue squarely at stake in the conflict over the SCA. Writers such as Stevenson (1997) and Sheth (1995) stress a homogenizing force at work in democratization that threatens the diversity of local cultures and local solutions to problems. The movement for the SCA represents both the challenges and opportunities presented by democratization and demonstrates that traditional forms of social movement organization are a potentially effective way to address the concerns of democratization's critics.

Globalizations 2: Poverty, Street Children, and the Economic Context

One of the movement's main branches involves street children, a growing feature of the poorer sections of the globalized city around the world, whether Manila, Cairo, Rio de Janeiro, or Belém. Although the SCA was written to apply universally to all children and adolescents in Brazil, much of the momentum behind the law came from movements for street children and the nongovernmental institutions that cared for them. In Brazil, *moleques de rua* (street urchins) have been a common feature of urban life for decades, but in the economic crisis of the 1980s their numbers appeared to skyrocket. One of the main intentions behind the SCA was to address the social conditions believed to be involved with the growing numbers of abandoned and street children in the country as well as increasing rates of youth crime. The polemic in Brazil over the SCA is centered on these issues, and this section addresses some economic and cultural aspects of childhood in Brazil.

With the support of the actors and institutions outlined previously, the Movimento Nacional de Meninos e Meninas de Rua (MNMMR, the National Movement of Street Children) grew out of more localized efforts such as Father Bruno's República do Pequeno Vendedor (RPV, Republic of the Little Vendor) in Belém. The RPV provides youth street vendors with classes, activities, counseling, and an experience of democratically organized social life in which the children are asked to make collective decisions about their lives. Social workers and psychologists from the RPV also run an art education program of outreach in which counselors from the RPV go to areas where street children congregate to engage them in educational street theater and in the end bring them into the orbit of the RPV and its programs. The MNMMR was one of a number of similar organizations that were emerging in many countries within and outside of Latin America, reflecting increased international concern with the growing numbers of abandoned children living on the streets in Latin America and the developing world generally. In this respect, the international movement for street children resembles what Keck and Sikkink (1998) call "transnational issue networks."

Another organization founded by Father Bruno is the Cidade de Emaús. It takes its name, City of Emmaus, from the New Testament story in which Jesus takes the apostles to a town called Emmaus, Father Bruno's intention being that the Cidade is an attempt to realize the discipleship of the Gospels with children who are at risk of being abandoned by their society. The Cidade has a large compound in the neighborhood of Bengui, a working class suburb on the outskirts of

Belém. There children attend classes and work attending gardens from which they harvest food and herbs. The Cidade includes a pharmacy that grows and uses the herbs to make natural remedies that some of the children sell on the streets for profit. The RPV, Cidade de Emaús, and organizations like them in other regions of Brazil seek to provide some guidance, education, and material support to the boys and girls who eke out a life selling gum, candy, and other small items on street corners and at bus stops.

Brazil's endemic conditions of poverty and social inequality, together with the economic crisis of the 1980s—known generally among Latin Americans as the lost decade—both exacerbate and contribute to the problems afflicting the country's youth. Of about 146 million Brazilians, some 60 million (41 percent) are seventeen years of age or younger. Children, not only in Brazil but in many societies (including those in the developed world), are among the country's poorest citizens. As many as 53.5 percent of Brazilians seventeen years of age and under live in families with a per capita monthly income of only up to half the legislated minimum salary, which stood at about $74 per month in 1991. Only 10.1 percent live in families with per capita monthly incomes over two minimum salaries, about $150.[13] In terms of the overconcentration of poverty among youths, the math is simple: the vast majority of Brazilians is poor, poor families have higher birthrates and more children than wealthier families, and the incidence of families headed by single or abandoned women is higher in the poorer classes.

Brazil has one of the most unequal distributions of income in the world. In 1980, 10 percent of the population earned close to 50 percent of the national income, while the lowest 50 percent earned a mere 14.2 percent (see table 7.1). By 1989, the share of the lowest 50 percent had shrunk to 11.2 percent (Soares 1995, 10).[14] These figures are even more compelling when Brazil's basic social indica-

TABLE 7.1. Distribution of Income, by Deciles, 1960–80

	Percentage of National Income		
Population Decile	1960	1970	1980
1	1.9	1.2	1.2
2	2.0	2.2	2.0
3	3.0	2.9	3.0
4	4.4	3.7	3.6
5	6.1	4.9	4.4
6	7.5	6.0	5.6
7	9.0	7.3	7.2
8	11.3	9.9	9.9
9	15.2	15.2	15.4
10	39.6	46.7	47.9

Source: Wood and de Carvalho, 1988, 76. The authors compiled these statistics from the Brazilian national censuses of the Instituto Brasileiro de Geografia e Estatística.

tors are compared with those of other countries (table 7.2). Although Brazil is the world's eighth largest economy and has a national income about equal to that of Hungary, social indicators such as literacy, life expectancy, and child mortality match more closely those of Honduras, which has a national income about one-third that of Brazil's.[15]

On the street, poor children often become vendors in the informal economy. They sell candy, gum, cigarettes, newspapers, magazines, toys, and, increasingly, drugs and their bodies. These children are usually barefoot and frequently shirtless. They may be dirty and covered with scars or open wounds. Shop owners consider these young people to be more than a simple nuisance; street children are perceived as dangerous criminals in development. Sadly for many youths on the street, these stereotypes ring true. Inside stores, these children often shoplift. Outside, they target watches and jewelry. An unsuspecting pedestrian may suddenly be surrounded by four or five kids who simultaneously distract his or her attention and abscond with various possessions. In general, people of all classes see these children as a festering sore on their society. Popular perceptions of the problem note that youth crime is on the rise, and not so surprisingly people recall that it was "not as bad" before the SCA was passed into law,

> *Woman, thirty-five, shop owner:* This is a relative thing, because there are a lot of those kids who are working [on the street], you know. But there are a lot who are there just to steal. A lot of *pivetes* [punks], even more because of this law that says you can't arrest or hit a minor. Now they're attacking in every which way. In other words, they may be selling stuff down there, but they really want to assault you.
>
> *Researcher:* What law are you talking about?

TABLE 7.2. Comparison of Basic Social Indicators, Selected Countries, 1990

Country	GNP per Capita (U.S.$)[a]	Child Mortality Rate[b]	Life Expectancy	Adult Literacy (%)
Belgium	16,220	9	75	n.a.
Venezuela	5,220	43	70	88
Portugal	4,250	16	74	85
Hungary	2,590	16	71	n.a.
Brazil	2,540	83	66	81
Panama	1,760	31	72	88
Jamaica	1,260	20	73	98
Honduras	900	84	65	73
Haiti	360	130	56	53
India	340	142	59	48

Source: UNICEF 1992.

[a]GNP per capita is based on 1989 data; all other information is for 1990.

[b]Child mortality is the number of children per thousand live births who die before the age of five.

Woman: It's a law for minors [the SCA]. I don't know how to explain it, but it's the law that you can't hit children up to sixteen years old. You can't arrest them. They're free to do whatever they want. They can kill since killing won't get them arrested. Nothing can be done to them. . . . And so they take advantage of this. (C101/41–42)

The generalized perception of impunity that people attach to the SCA is also related to the growing number of "death squads," often composed of off-duty police and shop owners. The July 1993 killing of 8 children sleeping in front of the Candelária Catholic church in central Rio de Janeiro garnered international headlines for its vivid cruelty. This incident, however, was not an isolated event. Throughout Brazil, numbers tell a sad story: in 1990, a common grave holding the bodies of 560 children was found in São Paulo; in 1991, the public morgue in Recife received 15 bodies of children each month, most of them damaged and mutilated; and between 1990 and 1993, 4,611 children were murdered in Brazil. These figures reflect Brazil's overall social conditions—most of these children were black and poor.[16] A noted case of execution by public mob occurred in 1993 when three boys running through a working-class neighborhood in Rio de Janeiro were mistakenly identified as thieves by locals. The teenagers were beaten and burned to death on the street.[17]

The economic and social contexts engendered by the growth of poverty and social exclusion during the 1980s challenged the movement for the SCA to focus and frame its emphasis on issues of citizenship. Rather than attempting simply to speak of the human or civil rights of street children, poor kids, or young offenders, the movement began to focus its public discourse on the notion that the SCA would create a definition of citizenship for minors that would outline both their rights and responsibilities within the larger context of the duties of state and society regarding young people. As a concept, citizenship allowed the movement to claim that it was speaking for all people under eighteen, as the movement and the SCA was aimed at developing a legislative outline of the *general* citizenship of all minors. Poor children, street children, wealthy children, youth offenders, and those who abided the law—all obtained the same rights and duties under the SCA. This framing, consistent with notions of citizenship generally accepted in democracies around the world, was crucial to the passage of the SCA.

Globalizations 3: The State, Citizenship, and the Statute

The globalizations and problems just outlined overlap and reinforce each other to render young people, for the most part, excluded from ordinary society. Poverty, age, physical size, malnourishment, violence, abuse, and poor education are the hallmarks of youth for a growing number of Brazilian children—not only the very poor but also the children of the working and lower-middle classes as well. The movement for the rights of children and adolescents built its legislative task on human and civil rights within the context of Brazilian citizenship and the notion that young people were citizens "in the process of development" (art. 15). Organizations concerned with the problems of street children and violence both against and caused by youths took the lead in lobbying and public action, but movement leaders and organizations framed their goals in more general terms: how to make Brazil a better, safer, more nourishing place for children to grow into mature and responsible adults.[18] As the statute states,

> *Article 4:* It is the obligation of the family, the community, society in general, and public authority to ensure with absolute priority the establishment of the rights that relate to life, health, nourishment, education, sport, leisure, job training, culture, dignity, respect, freedom, and family and community life.

The first step in dealing with youth violence was to acknowledge the citizenship of all young people. To that end, the movement eschewed the term *minor* and its connotations of inferiority and diminished capacity in favor of *child* and *adolescent.* The statute thus defines a child as any person between zero and eleven years of age and an adolescent as any person between twelve and eighteen years of age.[19] Yet acknowledging the citizenship of all children and adolescents never, in the movement's framing of the issues, denied the obligations of these people to society, especially when they break the law. As article 112 notes, all people under the age of eighteen are punishable and must answer for any illegal action, and the statute provides for ways to enforce the law with regard to youth violators in ways that punish crime within the context of developing ways to help these people become productive citizens.

The statute's 267 articles detail rights pertaining to *all* children and adolescents as well as the obligations incumbent on parents and guardians. Children and adolescents thus enjoy all the human rights of adults as stipulated in the Brazilian constitution, with the understanding that children and adolescents are "human beings in the process of development" (art. 15). Specifically, the statute delineates the young person's freedoms as (1) to come and go from public places in accordance with the law, (2) opinion and expression, (3) religious faith, (4) to play, practice sports, and enjoy oneself, (5) to participate in family and community without discrimination, (6) to participate in politics in accordance with the law, and (7) to seek refuge and aid (art. 16). All citizens have the obligation to "watch over and rescue" children and adolescents from "any inhuman, violent, terrorizing, abusive, or coercive treatment" (art. 18).[20] Parents and guardians are to guarantee, within their means, the sustenance of children, and the statute outlines the conditions and circumstances under which parents may be legally relieved of their authority over children as well as the process by which children and adolescents may be relocated to another home (arts. 22–24, 155–70).

The sections that deal with the treatment of youths who break the law were written to address the traditional manner in which adults, parents, and public authorities have disciplined young people. Corporal punishment has been the norm for minors, and in general physical abuse by the police and parents has long been tolerated in daily life. The goal of the statute's policies toward youth offenders is to enable authorities to correct the misbehavior of young people but completely in keeping with article 18's prohibition of inhuman and abusive treatment. In a deeper sense, these provisions of the statute are one attempt to address the violence in everyday life. The fact that about half of the statute's articles are devoted to dealing with youth offenders and the juvenile justice system is perhaps indicative of the scope of the problem.

The combination of endemic poverty and the diminished status of the minor has, for example, become manifest in the general suspicion that poor kids steal and pick the pockets of passersby. A person who becomes aware of a missing wallet or purse may, without pausing to think, point a finger at nearby kids, who then become the target of police action. The statute attempts to undermine such prejudice by providing that "minors under eighteen years old may not be attributed punitive responsibility subject to the stipulations provided in this law" (art. 104) and that "no adolescent will be deprived of his freedom unless caught flagrantly in the act of infraction or by written order of the competent judicial authority" (art. 106). In other words, young people will not be held criminally responsible for their acts in the same manner as adults and the methods of correctional treatment provided in the statute will apply only to those who are *caught in the act* or in cases where judicial authority has enough evidence to order a youth's arrest.

Youths who are apprehended in violation of the law are then subject to the following "socioeducational measures": (1) warning, (2) obligation to repair damages, (3) performance of community service, (4) freedom under the cognizance of others, (5) restricted freedom, (6) assignment to an educational institution, or (7) a number of more detailed regimes including removal from the family (art. 112). The point of these detailed legal stipulations is that children and adolescents, as "human beings in the process of development," must be given the guidance and supervision necessary to correct misbehavior and allow the youth the opportunity to mature in a way that will ameliorate and diminish the feelings of marginalization and discrimination that delinquent youths and gang members cite as reasons for entering street life.

Finally, the law provides for the establishment of several layers of advisory and assistance councils involving the participation of both public officials and representatives of organizations in civil society that are devoted to the youth issue. At the national, state, and local levels, Councils for the Rights of Children and Adolescents (hereafter, Rights Councils) elaborate policies to secure the implementation and provision of the rights of children and adolescents as laid out in the SCA (Pontes 1993, 20). These councils are composed of one-half state representatives appointed by current executives (the president, state governor, or mayor of the municipal district); the other half is made up of representatives from organizations in civil society such as the bar association or other organizations associated with the movement. Movement representatives on the councils are supplied by the movement organizations, which must meet in open forums to select their representatives. The NGOs or movement organizations that qualify for the selection process vary according to policy needs and local conditions, but in general these organizations must be "entities devoted to infant/juvenile issues . . . such as, for example, those that include among their institutional mission the direct servicing, research, promotion, or defense of the rights of children and adolescents" (51). The total number of members varies given local conditions; in Belém, the Rights Council consists of eighteen people, one-half appointed by the mayor and the other half coming from civil society.

These three levels of developing and implementing the SCA mirror Brazil's federal, state, and local governmental structure. The fourth type of movement participation in the statute's implementation is also at the local, *município,* level, in *conselhos tutelares.*[21] While the work of the Rights Councils involves the development of policy, the *conselhos tutelares* do actual casework that assists and accompanies claims of either the abuse of youth rights or the adjudication of youth offenders through the juvenile justice system.[22] The *conselhos tutelares* are popularly elected in each *município,* and candidates for these positions are usually from the movement that helped to pass the SCA. Each *município* is to have at least one *conselho tutelar* with at least five councilors sitting on it (Sêda 1992, 7). Although all *municípios* are to have at least *conselho,* the number varies across the country. The *município* of São Paulo, with about 10 million inhabitants, has twenty *conselhos tutelares;* Franca, a smaller *município* of 250,000 in the state of São Paulo, has two *conselhos;* and the similarly sized Maringá in the state Paraná has only one (Blanes n.d., 21). Belém, with its population of a little over a million, has four *conselhos* in existence today, with plans to expand that number to eight in the future.

The existence of these councils at all levels reflects the 1988 constitution's mandate for the "popular" participation of citizens in governance. The councils demonstrate an expansion of citizenship in postmilitary Brazil, as the councils not only work to secure citizenship rights but also to allow citizens—and the movement organizations they may represent—to enter into the administrative process in unprecedented ways.

This movement, which took advantage of democratization to pass comprehensive national legislation regarding the citizenship of a class of people, those under eighteen years of age, is built of classic, modular forms of social movement activity that can be found in any Western democracy, but it transcends older social movement models by its implication in several kinds of globalizations. By framing the issue in terms of citizenship, the movement took advantage of a discursive globalization that gathered steam on several continents and, with the end of the cold war, has become a prominent feature of social movement activity around the world. This trend is also evident in a renewed scholarly interest in T. H. Marshall's ([1950] 1992) work on citizenship (see Seidman 1994, 197–203; O'Donnell 1993; Klausen 1995; Somers 1993; Turner 1993; and Mische 1995). By using the state as a fulcrum between conflicting globalizations, however, the movement poises itself to depart from the usual, contentious movement repertoire to move inside the state, much in the manner of interest groups, by sitting on government councils and developing policy. The primacy of legislation itself is an effect of democratization and the establishment of the "rule of law" as a global feature of state discourse in the post–cold war era, and legislative aims are more and more part of social movement concerns.

All of this is not to say that the movement has abandoned in any way its nonlegislative activities. The MNMMR and Centros de Defesa do Menor around Brazil continue to work in and develop the kinds of programs started by Father Bruno and exemplified in the Cidade de Emaús or the RPV. These activities continue, but they are not the focus of this chapter, which is the way that the legislative part of the movement accomplished this goal and then dealt with movement-state relationships as movement goals came to include enforcing legislation—not a typical social movement activity—in a local context that does not universally accept the movement's understanding of youth citizenship and the duties of the state and society with regard to people under eighteen years of age. The next section takes up this struggle, exploring how the movement confronted and dealt with issues of how well the SCA and the movement's claims resonated with popular culture in Brazil.

Movement and Countermovement: Localizing the Struggle

Sidney Tarrow (1992, 176) identifies three general value structures that social movements must both confront and work with:

> (1) Societal Mentalities, "popularly held values and practices about private life and behavior . . . [that] are largely passive interpretations of the status quo detached from agency"
>
> (2) Political Culture, "more clearly molded points of concern about social and political relations, containing both system-supporting and oppositional elements"
>
> (3) Collective Action Frames, "purposively constructed guides to action created by existing or prospective movement organizers"

Tarrow's delineation of these structures of value is useful in discussing how social movements must position themselves (i.e., frame their agendas and goals) vis-à-vis the societies in which they operate in order to build the basis for collective action. In Tarrow's view, social movements contest both governments and the practices and values associated with societal mentalities. Movements develop collective action frames that attempt to take advantage of the political opportunity structure and, if movement activists so agree, elements of the political culture that augur for the movement's greater success. The movement for the citizenship rights of children in Brazil clearly fits Tarrow's ideal type, *but only until the passage of the Statute of the Child and Adolescent.*

With the passage of the SCA, everything changed. To use Tarrow's terms, the SCA is nothing less than the movement (1) using the political culture to (2) establish its collective action frame as (3) the legislated basis of changing societal mentalities. The SCA broadened the movement's scope. No longer was it sufficient to mobilize enough people to place items on the agenda of the constitutional assembly; with the passage of the SCA, the movement's continued success came to depend on mobilizing *society* on a much grander scale. One may guess at the numbers necessary to establish a piece of legislation as fundamentally accepted by a society, but if it is less than the whole or even an absolute majority, it is surely far in excess of the critical mass necessary to establish a social movement.

Lorena's statement cited at the outset of this chapter is one woman's attempt to understand how this law affects what she has always presumed her life to be. Although Tarrow perhaps overstates the passivity of societal mentalities, it is certainly the case that Brazilian mentalities regarding status and social position tend to be constructed to use and implement existing patterns of difference and hierarchy rather than to question them. At a basic level, children in Brazil (and most other places) are viewed as incomplete people who need to be shown what to do and what not to do. Punishment, from this perspective, is as much a part of childhood as love, care, and education; indeed, most parents appear to view punishment as a manifestation of love, care, and education. And in many societies, even some of the most "civilized" in the industrialized world, corporal punishment is believed to be appropriate except in cases of excess and cruelty. As these issues relate to the SCA, it should be noted that the SCA doesn't prohibit corporal punishment in explicit terms; rather, the statute prohibits "inhuman," "terrorizing," or "abusive" treatment—general terms that are open to contestation.

So how did Lorena and others come to see the SCA as taking authority from parents and prohibiting "the discipline of children"? If the movement's general goals—to see that children have the environment and opportunities to develop into mature adults—are in fact widely held in Brazil (and they are), how have people come to see the SCA as a major threat to social order and to children themselves?

The story of Lorena's position involves a pitched battle over children, crime, and the cultural context of the street. The lines of this struggle have been drawn by the SCA, which is a legislated attempt to translate the movement's collective action frame into a new, or at least improved, societal mentality regarding the treatment of those citizens who comprise more than 40 percent of the national population. In some senses, supporters of the SCA have left the realm of civil society because (1) their goals are enshrined in law and (2) through *conselhos tutelares* and other agencies movement activists have moved *into* the state as part of the executive apparatus of the law. If the movement retains in any way the properties Tarrow (1994, 2) identifies as "contentious collective action," it is in contention with social structures of value and not with state authority.

The signing of the SCA not only changed the political structure and context surrounding the movement for children's human rights in Brazil; it also provided the impetus for a countermovement against the law and the movement's goals.[23] The countermovement is not so highly organized; one cannot chart the layers of influence and their relationships as easily as was done in figure 1. Rather, the countermovement is one of public opinion, and as such key actors include "opinion leaders" whose discourse organizes and catalyzes popular perceptions of the SCA and its effects. The most important and widely heard voices in the countermovement are those of police officers, officials in state secretaries of public security, journalists, and broadcasters. In public statements, press conferences, and interviews, police officers and officials frequently criticize the SCA for creating a context of impunity in which youths already prone to violence feel free to act. When speaking in delicate terms, the police state that the SCA is problematic because, while it sets forth rights, obligations, and policies regarding youths, the government has not adequately created and funded the agencies to carry out these policies. As Paulo Tamer, secretary of public security for the state of Pará during 1993–94, put it in an interview with me, there is no place to "put minors who break the law" and this foments criminal activity.

Spokespersons for the countermovement usually adopt the stance of "victims," claiming that a small minority movement has usurped the goals of the democratic process to advance an agenda (human rights for children and adolescents) contrary to public safety. This framing of the issues surrounding the SCA resonates with the feelings of victimization that most people feel with respect to the growing problem of crime,

> *Woman, thirty, housewife:* I don't know—I think it's this business of human rights. This came about just to make our lives even more difficult. Because of this statute of the minor—of adolescents, abandoned children—this was a horror. Nowadays, boys walk around with pocket knives and handguns. And they shoot and kill because they won't get arrested; they won't get punished. Poor little things! They're minors, adolescents, and everyone feels sorry for them! Who feels sorry for the victims? Those who are mostly—90 to 99 percent—honest workers, human beings . . . useful people who work to make an honest living to survive? (C302/29–30)

The police, too, portray themselves as victims—they stress that they are at war with crime and place their lives on the line for the general safety of society.

On August 8, 1993, at a state-sponsored forum on youth and violence in Belém open to the public and attended by social workers, representatives of the street children's movement, academics, the police, and the public, Tamer drew rounds of applause from police in attendance when he thanked the organizers for "finally allowing the side of police" to be heard in public. He said that the goals of the police are to "combat street violence" and "confront 'the boys' when social policies fail." To back up his military-style discourse, he displayed a variety of dangerous martial arts weaponry that gang members employ, stating that the public needs to be aware that the police are not confronting mere children but well-armed and dangerous opponents. Speaking of gang members and criminals, Tamer criticized public policy for not recognizing that some people have a "criminal disposition," the implication being that the universal application of human and civil rights to all citizens allows such people greater latitude for criminal activity. When a member of the audience asked what Tamer meant by *disposition,* he responded by saying "people who commit crimes for pleasure rather than necessity."[24] This view is widely shared by ordinary people, who often distinguish between those crooks who steal out of necessity and those who "kill for pleasure."[25]

Police discourse about the SCA is echoed in the press by crime reporters and in sensational current events programs such as *Barra Pesada,* which is shown daily from noon to 3:00 P.M. in Belém. *Barra Pesada* centers on reports of crime and public disturbances in lower-class neighborhoods. A person with a dispute over a property line, for example, may call the show's reporters to ask for public coverage of his claim, and the show often broadcasts lively and colorful arguments between neighbors over such issues. Gang activity is a staple of the broadcasts, as is regular police news of arrests and violent crime. Reporters often interview criminals from their jail cells, and the reporters are frequently indelicate, asking prisoners, for example, if they feel sorry for their barbarous activity.[26] Also, daily newspapers usually contain two to three "police pages," which run down violent crime in the area and offer "crime columnists" a chance to discuss the advantages and disadvantages of public policies for dealing with crime, including the SCA.

The end result of this sort of publicity is reflected in daily conversation, as people talk to each other about "what's wrong with kids today." The cases reported in the news and publicized by the police become "vivid cases" that are told and retold and become part of urban legend. Below, a resident of a squatter neighborhood responds to the question, "Is it more violent today?" by invoking the formula of "children beating parents," which has become commonplace in urban discourse on issues surrounding the SCA,

> *Woman, thirty-eight, housewife:* I think so, yes. God help me—it's very violent! You see a twelve-, thirteen-year-old street kid spending day and night on the streets with his "partners." There he's smoking marijuana,

> sniffing glue, drinking *cachaça.* When he comes home, he's beating his mother, his father, sisters, and nieces. You wouldn't see something like this in the past, at least in my time. . . . Like I saw yesterday on *Barra Pesada,* some guy named Índio in Marituba [a nearby neighborhood]. Because his mother didn't give him money to buy marijuana, he took her butane gas tank and sold it. So she mentioned it to him, and he beat his mother. Tell me something—could a son like this be human? A hanger-on like this is an animal. . . . A person like this ought to be isolated, renounced by other people, by human beings. A person like this ought to die rotting in prison, because a creature like this, who did this to his own mother, isn't one of us. (AA05/64)[27]

Discussions of crime and violence often give way to images in which traditional patterns of authority are inverted, and for many the passage of the SCA represents one more event in the decay of authority and status. In the following statement, a man notes how the SCA has turned upside down the status relationship of men and boys, such that men now fear children,

> *Man, thirty-five, cobrador* [bus fare collector]: We men don't fear other men. We fear *pivetes* [punks]. When we're passing another man on the street, nothing happens, but when we walk by two *pivetes* we're afraid of assault. . . . They can kill, steal, and do whatever they want, and they won't be arrested. They'll just be detained and released again a little while later. We're afraid of walking by these kind of people.
>
> *Researcher:* But why do the *pivetes* get released?
>
> *Man:* The *pivete* gets released because of this constitutional law that's come about recently. (BF04/56)

The countermovement's discourse resonates profoundly with the everyday values of all classes. For the poor and working class, the SCA inverts the two basic kinds of status and authority available to those with limited incomes and mobility: adulthood and parenthood. Violent teenagers and youth criminals threaten an already precarious struggle for lower-class people to make ends meet. For the middle and upper class, the law seems to set free the worst and most uncontrollable elements of the dangerous classes, boys. As a university professor and well-to-do businesswoman put it in a comment on Brazilian democracy post-1985,

> *Woman, forty-seven, accountant and university professor:* We've noticed that people don't really know how to live with this freedom. Already, they confound liberty with libertinism . . .
>
> *Researcher:* What should be done?
>
> *Woman:* It should be stricter, more serious. For example, if you were caught

putting graffiti on someone's house, you should be punished. There's too much impunity today.

Researcher: Aren't there penalties these days?

Woman: There are, but it should be said that minors have the law of the minor. They can do various things without being punished. If you're sixteen years old, you've got the right to kill, put graffiti on someone else's house, to rape, and much more. I think this is wrong. (C401/89–90)

At the end of the day, the countermovement's version of the SCA and youth impunity resonates with wider fears that Brazilian society as a whole has become a lawless arena in which the wealthy or anyone with any sort of power—a knife and the protection of the SCA, for example—can take advantage of the powerless without fear of repercussion. The signal event that provokes livid and angry debate over the decay and corruption of contemporary society is the impeachment of President Fernando Collor in 1992 on charges of political corruption. Along with his former campaign treasurer, Collor was alleged to have set up a wide-ranging operation to extort millions of dollars from businesses desiring access to presidential policy making. As one man claimed, "Everybody's discovered that [the president] was a thief. So now? Everybody wants to steal" (BF04/54–55). Given the countermovement's rhetoric of impunity and popular perceptions that moral decay begins at the top, it is more than simple irony that Collor was the president who signed the SCA into law.

In sum, the SCA challenges popular notions that criminal activity places one outside of the ordinary definition of citizenship—that is, that upon committing a crime one surrenders one's citizenship rights. And for many people in Brazil, criminals not only fall outside commonplace notions of citizenship but they remove themselves from their status as human beings. People who break the law, especially in violent crimes, are referred to as animals and less than human. For children and adolescents, whose citizenship is already attenuated by their youth and constitutional status as people "in the process of development," the effects of breaking the law upon popular consciousness is even worse; for many people like Lorena and the countermovement to the SCA, these youth offenders are completely outside of the system and should have no rights in decent society. The movement's challenge is thus to emphasize the culpability of these offenders while at the same time emphasizing their continuing rights as citizens and the duty of state and society to work for their rehabilitation.

The State, Resistance, and Framing the Movement's Goals

The struggle for the citizenship rights of children as it is carried out by the movement for the SCA in Brazil highlights important ways in which competing discursive globalizations converge and present local actors with important opportunities to organize and address local or national grievances. Economic changes in the world economy have given rise to global cities that tie together the postindustrial capitalist system. There are different "levels" or layers of global cities—London, São Paulo and the like at the top, followed by national and regional centers such as Belém—but spread across them are consistent features (Sassen 1996; Armstrong and McGee 1985; Knox 1997). A privileged global professional class oversees the connections between different nodes of the global economy. The financial districts and their glassy high-rises are distinctly similar from city to city, as are the slums and informal economies that emerge alongside them. The global cities hold a promise of better communication, opportunities, and economic citizenship for some classes, while they also represent a localized means of exclusion within given territories—O'Donnell's (1993) "low-intensity citizenship" for poor and working people as contrasted with Sassen's (1996) picture of "economic citizenship" for the wealthy and corporate actors. At the same time, however, globalized discourses of democracy and human rights offer all inhabitants of global cities, at whatever level in the hierarchy, ideological resources and political opportunities to address grievances, whether those grievances are created by local or global conditions. Empirically, democracy and human rights promise to counteract the exclusion inherent in today's economic structure; the extent to which democracy's promise is realized is dependent on the effectiveness of local organizations—that is to say, on social movements and SMOs.

The nexus through which these globalizations interact is the state. The state is limited in important ways in this problematic. It cannot act alone against the international economic changes that have resulted in the deepening of urban poverty by changing the rules of entry into the national economy. Those that have tried to do so since the early 1980s—for example, Peru under Alain-Garcia or hyperinflationary Brazil under a variety of presidents and economic ministers up to 1994—have failed. Those states that have adjusted to neoliberal changes have perhaps emerged in a stronger position vis-à-vis their own societies and the international order—the case can be made, for example, that for all the problems faced by the Mexican state its economic restructuring has contributed to its ability to further the transition from a one-party state to a competitive democracy. In the case of the SCA in Brazil, a globalized discourse concerning democracy and the citizenship of children limits the state through its use of internationalized standards for the treatment of children—that is, the state is held to standards of citizenship that were developed outside of its sovereign jurisdiction. At the same time, the movement and its discourse take advantage of the Brazilian state's sovereign role as protector of its citizens against abuses of any kind. At this global crossroads, the state remains a powerful and important actor.

At the local level, a parallel struggle is being fought over the ways citizens might deal with these globalizations, and important features of this struggle involve the cultural framing of movement aims and resistance at the level of everyday life—a not-so-passive aspect of "societal mentalities." The movement's structure, use of resources, and methods of framing exemplify the successful cases to be found in social movement literature. The problems it faces on the ground as activists search for ways in which the SCA might "resonate" (Snow and Benford 1988) more fully with the values of ordinary citizens involve the contradictory nature of power among subordinate classes (see Ortner 1995). The struggle between local police, ordinary citizens, and movement activists doesn't pit people from distinct class backgrounds against one another. Actors in the movement and the countermovement come from all class backgrounds. Frequently, poor people find themselves bewildered and even belittled by the SCA and what they see as an assault on their values about family life, even if Father Bruno and the movement would portray the movement as one that empowers lower-class people. The objections raised by poor people to the SCA (that it devalues the roles of parents) and the problem of street children (that they are criminals who must be punished) are the same as those raised by the middle classes and the professionals who are at the upper end of the global city's hierarchy. Popular resistance against the movement and the SCA concerns values and ideologies grounded in global and local discourses that cut across class, and all of this hinges upon how Brazilians—within the movement and without—choose to define the citizenship rights and duties of youths, both when they abide by and when they break the law.

To this extent, the case demonstrates how globalizations alter the familiar class terrain of resistance studies and the position of the state in that struggle. In the Brazilian movement for the rights of children, class is recognized as a prominent reason for the SCA; activists from any class in the movement understand and acknowledge that poor children bear the brunt of the problems addressed in the statute and that empowering poor families to raise and educate their children in a manner closer to that enjoyed by the middle and upper classes is an objective. As the movement resists the societal mentalities that reject the SCA's vision of citizenship as it applies to young people, the movement's *resistance frame* is decidedly non–class based and relies on a universalism like that of the larger human rights movement, a frame of citizens and citizenship resisting the prejudicial power of either the state or other citizens. The movement's resistance frame pictures the state not only as a potential violator of youth citizenship rights but as a defender of citizenship, a useful partner in developing broad-based, egalitarian values about the nature of citizenship, regardless of class and age status, as well as the citizenship rights that remain even when one is accused of breaking the law.

Cultural framing and the concept of resonance in social movement theory allow an analyst to confront the power cleavages that exist among subordinated classes. These cleavages are evident in the following statement by an unskilled minimum wage worker, who discusses how street kids are different from other children and, importantly, how the apparent impunity of these children under the SCA seems to diminish the citizenship of law-abiding people, young and old. The following statement about street children is from a man who makes less than one hundred dollars per month working for the city of Belém.

> *Man, thirty-seven, municipal employee:* The way I understand it is the weakening of the law. I think that minors ought to be protected but without forgetting the right remedy as well. This law ought to be applied to kids who live at home and not to street children. There should be some change made to punish street kids.
>
> *Researcher:* So do you think that street kids and kids who live at home are different?
>
> *Man:* Yes, I think so. . . . Different, for example, because a person who is accustomed to living at home has another way of thinking. Those who are used to living on the street lack direction, and so they become rebellious children. We don't have any kind of service that would make those children see the path they have to follow. We don't have this, and this is the big problem. (BF06/32–33)

Through a class lens, both this man and street children or children who break the law are victims of structural adjustment and economic marginalization. They share a similar location in the changes being wrought by the neoliberal economic order that has been in place in Brazil since 1989 and has intensified with the implementation of the Plano Real in 1994. The target of their frustration could be the same elite class, but the above speaker sees it differently. The relevant distinction for him in this case is not class, for he knows these children and he is from the same class; the distinction is one of order and decent behavior.

To the social movement, the widespread nature of the values the speaker discusses are a major problem. For some social movements, forms of localized resistance might present a generative basis for collective action—as in a neighborhood movement of the kind examined by Berner and Korff (1995)—but in the case of the SCA localized resistance is a barrier to movement objectives. But it is a barrier that can be overcome as movement activists work to frame the issues of child abuse around issues of poverty in much the same way that labor activists and neighborhood movement leaders were able to bring together their concerns by framing their different problems as having a common base in the authoritarianism of the military government during the 1980s (Seidman 1994, chap. 5).

The following statements about the problems of street kids and the SCA demonstrate some common ground between the movement and Brazilian social mentalities, since these speakers understand the importance of poverty to the problem, and they point to the role of the state in addressing issues that affect youths. The first is a middle-class businessman, the second a community leader in a poor squatter invasion neighborhood, and the third another woman from the same neighborhood as the second.

Man, thirty-three, entrepreneur: I think it's because a guy has a kid and can't feed him. The kid goes into the street to beg, and he turns into that street kid. [It's] the government's fault. Today, they've got to arrange some solution for those [kids] already here, these street kids, you know. . . . The state military police do a lot of things here. They created the "Little Guard," have you heard of that already? . . . There [in the Little Guard], they give the children food, leisure activities, physical education. They have swimming. Beyond that, they put the kids in public squares for watch duty, helping people park. (C301/17–18)

Woman, thirty-eight, housewife and community leader: I'm not against the statute and what it says. I'm against them not executing the statute because the statute has very good things. If it were truly in practice, we would have no problem. But it just exists on the books, not in reality. The government hasn't developed it. (BF11/49)

Woman, fifty-three, housewife: [My father] was very good hearted, my mother too. Everything he had he gave to his relatives and neighbors. He always showed us the path we would have to choose. He counseled us and wasn't the type to beat us, you know. . . . So parents are the ones who should accompany their children and open the door for them. . . . There are some parents who are bad. They're very violent with their children. The kids become revolted by it, and they go off with those who've lost their way. This is why there's so much violence here. (BF02/41–42, 53–54)[28]

In all three passages, a concern for the care of children in contexts of poverty is evident, and in the first two the role of the state in this process is explicit. The task for movement activists has become to frame the SCA's objectives as a viable method of countering the effects of poverty that are grounded, in part, in the global economic restructuring that all poor people in Brazil experience on a daily basis. The movement thus uses its position inside the state, via the organs (e.g., the *conselhos tutelares*) through which citizens and movement activists may participate in the development and implementation of the statute.

The Changing Relationship of Movements and States

The importance of the state in turning the movement's goals into reality is evident in the ways Brazilians talk about the law and its potential. Like the speakers just cited, the vast majority in Brazil recognize the problems that youths of all classes face in contemporary society, and they are not opposed to developing some way to ameliorate the conditions that lead to the existence of street children, youth crime, or the abuse of otherwise "good" kids. These opinions are echoed in all classes, and criticism of the state (whether for passing the SCA or for not enforcing it) is matched by an understanding that the state could—and should—play a role in addressing the problems of young people. Brazilian popular discourse about the role of state in society thus creates a potentially powerful opportunity for the movement to use the Rights Councils and *conselhos tutelares,* along with the movement's nongovernmental activities, to try to sway public opinion regarding the SCA. The continuing programs of NGOs and SMOs such as Father Bruno's RPV are important to the movement's challenge in the face of popular opinion, but the ability of the movement to use the state in this regard is an important development that challenges both movement theorists and activists to understand this new, less than contentious relationship to the state.

In terms of both the globalizations implicated in the SCA's development and the countermovement and popular resistance to the statute, the movement and the state find themselves as allies. This is a new situation for both the state and movement actors. As José Oeiras, a community activist and former member of the Municipal Council for the Rights of Children and Adolescents in Ananindeua, a suburb of Belém, put it, "[T]he SCA made it possible for the state and civil society to participate without the old conflict" that had pitted movements against the state in the past.[29] The opportunity offered by the development of the various layers of councils involved in the SCA's implementation also exists for other movements, in particular the women's movement and the movement for human rights. In both cases, councils like those mandated for the SCA operate at various levels of government, and, like the SCA, movement activists who once viewed the state as an enemy now find themselves on councils and in official positions that allow them to affect the implementation of policy.

This is the fruit of Brazil's democratization process, both in its specific historical and local development and in the context of the transnational movement for "popular participation" in government that grew out of the reawakening of Latin American civil society during the democratization of the 1980s. The imperative for popular participation—most commonly through representatives of SMOs and NGOs in civil society—is felt even as far as development projects being sponsored by the World Bank and the Inter-American Development Bank, whose loans and programs increasingly incorporate advisory councils of the kind mandated in the SCA. Also implicated in the transnationalization of the popular participation discourse are journalists, movement theorists, and academic analysts, who have accompanied the growth of Latin American civil society beginning with the community and other movements that resisted the military dictatorships of the 1960s and 1970s. By exposing the social, political, and economic grievances of various classes and groups during the period of military rule, Latin Americanists helped fuel transnational discourse about the relevance and potential of opening governing processes to more democratic forms of participation than simply voting.

As the Brazilian state opened itself in the process of democratization, various movements faced questions of becoming involved with their former antagonists. Keck (1992) traces the disputes in the "new union movement" of the late 1970s, and later the Workers' Party that grew out of that movement, as movement and party actors differed over whether they should take advantage of or reject the possibility of working inside the state (and by extension cooperating with other parties in the legislature and other branches) by competing for and winning elective offices. Alvarez (1990) does the same for the women's movement in Brazil. The stakes of participation in state organizations can be quite high, and the possibility that the movement may be sacrificing its autonomy by placing members on state councils or in official political positions is a very real one. The Brazilian labor movement's experience with state participation or the "generosity" of political leaders is a history of state co-optation from the time of populist dictator Getúlio Vargas's Labor Code of the 1930s through the military dictatorship's use of the code to silence labor opposition in the 1960s and 1970s. Little in Brazilian (or Latin American) political history suggests that working within the state will do anything but place the movement in the hands of politicians who seek to use it for political gain or to strip it of its ability to resist the state.[30]

But the changes of the 1980s called for new strategies. In Latin America prior to the 1960s, organized labor was the most important social movement with great political impact inside countries, followed by Catholic Church organizations such as Catholic Action. The relationship of these movements to states tended to be very contentious unless or until political parties or public officeholders managed to co-opt their organizations. A couple of factors opened the way for movements to begin to reevaluate their relationship to states. By the 1970s, the growing transnational linkages of a number of newer social movements—human rights, women's, environmental, community, religious, and even indigenous—provided movement organizations with resources independent of the state; in effect, through the transnational public sphere movements gained a hedge against the potential loss of autonomy by means of involvement with the state. At the same time, with the deepening of economic globalization, states faced, and continue to face, grave challenges to their capacities to create social and economic policies. States were now in a position to turn to the nongovernmental sector in the development of social policies; movements had developed diverse bases of organization, resources, and mobilization that rendered states less threatening. The international discourse of democratization that blossomed in the 1980s provided the ideological reasons and alternatives that brought these two once antagonistic actors together.

This process of state-movement approximation blurs the lines between public sectors and government agencies; between movement proposals, legislation, and policies; and, as movements are ever more implicated in transnational processes, between transnational public spheres and the domain of state sovereignty. Within the Rights Councils of the SCA and other councils devoted to the women's or human rights movements, the Brazilian state in the late 1980s and early 1990s began for the first time to sit at the same table with organizations in civil society and negotiate policy.

This new "usefulness" of the state has impacted different movements with varying levels of importance, but there is no doubt that the state, with the passage of the SCA in 1990, became extremely important to the movement for youth citizenship rights in Brazil. But this usefulness is not completely uncontentious. Issues of co-optation remain; many movement activists rightly fear how reliance upon the state might affect the way nongovernmental organs of the movement carry out their role of monitoring the abuse of youth rights. As movement actors take up positions on Rights Councils or in other governmental agencies, movement organizations lose, at least in part, the service of these actors. Also, involvement with the state could bring party-related and other political controversies into the movement, diminishing its capacity to present a united front for social action across the diverse organizations that compose it. But the risks that come with state involvement are simply part of the political landscape of contemporary Brazil; this is how movement activity is done now, at least among movements that have gained the kind of prominence that labor, women's, environmental, and children's rights enjoy today.

A more important challenge, however, in terms of social movement ideologies in Brazil concerns the relationship of movement activity to the development of citizenship. One of the key principles of movement development from the 1970s on was the development of an "active citizenship" by individuals and groups in civil society. Movement actors saw as part of their objective to enable ordinary people to stand up and demand that their rights be respected, whether through the provision of channels of access to these citizens or through the movement's example in contesting the state.[31] The risk with state involvement is that the development of this autonomous practice of citizenship might diminish as people expect the state to fulfill this role for them. As João Gomes, a community and NGO activist and former member of a *conselho tutelar* in Belém (June 1995–April 1997) put it, civil society in Brazil has traditionally been rather weak when it comes to holding politicians and the state accountable for their actions. "We live in a society where we don't have an 'active citizenship.' People always wait for the dominant classes to take the initiative. They always wait for government officials to take the initiative."[32]

However, this risk is diminished somewhat simply due to the amount of time and struggle it is taking to develop the councils that help implement the SCA. To say that the state has become useful, is to recognize a potential that is only minimally developed at present. Among scores of *municípios* in the state of Pará, only twenty-four *conselhos tutelares* were functioning by mid-1998 in the state of Pará, four of these in Belém alone. All of these operate at a "precarious" level according to Gomes, who in his current role as an administrator in the national NGO, Federation of Organs for Social and Educational Assistance (FASE), works in the nongovernmental sector to monitor the state in various policy areas. Even in states where the *conselhos* and Rights Councils are more numerous and active—principally in the more highly developed regions in southeastern and southern Brazil—the tasks facing these bodies are daunting. The existence of more than twenty *conselhos tutelares* in São Paulo seems paltry in the face of the continuing violence against children in that city. The movement in Belém managed to force the conservative city government of Hélio Gueiros to establish two *conselhos tutelares* by the mid-1990s but only several years after the passage of the law in 1990; Gueiros's administration also resisted the establishment of other state-society councils mandated by the constitution in areas such as health care and urban development. Plans to increase the number of *conselhos* had to wait until Edmilson Rodrigues of the left-wing Workers' Party was elected mayor in 1996.

The struggles that the movement for the SCA faces in terms of the political indifference of local officials reluctant to share power through advisory or other types of participatory organs allow it to continue to frame its objective as an effort to build "active citizenship." That process in itself helps it to hedge against the development of complacency that movement activists fear. The state may have become useful in this contest, but it has in no way become an actor that should diminish the incentive for groups and citizens to monitor its activities. In the end, movement organizations that wish to use the state face a constant struggle to force politicians to abide by the participatory provisions of the constitution and the SCA, and in that struggle the nongovernmental parts of the movements and movement organizations continue to have an important role in sustaining the movement, framing its objectives for the general public, and recruiting and training new activists in either the governmental or nongovernmental domains of movement activity.

The new context of state-society relations, the rebirth of civil society after dictatorship (and during its demise), and the ways that different globalizations push the state and movements together in an effort to realize their goals and the capacity to create policy—all of these factors have provided movements with great opportunities for development in the 1980s and 1990s. In the case of the SCA, the movement was solidly developed by the time of the constitutional assembly of 1986–88, and it has been a focal point of collective action in civil society. The movement has been not only a model for other movements but in opening up the state to movement penetration through the councils mandated in the SCA it has allowed for something of a cross-pollination effect among movement organizations in a variety of domains.

SCA movement activists such as João Gomes or José Oeiras are involved in many different kinds of action that cross the boundaries of different social movements. In particular, SCA activists are usually linked to neighborhood and community movements. Gomes, thirty-eight years old and with a high school education, was introduced to the children's rights movement through his own upbringing as a poor youth who became involved in Father Bruno's RPV and the Cidade de Emaús; later, as an adult, he became a leader in his neighborhood of Benguí, serving as president of the local neighborhood association and eventually as president of the metropolitan Belém Neighborhood Commission, a progressive organization that unified the diverse neighborhood movements that arose in the 1970s during the waning years of the military regime. Presently, Gomes works as an administrator and educator for a major national NGO, FASE, which develops research, literature, and educational programs that bring together activists from a diverse array of movements, including women's, labor, environmental, indigenous, community, religious, human rights, and children's rights.

Oeiras, thirty-six years old and with some experience in college, came to his involvement in the movement for the SCA and the neighborhood movement of Ananindeua through his participation in the party activity of the Left, which began to flourish after the party laws were relaxed in 1979. Oeiras has been able to work between the neighborhood movements and the movement for the SCA, building bridges between them and the progressive Left. He has been president of the Federation of Community Centers for Ananindeua, an umbrella organ that unified neighborhood associations in this suburb of Belém, and through his work in the federation he was able to participate in Rights Councils and meetings at the state and local levels and to become a representative on the Rights Council in Ananindeua. As he surveys his experience in these different movements, he places the SCA and the movement behind it in a central place, as it allowed other social movements to come to the fore when representatives such as himself, with experience in different organizations and movements, began to envision ways in which different movement concerns—in neighborhoods, women's groups, and other organizations—came together in the same struggle for democracy and citizenship. "The SCA [and its forums and Rights Councils] made it possible for other subjects to be heard" such as the neighborhood movement concerns with which he was also involved.[33]

To conclude, the story of the SCA and the struggles it faces provides a number of ways in which to examine the impact of globalizations, the development of public spheres at local and transnational levels, and the changing relationship between the state and social movements. The movement shows how a number of globalizations—such as democratization, demands for a more active citizenship, demands that the state secure and safeguard citizenship, and the economic changes ushered in by structural adjustment and the hegemony of neoliberalism—have converged to change the ways in which states and movements regard each other. In the blurring of public spheres, public officials and movement actors become allies in a contest to bring some parts of the state (notably, the police) and public opinion over to the movement's position that children and adolescents, even those who break the law, have citizenship rights that must be respected. As it stands, the movement's struggle is far from over, and the state remains a reluctant partner in this process. But opportunities exist now that did not in the past, and actors from a variety of Brazilian social movements find themselves redefining their relationships to the state on a daily basis, using the discourses and resources available in the local and transnational public spheres to enlist the state in activities that were once the province of movements alone.

NOTES

Field research in 1992–93 for this chapter was assisted by grants from the IIE Fulbright Program and the Joint Committee on Latin American and Caribbean Studies of the Social Science Research Council and the American Council of Learned Societies with funds provided by the Andrew W. Mellon Foundation and the Ford Foundation, in 1995 by a Hewlett International Travel Grant, and in 1998 by Augustana College. The author is also grateful for the comments of the Sawyer Seminar at the University of Michigan's Advanced Study Center in 1996, my coeditors, the reviewers for the press, and Peter Kivisto.

1. From the pamphlet "Estatuto da Criança e Adolescente: Coisa de Gente Grande" (UNIPOP n.d.). All translations from Portuguese texts and field interviews are my own.

2. Interview with the author (AA10/38). Unless otherwise specified, all names of respondents are pseudonyms. Interview codes signify the following: letters and numbers to the left of the slash indicate neighborhood and sequence in the series of interviews there; the number to the right of the slash is the page from the interview transcript where quoted material may be found.

3. The SCA applies to people under eighteen years of age (with some special provisions for people up to twenty) who are legally defined in the statute as a child (zero to eleven) or an adolescent (twelve to eighteen). To avoid redundancy or awkward repetition, I will refer to people up to eighteen years of age as young people, youths, or kids, using *child* and *adolescent* when specificity is required.

4. Watkins (1995) presents a thorough picture of the linkages between these phenomena and their impact on poverty, especially for women and children.

5. O'Donnell (1993) has analyzed the democratizing states of Latin America and notes that while freedom of expression and association are respected and elections are competitive and frequent, citizenship rights are not equally distributed because of widespread poverty and an inability (or lack of desire) by states and elites to address this problem. He calls this situation "low-intensity citizenship" and maintains that it is the main impediment to consolidating democracy in Latin America.

6. Pontes (1993) lists some of the accords that followed the 1959 declaration—for example, the United Nations Minimum Guidelines for the Administration of Child and Juvenile Justice (1985), the United Nations Convention on the Rights of Children (1989), and the United Nations Guidelines for the Prevention of Juvenile Delinquency (1990).

7. My examination of the contexts surrounding the movement for children's rights, the passage of the SCA, and the lives of the children and adolescents themselves draws on many sources. Dimenstein (1990, 1992, 1993) is the best-known author writing on the subject of youth life, the streets, gangs, violence, and child prostitution in Brazil. Zaluar (1994) provides an overview of the culture of *favela* (squatter neighborhood) life in Rio de Janeiro and the pathways and factors that lead children into a life of crime. Movimento Nacional de Meninos e Meninas de Rua et al. 1991, Ordem dos Advogados do Brasil 1993, Marques 1976, and Campos 1984 together provide an examination of the state of youth offenders, street crime, and violence from the 1970s to the present. For Amazonia, where my field re-

search was based, the Associação das Universidades Amazônicas has published an exhaustive five-volume series (Lèna and Silveira 1993; Moura et al. 1993; Jatene et al. 1993a, 1993b; and Costa et al. 1993), which addresses the life of young people in the region. Miranda 1992 and Diniz 1994 provide an in-depth look at youths and street life through long, open-ended interviews with children in the region. My own field research in 1992–93 and 1995 was based on: (1) neighborhood studies; (2) a series of interviews with officials of the local branch of the Movimento Nacional de Meninos e Meninas de Rua, the Centro de Defesa do Menor, República do Pequeno Vendedor, Ordem dos Advogados do Brasil, and police officers and state agencies treating the problems of youth and implementation of the SCA; and (3) a series of seventy open-ended interviews with people of all classes in Belém.

8. This literature is voluminous. Some prominent examples include Alves 1985, which examines the *abertura* as a strategy for the regime to leave power without turning the government over to the Left. Keck (1992) turns to the formation of the PT (Workers' Party) and shows how party leaders were concerned that splitting from the rest of the opposition, which the PT eventually did, might be playing into the military's grand plan of dividing the opposition. Stepan (1988) looks at the institutional and structural constraints on demilitarization in Latin America, Brazil in particular. Von Mettenheim (1995) examines Brazilian voting trends during the 1970s and 1980s to show how both pro-military and opposition parties used the *abertura* to position themselves vis-à-vis the voters.

9. The opposition PMBD won 257 (52.9 percent) of 487 seats in the national congress in the 1986 elections. The PFL (Liberal Front Party), formed by politicians who deserted the pro-military PDS (Democratic Social Party) toward the end of the regime, won 118 (24.2 percent) of the seats. The PDS won 33 (6.8 percent). At the state level, the PMDB won 22 of 23 gubernatorial races. See Rodrigues 1995, 79, and Von Mettenheim 1995, 118–20.

10. Keck (1992, 225) notes that the petition process led to 122 amendments bearing 12,265,854 signatures.

11. Movimento Nacional de Meninos e Meninas de Rua, n.d., 13.

12. On the importance and effectiveness of international linkages in enabling national groups to make their claims, even under repressive political regimes, see Keck and Sikkink 1998.

13. These figures are close approximations intended to give the reader some idea of the general situation of Brazilian children. The total Brazilian population according to the 1991 census was 146,154,502 (IBGE 1992a). The number of those under eighteen years of age, 59,343,041, was drawn from the government's 1989 survey of households (IBGE 1989; see also IBGE 1992b, 14, 144; and Jatene et al. 1993b, 65). The value of the monthly minimum salary in June 1991 was stated by the Departamento Intersindical de Estatística e Estudos Sócio-Econômicos at seventy-four dollars (DIEESE 1991, 18). The real value of the minimum salary during the 1980s and 1990s is a matter of great debate, given Brazilian levels of inflation, but what is certain is that it has been in a state of declining absolute value since the early 1960s (DIEESE 1993, 9).

14. Throughout Latin America, the 1980s are called the "lost decade" because of a regionwide economic contraction resulting from the debt crisis and the structural adjustment programs implemented to deal with it. The growth in the income gap seen in Brazil has been repeated around the region, most notably in Mexico.

15. Jatene et al. (1993a, 1993b) provide an authoritative, current study of the relationship among poverty, youth, and family in the Amazonian region of Brazil. Though Amazonia is relatively poorer than the rest of the country (except the Northeast), the relation-

ships and trends examined in these volumes tend to hold for the rest of Brazil, the regional case being an exaggeration of national patterns.

16. See Scheper-Hughes and Hoffman 1995, 147; and Jeffrey 1995, 155.

17. See Auler 1993. The execution was led by shop owners and men who control the local vending points of the *jogo de bicho,* Brazil's popular and illegal numbers game. Dangerous youths are bad for business, legal or illicit.

18. It is important to note that street children are only a small segment of Brazilian youth. In the popular perception, the poor kids who work and play in the street are street kids, but most of these children do live at home with their families.

19. Estatuto da Criança e do Adolescent, art. 2. The texts reads, "A child is considered, for the effects of this law, the person up to twelve years of age, incomplete, and the adolescent those between twelve and eighteen years of age." The stipulation for children up to "twelve years of age, incomplete," means that on a child's twelfth birthday he or she legally becomes an adolescent.

20. Article 18: "É dever de todos velar pela dignidade da criança e do adolescente, pondo-os a salvo de qualquer tratamento desumano, violento, aterrorizante, vexatório ou constrangedor."

21. In territorial terms, the *município* in Brazil is roughly equivalent to the county in the U.S. system; in structure and governance, it operates like a U.S. municipality, with a mayor (*prefeito*) as the executive and a municipal council. Because of the specific nature of the *município,* I will not translate it, and *município* and *local government* in this chapter are used interchangeably. The term *conselho tutelar* can be understood as an advisory and assistance council, but the translation is cumbersome and I will leave it in the original Portuguese.

22. Specifically, the *conselhos* are to oversee the application of the SCA's correctional provisions, when the rights of children and adolescents are violated (1) "by action or omission of the society or state," (2) "by the negligence, omission, or abuse of parents or guardians," and (3) "by reason of [the youth's] own conduct" (art. 98). Functionally, the *conselho* is one authority to whom people (of any age) may turn if, for example, they know that a neighbor is physically abusing his or her children. The *conselhos* should also oversee the correctional measures applied to youths who break the law. As for the juvenile justice system, it is set out as an administrative apparatus to execute the statute and prevent young people from becoming involved in the regular penal system, where it is understood that they will be abused, victimized, and inaugurated into a larger life of crime.

23. For discussions of movement–counter movement dynamics, see Zald and Useem 1987 and Meyer and Staggenborg 1996.

24. Police characterizations of youth offenders and gang members tend to be more vivid when used in conversation among police or with sympathetic companions. As one city council member put it in an interview with me, Tamer has stated that the job of the police is "to prepare themselves to confront animals" (FN12/127).

25. One of the striking consistencies of interview responses in discussions about crime and violence was the indignity over criminals who "kill for pleasure" (*matar por prazer* or *matar por que gosta de matar*). It cropped up in the great majority of the seventy field interviews, cited by both men and women of all classes as another sign that violence is completely out of control. When asked to explain *why* people would kill for pleasure, answers were not always of the dispositional type cited by Tamer, which in ordinary conversation would be rendered often as simply the "lack of love for others" (*falta de amor pro próximo*). More frequently, respondents would explain how people who killed for pleasure probably did so because of poor family upbringing and an unfavorable social environment that had left them "in revolt" against the norms of society.

26. The show's title, *Barra Pesada,* is slang for "tough place" or "bad neighborhood"; in commonplace parlance, it refers to working-class neighborhoods known for crime and violence. Violence and local disputes are not, however, the only sort of material *Barra Pesada* covers. The show also lists birthdays and runs raffles. Even more notably, the program covers some neighborhood demonstrations such as blocking a road to attract attention to sanitation problems or traffic accidents and injuries.

27. *Cachaça* is a liquor distilled from sugarcane. It is widely consumed in Brazil by people of all classes, although the middle and upper classes tend to regard it as one of the markers of diminished class status and usually drink it mixed with lime, sugar, and ice as *caipirinha,* the national drink. One brand of *cachaça,* "51," is actually the best-selling alcoholic beverage in the world. The butane gas tank (*butijão*) in the story is a common feature in Brazilian households of all classes. Except in the more industrialized areas of the south and southeast, where gas for stoves and heating is often piped into middle- and upper-class neighborhoods through a public utility system, people must purchase a gas tank to fuel their stoves and ovens. Companies providing the service send a truck with tanks through neighborhoods on a regular schedule. At the outset, however, one must buy the tank itself, for later exchange and refill, and the tank costs quite a bit more than the gas.

28. Although most of the physically harmful and violent abuse of children is practiced by males (stepfathers, fathers, and uncles, in that order), respondents cite the violence of mothers as well, particularly in terms of beating young children. Understanding these claims is a difficult matter. Every interview contained some conversation about gender, family issues, and the relationship between men and women, and respondents were always careful to state that women are just as capable of violent acts as men. The typical sort of response began by citing male violence and its ubiquity, closing with a statement that women behave this way as well, even if not as often as men do. I understand the add-ons about women to be more a nod toward commonplace egalitarianism, for, although people are well aware of the structures of status and power in households, they are careful to present the household as a collaborative project in which the capacities, good and bad, of all members are somewhat equal. And, to be certain, ordinary people and social workers alike can cite examples of cruelty practiced by mothers, which helps lend veracity to the notion that women are not universally or essentially kind and gentle.

29. Interview with the author, Belém, Brazil, August 14, 1998.

30. Collier and Collier's (1991) eight-country comparative study of Latin American labor movements and their relationship to the state or politics shows that in just about every instance interaction between labor movements and states or parties, no matter how radical, tended toward the moderation of labor demands in exchange for the freedom to operate or a voice in the political system. In the Brazilian case, they show that "state-led incorporation" of the labor movement into the political arena kept labor quiescent from the 1930s through the mid-1970s, when the "new unionism" analyzed by Keck (1992) and Seidman (1994) emerged.

31. Stokes (1995) studies neighborhood movements in Peru and demonstrates how progressive movement organizations struggled against the more passive visions of citizenship rooted in clientelism. Gay (1994) provides a similar contrast in Rio de Janeiro. In general, movement organizations with more active notions of citizenship tend to find themselves engaged in struggles with other local groups that are more closely tied to clientelist practices that emphasize citizen passivity.

32. Interview with the author, Belém, Brazil, August 13, 1998.

33. Interview with the author, Belém, Brazil, August 14, 1998.

PART III

Movements, Identities, Cultural Transformations

CHAPTER 8

Refugees, Resistance, and Identity

Julie Peteet

"Arafat! Arafat is not a Palestinian! A Palestinian is one who struggles," Khalid, a former commando and leader in the Palestinian resistance movement, spat with contempt. "She's a Palestinian!" he said with a triumphant wave of the hand, indicating Christina, a foreign woman who had worked in Palestinian refugee camps for years. In Beirut in the summer of 1995, the three of us had been discussing the peace accords between the Palestinians and Israelis. I tell of this incident to bring to the fore the way in which resistance figures so prominently in the contemporary production and reproduction of Palestinian identity. It suggests not simply the now commonplace assumption of the negotiability of identity but also the need to locate it in specific historical junctures. Most significantly, it directs attention to questions of agency as critical to discussions of identity.

The process of human displacement, resistance to it, and implications for identity are examined here as they are locally configured and experienced. Operating at the intersection of globalizations and movements, as outlined by the volume's editors, this chapter attempts to problematize and explore the highly complicated relations between dispossession, misrecognition, resistance, and identity. Dispossession and recognition were the immediate, far-reaching effects of a larger global process of colonialism eventuating in partition at the end of empire. The specific point of departure is the constitution of Palestinian identity in exile and in the midst of a diasporic social movement to resist dispossession and organize for the achievement of national sovereignty. The question arises as to what is the relationship between a diasporic social movement and identity. What is the nature and direction of this relationship? How were identities enabled and nuanced by the resistance movement?

My point of departure in discussing identity is a conceptualization of it as a cultural product of peoples' sociospatial location and their practices within a shifting field of power relations that is historically and culturally specific. Location is a beginning, not necessarily an end, in the trajectory of identity. I highlight the historical and the spatial rather than the cultural because culturally specific frames for understanding identity can, if one is not careful, gloss over the complexity of agency and history. My chapter, on what the editors insightfully note as the relatively underresearched area of social movements and identities, highlights the way identities can shape social movements and yet are themselves, in the process of this interaction, sites of rearticulation.

As cultural products grounded in histories, identities are always shifting and emerging and aspects of identity are variously denied, suppressed, mobilized, celebrated, and given organizational and institutional expression. I will argue that the very form of identity used as a mobilizing frame can be transformed during the course of social movement participation. Thus, I do subscribe to the notion that social movements mobilize around certain assumed to be given aspects of identity. However, I carry in a somewhat new direction this relationship between identity and social movements. Ethnographic research among Palestinians in Lebanon suggests that while social movements can mobilize around and reaffirm identities they have the potential to transform them as well. The chapters by Lo, Perales, and Uehling address the issue of how participation in social movements can be transformative of identity.

The theoretical issue this chapter advances is that the specific parameters and content of identity were not given but were continuously emergent, in this instance, through resistant practices that could transform individual and collective identities. Further, identity was not simply constructed vis-à-vis an other but through the process of resisting the power and dominance of this other, the assumption being that the existence of an other implies and denotes hierarchal difference. Local identities, as an aspect of cultural production, can in and of themselves be interventionist in projects of domination. Furthermore, they are more than just sites of intervention by dominant forces or sites of social movement mobilization; they are themselves a means of resistance, and in the process identities themselves can be sustained, reaffirmed, or, as I argue, can take on new contours. This is certainly the case with the Palestinians, whose national identity in a global area was long denied and yet whose expression could incite violence and repression. It was around this identity, negated and suppressed on a global level, that the Palestinian resistance movement was organized and mobilized and, in the process, reconfigured.

I would like to note and comment on a certain tension this work contains between the possible essentialization of the identities of Palestinians in exile, the resistance movement and its meaning for Palestinians, and the particular places from and in which they experience exile. Neither identities nor places are single, unitary, and stable entities with fixed meanings. Identity is embedded in and takes off from a multiplicity of places, experiences, and positions in life that are variously accommodated, celebrated, and resisted. The meaning of place not only is vastly different depending on one's social and political location, but it fluctuates radically depending on its location in arrangements of power that write and rewrite its scales. Yet there are historical moments when the construction and presentation of self and collectivity are overwhelmingly referenced to a particular aspect of identity, place, and experience and the way they are produced by an arrangement of power.

In terms of diaspora politics, Palestinian identity can accommodate Appadurai's (1993) postnational cosmopolitanism, which emerges from political collectivities organized around transnational issues such as the environment and human rights rather than narrowly defined national interests and identities. One could argue that the "struggle" component in Palestinian identity, a way of being and acting on the world, is hardly a narrow national issue. *Struggle* in this instance references a continuing mobilization against local manifestations of a global form of colonialism with its dislocating impulse. As the opening scenario illustrates, identity is more hitched to agency and consciousness than narrowly conceived sentiments of national identity. Diasporic politics can take multiple forms and should always be located in, among other things, the causes propelling dislocation, the elements of choice, and conditions in the homeland and host country. Moreover, a Palestinian diasporic politics,[1] while organized around the obvious issue of national sovereignty, is further complicated by the fragmentation that ensues from exile in different regions and various states. Fragmentation, with its multiple geographic and cultural sites of exile, has fostered in Palestinians transnational identities and increasingly a sense that the future will be less one of identifying oneself as other and more a seeking of common ground on a variety of levels of affiliation.

If we zoom in on the refugee camp as a particular local manifestation of a larger process of global politics, our picture of diaspora politics is complicated in productive ways. The increasing literature on diaspora identities rarely deals with refugee camps,[2] particularly those with longevity, being more focused on diaspora communities in larger, urban centers in the West. As living spaces that are the outcome of powerful displacing forces, they embody the capacity to affect identities in particularly acute ways, ways that can at one historical and spatial moment be conducive to essentialized identities and at another spawn cosmopolitanism. Periods of near incarceration contribute to a sense of self and community as bounded. Yet a diasporic social movement with international ties and a civil war in Lebanon (1975–90) that forged militant solidarity with local forces loosened these same spatial boundaries and induced a kind of transnational cosmopolitanism revolving around anticolonial political activism and sentiment. Essentialism then becomes a political and cultural necessity, a construct if you will, pointing to the notion of such essences themselves as contingent.

"Everything that will happen to my people will happen to me." When Rashidiyyeh, a Palestinian refugee camp on the outskirts of the southern Lebanese town of Tyre, fell to the invading Israeli forces in the summer of 1982, a Palestinian woman, standing in the rubble, screamed the above statement at a journalist.[3] This embedding of the self and worldview in a national and cultural identity and social location as a refugee is not at all unusual for Palestinians. Daily existence for Palestinians in Lebanon, with its crisislike atmosphere and multitude of problems, is constantly referenced to place and national identity—to being stateless and Palestinian.

Taking off on a strand of feminist thought, Calhoun suggests that we might at certain times and "under certain circumstances," mainly political but also intellectual, "risk essentialism" (1994, 17). He sums up the argument this way: "At its simplest, the argument suggests that where a particular category of identity has been repressed, de-legitimated or devalued in dominant discourses, a vital response may be to claim value for all those labeled by that category, thus implicitly invoking it in an essentialist way" (17). Palestinian in-group essentialism is hardly a surprise given that their nonrecognition, denial of a right to their homeland, and denial of a right to national expression of identity have played a central role in neocolonial projects that grant recognition, homeland, and national expression to an other in Palestine. It has been produced in a context of violent displacement and exile and a continuing project to deny return. Indeed, it is precisely at the intersection between displacement from a homeland claimed exclusively by an other and transformed by them to erase a Palestinian presence and everyday life in refugee camps that Palestinian identity is being constituted. Experiences of domination, violence (displacement, denial of return, and sovereignty), and place (exile and refugee camps) emerge as the significant factors for locating contemporary Palestinian identity.[4] Yet alongside these intermittent expressions of essentialism one finds a cosmopolitanism openly iterated or a suppressed desire for a past cosmopolitanism that was severely restricted by the end of the civil war in Lebanon and the reimposition of government controls over the camps.[5]

Evoking Palestinian national identity in definitions of self and community is central to resisting a project in which nonrecognition was pivotal—the myth of the empty landscape or, in other variations, of people who could be moved at will to make way for those possessed of both more rights and the technologies to render them possible. Calhoun's point that "self-critical claims to strong, basic and shared identity may be useful" (1994, 17) certainly warrants serious consideration. Indeed at some historical points, the very identity "Palestinian"—being and voice—constituted a form of resistance. I am well aware of the very real dangers associated with positioning the national as an essentialist aspect of identity both academically and politically. It can be implicated in actions that target a populace. Libya's recent expulsion of Palestinians, Israeli policies of collective punishment, and Kuwait's campaign of terror and expulsion of resident Palestinians during the Gulf War are reminders of such dangers. Yet it is in these everyday spaces of violence that a sense of collective identity is reinforced and strengthened in narratives of self and collectivity.

Locating the Local

Locating the local is not meant to imply a simple juxtaposition of the local vis-à-vis the global. Positioning the local in a spatial arrangement of global power should facilitate a more dynamic view of the local as constituted at the intersection of an array of forces and interests on a global (as well as regional) level and the internal arrangements of structure, power, and culture. Resistance to global positioning is highlighted here as it plays into and nuances identity. In the process of resisting (as well as accommodating) such positioning, identities are constantly reconfigured in substance, form, emotive content, and enactment.

The local in this instance is the Palestinian refugee community in Lebanon. As a whole, the Palestinians are one of the largest refugee populations in the world; nearly half of the population of 5.2 million Palestinians are refugees. Lebanon is home to 300,000 to 400,000 Palestinians. With the establishment of the state of Israel in 1948, nearly 100,000 Arabs from the northern areas of Palestine were expelled or fled to Lebanon. Denied the right to return and compensation for lost livelihoods and property, the refugees gradually settled into the fifteen refugee camps established by the United Nations Relief and Welfare Agency (UNRWA) or into Lebanese towns and the capital city of Beirut. The UNRWA provided rations, shelter, education, and medical services. Initially impoverished, fragmented, dispirited, and unable to muster a leadership capable of addressing their needs or political aspirations, this state of affairs gave way to a significant transformation in the late 1960s. The gradual emergence of Palestinian political organizations resulted in their supplanting UNRWA and conflict with the Lebanese state and emerging militias. In November 1969, following a series of clashes with the Lebanese army, the government accepted an open, armed Palestinian presence in an agreement known as the Cairo Accords. The resistance movement assumed daily management of the refugee camps, providing security as well as a wide variety of health, educational, employment, and social services. This period of autonomy from Lebanese authority was short lived, as the camps and individual Palestinians came under increased military attack from various Lebanese militias and continued Israeli incursions and bombings of the camps. The period of autonomy came to an abrupt and rather dramatic end in the summer of 1982 with the Israeli invasion and siege of Beirut. With the evacuation of the Palestine Liberation Organization (PLO) forces from Beirut, the Palestinian community was left traumatized, impoverished, and exceedingly vulnerable.

The West Bank and the Gaza Strip are the areas of Palestine that were not occupied by Israeli forces in 1948. In 1950, the West Bank was annexed by Jordan, while the Gaza Strip was administered by Egypt. Residents of these two areas consisted of the indigenous Palestinian inhabitants and refugees displaced during the 1948 war. In 1967, both areas came under Israeli occupation (along with the Syrian Golan Heights and Egypt's Sinai Peninsula). While resistance was commonplace from the beginning of the occupation, it was only with the *intifada* in the late 1980s that a somewhat coherent and sustained movement emerged to challenge the occupation. Following the Palestinian-Israeli peace accords, these two areas are now in the process of gaining a highly debatable and contested degree of autonomy.

Individuals in any society carry the potential for multiple and imbricated forms of identity comprised of gender, age, class, ethnicity, regional origins, kinship, religion, political affiliation, sexuality, and so on. While nationalist movements and narratives may insist on a single unitary subject (especially in the sense of an active subject), adherents are always part of a multiplicity of networks and have sentiments of belonging that may compete with, or at times coincide with, nationalist sentiments. In the Palestinian national movement as it existed prior to the peace accords, the pressure was to gloss over or deny the presence and validity of some forms of identity as sites of political organizing autonomous from the PLO umbrella, particularly gender.

Before outlining the parameters of Palestinian identity, I would like to refer briefly to historical antecedents. Palestinian identity has been produced in a particular space and history and in a field of power relations that has a specific historical depth. A brief overview of Palestinian identity formation and consciousness in the pre-1948 period will help to locate and frame post-1948 developments. Palestinians do not differ from most people in having multiple identity referents. What does distinguish them from many, however, is the absence of national independence in their homeland despite a distinct form of national identity. Notions of Palestinian nonexistence, or the emergence of their national identity as a response to Zionism and the formation of the Israeli state, have been rather standard in Zionist discourse and scholarship.[6] These notions have now been sorely tested, if not put to rest, by recent Arab and Western scholarship (Khalidi 1997; Muslih 1990; Scholch 1993).

Palestinian identity, in the "incipient sense of community-as-nation" can be traced to the late nineteenth century (Khalidi 1997, 28). Palestinians had a distinct sense of the geosocial territory of Palestine, particularly from a religious perspective, as sacred space dating back, in the historical literature recovered so far, to the sixteenth century. The presence of an external threat has long been present in Palestinian identity going back to the Crusades, which often serve as a historical referent for modern day projects that have laid claim to the space of Palestine.

During the British Mandate (1921–48), Khalidi argues, the foci of identity shifted. With the demise of the Ottoman Empire and the prominence of religion in daily life, the British Mandate in Palestine, the expanding secular educational system and press, the intensified Zionist project, and nationalist sentiment in other parts of the region, a distinctly modern form of Palestinian national identity began emerging among large segments of the population, although it was particularly evident among members of the elite (who leave historical records far more frequently than do nonelites). The presence of "another" certainly gave Palestinian nationalism its intensity and revolutionary dimensions, particularly as it obstructed Palestinian national aspirations, but the emergence of Palestinian national identity, which had clearly been in formation for several decades before the gravity of Zionist intentions were realized, cannot be referenced primarily to the Zionist movement in Palestine.[7]

What happened in 1948—the loss of Palestine, the expulsion and flight of the overwhelming bulk of the population, the denial of return or compensation, and the beginnings of the diaspora—forged a collective consciousness of shared experiences of statelessness, suffering, and the trauma associated with a rupture with place. A Palestinian national identity that encompassed the elites as well as the mass of now dispossessed peasants resurfaced with organizational vigor in the 1960s as they organized for return under the auspices of the various constituent groups of the PLO. I would not go so far as to call the *al-nekba,* the disaster of 1948, the great leveler, as does Khalidi (1997), but I would position it as a common denominator, an overwhelmingly pivotal one. On some level, exile glossed over many of the differences that made for conflict in pre-1948 Palestine such as rural-urban and class differences. Yet these same differences themselves traveled and were replicated in diaspora society. Camp/noncamp residency became a signifier of social class and origins. Even village rivalries and feuds were carried into exile and reconfigured in the refugee camps. What gave Palestinians a sense of collective consciousness was attachment to place and its violent denial and rupture. Moreover, the sense of being in exile, of being homeless and stateless, and the acute sense of vulnerability associated with that condition, while attenuated by class and capital, pervaded the sense of being of all refugees.

With the fragmentation of the Palestinian community after 1948, Palestinian national identity took root in the various places of exile, although it had to wait until the mid-1960s to take on organizational form and expression. While quiescent after the trauma of 1948, a Palestinian sense of community was being reenacted wherever they found themselves in the diaspora. At the most basic level, in the camps pre-1948 Palestine could be read in the organization of space by village boundaries. The camps resembled microcosms of northern Palestine in their layout according to pre-1948 villages, spatializing a desire to re-form a physical and social geography of trust (Peteet 1995). Local community relations continued and indeed were often intensified spatially through sheer proximity, socially through long-established networks, and new networks of social affiliation emerged as people from different villages forged relations with each other in their new environment.

Something else happened in the diaspora that had resounding implications for identity. For the refugee, the way of being in the world was transformed and the presence of others became highlighted. Knowledge of place, the built environment, livelihood, community relations, social networks, and power had all been part of a familiar routine that peasants engaged in during the course of their daily lives without much conscious elaboration. In exile, the notion of the familiar becomes strained. The terrain, both geophysical and social, have to be relearned and navigated. In spite of similarities in language, culture, and religion, Palestinians were acutely aware of difference from the host population.What set the Palestinian refugee apart from the Lebanese host was neither language nor culture but relation to place and the absence of citizenship and the rights it entails. When Palestinians in the diaspora in the Middle East speak of alienation, it is doubly meaningful. It refers to the alienation of being severed from place but also from the host Arab population that treated them with disrespect and eventually outright hostility and violence. The severance of belonging in place, and the social honor that accrues from a recognition of one's grounding in particular place, meant learning anew, in a new context, how to carry oneself, present oneself to others, and reconstitute social honor.[8]

Place and Identity

The common denominators in denoting contemporary Palestinian identity are origin in and continuing attachment to the space and particular places of Palestine; the collective loss and trauma of exile (or occupation); outrage over the injustice of dispossession, misrecognition, and international complicity; the idea of return; and the concept and practice of resistance.

The meaning of place is neither constant nor essential, and as the power nexus that gives meaning to places shifts identities can be unsettled and reconfigured. The shifting nature and meaning of place has serious implications for identity formation. As people and communities live these particular articulations of power relations embedded in and through places, their notions of self and community shift, both accommodating and contesting the kinds of identities that may be imposed by place and, in the process, constructing and reconstructing their own identities. This work inserts a historical and spatial component to the process of displacement and the constitution of identity by tracing their ever shifting configurations and interstices in particular places and times.

Place is implicated in a number of ways in the formation of identity. Fifty years of exile in a particular host country and the specificities of host population–refugee interaction have certainly been salient factors in Palestinian identity, particularly feelings of marginalization, otherness, and discrimination. Arab host country policies toward Palestinians in terms of rights and restrictions are variable. Jordan gave Palestinians citizenship but not the political right to organize for return; Syria gave Palestinians a number of civil rights, such as the right to be employed, but it tightly controlled, severely suppressed, and/or manipulated Palestinian political organizing. As a weak state unable to effectively oppose Palestinian political and military strength, Lebanon, once host (although with great reluctance and much eventual opposition) to the resistance, is now, after years of violent attempts to contain Palestinian political expression, intent on containing and controlling them in tightly bounded and strictly surveilled refugee camps.

Popular self-categorization associates particular forms of Palestinian identity with places of exile so that one can speak of the Palestinians of Lebanon, the Palestinians of Kuwait, and so on based on their specific experiences of arrival and reception by host countries (but most critically by host populations), their legal status and rights, and host country policy on political activities and expression. The

Palestinian presence in different locales strongly points to the emergence of a Palestinian national identity that is multisited or transnational. This raises such interesting questions as whether *multisited* means fragmentation and how one works beyond and within multiple sites. What is the relationship between national identity and nationalism? These are questions that can't be adequately addressed here, only raised. In any case, the point is that the Palestinian subject is involved in multiple fields of interaction and meaning that need not be in open tension but certainly can be (as is the case with feminist identities and nationalist politics and ideologies or Jordanian and Palestinian identities).

Refugee camps, as technologies of power,[9] are a peculiarly twentieth-century phenomenon. They are places, often bounded, devised to contain, manage and reinvent the identities of refugees. Yet, I would posit, they are also sites of resistance to displacement and the construction of desired identities. Indeed, they are heavily implicated in a process of identity formation in which resistance is prominently positioned. What is the location and meaning of the refugee camp, with its multiple meanings, for Palestinian refugee identities? And, how was the resistance movement, heavily present in the camps, decisive for Palestinian identity? For a period of over a decade (1968–82), the refugee camps in Lebanon were arenas in which the Palestinian resistance movement had an extraordinary presence and a high degree of autonomy. So closely associated were the camps and the resistance movement that *camps* became a signifier of resistance and political activism (and not solely to the Palestinians). For decades, the Israelis have bombed the camps, employing the mediated image of them as military bases, which again draws our attention to the dangers that can inhere in the process of essentializing identities as well as place.

As a spatialized intersection of power, place is a critical component of Palestinian identity. Palestinian identity, however, is not be to indexed simply to place, either originary (Palestine) or exilic (the refugee camps or exile in urban areas). Correspondingly, identities are so complex as to preclude a simple referencing to one experience, locale, or individual or group characteristic such as gender, age, race, religion, ethnicity, nationalism, or class. The identity of any one individual is a study in imbrication; at specific historical and political junctures, aspects of identity may be in tension, as can be the case with feminism and nationalism. The spatial arena is privileged primarily because it figures so largely in the constitution of Palestinian identity in exile. The refugee camp, as a space of confinement, control, and the reconstitution of self and community, and the resistance movement, which was deeply rooted in camp lives and experience, both played and continue to play critical roles in the formation of identity.

In exploring the complexities of identity formation in refugee camps, one can liken those in Lebanon to a borderland: "a territory defined by a geopolitical line: two sides arbitrarily separated and policed but also joined by legal and illegal practices of crossing and communication" (Clifford 1994, 304). Borderlands are places where two cultures intersect and rub against each other. In them, people engage in the process of reassembling ideas and practices of self and community in the face of past and present traumas and the will to survive.

To understand the process of identity formation and (re)formation requires zooming in on the intersections of past and present, homeland and exile. First, overlaying, or intersecting, with this spatiotemporal frame for locating exilic identities is the presence of the resistance movement in the daily lives of refugees. These intersections point to the need to explore the nature of a borderland and how its boundaries are formed and continuously (re)formed against a backdrop of power relations between refugees and the host country and military forces. Second, they point to the relations between past and present and how they are constituted by memories and imaginings of the past. Last, they point to the resistance movement as the body that gave institutional and community expression to Palestinian identity.

The following two kinds of routes to identity can be mapped onto spatial transformations. First, conceptualizations of self and identity are constructed on a continually shifting spatial plane. Experiences of continuing displacement within Lebanon point to the multiplicity of places entailed in the production and (re)production of Palestinian identities. Rather than identity being referenced solely to a single place of origin, what emerges is a sense of identity that is multireferenced in terms of places of exile. What we need is an analytical approach that bypasses a direct line to the past in identity formation and sets its sights instead on locating the connections with and nostalgia for multiple places.

For refugees, place is a lived experience that is carried from one site to another. As it travels, originary place intersects with new places to nuance identity. My research suggests that identity remains territorialized in a globalizing world on the move but in a way more complex than usually imagined. It is grounded in specific villages and regions or cities—and yet deterritorialized and reterritorialized. As it travels, it is (re)configured in new places and takes on new contours. Exile is a messy affair; linear movement is difficult to discern as people move in seemingly haphazard fashion from one site to another. Memory of place and the mapping of identities to place are not linear. Rather, memory and identity are multisited, shifting uneasily between the original village and a trajectory of exilic places. This is apparent in the nostalgia for and attachments to places of origin as well as particular places of exile. Indeed, refugees become identified by other Palestinians through various places and the various, but specific, experiences associated with life in them. People who survived Tel al-Za'ater are still known, nearly twenty years later, as Tel al-Za'ater people. A new building in Chatila camp, built to accommodate refugees whose camps were destroyed in the war, houses refugees from a number of camps but is popularly referred to as the Za'ater building. Chatila residents, themselves from a number of other camps, can identify

Za'ater people, their villages of origin, and where they now reside in the camp. Thus identity formation is highly variegated, multisited, dialogic, and traveling.

Second, for Palestinian refugees, identity is very caught up with spatial boundaries and the way they produce and are reproduced by relations of power and disempowerment. Refugee camps, by their very design, imply a transformation in identity in a situation of relative powerlessness on the part of refugees. They are sites where national identity and relation to place are both to be denied and in the process dismantled. It is critical to pay attention to how refugees define themselves especially vis-à-vis bureaucratic and administrative designations of them as refugees.[10] In particular, there is correspondence between terms of reference and categorization and the relations of power in which a group is enmeshed.

During the period from 1948 to 1968, Palestinian refugees were dependent on UNRWA for basic food rations, education, and medical services and were fairly powerless on the Lebanese scene. The borders of the camps were quite distinct, marked by barbed wire and spatial demarcation from Lebanese areas. Exit was often subject to control and surveillance; in some camps, Palestinians had to register their names on a list with the Lebanese police in order to leave the camp. Tales of experiences of discrimination circulated easily and do so again today. While they did not like being referred to by the word *refugees,* with its implications of powerlessness and marginality, their sense of selves as *returnees* was quite ambiguous, having little structural force to embody and express it. Identity was clearly referenced to the past and one's place in it but was increasingly liminal in terms of space and place as the past and past places became more and more distant, not in terms of memory or attachment but in terms of accessibility and immediacy of meaning. What was just across the border was a million deathly miles away. But the spaces of exile—the harshness of life in the camps, the daily interactions with the host population (which reminded one of marginality and otherness), dealing with the refugee bureaucracy, continuing displacement, and attacks on the camps—were immediacies that directly and often violently impinged on identities, mediating the linearity of exilic ties to the past.

Refugees and Resisters

"Without struggle—without the resistance movement—we don't know who we are. It was through struggling that we found our identity," Muna, a Palestinian administrator in a foreign NGO assisting Palestinians and Lebanese, said with exasperation. "Of course, we know who we are, but we struggled for years and made all those sacrifices—all those people killed and displaced. We kept 'Amal out of the camps. Now, we have no sense of belonging. We don't know who we are! What will happen to us?! Are we animals to be moved around? They talk of moving us to various parts of Lebanon. The Lebanese authority is always giving statements against implantation and naturalization. Where do we belong?" Muna made these statements in the summer of 1994, when Arafat made his entrance in Gaza and Jericho, when the Lebanese government publicly iterated its refusal to consider naturalization of Palestinians, and rumors were flying that the camps were to be moved to remote parts of Lebanon.

While relation to place was almost a given of Palestinian identity in exile, what transpired during exile pushed to the forefront aspects of experience, mainly suffering and resistance. Agency, in this instance the practice of resistance, was to become critical to Palestinian identity in Lebanon during the era of resistance.

When I first engaged in fieldwork among Palestinians in Lebanon, I was working on issues of gender and political activism. I often approached political activism in terms of formal belonging to a constituent group of the PLO. Unwittingly, I was imposing an analytical framework of active/nonactive or formal/informal that had minor relevance either to one's identity as a Palestinian or as one who is a participant in resistance activities. What is of significance here is the relationship between formal political activism and the informal that drew in the domestic sphere, mothers, the elderly, youth, and children, sectors of society not always easily mobilized. The pervasive sentiment of resistance was only made possible by the presence of the formal organized resistance movement. It was able to mobilize vast numbers of members and supporters around the issue of return and national sovereignty as expressions of a Palestinian national identity. Its very presence in the camps, its control over various aspects of daily life, and its authority to protect and defend camp residents meant that Palestinian identity became intricately entangled with resistance. The Palestinian resistance movement was the public and international expression of a Palestinian identity. It endowed that identity with resistance qualities. It was identity giving in two ways. First, the resistance endowed Palestinian identity with celebratory qualitites. As people in a state of resistance to a contemporary colonial presence in the region, Palestinians for a while were seen as embodying the Arab spirit of struggle against foreign control in the region. Palestinian identity was a source of pride easily displayed, for example, through aesthetics such as gold medallions in the shape of the Palestinian map and in an accent openly used in non-Palestinian areas. The dissimulation prevalent now is in marked contrast to the once open displays of Palestinian identity. Such displays were made possible by a combination of factors. The military strength of the resistance movement in Lebanon accorded Palestinians a well-founded sense of protection, and initially their cause garnered fairly widespread sympathy and support for their cause among some sectors of the Lebanese populace. The resistant qualitites of their identity were thus endowed with organizational expression, support, and protection in the resistance movement.

Second, the various political groups that comprised the resistance movement and with which nearly every family was affiliated, whether formally (as full-time, salaried activists) or by means of what is called "friendship" or ideological affiliation, conferred a specific aspect of one's Palestinian identity. People were thus known by their political affiliations. Indeed, these affiliations were so strong that endogamy was encouraged among members of particular groups. Last, as a transnational movement with branches all over the world, Palestinians in the diaspora enjoyed a connection based on political affiliation and commitment with Palestinians in a variety of other places.

Militancy and struggle were such a part of one's identity that to withdraw was to lose stature as a "true" Palestinian. In the camps, I often heard people referred to as true Palestinians by virtue of their political activism, particularly but not always necessarily, in the form of militancy. The Israeli-Palestinian peace process, which excludes the refugees in Lebanon, was seen by them as a betrayal, especially in light of the long and very deadly years of conflict in support of the resistance movement. And that helps to explain why a camp resident could exclaim that "Arafat is not a Palestinian!"

Muna's statement captures some of the tension inherent in the term *resistance* in this, and perhaps in other, anticolonial, mass-based social movements. She says, "Without struggle—without the resistance movement—we don't know who we are." The resistance movement refers to institutional, organized resistance under the PLO umbrella. But resistance also embodied a far more pervasive and deeper meaning. *Struggle* refers to the latter kind of resistance, which extends beyond the boundaries of the PLO. Everyday existence was perceived as enacting resistance, as a form of struggle (Peteet 1991). People would respond to my questions about their activism: "We are all in the resistance. Just to sit in these camps is a way of resisting," registering a refusal to go away or, more precisely, to be moved. For some women, child rearing was also rhetorically conceptualized as an act of resistance: "This is my contribution to the cause."

Aspects of daily life in a crisis situation became identity endowing and affirming. The refusal to move has a certain resonance to it among refugees in Lebanon. Until the demise of the resistance movement in Lebanon in 1982, the subsequent Sabra-Chatila massacre, and the camp wars of the 1980s, Palestinians pondered and debated what their parents' generation did in 1948. They wondered what would have happened if people had simply stayed put at the border or in their villages—sort of a mass sit-down strike. It was not until the generation born in exile underwent similar attacks, massacres, and systematic removal during the course of the civil war in Lebanon that they gained some understanding of the complexity of actions during wartime.

The concept of *sumud* has been central to self-definitions both in exile and later during the *intifada*. As a way of being in the world, *sumud* illustrates some of the problems involved in the imposition of an overly rigid distinction between membership in a social movement and more informal expressions of political activism and sentiment. *Sumud* means, in the simplest terms possible, steadfastness and endurance. Resistance leadership rhetoric exhorted camp residents to be steadfast during military assaults, and people explained their own behavior as steadfastness. Steadfastness as a category for interpreting one's own actions and those of others during times of crisis underwrote a cultural and political recoding of action as resistance, even the passive action of staying put. Steadfastness takes on a connotation of survival for Palestinians, who see themselves as victims of a neocolonial movement in which their displacement defined the possibility of the project. *Sumud* registers a refusal to acquiesce. Highlighting the concept of *sumud* also calls attention to the issue of violence. *Sumud,* as an act of resistance, is only meaningful in the context of an exceedingly powerful, well-equipped other in possession of and willing to unleash the means of mass destruction. Edward Said laments that "the one thing none of us can forget is that violence has been an extraordinarily important aspect of our lives . . . and [has] exacerbated our self-awareness as a community set apart from others" (1986).

Equally significant in their narrative of self and community has been their forced disappearance. International discourse and public opinion initially cast them as nonexistent, eventually (if they did exist) as terrorists, and more recently as Islamic fanatics, each a representation or discourse that locates them beyond the bounds of civilization, international law, and diplomacy and therefore beyond political recognition and national sovereignty. Identity through resistant enactment may be related in significant ways to attempts at a forced disappearance. Certainly the early spectacles, such as international airplane hijackings, can be seen in this light.

By 1968, in the newly emergent political situation of the Palestinians in Lebanon, the term *refugee* was avoided in self-characterization and public presentation; it embodied an image of passivity and denationalization. Outsiders were quickly corrected if they used the term in reference to camp residents. In the early 1970s, when I first arrived at the American University of Beirut, I casually referred to Palestinians as refugees in conversation with my Palestinian roommate. She promptly chided me for this injudicious choice of words and told me in no uncertain terms that they were not refugees. They were, she informed me, returnees, militants, and revolutionaries. Rather than choosing terms of self-definition that indicated where they were (seekers of refuge in), they defined themselves as people seeking to return. The distinction hinges on action as well as belonging. The "returner" implies a political commitment that underwrites agency, for return is contingent upon political participation. Such a deployment of terms defines present time and place as liminal and fixes identity to the practice of resistance and a future time, however ill defined.

At that time, the term *refugee* was demeaning to Palestinians' sense of self, community, and agency, denying relation to place and national identity. It implied a passive acceptance of the status quo and suggested the possibility of resettlement in a third country. In addition, it had little relevance to daily material existence. UNRWA's provisioning of rations and medical care had been superseded by the resistance's institutional infrastructure, which provided welfare, medical care, and a host of other services, and a civil war that rendered the legality of residency irrelevant. The regional economy of the oil boom years as well as the economic opportunities opened by employment in resistance institutions enhanced the standard of living so that rations were hardly the necessity of life they had been in the 1950s and early 1960s.

During this era in Lebanon, Palestinians referred to themselves as strugglers, militants, activists, revolutionaries, or simply Palestinians. *Refugee* was not often used; it encoded passivity and, at that time in its international meaning, it suggested humanitarian rather than political solutions. Identities were very much caught up in resistance activities and the organized resistance movement. People describe the takeover of the camps as "a new beginning." The formal, organized movement was deemed to be the institutional and militant expression of mass sentiments of resistance. They tell of a "euphoria" and a new way of being in the spaces outside the camps. Whereas previously they had felt vulnerable, they were now incredibly empowered by a movement prepared to defend them—as individuals or as a collective—and their own open bearing of arms. While the Palestinians were hardly significant players or a factor in the regional balance of power, militancy had a deeper resonance internally. The gun became a potent symbol of agency and empowerment, and it was incorporated into a wide variety of forms of cultural production such as poetry, the visual arts, songs, and dance. People talk of carrying weapons as an absolutely overwhelming experience, endowing them with self-esteem and pride. Women, when they were first mobilizing and entering the ranks of the resistance, often insisted (the young, unmarried ones) on weapons training and military duty. Military training was an arena for a rite of passage into militancy. It credentializd their ability and commitment not only to the community but to themselves; training and its requirements of distance from home unsettled family control over young women and strengthened them to challenge their families.

The guerrilla forces in Lebanon drew mainly upon the refugee camps for recruits. The bulk of the fighting forces were thus of peasant background. The camps also were the targets of attacks on the Palestinian community. They were spaces in which the resistance had autonomy, a good deal of internal control, and many offices and institutions. As such, they became sites embodying the notion of resistance and a pure Palestinianism. Urban Palestinians perceived camp residents as endowed with an identity less sullied by contact with the exterior and thus as spaces of Palestinianism contrary to their own cosmopolitanism. Similar to the quintessential peasant, camp residents, as descendants of peasants, were elevated to the position of signifiers of central motifs in Palestinian culture, particularly in relation to the land and modes of resistance.

The meaning of legal refugee status was not constant. Although it is a category of persons with international recognition, the meaning can be a contingent one for both the refugee and the host. In this instance, it shifted in tandem with shifts in the power of the resistance movement. Representations of authenticity were imposed on the camps and their residents. While they were sites of suffering and a celebration of national and cultural identity, they were not spatially isolated. Indeed, they were sites of some cosmopolitanism, as families sent male migrants out to labor in Europe or the Gulf and the resistance movement had relations with a multitude of foreign supporters who visited the camps and frequently worked in camp hospitals and clinics. With the violent disempowerment of the resistance movement and the reestablishment of the camps as tightly bounded spaces in the wake of the 1982 Israeli invasion of Lebanon, the PLO's evacuation from Beirut, and the Palestinian-'Amal wars of the late 1980s, Palestinians began referring to themselves as refugees. Suffering is now accompanied by a spatial isolation that works against cosmopolitanism. Now camp residents hardly interact with urban Palestinians. With the safety net provided by the resistance movement pulled from beneath them, claims of refugee status were quickly resurrected. Not only did they entitle holders to rations, medical care, and education, but they provided the documentation necessary for legal residence in Lebanon. This is a referencing of self and community that is highly present oriented and reverberates with disempowerment. The acceptance and self-characterization of *refugee* is a barometer of sorts, indexing power, dependency, and (more ominously) vulnerability to mistreatment by the host population and government. In the 1990s, the term *refugee,* as an appellation for camp residents, does not arouse much reaction. The power frame in which this is occurring is one in which refugees in Lebanon are being reconstituted as a legal minority subject to restrictions on work, residence, travel, education, and political organizing and expression. With the absence of alterative structural and institutional services in the face of the impoverishment of the refugee community and their recasting as a tightly controlled and surveilled community, belonging to the category of "refugee" was a strategic necessity. In the wake of the PLO's demise in Lebanon, refugee status offered some services, however minimal, from UNRWA. In addition, it offered a starting point, as a legal status, for bargaining with the Lebanese government for some sort of rights.[11] This calls attention to the way the legal category of "refugee" identity can be crucial for survival and suggests some of the ways in which identities are hitched to changes in the power structure that frame everyday life.

Turning back to the effect that the resistance movement had on the formation and content of identity, what the resistance movement transfigured was the way of being a Palestinian in the world, particularly in relation to others in the world of exile (or occupation). Empowerment, personal and collective, was the key component of this transformation. Palestinians described the years before the resistance movement as ones of marginality and insecurity in Lebanon and of being under the control of others. This was often expressed in the stories that still circulate to describe the preresistance era of hostile encounters with Lebanese authorities and the derogatory remarks directed toward them. During the resistance era, Palestinians were perceived as so empowered that people were easily intimidated by them, deferring to them in public encounters. During the civil war in Lebanon, where a large number of people, Lebanese and Palestinian, belonged to a militia and were armed, identities became exceedingly entangled with national and or sectarian communities in a way that points to the dangers of essentializing identities or, perhaps more appropriately, the way conflict can act on identities. A person could be killed simply on the basis of the national or religious identity noted on his or her identity papers or according to accent. Whole sectors of the city defined as Muslim or Christian, regardless of their actual social composition, could be the target of military assault or siege. One need only think of Bosnia, where once fairly fluid lines of identity and community have become rigidly drawn lines.

Since 1982, the way of being a Palestinian in Lebanon shifted in a dramatic way. Once the PLO was removed, and in spite of U.S. guarantees to protect the Palestinian civilian community, a massacre occurred in the Sabra-Chatila camp. This was the opening act in a new scenario for Palestinians in Lebanon. It was followed by a decade of mass terror directed specifically at reducing the Palestinian population in Lebanon and their reincarceration in camps. The meaning of Palestinian identity has been reconfigured to focus even more intensely on suffering and again disempowerment, and now abandonment, by their own movement. Rather than Palestinian identity being a source of pride and public display, Palestinians now often engage in dissimulation to protect themselves and minimize their presence in public. The accent is disguised upon leaving the camps as Palestinians attempt to pass as Lebanese.

With the defeat and evacuation of the resistance movement and their reincarceration in camps, Palestinians are engaging in a different sort of politics. The primary arena in which the Palestinian community is trying to defend itself is legal. They are attempting to secure civil rights without asking for citizenship. With their ability to work heavily circumscribed—they are convinced the Lebanese government is engaged in a strategy of exclusion comprised primarily of an economic war of strangulation to force them out of Lebanon—they are directing their energies toward gaining the rights to work, to education, and to rebuild their camps.

The term *resistance* evokes different meanings now. Daily life in the camps—simply being there—is still considered a form of resistance, as is having survived the horrors of camp life since 1982. With the organized resistance movement gone and seen as engaged in a politics of surrender that verges on betrayal, camp Palestinians in Lebanon see themselves as the true resisters, embodying two qualities of true Palestinians—suffering and struggle. The leadership is berated and bitterly critiqued for its political failures and abandonment of the Lebanese arena (see Peteet 1995b, 1997). That is why "Arafat is not a Palestinian." He has given up the struggle.

Within the camps, the recent establishment of village associations, which are seen by some as a way to enhance Palestinian identity as it relates to place and the social relations and ties associated with former places, is considered by some a form of continuing resistance to displacement and a denial of relation to place.

Community in Exile

Traditional anthropological notions of community tied it closely to place. Community was delimited by geography. This notion, once taken for granted, has been undermined by a realization that historically not all communities are tightly confined by place. The increasing rapidity with which people and culture move through time and space and the constitution and reconstitution of social relations and communities in new locales and/or their continuity over long distances undergird the move toward transnational analytical frames. Thus, in the contemporary era one can hardly say without raising serious questions that communities are bounded by place. As a diasporic people, Palestinians form communities in multiple places, from refugee camps in Lebanon to working-class sectors in Detroit and the communities of the elite who conduct business from London, Geneva, or Kuwait. Refugee camps are recognized as communities by Palestinians both inside and outside of them and by members of the surrounding Lebanese host population, who can identify their boundaries and know them as dangerous places. What I attempt to do in this section is less ambitious than dealing with the globalization of the Palestinian community. I deal only with the formation and reformation of community among refugees in Lebanon.

In camps, as elsewhere, the bases of community have not been fixed; they have undergone a number of distinct shifts, as have the physical boundaries of the camp. The meaning of the space within which community is constructed, performed, and felt is in flux as well. While one can speak of the Palestinian community in Lebanon, one must be cautious not to overgeneralize and to note the multilayered nature of both community and identity. Seemingly local, community, like place in general, is constituted, both in its form and in the kinds of identities it might generate, in intersections of local and global structures and relations. Over the course of a nearly fifty-year period of exile, refugees in the camps in Lebanon have developed a distinct sense of themselves as a community, with a set of shared experiences and expectations. The resistance movement took hold in a community with a strong collective consciousness but a weak institutional framework in which to organize for its enactment and expression. The resistance's presence enhanced and strengthened this consciousness into a form of collective empowerment and action.

Given that community formation is a multilayered process, what are these different layers?[12] How is the Palestinian community marked off from the larger host society in which it is sited? What makes for community? How is it expressed such that we know it exists? What were the connections beyond particular refugee camps that made for a community of Palestinians in Lebanon? And what role did the resistance movement play in defining community?

First, one can identify the coming to Lebanon of refugees from a variety of villages and towns in northern Palestine in the wake of the events of 1948. A common point of reference for refugees is the past and origins in and a sense of belonging to the physical and social territory of Palestine. The past is hardly distant from the present, undergirding and giving meaning to one's historical sense of self. In others areas of Palestine, refugees fled to the Gaza Strip, Jordan, or Syria, and one could argue that they also developed a sense of themselves as a community, however loosely, in Jordan or Syria. The refugees who came to Lebanon eventually formed a community of refugees who shared an experience of displacement and exile in a particular location.

Second, in terms of self-identification and later resistance organizing, there was a coalescing of all camps in particular areas of Lebanon into groups fostering the notion of communities of refugees in South Lebanon, North Lebanon, and the Beirut camps. Before the emergence of the resistance in the late 1960s, spatial proximity and visiting between camps facilitated the foundations for identity formation based on the general geographical location of the camps.

In exile, the resistance movement further fostered a sense of community, and these sentiments were then given organizational expression in the political, social, and military activities and institutions of the movement. The resistance also linked regional groups of camps into units that were cohesive and able to act in unison, particularly militarily.

Third, the formation of a sense of community and identity as a people who live in refugee camps as distinct not only from Lebanese but from Palestinians who do not reside in camps has been an exceedingly salient and formative aspect of refugee identity. Those who settled in the camps were by and large peasants without the capital or kin relations necessary for settlement in Lebanese cities and towns. As previously mentioned, the pre-1948 rural-urban division in Palestinian society was carried into exile and replicated in spatial form. Experiences as refugees could be markedly different for camp residents than for refugees who lived in urban Lebanese areas and were not subject to surveillance and control over movements. Middle- and upper-class urban Palestinians possessed the material means to escape or at least soften the worst aspects of being a refugee. Their capital assets and skills have allowed them to reside outside the camps and to emigrate. During attacks on the camps, they are physically distant. In short, they have more options. Nor were they ever to face the kinds of incarceration that camp residents faced in the first years of exile and in the late 1980s.

The assaults on the camps and their leading role in resistance activities—as headquarters, sites of mobilization, the source of the bulk of the fighting forces, and the defenders of the resistance movement against external attack—spawned among the refugees a sense of being different, not at all in a negative sense but as the guardians of resistance and Palestinian cultural authenticity. The camps, as they are endowed with meaning by Palestinians, are places of belonging, places where a particularly Palestinian sense of identity is fostered and sustained and can be openly enacted. Their experiences of the civil war in Lebanon (1975–91), in all its various stages and permutations and the ways in which its everyday practices impinged upon camp residents, foregrounded an identity deeply shaped by trauma, discrimination, marginality, and yet resistance and survivability.

Last, the most immediate sense in which all Palestinians form a community in Lebanon is in their legal status as refugees lacking citizenship.[13] There is a community of Palestinians in Lebanon that cross-cuts camp/noncamp residency: the absence of civil rights consigns them to a space of nonbelonging in the national order of things.

The process of othering by Lebanese has not been consistent over time, nor is it totalizing. But it has reached a stage at which Palestinians, in camps or not, are openly discriminated against and are the subject of physical and verbal attacks in their daily lives without arousing much, if any, sympathy or support from the Lebanese. These days in Lebanon one hears frequent complaints about "foreigners." Crime and dirty Beirut streets are attributed to the large numbers of them. Palestinians are now included in the list of foreigners along with the Syrians, Sri Lankans, Filipinos, and Kurds—sources of cheap manual labor imported from the global labor market. The Palestinians have been defined as a minority with severely limited rights. After years of assault, sieges, massacres, and reincarceration in camps; the enforcement of legal statutes that severely restrict Palestinian economic and political activities in Lebanon; and a general sense of being disliked and discriminated against even if they possess Lebanese citizenship, Palestinians as a community bounded by origins in Palestine, fifty years of traumatic exile, and a process of othering by the Lebanese are keenly aware of who they are and the dangers of that particular national identity. National identity is being further reinforced in this specific locale and embodies and encodes the experience of exile in a particular place. A peace process that leaves them out has served to refine this development of a nationalism in which multiple places are implicated.

I have argued that the relationship between community and place is ambiguous, that communities need not be tied to place but are rather, in many cases, multisited. Palestinians clearly constitute a transnational community. So how does one read and know both local communities and the transnational community? One way to read local community is through an array of spatial signifiers. Camp residents' mapping of the camps and their conceptualization and naming of space and place point to community. More than fifty years after 1948, Palestinian camps are still spatially organized by pre-1948 village. Bourj al-Barajneh camp in the southern suburbs of Beirut, known as one of the most urban of camps, is composed, in the main, of the villages of Kweikat, Tarshiha, Kabri, and 'Amqa. They reside in quarters named according to the village. When I first visited the camp, I would find my way around by asking for directions to a particular village. Village boundaries and reference points gradually became overlaid with sectors and markers of the resistance movement such as its office, schools, and co-ops. Now, with the demise of the resistance movement in the camps, space is more univocal, marked primarily by villages with occasional references to past resistance markers. Community can be located at another level as well—that of the camp itself. Each camp in Lebanon has a set of lore about its history, its resistance to displacement and assault, and its heroes. Bourj al-Barajneh and Chatila camps' borders are now exceedingly marked, the end result of the reimposition of a border crafted through demolition, shelling, and terror in the war with 'Amal and the Syrians. What this suggests is that, while communities are not bounded by place, there are historic instances, such as this one, when communities can be given highly distinct spatial and relational definition (while still being connected to other, similar communities). Indeed, refugee camps by their nature are spatial technologies of control and management. Local conceptualizations of the uniqueness of place do not in any way deny the global production of these places.

The resistance movement was a crucial factor in linking camps with one another and with the Palestinian community outside their boundaries, thus playing a strategic role in community formation. The resistance movement structure was such that camps in a general region such as the South or the North were under regional command. Activists in the movement traveled from camp to camp to organize and staff offices. Meetings, both regional and in Beirut, brought together people from different camps. The international diplomatic activity of the PLO connected Palestinians in refugee camps to regional Middle Eastern centers and globally to the networks of solidarity activists. Camp residents hosted a large number of foreign solidarity visitors, activists, and delegations, establishing linkages with a world far beyond their boundaries. The formation of institutions that cross-cut camp boundaries formed the bases for resistance and the sites around which new identities would emerge.

Tensions with Gender

The Palestinian women's movement has posed a serious challenge to the logic that privileges national identity. If people occupy multiple subject positions, gender, like religion, is one such identification that is not coterminous with national boundaries.

Initially organized around national issues, women began to question the argument of the primacy of both national identity and forms of struggle, and they have worked themselves toward a feminist-nationalist stance and agenda focused on the intersection of national and gender subordination. The trajectory in women's identity, consciousness, and organizing has been grounded in national struggle.

The tension between nationalism and feminism, which was incipient in the Lebanon era and reached its most salient point in the West Bank in the transition to autonomy, arose in the context of resistant practices. Palestinian women's political organizing dates back to the first decades of the twentieth century and was in response to national issues such as the Balfour Declaration and increasing Zionist immigration to Palestine; at that time, their own subordination was conceptualized as an issue. Feminist issues and discourse were not to surface until the 1980s and 1990s. When I did research on women in the resistance movement in Lebanon in the late 1970s and early 1980s, there was a very apparent, although subtly expressed, tension between the resistance ideology and mobilizing strategies and the growing feminist consciousness of Palestinian activist women. With a few exceptions, the leadership and ideologues of the movement insisted on the primacy of national identity and national struggle. The mobilization of women was encouraged not to gain women' rights or liberation but as part of a policy to mobilize for patriotic action large sectors of the population across class, gender, and age lines. Women joined the movement as nationalists.

Yet in the process of mobilizing women for nationalist activism women's issues constantly arose. How could women be mobilized if they were responsible for child care and housework? Codes of behavior governing women's mobility and interaction with men were obstructing their nationalist potential. To mobilize women, these issues continually had to be confronted. What occurred during the mobilization process and later during activism in the resistance movement was that feminist consciousness begin to emerge as women became aware of the obstacles to their nationalist activity imposed by male/familial domination and women's subordination in society (Peteet 1991). To be active, women first had to face their families' opposition and that of male comrades. Feminist rhetoric and analysis, however, remained fairly muted until the *intifada.* In Lebanon, the site of the greatest resistance, autonomy, and power, the women's movement often functioned as an appendage of the larger national movement, replicating its factions and interests. Feminist issues were talked about quietly and without mentioning the word *feminist,* which at that time was cast as a foreign import and functioned as a verbal weapon pulled out to keep women activists in line. It must be said, however, that the military situation in Lebanon prominently played into these tensions. It was difficult to address specifically women's issues that went beyond the nationalist framework—for example, women's legal status—in a time of constant military alerts, massacres, sieges, and bombings, in short, all the trappings of modern warfare.

Crisis has ambiguous meanings for women. On the one hand, it can and often does mobilize them out of the house and into political activities that denote a marked challenge to traditions governing women's behavior. But on the other hand it tends to deflect attention from what are called "women's issues." It does so in two ways. First, it casts them as secondary and promotes to the forefront militancy of a military character—which, I would emphasize, reaffirms masculinity but not necessarily femininity. Second, it serves as a convenient excuse to relegate feminist issues to the back burner (Peteet 1991, 128–31).

A somewhat different trajectory was evident in the Occupied Territories and was eventually marked by the emergence of a self-proclaimed feminist-nationalist movement. Distance from the centers of the PLO, then based in disarray in Tunis, certainly gave an impetus to local leadership development. In addition, grassroots organizing among women in committees that maintained a degree of autonomy from the national movement while working with it to benefit from its legitimacy, greater resources, and mobilizing appeal certainly was crucial in propelling this shift. In the late 1970s, urban, middle-class, and often university educated women began organizing women's committees in the West Bank and Gaza Strip. While attached to various Palestinian national movement factions and working to mobilize women into their respective organizations, these committees soon developed a spirit of autonomy from the larger movement, which itself was soon to face disarray following its defeat in Lebanon and its exile to Tunis, far from the borders of Palestine. The committees focused heavily on rural women, who had not previously been actively involved in the women's movement. Until the 1970s, in the Occupied Territories the women's movement had a heavy component of the old charitable, elite women's cast to it. The committees mobilized rural and camp women into cooperatives and provided day care centers, vocational training, and political education among other things. They were unable, however, to completely transcend the factionalization of Palestinian political life.

The *intifada* turned out to be the time and space in which women made a transition to a more openly feminist platform and form of organizing. Interestingly, some of the women who began this process were political independents. Thus distant from organizational agendas and restraints, they founded a number of women's research centers and study groups in the early 1990s. Conferences organized by these independent study and research centers drew large audiences to discuss topics such as domestic violence. These kinds of issues quickly broke the taboo on raising what had been, in nationalist discourse, private secondary matters that were labeled as divisive and consigned to matters to be taken up after statehood. With the example of Algeria in mind, women were careful not to lose sight of the possibility that they would be bypassed in the coming autonomy process. With some vague form of autonomy on the horizon after years of revolt, women quickly took action to prepare themselves. Activists were well aware that they had made women a critical part of the grassroots organizing that buttressed and sustained the *intifada* for several years. The Unified National Leadership (UNL) was not oblivious to their demands and concerns and had made attempts (however uneven) to include women's issues in their political communiqués (their main form of communication with the populace). What concerned women was that the forthcoming arrival of the *abuwaat* (fathers)[14] from outside would undermine their gains by imposing a Beirut/Tunis mode of political and social operation in which women's interests had fairly consistently been relegated to the secondary. They also feared that the exiled leaders would try to impose themselves and their style on the local leadership.

Moreover, they were vividly cognizant of the possibility of being handed to the Islamists as a gesture of reconciliation and appeasement, as had nearly happened during the infamous *hijab* saga in the Gaza Strip in the late 1980s. The contest between the emerging Islamist movement and the secularist nationalists was played out in public on the issue of the veil and women's identities. In Gaza in the spring of 1988, graffiti, a form of cultural intervention and means of communication and debate during the *intifada* (Peteet 1996), began mandating veiling and calling for Islamic-scripted roles for women. This was accompanied by a campaign of violence and intimidation directed at unveiled women by young boys and men associated with the Islamist organizations (Hammami 1990). The UNL was slow to respond, and by the time it did so, in graffiti and communiqués, nearly all the women in Gaza had donned the head scarf, most unwillingly.

What is strikingly different in the 1990s is the issue of citizenship. The feminist-nationalists in the Occupied Territories realized that ways of being a citizen are heavily gendered and that if they were not active participants in drafting the constitution and the legal code they would end up with second-class citizenship (however sketchy the whole notion of citizenship is in the Occupied Territories). A broad-based group of women drafted a women's charter entitled "Principles of Women's Legal Status," which draws heavily on United Nations' conventions, including the Convention to End Discrimination among Women (CEDAW) (Gluck 1995). In it, they called for "equality in civil rights, including the right to obtain, maintain, or abdicate citizenship and in a woman's right to grant it to her spouse and children,"[15] in addition to a call for complete equality in political and economic rights. Most significantly, they call for "equality in personal rights on the familial and societal levels which guarantees equality between women and men in the right to choose a spouse, provide care for the family, ownership rights, and the protection of family property." While not explicitly challenging Islamic personal status laws, they are calling for a secularization of family law and are thus confronting, through bypassing, Islamic legal strictures that set out women's rights, identity, and social roles. The right to citizenship as individuals rather than as gendered persons embedded in kinship and religious communities clearly points to a conception of women's identities, at this embryonic stage, as a critical commentary on the kinds of notions of state and citizenship being put forth by the Palestine Authority and the Islamists.

Conclusion

Palestinian refugees in Lebanon are well aware that a return to Palestine is hardly imminent. They do not have a nostalgic longing for pre-1948 Palestine, which in this third generation of exiles most have never seen. They can describe their villages, having learned their landscape, smells, history, and daily routines from their elders, and socially they are intimate with the village because they have lived its spatial and social re-creation in the camps. But they are also aware of the transformation of their villages. Palestine is envisioned not in a nostalgic longing for pre-1948 life-styles but in the longing for security of place and the rights entailed in being a citizen.

A curious story is circulating in the refugee camps in Lebanon, one that captures well the intersection of the forces of globalization, social movements, and identity. People tell this story to describe themselves and the kind of future they envision. A young boy has a dream of the return to Palestine. All the refugees in Lebanon board buses and head for the border. Once in Palestine, the people of Tarshiha go back to Tarshiha, the people of al-Bassa go to al-Bassa, the people of Suhmata go to Suhmata, the people of Khalsa go to Khalsa, and so on. But a busload of people from Chatila camp stay together and build a new village. This futuristic narrative of return does not evoke a nostalgia for a past that is no longer attainable and therefore underscores the ways in which exile and social movements forge new relationships and ideas of community. The most authoritative source of the story claims that a researcher in the camps in Lebanon was collecting children's dreams and this was one of them. I first heard this story in Chatila camp in 1994 and also among urban Palestinians in Lebanon talking about people in the camps. The people in the camps tell it both with amusement and as a commentary on who they are and the multiple places implicated in their identity and aspirations. I found it amusing and poignant but didn't give it much thought. But when I heard it told by a Palestinian acquaintance in Michigan I saw its potency in a new light. It has currency as a narrative for Palestinians across a number of borders. It locates the refugee camps as places on the border, not just spatially between Palestine, Lebanon, and Israel but as places where spatialized experiences of incarceration and suffering mediate the linearity of exile. It also points to the capacity of exilic-based social movements to transform identities in the process of struggling for social justice.

Identities are formed at multiple intersections of history, place, and experience. A social movement, while it mobilizes on the grounds of particular identities, and in this case to be able to realize an identity in place, in the process has the capacity to endow that identity with new attributes and meanings.

NOTES

This research was made possible by grants from the Joint Committee on the Near and Middle East of the American Council of Learned Societies and the Social Science Research Council, with funds provided by the National Endowment for the Humanities and the Ford Foundation, and the Graduate School of the University of Louisville. The writing was supported by a Mellon (Sawyer) Fellowship at the Advanced Study Center, International Institute, University of Michigan, Ann Arbor.

1. Palestinians pose many problems for the study of social movements and identity related to their uniqueness in the postcolonial order of things. Appadurai, in trying to develop a vocabulary for framing transnational identities and movements avoids the term *culture* and suggests instead *culturalism* as the "conscious mobilization of cultural differences in the service of a larger national or transnational politics" (1996, 15). Culturalist movements, he argues, "are self-conscious about identity, culture and heritage, all of which tend to be part of the deliberate vocabulary of culturalist movements." Examples of such movements are the Algerians in France, the Pakistanis in Britain, and the Sikhs in Canada, among others. While the Palestinian movement is transnational, I have serious doubts that it could fit into the category of a culturalist movement, particularly as it exists in the Middle East, where the bulk of Palestinians reside. By and large, Palestinians reside as refugees or exiles in host countries where cultural differences are minimal and a distinctly Palestinian cultural identity coexists in complicated but not necessarily tense ways with local Arab cultures. Appadurai's schema would perhaps find resonance if one were to look at the Palestinians in Israel, who more closely approximate a culturally different minority.

2. Malkki 1995 is an exception.

3. I used this quote in the introduction to my book on the Palestinian resistance movement and gender (Peteet 1991).

4. Refugees outside the camps are beyond the scope of this chapter except in a very cursory way. See Malkki 1995 for a similar process of identity formation among Hutu refugees in camps.

5. The issue of diaspora cosmopolitanism has been taken up by Malkki (1992, 1995). She draws a distinction between the more flexible, unbounded, and cosmopolitan identity of Hutu refugees residing in towns and the more intensely bounded Hutu identity of camp refugees. My work indicates that cosmopolitanism is less a matter of location and more a historical product occurring at specific junctures. Refugee camps in Lebanon were sites of intense national identity and yet simultaneously sites of cosmopolitanism as camp Palestinians worked and fought in a diasporic social movement with ties of solidarity and support in other parts of the world.

6. For an example, see Curtis et al. 1975.

7. Khalidi argues that, among other things, in the post–World War I era of partitions of the region, neighboring Arab nation-states developed their nationalisms in the absence of a Zionist challenge.

8. See M. Hirsch 1994 for a poignant self-reflection on displacement.

9. The notion of refugee camps as technologies of power derives from Foucault's work (1979) on the prison and other disciplinary regimes. But I conceptualize them as places from which, and through which, people struggle to overturn these regimes.

10. Palestinian Mahmud Darwish's 1964 poem "Investigation," which begins "Write down I am an Arab/My card number is 50,000," and Rashid Husayn's poem "Tent #50, (Song of a Refugee)," which begins "Tent #50, on my left, is my new world," evoke in desperate verse the wrenching alienation of numerical, bureaucratic designations of home/place/identity. Darwish's poem, written while he was still in Palestine, refers to Israeli registrations of the now "foreign" Palestinians and found widespread resonance among exiled Palestinians.

11. Legal restrictions on Palestinians forbid employment except in the most menial of jobs. International law gives refugees the right to employment.

12. Sociological research conducted by University of Michigan graduate student

Deborah Billings among Guatemalan Mayan refugees in Mexico suggests a similar process of community and identity formation. I am grateful to Deborah Billings for sharing her insights with me.

13. Palestinian refugees in Lebanon are predominantly Muslims. The Christians who arrived in the wake of the 1948 war were given Lebanese citizenship in a move by the government to increase Lebanon's Christian population. Some small number of Muslims did obtain citizenship, often, it is said, by paying for it.

14. In Arabic, an adult man is called after his firstborn son. *Abu,* or "father of", is added to the firstborn son's name, and the father becomes known as "father of." The leadership of the resistance adopted these as noms de guerre such that Yasir Arafat is more popularly referred to in Arabic as Abu Ammar. In some cases, leaders did have sons with these names; in other cases, such as Arafat's, the name was fictitious.

15. For the text of the document, see the "Declaration of Principles on Palestinian Women's Rights" (1995).

CHAPTER 9

Confronting Contradictions and Negotiating Identities: Taiwanese Doctors' Anticolonialism in the 1920s

Ming-cheng M. Lo

While it is often agreed that Japanese colonialism in Taiwan succeeded in modernizing the colony, it is intriguing that this "success" transformed the colonial project itself. As the designs of Japan's "scientific colonialism" (discussed below) involved various mechanisms of rule, the intersection of these mechanisms produced structural constraints, which—though powerful—were multiple, incoherent, and often contradictory. The social consequences of scientific colonialism were thus beyond the original expectations of the colonial state.

This chapter analyzes one unexpected outcome of Japan's scientific colonialism—the development of Taiwanese physicians' liberal anticolonialism in the 1920s. After a brief discussion of the content of scientific colonialism and the development of colonial medicine in Taiwan, I will delineate a specific structural conjunction produced at the intersection of the medical profession, the Taiwanese ethnic community, and the colonial state in Taiwan. Then, I will explain how the nascent Taiwanese civil society provided a space where these specific structural forces became important not just to Taiwanese doctors but to the general public. I trace how physicians experienced tensions within this structural conjunction, how they forged for themselves a meaningful understanding of their environment, and how they struggled to formulate and present a socially salient public identity that did not come readily from their preexisting cultural "toolbox." In the process of constructing and reflecting upon their identity, these doctors—initially trained by the Japanese as a hegemonic tool—became mobilized on behalf of their ethnic and professional communities and thereby mutated Japan's imperial project.

I. Japan's Scientific Colonialism and Colonial Medicine

After the Meiji Restoration of 1868, the Japanese Empire completely reversed its two-century-long policy of seclusion[1] and eagerly sought to rank itself among the "modern" nations of the world. Modeling itself after Europe and America, Japan adopted the road of imperial expansion as a "reasonable" way to strengthen itself. The empire acquired its first colony, Taiwan, after the Sino-Japanese War of 1894–95. Although there has been much debate as to whether Meiji imperialism was planned or unplanned,[2] it is commonly agreed that Japan carefully designed its colonial policies toward Taiwan with the hope that it would become a "model colony."

To be sure, this was no easy task. When the Japanese arrived in 1895, Taiwan was an immigrant community with a turbulent history.[3] Conflicts among different clans and communities prevailed on the island (Mukōyama 1987). For generations, Han settlers from China had acquired lands from the tribal aborigines largely through forceful dispossession, and the aborigines often raided Han settlements in revenge. In addition, the Han community itself was divided. Settlers originating from different parts of China formed opposing factions. Whatever political differences they had were reinforced by their distinct dialects and lifestyles. So when the Japanese came in 1895 they were faced with the task of stabilizing the social order and singularizing hegemony.

Strategies of police control and co-optation allowed the Japanese to gradually establish a measure of social order in Taiwan.[4] But in order to truly transform the island into a model colony, the colonial government needed more complex policies. The first few years of Japanese rule had testified to the difficulty of the task. "Without a colonial tradition, literature, or policy, or a corps of trained administrators, it was difficult to translate self-satisfied pronouncements into effective colonial policy, as the first chaotic and haphazard attempts to govern Taiwan quite dismally revealed" (Peattie 1984, 83). With the appointment of the third governor-general, Kodama Gentarō, and his civilian administrator, Gotō Shimpei, the Japanese at last adopted a policy of scientific colonialism geared toward building a modernized and Japanized model colony (85).

Governor Kodama's civil administrator, Gotō Shimpei, a German-trained physician, first developed the theory of scientific colonialism based on his knowledge of German colonial policy.[5] He adopted a systematic and research-oriented approach to the development of Taiwan, conceiving of the island as a laboratory. Research into the natural, social, and political environment of the colony would supposedly yield an understanding of its course of social change and evolution (Peattie 1984). To carry out his plan of scientific colonialism, Gotō enlisted outstanding Japanese scholars to carefully and extensively study the customs and laws of Taiwan. At his initiative, Tokyo University established a chair in colonial studies in 1908.[6] A deep, scholarly understanding of the colonies, Gotō believed, was essential to the making of policies that would commence the modernization and Japanization of the territories with the utmost naturalness and ease. The idea of scientific colonialism left a clear imprint on Japanese colonial attitudes and served to legitimize the domination of Taiwan and other Asian colonies as a form of paternalistic guidance. Those in the mainstream of Japanese colonial thought argued that "Japan's subject peoples should be introduced to the benefits of modern civilization—hospitals, railways, the telegraph, basic schooling—under the careful scrutiny of colonial authority" (94).

After assuming control of Taiwan, the Japanese thoroughly and meticulously planned the construction of a modern infrastructure. Colonial officials invested heavily in railroads, harbors, roads, warehouses, and banking. Throughout the colonial period, "transportation and communication projects consistently absorbed the largest share of the colonial governments' investment" (Ho 1984, 352). The colonial government also initiated economic programs and as a result became financially independent of the central government's subsidies in 1905 (Ho 1984; Ng 1989). Most of the groundwork for scientific colonialism was laid during the Kodama-Gotō era (1898–1906).

In addition to the development of local infrastructure and economy, scientific colonialism aimed for the gradual transformation of the native population. Through education, colonial officials carefully engineered the composition of Taiwan's elite strata. It is widely known that the Japanese colonial government worked diligently to raise the literacy rate in Taiwan, but it proceeded with great caution. These officials observed in other colonies specific points to be avoided, as they "were particularly keen students of comparative colonialism" (Tsurumi 1977, 47). Their comparative study of colonial situations convinced them that "to import systems, especially systems of education, from the mother country spelled disaster. To disseminate knowledge which encouraged an individualistic mentality was to poison the social order" (48). Thus, the colonial government was as determined to avoid these problems as it was committed to the training of native agents. The colonial officials built schools at various levels in Taiwan, and yet it strictly controlled both the curriculum and the student body of them. Although almost all Taiwanese children were encouraged to receive their elementary education at the "common schools" (*kōgakkō*), only a handful of the most outstanding common school graduates were encouraged to apply to medical or normal schools (Wu 1992). The rest of the common school graduates were encouraged to return to commerce or agriculture. Before 1918, "teaching and medicine were the [only] two main safety valves by means of which a small number of Taiwanese might legitimately seek upward mobility" (Tsurumi 1977, 77).[7]

The state-engineered system of education produced major changes in the structure of Taiwanese elites. While in the past two groups of social elite (landlords and gentry) were predominant on the island, the new schooling system gradually changed the basis of social power for the indigenous population. In the first decade of the century, landlords and gentry (known as the "old elites") had begun to give way to rising groups of trained professionals working in colonial institutions. By the early 1930s, these new elites outnumbered the old, and the growth of new groups continued until the end of the colonial era.[8] Two professions largely accounted for the rise of the new educated elites: medicine and teaching.

Among Japan's various modernization projects in Taiwan, the achievements in public health probably most clearly illustrated Gotō's theory of scientific colonialism. The Japanese were the first to institutionalize cosmopolitan medicine in Taiwan.[9] When Japan occupied Taiwan in 1895, more Japanese soldiers died from disease than perished in battle. Therefore, the colonial government soon found it necessary to improve health conditions in the new colony in order to transform it into an "inhabitable land" for the empire (Chen 1992; Oda 1974). As early as 1896, the government promulgated a series of health-related rules and regulations.[10] These addressed various aspects of public health, from disease prevention to the prohibition of opium.[11]

When Gotō Shimpei—himself a medical doctor—assumed the position of civilian administrator in Taiwan, he further developed health and sanitation plans for the colony. Most notably, he built the first islandwide water supply and sewage system, formalized the harbor immunization system and other immunization measures, established the system of "police physicians" and "public physicians," and successfully implemented a gradual policy of prohibiting opium (Hsieh 1989; Ide [1937] 1988; Li 1953). Subsequent colonial officials built upon Gotō's groundwork. By 1920, a number of significant institutions and controls had been created. These included the well-established state regulation of the medical profession, the development of a medical school and several hospitals that regularly served the Taiwanese, and the close supervision by the police and public physicians of the sanitary conditions of private residents, slaughterhouses, graveyards, public bathhouses, parks, and other public gathering places. In addition, major epidemic diseases, such as pestilence, malaria, and cholera had been brought under control (Hsieh 1989; Ide [1937] 1988; Li 1952). Overall, the Japanese created a visibly healthier environment in Taiwan during the colonial period. This achievement, seen as an important benchmark in the modernization of the island, pleased the government, the educated Taiwanese, and eventually also the general Taiwanese population (Chen 1992). From the Japanese perspective, Taiwan was transformed from a "sick" to a healthy land. It came to be considered a "central base for tropical medicine" during World War II. In this sense, improvements in health conditions in Taiwan appeared to embody the success of Gotō's scientific colonialism.

II. The Physicians' "In-betweenness": Structural Contradictions

From the perspective of the Japanese state, these achievements in public health were meant to be a tool both in civilizing the colonial subjects and in legitimizing the colonial regime. In his postwar writings, a former dean of the Medical College at Taipei Imperial University reported Gotō Shimpei's 1901 speech at a medical conference in Taiwan:

> If we take a look at colonial policies in other countries, we find that there is no country that does not use religion to facilitate its rule. In other words, the aim is to increase the regime's popularity by resolving mental confusion for,

> and providing spiritual comfort to, the colonized. However, the native religion in our country [Japan] has not been fully developed. But physical diseases, like mental confusion, are also a human weakness, which provides a space [in which the regime can alleviate people's pain in order to] enhance approval in the popular mind. That's why we adopted the system of public physicians. . . . Physicians will function in our colony the way missionaries did [in other colonies]. (Oda 1974, 51–52)[12]

This statement reveals the overt nature of the colonial regime's attempt to legitimize its rule through medicine.

The implementation of Gotō's plan, however, brought together multiple social domains in Taiwan and fused them in new and unpredictable ways. As the state trained and employed Taiwanese physicians to help carry out its health projects, doctors were gradually incorporated into the professional community of medicine. The state tried to control them; the medical community was meant to assimilate them. While both attempts succeeded to some extent, doctors' social identities remained grounded in their Taiwanese community. Gotō's project of "medical missionaries," therefore, quite unexpectedly situated its Taiwanese agents between the domains of the state, the medical profession, and their own ethnic community.

Three sets of structural contradictions become particularly salient when considering Taiwanese physicians' opportunities and constraints in their in-between position. First, the regulatory power of the state and the organizational autonomy of the medical profession were often in competition. Second, within the medical community professional organizations institutionalized ethnic inequalities between Japanese and Taiwanese, whereas the professional *culture* tended to challenge these inequalities. Third, within the Taiwanese community, Taiwanese physicians shared a cultural tradition and a sense of solidarity with their ethnic group, but their professional culture and class position sometimes distanced them from other Taiwanese. I will discuss these three contradictions in the following section.

The Profession versus the State: Organizational Autonomy and State Regulation

As it was carrying out the medical project under the banner of scientific colonialism, the colonial regime actively supported but closely regulated the medical profession in Taiwan. It facilitated the growth of the medical profession through education, funding, and technical exchange, and retained the authority to coordinate the occupational division of labor. Therefore, the medical profession, despite its early arrival in Taiwan, failed for many years to develop a significant degree of organizational autonomy. How did the state manage to uphold direct and unmediated control of the medical system and yet cultivate its instrumentality and efficiency?

The state did so through the implementation of two systems during the first half of the colonial period (1895–1920): the system of the police and public physicians and the system of medical education and licensing. With the former, the state directly assigned and supervised physicians' tasks; with the latter, it regulated physicians through education, licensing, and examinations. In 1897, the Japanese government added the position of police physician to local governments in Taiwan. Police physicians served as state agents who carried out health policies in local communities. In addition, they oversaw a wide variety of health-related affairs, ranging from administration of public health to the practice of medical jurisprudence (Li 1952, 57–60). A law was passed in 1909 to establish these positions as a mandatory part of the regular government staff.[13] It is interesting—in terms of both structure and metaphor—that the colonial state used the communications networks of the "real" civil police to communicate with its local police physicians.

Just prior to this, in 1896, the colonial state promulgated the "Rules and Regulations for Public Physicians in Taiwan." Eighty public physicians were recruited from Japan (though the original goal was to recruit 150) and underwent three months of special training in basic Taiwanese and immunization procedures for the most life-threatening diseases in Taiwan at the time such as malaria, cholera, and bubonic plague. Public physicians were not state employees, but they received state subsidies and were appointed by the state to practice medicine in designated areas of Taiwan. They took charge of general local sanitation, immunization, and corpse examination as well as serving as the state's agent in the regulation of pharmacology and Chinese medicine (Hsieh 1989, 53–55; Oda 1974, 52; see also Li 1952).

In addition to assigning police and public physicians to work in designated areas, the colonial regime recognized that private physicians would be indispensable to the thorough implementation of its medical policies in the colony.[14] Most private physicians in Taiwan graduated from the Medical Training Institute of Taipei Hospital,[15] which was established in 1897 by the government-general of Taiwan in order to provide basic training in cosmopolitan medicine to the Taiwanese. Graduates from the medical school were licensed to practice medicine throughout the island.[16]

Before 1920, the colonial state was also able to exert unmediated control over the medical profession without jeopardizing its efficiency. The state skillfully maintained this position by creating an environment that offered very little political autonomy but abundant economic resources to the medical community. On the one hand, the colonial regime's broad-based health system, staffed by police physicians, public physicians, and medical school graduates, essentially remained part of the state apparatus. On the other hand, the state also generously funded the medical system with state-controlled assets and revenues from local taxes (Li 1952, 49–54).

The state's regulatory power also extended to the realm of medical education.

Upon the founding of the Taipei Medical School, the governor-general, Kodama Gentarō, his chief civilian administrator, Gotō Shimpei, and other colonial officials, agreed that education should remain instrumental to the political designs of the regime. As Tsurumi puts it—and as I explained earlier in this chapter—"irresistible Taiwanese demands for higher education were to be channeled into professional studies, which would produce the kind of trained natives the colony required" (1977, 214). After founding the Medical School, colonial officials explicitly warned the government in Japan about the danger that the Medical School could become a source of political empowerment for the natives, as had been observed to happen in India, Indonesia, Algeria, and the Philippines (Wu 1992, 97–98; Chen 1992, 27). In response to these warnings, the colonial state designed a policy to selectively recruit students for the Medical School (Tsurumi 1977).

The subordination of professional to political authority did not, however, last as long as the state had expected. As the medical profession expanded, it inevitably cultivated its own internal logic. Within the medical community, the continual development and improvement of the field became a driving force. Increasingly, the betterment of medical practice and education was prioritized over the fulfillment of state policy. For example, despite the state's express intent to provide only a limited education to the colonized, Dr. Yamaguchi, the first president of the Taipei Medical School, declared as early as 1899 that the simplified curriculum at the school was a temporary measure and in due course the training program would be upgraded (Senmon gakkō kōyūkai 1924, 16–20). Likewise, the next president of the Medical School, Takagi Tomoeda, opposed the regime's policy of ethnic segregation in order to provide better training for his students. He attempted to bargain with Taipei Hospital, which was run by the state and accommodated almost exclusively Japanese patients, in order to gain internships for his Taiwanese medical students (78). After these attempts failed, he successfully requested that the Japanese Red Cross consider establishing a branch hospital in Taipei and allow his Taiwanese students to complete their internships there (Tu 1989).

Furthermore, health care gradually moved beyond the initial stage of institutionalization, inevitably producing an increased sense of autonomy among its Taiwanese agents. After 1920, the state turned its attention to the distribution of health care in remote towns and villages and the dissemination of general medical knowledge among the Taiwanese. In doing so, the Japanese found that the language, rules, and in fact the very "otherness" of Japanese doctors at public hospitals often alienated Taiwanese patients and even discouraged them from seeking treatment.[17] In order for cosmopolitan medicine to thoroughly penetrate the colony, they discovered, it had to be practiced in more familiar ways by more familiar people. The state therefore encouraged Taiwanese physicians to open their own clinics and began to rely on them as an important supplement to the public health care system. Though some native graduates of the Medical School continued to work for the public health care system, many went into private practice. As the number of private physicians increased over time (see table 9.1), they came to constitute a (relatively) autonomous social force.

In short, in the 1920s the medical profession finally gained some degree of authority to coordinate its own internal division of labor, and in this sense it achieved a measure of organizational autonomy from the state. The professional authority of the medical field now had the potential to compete with, keep in check, or even challenge the colonial political authority that had promoted its very creation.

Tensions within the Medical Community

Japanese scientific colonialism was articulated and justified through a diffusionist model, which naturally situated the metropole at the center of all modernizing forces. In this model, the colonizers occupied the position of benign mentors and the colonized that of eager pupils united in the goal of modernizing Taiwan. And it should be noted that the medical system accommodated colonial hegemony very well. In his speech at the first graduation ceremony at the Taipei school in 1902, Gotō Shimpei made an explicit analogy between teacher-student relationships at the school and relations of colonial hegemony in Taiwan:

> Ever since Taiwan became a territory of the Japanese Empire, the empire has kindly been exposing the Taiwanese people to modern civilization. You graduates are the especially fortunate ones among the three million Taiwanese; you have learned about, and are now ready to practice, the most advanced knowledge and skills. Does this not bring your ultimate happiness and honor? You have received a special favor from the Japanese state and the governor-general of Taiwan. (Senmon gakkō kōyūkai 1924, 25)

TABLE 9.1. Numbers of Private Physicians in Taiwan, 1910–42

Year	Physicians at State and Public Hospitals and Other Government-Run Organizations	Private Physicians	Public Physicians	Total	Percentage of Private Physicians
1910	124	179	80	383	47
1915	155	329	94	578	57
1920	156	508	99	763	67
1925	154	649	169	972	67
1930	206	857	209	1,272	67
1935	323	1,103	248	1,674	66
1940	573	1,537	291	2,401	64
1941	422	1,513	293	2,228	68
1942	492	1,665	284	2,241	74

Source: Chen 1992, 39.

The organizational structure of the Taipei Medical School and hospitals[18] embodied this master-apprentice "ideal." At the Taipei Medical School prior to 1919, all professors were Japanese and all students Taiwanese. Japanese professors possessed both knowledge and authority. After their graduation, at hospitals and in state-headed health projects Taiwanese physicians found themselves continually playing the role of disciples led by Japanese physicians or policymakers.[19] At public hospitals, Taiwanese physicians were almost exclusively placed in low-ranking positions, serving as assistants to their Japanese colleagues (Fan 1993). The Japanese teachers' knowledge justified their authority; the humanist discourse of medicine, in turn, justified the power structure at the Medical School and hospitals. Interethnic mentorship both disguised and embodied the colonizers' paternalistic intentions, and it also served to justify, to a large extent, institutionalized ethnic inequalities within the medical community. Numerous accounts illustrate how favorably Taiwanese medical students at this time regarded their Japanese teachers (e.g., Chen 1992; Tu 1989). For example, a 1932 Taiwanese graduate of the Medical School commented that long after the collapse of the Japanese rule he and his classmates "respectfully thought of Dr. Horiuchi Tsukio [the third President at the Taipei Medical School] as a kindhearted father figure" (Tseng 1995, 269). Another Taiwanese physician fondly recalled another "good" Japanese mentor in his autobiography:

> In 1919, I started to work at Tainan Hospital. The president at the hospital then was Dr. Akiishi, one of the Japanese I respected. . . . He never was discriminatory toward Taiwanese. . . . [According to the regulations in the hospitals at the time, as a medical assistant] my duties were limited to copying prescriptions, carrying out examinations, and checking patients' medical records. Not being involved in the treatment of patients accounted for my lack of interest in my work. In the end, Dr. Akiishi went along with my request and charged me with the responsibility of primary care for a number of patients. My job began to involve office practice, provided that there were patients who wished to see me. [Dr. Akashi's decision] was made with unprecedented insight, but numerous complaints about this came from the Japanese staff. (Han 1966, 25)

Like many others, Dr. Han eventually left the public hospital to open his own clinic. Institutionalized ethnic inequality encouraged many Taiwanese physicians to do this. Noticeably, these private physicians did not use their autonomy to question the discriminatory organization of public hospitals. The option of establishing private clinics encouraged Taiwanese physicians to distance themselves from the ethnic inequality in the profession rather than directly challenging or transforming it. Perhaps largely as a result of this condition, the data do not seem to suggest the existence of major interethnic conflicts within the medical community prior to 1919.

After 1919, however, the heightened emergence of a liberal culture at the Medical School and hospitals began to destabilize discriminatory practices and forms of organization. The medical community in Taiwan had always demonstrated a liberal humanist culture, but this culture did not come into direct conflict with discriminatory regimes until the 1920s. From the start, the presidents of the Taipei Medical School all seem to have been liberal thinkers (Tu 1989). For example, President Takagi openly encouraged humanist thinking. He ignored the common school rules regarding language in the colony and allowed his students to speak Taiwanese at school (ibid.). His famous edict—"Become a human before you become a doctor"—was quoted repeatedly by his Taiwanese students.

Ironically, when the government-general did at last attempt to create an ethnically integrated system of education, the attempt only served to trigger discontent among these liberal students. In 1919, the government-general issued the "Command for Integrated Education" (*kyōgaku-rei*), which loosened its political grip on medical education.[20] The Integration Rescript of 1922 further extended the practice of ethnically integrated education to different levels of schooling. Although the new policy was intended to improve education for the Taiwanese, it was often used by colonial officials to serve the interests of Japanese residents in Taiwan.[21] This situation intensified the contradiction between liberal culture and ethnic inequalities in the medical community. Taiwanese students began to argue that school authorities had formalized an ethnically integrated education but had not provided for the equal treatment of both ethnic groups.

For example, in 1924 the Medical School promised to change its segregated educational system. With this change, the preparatory course for the Taiwanese students was extended from four to five years and future graduates of the five-year preparatory course were promised admission to the Medical School without entrance exams, just as was the case with Japanese students on the island. However, as the graduation date for students of the new preparatory course approached, the college suddenly decided that Taiwanese graduates would still have to pass the old entrance examination in order to enter the school. Though all the graduates of the preparatory course passed the exam, students expressed serious discontent and severely criticized the Medical School (see *Taiwan Minpō*, hereafter MP, 2 (6): 12). Similarly, Taiwanese physicians began to complain about unequal treatment. For instance, they openly denounced the ethnic distribution of promotions, pay raises, and allocations of internships to medical school graduates (see MP, no. 261, 4; no. 408, 13).

Thus, in the 1920s the medical community was increasingly affected by contradictory trends. On the one hand, interethnic mentorship continued to structure the organization of the medical community. On the other hand, the ideal of equality undercut this structure. The experience and awareness of institutionalized ethnic inequality began to mobilize a group consciousness among Taiwanese physicians. Gradually, they emerged as a subgroup within the medical community, and members of this subgroup developed an ethnicity-based solidarity. However, the relationship between Taiwanese and Japanese physicians remained ambiguous. To Taiwanese medical students and doctors, their Japanese colleagues simultaneously embodied two identities, oppressor and mentor, a paradox never resolved throughout the colonial period.

Tensions within the Taiwanese Community

As Yanaihara Tadao points out in his classic *Taiwan under Imperialism* (*Teikokushugika no Taiwan*), "Class antagonisms and ethnic conflicts in [colonial] Taiwan were rival forces which nevertheless were intertwined" (1929, 117). Because of the market position of the medical profession, Taiwanese physicians, perhaps more than any other social group, experienced the contradiction of these two forces in their lives.

On the one hand, physicians and nonelite Taiwanese faced the Japanese as a common oppressor, and they joined together at distinct points in their resistance to colonial rule. On the other hand, physicians were often viewed by nonelites as the "typical native bourgeoisie." They occupied a privileged market position, and low-income people had to plead with them to reduce their charges to obtain medical care. Some information regarding physicians' incomes should illustrate this point. In 1908, for example, a private Taiwanese physician's monthly income ranged from 200 to 500 Japanese yen, while teachers—the other major group of educated native elites—earned just 12 to 45 (Chen 1992). Doctors clearly formed a distinct class in the colonized population. Therefore, the colonial system at the same time promoted ethnic solidarity among all Taiwanese and class conflict between Taiwanese physicians and the nonelite. Taiwanese doctors were caught between two sets of inequalities: ethnic inequalities between Japanese and Taiwanese and market inequalities between professionals and their patients. In short, they had an ambiguous relationship with the larger Taiwanese community.

III. Activists in Taiwanese Civil Society: Why Doctors?

Thus far, I have sketched the ways in which various dimensions of colonial rule, the medical profession, and Taiwanese ethnicity intersected and contradicted one another. It is important to note that these interacting structural forces played out not only within the domains of the medical system or the local communities but also in a relatively open space that was, at least in principle, accessible and influential to all the people in Taiwan.

Ironically, the Japanese helped to foster the growth of such a public space in Taiwan. Islandwide police forces, administrative systems, modern infrastructures, and formalized education—in short, measures of control, co-optation, and scientific colonialism—established a strong and singular political and social order in

Taiwan. The Japanese government unified and homogenized the society of Taiwan to a great extent and thereby facilitated the development of a Taiwanese consciousness. As Ng argues, "the residents of Taiwan did not develop a 'Taiwanese consciousness' until the Japanese era" (Ng 1989, 40). Ng points out that a Taiwanese consciousness among Han immigrants first developed in response to the recognition of the Japanese as obvious outsiders. Growing in the course of guerrilla wars waged against the Japanese, ethnic consciousness finally matured through constant social interaction between different local communities, which was facilitated by the islandwide roads and communications networks built by the Japanese (40). Other researchers also note that a formalized Japanese education provided a common language and thereby facilitated associational activities among educated Taiwanese of Fukien and Hakka ancestry (Chen 1992, chap. 5). Taiwanese consciousness signaled the beginning of an "imagined community" among the Taiwanese people. By 1920, when military rule was succeeded by a civilian government, the space of that imagined community, at least on the surface, was protected as well as limited by the law. One can argue that Taiwan developed a nascent civil society during the first twenty-five years of colonial rule.

In the increasingly liberal atmosphere of the 1920s, this nascent civil society nurtured new forms of social action that might be recognized as modern social movements. In contrast to early anti-Japanese uprisings, which were typically patronized by local Han landlords or aboriginal tribal heads and appealed to limited ethnic groups, these new movements were meant to mobilize the entire Taiwanese populace, and they developed through autonomous associations. These modern social movements fell into two large categories: those aiming for the full development of civil society and those suspicious of the capitalist and imperialist elements of civil society. The former included the campaign against Law no. 63, the Home Rule Movement, and the Campaign for the Attainment of Local Autonomy; the latter included the Taiwan Communist Party and other leftist groups. The most influential of these organizations, the Cultural Association (Taiwan bunka kyōkai), interestingly enough, accommodated both trends.

Who were the key actors of these movements in the nascent civil society? Despite the differences in their political platforms, these were mainly movements of the educated elite, sometimes supported by landlords. Yanaihara (1929) identified these dissidents as the middle class and intellectuals, Wakabayashi (1983) as native landlords and nationalist intellectuals, and Chou (1989) as emerging intellectuals. Tsurumi nicely summarizes the role of Taiwanese educated elites in anticolonialism:

> Conservative or radical Taiwanese anticolonialism was a product of Japanese education. Modern Japan no longer held mysteries for the Taiwanese. Their rulers, by school, teachers, and the printed word, had thoroughly acquainted them with a society once alien but now understood only too well. If educated

> Taiwanese accepted the premises upon which this society stood, they soon discovered that they, who in competition had proved themselves capable of first-class performance, were treated as second-class citizens. This discovery turned many intellectuals into anticolonialists. (1977, 211)

Taking these observations as a point of departure, I wish to underscore the double role of these Japanese-trained Taiwanese elites. It is true that Taiwanese anticolonialism was largely a movement of intellectuals. But let's not forget that these Japanese-manufactured elites also cooperated with the colonial system in various ways. It is an ironic outcome of colonial education that native elites were trained to facilitate the colonial system but they sometimes used their power in ways unanticipated by the state. In colonial Taiwan, these educated natives manifested an ambivalent social power.

These people mainly consisted of doctors, teachers, and common school graduates. Japanese-trained Taiwanese doctors and teachers, who emerged as the first and major professional groups in Taiwan, were more influential than common school graduates. Of the two groups, doctors achieved higher status in both the colonial and the anticolonial domains. From the beginning, doctors were at the same time more integrated into and more autonomous from the colonial system than were teachers. Doctors were more integrated in the sense that they benefited more from the system: they received more years of education, higher incomes after graduation, and a more elite status than did teachers (Chen 1992; Wu 1992). They were more autonomous in the sense that they were subject to less state control. While all teachers worked as government employees under the close supervision of Japanese superiors, many doctors opted for the relatively autonomous career of private practitioners. Similarly, doctors received more positive evaluations than did teachers from both Japanese and Taiwanese. The Japanese valued native doctors' contributions to the improvement of public health in Taiwan,[22] and the Taiwanese also praised Taiwanese doctors' leadership in anticolonial activities (see Chen 1992). In contrast, the government-general felt that Taiwanese teachers lacked enthusiasm in promoting the goal of colonial education, while the Taiwanese public complained that these teachers showed little courage in sponsoring activities organized in the Taiwanese public sphere (Wu 1983). In short, Taiwanese doctors were presented more heroically in both colonial and anticolonial activities than were other educated elites. Their paradoxical position probably best characterized the ambiguous and contradictory nature of the social power of native elites in colonial Taiwan.

As members of a mature profession, doctors distinguished themselves in one important way: they were much more clearly located in a developed institutional base than were teachers or other educated natives. The doctors' institutional base granted them resources, autonomy, and power to challenge the colonial system. By the same token, they were invested in defending this institutional base, which was part and parcel of the colonial system. In this sense, doctors were the most powerful native elites in colonial Taiwan, but their in-between position was also most accentuated.

How, then, did they negotiate the dual pressure to support and oppose the colonial regime? Let us take a close look at the mechanisms within Taiwanese civil society that enabled physicians to act upon the structural contradictions they confronted.

1. Social Movement Organizations (SMOs)

In 1921, several graduates from the Taipei Medical School founded the Taiwan Cultural Association in Taipei. The Cultural Association declared itself to be dedicated to cultural self-improvement among the Taiwanese. But its activities actually spanned a wide range: it functioned as an island base for the home rule movement, offered several series of public lectures, and sponsored newspapers, study groups, and other cultural activities (Tsai et al. 1983, chap. 6). In 1927, those who supported a socialist revolution took control of the Cultural Association and began to actively sponsor labor and peasant protests. The liberals split off to found the Taiwan People's Party (Taiwan minshūtō), which continued to promote a liberal, reformist platform until its disbanding in 1931. In 1930, tensions between the radicals and the liberals also split the People's Party; those members who insisted on a reformist agenda left the party and founded their own League for the Attainment of Local Autonomy (Taiwan chihōjichi renmei), which lasted until 1936.

The Taiwan Cultural Association was the central locomotive for Taiwanese cultural and political activities. In sponsoring them, it hoped to modernize Taiwanese society and improve its international status. Despite the resonance of these goals with the colonial regime's own policies, the colonial police viewed the Cultural Association as an anticolonial, antigovernment organization and monitored its activities closely (see *Taiwan she-hui yün-tung shi* [*Taiwan sōtokufu keisatsu enkakushi*], hereafter KE).

Physicians constituted a significant portion of the organizers of the Cultural Association, as is well documented by police records of the period. According to these records, there were fourteen physicians among the fifty-two core members of the Cultural Association. Table 9.2 shows that physicians and landlords were statistically overrepresented in the Cultural Association in comparison with other groups such as journalists, small business owners, lawyers, or teachers. It is important to realize, however, that physicians were the ones who took the lead in most activities of the Cultural Association such as organizing public lectures, writing journal articles, and negotiating with the police. Landlords were not very active in these areas.

Another study points out that physicians consistently made up about 30 percent of the rank and file of the Cultural Association until the internal split between the liberal and radical wings in 1927 (Chen 1992, 136). By the end of 1931, among the 1,138 native physicians in Taiwan, at least 116 had participated as leading activists in anticolonial activities and many more supported these activities (143).[23]

TABLE 9.2. Occupations of the Core Members in the Cultural Association

Occupation	%	*N*
Landlord	28.84	15
Physician	26.92	14
Journalist	13.46	7
Small Business Owner	9.61	5
Lawyer or Teacher	5.77	3
Other	15.38	8
Total		52

Source: Lin 1993, 77–79.

2. *Communicative Mechanisms*

One major contribution of the Cultural Association to the development of native civil society lay in the creation and strengthening of islandwide communication mechanisms. The Cultural Association sponsored the only non-state-affiliated newspaper, *Taiwan Minpō;*[24] organized reading groups; and, most importantly (and most problematically for the state), planned several intensive series of islandwide public lectures.

Physicians actively participated in these lectures. Their discourse centered on the theme of modernization, drawing heavily on their role as scientists and their exposure to Western and post-Meiji Japanese societies. Some physicians spoke on very provocative topics such as "Politics in Taiwan: Where Public Opinion Doesn't Matter." But many physicians seemed to gear their talks toward disseminating new information rather than cultivating anticolonial consciousness. Topics included "Glimpses of Foreign Countries," "Meiji Restoration and Japan," and so on (see Lin 1993; Tsai et al. 1983). Regardless of their topics, the police found these public lectures threatening. One police record states:

> These public lectures are the most serious problem with the Cultural Association. Since the level of education in contemporary Taiwan is fairly low, [the Cultural Association] can hardly rely on written materials to advocate its political agenda. So the public lectures become the major means through which to gain public support. . . . Local members of the Cultural Association invite speakers [from its headquarters in Taipei] whenever there is a chance. They mobilize local people to welcome the speakers, but it is really a form of demonstration. (KE, quoted in Lin 1993, 117)

Although it is impossible to recover the content of the majority of these lectures, the attitude of the police toward them suggests the political nature of even those lectures with apolitical titles. The few examples preserved by the KE seem to support this point. In "Glimpses of Foreign Countries," for example, Dr. Wang "introduced" to the Taiwanese people the story of the German occupation of two French provinces, Alsace and Lorraine. He then concluded that "the Germans forced the people in these provinces to use German instead of their own language, French. As a result, their cultural development was impeded during German occupation. It seems that we Taiwanese should think about what this story means" (see KE). Obviously, the talk carried political content that its title did not suggest.

3. Social Networks within Native Civil Society

The Cultural Association also extended its influence through informal social networks. Since many physicians were members of the association, they could mobilize their colleagues in the medical community to support it in various ways.

The distribution of medical care is a good example. The Cultural Association sponsored community clinics that provided medical care at low cost. Due to its influence, many physicians who ran private clinics also offered *shih-fei chuan,* essentially tokens for discounted medical services, to low-income patients. Since poverty was one of the few general defining features of the colonized population, the Cultural Association considered extending medical care to the poor to be a form of resistance. Such actions, which interfered with the state and market control of the distribution of medical resources, may or may not have been considered by all physicians to be a political activity, but both the public and the physicians themselves recognized it as a social mechanism within native civil society.

4. Networks between Colonizers and Colonized

The native public sphere sometimes became a space where the mediation of colonial relationships took place. Confrontations between the police and Taiwanese provide a good example. The police during the colonial period penetrated every corner of Taiwanese society. As the patrolling agents of the state, they were notorious for abusing Taiwanese suspects. Physicians, however, were able to "measure" and document police violence scientifically. They could issue a documented diagnosis to a suspect who had been victimized by police, and the suspect could then bring the case to higher authorities. More frequently, physicians would be called in to mediate between the police and a suspect who had been abused, and they would solve the dispute by withholding the documented diagnosis in return for some compensation for the suspect. I will return to a detailed discussion of this issue later.

IV. "Narrative Identity": Experiencing, Making Sense, and Recognizing

I have analyzed how various structural forces intersected within the medical and the Taiwanese communities. I have also discussed the mechanisms within Taiwanese civil society that enabled physicians to act upon the structural contradictions they confronted. But the structural conditions and social space could not dictate their *roles;* the physicians had to experience and interpret their environment and in the meantime formulate an identity recognizable to themselves and others. These structural tensions became meaningful only when they were meaningfully integrated into personal and group life.[25]

A Compound Identity: Ethnic Professionals

In terms of group identity, these physicians increasingly attempted to integrate their ethnic and professional roles by constructing a compound identity. In the early 1920s, they began to call themselves Taiwanese physicians or ethnic physicians (*minzoku ishi*)—a label that served to differentiate them from Japanese physicians. In 1925, a group of Taipei Medical School graduates who were pursuing higher degrees in Japan held a formal gathering and, describing themselves as a collective of Taiwanese physicians, initiated contact with the Japanese medical community (MP, no. 84, 13). In 1927, forty some Taiwanese physicians and medical students in Tokyo, together with a few in Kyoto, established a new organization, the New East Asian Medical Association (Shintōa igakkai), which formally declared that its members should "perform the duty of a Taiwanese physician" (MP, no. 149, 5). Thus, these physicians explicitly articulated and embraced a new communal identity as Taiwanese physicians, and they continued to share this communal identity after they returned to Taiwan.

But what did this communal identity mean? These doctors saw themselves not only as physicians who were Taiwanese but as "physicians for the Taiwanese nation." In addition to offering free and low-cost medical services to the poor, numerous Taiwanese physicians volunteered to write articles on health issues for the opposition newspaper or gave public lectures on medical topics. Local medical associations often stated in their charters that they assumed the responsibility of improving health conditions for the Taiwanese community at large. Furthermore, the labels "physicians for the nation," and "national physicians," gained wide social and political resonance. Many doctors came to believe that national physicians should also cure the "social diseases" of Taiwan. Some medical associations explicitly drew an analogy between themselves and Dr. Sun Yat-sen, the physician "national father" of the Republic of China. They declared that "to live up to the role of Taiwanese physicians, one needs to cure the physical *and* the social diseases of the nation" (MP, no. 179, 4).

A famous example nicely illustrates how an analogy was drawn between physical and social diseases. Dr. Chiang Wei-shui, a founding member of the Cultural Association, wrote a social critique of Taiwan in the form of a medical diagnosis. His document, entitled "Clinical Diagnosis," was initially published in the first issue of the *Cultural Association Newsletter* (*Bunka kyōkai kaihō*) in 1921. A few sections from the "diagnosis" are worth quoting at length:

> **Name:** Taiwan Island
> **Sex:** Male . . .
> **Symptoms:**
> Immoral . . . impoverished spiritual life, . . . superstitious, reactionary, unsanitary
> **Causes:** Intellectual malnutrition . . .
> **Prescription:**

Basic education	maximum dose
Supplementary education	maximum dose
Preschool education	maximum dose
Libraries	maximum dose
Reading groups	maximum dose

This document, interesting in and of itself, became very important in the history of anticolonialism in Taiwan and has been cited on many occasions. No other document articulates more explicitly the analogy that was drawn between physical and social diseases in the Taiwanese doctors' modernist critique of colonialism. Other doctors continued to elaborate on the theme of this document, thus firmly establishing in the public imagination the basic analogy between their medical and social responsibilities.

By the second half of the 1920s, the general public in Taiwan had also widely accepted the implications behind the label "national physicians." For example, a survey of articles in the *Taiwan Minpō,* the only opposition newspaper at the time, shows that it devoted an unusually large amount of space to the professional activities of Taiwanese doctors. It published frequent reports on the establishment of new clinics, the conferring of medical degrees to Taiwanese students, and so on. Essentially, these matters were considered community news. The Taiwanese public saw their doctors as public figures worthy of great respect, and they were ready to make claims on them accordingly.

Challenging State Power

Once Taiwanese doctors had articulated an identity as national physicians and come to be recognized as such, they began to use this formulation to reason through the other structural contradictions they faced. In particular, this new identity significantly impacted their position between the colonial state and their ethnic community.

As previously noted, the colonial regime and its agents, especially the police, had at their disposal the institutional power and means to abuse the colonized. Medical institutions, on the other hand, had by now achieved relative autonomy in their organizations and a certain legitimacy based on professional knowledge. The national physicians now used this professional autonomy and knowledge to challenge the state's abusive acts. They could, as discussed earlier, issue a documented medical diagnosis and "scientifically" assess police violence. Often, however, the police would offer compensation or an apology, or at least release the victim, before the incident was reported to the court. Many such instances were reported in the *Taiwan Minpō.*[26]

Such encounters between physicians and the police helped to further consolidate the nascent group consciousness of Taiwanese physicians. Especially when the police or legal authorities rejected a documented diagnosis, they were quick to act in defense of the legitimacy of their professional knowledge.[27] More importantly, the task of "measuring" police violence led many of them to critically and publicly discuss the issue of human rights. For instance, a report in *Taiwan Minpō* in 1928 indicated that, according to the results of an autopsy, a certain suspect had been strangled to death while in detention. But the report in the government-controlled *Taiwan News* (*Taiwan Shimbun*) indicated to the contrary that no traces of torture or physical mistreatment were discerned. Upon reading the report in *Taiwan News,* the two physicians who had performed the autopsy immediately made a request to the appropriate authority to repeat the autopsy. In this case, the physicians were not only struggling with the political authorities for the legitimacy of their professional knowledge but also attempting to support the counterdiscourse of the opposition press.[28]

If confrontation with the abusive power of political authorities was part of the physicians' everyday life, how did they transform such experiences into collective action? This question can be answered through a close look at an important event in the 1920s: the Opium Dispute. Opium prohibition was a major goal of the colonial regime from the beginning of its rule. In 1929, the government-general revised and relaxed its policy on opium prohibition, declaring that the new policy would be more practical and humane (Ryū 1983, 159–160). But since the Japanese government had a monopoly on opium sales, the People's Party suspected that the government simply wanted the Taiwanese to continue to smoke opium so that it could benefit financially. The People's Party accordingly protested the new opium policy for over a year, not only filing formal petitions with the regime, but also communicating their opinions to several international organizations. This probably hastened the regime's decision to ban the Party (ibid., 170–171).

Taiwanese doctors saw the Opium Dispute as a crisis for the national health of Taiwan. Islandwide Taiwanese medical associations[29] submitted written protests to the government-general in support of the People's Party's stand. Their written protests were prepared with abundant citations from the medical literature, and their scientific discourse worked to shift the dispute from a political event to a medical issue (MP, no. 296, 12; no. 298, 10; no. 300, 10; no. 302, 11). These physicians invoked their professional expertise as a legitimate tool in evaluating the "humaneness" of the new opium policy. Their scientific discourse concerning the body of the colonized raised challenges that the state could hardly meet (Ryū 1983, 162). (The Japanese medical community, in contrast, remained silent throughout the event.) Although the new opium policy was eventually implemented, the physicians and the People's Party did have an important impact in two ways. First, they managed to enlist the support of international organizations in exerting pressure on the government-general. This helped pressure the regime to implement plans for the treatment of the addicted (174). More importantly, their critical discourse inserted itself into the Taiwanese public sphere, and the new generation widely adopted the opinion that smoking opium was a shameful deed rather than a "traditional" habit (174). This discourse may have been as effective, if not more so, than state policies to combat opium addiction.

In the course of taking action against the opium policy, Taiwanese doctors seriously debated their own roles. Should they act in accordance with state regulation and respect the state's policies on opium or could they act as autonomous professionals and defend their ethnic community in ways they saw fit? Doctors were torn between these two positions, and the debate was heated. Eventually, most Taiwanese medical associations concluded that as national physicians they had a responsibility to defend the nation's health, even at the risk of state sanctions.[30]

Furthermore, they confronted the contradictions between their ethnic tradition and modernist culture. A concrete example arose in the Ping-tong Medical Association. One member tried to persuade the association to withhold its critique of the new opium policy because his own father was an opium dealer and addict. This issue stimulated much discussion within the association and forced its members to take a stand. In the end, most members disagreed with the opium addict's son, and the debate itself served to reinforce their reformist attitudes (MP, no. 303, 11). Similarly, Taiwanese physicians' professional ties with their Japanese colleagues or seniors were called into question. The head of the Taipei Medical Association, for example, decided to withdraw the association's "propositions" on the opium problem, on the advice of Dr. Horiuchi, the Japanese principal of the Taipei Medical School. Though Horiuchi enjoyed a close relationship with, and the respect of, most Taiwanese physicians (many of whom were his former students), most members of the Taipei Medical Association expressed strong criticism of his "malleable stand" and some even threatened to break away from the association (MP, no. 300, 10). These instances show the doctors' efforts to further delineate their public identity against the ethnic and colonial backgrounds in which it was embedded. During the Opium Dispute, physicians united their professional autonomy and knowledge with an alternative political legitimacy in the form of opposition organizations in order to protect their ethnic community. Through such collective actions, they also developed a more coherent group identity.

However, it is noteworthy that sometimes interethnic professional ties did compromise Taiwanese doctors' political stand during the Opium Dispute. Some local medical associations were eventually persuaded by their Japanese colleagues to modify their political actions. Similarly, internal conflicts within the Taiwan Dental Association in 1930 provide another example. Taiwanese dentists raised concerns of ethnic inequality and threatened to form an independent organization. But their Japanese seniors and friends persuaded them to honor their personal ties and refrain from radical action. In the end, Taiwanese dentists abandoned their plan for an independent association (MP, nos. 339, 355, 359). In this regard, systemic problems were sometimes mediated by personal relationships, which to some extent pacified the national physicians.

Defending the Professional Market

The previous section illustrates how Taiwanese physicians acted as national physicians and used their professional autonomy and knowledge to defend their ethnic communities against ill-conceived state policies. In contrast, this section shows how these national physicians thought and acted much differently in facing contradictions between their ethnic identity and market interests.

As indicated earlier, physicians constituted a substantial portion of the new national bourgeoisie by the 1920s. Their education and economic potential granted them the position of a national elite in Taiwan during this period. This elite positionality was precisely what enabled them to identify as "physicians for the nation." Physicians were able, because of their relative wealth, to voluntarily compromise their economic interests in sponsoring community clinics or providing low-cost medical care. Returning to a previous example, many physicians who ran private clinics issued *shih-fei chuan,* a token for low-cost medical care, to low-income patients. Their actions amounted to the creation of a social welfare mechanism within native civil society.

But just as they were economically privileged under the colonial system these doctors were culturally more assimilated. And for this reason they joined the Japanese in reforming—and criticizing—Taiwanese customs. For example, physicians often criticized conventional weddings and funeral ceremonies as superstitious, feudalistic, and meaningless (Chen 1992, 76–78). Many were also critical of the gender inequalities implied in many Taiwanese traditions. They often voiced their liberal opinions in the MP (Chen 1992; Yang 1993). Many also directly participated in the public lecture series organized by the Cultural Association.

Furthermore, the elitist positionality that allowed doctors to make substantial gestures of solidarity with the Taiwanese poor also brought them into a market-based conflict with nonelite Taiwanese groups. During the economic depression of the late 1920s, economic differences between the physicians and their poor patients—including workers and peasants—intensified. At first, a number of working-class and peasant organizations appealed to the "social responsibility and conscientiousness" of Taiwanese physicians, asking that they reduce their medical fees (MP, nos. 120, 220, 237, 333, 334, 335, 337). Initially, the physicians responded positively. Some doctors issued more *shih-fei chuan;* others, with the help of charity organizations, established more nonprofit community hospitals (Chen 1992; SMP, nos. 328, 338, 362).

However, these concessions proved to be inadequate as a solution to the health care problem. While members of the low-income class demanded a new distributive system of medical resources based on need, physicians responded with modifications to the existing distributive system based on the market. A careful reading of two articles that appeared in the opposition newspaper in 1930 serves to illustrate the basic difference in these two positions. In an interview with the newspaper, the head of the Taipei Medical Association emphasized Taiwanese physicians' sympathy for the poor. He stated that "the medical charges set by our association are usually 20 percent lower than those set by Japanese practitioners on the island. We have always been concerned about the well-being of the poor and have tried to provide treatment to them" (SMP, no. 335, 2). In the second article, the People's Party explicitly criticized the "special treatment" of the poor on which the physicians prided themselves. They argued that Taiwanese physicians' common responses to the societal demand for reductions in medical costs had the following problems: (1) they usually became a marker of poverty and shame; (2) thus, most people were reluctant to rely on them for medical treatment; (3) the recipients of special treatment usually received discriminatory treatment from physicians; and (4) physicians often exhibited a condescending attitude toward their patients (SMP, no. 340, 2). In order to avoid these problems, the People's Party advocated a *general* reduction of medical charges. Most doctors and medical associations disagreed and refused to compromise further. Their reasoning was that, even though they felt responsible for the well-being of their Taiwanese patients, they were also entitled to a reasonable profit. The fundamental difference between the logic of social needs and that of the market placed a satisfactory compromise ultimately out of reach. Although these doctors did sacrifice their profits to some degree, and they compromised with the poor much more than their Japanese colleagues did, their market position placed limits on their willingness to make greater sacrifices (see MP, nos. 174, 371, 383).

Interestingly, while these national physicians were willing to take political risks in challenging the state policy on public health, they obviously never felt compelled to reform the system of health care. It seems that the role national physicians, in these doctors' understanding, did not involve questioning the medical system itself, even though it might demand the exercise of professional expertise against state policies. Taiwanese groups, especially peasant and working-class organizations, gradually grew critical of their national physicians, as negotiations proved unfruitful (SMP, nos. 324, 2; 336, 3; 341, 3; 337, 9; 377, 4). But their criticisms also centered on questions of the social responsibility and conscientiousness of their national physicians; almost no one viewed it as a systemic problem.

Ultimately, the attempt to solve a systemic problem through appeals to ethnic solidarity was ineffective; it channeled political energy away from systemic reforms. These unresolved tensions between the national physicians and their nation, together with Japan's increasing militarization, eventually demobilized all powerful oppositional movements in Taiwan in the beginning of the 1930s. After that, the history of colonial Taiwan entered a completely different phase.

Scientific Colonialists, National Physicians: Professional Powers and Hybrid Identities

Many studies have documented the presence of physicians in anticolonial activities in Taiwan in the 1920s. These studies accentuate the relationship between modern education and anticolonialism. However, they have rarely bothered to differentiate between professionals and intellectuals. As a result, little has been said concerning the complex role of Japan-trained professionals in Taiwanese anticolonialism.

Chen's study (1992) of Taiwanese physicians' social status was probably the first major contribution to this topic. His research revealed a significant finding: in disputes between liberal nationalists and left-wing radicals within Taiwanese anticolonial organizations in the late 1920s, physicians were generally inclined to identify with the liberals.[31] However, Chen treats physicians as a homogeneous social category, and he assumes that their political attitudes reflect the expression of a bourgeois modernist mentality. He did not examine the contradictory structural forces surrounding these doctors and hence misses the complexity involved in the evolution of physicians as a group.

The analysis in this chapter has focused instead on the "in-between" position of physicians. I have explored the ways in which Taiwanese physicians, by interpreting and acting upon structural contradictions, developed the identity of "national physicians." Within the space of the Taiwanese civil society, these national physicians acted as anticolonial liberals, public health-care providers, and middle-class professionals, but their roles were qualified and contained by their largely uncritical trust in the institution of colonial medicine. My analysis in this chapter suggests that the real puzzle of Taiwanese physicians' actions does not lie in the contrast between their privileged social positions and oppositionist attitudes but rather in the mixture of their opposition to the colonial state and their incomplete critique of colonial medicine.

In this sense, Taiwanese physicians in the 1920s present an interesting case for us to reconsider the powers of professionals. According to the theories of Abbott (1988), Freidson (1970, 1986, 1994), and others, professionals are highly motivated to defend their market positions. However, an emergent scholarship has posed challenges to this dominant assumption in the profession literature, suggesting that professionals are largely rational, elitist, and market oriented. Recently, Hoffman (1989), Kennedy (1990, 1991), Brint (1994), Johnson (1995), and Brooks and Manza (1997) have centralized the social and political roles of professionals and proposed different ways to understand them. Adopting a Foucauldian perspective, Johnson (1997) argues for the need to view expertise, as it became increasingly institutionalized in its professional form, as part of the process of governing. In other words, he sees professions as very political, as they are indeed part of the disperse power of the state apparatus.[32] In contrast to this view, Hoffman (1989) and Kennedy (1990, 1991) show that professionals can draw upon the values and worldviews of their professions to critique the inequalities within and surrounding their occupations. Brint's (1994) careful survey of U.S. professionals suggests that they generally display a liberal attitude toward social issues. However, Brint also qualifies his argument with an observation on the source of this liberalism. He argues that professionals' liberal attitudes tend to come from their demographic backgrounds rather than the inherent values of their professions: "Professional people are more likely to be relatively young, highly educated, urban, and nonreligious" (102).[33] At least partly overcoming this doubt about the strength of professionals' liberalism, Brooks and Manza (1997) seek to locate a stable expression of criticality in the professional strata. Their empirical research indicates that U.S. professionals display increasingly liberal attitudes toward social issues and a growing tendency to vote Democratic in the past few decades. These studies present a powerful challenge to the assumption in the conventional Marxist map of class relations that the rise of professionals is an interesting historical footnote but ultimately not very significant. They quite accurately reinsert professions into the heart of civil society.

In this sense, my study of Taiwanese physicians seeks to join and advance these scholarly efforts. My analysis shows that these doctors displayed both the tendency to defend their market position and the potential to resist social inequalities. Consistent with Freidson's and others' views, the national physicians in our case were strongly invested in protecting their professional domain and market interests. On the other hand, like the liberal professionals in the studies just mentioned, the Taiwanese national physicians contributed significantly to critical discourse and political activities in Taiwan. They helped shape what Habermas would call the criticality of Taiwanese civil society, although their criticality was circumscribed by their collective market project and exclusive membership. Taken together, in civil society these national physicians acted collectively to disrupt a system that they perpetuated in other ways. In short, they manifested an interesting mixture of what may be called imperialist and ideological powers,[34] showing that professionals are *both* market-oriented and critical social actors. The recognition of this ambivalent position brings to the fore the unpredictability in the public roles of professionals. Thus, in our examination of professions as sites of political contention it becomes crucial to study the patterns in which professionals mixed their imperialist and ideological powers.

The manner in which physicians experienced systemic and antisystemic parameters as alternatively empowering or limiting constitutes another significant theoretical issue. As Peter Sahlins (1989) suggests in his study of the negotiation between local and national identities in the Pyrenees, communities can make use of the penetration of the center to strengthen their local identities, though the latter may be transformed in the process. Likewise, Taiwanese physicians accepted the system of modern medicine imposed by the colonial regime. But to the extent that they managed to use it to increase the strength of native civil society they also transformed the valence of colonial policies. Likewise, their identification with the medical system limited the emancipatory potential of their participation in civil society, even while their professional experiences informed their actions and discourses in civil society. Hence the surprising strength *and* the surprising limits to their political imagination.

An understanding of this "in-betweenness" is important for studies of Japanese imperialism in particular and non-European colonialism in general. In their in-between position, Taiwanese doctors internalized certain institutional and cultural aspects of Japanese colonization, but at the same time their creative articulation of the identity of the national physicians empowered them vis-à-vis Japanese rule. Similarly, the Japanese colonizers were also a hybrid category themselves, in the sense that they tried to imitate Western colonizers in order to effectively resist them (Robertson 1995; Tanaka 1993). In so doing, they diligently studied European colonialism and then creatively designed their own "scientific colonialism." In this light, we can see that Japanese imperialism represented neither a mere reproduction of Western hegemony, nor complete control of its own colonies, but a chain of colonialism and hybridization.

Placing both the Japanese scientific colonialists and the Taiwanese national physicians in the chain of colonialism, we become more aware of the complex political potential of the hybrid. It is true, as Bhabha (1994) points out, the "hybrid," or the category that merges forces from the colonizers and the colonized, can be creative and disruptive. The contradictions it embodies, while preventing the hybrid from conceiving *complete* resistance, often stimulate new imaginings of identity. With the limited possibilities of resistance among the colonized, the hybrid—for example, the physicians in colonial Taiwan—represents an important form of power to mediate the "colonial gaze" fixed on a native society. However, what must also be recognized is the potential of the hybrid to perpetuate colonialism as a way of articulating its new identities. As the discussion of Japan's scientific colonialism brings to mind, Japanese imperialism represents the successful creation of a hybrid identity that attempted to assert itself against European and American imperialist forces. The contrast of these different hybrids replaces the postcolonial celebration of hybridity with a question: how are we to theorize the different types of hybrid power? How do we, for example, theorize the different positions occupied by the Japanese scientific colonialists and the Taiwanese national physicians on the chain of colonialism without losing sight of their common hybrid identity? In our thinking about the interactions between globalizing forces and local resistance, this question remains an important challenge.

NOTES

The research for this study was supported by the Chiang Ching-kuo Foundation for International Scholarly Exchange, the Center for Chinese Studies and the International Institute at the University of Michigan, and a Faculty Research Grant from the University of California, Davis. I gratefully acknowledge the helpful comments that I received from Michael Kennedy, Jennifer Roberston, Mayer Zald, Martin Whyte, Renee Anspach, Fred Block, Vicki Smith, Diane Wolf, Susan Mann, Chris Bettinger, and Margaret Weigers. I would also like to thank Naomi Galtz and Eileen Otis for their editorial assistance.

1. "From the 1630s Japan was virtually cut off from outside contact, with the exception of some trade with China and Holland through Deshima (Nagasaki). From the 1790s increasing Western attempts were made to break Japan's isolation, but it was not until the mid-19th century that the increase in Pacific whaling and trading made the US determined to secure from Japan coaling stations and supply and help facilities. . . . Eventually under the 1854 Treaty of Kanagawa Japan agreed to open ports, provide supplies, help castaways, and later on exchange consuls. This is followed by treaties with other powers and renewed pressures to extend intercourse" (Hunter 1984, 192–93). These foreign pressures caused major domestic crises in Japan and eventually led to the Meiji Restoration of 1868.

2. For example, see Wray and Conroy 1983, chap. 5: "Meiji Imperialism: Planned or Unplanned?" See also Jansen 1984.

3. The oval-shaped, mountainous island of Taiwan measures about 240 miles from north to south, and 90 miles from east to west at its broadest point. Although small in size (13,807 square miles, slightly larger than the Netherlands), Taiwan's location attracted visitors from an early age. The earliest inhabitants of the island, who came from Malay-Indonesian-Philippine areas, left traces of civilization from as early as 3000 B.C. Historians believe that Chinese and Japanese pirates and sailors stopped off at Taiwan before any authorities laid claim to it. In the fifteenth century, Chinese and Japanese pirates set up headquarters in the south and the north of Taiwan, respectively (Office of the Chief of Naval Operations 1944, 162). In the next century, Taiwan was occupied first by the Dutch and then by the Spanish in the course of these nations' imperialist expansions. Of the two European powers that did occupy Taiwan, the Dutch arrived earlier and stayed longer than the Spanish, gradually turning Taiwan into an "important entrepôt in Holland's worldwide trading network" from 1624 to 1662 (Tsurumi 1977, 4).

In 1662, the Dutch were expelled by Koxinga (Cheng Cheng-kung), a Chinese general who settled in Taiwan and attempted—unsuccessfully—to overthrow the mainland Ch'ing regime in the name of resurrecting the heritage of the Ming dynasty. Under the Koxinga family, Chinese-style schools were opened and the Chinese legal system was adopted. Foreign trade with Japan, the Philippines, Indochina, Siam, and the East Indies was promoted (Copper 1993). In 1683, Koxinga's grandson surrendered Taiwan to the Ch'ing regime. After Taiwan was formally incorporated into Chinese history, it remained politically and culturally marginalized in the Chinese empire. Not until 1887 was Taiwan made a formal province of China; eight years later it was ceded to Japan.

4. For a discussion of these measures of control and co-optation, see Lo 1996, 38–46. See also Mukōyama 1987, 164–304; Chen 1984; and Wu 1992, 24–42.

5. See Peattie 1984, 85, n. 13, for a brief outline of the similarities between German and Japanese colonialism.

6. Gotō was the president of the South Manchuria Railroad Company at this time.

7. Furthermore, the colonial government limited the expansion of higher education in Taiwan, despite increases in demand. Throughout the entire colonial period, only one medical school existed in Taiwan. A few vocational schools were founded after 1919. A university was finally opened in 1928, mainly to accommodate Japanese youths on the island. In addition to ensuring the slow pace of the expansion of higher education, the colonial government controlled admission to most schools and reserved many spaces for Japanese students.

8. Of the existing literature on this topic, Wu Wen-hsing's study (1992) probably most tellingly captured the transition from old to new elites. Wu's analysis indicates that by the early 1930s the new educated elites had grown to represent 64 percent of all elites, while the old elites had fallen to 23.9 percent. Doctors and teachers were the most important educated elites, making up 17.0 percent and 18.9 percent of all Taiwanese elites, respectively. Wu's analysis of the 1943 *Who's Who in Taiwan* confirms the continuation of this trend. At this point, doctors constituted 17.9 percent of all Taiwanese elites and teachers 16.6 percent.

9. I follow Dunn (1976) and Leslie (1976) in using the term *cosmopolitan medicine* to refer to what is alternatively called modern medicine, scientific medicine, and Western medicine. Dunn and Leslie caution us against the biases implied by these terms. Leslie explains that the terms *modern medicine* and *scientific medicine* carry the assumption that all medicine other than cosmopolitan medicine is antimodern or unscientific. The term *Western medicine* is even more problematic. According to Leslie, "The scientific aspects of Western medicine are transcultural. Ethnic interpretations of modern science are the aberrations of nationalistic and totalitarian ideologies or, in this case, a reflex of colonial or neocolonial thought. . . . The social organization of cosmopolitan medicine . . . is as Japanese as it is Western" (8). For these reasons, Dunn proposes the term *cosmopolitan medicine* and Leslie favors it over alternative terms. Susan Long (1980) later employs the term *cosmopolitan medicine* in her study of the careers of Japanese physicians.

For all these reasons, I also use the term *cosmopolitan medicine* (or *cosmopolitan physician*) in my study. However, it would be wrong to paper over the fact that many Japanese health administrators and Taiwanese physicians assumed that "good" medicine was distinctly modern and scientific. Thus, in order to avoid confusing these people's self-description with my analysis of them, I will preserve the terms *modern medicine* or *scientific medicine* in their narratives and use the term *cosmopolitan medicine* in my own.

Western missionaries had introduced cosmopolitan medicine to Taiwan thirty years prior to the arrival of the Japanese. In 1865, Dr. James L. Maxwell, dispatched by the British Presbyterian Church to introduce Christianity as well as to provide medical services in Taiwan, opened the era of "church medicine" on the island (Hsieh 1989). Dr. Maxwell founded a hospital in Tainan, and in the following years Rev. George Leslie Mackay of the Canadian Presbyterian Church and Dr. Calvin Russell of the British Presbyterian Church established hospitals at Tan-shui and Chang-hua. These hospitals, like the church itself, were greeted with mistrust and hostility at first, but the missionaries persisted. Gradually they attracted many Han Taiwanese as well as aboriginal patients, and they converted some of these patients to Christianity.

10. These rules and regulations included the "Official Organization of the Pharmacy of the Taiwanese Government-General" (Taiwan sōtokufu seiyakujo kansei), "Regulations of the Medical Occupation in Taiwan" (Taiwan igyō kisoku), "Rules for the Prevention of Contagious Diseases" (densembyō yobō kisoku), "The Opium Law of Taiwan" (Taiwan ahen rei), and "Regulations of the Taiwan Central Hygiene Association" (Taiwan chūō eiseikai kisoku) (*Taiwan sōtokufu minsei jimu seiseki teiyō* [hereafter MJST] 2:240–58).

11. In contrast to the church hospitals, whose service only covered three sites (Tainan, Tan-shui, and Chang-hua), the government's health program was meant to affect life islandwide.

12. Unless otherwise indicated, quotations from Chinese and Japanese materials in this study are my translations.

13. The position of police physician was changed to that of sanitary technician in 1944.

14. See Taiwan Kyōiku-kai 1939, 926–27.

15. In 1899, the name of the institute was changed to the Taiwan sōtokufu iggakō (Medical School of the Government-General of Taiwan). In 1918, the school began to admit Japanese students, but it kept them segregated from Taiwanese. In 1919, the Taiwan Medical School was upgraded to a college, called the Taiwan sōtokufu igaku senmon gakkō (The Government-General's Medical College of Taiwan), and in 1922 it adopted the policy of "integrated education" for the two ethnic groups. In the same year, it finally acquired equal status to the medical colleges in Japan and was changed to Taiwan sōtokufu Taihoku igaku senmon gakkō (Medical College of the Government-General of Taipei) (Li 1953, 328; Chen 1992, 29). Despite the changes in name, I will refer to this school as the Medical School or Taipei Medical School throughout this chapter.

16. In addition to regular private physicians, the government-general of Taiwan also recognized "practicing physicians in restricted locations." This term applied to doctors who obtained their licenses through a state-administered examination instead of a regular medical course. They were allowed to practice only in specific, usually remote areas (Li 1952, 64–66).

17. Fan Yen-ch'iu's (1993) work on I-lan Hospital is an excellent case study that illustrates this point with rich data and examples.

18. At this time, professional associations had not yet emerged in Taiwan. The formation of a medical professional identity, then, mainly transpired in the training process and the practice of medicine, that is, at the site of medical schools and hospitals.

19. For example, Dr. Lin Yu-hsu, who graduated from the Medical School and later worked for a state-headed medical project, comments in his memoirs on the similarities between the mentorship he received at school and the mentorship he was placed under at work (Lin 1935).

20. The Medical School was originally supervised by the Police Bureau. With the reform, it was placed under the supervision of the Internal Affairs Bureau (Taiwan Kyōiku-kai 1939, 926–28).

21. The integration policy was not closely observed at the level of elementary education. In Taiwan, Japanese children still received a better elementary education than did their Taiwanese counterparts. Because they were trained differently at an early stage, ethnic integration in higher education actually disadvantaged the Taiwanese. Formerly all-Taiwanese facilities were now open to Japanese students, and thus Taiwanese students faced stiff competition for these slots. For a detailed discussion of this, see Tsurumi 1977, 91–106.

22. For example, Governor Uchida Kakichi (1923–24) gave a very positive evalua-

tion of native physicians in a speech delivered at the twenty-fifth anniversary of the Medical School. Even for a speech on such occasions, his praise of native physicians seems unusual. He noted that these doctors "contribute to the public health everywhere on the island, and furthermore, some of them work diligently in far and foreign places such as South Manchuria, southern China, and the South Seas" (Senmon gakkō kōyūkai 1924, 7). See chapter 7 in Oda 1974 for similar evaluations of Taiwanese medical students.

23. Furthermore, the police record showed that the most active physicians usually participated in several political or cultural organizations in addition to the Cultural Association. They played an important role in both the liberal reformist organizations and the agencies of the emergent public discourse such as journals and study groups (see KE). Their membership across these two types of organization—the political and the cultural—is evidence of the direct linkage between the emergence of a liberal civil society and the rise of anticolonialism.

24. In 1920, a group of Taiwanese students in Tokyo (most of whom belonged to the New People's Society) founded the journal *Taiwan Seinen. Taiwan Seinen* was renamed *Taiwan* in 1922. In 1923, the founding members of the journal established a publishing company in Taiwan, but the journal continued to be published in Tokyo. In the same year, *Taiwan* transformed itself from a journal into a newspaper called *Taiwan Minpō.*

But even if MP called itself a newspaper, it only appeared biweekly in the beginning and later every 10 days. Starting in 1925, MP was published once a week. During these years, its readership in Taiwan continued to grow, but its headquarters were still located in Tokyo. Although the core members of MP had many times negotiated with the government-general, the latter did not approve the plan for MP to move to Taiwan until 1926. Starting in August 1927, MP was formally published from its offices in Taiwan. The move significantly enlarged its readership. In 1930, MP was renamed *Taiwan Shinminpō,* in anticipation of becoming a daily newspaper. With the governor-general's final approval, *Taiwan Shinminpō* (hereafter SMP) published its first issue as a daily on April 15, 1932. For a detailed discussion of this history, see Tsai et al. 1983.

25. For a discussion of the concept of "narrative identity," see Somers 1992, 1994. Somers argues that social identities are largely shaped by the process in which human actors imbed themselves in a web of social and discursive relationships. "A narrative identity approach assumes that social action can only be intelligible if we recognize that people are guided to act by the structural and the cultural relationships in which they are embedded and by the stories through which they constitute their identities—and less because of the interests we impute to them" (1994, 624).

26. For example, see MP, nos. 120, 13; 188; 389, 8. See also Chen 1992.

27. For example, a Taiwanese physician was once arrested by the police because they deemed one of his diagnoses to be invalid. Although he was eventually released, local physicians were mobilized to express their discontent collectively (see MP, no. 389, 8).

28. In another example from 1929, the same two physicians carried out an autopsy in a possible case of police violence. Convinced that the case involved the violation of human rights, they forwarded their concerns to the Taipei Legal Association (Taihoku Bengoshi-kai). Meanwhile, their actions attracted much attention from the opposition newspaper and motivated the People's Party (Minshū-tō)—a short-lived Taiwanese opposition party—to plan several public lectures on police violence and human rights (MP, no. 246, 10).

29. In the early 1920s, local medical associations in Taiwan typically accommodated both Taiwanese and Japanese physicians. As a result of the Cultural Association's mobilizing efforts, many Taiwanese physicians formed their own medical associations at different sites on the island (see Chen 1992; Oda 1974; and Ryū 1983).

30. The state did punish the physicians most active in this event. In many instances, they were harassed by the police through unfounded charges of malpractice, unauthorized supervision of their clinics, or suspension of their licenses. See MP, nos. 7, 142, 184, and June 2, 1931.

31. Chen also points out that some physicians were leading members in the peasant or worker unions. However, his analysis of the memberships in different political organizations shows that the majority of the political physicians tended to join the liberal camp.

32. Johnson uses the concept of "governmentality" to explain the role of professional expertise: "Foucault redirects our attention to the place of expertise in the politics of governmentality: to the recognition of changing spheres of neutrality and technicality, as identified by Starr and Immergut; to the generation of novel disciplines that both define and render governable realms of social reality, as undercored by Larson; to the establishment of these disciplines as part of a process of struggle over jurisdictional claims and occupational strategies, as outlined by Abbott" (1995, 21).

33. Brint explains this in detail: "The most consistent predictors of social conservatism were advanced age, lower levels of education, high levels of religiosity, and residence in the South. Other anchoring variables—residence in small towns and suburbs, marriage and child rearing, membership in the dominant gender and racial groups—all showed the expected associations with conservative views. Of the employment-related variables, lower incomes, human services occupations, and location in the manufacturing and trade sectors were associated with conservative views, while the more intellectual social and cultural professions were associated with greater liberalism" (1994, 99).

34. Freidson (1994) argues that professional power is both imperialistic and ideological. It is imperialistic insofar as it works to claim a broader jurisdiction for the profession and ideological insofar as it strives to maintain a worldview consistent with the profession's system of knowledge.

CHAPTER 10

Politics and Play: Sport, Social Movements, and Decolonization in Cuba and the British West Indies

José Raul Perales

'You see dat show?' the people was shoutin';
'Jesus Chrise, man, wunna see dat shot?'
All over de groun' fellers shaking hands wid each other
as if *they* wheelin' de willow
as if was *them* had the power

—Edward Kamau Brathwaite, "Rites"[1]

That is why, now that I see that all the boys are busy playing such a useful and healthy game as baseball, I would like to get together with my girlfriends of that time and tell them: 'The youth of my country also play like those in your country.'

—"Elena E.," Cuban student in Havana, reflecting on boarding school in New York, *El Base-Ball* (Havana), October 23, 1881[2]

How is homogeneity produced from a variety of groups such that a single notion of what a nation-state should be is created? This question, dating back to the writings of Karl Deutsch on social mobilization, nationalism, and development,[3] has received numerous responses from anthropologists, historians, social and cultural theorists, sociologists, and some political scientists, whose views on "nation" have centered mainly on symbols, traditions, discourses, and values that have been socially constructed and coded and perpetuated through relationships of power and repression of hegemonic groups against subdued segments of the social system. Even the meaning of resistance (in terms of this imposition), especially in colonial and postcolonial settings where the debate about "the nation" is continuously contested and redefined, has been challenged by revisions of what is resistance and where it is to be located. Categorical divisions along the lines of colonizer and colonized, oppressor and oppressed, have changed meaning as new forms and sites of political resistance have been "discovered" in the activities of everyday life, even those which to the "naked eye" seem to be reproductions of the subjugated condition.[4]

This chapter is about one of those practices—sport—and its important political power in terms of creating a feeling and a common vision of nation for two decolonization movements in the Caribbean in two different centuries: Cuba's fight for independence in 1868, and again in 1895, and the march toward independence for the British West Indies in the 1960s. The similarities between these two cases do not merely arise from their having shared the same geographical context and arguably similar socioeconomic patterns of colonization. Similarly, discrepancies between Cuban and West Indian decolonization are not necessarily related to differences in size, epoch, and colonizer. In this sense, however, it is important to point out that while the West Indies obtained its political independence from Britain partly as the result of a combination of the collapse of the British colonial administration system and popular grievances in the Caribbean islands, Cuba obtained its independence from Spain after two bloody wars (the Ten Years War of 1868–78 and the War of Independence of 1895–98) and the intervention of a third actor (the United States). Nevertheless, as will be demonstrated, the common ground between the two cases is the role of sport (baseball in the case of Cuba, cricket in the case of the West Indies) as a vehicle for constructing an idea, a cohesive project, and ultimately a collective vision of "nation" without which generalized social mobilization in favor of independence would have been almost impossible. Sport became a socially instituted space in which popular grievances against the colonial order were played collectively (by people seemingly representing all strata of the colonial society), where the social contradictions and the political capabilities of Caribbean societies became at once recognized and developed, and where ideas about a new "postcolonial" political and social order had their popular origins.

This claim is not devoid of assumptions about key concepts that help define a specific set of actions, actors and circumstances in the emergence of decolonization movements in the Caribbean, or for that matter the importance of sport in this process. For instance, it must be clarified what a social movement is in the first place, in contrast to rebellions or revolutions. Also, we must understand what "nation" is, especially as a condition of certain social practices (e.g., national movements, national sports, and even the nation-state as opposed to the colonial state) in which this identity is generated and reproduced.

Consequently, the first section of this chapter examines some of these topics in light of theories about social movements and their adequacy in accounting for mass mobilization and support for political independence in Cuba and the West Indies. It will be demonstrated that the social network underlying the success of this mobilization could not have been possible without a generalized idea about these Caribbean societies as nations (rather than colonies or political appendages).[5] This, in turn, was enabled by the powerful catalyst of sport. The second section of this chapter elaborates on the link between sport and the Caribbean masses along issues of values, traditions, and rituals. It was a combination of these elements in

Cuban baseball and West Indian cricket that made such games an exercise of resistance to colonial domination and construction of new social imaginaries and visions of collectivity. The third and fourth sections of this chapter elaborate on the case studies of Cuba and the West Indies, respectively. The focus is on social and political conditions during late colonial times and the patterns of interaction among different segments of these societies that were radically transformed by sport, thus resulting in movements demanding *national* independence. The concluding section reflects on theoretical considerations and questions arising from our reflection on sport, the generation of national identities, and the formation of social movements, in particular, whether "success" is a crucial variable in our understanding of how identities can generate discursive opportunities for mobilization.

Social Movements and Social Projects: Sport as Political Vehicle and Catalyst

In his book *Power in Movement,* Sidney Tarrow defines social movements as "collective challenges by people with common purposes and solidarity in sustained interaction with elites, opponents and authorities" (1994, 4). Tarrow notes that this definition is based on four basic empirical properties of social movements: a collective challenge through disruptive direct action, a common purpose based on overlapping interests among participants in the movement, solidarity as recognition of such interests, and sustained interaction against an opposing force. Collective action presents a problem for social movements, but the explanation offered by Mancur Olson in *The Logic of Collective Action* (1965) in terms of selective incentives can only account for one aspect involved in such a decision. In accordance with Charles Tilly, Tarrow contends that social movements motivate people into collective action through known "repertoires of contention," which, in their "modular" version, reflect the variety of protest and grievance mechanisms that can be employed similarly by often distinct groups over an extended geographical area. Tarrow's theory about the emergence and prospects of the success of social movements is that "changes in the political opportunity structure create incentives for collective actions. The magnitude and duration of these collective actions depend on mobilizing people through social networks and around identifiable symbols that are drawn from cultural frames of meaning" (1994, 6).

The importance of political opportunity is crucial for understanding why groups lacking financial resources and institutional capabilities often succeed in pursuing their agendas while other groups endowed with better resources and capabilities fail in their objectives. For Tarrow, the key element of social movements is the ways in which organizers use contentious collective action to take advantage of political opportunities, to create collective identities on the basis of these opportunities, to conduce people into organizations, and to further mobilize "organized people" against overwhelming opponents. In this sense, the state serves two purposes: it is simultaneously an object of contention for less powerful actors (the movements) and the fulcrum through which modular repertoires of collective action can successfully emerge.

Where does recognition of political opportunities come from? Tarrow's analysis of social movements is quite explicit in discussing the tools and mechanisms available to social movements for successfully achieving their purposes. For instance, opportunities are ideally seized and created by social movements through the diffusion of collective action by means of social networks and coalitions, through the creation of political space for associated movements and countermovements, and through the provision of incentives to which political elites will respond (1994, 82). However, Tarrow is less explicit about how these purposes are arrived at and ultimately agreed upon. If his theory of social movements is dissected through a levels of analysis approach, the importance of social networks and cultural symbols marks the basis of the patterns of social relations upon which collective action is built. But how do these networks and symbols come into existence?

The recognition of political opportunities cannot be possible without two previously existing conditions: a collective identity and a definition of interests. While identity is almost always linked to a reference point (e.g., racial, sexual, or economic identity), in terms of political identification, contestation, and mobilization "identity" could be looked at through the functional lens presented by Linda Alcoff in her discussion of identity politics. For Alcoff (1994, 115), identities are assumed and defined as "a political point of departure, as a motivation for action, and as a delineation of one's politics." This perspective can be potentially tautological, for one could run into the problem of claiming that a social movement's identity is the result of the political opportunity that the movement is seeking to take advantage of but could not otherwise be recognized unless some identity was already in place. In order to avoid this explanatory trap, one could look at the origins of a *collective* identity in terms of the ways in which it emerges out of common historical experiences and the interaction of people in interpreting and redefining those experiences. As noted by Dirks, Eley, and Ortner, "'Identities' may be seen as (variably successful) *attempts* to create and maintain coherence out of inconsistent cultural stuff and inconsistent life experience" (Dirks et al. 1994, 18). A social movement cannot emerge as such until collective experiences are built and interpreted as an identifying bond between members of the group (or, as Dirks et al. put it, until the "nonfixity" of identity somehow becomes temporarily fixed so that individuals can behave in some kind of political agency. This interpretation is not spontaneous but is actually mediated by rituals, traditions, and other cultural factors that together serve as the lens through which societies create their own history and sense of purpose. For West Indian, and to a lesser degree Cuban, societies, sport acted as an important lens through which fragmented social knowledges (of slaves, workers, merchants, mothers, etc.) were transformed into a single national experience prior to (and even simultaneous with) their engagement in decolonization processes.

The notion of interest is equally important in identifying political opportunities. Interest is a problematic category since a social movement often involves at least two sets of interests—those of the collectivity and those of its leaders—which may not necessarily coincide. Tarrow's prescription for a successful social movement includes the presence of a common purpose among participants and widespread solidarity behind this common interest. Yet Tarrow also recognizes that the mechanics of effective social movements are defined by the extent to which organizers use the potential for contentious collective action to exploit political opportunities, create new collective identities, bring people together in organizations, and mobilize them against more powerful opponents. To what extent do leaders' interests represent those of the movement? In other words, it seems that it is not so much the objective condition of a political opportunity or the relative mobilizational capabilities of a collectivity that determine a social movement's success: equally important are other factors such as the leader's discount rate or his or her ideas about the political system in general and the movement in particular.

Where does the leader's "interest," or for that matter the movement's, come from? If one claims that it is the social movement that creates interests, one runs the same tautological danger as with the concept of identity. *Interest* should not be defined in essentialist terms. It is often the case that a group's interests become redefined and rearticulated as new experiences shape attitudes and perspectives of individual segments of the collectivity. For instance, the first wave of labor protest in the West Indies during the early 1900s started as a series of local protests and rebellions claiming wage increases at a time when worker unions were illegal. By the end of the 1930s, these protests had changed the political and organizational landscape of the West Indies in such a way that political grievances besides worker rights became mediated by labor associations.[6]

Interests are inextricably linked to the political character of a movement's identity, within which can be found the parameters that demarcate "acceptable" fields and practices of collective action. It follows that not only interests are subject to some degree of change (much in the same way as identities are inherently constructed and subject to variation) but that they seem to be "path dependent" to the extent that a movement grows in scope and power. Political opportunities cannot be regarded as absolute or essential in this sense, since a movement can perceive political opportunity differently at different stages of its development. This development, in turn, is not objectively defined at the movement's inception but is subject to change and contestation.

The role of the state, in our case the colonial state, is a key element in the creation of collective identities and interests and ultimately in shaping nationalist independence movements. As stated by Tarrow, for social movements the state is both the target of their collective action and, because of its extensive capability to penetrate widely divergent social sectors (thus unifying otherwise disparate social groups through common, *national* policies and institutions), the pivot around which national social movements emerge in the first place. Yet the state should not be seen as an actor outside the society upon which it is built. Rather, it is imbued in contests for power with its own interests, playing actors against each other and allocating property rights among them (Douglass North's discriminating monopolizer theory of the state). As noted by Susan Stokes (1995), states create patterns of interaction with groups in civil society that not only change the course of state-society relations, or even these groups' interpretation of political opportunities,[7] but also help to mold social organizations' goals and perceptions of themselves. For colonial societies, the problem in the formation of social movements is that the administrative and ideological presence of the state is so pervasive that it can effectively destroy the preconditions Sidney Tarrow claims are fundamental for the emergence of social movements in the first place. In colonial societies, the political structure is such that decolonization movements not only have to devise a collective consciousness for the population—a vision of nation[8]—but they also have to create some of the preconditions for mobilization (like organization of opinion) that social movements whose reference point is a different kind of state—even a totalitarian one—only have to put together.[9] Where such an overbearing presence of political power impedes the development of any kind of resources or preconditions for venting social grievances from diverse social segments, the only space reserved for political manifestation becomes culture: rituals and practices charged with political symbolism. One such practice in colonial Cuba and the West Indies was sport.

Values, Traditions, and Rituals: The Popular Power of Sport

Reflecting on the work by Raymond Williams on the politics of cultural production, Dirks et al. note that

> culture is seen as political not only (or not even) in the sense that is produced to serve certain specific interests, but rather more generally (and usefully) in that it constitutes the terrains of meaning and feeling that are central to the securing of consent and/or the incitement of rebellion in a world where brute power is only part of the story. . . . [C]ulture has to do with meaning, with the way the experience is construed rather than with some unmediated notion of experience itself, with the centrality of symbol for formulating and expressing meanings that are pervasive as well as shared. (1994, 22–23)

Culture, in other words, is inherently political; it is the common knowledge through which "repertoires of contention" are constructed and identified. This culture is not static but rather dynamic; it is constantly reformulated with new meanings emerging out of practice, including contentious politics and mobilization. In turn, culture defines what is contentious and what is mobilization; it is a symbiotic relationship in which practice and category become mutually reinforced through experience.

Culture is an ample word, and it would be devoid of much meaning if it were not linked to specific practices imbued in particular social contexts. For the present discussion, these practices will be limited to the ones Raymond Williams claimed do not "articulate with the current regime of the ordinary" (quoted in Dirks et al. 1994, 16), in other words, to those areas within a system of social domination (in our case colonial domination) wherein actors are not completely subjected. More specifically, our concern here should be with the ways in which the politics of culture become crystallized in action, with the ways in which particular symbols come to embody those aspects of contestation that social movements seek to materialize through collective action.

But why sport? After all, Caribbean societies are, in the words of Franklin Knight (1990, 308), "an eclectic blend of almost all the peoples and cultures of the world." Cultural symbols for mobilization should abound; however, they ought not be so particularistic as to prevent the building of connections between disparate social groups. Based on our operational definition of *culture,* sport needs to be framed in both the structure of social relations from which it became an acceptable (in fact, commendable) practice and the structure of social domination (colonial systems in Cuba and the West Indies) in which it became a form of resistance and of nation building.

Sport, as opposed to games, pastimes, recreation, or play, became a favorably sanctioned social activity during the Victorian Age in Britain. The reformation of the educational system during this period of British history created an image of education as not just that of the intellect but of the body and the spirit as well. Based on ideas about social Darwinism, British theories of education came to associate a strong body with strong character. A complete and proper education, then, should include not only mastery of great works of art, literature, and philosophy but dexterity in a physical activity that requires skill, discipline, and a sense of honor. Sport, especially team sport (most notably cricket), was regarded as one such activity. By emphasizing discipline through a physical activity encoded with rules of practice and principles, it was believed that students would develop the necessary strength of character, perseverance, and spirit to become adequate citizens of the British Empire.

British international hegemony during the nineteenth century (indeed, during the entire Victorian period) was responsible for the spread of these ideas throughout many parts of the world. Indeed, British mores and sense of "fair play" permeated the adoption and practice of sports in other parts of Europe to the point that, even in 1990, the often rejected ethic of "fair play" (given its ethnocentric and moralistic overtones) became the official exhortation in the European Soccer Cup

(Mangan 1996, 3). Sport also became an instrument for British imperialism in its colonial territories. Because it emanated from British public schools, which were reserved for the children of the upper bourgeois class and the aristocracy, colonial elites throughout the British Empire saw in sport a way of becoming more identified with British social values and the upper echelons of British society. In the same fashion, these colonial elites believed sport would complement the *mission civilisatrice* of colonization through the teaching of moral and spiritual values, of virtue and of social discipline, to colonial masses. It became a system through which people would learn to respect authority, honesty, courage, and humility. While in Europe the discipline of sport was seen as "building the body's performance as the outer and visible sign of an inner, personal excellence" (Faure 1996, 80), in colonial empires it was a way of keeping the masses divided through their ability to engage successfully in it.[10] It is perhaps C. L. R. James who best captures this feeling among colonial subjects when he discusses sport and education in the British West Indies:

> It was long years after I understood the limitation on spirit, vision, and self respect which was imposed on us by the fact that our masters, our curriculum, our code of morals, *everything* began from the basis that Britain was the source of all light and leading; and our business was to admire, wonder, imitate, learn; our criterion of success was to have succeeded in approaching that distant ideal—to attain it was, of course, impossible. Both masters and boys accepted it as in the very nature of things. The masters could not be offensive about it because they thought it was their function to do this, if they thought about it at all; and as for me, it was the beacon that beckoned me on. ([1963] 1993, 30)

Indeed, even in Europe these two interpretations of the social virtues of sport and physical activity became powerful instruments for governing elites interested in building a sense of duty and a moral responsibility to the nation in preparation for future warfare. For instance, in late-nineteenth-century France it was not uncommon for military planners to compare the soldier to the gymnast: "The gymnast and the soldier are similar in character: a controlled fighting spirit, voluntarily prepared and always available 'for the struggle for existence, as for the struggle between peoples'" (Faure 1996, 78). Yet this fighting spirit, as noted by Faure, is a form of correction to otherwise belligerent and irresponsible social conduct—in other words, the opposite of violence. Organized sport, with its rules and constraints, was believed to provide the school in which the French soldier would learn to discipline himself and to assimilate the rules of desirable social behavior. In turn, popular competition in organized sports would allow such rules and moralizing ideas to disseminate among a nation of spectators. It was hoped that by witnessing organized competition the French masses would become educated in the social values and pursuit of personal excellence that national political elites wanted to instill in the population.

How can sport become resistance, then? In Gramscian terms, the notion of resistance is based on the production of a counterhegemony that would break the ideological grip of socially dominant classes. The development of such a counterhegemony through sport seems all the more contradictory given that, as noted earlier, sport was widely regarded as a tool among ruling elites for producing "an individual who would be capable . . . of governing himself so as to be able to govern others" (Faure 1996, 78). In the context of colonial societies, then, the link between sport and resistance must be explained in terms of how sport, both as organized competition and as social more, became an instrument and a site for subverting the political, and in fact the psychological, relationship between metropolis and colony. While in the case of Cuba the adoption of baseball was in a sense a matter of counterhegemony (since the sport fostered by Spanish colonial authorities was bullfighting, as will be discussed later), in the West Indies resistance was produced through cricket, the sport of the colonizer and therefore a part of the latter's ideological control over colonial societies.

At this stage, it would be useful to reintroduce the notion of everyday resistance that has been widely reviewed in the social sciences.[11] Because the subjugating effects of power are not totalizing, several social pockets are left out of the sphere of domination, where common daily practices that would otherwise be perceived as normal are charged with meanings of defiance and self-affirmation. For colonial subjects without a social project of "nation," transformation at these initial stages of resistance is not a matter of reformulating the constituted system but of gaining some access to it. It is, as Marshall Sahlins (1994) points out, a matter of reasserting existing cultural forms and adapting European practices and objects to the fulfillment of traditional ends. In this sense, one could see in cricket not just the imposition of British social mores on West Indian peoples but the witnessing of resistance through the incorporation of (socially incorrect) festive rituals and cheering among the (predominantly black) crowds witnessing cricket matches. In Cuba, baseball became a way of emulating an orderly society and a respectable code of conduct radically different from the violent, sanguine, and demeaning spectacle of bullfighting.[12]

The importance of ritual as a vehicle for expressing resistance and constructing powerful social ties among the colonized lies in its ability to build an alternative "language" encoded with particular meanings based on the social experiences of the subjugated. Ritual is often overlooked in analyses of everyday forms of resistance, since it has been typically associated with the reinforcement of traditional social ties and roles (Dirks 1994). Yet, assuming that power is not a totalizing phenomenon, there is little consideration of how rituals can become instruments for distilling dissent through "a subtle but systematic breach of authoritative cultural codes" (Comaroff, quoted in Dirks 1994, 487), an "unconventional domain . . . through which the values and structures of a contradictory world may be addressed and manipulated" (Dirks 1994, 487). It may be precisely because of the fact that ritual bears a significant element of authority (given its importance in the construction of social order) that it is a crucial site where conflicts over authority may take place (Dirks 1994). Thus, rituals could be regarded as vehicles for imposing particular types of authority over others. For instance, in the case of the British West Indies, mimicry and parody, two of the main sources of traditional Afro-Caribbean culture, became the instruments through which a free black population took over carnival in late-nineteenth-century Trinidad and transformed this traditionally white elite activity through a set of activities and symbols based on the experience of a new social status. In short, what used to be a pre-Lenten festivity quickly became a popular black festival of liberation (Burton 1995.)

It is in this light that sport in the Caribbean became encoded with rituals and symbols and generated a tradition of common gatherings, languages, and activities around the only seemingly "democratic" social practice permitted by colonial rulers. As a ritual, while officially sanctioned by colonial authorities, sport quickly became a social drama in which collective experiences of racial, economic, and political conflict were literally "played" through the symbolism of organized confrontation. As opposed to dance, festivals, and other public displays of mass culture (including the important example of Caribbean carnival), sport was capable of generating the social bases for a common project of nation because, according to Eric Hobsbawm, "what has made sport so uniquely effective a medium for inculcating national feelings, at all events for males,[13] is the ease with which even the least political or public individuals can identify with the nation as symbolized by young persons excelling at what every man wants, or at one time in life has wanted, to be good at. The imagined community of millions seems more real as a team of eleven named people. The individual, even the one who only cheers, becomes a symbol of the nation himself" (1990, 143).[14] Moreover, as noted by Richard Holt in his analysis of French sport and militarism, national self-image may be crucially determined through the perception of the ethnic qualities of rivals in organized competition (Holt 1996). In the Caribbean, as will be demonstrated, the powerful social imaginary potential contained in sport became crystallized through competition with outside *national* teams. For the West Indies, it was the cricket test matches against Britain (especially its 1950 victory over the British team in London, its first such victory ever); for Cuba, it was the baseball games against North American teams during the Spanish colonial period of the late 1800s.[15]

Cuban Baseball and Alternative Social Order as Colonial Grievance

It is generally observed that baseball entered Cuba through various simultaneous channels. One of these was the continued commercial interaction between Cuba and the United States during the second half of the nineteenth century (especially after the American Civil War), through which Cuban merchants learned some American customs and pastimes, including baseball. Baseball also became a part of Cuban social life as the result of the children of elite bourgeois families who returned to Cuba from boarding schools in the United States and thus brought with them a new practice of social legitimacy for what was to be regarded as superior and modern. Thus, from the beginning baseball in Cuba became assimilated at different social levels through various cultural channels at a key time when social class structures in Cuba, as the result of the Ten Years War with Spain (1868–78), were in a transformational stage.

The social and political context into which baseball arrived in Cuba was one of a confused, distraught, and decaying colonial society. After the 1878 Peace of Zanjón, which ended Cuba's first independence struggle against Spain, Cuban society became immersed in economic chaos and political confusion. The war had disrupted sugar production, which resulted in an economic depression. Banks and businesses closed, trading companies failed to meet their credits, and planters became increasingly indebted through heavy mortgages in order to subsidize sugar production in the absence of buyers. Government revenues decreased, so crucial social services ranging from education to sanitation, health, and public works declined or disappeared (Pérez 1985). The lack of employment opportunities in the private and public sectors (Spanish officials controlled civil service positions) generated an immense beggar and vagrant population in Havana and other Cuban cities. Petty theft evolved into complex systems of extortion and blackmail, which not only corroded Cuban society but were regarded by many as open resistance to colonial law at a time when confrontation with Spain was still on everyone's mind in spite of the 1878 defeat. Finally, a burgeoning labor movement introduced popular education among workers, challenged divisions between free and unfree labor (slaves and indentured Chinese workers), and confronted colonial authorities with demands for higher wages (Casanovas 1995).

It is precisely the defeat of 1878 and the subsequent disruption of Cuban society that evidenced one of the crucial aspects of Cuba's failure to win independence from Spain after the Ten Years War. The "independence" project of 1868 was fraught with social incoherence and divisionism. For example, the creole elite was split over the important issue of slavery. In addition, Spain's vague promises of economic and political reform (e.g., the 1865 election in Cuba and Puerto Rico of a reform commission—the Junta de Información—to discuss colonial policy in Madrid) split much allegiance among independence supporters. Even the Guerra Chiquita of 1879–80, which enjoyed more popular backing than the Ten Years War, involved more than just a conflict over political independence. It was actually a confrontation between the institution of slavery and privileged classes and those who sought a different political, economic, and social order (Ferrer 1991). In the end, class, color, and race fragmented a small nationalist movement that had failed to encapsulate most of Cuban society in the first place (Knight 1990).

It is because of the perceived divisionism of Cuba's independence movement, of the desire to transform Cuban society with its problems of rampant banditry and lawlessness, that the struggle for independence after 1878 gained an aura of social reformism, leading all the way into the island's second war of independence in 1895 (Pérez 1985). Cuba's increasingly closer relationship with the United States, especially as a result of sugar exports to that country, fulfilled the island's need for capital, technology, and markets, and it also presented the island with an alternative to the inefficient political and economic order of Spanish colonial administration. Creole elites and other social sectors who had been exposed to American society came to regard the United States as a model of order and a vision of material and social progress. Baseball became a cultural symbol of just such an imported order; a replicable activity through which people in Cuba felt themselves to be participants in "modernity." It created a new way of being Cuban, distinctively different from whatever was embodied in Spanish legacies.

Baseball was becoming very popular in the United States at this time, and some of the Victorian values of sport alluded to earlier became a part of the baseball culture, of which Cuban émigrés in the United States were an important element.[16] Thus, when Cubans brought baseball back to Cuba they brought with them not only a sport but a system of social values and rules of conduct that could impose a vision of progress and order on the chaos prevailing in Cuban society. At a time when alternative symbols were missing on the island, baseball's appeal as a seemingly democratic activity that allowed all classes and races to come together as a group made this sport a powerful instrument for creating a national community out of the amalgam of races and classes that fragmented Cuban society under the Spanish colonial administration. Because of the structure of the sugar economy, which left the summer months of *tiempo muerto* (dead time) in sugar production free for various kinds of activities, the progress in Cuban railroads and communications during the second half of the nineteenth century; and the expansion in economic ties with the United States, baseball quickly spread throughout Cuba and became a common fact of life on Sunday afternoons by the late 1880s (Pérez 1994).

Baseball embodied some of the social characteristics that were missing from Cuban society and independence struggles. For instance, it was characterized by a team ethic of working closely together and in consultation that was lacking in Cuba's decolonization movement. Baseball gave the impression of a new vision of social democracy through the ways in which teams were constituted and labeled (especially by geographical location, such as Matanzas and Cienfuegos, and by "revolutionary" symbols, such as Yara and Anacaona).[17] The sport produced a distinctive space that allowed many Cubans to find an outlet for their disaffection with Spanish colonial administration in a way that was distinctly not Spanish. These elements gave Cubans a sharper sense of place and identity in preparation for other kinds of challenges. In the Victorian sense, it became a practice through which civil and moral values of a new *patria* (fatherland) could be learned and practiced.

Spanish authorities were obviously aware of the spread of baseball throughout Cuba, but they could never point exactly to the symbolic characteristics of the game given it by Cubans. This can be explained partly by the fact that baseball, like many other sports, generates its own language and codes. While Spaniards recognized some sort of subversion in baseball, it became more difficult to suppress than other, more confrontational forms of resistance. Moreover, part of the Spanish colonial administration of the Antilles had been the notion of *baile, botella y baraja* (dance, drink, and play), which represented activities fostered by these administrations as an inexpensive, popular way of keeping people's attention away from political concerns (especially separatism). As a game, baseball potentially fit into several aspects of this rationale, and so it could divide Spanish reactions to the spread of the game. Yet the fact that it was a game derived entirely from North America made Spanish officials and residents in Cuba uneasy. This resulted in frequent petitions to the central government to have baseball clubs disbanded (Pérez 1994).

Baseball's popularity thus served as a unifying mechanism in Cuban society through which a national consensus about the virtues of what the Cuban nation should be like became a common purpose and vision. This perception proved essential to the Cuban decolonization movement, allowing it to consolidate popular support for independence and channel political opposition to Spanish colonial rule into the successful second war of independence. Beyond actual team play, it is interesting to observe that baseball games involving Cuban teams outside of Cuba became centers for the collection of funds that supported the revolutionary juntas organizing immediately before the 1895 war (Pérez 1994). Such activity demonstrates how the power of culture and play can become a vehicle for direct social and political action beyond the game itself, can transform play into an instrument of mobilization (indeed, almost converting sport, in the words of Sidney Tarrow [1994, 19], into a modular repertoire of contention).

West Indian Cricket and the Birth of Nationalist Independence Movements

Previous sections discussed how cricket became a crucial part of British colonial rule and imperialism. What still needs to be addressed is how this symbol of colonial domination became a part, in fact one of the pillars, of West Indians' repertoire of contention before independence.

The contradictions of cricket culture in the West Indies are problematic, especially when one looks at the strength with which cricket became a part of the social code of virtuous practices among a largely black population, which was excluded from playing the game at the established clubs in the first place. This characteristic was even more evident in the case of Barbados, which retained the full extent of the Victorian ethic code of cricket even after other island societies in the Caribbean had adapted the game to their social realities *after* independence. A possible explanation for this apparent contradiction has been offered by Brian Stoddart (1995) in terms of coexisting cultures in the English-speaking Caribbean: the British-originated culture, identified with the white ruling elite; and the folk culture of predominantly black populations, which retained key symbols of its origins through bush medicine, tuk band music, and community dances and festivals. The pervasiveness of cricket stems from the aspirations of a black population that sought social betterment through the channels provided by the economically dominant white elite. As a highly regarded social activity, cricket became a part of the socialization experiences of "socially ascending" blacks, especially after slave emancipation in 1838.

But precisely because of these competing cultures cricket was assimilated into the black population in a version different from its British ancestor. Socially deprived blacks adapted the tools of cricket to their "technological environment" (Beckles 1995a). Because of the theatrical elements and participatory festiveness of black rituals (which combined comedy with heroism and tragedy), the artistic and performative aspects of cricket were enhanced in the creolized version of the sport. Burton compares it to another performative festival important to West Indian culture:

> carnival is a phenomenon of the street, and it is also to the street that, in the first instance, West Indian cricket belongs . . . the values, mentalities and ways of behaving in evidence among West Indian crowds are an extension . . . of the already stylized values, mentalities, and ways of behaving characteristic of West Indian male street culture in general: expansiveness, camaraderie, unruliness, jesting, joking—verbal and bodily bravado, clowning—in a word, *playing*. . . . [T]he qualities that West Indians most prize in their cricketers are essentially "street qualities." (Burton 1995, 90)

The discriminative aspects of colonial administration, especially the dominance of a white minority, created social constraints, and potentially aggressive pressures, whose only outlet was the officially sanctioned game of cricket.[18] C. L. R. James did not have "the slightest doubt that the clash of race, caste and class did not retard but stimulated West Indian cricket. . . . [I]n those years social and political passions, denied normal outlets, expressed themselves so fiercely in cricket (and other games) precisely because they were games. . . . The class and racial rivalries were too intense. They could be fought out without violence or much lost except pride and honour. Thus the cricket field was the stage on which selected individuals played representative roles which were charged with social significance" ([1963] 1993, 66). Excellent (in fact, spectacular) performance in the game thus became recognized among socially disenfranchised West Indians as the only way of asserting their presence in colonial societies beyond their roles as workers on sugar plantations. The development of a particular West Indian style of cricket through athletes' individual accomplishments became the seed of a "national" style of the sport, which only became evident through test matches against teams from other parts of the British Empire.[19]

This was true not only of the players but, equally important, for the crowds witnessing cricket matches. Victorian etiquette for cricket spectators dictated order, seriousness, moderation, and a socially approved range of comments about players' performances and moves. For West Indian crowds watching their black players in matches against colonial elites and administrators, a new set of values and emotions dictated behavior as they observed the match. These crowds (literally, crowds, for the number of spectators at any West Indian cricket match is almost always larger than the park's capacity) not only witnessed the match; they became a part of it as they "acted out many of their frustrated emotions originating in the social experience of a colonial people" (St. Pierre 1995). Crowds became passionately identified with black cricket players, who for them represented the efforts of a subjugated people to defeat the source of their oppression. The repertoire of popular participation in cricket has been typically symbolized through acts such as cheering, booing the umpire, singing, dancing, and even throwing bottles, all the way to rioting.

Achievement in cricket became a crucial element in the "politicization" of the game, for black cricketers' excellent performance created pressures on West Indian cricket clubs to open up membership, and in fact captaincy (though not into the 1960s), to blacks, all in the name of athletic competitiveness. In this way, entrance to cricket clubs not only became a symbol of social achievement within West Indian societies, but because of regional and international matches (starting in 1900 when the first West Indies cricket team toured England) players were able to visit other territories in the Caribbean and establish social links with them. Based on recruitment from public schools modeled after those in Britain, "national" teams emerged in open, regular competitions among British territories in the Caribbean. A regional team was selected to play internationally after the intraregional matches, thus helping to create a sense of region and community throughout otherwise dispersed and isolated British colonies along the Caribbean Sea. Cricket heroes became identified with the region or island they came from, thus enhancing the sentiment of belonging that is crucial for definitions of nation and nationalism.

The crucible of national teams, local heroes, audience participation (indeed, similar to religious attendance), and international confrontation enabled cricket to create, and reformulate, a sense (an *identity*) of group solidarity and community consensus that was nonexistent in West Indian political culture. As noted by Maurice St. Pierre, "in a society desperately short of indigenous heroes, cricket provide[d] young West Indian boys with the chance to grow up with a sense of national pride by identification with the exploits of West Indian cricket 'stars'" (1995, 131). Cricket slowly transcended its role as a mediator of West Indian racial and political grievances: it assumed its role as "transubstantive symbol" and became "inherently meaningful . . . the thing to be mediated." In other words, "Cricket, as an ordinary substantive symbol, mediates and symbolically resolves certain basic conflicts within Jamaican society. It is also, however, a transubstantive symbol and acquires the quality when it ceases to mediate and canalize social conflict and instead becomes identified with such conflicts" (Patterson 1995, 141). An emerging black leadership in the 1940s West Indies thus linked three issues in their political agenda: the politics of black nationalist decolonization, a movement toward a nation-state (singular or a federation of all British West Indies colonies), and black leadership of West Indian test cricket, given the absence of such leaders among clubs (Beckles 1995b). This increasingly politicized cricket culture found its zenith in the 1950 defeat of the British team in England, where the process by which the opposing team slowly was becoming regarded as the outsider to be defeated suddenly became embodied in the political sovereign.

The full extent of the social impact of this victory cannot be understood if it is not framed within the political cleavages of those years in the West Indies. A powerful workers' union movement had been evolving in the English-speaking Caribbean since the early years of the twentieth century. The British colonial administration was slowly becoming incapable of (and to a certain extent unwilling to undertake) handling the economic and political problems plaguing the post–World War II Caribbean. A series of clumsy administrative measures to reduce colonial costs ended in the disastrous West Indies Federation of 1958, which collapsed after only four years of existence. Churches, which up to the 1930s had been "psychological havens" for the black masses (Knight 1990), thereafter became centers for grassroots organization and political mobilization around economic grievances. The victory in cricket over Britain became a powerful popular symbol of the social capabilities West Indians possessed not just as blacks, workers, or faithful, but as *nations.* These events soon led to the chain of successive political independence from Britain among the Caribbean's tiny island nations, starting with Trinidad and Jamaica in 1962.

Conclusion: Sport, Identities, Collective Action, and Decolonization

Pierre Bourdieu observed that:

> the subjective necessity and self-evidence of the commonsense world are validated by the objective consensus on the sense of the world, what is essential

> *goes without saying because it comes without saying:* the tradition is silent, not least about itself as a tradition; customary law is content to enumerate specific applications of principles which remain implicit and unformulated, because unquestioned. . . . The adherence expressed in the doxic relation to the social world is the absolute form of recognition of legitimacy through misrecognition of arbitrariness, since it is unaware of the very question of legitimacy, which arises from competition for legitimacy, and hence from conflict between groups claiming to possess it. (1994, 163)

For Caribbean societies, sport became a crucial vehicle for reformulating and creating new identities, for imagining communities where previous links had been absent, and for ascribing meaning to social practices and experiences that formerly had been devoid of concrete political articulation. In their effort to build nations and states, Caribbean societies legitimized a particular kind of knowledge, crystallized in baseball and cricket, and in the process suppressed other kinds of knowledges and practices that claimed equality in defining a vision of nation and collectivity but did not fit into the "legitimate" mold determined by the hegemonic discourse of independence. In this sense, as noted by Louis Pérez (1985), the new patterns of social relations after independence ended up in many senses replacing the colonial perspective but not its methods and practices. Racial, economic, political, and social inequalities were incorporated (oftentimes expressly, as in the case of gender discrimination) into decolonization movements and ultimately into the new forms of political organization that resulted from them. While this reflection is not intended to delegitimize the decolonization struggle of the Caribbean peoples, it is nevertheless necessary to take into consideration that these were not unilinear nor coherent processes. Many victims fell along the way, and sometimes the end result of the struggle differed little from the previous order. Perhaps other revolutions, such as Fidel Castro's in Cuba and Maurice Bishop's in Grenada, could be understood as actions necessary to break with racial, economic, and political legacies of an oppressive past.

As a final note, our understanding of how sport became a source of new identities and discursive opportunities for mobilization in the Caribbean must be placed within the context of our own expectations regarding globalizing discourses and contestation. The story of popular mobilization through baseball and cricket can be narrated as an example of counterhegemony and social movements because of events that we know, with the benefit of hindsight, happened after the formation of new identities in Cuba and the West Indies. But we should also question why we have found the source of specific repertoires of contention in sport.[20] While several characteristics of sport have been related to the formation of national independence movements—for instance, the logic of team participation and organized competition as a staging of actual confrontation between colonizers and colonized and the language of popular sport as both symbol and instrument of resistance—we must nevertheless reflect on whether there is something intrinsic about sport that generates alternative discourses of popular mobilization and builds social networks to such effects, or if sport is just a space—a valve—in these networks where grievances can be "played." For example, even in the Caribbean contemporary Puerto Rican prowess in basketball, while affording the country one of its few opportunities to assume a distinct international identity, has not generated a set of discursive repertoires for decolonization to the same extent that prowess in cricket did in the British West Indies during the first half of this century or playing baseball did for Cubans in the nineteenth century. It would thus seem that sport can be an important catalyst for contestation only in particular cases in which the lack of political institutions consigns resistance to what Nicholas Dirks calls "unconventional domains" such as rituals. In other words, sport can play an important role in contexts in which it can allow the "manipulation of values and structures" as a means of subverting a power relationship "in a political world of hegemony and struggle [where] representation itself is one of the most contested resources" (1994, 487). This specific instance in which sport can become resistance should make us cautious about the terms in which we discuss the practice of resistance itself, for such terms ironically pertain to a globalizing and hegemonic discourse that scholars might employ in ways that do not necessarily reflect the practices and the means of "resisting" but rather the ends and the results.

NOTES

I would like to thank Daniel H. Levine, Rebecca J. Scott, John A. Guidry, Mayer N. Zald, and Michael D. Kennedy for their comments and suggestions throughout various phases of this essay.

1. Quoted in Beckles and Stoddart 1995, reprinted from Edward Kamau Brathwaite, *Islands* (London, 1969), which, according to the authors, is a fundamental reading for understanding the social psychodrama of the cricket match in the West Indies.
2. Quoted in Pérez 1994.
3. See, for example, Deutsch 1961.
4. Among works that have provided challenging views on the concept and praxis of resistance, see Dirks 1994; Lüdtke 1995; and Levine 1992.
5. As will be discussed later, it should be noted that the case of Cuba differs somewhat from that of the West Indies in this respect. For the most part Cubans had an idea of "nation," but it was not a coherent or generalized one. It seems sometimes as if Cubans defined the limits of the Cuban nation as that which was not Spanish, which could mean independence but could also mean annexation to the United States. As an American sport, baseball's influence on Cuban society simultaneously generated and changed some of these perceptions. In the West Indies, however, the case was one of the classic colonial syndrome, wherein the islands recognized themselves as different from Britain, but did not conceive of those differences as sufficient grounds for legitimizing a sovereign status. Difference, however, must be qualified by class, gender, and race, which themselves enhance the sentiment of fragmentation that only cricket could overcome.

6. On the history of the social and political development of the West Indies around the labor movement, see Lewis 1968.

7. In fact, these changes reduce the possibility of any group seizing political opportunities for collective action in the sense Tarrow discusses in his theory. Tarrow defines the structure of political opportunities as the "consistent—but not necessarily formal or permanent—dimensions of the political environment that provide incentives for people to undertake collective action by affecting their expectations for success or failure" (1994, 85). If states change the most fundamental dimension of the political environment—their links with society, from corporatism to clientelism, for instance—the ability of different groups to perceive their opportunities for becoming successful by taking advantage of resources and opportunities is significantly reduced, for there is no stability in the institutional structure from which these resources can emerge in the first place. In fact, based on Charles Tilly's definition, this could be considered an indirect, very expensive form of repression. It should also be noted that this type of state behavior is also consistent with North's characterization of the state as a discriminating monopolizer.

8. It should be quite interesting to compare these two notions of nation—one, the decolonization movement attempting to build a sense of nation as the bridge uniting collective experiences under colonial rule; the other, a state creating "national" social linkages by enacting policies and extracting resources over a territorially defined area (thus becoming a national state). It can be said that in the former a state was already in place (to the extent that it was capable of extracting resources from the population) but it was not a national state (to the extent that those extracted resources ended up in the hands of outsiders), while in the latter a political hierarchy existed before the national state, but it had no binding value for different social segments because it lacked the legitimacy and the capability to build bridges among different groups in order to extract resources from its claimed constituency.

9. This is not to say that in totalitarian states such preconditions do not have to be created as well. For the purpose of our discussion, the difference between colonial states and totalitarian ones lies in the level of political development, thus in the forms of social mobilization that are within reach of these societies. The type of organization that can result from a totalitarian state, where a sovereign, national state with links to a social structure have reached a particular level of development, is much more advanced than the one that can result from colonial administrations for which political organization is a functional response to the demands for extraction of profits from the colonial territory. Any type of endogenous social links in colonial societies would be anathema to the goals of the political system and the ruling elite.

10. The importance of sport for quiescing potentially disruptive masses was not unique to colonial empires. For instance, in his reflection on the role of baseball in early-twentieth-century American society, Alen Sangree noted in 1907 that "the fundamental reason for the popularity of the game is the fact that it is a national safety valve. Voltaire says that there are no real pleasures without real needs. Now a young, ambitious nation needs to 'let off steam.' Baseball furnishes the opportunity. Therefore, it is a real pleasure. . . . That is what baseball does for humanity. It serves the same purpose as a revolution in Central America or a thunderstorm on a hot day. . . . A tonic, an exercise, a safety valve, baseball is second only to Death as a leveler. So long as it remains our national game, America will abide no monarchy, and anarchy will be too slow" (quoted in Okrent and Lewine 1991).

11. See note 3.

12. For an example of late-nineteenth-century Cuban popular attitudes about the virtuosity of baseball, see the epigraphs at the beginning of this chapter.

13. Hobsbawm's observation about the sexist character of sport practice (not in the

sense of viewing the event) has some very interesting varieties, and possible exceptions, in the Caribbean. In Cuba, baseball was actually lauded as a public sport that could be witnessed by women. According to Louis Pérez, this ennobled baseball in the eyes of Cuban society, and it also made women participants in a part of local social life that was slowly becoming perceived by everyone as distinctly Cuban (as opposed to Spanish) (1994, 507). In the West Indies, the gendered nature of cricket came to be regarded as a natural extension of the plantation society of workers, owners, and managers. While cricket was openly discouraged as an inadequate activity for women (especially by the cricket clubs), it was black women who, through claims about democratic life and practices, challenged men's clubs through their own organized cricket. This situation is also evidence of the potent impact of cricket as a symbol, and often embodiment, of political life and of the social system in the West Indies.

14. In this sense, the importance of symbols and practices in the matches themselves—everything from chants, cheers, and athletic styles to more formal ones such as anthems and flags—for consolidating a "national" community must also be underscored. The incorporation of national symbols for political purposes in sporting activities has been analyzed in the cases of Nazi Germany, the Soviet Union, and authoritarian Argentina (see Krüger 1996; Mason 1995). In the absence of such symbols among colonial masses, the case of athletic style—for instance, characteristic or extraordinary moves by a particular player—became an important element in the popularity of cricket in the British West Indies. As will be discussed later in the chapter, such unique styles were in fact one of the most open manifestations of resistance (by both the athlete and the crowds that cheered him) to colonial rules as embodied in the "code" of cricket.

15. It is here, also, that one could make the distinction between sport and *national* sport. For instance, when looking at the United States it is somewhat difficult to pinpoint which is the national sport. In terms of tradition, it could be baseball; in terms of audiences and "rites of passage" for young males, it could be football. Perhaps the difference might lie in this capability of the national sport to organize a wide variety of collectivities into a single "cultural" system, for becoming a channel through which other social symbols of political life (like national pride, honor, etc.) can be articulated in concrete circumstances. The case of soccer in Brazil and Argentina is representative of this claim.

16. See Kirsch 1989 for interesting discussions about the emergence and consolidation of baseball in the United States through the incorporation of Victorian values.

17. Yara is the name of the proclamation of colonial rebellion that initiated the Ten Years' War. Anacaona is the name of a Taina Indian princess who died while fighting Spanish colonization in the fifteenth century.

18. Indeed, as noted by L. O'Brien Thompson (1995), changes in the history of West Indian cricket were often the reflection of social disturbances and conflicts among the general colonial population. For example, in the late 1930s spectators from the lower classes were first allowed into the cricket parks, where "official" clubs played, only after the masses revolted, with the support of the nonwhite middle class, against the colonial system.

19. A similar point regarding this nationalistic element of cricket culture among former British colonies is raised in Appadurai 1996.

20. I thank the editors of this volume for bringing this point to my consideration.

CHAPTER 11

Social Memory as Collective Action: The Crimean Tatar National Movement

Greta Uehling

Memory, as transmitted through folk songs, epic poems, and oral traditions has the power to destroy empires, as water has the strength to crack stones.
—Vladimir Dedijer

Relying primarily on documents and statistics, and working without the benefits of field research, many Soviet area specialists have left relatively unexamined the stories, songs, jokes, and performances that formed a rich oral tradition and fed counterhistories even before the collapse of the Soviet Union.[1] Control over the writing of history—and its interpretation—was not as effective as totalitarian models would suggest. Sovietologists have therefore typically overestimated the number of "blank pages" created by Soviet authorities' eclipsing of non-Russian history. The more quotidian aspects of resistance such as memory and the family were until very recently consistently underanalyzed. This is unfortunate because the results of such studies could have begun to fill a noted gap in the literature on social movements. Scholarship on social movements suggests that collective processes of interpretation provide a link between changes in political opportunities and mobilizing organizations. As Zald observes, however, the literature on culture and framing in social movements has been relatively vague (1996). This chapter attempts to bring greater conceptual clarity to the process of cultural framing through an ethnographic exploration of the memories and stories animating the Crimean Tatar National Movement.

Exploring this movement is not just a means by which to fill the "culture" lacuna in social movement research or provide data from a movement outside the West, although it may do both of these things. The central contention is rather that a productive trajectory for social movement theory is to see remembering as a form of collective action. This may seem like an equally amorphous approach because, to the extent that memory is part of thought, there is no means to directly observe it in operation. However, we do have access to the ways in which a society remembers through language and behavior. The physical, noncognitive aspects of memory may also be considered. In a social constructivist approach, memory gains meaning not in the mind or as a text but through usage. Viewing remembering as collective action is a fruitful path of investigation because it has concrete spatial referents and effects we can measure: in the Tatar case, the results are seen in their return migration and resulting demographic distribution across the post-Soviet landscape as well as the strong sense of collective identity that develops out of the practice of collectively remembering and commemorating the past.

The end of Communist rule was accompanied by a striking growth of national movements. Many were surprised because Marxist-Leninist ideas about the decrease of ethnic tension in socialist states did not materialize. Others held to modernization theories that suggest the importance of ethnic identity declines in modern developed societies. But the proliferation of national movements should not be surprising considering that one feature of the Communist system was to progressively eliminate sources of affiliation other than ethnicity, effectively channeling identification and resistance to the state along ethnic and national lines. As a result, nationalism has become a standardized method for gaining a political voice. In this sense, it is a global strategy having less to do with essentialized ethnic identities than maneuvering in the world capitalist system of nation-states or what has been referred to as the national order of things (Malkki 1992, 1995).

Like other national movements, the Crimean Tatar National Movement draws on an international discourse of human rights, including the UN designation of "indigenous people" and the rights that should be accorded to them.[2] Yet the Crimean Tatar movement stands out among movements in the former Soviet Union, having arisen long before glasnost and perestroika and continuing to this day. It represents a more uninterrupted effort in contrast to movements that have a short-term nature. The Crimean Tatar movement is also different because it has taken a pro-state or pro-Kiev position regardless of Kiev's stance toward movement. As one angle in a power triangle between Russia and Ukraine, the leadership has identified the interests of the national movement with the interests of the Ukrainian state, speaking against demands for independence from Ukraine made by Russian separatists. The Crimean Tatar National Movement is also distinguished by the strategies it has adopted, which will be discussed in this chapter: self-immolation and squatting. What drives this strategizing and accounts for both its meaning and success is social memory. In this respect, the Crimean Tatar National Movement vividly demonstrates the importance of cultural framing for social movements. Social memory is important to the movement because without it the young Tatars born in exile who are adamant about returning would not have the political consciousness, the will, or the desire to return. They would not give up relatively comfortable and secure lives in Central Asia to return to their parents' birthplace believing it to be the place where they, too, must live. The group (and their movement) are transnational in character but the social practice of memory serves to ground or reterritorialize the Crimean Tatars, who were forcibly deterritorialized.[3] The return migration takes on a sense of urgency as Tatars reestablish broken ties in Crimea. Through memory, the transnational movement localizes Tatars in Crimea by supplying the rationale that this is the place where they belong.

Since 1988, the Crimean Tatar National Movement has facilitated the mass migration of over 250,000 Crimean Tatars from settlements in Central Asia to the Crimean Peninsula (Forced Migration Projects 1996). This has taken place in spite of the fact that Tatars have received only minimal support from organizations like Ukrainian Popular Movement in Support of Perestroika (RUKH). Resistance to their resettlement has been so extreme that faced with opposition Tatars have resorted to squatting on land, which has brought them into violent confrontation with police, local authorities, and the Mafia. As social movement theory suggests, repertoires of contention are "modular" in the sense that a limited set of routines is learned, shared, and enacted. Tatars have been able to legitimize their action in the city mayor's office, or *gorispolkom,* by learning to make claims that it was their ancestors' home or land before they were deported. It is this instrumental use of memory that illustrates the sense in which social memory is a means of collective action. In the post-Soviet context, remembering the past is a form symbolic capital that can be converted into economic capital: land claims and requests for aid.

Social Memory

The social memory referred to in this chapter is somewhat different from Halbwachs's ([1941] 1992) "collective memory" because it is not based on a mystical notion of *conscious collective,* nor is it grounded in the Durkheimian tradition. While my approach departs from Halbwachs's in a number of ways, his work does have tremendous significance for the Tatar case because, even before the politics of memory came to occupy the center of attention in much current theorizing, Halbwachs pointed out that we are constantly reinventing the past in living memories and they are therefore highly unreliable for understanding what actually happened.[4] He was progressive for his time in recognizing, before *The Invention of Tradition,* that collective memory is continually revised to suit present purposes (Hobsbawm and Ranger 1983). However, by examining the persistence of social and power differentials *within* societies and their implication for what is remembered and forgotten, I will be extending this in a different direction than that of Halbwachs, who suggested that "society can live only if there is a sufficient unity of outlooks among the individuals and groups comprising it" (82).[5]

The relevance of memory to cultural framing is immediately apparent in Halbwachs's work: "[I]t is in society that people normally acquire their memories. It is also in society that they recall, recognize and localize their memories" ([1941] 1992, 40). What is remembered of experience is a reduction of particular memories into an idealized image. Such composite memories provide the conceptual schemes, or as Halbwachs puts it, the "social frameworks" in which individual memories come to be located (Hutton 1993, 7). However, we must stop short of Halbwachs's assertion that what follows is that individual memory is *bound* to conform to the model that the structure of collective memory provides. If this were the case, social movements would not take place, nor would we witness what could be metaphorically described as the "bending" or alteration of cultural frames. Crimean Tatars who were framed in the former Soviet Union as evil descendants of Chingis Khan and the Golden Horde are now seen as preserving social order.

What we mean when we talk about memory is continuously changing and therefore must be historically contextualized. Boyarin suggests that right now a good operative definition is "rhetoric about the past mobilized for political purposes" (1994, 2). This aspect of memory is connected to its role in the consolidation of group, community, and national identities. As Passerini suggests, testimonies are above all declarations of cultural identity in which memory steadfastly adapts received traditions to present circumstances (1987, 17). Memory is felt to be a site of struggle, a fluid ideological terrain where differences in power are played out. What has been less explored, as Swedenburg points out, is memory's *transnational* dimension. He argues that the Palestinian situation shows that we must think of memory as "a multidimensional, displaced, and local-global construction" (1995, xxix). Because they are a people in a diaspora, Tatar remembrance of the past affords just such an opportunity for exploring the transnational dimension of memory.[6]

Background

The national movement was precipitated by a forced deportation ordered in 1944 by Stalin. In the early dawn on May 18, just days after Soviet forces had liberated Crimea from Nazi occupation, the Crimean Tatars were deported en masse to the Ural Mountains and Soviet Central Asia. Those who were not interned in forced labor camps spent the ensuing years under a "special settlement" system that forbade them from leaving prescribed areas. Until 1956, it was necessary to check in with a commander on a monthly basis, and the punishment for violating the rules was imprisonment. In 1967, the Central Committee of the Communist Party issued a document rehabilitating the Tatars for allegedly having collaborated with the Nazis, but this "rehabilitation" represented a change in the rhetoric of the Soviet state, not its policies. Only in the context of glasnost and perestroika were Tatars successful in returning on a massive scale. To date, it is estimated that more than 260,000 have returned, and perhaps as many remain in Central Asia (Forced Migration Projects 1996, 8).

Scholars of other attempted exterminations such as the Holocaust tell us that such oppressive social conditions can effectively silence survivors.[7] For example, Greenspan suggests that survivors' experiences are fundamentally untellable (1992, 13). Felman and Laub (1992) tell of the destruction of the witness and the resulting silences that are created. Yet Crimean Tatars have constructed a narrative about deportation that has been consistently told and retold until the descendants of survivors know the story "like five fingers" or, as some informants put it, *better* than those who experienced it. Why haven't the painful memories been effaced as in the case of Argentina (Parelli 1994) or Japan (Yoneyama 1994)? My Tatar companion Nizami said "for the Soviet people, the thirties, the forties, the fifties—are *history.* For Crimean Tatars they are *now.* And in those villages where Tatars were killed they are *still* crying, still remembering. They live history." This aspect of the social construction of the past cannot be emphasized enough because it conveys how Tatars conceive of past events as being truly effective in the present—in other words, not really past. What matters for the exploration of the Tatar case is not whether particular memories are historically accurate but how Tatars construe *their own* memories. Situating Tatars in relation to their own traditions and asking how they interpret their past will yield more insight into cultural frames of reference than questioning the truth or historical validity of particular narratives of the past.

All across Eastern Europe and the former Soviet Union, history is being rewritten because, as Fanon so eloquently put it, "Colonization is not satisfied merely with holding people in its grip and emptying the native's brain of all form and content. By a kind of perverted logic, it turns to the past of oppressed people, and distorts, disfigures and destroys it" (1963, 170). In the Soviet case, the Communist regime attempted to erase the Tatar past in a massive project of human engineering. After the entire population was deported, place names were immediately changed from Tatar to Russian. Then Russians and Ukrainians were relocated to make Tatar homes their own. Nothing about the deportation was reported in the press. The vast majority of material printed in the Crimean Tatar language, even classics like the works of Marx and Lenin, were burned, as were books in Russian with anything but a select view of the past.[8] Tatars in exile who expressed interest in their history had their manuscripts confiscated and were sometimes executed (Allworth 1988; Fisher 1978). As a final means of erasure, cemeteries were plowed under and gravestones were used as construction material.

In addition to state-managed forgetting, there was a consistent misrepresentation of Tatars as "traitors who had sold the motherland" and invaders. These labels are used even today, such as in 1995 when a Tatar artist who accompanied me to the Pushkin Museum presented his artists' union card to gain admission and was rebuffed with epithets of "traitor" and "invader." Misrepresentation and falsification also involve Soviet texts. A 1951 history book edited by Nadinskii deployed typically ethnocentric rhetoric to claim that Tatars have a parasitic life-style. He said that the Crimean Tatars were "accustomed to living on profits gained from plundering raids, have worked at productive labor little themselves, and unwillingly" (Nadinskii, quoted in Alexeyeva 1988, 53). The passion with which Tatars relate to their past is demonstrated by an informant who told me that he would show me a book in which Crimean Tatar history was blatantly falsified, but instead he shredded it and threw it in the trash after reading it. In addition to slanting history to serve its needs, the state can manipulate memory. If memories become collective not in the mind or the text but through usage, and if remembering certain pasts such as that of the Tatars is a punishable offense, the construction of social memory may be thwarted. Watson (1994) suggests that in socialist societies attempts are made to "privatize" memory and in so doing obliterate social memories. Without an opportunity to propagate memories, there is little chance of converting them into alternative histories.

Oral communication through stories, testimony, reminiscences, and artistic performances becomes especially important in socialist societies in which official history is automatically suspect and personal memory is more readily accepted as truth (Nora 1989). In pluralist systems such as the United States, history is seen as *more* trustworthy than personal memories, but the reverse prevailed under state socialism. Jones (1994) has argued that the intensity of memory politics under state socialism actually serves to keep the past very much alive, suggesting the use of personal memory or national narratives as forms of opposition has a strong correlation with socialist-type systems. When the official means of conveying the past are obviously manipulated, individual memories in particular gain added importance as a source of national history. Individuals anchor opposition to the Soviet regime in personal memories. But can we read this remembering as a form of resistance? Can we celebrate this memory as heroic? In *The Book of Laughter and Forgetting,* Milan Kundera writes, "The struggle of man against power is the struggle of memory against forgetting" (1981, 3). As in Kundera's novel, Tatars who kept letters, documents of historical relevance, or wrote memoirs took enormous risks. Kundera's book has become paradigmatic of the ideal of resistance through memory in the literature about memory and postsocialist states (Eschenbade 1995).

The life of Mustafa Jemilev, a leader of the Crimean Tatar National Movement, demonstrates how resistance is mobilized from memories. He was seven months old at the time of deportation, and, while he has no personal recollection of the deportation, he listened to countless stories from earliest childhood. These were not legends or epics but the testimonies of people who experienced the deportation. This was clearly a formative experience because after hearing the oral testimonies Jemilev spent time in the Tashkent public library trying to find an explanation for the deportation. His contact with the Tatar oral tradition was the first step on a path that ultimately led him to endure multiple prison sentences and become the leader of the national movement.

When Amza Imirov, another activist of the movement, was asked how he knew so much history, he replied that on one level he and his compatriots felt compelled to find out why they had been deported. On another level, it was necessary to beat the Soviet regime at its own game. The movement adopted a nonviolent orientation and attempted to point out how the regime had violated its own Marxist-Leninist principles about nationality. Ironically, the globalized and totalizing discourse of Marxism-Leninism was used as a weapon against the Soviet state.

Jemilev was successful in producing a counterhistory that earned him the accolades of contemporaries, but it also led to searches of his house, seizure of manuscripts, and imprisonment. The salience of alternative or counterhistories is emphasized in his story:

> For young people who had always read about their ancestors in the official literature as if about some kinds of barbarians and betrayers who were always being vanquished by the heroic Russians, it was of course pleasant to hear the news that the glorious Russian Czar Petr I was soundly beaten in 1711 at the river Prut by the Turkic-Tatar forces, that the Crimean Tatars had put things in order in Moscow more than once, and that the Crimean Tatars had institutions of higher learning already a millennia ago. (Jemilev, quoted in Alexeyeva 1988, 57)

Alexeyeva points out that "judging from the motifs Mustafa put forth in his lecture, he did no injustice to the truth, but he nonetheless concentrated attention on events that were flattering to the Crimean Tatars' sense of national pride. And in the end any evidence sufficed: both the creation of institutions of higher learning before the Russians, and the successful attacks on Moscow, which an objective historian would be loath to call a 'putting in order'" gave moral weight to the movement (57).

The difficulty with raising personal memory and national counternarratives to the level of the heroic is that, like the state, individuals suppress some memories and gloss over others. Individual constructions of the past are notoriously prone to slippage and omissions (Casey 1987). Perhaps even more relevant for this analysis, individuals' reiteration of the past within the framework of their *national* history can present an overly unified picture. We might wonder if in the midst of this heroic remembering there are not other, more subtle hegemonies at work. Jemilev, the politician whose interpretations of history are taken as authoritative, is included here. National traditions *need* a version of the past as a constitutive element of their identities. In fact, some form of discourse about the past is a prerequisite for a national project and memory can provide source material for that discourse. The Tatars who took the risk of collecting and recording their society's remembrances now treat their personal archives as a nest egg for the national future.

Because Halbwachs ([1941] 1992) believed that history begins where collective memory leaves off, he never considered some of the interconnections between the two. As Hutton points out, Halbwachs failed to recognize the full implications of what he had discovered about memory. He never considered history as a kind of official memory, a representation of the past that must acquire legitimacy (1993). History may record, dramatize, and order its material in a way that collective memory or oral histories do not. However, there are interesting connections, and if we were less interested in the differences between memory and history perhaps we would not be taken by surprise when the uses of personal memory are as inflected with power relations as the writing of history itself.

Domination, Resistance, and Other Misleading Dualisms

If, like Foucault, we build on Nietzsche's idea that heritage is "not an acquisition, a possession that grows and solidifies; rather, it is an assemblage of faults, fissures and heterogeneous layers . . . " (Foucault 1977b, 146) then we gain a different perspective on the social construction of personal narratives and national histories. This is a perspective that does not seek to restore an unbroken continuity. A view of memory as struggle or *resistance* valorizes a precarious human practice, but this is misleading because, as Abu-Lughod (1990) has suggested, those who "resist" often become entangled in relations of power that result in other, less obvious forms of domination. Memory is instrumental in social movements but too readily conflated with resistance: remembering is better understood as a practice or a social skill (Fentress and Wickham 1992). Like other social skills, it is exercised in various styles that can be investigated.

Jemilev's counterhistory is more accurately viewed as situated knowledge than resistance. It is not transcendent knowledge but partial, positioned, and therefore more responsible for a particular vision of the world. Otherwise, having "heroized" these practices of remembering and representing, we are disappointed when individual oral histories and national projects turn out to be fallible or hegemonic. In the past, Jemilev was charged with selecting students to participate in Tatar educational programs in a prejudicial manner. Some Crimean newspapers suggest he has become involved in the burgeoning Mafia himself, and he has been charged with mismanagement of humanitarian funds. This has prompted a special congress, or *Kuraltai,* and election to decide the fate of his position as representative of the Crimean Tatar political body, or, *Mejlis.*[9] Haraway's insistence that the standpoints of the subjugated are not innocent positions seems to be confirmed here (1988, 546). Recognizing all viewpoints as contingent enables us to avoid overromanticizing resistance. Romanticizing resistance, particularly seeing individual and national memory as resistance to the state, only obscures recognition of the contingent nature of all knowledge. The difficulty, as Haraway puts it, is how to have an account of the historical contingency of all knowledge claims (including our own) while maintaining a commitment to attempt to recount the "real" world, which can be at least partially shared (592).

The original dualism of domination and resistance has been refined to examine less institutionalized and more pervasive forms of both power and resistance. But I share Ortner's basic position, and the position taken in the introduction to this volume, that the dualism is falsely oppositional and that within a particular setting both terms must be simultaneously true (1992, 6). Crimean Tatar resistance involves a form of domination, just as the centralized power of the Soviet state proved to be not just capable of domination but vulnerable itself. The problem with dualist theorizing, Ortner suggests, is that it demands purity rather than recognizing how resistance is always part of larger social processes with their own complexities and contradictions (8). Another dualism that emerges in the literature on resistance is that between discourse and event or discourse and reality. Dirks provides a sophisticated analysis of resistance in ritual. However, he sees a site of struggle "between discourse and event, between what could be said and what could be done" (1994, 494). This, too, is an unhelpful dualism. Central to my contention that the practice of remembering constitutes a form of collective action is a belief that *what can be said is part of what can be done.* This cannot be overemphasized, for if one thing is learned from the Crimean Tatar National Movement it should be that the practice of social memory can become a form of collective action.

Social Memory and Collective Action

If we reject resistance as a useful concept for identifying the basis of national projects, what sorts of micropractices might constitute collectives? What sorts of microprocesses coalesce into movements? The following narratives illustrate how the remembrance of, and longing for, homeland that informs the movement is not a priori but socially constructed. The notion of "homeland" is a social construction that is connected to place both as a concept and as a physical experience. An informant I will call Nulifar returned to the peninsula for a vacation, having no idea that her memories would be so overwhelming. For Nulifar, the desire to return to the Crimea was not a preoccupation dating from childhood but something that evolved in connection with the circumstances and opportunities in her life. The return becomes imaginable only *after* she visits Crimea to show it to her daughters.

> You know, I always knew that I was *from* here. But when I lived there in the North, I still hadn't imagined. But after we had already left there, and came to Tashkent [pause] and moved here and there, I started to get the idea. Then I got the kids together, and we all came. When we came, I couldn't enter the house at first. It was so very difficult for me. After all, I understood that it was *here* that my mother lay. But when we came that [first] year . . . as we had left the house, everything remained as it was. Everything was there. Everything. Where mother lay, the bed—my mother had been confined for a long time—in a different spot there was a couch. Everything. What was on the floor, everything was lying there completely. I entered [head motioning] like that into the doorway but I couldn't go in. You see, I didn't have the strength. I

> started to cry. She said "come on in come on in," but how could I go in? After all, I was seven years old in that house. I had seen everything at my parents' house. Everything came up before my eyes, and I remembered everything.

Nulifar's statement illustrates that, rather than being a purely cognitive phenomena, there are also types of remembering that are sensory and linked specifically to physical place. Before arriving in Crimea, Nulifar wanted only to show her daughters where she had once lived. She did not anticipate how painful the experience would be—or how formative in her daughter's lives. Casey (1987) argues that memories are "selective" for place because they gravitate to place as a point of reference: place provides a context in which memories can unfold.

Halbwachs's thinking is germane to this because collective memory, he argued, is bound up with the problem of localization. In remembering, he suggests, we localize images of the past in specific places. The images produced in remembering have no clear or coherent meaning until they are projected into a concrete setting (1935). Setting provides us with our places of memory. This raises a question as to whether a transnational practice of memory is possible. In the Tatar case, the narrative framework and the stories are strikingly uniform across the republics of Ukraine and Uzbekistan, as well as the diaspora in the United States. Their social memory appears to be transnational but the specific forms of mobilization that it gives rise to are local. The practice of remembering ultimately serves to emotionally attach or "reterritorialize" Crimean Tatars in their ancestors' birthplace.

Nulifar's daughter Jemila brought up the *same* event in a separate interview in her home outside Simferopol of her own accord. She was born in the diaspora and reports a relatively secure and happy life in Sukhumi, where she worked as a piano teacher. How can she and countless others born in the diaspora be willing to "return" at any cost? Again, social memory is the foundation of mobilization. Jemila recalls the first time she came to Crimea:

> Well, you see, we came—Mama brought us. We came for vacation, and we needed to stay somewhere. We went to her village, Kokoz. To show us her Crimea. She even showed us . . . the cemetery where my grandmother . . . [beginning to cry]. When she went into the room, the curtains were still hanging and the *same* furniture was there as when she lived there. She started to cry and grabbed onto that table and started to sob. Mama! [crying]. We were little, and we grabbed onto mother and *also* started to cry. Because when we were little she told us her mother died on that very couch there. When her mother died [pause] they were getting ready to have the funeral and on the very same day they deported everyone. Everything got turned around.
>
> Mother said the furniture was sitting in the same place. It was all right there. When we were children, you see there was no way for us to understand the

> way we do now. Now we understand how it was *so hard* for our mother to see how [her] things were sitting there and the curtains were still in the window. She grabbed on and started to just *cry.*

After the interview, Jemila reiterated that she and her sisters empathized with their mother, but it was only later in life, after she had experienced personal losses of her own, that her mother's history and events of the Tatar past began to take on greater significance in her life.

Young Tatars like Jemila return because their parents' memories have become layered with their own. Still, young Tatars returning to the peninsula have their *own* representations and interpretations of past events and their current predicament. Steedman argues this point convincingly through a metaphor that resonates with Tatar place memory. She writes that the "point" does not lie in the past but in interpretation: "The past is reused through the agency of social information, and that interpretation of it can only be made with what people know of a social world and their place within it" (1994, 5). She suggests that we have to reject the received view that transmission of family patterns results from passive acceptance. It is only through interpretation that a landscape becomes historical: "[W]orked upon and reinterpreted, the landscape becomes a historical landscape, but only through continual and active reworking" (98).

Steedman's emphasis on interpretation dovetails with Foucault's notion that a genealogical method would record not events but a history of interpretations: "Genealogy does not oppose itself to history . . . it rejects the metahistorical deployment of ideal significations and indefinite teleologies. It opposes itself to the search for origins" (1984, 77). The genealogical notion of "effective" history as a history of interpretations frees us to accept gaps as part of history and part of memory. Paying attention to interpretations, and paying attention to the way that "knowledge was made for cutting" (88) brings the agentive aspect of collective memory back into focus and precludes us from becoming preoccupied with questions of accuracy.

Mobilization through Discourse: Homeland or Death

In the introduction to a volume that has become a touchstone for countless studies of the nation, Hobsbawm writes, "'traditions' which appear or claim to be old are often quite recent in origin and sometimes invented" (1983, 1). This concept has analytic utility for identifying the socially constructed aspect of the nation. But, as many have noted, it falls short on the grounds that *all* tradition is invented. And to say that all tradition is invented is still to assume a choice between invention and authenticity or discourse and "reality." In Hobsbawm's presentation, the distinction between authentic customs or traditions and make-believe is not clear. Much subsequent scholarship has therefore devoted itself to discerning the differences between them.

Rather than become entangled in the conundrum of whether the remembering that groups do is accurate recollection or retrospective reconstruction (and hence something artificial, a fabrication), it is more productive to focus on the tension between them, for memory is both. Similarly, demonstrating that tradition is invented as opposed to something originary or authentic misses the most productive site of investigation. We need to keep the past and the present, the way things are often prefigured yet constantly invented, in focus simultaneously. As Williams argues, "what we have to see is not just 'a tradition' but a selective tradition: an intentionally selective version of a shaping past and a preshaped present, which is then powerfully operative in the process of social and cultural definition and identification" (1994, 600). This is particularly useful to keep in mind in understanding the Crimean Tatar National Movement because it points to the way that the past shapes and is operative in the present, *at the same time* that remembering has a creative and imaginative component.

If there is agency in interpretation, can it be a source of social change? If memory is a shared and intergenerational activity, can we proceed to look for efficacy? A considerable amount of thinking points in this direction: "Spatial and temporal practices are never neutral in social affairs. They always express some kind of class or other social content, and are more often than not the focus of intense social struggle. . . . And from time to time these individual resistances can coalesce into social movements with the aim of liberating space and time from their current materialization (Harvey 1989, 238–39). Harvey amplifies the idea that representations of the past and sense of place are inherently controversial. In other words, peoples' interpretations of whose homeland is whose, who belongs in a given place and who does not, rarely concur. Tatars returning to the peninsula not only give up relatively secure positions in Central Asia, but they also face opposition when they arrive in Crimea. This affords an opportunity to observe how the proliferation of nationalist discourses all over the world are localized in concrete struggles over specific places.

We can understand battles over space as developing into battles over memory (Yoneyama 1994). This provides us with a way to think about attachment to place without relying on essentializing tropes of nationalism or insisting on a one-to-one, primordial correspondence between people, polity, and territory. Rather than relying on the ubiquitous metaphor of an identity that is so essential as to course through our veins like blood (Parelli 1994), we can focus instead on the ways in which memory is contentious. One reason why young Tatars carry their parents' memories with them is that these memories have become a symbolic resource in the chaos of economic restructuring. What is remembered or forgotten has less to do with an "inner" memory and more to do with cultural practices of remembering. If memory is sustained by social contexts, it is more accurate to think of it as something that is performed as a participant in a particular culture. The price of forgetting is not just linkage to previous generations but a stake in what is otherwise a very precarious future. The memories of the past that young Tatars make their own are a major part of what makes them who they are. But more is at stake here than identity itself because it is out of their interpretations of their parents' memories that they undertake squatting and self-immolation. When squatting brings them into confrontation with other contenders for the same land, it is parents' memories of who lived where that constitute symbolic ammunition and justify action.

To a certain extent, the Tatars who return "replay" the central event in their parents' narratives by placing themselves in a position to be evicted by the authorities. Just as their parents were evicted in 1944, Tatars returning to squat on land in Crimea (until very recently) were immediately deported. I am not suggesting a complete homology, for there are important differences. However, scholars of the Holocaust (Bammer 1994; Bar-On and Gilad 1994) have shown that children of survivors often try to live out parents' interrupted lives. In the case of the Crimean Tatars, they have done this, but most importantly they have *changed the ending* to success. Parents' memories create a cultural frame or schema that Tatars of the postwar generation bring with them when "returning" to Crimea. This cultural framing helps inspire the squatting or taking over of land as well as the all or nothing attitude that instigates self-immolation and characterizes the movement in recent years.

The case of an informant I will call Zaria demonstrates how young Tatars are willing to go as far as to risk death in order to return to their national homeland. I asked her what homeland is, and she replied that her daughter asks her the same question, pointing out that she was born in Central Asia. Zaria replies that "homeland is homeland. After all, you can also have a baby in an airplane, but that airplane is not your homeland. That's what I suggest." Zaria had to defend this notion at gunpoint when the authorities attempted to evict her:

> If they had opened fire that day, I would have said "go ahead and shoot." And the children were crying. Thinking, remembering right now I feel so . . . it's so hard. I shouted . . . "Go ahead and shoot, but we aren't leaving this place." That's the way that we stood there. They shouted at us the day OMON[10] came with semiautomatics. The Russian neighbors stood around and listened, but none of them came.

The rest of Zaria's story also dramatizes the contentiousness of former state property within the Newly Independent States. After beginning to squat, Zaria spent months raking the trash out of the dwelling, plastering, replacing ripped out light fixtures, and painting. Still, the owners who had abandoned the property to move into a new apartment building demanded payment:

> They say "so pay whatever price we say for it if you have supposedly relocated to your homeland." But what is there to give money for? It's not really

> a house. It was basically a pig sty. All the more considering I am a single mother with two children, no husband, and an invalid mother. The house would have stood empty one hundred years, probably. What am I supposed to do? Watch while it falls into ruins? My mother would never allow for my grandfather's house to stand empty and be ruined like that. I myself would never let that happen.

These interchanges, while highly contentious, are not without moments of painful, if humorous, reflection:

> Yes, I left everything there [in Central Asia]. I lived well there and gave everything up to move here. It was so hard for me. I got up every morning and cried. It was terrible. It was WORSE than a pig sty. But the new wife [of the legal owner] cried "I want to keep a cow there!" She wants to keep a cow there while she herself lives in an apartment with all the conveniences. I said "I won't give up my grandfather's house for you to keep a cow!"

The Tatar past is transmitted to successive generations in the form of narratives about homeland. As an informant, Fatma, encapsulated it:

> Homeland—it's our ancestors, first of all, it's our whole life, it's our elders, our parents, it's our soul, our blood, our bread, I'm telling you. For us, homeland is bread, water. Where we lived before? They said "go to your homeland." On account of homeland, we are already ready for anything. We're ready for death—for anything. If only to live in our homeland.

Zaria, Jemila, and Fatma's internalization of parents' memories and sentiments about homeland demonstrates the intensity of their connection to Crimean Tatar identity—otherwise, they would remain unmoved, both literally and figuratively. Moreover, the past makes sense as symbolic capital when the deployment of historical memories results in the acquisition of land, as the following discussion demonstrates.

The Cybernetics of a Movement and Repertoires of Contention

Squatting or land "captures" seem to appear on the post-Soviet scene from nowhere. As Guha (1994) points out in considering peasant rebellions, there is a tendency to naturalize movements as something primal and unpremeditated. But this actually amounts to remaining blind to agency in the subaltern by chalking it up to passion. Also, some of the literature on social movements places a great deal of emphasis on the political opportunity structure for the emergence of movements.

Crimean Tatars had their own story to tell about the movement. This is not the story that generally emerges in the popular press, which suggests that approximately 250,000 people who have been waiting quietly in Central Asia for the past fifty years have suddenly flocked to the Crimean Peninsula as part of the fallout of the Soviet collapse. The received view also suggests that the mass migration is occurring as part of the process of ethnic sorting. There may be tension in places like Uzbekistan, but on balance Tatars and Uzbeks work together, intermarry, and are only prone to conflict when provoked by authorities. The mass migration has also been explained by journalists and Sovietologists in the terms that finally they are "being allowed" to return. A different picture of the Crimean Tatar National Movement emerges from the "ground level." This perspective, while also partial, demonstrates how the strategic, planned, and concerted effort of Crimean Tatars over time is largely responsible for the accomplishments of the movement today.

The Beginning of the Movement

The Crimean Tatar National Movement experienced its first dramatic upsurge in the late 1950s and early 1960s, when young intellectuals like Mustafa Jemilev, Reshat Jemilev, Rustem Khalilov, and others emerged as leaders. Shemi-Zade, one of the founding members of the first "initiative group," explained that in the early 1960s he and other Tatar intellectuals saw that a moment had arrived in which the Soviet authorities were willing to at least listen. But as a result of the imprisonment, repression, and assassination of so many Tatar intellectuals there was really no active movement. What they needed, according to Shemi-Zade, was a concept, and the concept they found was that of a peaceful democratic movement. In this respect, the Crimean Tatar National Movement is a classic social movement framed in the globalized discourse of human rights, democracy, and self-determination. Its members are implicated in globalizing processes in the second manner described in the introduction to this volume: locally focused actors drawing on global circuits of imagery and resources to ameliorate the conditions facing them. The strategy was initially criticized by those who wanted to keep movement activities within the rules and regulations of the Communist Party. After much debate, the globalized concept was deployed by the Crimean Tatar movement in order to attract the financial resources of the international community. No less importantly, recalling the ideals of the transnational public sphere might embarrass the Soviet authorities enough to change their behavior.

Encouraged by the 1964 fall of Khrushchev, the initiative group began a permanent, rotating lobby in Moscow. On three occasions, this resulted in senior members of the party and state leadership receiving Tatar delegations. Out of the third meeting came a partial concession: the decree of 1967, which exculpated them from the false charge of mass treason during World War II (Reddaway 1988, 195). They were also encouraged by like-minded intellectuals such as Sakharov and Grigorenko, who told a group of assembled Tatars: "You must firmly seize what is offered by law, not request but demand! . . . Begin to demand. And demand not part, not a fraction, but all of what was illegally taken from you—the establishment of an autonomous Crimean Tatar Soviet Socialist Republic" (Alexeyeva 1988, 61).

There was a considerable amount of consultation among activists in various national movements in the former republics. For example, one of Jemilev's colleagues told me that activists came from Latvia to visit him in Uzbekistan (Jemilev was renowned as a defender of human rights) and exchange information. The Latvians wanted to form a united front, but Jemilev declined on the grounds that a "methodology" was not necessary. According to his assistant, he did not want a united front because he believed that each movement has its own specifics. Jemilev and other activists likewise traveled to Bulgaria and the Baltic republics. They brought material aid, helped to demonstrate, and offered moral support reflecting the global flow of information and capital. At the same time, Jemilev's logic reiterates that of this volume's editors by suggesting that context is critical and we must not allow the globalization of social movements to overshadow the specific meaning of movements and identities in particular localities.

The First Returns

Many Tatars either genuinely or deliberately "misunderstood" the 1967 decree as permission to return home. According to Allworth, this migration reached one hundred thousand, but almost all were physically prevented from settling in the peninsula (1988). An informant I will call Sultana is one of the few who succeeded in returning to her village, but she was redeported many times. She first arrived in 1967. She thinks the Soviet authorities suspected she had foreign connections and was spying.

> They would come, put me in a car, and drive me away. Of course I turned right around and came back anyway. They didn't want me to live here because Bakchesarai was a closed city. They didn't let anyone into this area. I think there were perhaps one or two families in the area. And when Tatars started migrating on a massive scale Bakchesarai was still closed. And they hassled my husband. I was young, I wasn't frightened. They would deport me, and I would return. If it was now, I would have had a coronary a long time ago, but then . . . then I was young and I could stand it.
>
> They came for my husband once at about eleven at night. They took him from home and drove him to Simferopol. I hid. They took him to the KGB. He said there was a big room with about twenty people sitting there, in the auditorium. They said "Why did you latch on to that Tatar? We'll find you a Russian, a Ukrainian to marry." He said "Well, she's my wife, we've been to-

> gether for five years, how could I just leave her? I don't want to—I love her." Then they said, "either you leave her, or we will destroy your house. We'll send a tractor and have it plowed under."

If he left her, she might stop returning, and they would be more successful in ridding the peninsula of Crimean Tatars. The local authorities' threat to plow the house under was not just a threat: there were quite a few occasions when they sent in tractors and other heavy equipment to destroy the homes that Tatars were building, sometimes with the occupants still inside. There were casualties from these confrontations, but in most cases the Tatars began to build again.

> So we got ready and went to Moscow to ask to be defended by the Council of Nationalities. We went from one person to the next, and finally there was this Kazanev. We went in to see him, and I couldn't say anything, I cried. But my husband explained everything. He asked me to write a petition, and I did, explaining. And he said you can go home, they'll register you. He gave us a letter on special stationary to give to anyone who approaches to deport me. Then he called Bakchesarai and said "What is going on down there? How could you? She's his lawful wife!" To make a long story short, I was finally registered.

Sultana's narrative suggests a disjuncture between local and national levels of authority. Sometimes other informants were also successful in playing these levels off each other. However, most people who migrated at that time ended up settling just outside the Crimean Peninsula in hope of moving closer to their native villages in the future. Sultana was successful in staying in part through her own perseverance and in part because her husband was a Kazan as opposed to Crimean Tatar. Even as the Newly Independent States of Ukraine and Uzbekistan are gradually drawn into the world capitalist economy, power is localized to such an extent that only the most ambitious are able to harness nonlocal resources to accomplish particular projects. In spite of the special relationships of ethnic minorities and states, most individuals must contest or make peace with the authorities who most directly confront them.

Demonstrations

Early migrations led directly to demonstrations. According to many informants, a watershed moment was the 1987 demonstration in Moscow. Tatars traveled from all over the Soviet Union to participate in a demonstration in Red Square. Informants described what it was like sleeping in dormitories by night and marching with banners on the bricks in Red Square by day. Taking into account the preliminary arrival of activists, this demonstration lasted almost a month, receiving fresh cadres as Tatars flowed in from various locations in the republics.

Other, smaller demonstrations took place in cities like Bakchesarai and Simferopol in Crimea. One woman told me that they were forced to squat when they were unable to buy anything. She said:

> They beat us up with police sticks—myself, and my children. They tried to chase us away, but all the same we stayed anyway. All kinds of things happened. All those troubles, difficulties. They wanted to dynamite the land capture (squatters' settlement). But for some reason, they didn't come to ours because our seizure was one that happened very fast, very organized. Then it quieted down.

She told me that if there was a meeting they all felt they needed to be there. At that time, people were spread out and vulnerable to harassment. Until they could become more organized, they tried to travel to support each other whenever dissension arose. "Then people started to hold meetings. We would all gather, and when they tried to try to chase us [off the land], it became clear that we're *not* going to leave." Her story illustrates the material as well as ideological dimension of squatting. Unemployment, chaos in the wake of privatization, and struggle over the remainders of the old command economy are prevalent across the former Soviet Union. In this instance, the local cultural schema of Tatars is mediated by material factors to produce the practice of squatting.

Self-Immolation

In 1979, a young father of three named Musa Mamut poured gasoline on himself and lit a match when police came to arrest him. After his tragic death, self-immolation became an institutionalized form of protest. A central obstacle to return migration has been the registration, or *propiska,* system: it is necessary to be authorized to live in a particular location. Without this registration, it is rarely possible to find employment, and without employment, it is difficult to become registered. The vicious cycle creates a form of social control that is difficult to escape. Mamut and his family were among the early returnees who came back following the 1967 "rehabilitation." He came back and bought a house but was refused registration, validation of his purchase, and permission to work. In 1976, Mamut and his wife were arrested. After serving his sentence, he returned to his home. Mamut and his wife again approached the authorities for a permit for the house but were denied. When the authorities threatened to imprison him again, Mamut warned them he had gasoline ready. A policeman arrived at his house to carry out the threat, and Mamut asked permission to change his clothes. He went into the barn, doused himself with gasoline and as he walked toward the policeman set himself on fire. Instead of attempting to save Mamut's life, the policeman ran away. Mamut ran after him, engulfed in flames.

During my fieldwork, the story of this self-immolation was told and retold to me, and it loomed large in the social imaginary. Since Mamut's death, self-immolation appears to have become a highly successful tactic when Tatars are in a standoff with authorities. While Tatars have not made this threat without the willingness to follow through, it is so successful that gasoline does not necessarily have to be present—the KGB, special forces, and local police know Tatars are serious. Law enforcement officials have been known to mistake canisters of water for gasoline. The following narrative demonstrates how stories of self-immolation have come to occupy the social imaginary and are played out in real life.

> It so happened that at the time we were doing the plastering in those two rooms, and they came and started to chase us out. The police were there with sticks. It was cold, there was snow, and at the time I didn't have running water, so there were twenty-liter containers sitting there with water in them. Two containers. I said "if you are going to evict me," I said "there's gasoline and I'm going to start you on fire and myself on fire. I don't have anything left to lose," I said, "I don't have anywhere to go, I don't have a home in Uzbekistan anymore, I don't have a house here," I said, "I'm just going to live here. You will die with me—we will blow up together!" He shot [a picture], and then they ran! The correspondent photographed me and then the missionary newspaper, after three, no, it was after four years [there] was a photograph of me in back of the table with the lamp and the two containers. The caption said: "away on holiday." That was what they wrote. They didn't print an article about what I said to them, how they were evicting us, how I said I'll blow you up, but wrote "Away on holiday" [laughing]. There was just clean water in the containers; they could have seen for themselves but got scared and didn't notice that it was water.

At this point in the retelling, her mood shifted and, crying, she said, "Where am I going to go? What we had, the rats had eaten, everything had molded. Nothing was left." While the photograph in the paper provided a moment of comic relief, the long-term effect of threatening self-immolation is that violence and self-sacrifice are normalized. As part of the repertoire of contention, self-immolation is a socially sanctioned act possible in a Muslim society that prohibits suicide only because it is not interpreted by the collective as a self-willed act. One informant urged me not to confuse causes and effects. In the Tatar interpretation, self-immolation is an *effect* of the social structure:

> From an absolute benevolent state, a peaceful state, to a state of extreme irritation and aggressiveness, apparently this process, this capturing, [and] the readiness to do something with yourself or with someone else—it caught these people from the outside, from the *outside,* and influenced their spiritual

> condition. The slogan "homeland or death" at a certain moment was not just thrown out as a slogan but concrete actions could follow it! Perhaps not from a huge number of people, but a completely concrete group of people.

Self-immolation is valorized as the ultimate form of protest.

A widely read book about Musa Mamut is entitled *Jivoi Fakel,* or "Living Torch" (1986), with the idea that he died pointing the way. Self-immolation remains an important part of the movement repertoire; the most recent instance took place in November 1997.

Squatting

The practice of remembering the Tatar past creates a discursive formation that young Tatars make their own. The memories are manipulated and acquire a use value in the context of post-Soviet restructuring. While conducting research in Simferopol in 1995, the family I lived with took over, or in their words "captured," property downtown on behalf of friends who had become homeless. Within half an hour, a racketeer appeared and told them that he had plans for the property and if they did not leave his "boys" would take care of them. They responded that they, too, have their "boys" and were not going to leave. After some discussion, they agreed to divide the property by building a wall down the center of the inner courtyard. Construction began immediately, but after several days the family was confronted again, this time by a city official who demanded money or he would have the building condemned. The man was from *Zhek,* the Ukrainian equivalent of building inspection. In the economic upheaval in Ukraine, he was well positioned to exert his influence to demand a bribe. Having accomplished more than twenty-five captures before this one, an informant I will refer to as Gulzar was savvy enough to delay him and planned to go to the mayor's office to try to get a registration permit.

Before she could do so, the family was approached again, this time by a Russian couple who claimed the property was built by the woman's relatives and should rightly pass to them. In scrutinizing the map that they had brought marking the apartment, Gulzar detected a number of irregularities. This upset the Russian woman, who exclaimed that Tatars had "sold the motherland" and "invaded" her property. The property they were arguing about had been badly burned and vandalized two weeks before. Through questioning, Gulzar realized that the night the couple had come to Simferopol concerning the apartment was the same night that the fire had occurred. She suspected that the couple had committed arson to devalue the property and justify acquiring an apartment in a newer neighborhood. When Gulzar and her friends could not agree with the couple about who the property belonged to, the couple called the building commission. An offical arrived almost immediately with the police to straighten the matter out. After looking at the map and the property, the official told them that the matter would have to be decided in court. But before he left Gulzar's suspicion about the couple was confirmed when the woman offered her the property and settlement out of court, provided that the commission would arrange for her and her husband to receive a more "appropriate" (i.e. larger and more modern) dwelling.

While the two cases of squatting show how it can be individually orchestrated, they are far from spontaneous or unpremeditated. Morally, the captures are backed by mobilizing structures such as the local *Mejlis,* the political body of the Crimean Tatars. Social movements can colonize personal memories and generate legitimacy for themselves through particular representations and dramatizations of events. The mobilization of memories elevates personal tragedy to a national problem, just as it makes the national problem an issue of personal importance. The organization Krim describes the necessity of Tatar land "invasions" or "captures."

> Naturally, this is an illegal way of deciding the national problem. It follows to select the peaceful and lawful path for the approval of the Crimean Tatar people on the peninsula. [However] in three regions, Crimean Tatar families arriving in Crimea and not being able to find employment, buy homes, or obtain an apartment turned to the unlawful seizure of land in order to acquire by force the right to speak with authorities as owners of their plots.
>
> The dispersal of the "invaders" of the land, and the use of force by the troops of the Ministry of Internal Affairs [MVD] while the Crimean administration and press remains silent is viewed by Crimean Tatars in Central Asia as the signal for the beginning of a more active and spontaneous return of Crimea to the former native people—Tatars.[11]

The statement that they had no other options left but to use force is particularly significant because the only language the authorities could hear was an aggressive one in which the stakes had been raised from litigation to life and death.

Political Opportunity and Action

One of the most striking features of the Crimean Tatar National movement is what it is opposing. One might hypothesize that with the dismantling of the Communist Party and the disintegration of so-called state socialism the political opportunity structure would open to the extent that the movement would cease to have a target. Nothing could be farther from the truth—or more revealing about the current situation in the Newly Independent States. Gorbachev's reforms created an "opening" for Crimean Tatars to return when he publicly stated that every national minority should have a territory or homeland. This, along with the massacre of the Meskhetian Turks, helped determined the "when" of the mass migration from Central Asia. The attendant relaxation of social control assured Tatars that it was time to return and legitimated a move that had been planned and dreamed about for decades.

In order to understand the specific form that the movement has taken, it must be remembered that the political opportunity structure generates constraints as well as opportunities. The particularities of the local context are extremely important because they have been very influential in shaping the movement since its arrival in Crimea. The movement has been "criminalized" by the vicissitudes of operating in a severely depressed, crime-dominated economy that is largely dependent on the tourist industry and small-scale agriculture.

Crimean Tatars returning to the peninsula typically do not find employment in the depressed economy of the Ukraine. It is estimated that roughly 80 percent of Tatars survive on the proceeds from produce grown on private plots of land. Others travel long distances to barter and trade. Because they are involved in the informal economy, they are exposed to the pressure of the Mafia and the issue of protection money concerns a majority of the population. But what *is* the Mafia? In Soviet times, the Mafia was what Verdery (1996) and Reis (1996) have referred to as the Communist Party and Soviet state in its extralegal activities. It therefore reflected the composition of the legal apparatuses of power and the elites associated with them. Now its composition appears to be changing. The Mafia in Crimea is still believed to be one of the strongest in the former republics. Following the return of Crimean Tatars to the peninsula, the balance shifted and the Mafia went through a phase of being increasingly ethnically oriented. Crimean Tatars reported that it was as though everything was "already taken." When they were unsuccessful in either avoiding or controlling a Mafia-dominated local economy, conflict became increasingly likely.

In the summer of 1995, a spiral of small conflicts led to a large Tatar riot, now referred to as the Feodosia-Sudak events, which damaged the Feodosia city hall and destroyed Mafia-owned kiosks, cafes, homes, and businesses along the southern coast. Two Tatars were killed and many wounded in the course of the raiding by a group that formed at the funeral of two Crimean Tatars killed in earlier skirmishes with the Mafia. The riot escalated to involve more than eighty cars, two buses, and an estimated five hundred Tatars (Korobovaya 1995). A number of incidents led up to and fed into the disturbance, which help contextualize it in the overall sociopolitical climate of Crimea. A May 1995 article in *Express Chronicle*[12] observed that a wave of hired killings in Crimea demonstrated that private and government businesses and collective and state farms have all fallen into the grip of racketeers. The article ascribed a recent *drop* in the overall crime rate to the arrival of Crimean Tatars whose opposition to paying protection money and refusal to capitulate to organized crime helped frame them as a stabilizing influence (Korneva and Izumov 1995).

The large riot was preceded by a smaller conflict that erupted when racketeers asked Odju, a Tatar selling cigarettes, to raise his prices or they would "chase all the Tatars from Crimea." Odju refused, and the next day four cars filled with racketeers arrived at his house accompanied by a police sergeant. They severely beat Odju and threw him in a dumpster, believing him to be dead. In retaliation, Tatars raided a trading area controlled by a local Mafia group and then proceeded to the bazaar. When they arrived, a brawl between Tatars and racketeers broke out. Rather than arrest all the participants, the police took only the Tatars into custody. Tatars were incensed that in these and other instances local authorities consistently failed to defend them and obviously worked in collusion with Mafia structures.

Following this incident, Tatars held a massive demonstration in Simferopol, demanding that the authorities confront the spread of organized crime on the peninsula. They demonstrated in front of government buildings and appealed to the authorities but did not receive any response or commitment from government or law enforcement officials. Tatars then gathered at the Simferopol *Mejlis,* or political organization, for an emergency meeting and produced a statement maintaining that they had been forced to defend themselves from different kinds of criminal groupings. They stated that the most recent incident had convinced them not to rely on the authorities but take independent measures to defend Crimean Tatars. They also stated that from that time on no crime against a Tatar would go unpunished. Mustafa Jemilev commented that "We are not at all happy that we have to resist bandits. It's the work of the police and law enforcement agencies. But if they aren't going to fulfill their duties we will have to defend ourselves. In the future, Crimean Tatars will not pay the racket. If we find out that a Crimean Tatar is paying tribute, he will be called a traitor" (Korneva and Izumov 1995, 6).

The meeting and the call by Mustafa Jemilev mobilized Tatars and shaped subsequent interactions. Less that a month later, a Russian woman selling cherries in the market was approached for protection money. Two Tatar men who observed what was happening confronted the racketeers. The altercation developed into a fight, and two Tatars died. One interpretation frames the event within the globalized discourse of indigenous people and their human rights. The Tatars defended a Russian woman, it is felt, because when "moral" or human rights issues are concerned the movement's ideology ceases to be confined to the ethnic group and applies to all kinds of interaction. When I asked Jemilev in a personal interview why he thought the Tatars had defended the market seller, he replied, "Because it wasn't right." He stated that it is inappropriate for Russians to demand protection money when Crimea is not their homeland. And it is wrong to demand protection money from the indigenous people. A less idealistic interpretation frames the altercation as part of the criminalized Crimean economy: it is an instance of one criminal grouping coming into conflict with another. According to this interpretation, the Russian woman selling cherries was probably working for or being protected by the Tatars, who came to her defense because they had formed a Mafia of their own.

On the eve of the funeral in the village of Shebetkova, Tatars gathered and held a meeting. While this meeting was described by journalists as "spontaneous," funerals and *pominki* (the "remembrances" of the dead) are strictly observed. In other words, it is inaccurate to describe the meeting as spontaneous insofar as Tatar funerals are always a magnet for social gatherings of other types. One informant estimated that more than four thousand Tatars assembled. At approximately noon the next day, a group formed a motorcade of about ten cars and drove north from the city of Feodosia to Sudak. Along the way, they stopped and raided the businesses they knew to be linked to the local Mafia. Their first stop was a Mafia-owned restaurant and bar called Kommeria. Tatars threw hand grenades through the windows, burning the first floor. About seven cars in the parking lot were also damaged. The motorcade proceeded to the city of Feodosia where an estimated seventy to one hundred Tatars surrounded the local police station and demanded that the Tatars who had been taken into custody for an earlier incident be released. Even though they were released, this did not stop the riot. In fact, it gathered momentum. At this stage, an estimated four hundred Tatars began destroying kiosks and cafes. The head of the Feodosia police was taken hostage. Tatars surrounded and began breaking the windows of the city hall into which the Feodosia police had retreated. The motorcade then proceeded to the village of Koktebel, burning down a Mafia-owned roadside grill and taking a bus hostage. The Tatars released the passengers but used the bus as a means of transportation. In Koktebel, Tatars burned the home and cars of the purportedly corrupt director of the collective farm. A *Literaturnaya Gazeta* article claims that up to five hundred Tatars participated in the action in Koktebel, arriving in two buses and fifty cars (Korobovaya 1995). On the way to the city of Sudak, the motorcade broke into three groups and began raiding kiosks and commercial enterprises. On the way from the city of Sudak, the motorcade took control of a gas station to fill their cars. Here, Russian special forces moved in and began shooting. According to police reports, two Tatars were killed and six wounded in this interchange. A sergeant of police was also wounded.

Following the riot, a member of the Feodosia police reported to the *Literaturnaya Gazeta* journalist that "It was strange to supposedly be the preservers of law and order and find a crowd of us chased into the local station like a bunch of chickens. We're morally beaten. Here, the Tatar victory is complete" (Korobovaya 1995, 11). Refat Chubarov, a representative of the Tatar *Mejlis,* reinforced the sense of victory, stating that "Today, Crimean Tatars stood up to the spread of banditism and lawlessness. Tomorrow, others may unite against the insolent racketeers" (Korneva and Izumov 1995, 11).

The head of the Police Department of Crimea asserted in an interview with a journalist that this was the first instance in the Newly Independent States in which "an entire uncomprehending population" was drawn into settling a Mafia dispute (Korobovaya 1995). There are certainly many unanswered questions about the orchestration of conflict by elites in the former republics. However, it seems that if the Tatar population had been mystified as opposed to mobilized it would not have been prepared with explosive material. It is reasonable to believe that the riot was less spontaneous and more organized than journalists and politicians think. In fact, there is every indication that it was not an anomalous event but one that fits into and perpetuates the cybernetics of this movement. One informant's comment is particularly suggestive: "Bandits?" he said, "We ourselves are bandits!"

The Tatar disturbance is important to understanding crucial socioeconomic dynamics in the Newly Independent States because it highlights the way in which, rather than being part of an "underground" structure, rackets are part of everyday functioning (Verdery 1995, 1996; Handelman 1995). In some respects, the collapse of so-called state socialism and the Tatars' subsequent attempts to penetrate the economic and political structures of Crimea reveal the degree to which the authorities are implicated in crime. Crimean Tatars have now acquired their own mayor's office, or *gorispolkom,* to administrate housing. While the issue of registration, or *propiska,* has become less important, new difficulties have arisen in the internal politics of the movement with respect to this *gorispolkom.* As Haraway, Ortner, and Abu-Lughod have observed about social movements, there are no innocent positions.

Conclusion

Like the riot against the Mafia, the allegorical use of *capture* to describe the squatting strategy points to possibilities for social transformation. Narrative analysts like Passerini (1988, 1992) suggest that people resort to the stereotypes that they know their culture requires. The Tatar use of the word *capture* draws on a pejorative stereotype conjuring images of thirteenth- and fourteenth-century Tatar raids such as those portrayed in popular films like *Andrei Rublev.* The term may be selected out of necessity, but as Tatars gain symbolic power it is used with new meaning to legitimize their behavior. The most significant effect of the riot was the changing meaning of the old cultural frame in which Russians perceive Tatars as the evil descendants of Chingis Khan and the Golden Horde. The epithet is becoming increasingly polyvalent now that Tatars are being hailed as the defenders of law and order. The Ukrainian president, Leonid Kuchma, thanked the *Mejlis* for its role in stabilizing Crimea. Articles in *Izvestia, Literaturnaya Gazeta,* and *Express Chronicle* describe Tatars as a source of stability and one of the few remaining sources of opposition to the spread of organized crime. How this event will figure in the history currently being written is an open question.

Without the globalized discourse of universal human rights to draw on for inspiration and to use to shame the Soviet government into concessions such as the decree of 1967, the Crimean Tatars' movement would have been very different. They may have stayed with the early strategy of working within the rules of the Communist regime longer or broken away from this strategy without the support of the normative and normalizing standards of human rights. In particular, the set of rights of indigenous peoples recognized in the transnational public sphere and the right of freedom of movement stipulated by Soviet law were disregarded by authorities throughout the Soviet period. What is more intriguing is the way in which the discourse of human rights and democratic ideals is localized by Crimean Tatars through an idiosyncratic interpretation of history. According to many Tatars, and historians among them, they did not adopt the democratic ideals from the West *but the other way around.* Within the Crimean Tatar cultural framing, the West (Switzerland in particular) modeled its notion of democracy on the Crimean khanate, which formed in the 1440s and lasted until Russia annexed Crimea in 1784. While the khanate was not actually called a democracy, they believe the freedom to observe any religion, the equal rights of citizens, and a system of representation were an inspiration to democracies forming in the West.[13]

Here we come full circle to the importance of cultural framing for social movements because the ideals of democracy and human rights are not just a "legitimating" factor for the social movement but have become some of the building blocks of movement ideology. In Tatars' interpretation of their history and their movement, democracy and human rights do not originate somewhere in Europe but are already intrinsic to the way the culture, and hence the movement, operate. However perplexing this may sound to scholars of democracy who have never heard of Crimean Tatars or the Crimean khanate, it must be noted that after the demise of the Soviet Union, when conflict was raging in Sukhumi, Abkhazia, and numerous other "hot spots" on the post-Soviet map, the Crimean Tatar leaders consistently contained protest and pushed for nonviolent means of conflict resolution when all the ingredients for a bloody war were present. This suggests that democracy and human rights, the ideals of transnational public space, do run deeper for Crimean Tatars than something they simply read in a book or a United Nations report.

Recent scholarship on memory and history in the former Soviet Union has told us a great deal about how public and private acts of unsanctioned remembrance undermined the Soviet state (Watson 1994). Control over the writing of history was not as hegemonic or effective as totalitarian models would suggest. But we need to move beyond written history to oral traditions to understand how multiple versions of the past survived where one historical interpretation was meant to prevail. In this chapter, I have tried to attend not just to the idea that unapproved rememberings are now the material from which new histories are being created, but the specific mechanisms at work on the ground. Memory, I am convinced, has an instrumental role to play when it is reenacted in the Tatars' squatting strategy or when it mobilizes younger Tatars to "return" to a place they have never been before. It follows from this that we can also extend our line of inquiry from the now widely accepted notion that memory is necessary to the construction of individual and national identity to include the practices of memory that de- or reterritorialize *transnational* identities.

The idea of cultural framing processes enabled social movement scholars to take into account the significance of ideas and sentiments. Interpretation mediates the opportunities that arise and the actions that are taken. It also mediates the formal political opportunity structures and forms of organization like national movements. In order to reap the benefits of this thinking, we need to proceed from recognizing the importance of ideas and sentiments to exploring their concrete manifestation. Social movement theory can benefit from considering the practice of social memory as a form of collective action. As fallible as it is constructive, remembering and commemoration are daily practices among Crimean Tatars and a driving force in the Crimean Tatar National Movement. We need to include the everyday remembering of a people who "live history," as my informant Nizami suggested, because the micropractices of cultural framing are inseparable from, and constitutive of, macroprocesses of social change: memory has the power to destroy empires, just as water has the power to split stones.

NOTES

1. The 1995 and 1996 field research in Crimea was made possible by grants from the Margaret Wray French Fund for anthropological research and the Rackham School of Graduate Studies at the University of Michigan. The 1997 fieldwork in Uzbekistan was made possible by the Ford Foundation (Ford Foundation Grant no. 950–1163) and the National Council for Soviet and East European Research (NCSEER Research Contract 812–11). All names have been changed to pseudonyms except those of public officials and leaders. I have tried to choose first names that are widely popular as pseudonyms.

2. *Indigenous people* has two definitions. In international law, it is a people that subsists by means of its traditional way of life. Under this definition, very few groups qualify as indigenous. There is also a more common sense definition of *indigenous people* as a group whose ethnogenesis took place on a particular territory. The Crimean Tatars feel that this definition is most appropriate.

3. On the concept of deterritorialization, see Appadurai 1991; and Malkki 1992, 1995.

4. In addition to works cited pertaining to memory, see Boym 1995; Conway 1990; Hacking 1995; Hartman 1994; Langer 1991; Lass 1994; Le Goff 1992; Schwartz 1994; and Scott 1990.

5. Social memory differs from *personal memory* in the sense that it does not rely on a direct experience of the past. An event can be remembered by sharing the sets of images that have been passed on in storytelling or commemorative monuments. Social memories represent shared understanding that develops over time. One of the ways these shared understandings are concretized is through the localization of memories in place. Crimean Tatars, for example walk the garden paths their grandparents walked, touch the cracked stucco walls their parents plastered, and claim abandoned dwellings in "remembering" what they lost in 1944.

6. There are significant populations of Crimean Tatars in the United States, Turkey, the Baltic states, and Hungary, in addition to the highest concentrations in Ukraine and Uzbekistan.

7. Crimean Tatars claim that approximately 44 percent of the population perished during the 1944 deportation and many more died in the first years in Central Asia. Like *in-*

digenous people, the definition of *genocide* is contentious, and the term is not used here. While it troubles some scholars, the Crimean Tatar experience conforms to the United Nations' definition (see Deker 1958).

8. Among the books that survived is *Ocherki po istorii krima* (Notes on the History of the Crimea), Nadinskii 1951; see also Alexeyeva 1988, 53.

9. *Golos Krima* (Voice of Crimea), no. 47 (210), November 28, 1997; *Obrashenie k Delegatam III Kuraltai Krimskotatarskovo Naroda* (An Appeal to the Delegates of the III Kuraltai of the Crimean Tatar People), 1997, 2.

10. The Otriadi Militsii Osobovo Naznachenia: special, heavily armed forces similar to riot police.

11. Unpublished manifesto.

12. A Moscow weekly published since 1987 and financed by the Eurasia Foundation, the European Human Rights Foundation, and the National Endowment for Democracy.

13. What Tatars really mean by *democracy* is still contested. For some, but not all, it does not exclude giving priority to Crimean Tatar over Slavic representation in the government (even though Crimean Tatars are a vast minority) and polygamy, to cite just a few examples of contemporary debates.

CHAPTER 12

The Russian Neo-Cossacks: Militant Provincials in the Geoculture of Clashing Civilizations

Georgi M. Derluguian

As part of its ongoing coverage of the reemerging Russia, the *New York Times* ran a story romantically titled "Cossacks Ride Again along the Don." It described a new educational establishment in the southern Russia town of Novocherkassk, whose full name was the Emperor Alexander III Cossack Boarding School. Here the American visitor observed 158 teenage cadets dressed in World War I uniforms who were being instructed in the antiquated curriculum of equestrianism, marksmanship, the Orthodox religion, and ballroom dancing beyond the more usual prep school subjects. The journalist, who had done his required readings in Russian literature, had blended into the report classical quotations and evocative images of bygone Cossackdom—the dashing horseback warriors from the old Russo-Turkish frontiers, reputed for their traditional devotion to Christian faith, tsar, and Motherland. The story's message looked unambiguous to a Western reader. Behold, the ancient bedrock of old Mother Russia is reemerging from beneath the Soviet rubble although (alas!) alongside the chivalric traditions the Cossacks are passing over to the young generation "the dark side of their warrior ancestry: intolerance, violence and their role in leading pogroms against the Jews" (*New York Times,* April 4, 1996, A10). The description lies squarely within the time-honored Western tradition of awe bordering on fear of the Cossacks, who were seen as the epitome of Russian imperial grandeur. Anti-Semitism furthermore serves to establish an expressive cultural marker separating the heroes of the story from its American narrator. Nevertheless, the report is astonishingly flattering to the neo-Cossacks, who are presented as all they would like to be—but, alas, in mundane reality are not.

Typically of Western media reporting on the current spread of radical provincialisms (of the nativist or religious fundamentalist variety), the evocations of deep cultural bedrock and historical legacies obscure the more current context, in this case the legacy of the Soviet superpower-developmentalist project and the effects of its recent bankruptcy. For instance, the American journalist ignores the less heroic facts that the man featured in the story as the supreme commander of the Don Cossack Host, General N, in his previous life had never advanced beyond the position of police sergeant and that the school was not entirely new but in fact a Soviet military orphanage that the Ministry of Defense could no longer afford to maintain. True, the building is old. It was erected in 1883 under the august patronage of Tsar Alexander III to house the original Don Cossack Cavalry School, but it was disbanded in 1920 in the face of the advancing Red Army and ended up in Serbia, where it closed for good in 1933. What kind of curious continuity exists between the White emigrés of the Russian civil war and the Soviet petty-rank officials and Red Army officers who resurrect the Cossack spirit in Novocherkassk today? In the report, the town of Novocherkassk appears only vaguely as a timeless bastion of Cossack culture. In the post-Soviet reality, Novocherkassk is no longer the pre-1917 military and administrative center of a booming agrarian area populated with Cossack farmers. In the 1990s, it is a deindustrializing backwater that differs from other drab midsized towns in the post-Soviet rust belts only in the occasional appearance of a few and the same uniformed neo-Cossacks. They parade and pray in formation, adding flavor to electoral rallies, often in bizarre disregard of political partisanship. (A boss is a boss, after all, regardless whether he claims to be a Zhuganov Communist or a current official rallying behind President Yeltsin.) On occasion, the toughs in Cossack uniforms zealously assist the local police in hunting down illegal aliens, who are mostly recent Soviet compatriots from the now independent Caucasus and Central Asian republics. Almost invariably this would end in racist brutality and scandals widely publicized in the Russian postglasnost media, in the reports of human rights groups with connections outside Russia, and in (another novelty) lawsuits. Although the outcomes of these new (to Russia) forms of public activity are always inconclusive, the unwanted publicity and embarrassment make the Russian police and local governors treat the Cossack volunteers with caution. And so it has been for the decade since 1990.

Of course, journalistic reports can claim immunity on the grounds of lacking space to describe all the attendant ironies and complexities of the neo-Cossack revival. This excuse, however, hardly applies to the widespread analyses produced by the scholars and experts who subscribe to the same awestruck vision of primordial ethnic cultures that seem to breed nationalism, vicious conflict, and security threats as easily as the arrival of November breeds the flu virus. To continue the epidemiological metaphor, the authors who consider nationalist and fundamentalist movements largely on their own terms, that is, as products of elusive and deeply seated civilizational traditions unsullied by the time- and space-specific sociopolitical background, violate a basic rule of medical and social inquiry. They neglect to ask where the germ of nationalist militancy hides between the epidemics, whether it is indeed the same immutable variety, why it resurfaces only occasionally, and what conditions facilitate or, conversely, constrain the outbreaks. Yet, somehow such reports seem to perfectly satisfy the audiences of higher-status world media, including personalities in the positions of political, economic, and intellectual power. More so, it is this kind of "primordialist" cultural imagination that informs current debates and decision making in world politics, not the subtle explorations of Benedict Anderson's *Imagined Communities* (1983), which since the 1980s have set the tone of academic discussions. The success of Samuel Huntington's bestseller, very aptly, though misleadingly, called the *Clash of Civilizations* (1996) suggests that the reason is not mere lack of enlightened sophistication among the mass readership. Huntington articulated a *culturally* (if not theoretically) consistent position within the emerging field of post–cold war geoculture that resonates perfectly with the conservative political tradition and the broader Western worldview. One has to admit that the panoramic view of post–cold war world politics presented by Huntington is built in full accordance with the intimately familiar Newtonian laws of mechanics—clearly bounded, autonomous bodies (here states, movements, or civilizations) move within an essentially timeless (thus perfectly repetitive) space under the impact of forces (cultural traditions, power interests, competition for resources). They gravitate toward or away from each other and—naturally—they clash like the tectonic plates of the Earth's bedrock. Huntington's geological and geopolitical metaphor is rooted solidly in the modern mechanical view of the universe. It also provides a politically operational language for ordering and explaining the realities of political and economic competition in a world that is undergoing a major migration and restructuring of power generically called globalization.

It would be wrong to think that Huntington's audiences are only Western political elites. Far from that! Huntington's book is simply a more noticeable example of a much wider discourse that indeed can be seen as an *invitation* to global culturalist struggles. All over today we find social groups and regions whose previous ranking and position within the world system are being challenged and undone by the processes of globalization. The immediate interest of such groups and, if one wishes to be more expressive, their prerational instinct is to resist the effects of globalization by clinging to the erstwhile ideologies and institutions of power that aren't in fact so ancient. Only a couple decades ago, in the 1950s and 1960s, they were considered the cutting edge of progress—industrialization and national developmentalism through a strong state—until this model suddenly became obsolete and cumbersome in the 1980s and 1990s. Social groups that are most challenged by globalization are not the centrally located elites (elite positions and capital are great adaptation resources used by the children even if the generation of fathers gets stuck in the old order). They are rather middle classes, including certain strata of cadres and workers who are located in the more peripheral areas (provinces and poor suburbs that enjoy only virtual access to global flows). And they are likely mostly male. After all, to be downwardly mobile one must be positioned relatively high on the social ladder or at least perceive oneself to be entitled to superiority. Despite many claims, they are not the relics of traditional societies. These cadres grew and often were assiduoulsy cultivated by the developmentalist regimes to serve the purposes of state-led accumulation in the economy, ideology, and military. With the waves of bankruptcy suffered by virtually all developmentalist states (except those lucky ones that in the 1980s could turn themselves into the export-oriented "dragons"), the new educated classes that were massively created worldwide after 1945 almost overnight turned out to be redundant. In one possible response, they try to compensate for the waning economic and political viability of what used to be their power with vigorously conservative incantations of moral order and traditionally ordained discipline, reaching for symbolic resources further back in time. In brief, this is the formula of fundamentalism. Even if they do not read Huntington (although their ideologues may), they share the same modern mechanistic worldview and the same feeling of a world going wrong.

To state an alternative position in its briefest form, I prefer a very different view of social time/space wherein the world is a hierarchically organized, complex system. It is irreversibly evolving over historical time in numerous discernible patterns that form cycles and trends. Change in this world is constant but ocurrs unevenly over time, as instituionalization (hardly ever complete) punctuated with the periods of chaotic transition. This world encompasses the interrelated and overlapping arenas (or fields) of social action traditionally designated as politics, economy, and society that simultaneously exist (and likely have always existed) as global unity and a myriad of localized and mutually relational variations. Accounting for only one field or level without at the very least awareness of the others is a major methodological limitation despite its being common and in fact strongly prescribed by the discipline-divided modern social sciences. This isn't a theory but rather a paradigmatic perspective that should encompass a diversity of existing and potential theories and research programs. True synthesis remains a fairly distant possibility and in any event lies far beyond the scope of this chapter, which may be considered a call for such a synthesis growing from quite specific empirical and theoretical concerns that are generated by the current debates on identity politics, postcommunism, and globalization. In a manner that has to be theoretically eclectic, but, I hope, is not intellectually inconsistent, I have tried to produce a holistic account of the ethnically construed mobilization since 1990, which has been occurring somewhere in the Russian province of Krasnodar. The procedure required a combination of several spatial levels of analysis and time frames. First, I reconstructed the historically current (post-1945 and post-1991) structuration of the local scene, paying some attention to its deeper historical lineage, which reaches back into the Russian imperial past and the Bolshevik revolution, and the twisted ways in which these bygone realities endure (or fade) in social institutions and collective memories. I drew inspiration from the magisterial study of the Mediterranean in the time of Philip II by Fernand Braudel, who insisted on the importance of historically created landscape in analyzing fleeting political events. The necessary introduction to the local environment would allow us to meaningfully explain the sudden emergence and mediocre trajectory of the neo-Cossack militia movement (which I dare to claim is a more accurate term). The neo-Cossack movement is a good illustration of enduring Soviet-era social conditions and constraints that despite growing incoherence have continued to channel Russia's trajectory at least during the first decade following the demise of Soviet geopolitics and ideology. The analysis, however, should not stop at the level of the locally bound sociopolitical commentary and a paraphrase of postcommunist morass.

The story of the neo-Cossacks must be articulated with the larger picture of the attempts and strategies pursued by various groups of Russians that after 1989 unexpectedly found themselves forced into renegotiating their positions and their very identities within the world system. Movement organizing—or avoidance of social movements—is part of this repertoire. The choice of joining movements or avoiding them altogether is largely determined by the localized patterns of social power. In the recent scholarly literature, especially in the humanistically minded currents, localism is often celebrated as resource in dealing with globalization through identity construction. Krasnodar, the locality I explore, suggests that localism might also be part and parcel of provincialism, a condition in which social distance and mediated access between peripheral loci and the centers of power (imperial capital in Soviet period, the global nodes and flows now) becomes a mightily disempowering factor. Failure of movement organizing (which shouldn't be readily bemoaned considering what kind of movement prevails in Krasnodar) is only one of many failures to accrue new powers in the locality, which in effect is caught in the vicious circle of involution and further provincialization. What could be the further trajectory of provincial marginality in the globalizing world system remains a troubling question.

The Scene

The Krasnodar territory (*krai*), unofficially often referred by its historical name and the major river of the area, Kuban, is one of the most populous provinces of Russia. The population of five million (1995 estimate) is second only to the Moscow province.[1] The Krasnodar territory also enjoys an uncommonly warm climate, access to the Black Sea, and at least the reputation of prosperity. Since the disintegration of the USSR, the geopolitical environment of Krasnodar has become troublesome, reminiscent of the times before 1864 when Kuban served as the southern frontier of an expanding Russian Empire. Situated in the northern Caucasus, it borders on the Republic of Georgia, with its rebel enclave of Abkhazia, and two other Russian provinces, Stavropol and Rostov, which also experienced Cossack revivalism in the 1990s. The rebellious Chechnya lies only three hundred miles to the east. After the breakup of the Soviet Union, Krasnodar remained Russia's only territory with extensive resort and port facilities on the Black Sea. The major economic activity in the province, however, remains large-scale grain agriculture, which in various ways employs as many as two-thirds of its population. In the Soviet period, the unusually prosperous collective and state farms of Krasnodar were considered the showcase of socialist agrarian relations and were certainly helped by rich black soils and the warm climate. Nikita Khrushchev affectionately called Krasnodar "our Soviet Iowa." Such a reputation provided provincial leaders with serious political leverage at the Moscow planning agencies, which in the 1960s and 1970s allowed exceptionally high rates of agricultural investment.

The balmy southern climate, privileged geographic location, and relatively developed infrastructure of Krasnodar shaped its demographic and social peculiarities. Since 1945, the province, especially its towns, has been attracting retirees from among the more affluent and mobile civil and military servants of the Soviet era, including a high proportion of veteran officers and the former employees of the once generously paid industries of the Soviet far north. In 1994, as many as 1,249,900, that is, nearly a quarter of Krasnodar's population, were pensioners. In this respect, Krasnodar came to resemble Florida no less than Iowa. Even more than elsewhere in Russia, in the 1990s the once privileged pensioners favored the political forces of overtly nostalgic orientation, such as Zhuganov's neocommunists. The unusual concentration of grumbling stolid pensioners, however, was not conducive to explosions. In fact, the conservative attitudes of senior citizens, their prevalence in local politics and administration, their sheer numbers, and the custom of participating in state rituals like elections regularly frustrated the "adventurism" of various younger radicals.

Parallels to Florida may be further strengthened by the influx of legal and illegal immigrants of various ethnically non-Slavic origins. Despite increasingly stringent curbs on immigration, Krasnodar remains the principal destination for refugees fleeing economic devastation and armed conflicts in the former Soviet republics of Transcaucasia. The major component among the non-Slavic minorities of Krasnodar is ethnic Armenians, whose numbers in 1993 were close to 290,000, perhaps as many as one-third of them being undocumented recent arrivals (Ter-Sarkisiants 1994, 8). The immigrants were especially visible because in a shrinking labor market most of them ended up in street commerce and quite a few in criminal or semicriminal activities. Migrations, the attractions of the port cities and resorts, and geographic proximity to the warlord states in Caucasia (Abkhazia, Georgia, Chechnya, and Karabagh) are commonly blamed for the high incidence of crime in Krasnodar. One should be reminded, however, that Krasnodar was notorious for its criminality long before the Soviet collapse. Corruption in Krasnodar reached scandalous proportions in the 1970s during the long reign of the province's first secretary, Sergei Medunov, who boasted a personal friendship with Brezhnev. During the unperturbed Brezhnev period, the Communist nomenklatura of Krasnodar developed the ethos of corruption and developed an extensive symbiotic relationship of protection-extraction with the groups of embezzlers entrenched in mid- and low-ranking economic management. In retrospect, we are beginning to realize that Brezhnev era "corruption" was in direct anticipation of the post-Soviet managerial privatization of the state bluntly called "nomenklatura capitalism" after the administrative titles of the old Soviet system. More precisely, the nomenklatura *merchant capitalism* was rooted in the translation of the powers of administrative office into monopolistic control over the sphere of monetized circulation and state-ordered redistribution.

In 1982–83 Krasnodar suffered heavily from the KGB-directed purges mandated by Yuri Andropov in his effort to revitalize the Soviet state through drastic cleansing. Thousands of Krasnodar officials received unexpectedly harsh verdicts, in some instances the death penalty. For a couple of years, the local field of power and patronage networks remained in fear and disarray. This trauma conditioned the hostility of Krasnodar elites toward Mikhail Gorbachev, a new "disturber," ahead of any provincial conservatism. Ironically, the loathed policy of public glasnost unleashed by Gorbachev from the top allowed and even forced his potential victims, nostalgic for Brezhnev's placid 1970s, to transform their hostility and group solidarity into an explicitly conservative provincial opposition. In 1988–89, Krasnodar became one of the bulwarks of counterperestroika organizing. The ritual Soviet discourse of socialism and internationalism has been obviously dead and cold for some years. The conservative position in the emergent arena of Russian politics had little choice of rhetoric and ideological imagery other than some form of retrospective imperial patriotism. In its turn, departure from the official Soviet ideology opened a new field of conservative experimentation vacillating between the moderate incantation of Soviet achievements under the leadership of the party and the "pseudo-democratic chaos and ruin" (since 1994, this has become the mainstream of Russian parliamentary conservatism) and fringe radicalisms expressing themselves either in the form of popular Stalinism (defiant of both the despised "democrats" *and* the stolid neo-Communist officialdom) or the strictly paranoid xenophobic nationalism devoid of any socialist undertones.

Nikolai "Father" Kondratenko, the last Communist first secretary of Krasnodar before August 1991, and after a stint in opposition since 1996 its democratically elected governor, embodies the radical brand of post-Soviet conservatism. The populist discourse of Kondratenko (who is a typically stout and folksy local agrarian boss) boils down to the trademark aphorisms: *"I shall govern for the people despite all this democratic erotica [sic]; "Compatriots! Moscow betrayed us. Stockpile food and fuel, brace yourselves, brothers and sisters, for we are secretly besieged by the alien forces of evil";* and, more specifically: *"Future generations will never absolve us if we fail to fight back the most noxious political phenomenon of modern times—International Zionism!"*

The last phrase needs some clarification because Kondratenko means something more transcendental than the state of Israel. Dating back to the late 1960s, when the Soviet ideology lost its context and its remainig content, Russian nationalism first appeared in select dissident and literary circles. Contemporary observers commonly reduced the new phenomenon to vulgar anti-Semitism. Evidently, many observers of such matters belonged to antifascist watchdog groups and themselves were Jews who quite understandably felt traumatized by the invocations of old anti-Semitic formulas. Undisguised hate speech pervades the political discourse of the new Russian nationalists, including Kondratenko and the neo-Cossacks, but their anti-Semitic statements are more a sign of the lack of language than actual political targeting. The modern European clichés of anti-Semitism and traditions of conspiracy paranoia were exhumed and reintroduced in the former Soviet republics through the traceable activities of groups, personalities, and networks on the new nationalist fringes (not only in Russia but, for instance, in such unexpected places as Chechnya and Armenia). These were ready forms used in construing the hostile universes of xenophobe nationalisms, which emerged in the shattered sociopolitical environments of the post-Soviet states. Nowhere in the Eastern Europe of the 1990s did the residual and rapidly declining Jewish populations resemble the old communities of the turn of the century, which were clearly bounded by religion, legal codes, patterns of settlement, and internal solidarity. For even the most paranoid nationalists, Jews were no longer a real-life enemy but rather a timeless paraphrase of their world of woes, which helps to explain the pleasant puzzle of why the reemergence of Cossackdom hasn't led to a single pogrom. True, there were many instances of neo-Cossack brutality against individual non-Russians, but those were Armenians, Meskheti Turks, Chechens, and other recent immigrants to Krasnodar. Kondratenko and his ilk might even sincerily consider Israel a welcome trading partner and a state with a laudable record of war making. International Zionism is an entirely different, otherwordly matter.

Kondratenko's policy during the economic experimentation of perestroika was to hoard as much of the local produce as he could, to suppress independent economic enterprise or political organizing, and to heavily subsidize food prices within the province. The latter policy earned him enduring acclaim locally. At the same time, the administrative price controls invited foraging raids from the neighboring provinces with considerably higher prices. Since many of the neighboring territories were populated with ethnic non-Russians, the economic policy of local protectionism rapidly acquired a nasty xenophobic tonality and produced what Miroslav Hroch has called the "nationally relevant conflict" (Hroch 1993, 17). In 1990–91, the police of Krasnodar were deployed in virtual customs posts on the roads and administrative borders in a futile attempt to prevent the outpouring of subsidized produce. The numbers (and not infrequently the corruption) of the regular police proved woefully insufficient for the task, and in the fall of 1990 neo-Cossack volunteer patrols were introduced. Before long, newspapers and television ran the first sensational stories about the Cossacks flogging a suspected rapist in the market square. The ritualized violence, folkloric imagery, prayers in formation, the silver-clad daggers and rattling sabers, braided horsewhips, huge beards and mustaches, tall sheepskin hats, and World War I uniforms were a media smash that instanteneously advertised their arrival. To many, in Krasnodar, Moscow, and the West, these reinvented Cossacks came as if from a folk legend or the pages of Leo Tolstoy.

Cossack Myth and History

Most accounts of neo-Cossack revivalism treat it as a movement in a historically established ethnic community. To call it a social movement borders on insult. This thesis has been legally endorsed since 1991 by a succession of Russian legislative acts that listed the Cossacks among the peoples victimized by the former Communist regime.[2] This is, of course, a typical instance of a national movement claiming to be a nation or a nation in the making (Hobsbawm 1990). Outside the epic space of nationalist mythology, the question of Cossack historical roots appears to be a line in the historical trajectory of modern European states, especially the trend toward the monopolization of violence. The original Cossacks of the sixteenth to the eighteenth centuries were bands of land-based pirates that spread with the collapse of nomadic domination in the contested steppes between Muscovy, Poland-Lithuania, and the Ottoman Empire.[3] These frontier communities were largely Slavic in composition with a significant minority ranging from Tatars and Circassians to converted Jews. In Russian and Ukrainian folklore, Cossacks subsequently became symbols of rebellious freedom, manhood, and camaraderie, inseparable from the ideally Cossack occupation—honorable brigandage. Fierce allegiance to Orthodox Christianity crystallized over the seventeenth century as an ideological marker in ongoing confrontations with the Muslim Turks and Catholic Poles, although the Cossack Orthodox allegiance remained very nominal in the usual pattern of popular religiosity with its happy ignorance of basic Church norms and theology.

In 1815, when the Russian Cossacks pursuing Napoleon triumphantly entered Paris, the imagery of "untamed sons of the wild steppe" instantly captivated the romantically minded European public and, even sooner than other Western fashions, was imported back to Russian educated society. The Cossack mythology was translated from popular folklore and maintained in literary forms by a succession of titanic figures from Pushkin and Leo Tolstoy to the Nobel laureate Sholokhov (Kornblatt 1992). Ironically, the literary acclamation of the romantic Cossacks came at a time when the Cossackdom of primitive rebels had been giving way to the obedient imperial estate. Toward the end of the eighteenth century, especially after the suppression of the last major Cossack-led rebellion of Emilian Pugachev in 1773, the Russian monarchy resolutely broke up the hosts of independent Cossacks that had spread between the Urals and the lower Dnipro (Dnieper) River in Ukraine. Their remnants were invited to enter imperial service on special honorable terms as a separate estate alongside the nobility, clergy, town dwellers, and peasants. The new "loyal" (*vernye*) Cossacks of the tsar were exempt from taxes and other peasant obligations and were guaranteed lands on the newly conquered frontiers in exchange for lifelong service as cavalry and border guards.[4] In the nineteenth century, the Cossacks became an elite military and police force of the Romanov Empire, renowned for their exploits on the battlefield but also infamous for their later brutality in the pogroms and the suppression of revolutionary upheavals. The Kuban Cossack Host originated in 1793 as a permanently deployed, semiregular army along the newly acquired Russian frontier in the northern Caucasus. Its original core was formed by the Ukrainian Cossacks who were ordered by Catherine the Great to resettle in the northern Caucasus. The Ukrainian language endures in large tracts of the Krasnodar countryside to this day.

During the Russian civil war of 1918–20, the Cossack autonomous provinces (hosts) of Don, Kuban, Ural, and Siberia became bases for the White armies. Bolsheviks, who drew much of their imagery and inspiration from the example of French Jacobins, equated the Cossack provinces to a Russian Vendée and treated them accordingly. In the critical early months of 1919, Lenin and Trotsky ordered a campaign of Red terror explicitly called de-Cossackization (*raskazachivanie*). The stark episode, especially its casualty scores and motivation (whether Trotsky acted out of revolutionary or Jewish prejudice) remains bitterly contested among local historians. The focus on de-Cossackization, driven by the reemergent debate between Russian nativists and liberal Westernizers, almost completely obscures the main line of Cossack political history during the civil war.

In 1917–20, a majority of the Cossacks intermittently fought on two fronts—against the Bolsheviks and the Whites, who harshly opposed any signs of separatism for the sake of restoring the old empire. In the chaotic summer of 1917, the Cossack autonomists in Kuban sought to replace the defunct imperial authorities with a local political body typically called in Ukrainian a *rada.* This word means council, which is *soviet* in Russian. The Kuban Cossack Rada of 1917–19 interpreted the ideas of peasant socialism and national federalism, which were sweeping across the remains of the Russian Empire, in militantly parochial terms bordering on outright racism directed primarily against the "bootless" peasantry of greater Russia. This may look surprising considering the Cossack reputation as fighters against their Muslim neighbors and born anti-Semites, yet it was a rarely straightforward instance of ideology and politics following the economy and demography. The population of the Kuban Cossack Host grew from around 150,000 in 1864, at the time of the final "pacification" and forced emigration of the Muslim Circassian natives, to over 1.5 million in 1914, which is an impressive tenfold increase in merely fifty years. Since the 1890s, Kuban and other newly established agrarian provinces in southern Russia had been experiencing a tremendous boom in cash-crop production, which had fostered competition between the heavily entitled Cossack farmers and new immigrants, who had to lease their land from the Cossacks. By the time of the 1917 revolution, Cossacks already represented less than half of

Kuban's population (Ladokha 1924, 14). In this situation, the abolition of estate privileges and the looming introduction of market legal norms in land tenure were emotionally perceived in the Cossack settlements as imminent ruin and the end of social order. For an immensely tumultuous and violent moment, Cossack resistance to the capitalization of agriculture surfaced in a rather disoriented ideology and loose institutions that the Rada scrambled to create, until in 1919 the Rada itself was harshly suppressed by the Whites of General Denikin. A few months later, Denikin's White army was thrown into the Black sea by the Bolsheviks, who triumphantly renamed Kuban Krasnodar, which literally means "the red gift."

In the Soviet period, the Cossacks were undone in almost every aspect of their prerevolutionary existence—military, economic, political—as a peculiar rural culture and life-style. Bolshevik authorities considered the Cossacks an *estate* or, even worse, a *class* of "armed *kulak* servants of Tsarist despotism" (Likhnitsky 1931, 14). For this reason, the Cossacks were never granted even token ethnic autonomy, unlike the non-Russian minorities, who were recognized as nationalities. Furthermore, turbulent Soviet history and the calamitous socioeconomic transformation of the 1920s–1950s thoroughly changed the social, cultural, and demographic outlook of the Kuban population. Non-Cossack immigration continued throughout the Soviet period, especially under the impact of Soviet industrialization and World War II. The 1992 poll estimate, which was overtly generous to the neo-Cossacks, showed that only 18 percent of the "Slavs" (here a euphemism for Russians and Ukrainians) living in Krasnodar considered themselves Cossack descendants (Ter-Sarkisiants 1994, 9).

In 1942, Stalin sanctioned the formation of Kuban Cossack regiments as part of his effort to mobilize patriotic traditions. The desperately heroic charge of the historic cavalry against German tanks was at first successful due to sheer surprise, but overall it remained a propagandistic episode. Likewise the famous 1950 movie musical *Kubanskie kazaki* painted in accordance with socialist realism a fabulously fictitious picture of merry opulent life enjoyed by the collective farmers, who, in a folkloric twist, also happened to be dancing and singing Cossacks. Between 1945 and 1989, Cossack imagery survived in Krasnodar only as a residual part of a broader regional identity. Evocations of Cossack spirit were relegated to the art of state-sponsored folkloric choruses or to the cheering slogans of Krasnodar soccer fans–*Hey, Cossacks! Trample the bootless Russians!*—leaving one wondering if the history of agrarian conflict made any sense to Soviet soccer hooligans. The Cossack past was not simply forgotten, but it became unintelligible to the new, largely urbanized, Soviet generations. A few elderly women still kept faded photos of brave young men in World War I uniforms emblazoned with St. George's crosses, but they rarely showed these sad relics to anyone, not even their own grandchildren (including myself). The unbearably painful memories of the 1914–45 period remained firmly suppressed. So more surprising was the 1990 third advent of the Cossacks, this time as a revivalist movement.

Unrebellious Krasnodar

The appearance of the neo-Cossack social movement in 1990 may appear a further surprise considering that Krasnodar registered even less public organizing than most Russian provinces during the years of Gorbachev's perestroika. The conservatism and inertia of Russian provincial populations is the most commonly cited reason. It is not just a bad explanation; it is empirically wrong. When the opportunity arose during the 1990 parliamentary by-elections, Krasnodar awarded a landslide victory to former KGB General Kalugin who was an outsider and clearly the antiestablishment candidate among the two dozen local contenders. This totally unexpected outbreak of the protest vote, however, was a disservice to the nascent groups of Krasnodar political activists because Kalugin, like other Moscow celebrity democrats of the time, abandoned his constituency once he was elected. Moscow remained the exclusive field of emerging politics, which was reaching Russian provinces primarily through the Moscow-based mass media. This was a one-way and mostly ephemeral flow that helped to change attitudes but could never gain sufficient momentum to produce movement organizing. The high-status intelligentsia from Moscow and Leningrad forfeited what Sidney Tarrow (1994) has called the capillary work of movement organizing, preferring instead the immediate prestige of televised publicity. There was a structural reason for the predisposition of the perestroika era democratic personalities (like the dissidents before) to address their moral admonitions and conflicting practical recommendations to the Soviet leadership rather than the populace, which was taken for granted as the captive audience of the glasnost era media. The nascent field of politics was heavily centered around the figure of the last general secretary, Gorbachev, and later the first Russian president, Yeltsin. Thus, the new politics of Russia reproduced the highly centralized hierarchical lines of distribution of administrative power and intellectual status inherited from the Soviet era. Later attempts to extend into the provinces branches of new political parties invariably ended in frustration. The provincials remained incredulous and unresponsive even if not entirely uninterested.

The insights of social movement literature point at some immediate causes of such passivity. Unlike the countries of Eastern Europe and some republics of the USSR, where the revolutions of 1989 were a continuation and fulfillment of the rebellions of 1956 and 1968, in Russia the previous cycle of protest took place during the disastrous collectivization of 1929–33, whole epochs and generations away from the time of perestroika.[5] Furthermore, popular distaste for political mobilization was highly reinforced in Krasnodar by the experience of living in a socially segmented and pervasively corrupt environment where social goals were best achieved through personal networking and the cultivation of mutual dependencies. The alleged stagnant provincialism of Krasnodar is a misleading explanation, for it has to be explained. In fact, what makes a province provincial?

I would tentatively propose for the chief suspect the disempowering system of social controls inherited from the Soviet pattern of bureaucratization, which was at the same time parochial and territorially hierarchical. Three major characteristics of the Soviet enterprise system—a taut labor market; the rigid, ostensibly egalitarian, wage grid; and the distribution of social services through the workplace—shaped the managerial strategy of placing employees in a web of informally negotiated incentives and benefits conditioned on individual and group compliance.[6] The outcome was a paternalistic institution that resembled in its operations a sociopolitical community rather than mere enterprise. Ethnic and local ties were prominently reaccentuated in a "human-scale" environment of densely personal interaction. With a few exceptions, Krasnodar is hardly a province of gigantic enterprises and big towns where life develops impersonality and possibly even a cosmopolitan flair. Rural collective farms, small towns, and small to medium factories are social spaces where managerial control over production tends to coincide with control over the life conditions of employees. Local inhabitants are aware of this condition to a surprising degree. "Collective farm feudalism"—a caustic and sad expression that one commonly hears in Krasnodar—is a metaphor with a recognizable reality behind it. The continuity of social hierarchy and control in Russia's provinces is chiefly responsible for the tenacious survival of socialist agriculture following the demise of the Soviet system as well as accounting for the conservative voting patterns of Russia's rural inhabitants.

But the homeland of the neo-Cossacks is no longer entirely agricultural. Between 1945 and 1980, the population of the city of Krasnodar grew almost sevenfold, to nearly 700,000 people. The provincial capital boasts a decent university and a score of research institutes, several theaters (including a very respectable ballet), large hi-tech factories related to the military sector, many hospitals, several television channels and newspapers, and a literary monthly (which since 1988 has excelled at rabid nativism). In the Krasnodar territory, according to the 1989 census, the proportion of people with higher education was 9.2 percent (330,000 total)—only slightly lower than Russia's average—with almost half of this number residing in the territory's capital (*Krasnodarsky krai nakanune vyborov* 1995, 5). Nonetheless, the large numbers of intelligentsia, professionals, and students do not translate into political prominence, which is a direct result of the staunchly dependent configuration of intellectual fields in most provincial capitals of Russia. As in all bureaucratically centralized states, in Russia the intellectual field reproduced and accentuated the huge status dichotomy between the capital and the provinces. Provincial universities were considered peripheral in every respect. The local intelligentsia suffered chronically from low professional prestige, scarce material rewards, intellectual isolation, and stringent curbs on mobility. This situation engendered career stagnation along with cutthroat competition, vicious forms of ganging together, and bureaucratic intrigue. Withdrawal from public and professional pursuits into private life, hobbies, and friendships was often considered the best moral choice. To escape this shallow puddle and its blind-alley careers by becoming a party apparatchik or a KGB agent was an attraction that mightily demoralized the intelligentsia. Employment in the once comfortably subsidized but also far more disciplined military-industrial complex had similar effects on the inability of engineering cadres to foster a politically self-conscious intelligentsia. These factors must be earnestly considered instead of simply bemoaning the lack of civic "instincts" among Soviet provincial university-educated employees, critically contrasted today with the high moral standards of a Chekhovian provincial intelligentsia.

Barriers to collective action in the former Soviet Union were often trivial and therefore "naturally" invisible. The old institutions, networks, types of solidarity, and practices that sustained communities and the public sphere of prerevolutionary Russia were violently uprooted in the first decades of Soviet transformation, while the formation of a new civil society was continuously aborted by pervasive bureaucratic despotism, long-standing curbs on social communication, and the assiduous elimination of alternatives to the existing regime (Urban et al. 1997). The nuclei of civil societies emerged nonetheless within high-status professionalized fields such as literature, the arts, and academic science, but they were heavily concentrated in the capital cities (Moscow, Leningrad, and the centers of national republics). During perestroika, the high-ranking cities would become the typical sites of intelligentsia-led mobilizing, which was ideologically framed as a shifting mixture of democratic and nationalist demands (the former aimed at opening access to power locally, the latter at wresting power from Moscow). Like most Soviet towns of lesser rank, Krasnodar remained placid because its population, including potential leaders among the intelligentsia, was disempowered by the paternalistic networks while the nomenklatura who dominated such networks could resist the risky game of politicizing their administrative and economic power. As long as pressures on their positions from inside and below were diffuse while the normal bureaucratic channels and practices of bargaining with Moscow remained operational, the Russian provincial bosses preserved a clear interest in and the ability to keep their bureaucratic fiefdoms stolidly provincial. The monetization of the Russian economy in the 1990s reformulated and further reinforced the condition of provincialism. In the new configuration of power, Moscow has forcefully emerged not only as the central political arena but also as the hub of financial flows and the entry point to global networks.

The Spark

Despite the apparent immobility of provincial life, a single major exception took place in the city of Krasnodar in January 1990. Ironically enough for a place where *feminism* is universally considered a dirty word, barriers to collective action were overcome in a spontaneous surge of explicitly gendered women's protest, which led, in a further irony, to the creation of a male chauvinist movement. The protest erupted in response to the extraordinary summoning of army reservists for a secret mission that was, in another public relations blunder, described the next day as the "pacification of nationalist fanatics in Azerbaijan." Against the backdrop of the wildest rumors and muted media reports of Armenian massacres and general mayhem in Transcaucasia, army reservists had to be literally dragged out of their workplaces and homes all over Krasnodar. The rally brewed in the crowd of wives and mothers of the reservists who came to the Krasnodar Military Commissariat demanding information about the whereabouts of their family members. Emotions of frustration and anger, the urge to speak up and comfort each other, spontaneous organization for compiling lists of the men taken away, plus the sheer concentration of women downtown in front of an aloof official agency sparked furious action that largely followed the traditionally legitimized model of Russian women's revolt (*babiy bunt*). For three days and nights, frenzied women rallied in downtown Krasnodar until the reservists began to return home. The event produced a doubly antithetical identity in the crowds—against the "violent Caucasians," who should be left alone to sort out their ethnic conflicts, and distant Moscow, which was willing to sacrifice the lives of Kuban men in its political gambles. Speakers at the rallies in Krasnodar soon developed new rituals of addressing the audiences as "the people of Kuban" (*kubantsy*) and cheering them up with Cossack folk songs like they would at a wedding or village festival. After a moment of disarray, the Krasnodar officials decided to endorse the rally, provided it with live television coverage, and subscribed to its anti-Moscow and anti-Gorbachev rhetoric.

The January 1990 women's revolt in Krasnodar (similar protests took place in neighboring Rostov and Stavropol) showed that the Soviet military machine could not be automatically counted on to quell internal unrest. The military command and conservatives within the Soviet political leadership apparently drew their own lessons from this. In the spring of 1990, they sponsored a series of seminars to discuss the idea of restoring the Cossack frontier guard service. The details of such an odd project were certainly unclear to its authors. It was another of the apparat improvisations that abounded in those chaotic times. Still, the aim was transparent—to insulate Russia from the increasingly unruly and nationalist Transcaucasian republics with a buffer of loyal Russian subjects organized in paramilitary reserves.[7] In June 1990, the first All-Russian Cossack Congress was held in Moscow (the Ukrainian Cossack revivalists were not present because from the outset their movement was directed by the Ukrainian anti-Soviet nationalists). Following the all-Russian event in Moscow, neo-Cossack movements were established in a dozen Russian provinces and the contested, predominantly Slavic, northern provinces of Kazakhstan. The newly encouraged Kuban Cossacks held their founding congress in Krasnodar in October 1990, which created the permanent organization called the Rada (council), following the 1917 precedent. It was, of course, a very different Rada.

From Apparat Improvisation to Movement Organization

Small circles of Cossack enthusiasts existed in Krasnodar since before 1990. They consisted primarily of amateur local historians, collectors of military regalia, professional scholars, folkloric artists, and not an insignificant number of adolescent buffs of war history, weaponry, and equestrianism. Politicization arrived with the demonstration effect, indeed, the psychological pressure exercised by the non-Russian national movements in the Soviet republics. The urge to formulate a defensive discourse of Russian identity grew particularly strong in the borderland and multiethnic regions such as Krasnodar. Curiously enough, the historically Ukrainian origins of the Kuban Cossacks were largely ignored—Ukraine has become a national state whose independence in 1991 was perceived as a major blow to the messianic Russian *idea.* Organizers of the First Kuban Cossack Congress in the fall of 1990 put their eschatological sentiments together with the resources offered by the provincial Communist administration, obviously acting with the sanction of Moscow. For instance, the strictly checked invitation tickets barred a number of Ukrainophiles and "disorderly personalities" from participating in the founding congress. The same invitations entitled their carriers to purchase elaborate Cossack uniforms, including the traditional daggers, tall sheepskin hats, and silver-clad belts that were offered at a heavily subsidized price in a shop closed to the public. Impressive uniforms, marching in the streets, and praying in military formation would remain the major marker and mobilizing resource of the neo-Cossack movement, the vehicle of visual propaganda that worked infallibly in attracting curious spectators and visiting journalists from Moscow and abroad.

There are no reliable data on the social and professional backgrounds of neo-Cossack activists. In a tale-telling instance, they tore up the questionnaires distributed at a Cossack rally by a daring sociologist, shouting that sociology was "Jewish science." Field observations and personal interviews indicate that, like many radical movements in post-Soviet Russia, Cossack revivalism disproportionately attracted personalities with twisted life stories and problematic status in their social microenvironments. This may give credit to the widespread accusations of the lumpen and semicriminal character of the neo-Cossacks, which was indirectly acknowledged by their own leadership in numerous denials that they were "mere drunks, village ruffians, or gangsters in sheepskin hats."[8] These sort of men commonly blamed their personal woes, and by implication all the troubles of Russia, on the vile ethnic minorities. The racist tonality was most conspicuous in the Black Sea coastal districts and the city of Krasnodar, where ethnic Armenians and Greeks enjoyed sizable numbers and unwanted visibility in numerous entrepreneurial positions. Despite the scandalous notoriety of the debauchery-prone neo-Cossack racists, they were likely too volatile and politically destabilizing to become a leading group in the movement. The better disciplined core of the movement was composed of retired military and police officers (with some sympathizers still on active duty); former sportsmen, coaches, and similar members of Soviet-era professional groups that specialized in law enforcement or patriotic education; and especially members of the local intelligentsia, who obtained in the Cossack revival an opportunity to take nativist pride in their provinciality.

Field research suggests a singularly clear pattern in the emerging political preferences of the Krasnodar intelligentsia during the early 1990s. Political positioning in the early post-Communist period strongly correlates with the previous ideological status of career specialization. The choice of abstract and cosmopolitan pursuits (classical philosophy, theoretical science, linguistics, or anthropology) with few exceptions indicated a potential democrat, while their opponents came from the backgrounds that were either more "practical," and therefore allowed administrative advancement (engineering, agronomy), or "politically actual," in Soviet parlance (mainstream social sciences and law), and by definition patriotically inclined (e.g., the arts of socialist realism and party journalism, but the staunchest nationalists invariably were museum curators, who sought to compensate for the lack of academic tenure with ardent propagation of heritage). I want to stress that political preferences could be deduced from neither class, intelligentsia status, nor professional occupation or academic discipline. The picture is dynamic and relational, where one pole is provincialism associated with localized power and its opposite is the "impractical" choice of personal and professional prestige by association with larger, nonlocal intellectual fields. The history faculty at Kuban State University epitomizes this pattern in the confrontation between the chair of world history, which was home to Krasnodar's leading democrat, Dr. Zhdanovsky, once a Bronze Age archeologist, and the chair of Russian history, which gave the neo-Cossack movement its long-standing chief, Ataman, otherwise known as Associate Professor Gromov.

The rank and status earned in the Soviet era was directly transposed into the hierarchical organization of the neo-Cossack movement. This reproduced the familiar Brezhnev malaise—bureaucratic ossification, closed patronage, and a general lack of career mobility. The movement began to split under the pressure of ambitious younger activists shortly before its founding congress. The worst kind of loose cannons proved to be the new breed of businessmen, who sought to legitimate their capitalistic endeavors with the legal and moral sanction of Cossack patriotism under such fabulous slogans as "truly honest Slavic commerce." The stolid intellectual and military veteran leaders of the Rada desperately struggled to keep in line the entrepreneurs who considered their paltry financial contributions sufficient grounds for claiming high offices in the movement and employing its members as personal bodyguards. The differences were rendered irreconcilable by the divergent social experiences and the acquired sets of dispositions and practices. The Rada leadership belonged to the lower echelon and retirees of Soviet-era military and civilian cadres who were trained in apparat discipline and group solidarity. This also allowed them relatively easy rapport with and access to the acting state bureaucrats. The entrepreneurs, on the contrary, were fiery mavericks par excellence whose stormy careers were built on the habit of rule breaking and opportunistic alliances. Besides, in the corrupt and criminalized business environment of post-Soviet Russia, the aspiring entrepreneurs tended to acquire connections with organized crime and the demeanor of warlord tycoons or, in another often complimentary adaptation, the attitudes of populist politicos.

Framing, Boundaries, and Politics

The neo-Cossack movement suffered its most dangerous split in 1992 when the first post-Communist governor of Krasnodar, Diakonov, threw his weight behind a new organization, the Kuban Cossack Army. Diakonov was a good example of a momentously successful maverick. At the beginning of perestroika, he was the manager of the regional plumbing supplies trust, a lucrative position that controlled highly marketable commodities. This facilitated his conversion into a vocal proponent of the market economy and privatization. In 1990, Diakonov brazenly violated nomenklatura discipline by winning a seat in the Russian Parliament and joining the faction that was gaining strength—the Democratic Russia led by Yeltsin. The gamble paid off, and after the conservative coup attempt in August 1991 Diakonov returned to his native province as personal ally of the new Russian president and the first non-Communist governor. Diakonov's assault on the Rada was an attempt to monopolize the emerging political arena of Krasnodar as well as a purely personal revenge—in 1990, the backstage organizers of the neo-Cossack founding congress had eliminated his name from the list of candidates for the position of chief, Ataman. Highly emotional, authoritarian, and politically naive, Diakonov pursued his vendetta against what he called the "Communist impostors sullying the ancient Cossack uniforms," in the meantime utterly failing to build a political base within the real field of power, which still was the provincial nomenklatura. Within a year, he was toppled in a bureaucratic coup to which Moscow acquiesced. The main legacy of Diakonov's brief reign was the creation of an alternative neo-Cossack organization that established itself in opposition to the pro-Communist Rada as a self-alleged inheritor of the anti-Bolshevik White cause. In terms of numbers and influence, the Yeltsinite neo-Cossacks (whose rudimentary ideology never moved beyond personal attacks on the "Communists") remained a distant secondary organization. The field of neo-Cossack ideology, if not active politics, continued to expand. At least half a dozen groups, ranging from minor to embryonic, scrambled to constitute their own positions. Some claimed themselves to be "truly historical Kuban Cossacks" of Ukrainian stock opposed to the Great Russian chauvinists of either the Bolshevik or anti-Bolshevik kind, others rallied for an independent Cossack Nation, and still others purported to revive the memory of anarchist "Greens" (not at all in the spirit of European environmentalists but rather the "third-force" guerrillas of the Russian civil war, whose double-pronged slogan was: "Hit the Reds until they turn white, hit the Whites until they turn red!"). A circle of apparently no more than ten people, led by a former graduate student in chemistry, attacked in their sporadic newspaper "empire-imposed Christianity" for the sake of a return to Slavic pagan origins. A bit more seriously, several local chapters based in the rural towns and collective farms broke away from the Rada, accusing its urban-based leaders of having "lost the touch with native soil in the asphalt streets." A few neo-Cossack organizations espoused little ideological vigor, opting instead for pure business while boldly claiming tax exemptions as folkloric charitable associations. In a succession of protracted internecine struggles, the original leadership of the movement, still entrenched in the Rada, outperformed all factional challengers and solidified the core movement. They were certainly helped by the fact that most contenders were peripheral and provincial in relation to the Rada, which was situated in the administrative center of Krasnodar. In the end, the main neo-Cossack organization whose name was changed in the process from the excessively Ukrainian Rada into the all-Kuban Cossack Host, boasted 183 local chapters with nearly eighty thousand members. The membership remained relatively stable albeit nominal. At no moment was the Host Rada able to support its apparatus and propaganda with membership dues and subscriptions, which made it heavily dependant upon state subsidies. Therefore, cultivating political and personal relations with state officials at all levels remained a major resource and concern.

In the wake of the bungled coup attempt in August 1991, less than a year after its founding congress, the neo-Cossack movement faced near extinction. It suddenly lost patronage in high bureaucratic offices and much of its political legitimacy. Salvation came in the early months of 1992 with the wave of mass protests against the neoliberal policies of shock therapy. The emergent nationalist sector of the new Russian politics sought to present these reforms as a plot to destroy the great Motherland, a covert economic genocide against the Russian people by the world plutocracy. Economic hardship, however, proved to be insufficient to stimulate a truly massive mobilization, especially in a fertile territory like Krasnodar, where the population massively turned to subsistence gardening or, exploiting another geographic advantage of Krasnodar, to the cross-border petty trade with Turkey. The overwhelming majority of Russian citizens put their trust in the microlevel strategies of daily survival rather than the distant promise of political action. Besides, for a warrior nationalist movement it seemed awkward to protest against the high prices. The neo-Cossacks yearned for a patriotic war, which they found and actively promoted in Transdniestria.

Transdniestria is an industrial enclave within Moldavia with a high proportion of ethnically Russian workers who were imported during the Soviet era. The enterprise and municipal infrastructure of Transdniestria served to organize and direct the resistance of Russian settlers who found themselves trapped in the projected Greater Romania. Moldavia was a lesser among the former Soviet republics and, from the vantage point of national principle, likely the most artificial. The majority of its population was in fact ethnically Romanian, and much of its territory (with the notable exception of Transdniestria) had belonged to Romania before 1940. In the revolutionary utopian climate of 1989–91, popular emotions in favor of an enlarged Romania within a new Europe ran very high. Besides the perceived promise of honorable integration in the European sphere, student activists and intellectuals, in both post-Soviet and especially post-Ceaucescu Romania, ardently pursued the nationalist project as the shortest road to debunking their leftover rulers and assuming leadership of a new state. It turned out that the promoters of Greater Romania on either side of the former Soviet frontier badly overestimated the combative spirit of their supporters and the readiness of nomenklatura to surrender their positions within the existing state institutions. This largely explains why Moldavia remained an independent state and why its authorities fought an unwanted war with Transdniestrian separatists only half-heartedly.

The participation of neo-Cossack volunteers in this brief conflict was in every respect symbolic. The four casualties they suffered in the Transdniestrian expedition, including that of a well-known Krasnodar patriotic poet, may seem negligible. Yet each funeral of the movement's fallen heroes, staged with maximum pomp and solemnity, became an occasion to revive neo-Cossack organizations and establish nationalist legends. Romanians, however, proved to be imperfect foes. They were Orthodox Christians like the neo-Cossacks themselves; besides, they gave up too easily. Several months later, a neo-Cossack expedition sent to rescue neighboring Abkhazes from Georgian nationalist militias became an even more ambiguous cause. The Georgians, after all, were also Orthodox Christians, although their leader, Eduard Shevardnadze, was held to be responsible by Russian nationalists for ceding the Soviet East European acquisitions to NATO while serving as Gorbachev's minister of foreign affairs. Abkhazes openly sought Russian protection, scared by the Georgian attempts to scrap the political entitlements of their ethnic autonomy and (not a small consideration in this war) watching the Georgian warlords reward their retainers with booty looted from an exceptionally wealthy area. Still, they were awkward allies. Abkhazes were neither Christian nor fellow Slavs. In fact, they were mountaineers who were helped in this nasty war by native nationalists from all over the North Caucasus, including Chechens. In Nagorno Karabagh, the neo-Cossacks found no fit at all—to them Azeris were loathed Muslims, and Armenians were loathed traders, while neither side was particularly disposed to accept aid from amateur Russian nationalists. What remained was, of course, Bosnia, where Serbian brethren militias were eager to embrace the Russian neo-Cossacks for their symbolical value in this post-Communist conflict dressed in the antiquated garb. Yet, for reasons that aren't entirely clear, the neo-Cossacks preferred to bypass the invitation. The secret likely lies with the Russian state, especially considering that in both Transdniestria and Abkhazia the neo-

Cossack volunteers and mercenaries operated with the connivance of the Russian military and some members of Yeltsin's administration.

Except for a brief moment during the public funerals of March and April 1992, the neo-Cossack search for heroic performance left Krasnodar generally unperturbed. One might expect that in such a chaotic situation as the demise of the Soviet Union large sectors of the population would condone, even hail, vigilante justice and xenophobic ultranationalist rhetoric, yet this didn't happen. The Soviet disintegration wasn't experienced by the Russian population as a momentous and final catastrophe. State institutions did not collapse overnight, as they did in 1917, but rather lost coherence and mutated incrementally. The structures of everyday life were preserved, and the general social environment remained familiar. Economic hardship was either tolerable or uneven and in most instances insufficient to provoke rebellion. Unlike the former Yugoslavia, at no time did civil war or ethnic massacre appear to be a credible threat anywhere close to Russia's heartland. Neither should one underestimate the stabilizing effects of Russia's democratization. Independent media and regular relatively free elections permitted Russian citizens to vent their anger without gambling on violence. A perceived lack of realistic alternatives to existing conditions made inaction the best available politics for post-Soviet politicians, both those in power and those in the opposition (while the horrifying example of the October 1993 armed revolt in Moscow and the disastrous invasion of Chechnya showed what could be the price of recklessness). In the absence of practical possibilities to play the game of politics, Russian political life shifted into an endless cycle of symbolic confrontations.

The wars in Transdniestria and Abkhazia wound down into lasting stalemates like all separatist conflicts in the former Soviet republics. During the disastrous invasion of Chechnya, most neo-Cossacks either prudently opted to stay away or weren't requested by Moscow. The bloody confrontation between the Russian president and his parliamentary opponents in October 1993 ended before most neo-Cossacks could sort out their internal differences and choose sides. After that frightening moment, the reconstituted Russian political elites established largely unspoken rules of power struggles. Central to the compromise was the acceptance of elections as the mechanism of power redistribution, avoidance of popular and state violence, the restraint of radicals on all sides, and further prevention of boundary-pushing outsiders from penetrating the established political arena or gaining exposure in the mass media. (Zhirinovsky appeared at first a dangerous exception, but he soon proved himself to be a perfectly predictable opportunist and a useful lightening rod for diffuse forms of antiestablishment discontent.)

The neo-Cossacks could not find a place in this picture. For success in party politics, their popular support was too narrow and their organizations too ineffective and dependent on various (often feuding) local authorities. In every election, the neo-Cossacks faced competition from both the present (Yeltsinite) and the recent (neo-Communist) holders of state power, upon whose favors they depended, plus the omnivorous populist Zhirinovsky, who established in Krasnodar one of his strongholds. Culminating in a long sequence of bureaucratic project making and intrigues, which emanated mostly from the Russian Ministry for the Nationalities, in 1997 the neo-Cossacks were officially decreed a state service in the domain of law enforcement and patriotic education. The trajectory of neo-Cossack revival thus came full circle. The erstwhile nomenklatura patrons of the neo-Cossacks pushed back into the academia the progressive anthropologists who briefly rose to power in the disarray of liberal reforms in 1992. The personalities who regained control of Russian policies toward the nationalities were the same men who had helped to invent the neo-Cossacks in the first place, and they still stubbornly promoted the experiment in patrolling the frontiers, training preconscription-age teenagers, and cultivating patriotic feelings. Ideological and patronage allegiances aside, entering a new ethnic minority (the Cossacks of all provinces and stripes) in the roster of Russia's nationalities promised expanded bureaucratic positions, additional finances, perks, and benefits without the headache of negotiating prestige, power, and perennially insufficient subsidies with the unruly presidents of ethnic republics within the Russian federation. Alas, in full accordance with the famous Freudian aphorism dropped by Premier Chernomyrdin, "we hoped for the better, but it came out as usual." State registration of the neo-Cossacks immediately became a bone of contention between Moscow and the Russian provincial governors, who felt they were being cheated. (Nikolai "Father" Kondratenko of Krasnodar never missed a chance to go public with his struggles against the Moscow bureaucrats.) In the end, the scramble for control over the new state service and its funds ran into the drastic depreciation of the Russian ruble after the financial crisis of August 1998.

Conclusion: Globalization, Fundamentalist Voice, and Emigration Exit

In its first decade, the neo-Cossack movement neither perished in its infancy nor flourished. Rather, it stagnated. Its membership, main organizations, roster of leaders, and half-baked nativist ideologies have remained the same since its founding moment in the early 1990s (when the free uniforms and ranks were parceled out). Such a mediocre outcome of movement mobilization conforms to the general trend in the Russian political arena, which throughout the 1990s remained locked in a balance of mutual weakness. The underlying condition, however, belongs to the level of analysis at which Krasnodar and even the whole of Russia appear to be just particular instances in a much larger picture of current global transformation. At this level, the localized story of reemerging Cossacks is really part of the overall trend of globalization. This instance of radical provincialism was an immediate reaction to the collapse of the Soviet Union, which left such a place as Krasnodar directly exposed to global trends.

Globalization is an exceedingly generalized term that encompasses three mutually reinforcing trends. First, it is the secular reversal of the states' claim to the power to direct economic processes and check the social effects of markets both within their jurisdictions and beyond. This is known as the overburdening of the welfare state in core countries, the crisis of Third World developmentalism, and waves of democratization deriving from the moral and financial bankruptcy of various authoritarian regimes in the semiperipheries, including the demise of the Soviet bloc. In their own perceptions, the neo-Cossacks bemoan this as the loss of the great state and historical certainty. Second, *globalization* refers to shifts in the organization of world production (the latest technological revolution spurred by the search for new sectors with higher rates of profit, the rise of East Asia's capitalist archipelago, the demise of newly uncompetitive industries elsewhere, and the worldwide though uneven depreciation of labor). In the neo-Cossacks' demonology, this is a hideous plot hatched by the global plutocracy to rob Russia of its industrial potential and natural riches. Third, the economic and political turmoil of the last thirty years undid the gains the peripheral and semiperipheral developmentalist regimes made after 1945. The net result was the reconcentration of systemic power within select core states and in the hands of nonterritorial capitalist corporations, which dramatically changed the character of global power games. Instead of being able to act as a cartel and play one superpower against another, today the countries of the Third World have to compete individually among themselves and with the fragments of the former Soviet bloc to attract investments and aid.[9]

Globalization hit the Russian Empire particularly hard because its twentieth-century form, the Soviet Union, was shaped and geared toward the 1914–45 world of fierce military and ideological struggles. Besides, the Soviet model was developed in the country with a huge mass of despotically controlled labor that could be applied almost regardless of cost to the building of new industries or the winning of immensely destructive wars. The labor pool and the resource of state terror were exhausted by the USSR in the 1950s, which prompted the regime to turn to the policies of more tacit disempowerment and consumerist pacification of the populace. At its end, the USSR was likely the world's premier example of bureaucratically unified control over a sheltered and contained labor force and an increasingly obsolete industrial base. And, of course, the Soviet Union was still the most significant geopolitical node on the semiperiphery until 1989, when its leaders embarked on an improvised attempt to renegotiate their power within the rapidly changing domestic and international environment. The USSR was certainly not alone in its troubles during the 1980s. Unbound by the onset of economic contraction in 1973–79, capitalist globalization once again brought the heavy artillery of cheap goods (material and symbolic) to batter all kinds of walls, demolishing worldwide the institutionalized rigidities and ossified monopolies that dated back to the periods before and immediately after 1945.

The recent global transformation has annihilated for all practical purposes the historical ideologies and political projects of the Russian state, both imperial and state socialist. Political mass consciousness in Russia is struggling to identify the cause of the trouble. Nevertheless, the placid political outcome of the 1990s suggests that the Russian citizenry realizes firmly enough that neither the restoration of territorial empire nor the reimposition of an autarchic, centrally planned economy are feasible or desirable options. Notice how amazingly little resistance there was to the dissolution of the empire (even in such a painful instance as Chechnya) and how readily many Russians accepted the promise of capitalist conversion. The neoliberal belief in markets, however, unlike other matters of faith, requires sufficient means of payment in order to be sustained. It is probably unjust to accuse global capitalists of robbing former Soviet citizens. The robbers who directly profited from the inherited Soviet industrial park (oil, aluminum, military hardware, etc.) and the residual special status of the Russian state (which for a while allowed its ruling elites to plunder the priviliged credits of the International Monetary Fund) were certainly some of their best-known fellow countrymen. What is much worse, contrary to optimistic expectations, the period of plunder failed to become one of primary accumulation in Russia. Russians and other former Soviet populations were bypassed by the global flows of capital and left in the world's largest pool of structurally unemployed labor. The native robber barons, big and small, contributed mightily to this outcome by creating local environments impossible for foreign investment and barely tolerable for themselves. Of course, most Russians see and understand that. The questions are in what terms can they frame their understanding and in what projects can they place their hopes of coping with chaos when all projects seem irrelevant, utopian, or cruel mockeries?

Here we encounter the crucial difference between the current bout of creative destruction and the nineteenth-century waves of globalization. It is the apparent exhaustion of ideological optimism and, closely related, the critical insufficiency of political agency capable of advancing a new systemic order and institutions of sustained growth. After 1989, capitalism won in the sense that it appeared to be the system with no sensible alternatives—of course, the advanced, corelike imagery of capitalism promoted by the current geocultural mainstream. The problem is that for the majority of humankind the capitalism of wealth, middle classes, and liberal democracy has remained the virtual reality carried through global media. Therefore, the immediate reality of economic volatility, social decay, and political frustrations seemed all the more painful. The discrediting of socialist and national-liberation projects in the 1980s consolidated the field of geoculture to a binary opposition: capitalism and its rejections, expressed mostly in localized discourses. The demise of antisystemic movements rooted in the progressivist ideologies of 1848 further reduced the dimensions of geocultural struggles. If capitalism appears invulnerable as political economy, then antisystemic sentiments have to be expressed primarily in moral and culturalist terms. The most concise expression of the new geopolitics and the geoculture of the 1990s is indeed Huntington's "the West and the Rest."

Fundamentalism is not such a new phenomenon. It is a variation within the range of societal responses to the situation of wholesale crisis when society loses its economic, social, and political anchors. State-led developmentalism (or what Immanuel Wallerstein (1995) wryly called "Leninism with Marxism or without") has been the dominant political response throughout the twentieth century. What remains after its extinction is the forceful affirmation of a fundamental normative order discovered in the past or in worlds beyond. This was the starting point of all world religions. In the troubled beginning of modern times during the long sixteenth century, fundamentalist affirmation of normative order (in spite of chaos *and* obsolete traditions) assumed the recognizable features of movement ideology. Among the founding fathers of modern social movements were such fundamentalists as Martin Luther in Europe and Ismail Safavi in Iran. Religion is precursor of modern ideology and its obvious substitute in our postideological times. Yet, religion may prove insufficiently rooted (as happens in Africa, where many religions compete) or institutionalized in ways that prevent movement mobilization or render religion only a part (however important) of a larger national identity. In fact, Islam seems quite exceptional in its transcendence of secular identities and therefore in its mobilization potential. Russia belongs to the more usual pattern of religion being subsumed by national identity, although the national identity in this case is very difficult to separate from the imperial. The ongoing experimentation with Russian imperial patriotism, including the neo-Cossack movement, suggests that a fundamentalist-like hybrid of national consciousness and state socialism is possible and likely. In fact, the hybrid looks very recognizable. Its previous name was fascism, although fascism is usually studied separately from fundamentalism.

Is the Russia of the 1990s then, a replay of Weimar Germany in the 1920s, as is suggested by alarmist commentators? Detailed study of one of the most conspicuous fundamentalist movements (the neo-Cossacks) in one of the most promising provinces (Krasnodar) suggests that there is nothing automatic in the combination of movement organizing and recent historical humiliation and imperial legacy, economic hardship, social disagregation, traditions of political conservatism, and a weak state unable or unwilling to repress radicals. One crucial condition seems missing—acceptance of messianic heroism by a deeply disillusioned and atomized population—which renders the Russian neo-Cossacks an analytically interesting instance precisely because here the germ of fundamentalism remains relatively weak, constrained by its very provincialism. In a negative reversion, the Russian example highlights the conditions that enable fundamentalist movements elsewhere in the world.

The Russians today differ in almost every social parameter from their not too distant ancestors of 1917 and the contemporary populations of India or the Middle East. Post-Soviet Russians exist in a framework set by predominantly urban industrial occupations and lifestyles, profound (indeed, hitherto unseen) demographic decline, alienation coupled with massive dependency on a corrupt and inefficient state, the lack of modern civil society, and the general sense of disenchantment in any public pursuit. There hardly remains a shred of live traditional culture or the kind of local civilizational tradition that can sustain society, which is left with nothing better than maintaining to the greatest degree possible the social and institutional inertia of the Soviet period. This explains, for instance, the odd stubborness with which former Soviet populations report to work at near-defunct enterprises and offices without being paid for months. People living in such a place are very unlikely to spontaneously burst into collective action, be it fundamentalist fervor or imperial conquest. The impulse cannot come from the elites either because, despite regular pronouncements to the contrary, they are learning from experience how severely constrained their positions are. Doubtful and suspicious of any collective or state action, both the elites and common Russians rely on personal strategies. The most obvious is to migrate from the crumbling semiperiphery into the core countries, but this increasingly runs against strong cultural preferences (most Russians who managed to establish lives abroad prefer to think that they are there temporarily) and, far more importantly, Western policies and anti-immigrant sentiments. The alternative is building sheltered corelike enclaves within Russia. This is the once-celebrated story of the emerging Western-like middle class, but it ran into the hard realities of Russia's newly found dependency on the world financial markets and the hostile reaction of other Russians in the forms of cultural stigmatization and direct criminal violence. In the end, the majority of Russians remain where they are and what they are. This situation is conducive to the continued reproduction of relative stability at a low point amid social decay, family disintegration, crime, corruption, and substance abuse. The long-term outcome could resemble the dilemma of American inner cities—areas and populations largely redundant to the process of capital accumulation that are costly in every respect, resistant to social reforms, and just won't disappear. But Russia, unlike the inner cities, still preserves a set of state institutions and the memory of a strong army. In the long run, all prophecies, if they are repeated often enough, become self-fulfilling. By eliciting and structuring fundamentalist responses, the geoculture of the "West and the Rest" becomes itself a major factor of systemic instability. Fundamentalist reactions are one of the few currently available responses to the process of peripheral involution and the geoculture of globalization. At least in the short term, provincialization and fundamentalism reinforce the globalization trend by skipping over economically marginal areas and providing a rationale for doing so. What kind of effects this may bring in the long term remains within the range of contested possibilities.

NOTES

In the long process of conceptualizing this essay I benefited from the thoughts and suggestions of Julia Adams, Faruk Birtek, Valerie Bunce, Fatma Müge Göçek, Anatol Lieven,

Michael Kennedy, Michael Urban, Immanuel Wallerstein, David Woodruff, Mayer Zald, and the fellow participants in the 1995–96 Sawyer Seminar on Social Movements at the University of Michigan. This essay was completed during the tenure of a Jennings Randolph senior fellowship at the U.S. Institute of Peace. Special thanks to my assistant, Frederick Williams.

1. Here and below *Krasnodarskii krai nakanune vyborov-95* 1995.

2. This legal maneuver pursued a double-pronged goal. It entitled the Cossacks to state-sponsored "rehabilitation" programs along with other "punished peoples" of the former USSR, while presenting ethnic Russians with victims of communism no less and likely even more than any nationality of the defunct empire.

3. On the earliest Cossacks, see Gordon 1983 and Stanislavskii 1990. For a thorough and innovative discussion of the Razin uprising of 1670–71 from a perspective close to resource mobilization, see Khodarkovsky 1994, 1–19.

4. The imperial military-bureaucratic regularization of Cossacks is the subject of McNeal 1987.

5. The Polish example provides a useful contrast to the Soviet situation. In Poland, institutional conditions for the continued existence of a relatively vibrant though oppressed civil society were created by the peculiar sociopolitical compromise of 1956, which itself was the outcome of the larger crisis of post-Stalinist political transition in the Soviet bloc (see Ekiert 1996).

6. Crowley (1994) powerfully develops the argument of mutual dependency in Soviet heavy industry, although his explanation works even better for the small-scale productive and social environments of post-Communist Russia.

7. The project of Cossack revival was obviously consistent with the contemporary policy of sponsoring or facilitating pro-Soviet countermobilizations in the areas where anticommunist nationalisms threatened the integrity of the USSR: the Internationalist Fronts in the Baltic republics, Abkhaz, and southern Osset; armed opposition to the Gamsakhurdia in Georgia; Transdniestrian separatism in Moldova, Crimean Soviet patriotism in Ukraine; and so on.

8. See, for instance, an interview with Ataman Gromov in the journal *Kuban,* January 1992, 1.

9. The world-systems analysis of globalization may be found in Wallerstein et al. 1996; Arrighi 1994; and Derluguian and Greer, 2000.

CHAPTER 13

Religious Nationalism in India and Global Fundamentalism

Peter van der Veer

1. Introduction

Fundamentalism is a global phenomenon. That is to say, there is a global discourse about fundamentalism. Whenever we care to open the newspapers, fundamentalism stares us in the face from different corners of the world. Sadat was murdered by fundamentalists, Rabin was murdered by a fundamentalist, a mosque in Ayodhya was destroyed by fundamentalists, the metro in Paris was bombed by fundamentalists. The media suggest an outright attack on modern society on a world scale by movements that are called fundamentalist, because religion is a significant aspect of their ideology. It is a label that has global use for journalists who, for example (in my own experience), ask someone who specializes in religion and politics in India to comment on the electoral success of a fundamentalist party in Turkey. When one knows about one fundamentalism, one knows about them all is the assumption. It is important to acknowledge the globalization of a certain language by the Western media, in which *fundamentalism* covers a number of widely differing political struggles. Whatever disclaimers one might have, one is inevitably sucked into using this language, which is indeed made available for global use. This is even true for critical students of culture like Stuart Hall, who uses the term *fundamentalism* for all those "backward-looking movements" that are "either left out of 'modernity' or ambiguously and partially incorporated in one of its many forms" (1993; see also Saba Mahmood's 1996 critique).

This language is certainly not merely descriptive but has an emotive, mobilizing, rhetorical aspect that is crucial to the making of world politics. The fall of the Berlin Wall has opened up a space for talking about a new world order in which modern society, wherever it might be located on the map, has to defend itself against the forces of fundamentalist obscurantism. Samuel Huntington's writings on "the clash of civilizations" are a somewhat bizarre but highly influential instance of that language. The open demand by Newt Gingrich, former Speaker of the U.S. House of Representatives, that money should be reserved for destabilizing the fundamentalist government of Iran is another.

The term *fundamentalism* was first used in the United States in 1920 to designate a broad Protestant movement in defense of biblical literalism. Especially after the Iranian revolution of 1979, it gained wide currency among journalists and politicians to designate a wide variety of religious movements in the world. To say that this broad application of the word *fundamentalism* is a journalistic invention does not, however, weaken or depoliticize it. It is a crucial term not only in the media coverage of world politics but also in the creation of world politics itself. It has become impossible to simply throw it away and use other terms. A powerful language or discourse is not something one can choose to accept or reject; it can be critiqued and deconstructed, but that will not make it go away. I would suggest that the term *fundamentalism* designates what is seen as a threat to both reason and liberty. It thus belongs to a discourse in which a modern, open society tries to define itself as a liberating and progressive force in world history (see Harding 1991). While liberals in the United States may sometimes use *fundamentalism* to describe the Christian Coalition, there can be little doubt that the evangelical Christians who constitute it belong to the mainstream of American society and are an important element in the Republican Party. Their pro-life and antistate activism is seldom targeted in the strongly condemning language used by politicians and the mass media to attack fundamentalism. It is, for instance, striking that the initial response to the Oklahoma bombing was strongly anti-Muslim and that when it turned out that the perpetrators had been white American farmers there was a sense of being ill informed about the kind of groups to which these people belonged. Even Martin Riesebrodt's sociological analysis of modern fundamentalism in the United States and Iran compares Protestant fundamentalism between 1910 and 1928 with Shi'ite fundamentalism between 1961 and 1979 and thus leaves the impression that fundamentalism in the United States is a harmless thing of the past, while fundamentalism in Iran is a political thing of the present.

The greatest enemies of "the open society," for whom the language of utter rejection and condemnation is used, are located not in the West but "in the Rest." If they are found in the West, they are from the Rest. Mostly, they are "fanatic Muslims" who threaten the status quo in the Middle East, where Western industrial societies have vital interests in the production of oil. Not all Muslim fundamentalists are enemies, though. Saudi Arabia, Kuwait, and Pakistan, but also the militant groups in Afghanistan fighting Soviet imperialism are often exempted from the strong, condemning tone used for Sudan and Iran as well as for the militant groups fighting the state in Egypt, Algeria, and Palestine. A crucial characteristic of fundamentalism is therefore that it is anti-Western. Another is that it is against the secular state. These two characteristics are often conflated in the notion that these are movements that see the secular state as an alien, Western phenomenon. The "fanatic Muslim" serves as a template for talking about other fundamentalists such as the Sikh Khalistanis and Hindu nationalists in India.

It is certainly important to analyze the globalization of this discourse, but it cannot replace the critical interpretation of the religio-political movements that we encounter in our studies. Since the term *fundamentalism* is out there to describe these movements, what are social scientists doing with this term? As one might expect, they try to provide a clear definition that fits into some larger social theory. In his comparison of the United States and Iran, Riesebrodt (1993) argues that fundamentalism is a social phenomenon that occurs during rapid social change, is marked by a profound experience of crisis, and tries to overcome that crisis with a revitalization of religion and a search for authenticity. This revitalization is characterized by what he calls a "mythical regress to the revealed and realized order." Authenticity is realized in "rational" fundamentalism by a literalist reading of sacred texts and in charismatic fundamentalism by the experience of a gift of grace. Further, he argues that fundamentalism implies a rejection of the world, but that that can take the form of either fleeing the world or mastering it by forming a political party, religious movement, or secret society. Riesebrodt's central thesis is "that fundamentalism refers to an urban movement directed primarily against the dissolution of personalistic, patriarchal notions of order and social relations and their replacement by depersonalized principles" (9). He asks for attention to the ideology of these movements as well as to the movement's carriers, defined as social units formed in a particular "sociomoral milieu," that is, by the coincidence of several structural dimensions. This, then, is a theory of social transformation and the response to it by social movements of a particular type.

Riesebrodt's definition and theoretical approach are subtle and fairly typical of the sociological approach to fundamentalism. They are very similar to the guiding ideas behind Chicago's huge, multivolume, fundamentalism project, under the directorship of Martin Marty and Scott Appleby. This project covers Christian, Jewish, Muslim, Buddhist, and Confucian fundamentalism in a great variety of societies, ranging from the United States to China and Italy to the Andes. The idea is that fundamentalism is a global phenomenon insofar as it is a response to global processes of social transformation. One could say that it provides sociological support to the journalistic and world-political notion of fundamentalism. There is really something out there that is fundamentalism, and it is everywhere. Although there is some hesitation to use the term *modernization* these days, much of the theoretical framework is in fact not very different from 1960s modernization theory, which focused on processes such as urbanization, industrialization, and secularization.

"Rapid social change" is obviously something extraordinarily vague that can be invoked whenever one needs it, and it has been invoked for every social movement in every place and every epoch of which I am aware. There is something valid in the sociological analysis of these movements as resisting certain fundamental changes in society and in the argument that these changes are in the final analysis part of the dynamic of world capitalism. But the question is: what kinds of resistance and what kinds of changes do we see in particular historical situations? These situations cannot be subsumed in the universal teleology of world capitalism and "the open society." In the case of India, which I will be discussing, there are a host of contradictions to be considered in relation to the issue of globalization. On the one hand, India has been long and effectively colonized and thus integrated into the world economy and in the culture of the English-speaking world. On the other hand, the nationalist movement has been consistently struggling against a certain economic and cultural dependency inherent in this integration. Self-reliance has been one of the strongest slogans of Congress leaders like Mahatma Gandhi, Jawaharlal Nehru, and Indira Gandhi. Since independence, the economy has been consistently protected against foreign capital and despite considerable changes after the liberalization policies of the late 1980s and 1990s this is still the case that explains, incidentally, why India is less affected by the Asian financial crisis than Southeast and East-Asia. What has perhaps more direct political influence on the development of social movements in India is perhaps not the liberalization of the economy but the liberalization of the media, which has allowed global players like Rupert Murdoch's News Corporation to market "infotainment." The state is thus not able to control information and the production of national culture. The developments and movements I describe in this chapter are, however, not yet very influenced by this relatively recent phenomenon. While the globalization literature often takes the demise of the nation-state under the pressure of transnational capitalism for granted, I would emphasize that in a huge society like the Indian the state is still under larger pressures from inside than from outside.

In this chapter, I want to discuss two religio-political movements in India that resist the secular state, as they encounter it in India, and want to effect crucial changes in state-society relations. These movements are not in any sense antimodern or anti-Western. The Hindu movement I will be discussing is perhaps more urban than rural, but the Sikh movement is probably more rural than urban. Moreover, both movements do not resist globalization but in fact embrace it. They are very popular among transnational migrants and in general have often been more in favor of opening up India to the global market than their opponent, the secularist Congress Party, has been. They are against the secularism of the Congress Party but mainly because it is in their view a pseudo-secularism that privileges certain religious communities for electoral purposes. I will begin my story in 1984.

2. Sikhs and Hindus

The year 1984 was to have witnessed the final collapse of the Soviet Empire, according to the famous dissident Andrej Amalrik. He was right about the collapse but wrong about the year. Instead, 1984 turned out to be a crucial year for another huge, imperial state: India. In June 1984, the Indian Army attacked the Golden Temple Complex, the central shrine of the Sikhs, in an operation with the code name Blue Star. This huge complex contained a great number of buildings, including the Harimandir (Golden Temple) and the Akal Takhat (Eternal Throne). The latter was occupied and heavily fortified by militant Sikhs, who demanded the separation of a Sikh state, Khalistan, from what they described as Hindu India. The army encountered so much resistance in the complex that it had to bring tanks into the operation, which caused much greater damage to the religious buildings than the generals had expected. The operation lasted from June 4 till June 7. It destroyed the Sikh Library, which contained a great number of sacred manuscripts and objects from the lives of the gurus in the Sikh tradition. Obviously, the numbers game of counting the casualties on both sides has not been conclusive and leaves us with estimates ranging from a few hundred to a few thousand. On the Sikh side, the number of dead militants was greatly outnumbered by the number of dead pilgrims who were caught in the firing.

The leader of the Khalistani Sikhs, Sant Jarnail Singh Bhindranwale, was killed in the encounter, but this was not the end, but rather the beginning, of his importance, since martyrs are central to Sikh tradition. His ghost turned out to be much more effective than he had ever been alive. Operation Blue Star took its place among the founding massacres in Sikh historical memory: the precolonial massacre of Sikhs in the battle of Malerkotka by the Afghan war leader Ahmad Shah Abdali in 1762, the colonial massacre of peaceful demonstrators in Jallianwala Bagh in Amritsar by British General Dyer in 1919, and now in 1984 the postcolonial massacre of Sikhs in the Golden Temple. These memories repress a lot, but they end up constructing a narrative of Sikh suffering inflicted upon them by outside states. It conveyed the message that India was no longer a state Sikhs belonged to, which was exactly what the militant Khalistanis had in mind. The clearest and perhaps most threatening sign of this was the mutiny of Sikh soldiers in various regiments across the country, the significance of which becomes clear when one realizes the crucial role Sikhs in the Indian Army have played since the late nineteenth century.

Operation Blue Star turned out to be Mrs. Gandhi's last battle, as the title of a book by Mark Tully and Satish Jacob (1991) has it. On October 31, 1984, India's prime minister was assassinated by two Sikhs who were her bodyguards. The assassination was followed by a widespread pogrom against Sikhs and their property, especially in major North Indian cities with sizable Sikh minority populations such as Delhi and Kanpur. These pogroms were organized and led by political leaders of Mrs. Gandhi's Congress Party and meant to "teach the arrogant Sikhs a lesson they would not forget," as people said at the time. They were allowed, and sometimes assisted, by the agencies of the state such as the police and military. Trains and buses were stopped and Sikhs taken out and killed, and in the Punjab the reverse happened with the militants killing Hindu passengers. In the elections of 1984 Mrs. Gandhi's son, Rajiv, a former airline pilot, gained a landslide victory in what was called a "sympathy vote." The anti-Sikh pogrom and the following electoral success of the political party that had orchestrated it left a great number of Sikhs who had never even sympathized with the idea of a separate Sikh state in fundamental disillusion with the Indian state. Whatever happened afterward, Khalistani militancy had gained a permanent place in the Indian polity.

The year 1984 was not only crucial for Sikh nationalism but also for Hindu nationalism. In 1984, I happened to be in India, but fortunately far from the happenings in Punjab. I was finishing my fieldwork in Ayodhya, a Hindu pilgrimage centre in Uttar Pradesh, India's most populous state. My research concerned the organization of ritual specialists, Hindu monks and priests, who are the hosts of hundreds of thousands of pilgrims each year (van der Veer 1988). These pilgrims come to Ayodhya for the dual purpose of worshipping the god Rama and venerating their ancestors. Ayodhya is almost entirely a Hindu sacred place, with hundreds of small and large temples in which the selling and consumption of meat and alcohol is forbidden by local law. There are only small pockets of Muslims living in the city, though a larger community lives in nearby Faizabad. However, Ayodhya was a much more important city for Muslims in an earlier period when it was a seat of administration in the Mughal Empire and together with Faizabad the center of the regional realm of the Nawabs of Oudh in the early eighteenth century before the Nawabs moved a hundred miles away to Lucknow, which continues to be the state capital.

The most prominent sign of the earlier Muslim presence is a large mosque in the center of Ayodhya. According to an inscription on the mosque, it had been built by a general, Mir Baqi, in 1528. The mosque is locally known as Babar's mosque, because Mir Baqi was thought to be a general of the first Mughal emperor. This mosque has been a bone of contention between Hindus and Muslims for more than a century. It had been closed by government order since December 1949, when unknown Hindus had put an image of Rama in the mosque and subsequently had spread the rumor that the Lord had appeared in the mosque. When I did my fieldwork, it was commonly believed in Ayodhya that the mosque had been built on a destroyed temple of Rama and actually was situated on the birthplace of this god. Pilgrims did go to the mosque and worshipped on a platform in front of it, which had been raised by the colonial authorities in 1856. Nevertheless, despite the firmness of local belief that the birthplace of the god Rama was occupied by a mosque and the fact that there was an image of Rama inside the mosque, there was no concerted effort to replace the mosque with a temple.

This changed in September 1984 when the Vishva Hindu Parishad (World Hindu Council, or VHP), a religious movement led by Hindu monks and closely affiliated with a political party, the Bharatiya Janata Party (Indian People's Party, or BJP) started a demonstrative procession of trucks with the name Sacrifice to Liberate Rama's Birthplace. The procession began in Sitamarhi, the birthplace of Rama's wife Sita. The demonstration was thereby given the religious flavor of a pilgrimage tour, an impression that was enhanced by the fact that some of the trucks carried religious images and of course a great number of monks. The procession stayed for a day in Ayodhya, but its appeal was limited in comparison with the many other attractions for Hindu pilgrims the city had to offer. It went on to the state capital, Lucknow, where it did attract large crowds and was supposed to end in a huge rally in Delhi, which fell flat due to the assassination of Mrs. Gandhi. The anti-Sikh pogrom drew attention away from the Hindu-Muslim tensions focusing on Babar's mosque in Ayodhya but not for long. A surprise decision of a district judge in Faizabad led to the opening of the mosque to the Hindu public in 1986. This decision could not have taken place without the connivance of the central government. The opening of the mosque enabled Hindus to worship the 1949 images in the main prayer hall of the mosque. This simple move made the mosque into a Hindu temple. Despite a huge rally of Muslims opposing this desecration of their mosque, which took place in Delhi in 1987, the decision was not changed. It not only opened the mosque literally but also metaphorically for further political action. The Vishva Hindu Parishad and its political ally, the Bharatiya Janata Party, continued to make the removal of the mosque the main plank of their political campaigns.

In 1988, these two parties organized a number of demonstrative processions throughout the country (and even among migrant communities abroad), in which bricks were consecrated for use in building the temple meant to replace the mosque. These bricks were brought to Ayodhya in processions, which often caused riots en route since they cleverly passed through Muslim areas. The greatest massacre in connection to these Rama Shila Pujas ("building processions"; see van der Veer 1994, 4) occurred in Bhagalpur, Bihar, where hundreds of Muslims were killed. In the elections of 1989, the Congress Party of Mr. Gandhi lost its majority in Parliament and the oppositional Janata Party of Mr. V. P. Singh replaced it with the parliamentary support of the BJP. Despite its factual support of the new government, the VHP/BJP continued its agitation for the replacement of the mosque with a temple. In 1990, they organized a large procession, led by Mr. Advani, the leader of the BJP, which started in Somnath in West India and was meant to end in Ayodhya with the ultimate goal of destroying the temple. This procession was stopped in Bihar, and Mr. Advani and a number of his lieutenants were arrested. This led to the withdrawal of parliamentary support for V. P. Singh's government by the BJP. The 1991 elections brought the Congress again to power in the wake of the assassination of its leader, Rajiv Gandhi, who was killed by Sri Lankan Tamil separatists in South India. The BJP, which had gained enormously in the years of Ayodhya agitation and had now become the major opposition party and the governing party in a number of states, including Uttar Pradesh, in which Ayodhya is located, continued with its campaign for the destruction of the Ayodhya mosque.

On December 6, 1992, the VHP and the BJP organized another rally in Ayodhya. The publicly announced aim of the rally was to destroy the mosque. Despite this public announcement the rally was allowed by the authorities, and under the eyes of the gathered press and without much hindrance by the huge paramilitary police force present in Ayodhya, activists started to demolish the old structure till, after a day of hard work, only rubble remained. Why didn't the police intervene?

A high-ranking police officer told the press that the police could easily have intervened and prevented the demolition. However, they had not received orders to do so. Naturally, they did not get any orders from the state officials of Uttar Pradesh, since Uttar Pradesh was at that time governed by the BJP, the political party that was behind the demolition. The paramilitary forces, however, were under the direct command of what in India is called the Centre, that is, the Union government in Delhi. Why did the Centre not act? Well, the story goes that India's prime minister, Narasimha Rao (Rajiv Gandhi's successor), was just taking a nap and, since he is a very old man nobody wanted to disturb him. When he woke up, the demolition had already proceeded too far. I do not relate this story to show a certain indecisiveness on the part of the Indian government, since on the next day the Union government did act very decisively by dismissing the state governments of four states in which the opposition BJP ruled. It put the leadership of the two movements in jail for a few days and banned a few radical movements, on both the Hindu and the Muslim sides. Narasimha Rao's nap had been a strategic one that allowed the Union government to reestablish the supremacy of the Congress Party, which had been seriously challenged by the BJP. Nevertheless, all these political actions did not prevent civil war from breaking out in many parts of the country, in which thousands (mostly Muslims) were killed, nor did it do anything to prevent relations between Hindus and Muslims from reaching their lowest point since Partition. Very significantly, many Muslims had by now totally lost their confidence in the state and its institutions, since politicians seemed unwilling to protect the rights and lives of the Muslim minority.

The year 1984 thus set the stage for the introduction of two series of events that can be connected in a narrative that involves the destruction of sacred centers of religious minorities either by the state or with the connivance of it. This narrative raises related questions about the secularity of the state and the religiosity of the two movements involved. I will address these questions in the following sections.

3. The Secularity of the Indian Nation-State

The nation-state encountered by Sikh and Hindu activists is the successor of the colonial state. We have to start, therefore, by asking what kind of "secularity" we find in the colonial state in British India of the nineteenth and twentieth centuries. Religious neutrality was seen as essential first for trading purposes and later for British rule in India. Despite their official policy of religious neutrality, the British interfered with every aspect of Indian religion and society. Considering the nature of the colonial project, there was actually no choice, and the tropes of withdrawal, secularity, and neutrality only tried to hide that discursively. Let us, for instance, look at the state project of identifying and classifying communities in Indian society, which is immediately relevant to the religious nationalist movements introduced in the beginning of this chapter. The Khalistani movement of today cannot be understood without looking at the colonial recruitment of Sikhs in the Indian army. After the Mutiny of 1857, the British disbanded the Bengal army and shifted their recruiting to the Punjab.

In their recruiting policy, they acted upon a notion of "martial races," and the Sikhs were not only counted among these races but the superior example of it. The British were still impressed with the military resistance they had encountered from the Sikhs during their earlier advance into the Punjab. They introduced in the process the idea that there was a clear boundary between pure Sikhs and "not quite" Sikhs and stipulated that only pure Sikhs should be recruited. Pure Sikhs were those who belonged to the Khalsa (Sikh brotherhood) and wore the five signs of being a Sikh, including the unshorn hair (and thus the turban), the dagger, and the steel bangle. Clearly, this boundary already existed in the precolonial period, but it was now reinforced by the "secular state" in the crucial process of providing labor opportunities. Baptism in the Sikh Khalsa meant eligibility for entry into the army. There can be little doubt that the colonial reinforcement of Khalsa identity provided a basis for later mobilization to defend the "purity" of Sikh faith in the Singh Sabha movement and for the postcolonial development of Sikh mass politics round the symbols of purity (Fox 1985).

Even more important than "identifying" who were Sikhs and who were not was the imperial notion that India was divided in two large nations, one Hindu and the other Muslim. Again, Hindu nationalism, as we know it today, is largely a product of that notion and the projects connected to it. Most importantly, the British set out already in the eighteenth century to codify Hindu and Muslim law. The main issue here is that the "secular" principle of equality before the law is replaced by a principle of differential legal treatment of religious communities. This codification of communal difference had significant postcolonial consequences. In 1986, a major political crisis broke out in India about the Muslim Women (Protection of Rights on Divorce) Bill (Pathak and Sunder Rajan 1989). The new legislation was the answer of the Congress government to agitation by Muslim leaders, who protested against a decision of the Supreme Court in the so-called Shah Banu case. This case arose out of an application made by a Muslim woman, Shah Banu, for maintenance under section 125 of the Code of Criminal Procedure. The woman had been separated from her husband and demanded a monthly allowance. The Code of Criminal Procedure of 1872 was intended to prevent vagrancy, a problem for public order. It circumvented the legal fiction that Muslim civil law should be in accordance with the *shari'at* (Islamic law as derived from the Koran). Precisely this circumvention was challenged in litigation in the Shah Banu case, in which in the end the woman herself, under pressure from Muslim leaders, withdrew her demand, saying that she did not know that it was against the *shari'at.*

The new legislation departs from the assumption that Muslim personal law derives directly from immemorial religious law, as codified in the *shari'at,* conveniently forgetting that this immemorial law, as codified in civil law, is in fact a colonial construction. The government action was immediately condemned by the BJP as an attempt to appease the Muslim minority, as it indeed was. We had now the curious situation of Hindu nationalists asking for the secular application of a uniform civil code for all Indian citizens, while the secular Congress Party wanted to protect the minorities from this uniformity. This irony can possibly be explained by the historical fact that the Hindu personal code, derived from the *dharmashastras* (Hindu lawbooks), has never gained the foundational value for the Hindu community that the *shari'at* has gained for the Muslim community. This, in turn, has to do with the nature of textual authority in Hinduism as well as with the construction of community in the Hindu case. In the Muslim case, the law has become the public symbol of the integrity of the Muslim community and is thus directly linked to the political treatment of a "minority," either in terms of protection or in terms of appeasement. This has ossified Muslim personal law in India to an extent unknown in Muslim states like Pakistan and Bangladesh. It provided Muslim leaders with an issue to fight for, but it also gave BJP politicians an issue that they could use to show the "backwardness" of the Muslim community, especially in its treatment of women, and to show the willingness of the Congress Party to pamper the Muslim minority in order to get their votes. It is striking to what extent the political terrain for this had been laid out in the colonial period.

The colonial construction of the Hindu community did not proceed along the lines of homogenization, as in the Muslim case, but along those of differentiation. The Hindu "majority" was seen as endlessly fragmented and diverse. In their documentation of these differences in censuses and district gazetteers, the colonial authorities created long lists of castes, ethnic groups that were hierarchically linked. These hierarchical listings led to widespread agitation and the formation of caste associations on an all-India basis whose main purpose was to enhance the status of each caste. In South India, much was made of the racial distinction between Aryans (Brahmans) and Dravidians (non-Brahmans) which led to the formation of Dravidian parties that continue to dominate politics in Tamil Nadu today. In the rest of India, caste consciousness was also raised by the colonial project of enumerating the different castes. This has resulted in a constant dialectic of caste politics against the politics of Hindu unity (*sangathan*).

The greatest threat to "Hindu unity" was the possible formation of a separate, huge community of "untouchables." Outside of the caste hierarchies were large groups that were untouchable outcastes, that is, groups with culturally despised occupations, such as sweepers, and scavengers, as well as "tribes," groups mainly living outside of peasant economies in hill regions and jungles. In the twentieth

century, the British gave these groups preferential treatment to redress t[h]
mense social disadvantages. This was immediately seen by Hindu politic[ians]
policy meant to weaken Hindu unity. The British decision in 1932 to create separate electorates for untouchables was especially strongly resisted by the leader of the Congress, Mohandas K. Gandhi, who undertook a fast unto death to have it revoked. The legal historian Marc Galanter (1984, 31) argues that "it is evident that Congress opposition, if not Gandhi's personally, was inspired by fear that the great Hindu base of Congress support would be weakened." The result of Gandhi's fast was that Ambedkar, the untouchable leader, abandoned the idea of separate electorates for a system of reserved seats that is still in force today. The importance of untouchable participation in Hindu nationalism has to be seen in light of Hindu-Muslim conflict and competition. Their votes were and continue to be crucial to Hindu majoritarianism.

Again, colonial (secular) interventions set the stage for postcolonial politics. The ante was raised by extending the principle of preferential treatment and distributive justice from the so-called scheduled tribes and castes to a new category, the Other Backward Castes (OBCs). This came to occupy a large part of the political arena, since, for example, in the South Indian state of Tamil Nadu OBCs were all castes except Brahmans. It led to caste warfare, especially in Gujarat but also elsewhere. And in 1989 the decision of the V. P. Singh government to implement the recommendations of the so-called Mandal Commission, implying massive reservations for castes in the public sector and universities, led again to the pitching of caste against Hindu unity. This was well expressed in the slogan: "Mandal or Mandir" (temple), meaning that one was either for this policy of reservation or a Hindu nationalist striving for the building of the Rama temple in Ayodhya.

4. The Religiosity of Nationalist Movements

There is a common fallacy that religion and politics are two different fields of social activity. This leads observers sometimes to speak of the "politicization" of religion and to say that this is against the original intent of the founder of a religion or God himself. Undoubtedly, there are movements that try to steer away from the official political arena and call themselves apolitical, but even in these cases I am inclined to see this withdrawal as political. Much clearer, however, is the political nature of the Khalistani and Hindu nationalist movements. Both attempt to reshape state-society relations within the global form of the nation-state. In these cases, the common question is not whether these movements are political but whether, or to what extent, they are religious. I think that it is largely spurious to come up with old or new definitions of *religion, culture,* or *politics.* It is more useful to look at the imagination of *history, territory,* and *identity,* which characterize these movements, and to recognize the extent to which this imagination is rooted in religious institutions and sacred scriptures and formulated by religious leaders. I will try to do that for both Sikh and Hindu nationalism in what follows.

In a long and ultimately elusive search for origins, the current Khalistani movement might be traced to the founding of the Sikh brotherhood (Khālsa) in the early eighteenth century. A direct link can be shown, however, with the Singh Sabha movement of the colonial period. The first Singh Sabha was established in 1873 and preached the cleansing of the Sikh brotherhood of "Hindu" practices. One of the key issues was thus the assertion of boundaries between Hindus and Sikhs, clearly in reaction to reformist activities on the part of the Arya Samaj (a nineteenth-century reform movement). A major victory for the Singh Sabha movement occurred in 1905, when Hindu images were removed from the Golden Temple in Amritsar. In the early decades of the twentieth century, the Singh Sabha movement increasingly turned its attention to the management of Sikh temples (*gurdwaras*). These temples were the property of priestly families whose moral and ritual behavior did not conform to the purist standards of certain reformists who originated in the Singh Sabha movement but came to call themselves Akalis. *Akal* is the term in Sikhism for the ultimate, timeless reality. The most important campaign of the Akalis was a struggle for control over the temples. In 1925, the agitation succeeded in placing the temples under the authority of the Shiromani Gurdwara Parbandhak Committee, a representative body of the Sikh brotherhood. Since then, the control of this committee has become the most coveted prize in Sikh politics.

The slogan of the Singh Sabha was that Sikhs were not Hindus. The boundary between members of the brotherhood and those followers of Sikh traditions who were not members of the brotherhood was now transformed into a boundary between "real" Sikhs (members of the brotherhood with beards, turbans, and the rest of the markers) and Hindus. Religious groups, such as the Nanakpanthis, Nirankaris, and Namdharis, who followed the Sikh teachings but did not accept the brotherhood, were asked to declare that they were not Sikhs but Hindus, which they naturally refused to do. The guiding fear behind all this seems to have been (and continues to be) that the Sikhs would lose their sense of a separate identity and simply become one of the many sectarian movements in Hinduism. One of the main grounds for this abiding fear is the practice of many Punjabi families of initiating only one son into the brotherhood, while the rest of the family are clean shaven and follow Sikh and Hindu teachings as they see fit. The boundary between Hindus and Sikhs is thus constantly negotiated in the day to day practices of a large portion of Punjabis who are only potentially "real" Sikhs.

It is striking that the Khalistani movement began, in fact, not as a separatist movement but as a protest movement of a "purist" faction of the Sikh brotherhood against privileges given to the Nirankaris. According to the tradition of the Sikh brotherhood, there have been ten Sikh gurus, and since the last one Sikhs have had to rely on the sacred sayings of these gurus (*gurbani*), collected in the sacred book of Sikhism, the *Guru Granth Sahib,* and in dispute to trust the opinion (*gurmatta*) of the brotherhood. The Nirankaris, however, continue to have a living guru. This is considered a blasphemy by the brotherhood. On the day of the big festival of Vaisakhi, April 13, 1978, the Nirankaris staged a large procession in Amritsar and were confronted by a group of radical members of the brotherhood. A number of people were killed on both sides. The government arrested some Nirankaris, but they were later found to have acted in self-defense. This verdict is often quoted by Khalistanis as a sign that true justice could not be expected from a Hindu government. In April 1980, this led to the assassination of Gurbachan Singh, the Nirankari guru. The immediate origin of the Khalistani movement lies therefore in a conflict about religious orthodoxy framed in the narrative of true or false Sikhs and in the failure of the state to protect pure Sikhism, or worse, in the alleged conspiracy of the state to use the Nirankaris against the brotherhood.

An important role in the attack on the Nirankaris was played by the Damdami Taksal, a religious institution under the leadership of Sant Jarnail Singh Bhindranwale (1946–84). Bhindranwale felt strongly that the Sikh religion was under mounting pressure. After the assassination of the Nirankari guru, he was suspected of involvement in the 1981 murder of Lala Jagat Narain, the editor of the largest Hindu newspaper in the Punjab, the *Punjabi Kesari.* Bhindranwale was arrested, and his arrest led to the hijacking of an Indian Airlines plane to Lahore by Khalistanis who demanded his release. His arrest had made him a rising star in the growing separatist movement in the Punjab. After his release, he quickly became its leader. He and his followers entrenched themselves in the Golden Temple and launched terrorist attacks from there on Hindus and state institutions. This ultimately led to the events of 1984.

The narrative of Khalistani aspirations is framed in terms of history, territory, and identity. The history of the Sikhs as popularly seen and told by themselves is one of constant struggle against "foreign" state power. Early on, it is a struggle against the Mughals, later against the British, and finally it is a struggle against the Brahmans of the Congress Party, which dominates the Indian state. In these struggles, the Sikhs are portrayed as the courageous minority who fight against overwhelming state power. The stories dwell on massacres and martyrdom but also on ultimate superiority and victory. The events in the Punjab in the 1980s could have been scripted along these lines. The Khalistani challenge to the central state elicited a growing involvement of the state in the affairs of the Punjab. It led to a police state in which the prisons were filled with young Sikhs, innocent or not, who were subjected to torture and numerous atrocities, which set the stage for civil war (see S. Mahmood 1996). Finally, the attack on the Golden Temple and the killing of Bhindranwale made the latter into a textbook martyr for the Sikh cause and "demonstrated" that he had been right all along about the bad intentions of the Indian state.

A major feature of nationalism is the politics of space. Bordered territory mbolizes the fixity, stability, and sovereignty of the nation-state, so that borders have become the contested sites for international warfare, refugees, and immigration policies. Those who see themselves as a nation often seek a spatial, territorial expression of their nationhood. The Indian Muslim league spoke of a homeland for Muslims when it demanded Pakistan in the 1940s. This expression was adopted by Sikh leaders when the Punjab region was cut in two by the Partition of 1947, but it did not play a significant role in the negotiations that led to an independent India. In the 1960s, Master Tara Singh, the leader of the Akali Dal, began a movement demanding a separate state within the Indian Union, with a Sikh electoral majority. Not religion but language (Punjabi) was the basis of this demand, since language had been generally adopted as the marker for deciding state boundaries within the Union. This movement was successful in 1966 when the Punjab was divided in the largely Hindi-speaking (and Hindu) state of Haryana and the largely Punjabi-speaking (and Sikh) state of Punjab. As we have seen, however, a separate state within the Indian nation-state proved to be not quite enough for some in the 1980s.

While these territorial strivings are typical of all nationalisms, some of them at least are grafted upon prenationalist senses of sacred space. According to Harjot Oberoi (1987), Sikhs were not bound to the territory of the Punjab but to the lineage of gurus and then to the scriptural guru, that is, the words of the guru in the *Guru Granth.* In his view, the territorial demand is entirely a modern, nationalist notion that has nothing to do with religion. This transterritorial aspect of Sikhism made it easy to travel beyond the Punjab and build temples wherever one had a large enough community. It is at the same time true that this religious transcendence of local belonging makes it possible to tie religious identity to either nationalism or transnationalism. Both possibilities are fulfilled in the Sikh case, which has produced both a Punjabi territorial nationalism and a transnational diaspora. Where both nationalism and transnational diaspora are tied to the Punjab, however, is in the central place for Sikhism, the Golden Temple in Amritsar. No other place expresses so strongly the existence of a global Sikh community. That is why the attack on the Golden Temple by the Indian state "proved" that the Sikhs need a territorial nation-state to protect their sacred center. Besides that, Verne Dusenbury (1995) has recently argued that diasporic Sikhs also are interested in the Khalistan demand because of the fact that their identity and status in the countries of immigration are indexically related to their "country of origin." In that sense, even diasporic Sikhs who would not dream of going back to live in a newly established Khalistan might dream of having come from a recognizable, separate nation-state.

Identity politics is obviously the main element in the Khalistani movement. As I argued earlier, the guiding fear among Sikhs of the brotherhood is that they may backslide into Hinduism. This fear is clearly expressed in the exhortation to young people to show the visible markers of being a Sikh, as in this speech by

Bhindranwale: "If you do not want beards then you should ask the women to become men and you become women. Or else ask nature that it should stop this growth on your faces. There will be no need for me to preach, no need to break my head on it" (quoted in Das 1995, 127). This passage also shows the extent to which religious identity is tied up with gender identity, as Veena Das rightly observes in her comments on Bhindranwale's speech. The message is that to be a real man one has to be a visible member of the brotherhood. That allows one also to wear the dagger and protect the honor of the Sikh community (especially women) against attacks from outside. This emphasis on masculinity is crucial to Sikh militancy, but it does not produce the kind of "radical patriarchalism" that Riesebrodt (1993) sees as a defining characteristic of fundamentalism. It is an idiom of protecting masculine honor without policing the public behavior of women. The idea that Sikhs need their own state in order to maintain the social and symbolic boundaries that distinguish them from Hindus is not only found among extremists like Bhindranwale. In the 1960s, the period of the agitation for a separate Sikh Punjab within the Indian Union, the acclaimed Sikh writer, historian, and longtime member of the Congress Party, Khushwant Singh, wrote in the conclusion of his two-volume history of the Sikhs: "the only chance of survival of the Sikhs as a separate community is to create a state in which they form a compact group, where the teaching of Gurmukhi and the Sikh religion is compulsory and where there is an atmosphere of respect for the traditions of their Khalsa forefathers" (Singh 1966, vol 2, 205). Khushwant Singh writes about a separate state within the Indian Union, and he is anything but a Khalistani, but still one sees in this quotation the common ground shared by extremists and moderates.

Globalization has affected the Khalistani movement in a number of ways. The Sikhs are almost the paradigmatic migrants. A third of them live outside of the Punjab, and more than a million live outside India. Migration was strongly stimulated by recruitment in the colonial army, which opened a window to the subcontinent, the British Empire, and the world at large. Racial discrimination encountered in Canada and the United States in the early decades of the twentieth century led Sikh migrants to engage in nationalist activities centered on India. The Sikh diaspora continues to be a prime example of the influence of a worldwide, transnational community on religious nationalism in India. The Khalistan movement of today, for example, receives more support among migrant circles in England and Canada than among Sikhs in the Punjab. Cynthia Mahmood (1996) reports that Khalistani refugees in the United States bring their children up with the idea that they will return to the Punjab to fight for an independent Khalistan. This evidence at least contradicts Ben Anderson's thesis about "long-distance nationalism without responsibility" (Wertheim lecture, 1992). It has also led me to wonder about the refugee experience of the 4.3 million people who fled to the Indian Punjab after Partition. To what extent did the experience of having to leave everything behind in another man's nation-state affect Khalistani sentiments in the 1980s? Finally, the conflict ıe Punjab is seen by some observers as caused by or related to the effects of Green Revolution (perhaps one of the most striking global innovations in food production), which were stronger in the Punjab than in any other part of India. In 1984, Punjabi farmers (mostly Sikhs) produced more than half the grain on the Indian market. Agriculture had become thoroughly mechanized and led to growing social tensions in the countryside. Punjab remains an industrially backward state even today, and much employment is only to be found in the agrarian sector. Marginal and small agriculturalists, primarily Sikhs, have been pushed out of the countryside and into the small provincial towns. Migrant labor, primarily Hindu, has been brought into the state in harvesting seasons (Wallace 1990). These upheavals, which are direct consequences of the penetration of global capitalism, have doubtless contributed to the success of Khalistani militancy in the Punjab countryside.

The Vishva Hindu Parishad was founded in Bombay on an auspicious day, the birthday of Lord Krishna, August 29, 1964. One hundred and fifty religious leaders were invited to Sandeepany Sadhanalaya, the center of a Hindu missionary movement headed by Swami Chinmayananda. The host had been instrumental in organizing the conference and became its president. Shivram Shankar Apte, a worker of the militant Hindu Rashtriya Swayamsevak Sangh, was elected as its general secretary. The aim of the new movement was to strengthen Hindu society and spread Hindu values, not only in India but abroad. I have argued at length elsewhere that the VHP is primarily trying to formulate a modern Hinduism as a unifying, common religion of the Indian nation (1994). Prior to 1980, its project had only limited success, but this changed drastically in the 1980s.

The VHP received a considerable boost when an untouchable subcaste in Meenakshipuram in South India converted en masse to Islam. Conversion and petrodollars are the master-tropes demonstrating that the Hindu nation is under threat from world Islam. In historical terms, Islamic aggression is seen by the VHP as the reason why so many Hindus left their religion and converted to Islam. In its view, the unity and integrity of the ancient Hindu nation has been most fundamentally threatened by conversion by the sword. Indian Muslims are therefore constantly exhorted to "realize" their fundamental Hindu nature. While these conversions were in the past, the Meenakshipuram case "proved" that the Middle East was using its oil wealth to continue the conversion project. It is an instance of the globalization of the discourse on Islamic fundamentalism and its expansion across the world. This discourse may originate in Western media, but it feeds into anti-Islamic sentiments outside the West. Although the Meenakshipuram conversions were insignificant in terms of overall numbers, this case has become the most publicized issue in the VHP's defense of Hinduism. Its propaganda about the Islamic threat led to the organization of a highly successful nationwide "sacrifice for unity" in 1983, which in turn became the basis for the events of 1984.

Hindu nationalism, as found in the VHP, also expresses itself in terms of history, territory, and identity. Like their Khalistani counterparts Hindu nationalists describe Hindu history as a story of oppression by Muslim rulers, followed by British Christian rulers, and now by Indian pseudosecularists. Their story is less one of militant rebellion against "foreign" rule or martyrdom, although this is not entirely absent from it, but more one emphasizing Hindu tolerance and spiritual superiority in their relations with their oppressors. At the same time, however, the VHP argues that Hindus have been taken advantage of because of their tolerance and should now stand up to claim what is their right, namely, the Hinduization of the Indian nation-state. The Congress Party, which has ruled India for most of the period since independence is condemned by them as a pseudosecularist party. Its Nehruvian program of reducing the salience of religious beliefs and practices in politics as well as the state's projected neutrality toward religious difference—a stance inherited from the colonial state—are both seen to be contradicted by the policy of "pampering the minorities" and specifically by using the Muslim community as a vote bank and dividing the Hindu majority by setting the untouchables against the rest. Independence—as VHP ideologues keep reminding their audience—has not brought freedom for the Hindu majority. The state should express the Hindu values of purity and incorruptibility as found in the divine realm of the god-king Rama. History books should be rewritten to convey the proud heritage of Hindu civilization and the wrongs inflicted upon it by foreigners.

The territory of the Indian nation-state is in the VHP's conception also of Hindu sacred space. This notion of nationwide sacred space is based on the existence of Hindu centers all over the country connected to each other by intersecting pilgrimage routes. These routes have been utilized for the VHP's processual agitations and most elaborately in the Sacrifice for Unity of November and December 1983, when three large processions and at least forty-seven smaller ones traversed the country. Processions of temple chariots are an important feature in Hindu temple festivals. The VHP made use of brand new trucks, named "temple-chariots," which carried huge pots filled with Ganges water and smaller pots with local sacred water. In this way, all the rivers and sacred waters of India were symbolically connected to the Ganges as the unifying symbol of Hindu India.

The Sacrifice for Unity laid the groundwork for the ritual processions aimed at the destruction of the mosque in Ayodhya. The VHP's plan to destroy this mosque as the first of a series of similar mosques allegedly placed on Hindu sacred sites is in a way a reinscription of the national geographic in Hindu terms. Tellingly, Mr. Advani's campaign of 1990, which ended in his arrest in Bihar and the downfall of V. P. Singh's government, started in Somnath, perhaps the best-known Hindu temple destroyed by Muslim conquerors. After independence, a new Hindu temple was built there by Hindu activists, led by major Congress politicians. Mr. Advani's message was clear: what had been done in Somnath by Congress should have been followed up in other places, and the BJP/VHP combine was going to do just that.

The identity politics of the VHP movement are complex in nature. On the face of it, Hindus do not have to worry, as the Sikhs do, that they will fade away. They are a comfortable majority, but, to use Stanley Tambiah's phrase, they do have a minority complex. This is shown in the success of the VHP propaganda about the Meenakshipuram conversions, which blew this incident to unbelievable proportions. The pre-independence political rivalry and mutual antagonism between India's two major communities, Hindus and Muslims, is given a new lease on political life by the VHP. While conflicts between the two communities after the creation of Pakistan were confined to particular cities and localities, the VHP succeeded in making it again into a nationwide phenomenon. The other side of Hindu identity politics relates to the long-standing fear that the untouchable communities that make up a crucial percentage of India's population may not be part of the Hindu nation. Policies that focus on these disadvantaged communities are portrayed by the VHP and its political ally, the BJP, as aimed at dividing the Hindus against themselves. They are a "threat to unity." This is why for Hindu nationalists the debate about affirmative action is closely related to their cause of unifying the nation under a Hindu banner.

The Vishva Hindu Parishad translates its name into English as World Hindu Council. Processes of globalization are clearly salient to it. From the start, the movement has been intended to unify the Hindu diaspora in the project of Hindu nationalism. The founding session was attended by representatives from Trinidad and Kenya. The Rama Shila Puja (in consecrating the building blocks of the temple in Ayodhya) brought stones from the United States, Canada, the Caribbean, and South Africa, which are prominently exposed on the building site. Whenever I speak about Hindu nationalism on American campuses, students belonging to the VHP approach and interrogate me. The Hinduja—one of the great Hindu entrepreneurial families—supports not only Hindu nationalism in India financially but has also made huge donations to the universities of Cambridge and Columbia to establish centers for the study of Hindu traditions. In my view, this has a much longer history in the global discourse of Hindu spirituality initiated by Swami Vivekananda in the World Parliament of Religions in Chicago in 1894 and later in Boston. Also, as in the Sikh case, the plight of Hindu migrants abroad was important for Hindu nationalism at home in the early decades of this century (Kelly 1991).

It is extremely difficult to interpret the effects of developments in the world system on the rise of Hindu nationalism since it is supported by a cross section of the population from very different positions of class, region, and ethnic background. What is striking about the 1980s was the growth of a consumerism that was made possible by a gradual opening of the previously rather closed Indian market. There has been growth in domestic tourism, a media boom that enabled new forms of advertising and marketing, and new possibilities for leisure (Appadurai and Breckenridge 1995). It is tempting to connect these changes with the success of movements that use the modern media to stress religious authenticity, but the evidence is contradictory and unclear.

Conclusion

The year 1984 was an important one for religious nationalism in India. It saw Operation Blue Star fulfilling the hopes of Khalistanis by creating a very real divide between Hindus and Sikhs in the country. It saw the beginning of the agitation that led to the destruction of the Babar mosque in Ayodhya in 1992 and to a new phase of intercommunal enmity between Hindus and Muslims in India. Both of these conflicts have an international dimension because of the inimical relations between India and Pakistan. India accuses Pakistan of assisting Sikh terrorists in their actions in the Punjab, which borders Pakistan. Pakistan follows closely what happens to their fellow Muslims in neighboring India. This situation is obviously worsened by the tense standoff in Kashmir, where Muslim militants want a separate state.

Why 1984, or better, why the 1980s? There are a few general features in the development of Indian politics that can be pointed out to have contributed to the happenings of 1984 and their aftermath. Many political scientists (Kohli 1988; Frankel and Rao 1990) have argued that the 1970s showed the decline of the Congress system, which had governed India since independence. Mrs. Indira Gandhi had to fight off her rivals to succeed her father, Jawaharlal Nehru, who had made India into a largely one-party system. She definitely succeeded in doing so, as her landslide victory of 1971 shows, but only at the cost of a further centralization of power in the center at Delhi and by weakening rivals by playing them off in their home bases against their opponents. This strategy led increasingly to a decline of the ability of the Congress Party to govern India. The precariousness of Mrs. Gandhi's rule became evident when she decided to dispense with democracy when her seat in Parliament was challenged in court. The Emergency of 1975–77 politicized the police and the powerful civil service and led to a general erosion of the credibility and legitimacy of Congress and the state itself. Many politicians, including leaders of the BJP, were arrested and put in jail. There can be little doubt that the distrust Hindu nationalists feel toward Congress's secularist and progressive posturing was much strengthened in this period. Mrs. Gandhi was soundly defeated after her decision to return to democracy in 1977, but the coalition that succeeded Congress for three years under the name Janata Dal was too internally divided to be an alternative to the Congress system, which had at least a long history of containing and balancing factional strife. In 1980, then, Mrs. Gandhi again won the elections and came back to power, but now more than ever her government had a feeling of embattlement, of presiding over a system that was falling apart.

In the case of the Punjab, there can be little doubt that the political strategies employed by Mrs. Gandhi's Congress Party were a major element in creating Khalistani separatism in the 1980s (Brass 1988; Wallace 1990). Since independence, Congress and Akali Dal have been the main contenders for power in the Punjab. While Congress has been the dominant party over much of this period, the 1977 and 1980 elections were won by the Akalis. It is widely said in India that Bhindranwale came to be used by Congress in this context to weaken support for the Akali Dal. Evidence for this comes from the fact that Bhindranwale's men stood as candidates against Akalis in the elections for the committee that manages all Sikh shrines in the Punjab and is the main resource in Sikh politics. To many analysts, this explains also why Bhindranwale was soon released after his arrest in connection with the murder of Lala Jagat Narain in 1981. Interestingly, the Punjab also provides an excellent example of the way Mrs. Gandhi divided her own party at the regional level in order to prevent challenges to her central power. She made the leader of one faction of the Punjab Congress Party, Giani Zail Singh, first home minister in the Union government and later president, while she put his opponent, Darbara Singh, at the head of the Punjab government. These maneuvers explain at least partly the inability of the state to deal decisively with the growing separatist militancy in the Punjab until the moment that the army was brought into the Golden Temple, a self-defeating action by all accounts.

Uttar Pradesh, India's most populous state with more than a hundred million inhabitants, shows a similar picture of divisive politics and a growing willingness among all political parties, including Congress, to see religious nationalism, in this case the Hindu one, as a possible unifying force. The main contenders for ruling Uttar Pradesh were Congress, Janata, and the BJP. It is important to see that, as in the Punjab, the Congress had lost its dominance in Uttar Pradesh in the 1970s. Uttar Pradesh in this period is a good example of the mobilization of the middle peasantry, the Backward Castes. For example, the short-lived Janata government that ruled Uttar Pradesh after the Emergency implemented reservation policies that favored these Backward Castes. The BJP, however, saw this kind of policy as dividing the unity of the Hindu nation. As we have seen, the politics of caste reservations and Hindu nationalism played themselves out in the politics of the 1980s, and Uttar Pradesh was a crucial arena for that. Congress could not stay out of this, even if it had wanted, and, as in the case of the Punjab, it ultimately favored religious nationalism. The crucial decision in 1986 to open the mosque in Ayodhya to the Hindu public could not have been taken without the direct consent of the Congress leadership. This was clearly done to gain political advantage by acting according to Hindu populist sentiments, although it backfired in the end by giving the BJP more wind in its sails.

The politicization of the main institutions of the state, such as the police and the civil service, is one element of what Atul Kohli (1990) has called "India's growing crisis of governability." The gradual decline of the Congress system, which contains various regional and social conflicts, is another. A major element in this is the success rather than the failure of mass politics in that a growing number of groups have become involved in the political system. Their mobilization has taken shape in two types of mass movement: the Backward Caste and religious nationalist movements. Unfortunately, this enhanced participation has also led to a growth in political militancy and violence. The change in the political arena is undoubtedly among the most important elements in explaining the growth of religious nationalism among both Sikhs and Hindus in the 1980s.

Another element in the explanation of the events of the 1980s is the departure from the Nehruvian policy of economic self-reliance and political nonalliance. Nehru's daughter, Indira Gandhi, and especially his grandson, Rajiv Gandhi, became in the 1980s much more in favor of economic liberalization, privatization of the public sector, and the opening up of Indian markets to foreign goods and investments. It has been argued by the Indian political scientist Rajni Kothari (1991), among others, that the collective anxieties created by the rapid globalization of production and consumption in the 1980s were among the social forces behind the emergence of religious nationalist movements. This is very much in line with the "rapid social change" thesis of Riesebrodt, which I criticized in section 1. To me, it is not so much the upheaval caused by rapid social change that matters but, quite specifically, a fascination with foreign products, films, and entertainment, which came readily available when India opened itself up to global television and advertising. These media images created a strong sense among especially young, middle-class men that they were entitled to participate in this world of consumption but unable to do so. The movements I have discussed explain this "injustice" in terms of the unjust nature of the "pseudo-secularist" state, which privileges the religious Other. The success of religious nationalism in this regard is that it not only gives an explanation for the feeling of lack but also for that of loss, namely, the loss of cultural authenticity in a world of globalized images. An interesting aspect of this feeling of loss is that it is particularly acute among transnational migrants, whose movement is intrinsically tied up with processes of globalization. Both the Sikh and Hindu diasporas play a significant part in religious nationalisms at home. It is striking in India how often the desire for the "green card" that allows one to settle permanently in the United States is combined with a strong feeling of the religious superiority of one's own nation. Rather than a clear-cut, "fundamentalist" denial of modernity and postmodernity, we have here the typical ambivalences and ambiguities of responses to globalization.

The phenomenon of religious nationalism itself, however, is not explained by either the rise of mass politics or the effects of globalization. It is also not explained by oblique references to the global rise of fundamentalism. As I have argued, the Western discourse on fundamentalism is important not so much in explaining mass movements as in framing them in a global language of modernization that opposes

ıgion to secularity as backwardness to forwardness. As we have seen, the lan-
age of modernization prevents us from understanding the complicated histories of movements that are produced in "postcolonial modernity." For that, we need a long-term perspective that analyzes the colonial past of both the secularity of the nation-state and the religiosity of religio-political movements.

PART IV

Reflections

CHAPTER 14

Adjusting the Lens: What Do Globalizations, Transnationalism, and the Anti-apartheid Movement Mean for Social Movement Theory?

Gay W. Seidman

"On or about December, 1910," Virginia Woolf ([1924] 1950) once wrote, "human character changed. The change was not sudden or definite [but] a change there was, nevertheless; and, since one must be arbitrary, let us date it about the year 1910. All human relations had shifted—those between masters and servants, husbands and wives, parents and children. And when human relations change there is at the same time a change in religion, conduct, politics, and literature." Something in the air just before World War I, Woolf claimed, pushed Europeans to focus on psychological dynamics rather than external description, privileging individual perspectives over social status.

Just about a century later, a similarly intrepid observer might well claim that we are going through another major intellectual sea change, a shift in perspective. Somehow, the world appears to have changed: people everywhere seem to accept the once preposterous notion that local events can only be understood through a global lens and to view social processes primarily as local manifestations of global patterns. Internationally, human character and social relations appear to be going through a dramatic upheaval—judging by a sudden and overwhelming concern with the way local lives are shaped by global flows, as politicians, business leaders, and academics assume that globalization is a primary dynamic in all our lives.

This new sensibility appears to be as important to social scientists as to novelists and business leaders: increasingly, we focus on global dynamics rather than local ones, privileging *globalization*—a term that covers a multitude of technological, institutional, and cultural processes—over perspectives that emphasize the unique and distinct experiences of people in different locations. The implications of this paradigm shift are enormous, as much for the questions we ask and the assumptions we make in research as for the way we lead our daily lives: social scientists are only beginning to think through what it means for social theories and research projects to take a more global perspective on human character, human relations, and social institutions.

In this chapter, I will first briefly discuss some facets of what we often call globalization, insisting that it involves both material changes in the organization of our (global) society and changes in the way we perceive and talk about reality in the shift from a territorially defined understanding of social life to a social imaginary built up more through flexible networks, relationships, and institutions than organized around geographically bounded spaces. Then, after suggesting some of the ways these shifts might lead us to rethink our assumptions about social movements—using chapters from this volume to illustrate some challenges that globalization may pose for social movement theory—I will briefly describe what I consider to have been a truly transnational social movement, the anti-apartheid movement of the 1970s and 1980s, in an attempt to illustrate the ways in which transnational movements might require theorists to rethink basic assumptions about identity, mobilization, resources, and the targets of collective action. Finally, drawing on the chapters in this volume for guidance, I will suggest some of the directions that a more global social movement theory might take.

Globalization at the End of the Century

As many analysts have pointed out, globalization is hardly new: people in far-flung corners of the world have been linked for centuries by multifaceted social, political, and cultural exchanges. Many of the interconnected patterns currently attributed to new global forces have been in play for centuries (Arrighi 1994; Hirst and Thomson 1996; Wallerstein 1998). The same breathless sense of discovery and limitlessness in which business leaders speak of a new global economy infused nineteenth-century discussions of unregulated global financial flows (Helleiner 1994), while discussions of the promise implicit in new computer technologies often parallel the enthusiasm that greeted the pneumatic tire and the steam engine.[1] Modernity has long been global, and, for the world's elites at least, international linkages are not so novel. Furthermore, as the editors of this volume so elegantly point out, the processes commonly called *globalization* are so varied that the word should only be used in the plural. No single process can be labeled globalization except at the risk of severe oversimplification, serious misunderstanding, or both.

Yet for most of us the late-twentieth-century sense of global reach seems new and remarkable, at least at the level of daily experience. Innovations ranging from electronic mail to new financial instruments to new patterns of industrial outsourcing link the world in an ever-changing web, extending beyond the control of any single government. Although some authors argue that these changes simply mark a return to the unregulated international trade regime of the late nineteenth century, the sense that something significant has changed is remarkably persistent. For many analysts, the close link between territory, state, and political identity today seems almost a vestige from an earlier age; increasingly, it seems more appropriate to conceptualize human identity as fluid and changeable and human relations as organized through more or less intangible and flexible networks, sometimes detachable from territorial identities, than to think of local communities and traditions as bounded, static, or timeless (Appadurai 1996; Yanagisako 1995).

For social scientists, this paradigmatic shift must alter both the questions we ask and the assumptions we make about how communities experience change. Just as multinational corporations are linked through e-mail and air travel, so are diasporic ethnic communities or communities of activists who work on issues of international human rights, environmental degradation, or gender inequality (Keck and Sikkink 1998). Ideas and resources seem to move around the world with astonishing speed and intensity. Political actors no longer limit their claims to territorial localities: local concerns about environmental issues are quickly reframed in terms of global dynamics (Rothman and Oliver 1998), as are discussions about gender inequalities or even issues as parochial as ethnic conflict (Basu 1995; Brubaker 1996; Malkki 1994). Global linkages have taken on new prominence in our conceptualization of human possibilities as we reach the end of the twentieth century: a new awareness of what the editors of this volume call the transnational public sphere is transforming the way local actors visualize the stage on which they perform.

To some extent, this shift in perception reflects real changes in the way we experience the world. Globalization, whatever it is, has taken place on several levels. Rapid flows of information, technology, and trade give new immediacy to events far across the globe and make national economies increasingly vulnerable to international pressures (Castells 1989; Sassen 1998). The new organization of production is of course uneven and incomplete, and some areas are far more linked to global production processes than others; while more advanced industrial areas remain central to global production, for example, most of Africa remains marginal. Yet the discourse of globalization in business journals takes on a life of its own. Capital has a new sense of its own mobility, while governments seem ever more concerned about whether state policies will attract or repel those fickle international investors (Harvey 1989; McMichael 1996).

Large institutional changes alter the context in which local processes occur: global institutions have assumed new powers and a new visibility. While international bodies like the World Trade Organization (WTO) and the International Monetary Fund (IMF) continue to work through national governments, many observers suggest that the character of national sovereignty has changed in the process: especially for the last three decades of the century international organizations have assumed increasing power over global economic forces, and even over local political processes, even as they continue to proclaim their respect for national sovereignty (Barnett and Finnemore 1999).

For local actors, the transnational public sphere takes on new importance—both as a site for contestation and as a source of new resources, ideas, and support. Though some people respond by reasserting local identities—like the conspiracy-minded Michigan farmer who placed a sign in a field near Ann Arbor in 1996 demanding "UN Troops Out of the U.S."—most of us recognize the growing tendency for the international community, whatever that is, to take an increasingly active role in local disputes and policies, especially in places where weak national states have little leverage in international hierarchies. The Korean worker who interpreted rising unemployment in 1997 as the result of IMF policies—carrying a sign at a Seoul demonstration, in English, reading "IMF = I am Fired"—appears as aware of global forces as the refugee who measures his experience against international norms and laws, appealing for help to the "international community" (Malkki 1994). People around the world in the late twentieth century interpret local experiences in terms of international forces; they recognize that those forces impose real constraints on their choices, and many look beyond the local nation-state for resolutions to the problems they experience at a local level.

But even those of us whose lives are relatively untouched by international organizations can hardly ignore the extent to which the world is increasingly integrated: we are all touched daily by the cultural shifts linked to globalization—perhaps the most obvious, and least reversible, changes of all. Commercially, Hollywood films are as ubiquitous as McDonald's hamburgers, but just as importantly, serious musicians, novelists, and cookbook writers regularly repackage and hybridize local cultures in an appetizing bricolage for consumption across the globe—at least for consumption by those of us with the incomes required to purchase the world's varied flavors.

Of course, cultures have long interacted, and local consumption has been affected by imported products and possibilities since before silks and spices traveled overland from Asia to Europe and before the nineteenth-century hybridization that accompanied European colonial expansion. But in the late twentieth century it has become difficult even to claim that a particular cultural form is purely local. Increasingly, observers of specific cases point out the extent to which diasporic networks of migrants traveling, interacting, and returning have transformed and reshaped cultures across the globe in ways that undermine any serious discussion of a static cultural "tradition" of the sort that once informed anthropological studies (Cooper and Stoler 1998). If local tastes remain important in shaping how global cultural products are consumed in specific places, there is nonetheless a popular sense—in Brazil as in Beijing—that cultural processes involve global as well as local ingredients and ingenuity and that cultural meanings are in a state of constant flux and reinvention—just as local economies are in a state of constant vulnerability to the shifts and fluctuations of international investors and speculators.

These processes of globalization are uneven, incorporating people in different regions and different social strata in very different ways; the "global cities" that serve as the central nodes of global commerce and interchange involve as much exclusion and marginalization as inclusion, as much reinterpretation of global processes as reformulation of local ones (Sassen 1991). But in the late twentieth century the global seems to take on new importance, and understanding the human condition requires examining the global context as well as the local and considering how the interplay between the two reshapes both.

Social Movement Theory: Local Lens, Localizing Assumptions

This new awareness of global processes is visible throughout the social sciences and humanities, but perhaps it has provoked no more heated discussion than in debates about social movements. Social movement activists—and, although perhaps to a lesser extent, social movement theorists—have long been aware that local phenomena are linked to broader global processes, but in the late twentieth century that awareness seems to take on new importance. Social movements invariably involve the construction of collective identities and the mobilization of broad constituencies. This new global perspective on identities, networks, and communities—a perspective that emphasizes the interconnectedness between different localities and parts of the world and emphasizes the way international processes shape, constrain, and redefine local ones—has prompted social movement theorists to reconsider many of their basic assumptions.

These questions motivate many of the essays in this volume. When does a local social process become a global one? When does a local social movement become so linked into global networks that it is in fact a global social movement? What do global processes mean for the very local processes through which movements create collective identities and movement constituencies? Who represents movements on the global stage and how are those representations redesigned for international consumption? How do local movements change in response to global resources or audiences? What role do global norms and organizations play in provoking local movements? How might global political processes create new opportunities for local groups seeking to challenge powerful interests at home?

And then there is the other side. How do these global networks alter the internal dynamics of local social movements? How might global processes undermine local groups' abilities to set agendas and shape realities? How does differential access to international audiences—different access to computers and electronic mail systems, different abilities to reach the donors and professionals of the foundation world—affect local hierarchies of power? To what extent do these international linkages constrain the choices facing local activists?

Activists have long been aware of the way global dynamics and audiences might aid or constrain their causes—more aware, perhaps, than many academics. As several essays in this volume demonstrate, social movement activists have long appealed to a global vision of common humanity, and common universalistic norms, to build an international constituency for local movements: the antislavery campaign (Keck and Sikkink, this volume) as much as modern human rights movements (Ball, this volume) relied on international embarrassment and pressure for its efficacy, while concern with wrongs in far-off locations has long been the basis of international appeals for aid (Rucht, this volume; van der Veer, this volume).

International appeals and cross-border activism are not new. For centuries, activists have sought help abroad and internationalist activists have worked across borders: French activists aided the American Revolution, African-American missionaries publicized King Leopold's barbaric regime in the Congo (Hochschild, 1998), and trade unions have long sought to build an international alliance of working-class organizations. At least since the middle of the last century activists have appealed to an inchoate "international community," invoking universal norms to challenge long-established social practices. As the editors' introductory essay underscores, internationalism is perhaps especially visible in colonial and postcolonial settings: international hierarchies mean that activists in Asia, Latin America, or Africa are especially aware of the way global forces constrain possibilities. Historically, anticolonial activists could hardly ignore the role of global inequalities (Lo, this volume) any more than Palestinian refugees today can ignore the role of international politics in shaping the very space in which they live (Peteet, this volume). When environmental activists today invoke a common global destiny in efforts to protect whales or the rain forest—or when a Brazilian child advocates drawing on international norms to demand changes in local legislation (Guidry, this volume)—they echo the discourses of a shared global morality and the assertion of universal norms that have marked social movement activists' challenges to established social practices from at least the eighteenth century.

Yet, while activists have often acknowledged the importance of global dynamics in the way they understood and framed issues, academics have generally been more cautious—in all realms of thought, perhaps, but especially in terms of their views of social movements and collective action. Social movement theories have tended to view the world through a remarkably localized prism: local collective identities, campaigns, organizations, strategies. The fact that these appeals are never uncomplicated—that activists often disguise parochial interests in universal claims, that they often seek an audience that is not in fact listening, and that they often represent local issues in universal terms in order to gain international support in local struggles—this fact should not obscure the internationalist character of the claims of many social movements. If European workers abandoned the international socialist movement in the face of World War I, returning to nationalist jingoism just in time to support their countries' imperialist efforts, should that lead us to ignore completely the long history of attempts by activists to build an international workers' movement?

In part, I think, the academic emphasis on social movements as localized phenomena reflects the logic through which most social movement analysts have proceeded and the methods that researchers have used. In general, social movement studies have explored the construction of collective identities and the mobilization of social movements from the ground up, often beginning with individual participants and looking at factors that explain participation or abstention; or they use a case study approach to examine how local constituencies mobilize around specific issues and/or to explore efforts by local activists to initiate some kind of social change at the local level.

Perhaps not surprisingly given the close links between academics who study social movements and activists, this grounded approach—which looks at cases within territorially defined sites and tends to view mobilization and framing in local terms—parallels the discursive strategies employed by many activists. Activists commonly legitimate and represent collective identities through geographically defined collective histories—especially, perhaps, in nationalist or ethnically defined movements, even when believing in those common geographic histories requires a significant stretch of imagination (van der Veer, this volume; Derluguian, this volume; Uehling, this volume). But frequently academics trying to study movements rely on those geographic and historical definitions in thinking about movements' potential constituencies, unconsciously reflecting movements' self-definition. Indeed, academic observers who challenge those collective histories, those geographically defined identities, risk undermining their access to movements: academics cannot undermine activists' basic claims of identity and collective interest without risking inadvertently undermining the movement's local legitimacy, and most academics (who have tended since the 1960s to sympathize with the goals of the movements they study) would probably undertake that project quite reluctantly.

But this bottom-up approach may limit social movement theorists' ability to explore fully the transnational side of collective action or social movement mobilization. By defining case studies territorially, academics coincidentally tend to underscore the local side of identities and strategies. Even with an eye to global processes—as with, for example, the diffusion of sport in the Caribbean (Perales, this volume)—many of the studies in this volume reflect a methodological choice that emphasizes the local identity of activists: the viewpoint of the researcher always starts from a geographically defined space, and so even globally oriented researchers are prone to describe local reactions to global processes rather than the global processes more broadly (see, however, Burawoy, forthcoming). This approach has often given a textured understanding of the processes of mobilization and the character of collective identities, but it has perhaps limited analysts' vision of broader changes in the character of collective action.

A second methodological choice is perhaps equally likely to lead to a local focus: many social movement theorists define movements in terms of their political targets rather than in terms of the universalistic appeals that activists make in the course of mobilization. Thus, for example, the civil rights movement is often viewed as especially American because American activists framed their demands in terms of inclusion in an American polity—at least when they were addressing American audiences. But as historians are increasingly recognizing (Frederickson 1995; Singh 1998; von Eschen 1997) a far more global vision motivated most activists. Not only did its leading figures speak in universal terms of a global humanity but they actively promoted links across borders, speaking to international as well as domestic audiences and raising international issues as well as U.S.-specific ones. Many activists viewed their struggle in terms of an international campaign to end racial inequality globally, not just within the borders of the United States—although they certainly targeted the U.S. government as the site where their mobilization would most directly affect policymakers. Given the extent to which the American civil rights movement stands as an archetype in American social movement theory,[2] it is worth noting the extent to which a research focus on the broader vision of the project of the civil rights movement—beyond the immediate policy targets located within the American state—immediately opens up larger issues: Pan-Africanism, decolonization, or links between diasporic communities of people of African descent.

In an international system in which states are viewed as the only legitimate actors, the researcher's decision to define a movement's goals in terms of its policy targets—rather than a movement's larger claims of inclusion and global reach—leads almost inevitably to a focus on activists' identity as it is defined in national terms. Sidney Tarrow (1994), for example, insists that for all but a tiny network of intellectual activists national identities remain more significant than any global sense of solidarity, even in the globalized 1990s. In a case involving debates about overfishing the Grand Banks, Tarrow (1995) argues that, while fishermen from around the world may understand that they share the seas with fishermen from other nationalities, ultimately they define their interests in nationalist terms. But does this not risk confusing the character of collective identity with the state-centered institutions through which transnational identities must be expressed? If fishermen must channel their political demands through national channels in order to reach the international arena, does that negate any possibility that in a different institutional framework the same concerns might be expressed in more transnational terms?

Obviously, under the current state system social movement activists who seek to change existing reality tend to frame their demands in nationalist terms as a way to appeal to policymakers. If we focus only on those expressions of interest, local nationalisms will always tend to trump universalistic claims, and claims of global solidarity are mere chimera—as the collapse of the international socialist movement before World War I, when national jingoism trumped universalistic socialism, demonstrated. It is tempting to suggest, in response to Tarrow's example of the fishing rights conundrum, that the persistence of national identities within global social movements may simply reflect a realistic understanding on the part of activists that the institutional frameworks through which political aspirations must be channeled are primarily national ones in the current state system—rather than reflecting national limits to activists' visions.

Moreover, the assertion of national identities in international debates may well reflect what the editors of this volume rightly point out has been a long-standing tendency on the part of social movement theorists to restrict their vision to the industrialized countries of the world, to look at movements that can appeal to states that are relatively powerful on the international scene, and to look at the movements that have emerged under relatively open, democratic conditions. Most social movement activists are strategic in their choices of targets and institutional representations: if activists in relatively open states—and in states that are relatively powerful on the international stage—tend to turn to national-level institutions in their search for new policies, activists in relatively repressive ones frequently go outside the nation-state, appealing to global constituencies rather than local ones for support. Similarly, activists who view their "own" national states as relatively powerless in the international arena or unresponsive on a particular issue may well stress global identities, hoping to attract international support for issues that might in a different context have been considered a purely local affair.

Most people are capable of viewing the world globally even while they pursue strategies through local institutions or couch their concerns in nationalist terms to achieve those narrower goals. In a world where global goals can only be met through national states, activists may 'think globally, act locally' to a greater extent than academics recognize. Thus, in Tarrow's example, if international organizations were not organized as a collection of state representatives might Portuguese fisherman perhaps join Canadian ones in their appeals for assistance, emphasizing collective cross-border concerns as fishermen rather than national identities as Portuguese or Canadians?

But, as I will try to show using illustrations from the anti-apartheid movement, the institutional fact that international bodies are generally composed of national representatives forces potentially global identities into national frames. But it need not blind us to the possibility that activists might under other circumstances frame their concerns more globally. As academics begin to take more seriously a global perspective on collective action, perhaps they will begin to see the limitations inherent in a vision that views international activism as the work of a "principled issue network" of individuals rather than as a reflection of a sense of collective identity that transcends geographic borders. A focus on national identities may be inadequate to the complicated reality in which activists live, where identities and interests may be simultaneously defined in transnational and national terms: a "transnational public sphere" is simultaneously national and transnational, and activists with any sense will work in both spheres, using both identities simultaneously and strategically.

This possibility poses a real puzzle for social movement theorists. If social movements are defined in part by the targets they address, and if local activists understand that the nation-state remains the most accessible site for policy intervention, then social movement theorists who define movements' constituencies partly in terms of appeals to policymakers will almost always see national citizenship as a kind of paramount identity for activists.

What happens to social movement theory if we avoid privileging local or national identities, looking instead at the relationship between global processes and local ones? What does globalization mean for how people understand issues, for how they mobilize? What does globalization mean for the kinds of alliances activists form or the institutions to which they appeal? What resources are available for activists in a global world, and how do these resources shape or constrain local movements' strategic choices about framing and targets?

Global Identities: The Anti-apartheid Movement

What might a global identity mean, and what would a global movement look like? In this section, I would like briefly to turn to the international anti-apartheid movement of the 1980s. Discussions of global social movements rarely include a sustained discussion of this remarkably global movement that emerged in the 1970s and 1980s. From the end of World War II, as former colonies took their seats in the United Nations General Assembly, apartheid was internationally condemned and finally declared a crime against humanity: as a system of laws imposed by a whites-only government, apartheid denied all political rights to the country's black majority, using legal racial classification to determine where individuals could live, attend school, hold down jobs, and even whom they could marry. But this international condemnation was not limited to the level of states' representatives or debates in the General Assembly. Over thirty years—generally in response to visible protests by black South Africans facing police bullets, imprisonment, and torture—the anti-apartheid movement gradually developed a grassroots constituency around the world. Within that movement, I will argue, activists developed a global antiracist identity that transcended, even challenged, state borders. More importantly, I will suggest, participation in that movement changed the way many activists viewed politics at home and added a global dimension to many discussions of racial inequality.

Admittedly, my view of this movement's importance is colored by my experiences within it. Like many academics who write about social movements, my interest comes in large part from my participation in a specific one; the line between activists and academics is as blurry in this realm as in any other area of sociology. From the mid-1970s to the mid-1990s, when South Africa finally held its first democratic elections and the country's black majority finally attained full citizenship, I participated actively in the American and international anti-apartheid movement. As an American undergraduate, I joined debates and demonstrations, writing articles and editorials urging universities to sell their stock in companies that had invested in South Africa. After college, I taught high school and wrote textbooks in Swaziland, Botswana, and Zimbabwe. When I returned to graduate school in the United States in the early 1980s, I was already part of what Keck and Sikkink (1998) might call a principled-issue network, committed to supporting anti-apartheid activists inside South Africa and to raising international concern about what was happening in the distant corners of South Africa's *bantustans.*

For most of the 1960s and 1970s, the Western anti-apartheid movement—located mainly in Sweden, Britain, the United States, Canada, Holland, Australia, and New Zealand but also visible in countries as unlikely as Italy, Norway, and even Japan—focused on raising public awareness and changing international policies toward South Africa. Each national group worked to change their local national policy, but they were explicitly linked to a broader, somewhat amorphous set of organizations and loosely coordinated activities around the world. These activists can hardly be described as nationalist; clearly, the focus on national governments stemmed entirely from the recognition that international pressure on South Africa would have to come through the actions of sovereign states. Even at the local level, the general purpose of anti-apartheid groups was international: local groups sought to redefine the relationship of their local entity—whether it was a university, a city, or a religious body—to South Africa as a way to put pressure on the white minority to change.

At moments when the movement was merely stagnant, anti-apartheid groups involved a rather motley crew, the kind of principled-issue network described by social movement theorists who reject the idea that social movements can construct a truly global identity. Generally, activists included South African exiles and expatriates concerned about events in their home country, former civil rights activists offended by racist practices in South Africa, and liberal do-gooders looking for a relatively safe cause to champion. Although there were many moments of high excitement—when the South Africans tried to sneak yet another sports team into an international sporting event in contravention of an international sports boycott or when yet another massacre of black South Africans provoked an international outcry—the anti-apartheid movement generally seemed rather peripheral to local politics. Our meetings and campaigns were always well intentioned and serious, but in general we were hardly at the center of international policy debates.

But through the 1980s this small network mushroomed into what can only be described as an international social movement in which people literally knocked on our doors to ask what they could do to help. In 1984, a new constitution in South Africa prompted widespread uprisings in black townships; images of unarmed black protestors at funerals, facing tanks and live ammunition, provoked widespread condemnation. Since the early 1960s, South African anti-apartheid leaders had called on Western governments to impose international sanctions on South Africa, but—especially while the cold war was at its height—Western governments continued to treat South Africa's white minority regime as an ally, despite its racist practices. By the mid-1980s, as South Africa enforced a draconian state of emergency on an increasingly militant uprising, anti-apartheid groups around the world publicized events, using any tactic possible to undermine the regime, from putting pressure on multinational corporations who invested in South Africa through shareholder resolutions or divestment motions to publicizing the ties between Western governments and the South African military.

In the process, the small principled-issue network that had once held the anti-apartheid movement together was literally overwhelmed, as ordinary citizens in an extraordinarily wide range of localities sought ways to demonstrate their opposition to apartheid's particularly virulent forms of racism. It is here, I would argue, that a new collective identity was constructed, giving participants a sense of belonging to something far broader than the local or national groups in which they participated. In Italy or France, no less than in New Zealand, participants viewed themselves as part of a *transnational* anti-apartheid movement. Although they always belonged to locally based organizations, their concern was with the transnational expression of opposition to South Africa's apartheid policies; even when they focused on local state policies—or even the policies of their local university or pension fund—they identified themselves as part of a transnational antiracist community.

For these grassroots participants, the impulse behind the anti-apartheid movement was clearly a universalistic one, asserting membership in a global community rather than in a local or national one; its activists appealed to a global vision of morality and community, and participation in the movement clearly reflected, at least for one moment, a sense by individuals of an identity that went beyond local borders. To use the editors' term, they clearly understood their participation in terms of a "transnational public sphere." Looking at any one part of the anti-apartheid movement, a researcher would have seen activists focusing on local issues, local concerns; and yet the impulse behind the mobilization involved an antiracist identity that cannot be understood in nationalist terms.

Obviously, not all participants in the anti-apartheid movement were equally involved in this transnational identity, and many of them would have instantly acknowledged the presence of hierarchies of commitment to that transnational identity within their groups. The small network of activists for whom the anti-apartheid movement had long provided a primary identity was clearly distinguishable from most participants; with ties to other activists, with a greater store of knowledge about the issue and the movement's history, they—or rather we—clearly had undue influence in directing and shaping the movement's strategies and discourse. Yet I think it would be inaccurate to dismiss the less knowledgeable, or less involved, participants from the picture: by focusing only on the network of activists and organizations that tended to speak for the movement, social movement theorists ignore the many thousands of participants who were clearly mobilized in the anti-apartheid movement and whose commitment to the global goal of ending racial inequality should be taken seriously.

The construction of a transnational collective identity does not, of course, imply that all strategies and targets were transnational. At the national level, activists focused on national policies toward South Africa, but when national politicians insisted that cold war loyalties to South Africa's regime were more important than targeting racial oppression activists often focused on more local links to South Africa as their only accessible targets. In the United States, this pattern was especially visible. Through the 1970s and 1980s, when American presidents generally refused to support most economic sanctions against Pretoria, anti-apartheid activists turned to universities, municipalities, and pension funds, insisting that stocks held in companies that invested in South Africa linked local institutions to a far-off system.

This strategy of finding local links to apartheid became even more visible in the mid-1980s, when the Reagan administration refused to impose sanctions although the uprising in South Africa made the nightly American news. In Washington in late 1984, the South African consulate made a strategic blunder: it called upon the police to arrest Randall Robinson and several other activists who had asked to speak to the consul. The episode triggered a new strategy for anti-apartheid activists: they began to engage in civil disobedience around the country, and Americans who wanted to find some way to express their outrage at apartheid sought out ways to get peacefully arrested. In many cities where there were no consulates, people displayed great creativity in identifying potential sites for displaying their concern about apartheid. In Berkeley, for example, people had to sign up in advance to be arrested for blocking the university administration building, as university students and ordinary Californian citizens objected to their taxes going to buy shares in corporations that did business in South Africa. On many college campuses, students erected shanty towns illegally, seeking to provoke almost the same images of bulldozers and forced removals in the United States that were familiar from apartheid South Africa. Lacking targets that could be directly linked to national foreign policy-making mechanisms, people across the United States found local links to South Africa and tried to cut them.

This was, then, a transnational movement, operating on a transnational stage, with transnational goals and strategies as well as national ones. Building on a transnational network of activists, it involved people around the world in a collective movement aimed at a global objective. Often involving transnational exchanges of ideas and resources, as well as personnel, the anti-apartheid movement built a transnational constituency for an international issue, treating the eradication of apartheid as an important step toward creating greater racial equality internationally.

But, like most collective identities, the collective identity involved in the anti-apartheid movement was fluid and multifaceted, and activists could shift the ground from which they spoke at different moments. Frequently, issues raised by the anti-apartheid movement had domestic as well as international implications, and activists often included domestic concerns as well as international ones in their agendas. Almost invariably, where the anti-apartheid movement really became a grassroots movement, anti-apartheid campaigns played into domestic debates as well as international ones. In the United States, civil rights activists explicitly suggested that the anti-apartheid movement could play two roles, one international, one domestic. Protesting American policy in South Africa was important as a way to bring apartheid to an end, but it also allowed activists to introduce discussions of racism in a nonconfrontational way, strengthening an American constituency for an antiracist project at a time when the American body politic seemed to have turned away from affirmative action and civil rights.

Other branches of the international anti-apartheid movement had similarly Janus-faced agendas. The anti-apartheid movement had long been a fixture on Britain's postcolonial scene, staffed largely by South African expatriates and exiles but with strong ties to Britain's Labour Party. In the 1980s, however, it took on a newly visible militance; British participants, like their American counterparts, were certainly responding to events inside South Africa, but the movement's appeal was also strengthened by a deepening concern about racism inside Britain. These local issues rarely created direct conflicts between the movement's transnational segments—unlike, for example, the situation in the international labor movement, where debates over setting fair international wage standards frequently deteriorate into struggles over protectionism and competition for jobs and markets. But ignoring the importance of these local issues in explaining the character of the transnational movement in the 1980s would, I think, lead observers to overlook one of the more intriguing aspects of transnationalism.

And in both these cases—along with others, such as that of New Zealand—widespread participation in the transnational anti-apartheid movement rebounded onto domestic politics, as activists rethought domestic issues in light of what they had learned in the international movement. In the United States, many white participants joined the anti-apartheid movement out of revulsion for racism, but as they began to identify with an antiracist transnational movement they often began to look more closely—and critically—at racial practices in their backyard, reassessing the extent of segregation and the persistent impact of racial inequality on American lives. Conversely, many black civil rights activists claimed that involvement in anti-apartheid activism—particularly their exposure to the "non-racialism" of the African National Congress, the leading South African political group in the 1980s—prompted a rethinking of separatist attitudes toward white participation in antiracist movements and a reevaluation of the importance of international policy.

What does this example suggest for discussions of transnational social movements? Above all, I think, it underscores some of the methodological challenges posed by transnational movements: neither a locally oriented case study approach nor a focus on targets would reveal the extent to which participants assumed a transnational identity or viewed their actions as oriented toward transnational goals. But it also reveals some of the complicated questions involved in transnationalism. It would be erroneous, I think, to ignore the transnational character of this movement or to argue that activists and participants were not concerned with the movement's transnational goals. Yet it would be almost equally silly to overlook the local dynamics within different parts of the larger movement.

Confronting Globalization, Rethinking Movements

The anti-apartheid movement is hardly the only transnational movement of the late twentieth century. Although social movement theorists have been generally reluctant to label movements as transnational, activists in many movements of the 1990s—from the explicitly globally oriented environmental movement to movements that draw on universal principles but act almost entirely locally such as the women's and indigenous peoples' movements—are far less restrictive in their claims. Repeatedly in an era of globalization social movement activists define their constituencies, their audiences, the resources on which they draw, and, above all, the principles to which they appeal in global terms. What does this mean for social movement theory, and where should we locate the starting points for examining transnational movements?

Although each of the chapters in this volume pursues its own logic, analyzing a particular social movement rather than a larger set of issues, as a whole they point toward some possible answers as well as toward some of the puzzles for social movement theory raised by a more global perspective.

Perhaps this volume's most obvious contribution lies in the descriptions of several social movements whose members span borders and whose collective identity seems to surpass any single national territory. The antislavery, Solidarity, and human rights movements (Keck and Sikkink, this volume; Rucht, this volume; Ball, this volume) involve participants who have redefined their sense of moral obligation to include a larger community.

But the cases in this volume suggest that transnationalism is more complicated than simply an appeal to universal norms. Social movements that involve appeals to international audiences, draw on international resources, and target international bodies—surely these all beg questions about the relationship between the global and the local and about transnational identities and movement. Social movements that consistently draw on international norms to challenge local practices (Guidry, this volume), address international audiences through universal images (Bayard de Volo, this volume), use globalized frames of discourse to delegitimize their opponents in local arenas (Kubik, this volume), or define participants' identities in terms of international legal norms and sites created by international organizations (Peteet, this volume)—surely these cannot be understood only in local terms any more than the anti-apartheid movement can. If, in the late twentieth century, even nationalist movements can really be understood only in the context of international flows of resources and ideologies (van der Veer, this volume; Uehling, this volume), then it seems reasonable to ask about the global side of any social movement and to assume that global dynamics have something to do with the way these movements mobilize participants, mobilize resources, and frame their strategies and goals.

The authors in this volume are careful to acknowledge that national frameworks continue to shape political action for most of us; and yet, based on the material they present, something important seems to be happening in the realm of social activists' vision of their constituencies and audiences. The shared networks, shared information, shared strategies—above all, the shared sense of moral connectedness and the construction of an identity that extends beyond national borders—suggest that somehow activists in these movements are increasingly likely to define their concerns in a way that is emphatically not limited to the single territorially defined community. There is at least a normative vision of a collective identity that goes beyond borders.

But these chapters also raise further questions about what it would mean to construct a global social movement. How might a new sense of global community affect social movement behavior in the future? Perhaps the first obvious impact on globalization is in the way social movement activists conceive of their constituencies and audiences and in their vision of who they represent. Increasingly, social movement identities are explicitly constructed to include people from many areas. In Brazil as well as in Europe, social movement activists have defined their concerns in universalist terms and sought to construct identities and constituencies that were consciously cross-border and internationalist in scope. Moreover, within many of these global movements, activists worked hard to prevent conflict among people of different nationalities, often reframing their concerns in ways that would be inclusive, rather than exclusive, in response to concerns about the perpetuation of global inequalities. Without denying the persistence of national interests, social movement theorists in the late twentieth century must nonetheless acknowledge the extent to which a new "new social movement" pattern has emerged, cutting across national boundaries.

Globalization offers new strategic options as well as new constituencies. Even in movements as persistently localized as the demand for land reform in Chiapas, Mexico, activists have proved astute at framing their concerns in ways that appeal to broader audiences, seeking resources and support far beyond national boundaries. And international activists have provided crucial resources for these local movements: ideas, funds, and international observers whose intervention can prevent repression—all these have become part of the repertoire on which social movement activists around the world can draw, and these concerns begin to play some part in how local activists frame the issues they raise locally.

If activists begin to conceive their constituencies in larger, cross-national terms, and if they begin to conceive of the issues confronting them in terms of global dynamics, how will that affect social movement strategies in the future? Social movement theorists are just beginning to look critically at the construction of global social movements, exploring these processes without romanticizing them. If it is true that social movement activists are beginning to use new technologies to construct new identities, to frame their concerns in terms of a larger community, what kinds of resources are they drawing on and how do they gain access to them? The chapters in this volume begin to lay the groundwork for addressing some of the most pressing questions in transnational social movement theory. How do activists build these cross-border identities? What kinds of appeals seem to resonate most across borders, and what explains activists' decisions to frame local struggles in internationalist terms? Are these appeals increasing in the late twentieth century, with the use of new technologies, or have these larger appeals always been part of social movement mobilization? Who gives shape to these collective identities and under what circumstances do internationalist identities collapse and give way to more localized concerns? How do these global movements, if they exist, behave differently from more localized movements? How best can we study these movements, given the obvious problem that individual researchers tend to remain located in a specific spot and so their observations are refracted through a particular local lens?

And the transnational character of social movements at the turn of the century begs social movement theorists to consider the hierarchical character of global society. For example, several chapters in this volume illustrate local activists' conscious use of international resources—both international ideas and international donor funds—in framing their concerns and shaping their strategies and the effort to address international audiences as they mobilize. Activists as well as academics might ask whether the request for international funds limits local activists to issues that fit with donor agencies' aims. Do local activists' desires for external funding shape their demands in ways that undermine activists' ability to represent faithfully the concerns of local participants? Even if global forces do not redirect local groups, we must ask whether globalizing processes re-create local inequalities. Who gains access to these new technologies, these new audiences, these newly interventionist international organizations? What will determine the outcome of those tensions and how will that affect the ability of movements to mobilize in the future?

Finally, if in the 1990s the transnational public sphere seems to be taking on importance, it is worth remembering that this shift is neither inevitable nor irreversible. The history of the international labor movement is replete with examples of the resurgence of nationalism: despite a rhetoric of internationalism, national unions tend to frame identities and issues in ways that assume that workers in different countries stand in direct competition with each other, reinforcing a nationalist worker identity rather than an internationalist one. For over a century, the international labor movement has struggled with the problem of how to balance national labor movements' local concerns with those of a broader international worker movement. Can social movement theorists predict the collapse of transnational ties within apparently global movements? Lurking in the background, too, are movements that emerge as a challenge to globalization. In the late twentieth century, globalization often appears to be the result of a hegemonic project, a process largely driven by those who are powerful and wealthy. Global social movements, on the other hand, often seem to embody local resistence to that project. What does that mean for the development of a transnational collective identity?

For activists as well as theorists, the relationship between global and local is fraught with tension. If activists must figure out how to negotiate the complicated strains that arise between local and global constituencies, social movement theorists must consider how to examine those tensions without exacerbating or exaggerating them and without treating all social movements as either homegrown novelties or new versions of cultural imperialism. How to raise internationally legitimate issues without undermining local legitimacy? How to address international audiences while still resonating with constituencies at home? How to attract international resources and activists without losing local control?

At the end of her essay on early-twentieth-century literature, Virginia Woolf warned her readers not to expect too much. "Do not expect just at present a complete and satisfactory presentation," she wrote. "Tolerate the spasmodic, the obscure, the fragmentary, the failure." A similar warning might well be posed to readers who are looking for global social movements in the late twentieth century—and to readers who are looking for a theory of global movements. We can barely distinguish a global from a local movement, and we are only beginning to understand that we might have other questions to ask. But rather than turning away from the challenge of reconstructing theories in the light of whatever it is that we call globalization, this volume invites us to enter the fray.

NOTES

1. In a relatively late example of technological euphoria, for example, the renowned sociologist Robert Parks ([1937] 1961) used language almost identical to the 1990s discourse of globalization but about an earlier generation of innovations: "Now that the aeroplane has . . . abolished the distances that once separated the nations and peoples and the radio has converted the world into one great whispering gallery, [the] great world—intertribal, interracial, and international—the world of business and politics—has grown at the expense of the little world, the world of intimate, personal loyalties in which men were bound together by tradition, custom, and natural piety."

2. American social movement theorists often seem to be thinking about the civil rights movement when they think about social movements generally—in sharp contrast to European social movement theorists, who frequently virtually ignore movements organized around racial inequality when they talk about "new" social movements. This difference may help explain some of the different perspectives exhibited by American and European social movement theorists in the 1980s. Generally, American theorists tended to take questions about the construction of a collective identity more or less for granted, focusing instead on questions of resource mobilization and strategies—perhaps because mobilization around

racial identities and racially motivated collective grievances appeared relatively straightforward in the United States, where a fairly rigid racial ideology meant that racial identities were relatively unquestioned until recently. In contrast, European theorists, who focused more on the student, peace, and women's movements, considered the construction of collective identities a far more thorny issue (e.g., McCarthy and Zald 1979; McAdam 1988; Melucci 1989; Morris and Mueller 1992).

Bibliography

Abbot, Andrew. 1988. *The System of Professions: An Essay on the Division of Expert Labor.* Chicago: University of Chicago Press.

Abel, Annie, and Frank Klingberg, eds. 1927. *A Side Light on Anglo-American Relations, 1839–1858: Furnished by Correspondence of Lewis Tappen and Others with the British and Foreign Anti-Slavery Society.* Lancaster, PA: Association for the Study of Negro Life and History.

Abel, Richard. 1995. *Politics by Other Means: Law in the Struggle against Apartheid, 1980–1994.* London: Routledge.

Abu-Lughod, Lila. 1990. "The Romance of Resistance: Tracing Transformations of Power through Bedouin Women." *American Ethnologist* 17 (1):41–56.

Afshari, Reza. 1994. "An Essay on Islamic Cultural Relativism in the Discourse on Human Rights." *Human Rights Quarterly* 16:235–76.

Alcoff, Linda. 1994. "Cultural Feminism versus Post-structuralism: The Identity Crisis in Feminist Theory." In Nicholas B. Dirks, Geoff Eley, and Sherry B. Ortner, eds., *Culture/Power/History: A Reader in Contemporary Social Theory,* 96–122. Princeton: Princeton University Press.

Alexeyeva, Ludmilla. 1988. "Mustafa Jemilev, His Character and Convictions." In Edward Allworth, ed., *Tatars of the Crimea,* 51–69. Durham: Duke University Press.

Allworth, Edward. 1988. Introduction to Edward Allworth, ed., *Tatars of the Crimea,* 3–8. Durham: Duke University Press.

Alvarez, Sonia. 1990. *Engendering Democracy in Brazil: Women's Movements in Transition Politics.* Princeton: Princeton University Press.

Alves, Maria Helena Moreira. 1985. *State and Opposition in Military Brazil.* Austin: University of Texas Press.

Anderson, Benedict. 1983. *Imagined Communities.* London: Verso.

———. 1998. *The Spectre of Comparisons: Nationalisms, Southeast Asia, and the World.* London: Verso.

Anzaldua, Gloria. 1987. *Borderlands—La Frontera; the New Mestiza.* San Francisco: Aunt Lute Books.

Appadurai, Arjun. 1991. "Global Ethnoscapes: Notes and Queries for a Transnational Anthropology." In Richard G. Fox, ed., *Recapturing Anthropology,* 191–211. Santa Fe: School of American Research Press.

———. 1993. "Patriotism and its Future." *Public Culture* 5 (3):411–29.

———. 1996. *Modernity at Large: Cultural Dimensions of Globalization.* Minneapolis: University of Minnesota Press.

Appadurai, Arjun, and Carol A. Breckenridge. 1995. "Public Modernity in India." In Carol A. Breckenridge, ed., *Consuming Modernity,* 1–23. Minneapolis: University of Minnesota Press.

Aptheker, Herbert. 1989. *Abolitionism: A Revolutionary Movement.* Boston: Twayne.

Armstrong, Warwick, and T. G. McGee. 1985. *Theatres of Accumulation.* London: Methuen.

Arrighi, Giovanni. 1994. *The Long Twentieth Century: Money, Power, and the Origins of Our Times.* London: Verso.

Ashworth, John. 1987. "The Relationship between Capitalism and Humanitarianism." *American Historical Review* 92 (October) 813–28.

Auler, Marcelo. 1993. "Sangue dos Inocentes." *Veja,* 14 July, 40–42.

Balcerowicz, Leszek. 1995. *Wolnosc i rozwoj: Ekonomia wolnego rynku.* Krakow: Znak.

Ball, Patrick. 1998. "Liberal Hypocrisy and Totalitarian Sincerity." Ph.D. diss., University of Michigan.

Ball, Patrick, Paul Kobrak, and Herbert F. Spirer. 1999. *State Terror in Guatemala, 1960–1996: A Quantitative Reflection.* Washington, DC: AAAS.

Balsen W., and K. Rössel. 1986. *Hoch die internationale Solidarität.* Cologne: Kölner Volksblatt.

Bammer, Angelika. 1994. "Mother Tongues and Other Strangers: Writing Family across Cultural Divides." In Angelika Bammer, ed., *Displacements,* 90–109. Bloomington and Indianapolis: University of Indiana Press.

Banner, Lois W. 1980. *Elizabeth Cady Stanton: A Radical for Women's Rights.* Boston: Little, Brown.

Barnett, Michael, and Martha Finnemore. 1999. "The Politics, Power, and Pathologies of International Organizations." *International Organization* 53(4).

Bar-On, Dan, and Noga Gilad. 1994. "To Re-build a Life: A Narrative Analysis of Three Generations of an Israeli Holocaust Survivor's Family." In Amia Lieblich and Ruthellen Josselson, eds., *Exploring Identity and Gender,* 83–112. Thousand Oaks, CA: Sage.

Barsh, Russel Lawrence. 1993. "Measuring Human Rights: Problems of Methodology and Purpose." *Human Rights Quarterly* 15:87–121.

Basu, Amrita, ed. 1995. *The Challenge of Local Feminisms: Women's Movements in Global Perspective.* Boulder: Westview.

Bayard de Volo, Lorraine. 1998. "Drafting Motherhood: A Comparative Analysis of Maternal Mobilization in W.W. II and the Nicaraguan Revolution." In Jennifer Turpin and Lois Lorentzen, eds., *The Women and War Reader.* New York: New York University Press.

Becker, G. S. 1976. *The Economic Approach to Human Behavior.* Chicago: University of Chicago Press.

Beckles, Hilary. 1995a. "The Origins and Development of West Indies Cricket Culture in the Nineteenth Century: Jamaica and Barbados." In Hilary M. Beckles and Brian Stoddart, eds., *Liberation Cricket: West Indies Cricket Culture,* 33–43. Manchester and New York: Manchester University Press.

———. 1995b. "The Political Ideology of West Indies Cricket Culture." In Hilary M. Beckles and Brian Stoddart, eds., *Liberation Cricket: West Indies Cricket Culture,* 148–64. Manchester and New York: Manchester University Press.

Beckles, Hilary M., and Verene Shepherd, eds. 1993. *Caribbean Freedom: Economy and Society from Emancipation to the Present.* Kingston, Jamaica: Ian Randle.

Beckles, Hilary M., and Brian Stoddart, eds. 1995. *Liberation Cricket: West Indies Cricket Culture.* Kingston, Jamaica: Ian Randle.

Bergensen, H. O., and G. Parmann. 1994. *Green Globe Yearbook: International Co-operation on Environment and Development.* Oxford: Oxford University Press.

Berkovitch, Nasa. 1995. "From Motherhood to Citizenship: The Worldwide Incorporation of Women into the Public Sphere in the Twentieth Century," Ph.D. diss., Stanford University.

Berner, Erhard, and Rüdiger Korff. 1995. "Globalization and Local Resistance: The Creation of Localities in Manila and Bangkok." *International Journal of Urban and Regional Research* 19 (June):208–22.

Berry, J. M. 1977. *Lobbying for the People: The Political Behavior of Public Interest Groups.* Princeton: Princeton University Press.

Bhabha, Homi. 1994. *The Location of Culture.* New York: Routledge.

Bibo, Istvan. 1991. *Democracy, Revolution, Self-Determination: Selected Writings.* Edited by Andras Boros-Kazai. Highland Lakes: Atlantic Research and Publications.

Bjarkman, Peter C. 1994. *Baseball with a Latin Beat.* Jefferson, NC: McFarland.

Blalock, Hubert M., Jr. 1960. *Social Statistics.* New York: McGraw-Hill.

Blanes, Denise Neri, Maria do Carmo Brant de Carvalho, and Maria Cecília R. Nobre Barreira. N.d. *Trabalhando Conselhos Tutelares.* São Paulo: Instituto de Estudos Especiais, Pontífica Universidade Católica de São Paulo.

Boli-Bennett, John. 1981. "Human Rights or State Expansion? Cross-National Definitions of Constitutional Rights, 1870–1970." In Ved P. Nanda, James R. Scarritt, and George W. Shepherd, eds., *Global Human Rights,* 173–94. Boulder: Westview.

Boli-Bennett, John, and John Meyer. 1978. "The Ideology of Childhood and the State: Rules Distinguishing Children in National Constitutions." *American Sociological Review* 43 (December):797–812.

Bosch, Mineke, and Annemaire Kloosterman, eds. 1990. *Politics and Friendship: Letters from the International Woman Suffrage Alliance, 1902–1942.* Columbus: Ohio State University Press.

Bourdieu, Pierre. 1994. "Structures, Habitus, Power: Basis for a Theory of Symbolic Power." In Nicholas B. Dirks, Geoff Eley, and Sherry B. Ortner, eds., *Culture/Power/History: A Reader in Contemporary Social Theory,* 155–99. Princeton: Princeton University Press.

Bowen, Rowland. 1970. *Cricket: A History of Its Growth and Development throughout the World.* London: Eyre and Spottiswoode.

Boyarin, Jonathan. 1994. "Space, Time, and the Politics of Memory." In Jonathan Boyarin, ed., *Remapping Memory: The Politics of TimeSpace,* 1–38. Minnesota: University of Minnesota Press.

Boym, Svetlana. 1995. "From the Russian Soul to Post-Communist Nostalgia." *Representations* 49 (winter):133–66.

Brass, Paul. 1988. "The Punjab Crisis and the Unity of India." In Atul Kohli, ed., *India's Democracy,* 169–214. Princeton: Princeton University Press.

Bräuer, R. 1994. "Zwischen Provinzialität und Globalismus: Die westdeutsche Dritte-Welt-Bewegung in den 80er und 90er Jahren." *Forschungsjournal Neue Soziale Bewegungen* 7 (3):32–48.

Brennan, G., and L. Lomasky. 1993. *Democracy and Decision: The Pure Theory of Electoral Preference.* Cambridge: Cambridge University Press.

Brint, Steven. 1994. *In the Age of Experts: The Changing Role of Professionals in Politics and Public Life.* Princeton: Princeton University Press.

Brockett, Charles D. 1992. "Measuring Political Violence and Land Inequality in Central America." *American Political Science Review* 86 (1):169–76.

Brooks, Clem, and Jeff Manza. 1997. "The Social and Ideological Bases of Middle-Class Political Realignment in the United States, 1972–1992." *American Sociological Review* 62:191–208.

Brown, J. F. 1993. "Eastern Europe: The Revolution So Far," *RFE/RL Research Report* 2 (1) (January):69–74.

Brubaker, Rogers. 1996. *Nationalism Reframed: Nationhood and the National Question in the New Europe.* Cambridge: Cambridge University Press.

Brysk, Alison. 1993. "From Above and Below: Social Movements, the International System, and Human Rights in Argentina." *Comparative Political Studies* 26 (3):259–85.

———. 1994. *The Politics of Human Rights in Argentina: Protest, Change, and Democratization.* Stanford: Stanford University Press.

Buchsteiner, J. 1995. Wenn Helfer zuviel helfen. *Die Zeit,* July 7, 1995, 3.

Buhle, Mari Jo, and Paul Buhle, eds. 1978. *The Concise History of Woman Suffrage: Selections from the Classic Work of Stanton, Anthony, Gage, and Harper.* Urbana: University of Illinois Press.

Burawoy, Michael. Forthcoming. "Reaching for the Global." In M. Burawoy et al., eds., *Global Ethnography: Forces, Connections, and Imaginations in a Transnational World.* Berkeley: University of California Press.

Burgers, Jan Herman. 1992. "The Road to San Francisco: The Revival of the Human Rights Idea in the Twentieth Century." *Human Rights Quarterly* 14:447–77.

Burton, Richard D. E. 1995. "Cricket, Carnival, and Street Culture in the Caribbean." In Hilary M. Beckles and Brian Stoddart, eds., *Liberation Cricket: West Indies Cricket Culture,* 89–106. Manchester and New York: Manchester University Press.

Butler, Thomas. 1989. "Memory: A Mixed Blessing." In T. Butler, ed., *Memory, History, Culture, and the Mind,* 97–113. Oxford: Blackwell.

Calhoun, Craig. 1989. "Tienanmen, Television, and the Public Sphere: Internationalization of Culture and the Beijing Spring of 1989." *Public Culture* 2:54–70.

———. 1994a. *Neither Gods nor Emperors: Students and the Struggle for Democracy in China.* Berkeley: University of California Press.

———. 1994b. "Social Theory and the Politics of Identity." In C. Calhoun, ed., *Social Theory and the Politics of Identity,* 9–36. Cambridge and Oxford: Blackwell.

———. 1995. *Critical Social Theory.* London: Blackwell.

Campos, Angela Valadares Dutra de Souza. 1984. *O Menor Institucionalizado: Um Desafio para a Sociedade.* Petrópolis: Vozes.

Carleton, David, and Michael Stohl. 1985. "The Foreign Policy of Human Rights: Rhetoric and Reality from Jimmy Carter to Ronald Reagan." *Human Rights Quarterly* 7:205–29.

———. 1987. "The Role of Human Rights in U.S. Foreign Assistance Policy: A Critique and Reappraisal." *American Journal of Political Science* 31 (November):1002–18.

Carroll, William K., and R. S. Ratner. 1996. "Master Framing and Cross Movement Networking in Contemporary Social Movements." *Sociological Quarterly* 37 (4):601–25.

Casanovas, Joan. 1995. "The Cuban Labor Movement of the 1860s and Spain's Search for a New Colonial Policy." *Cuban Studies* 25:83–99.

Casey, Edward S. 1987. *Remembering: A Phenomenological Study.* Bloomington: Indiana University Press.

Castells, Manuel. 1989. *The Informational City: Information Technology, Economic Restructuring, and the Urban-Regional Process.* Oxford: Blackwell.

Cerny, Philip G. 1995. "Globalization and the Changing Logic of Collective Action." *International Organization* 49 (4):595–625.

Chamoiseau, Patrick. 1998. *Texaco.* New York: Vintage.

Chatterjee, Partha. 1993a. *The Nation and Its Fragments.* Princeton: Princeton University Press.

———. 1993b. *Nationalist Thought and the Colonial World.* Minneapolis: University of Minnesota Press.

Chatterjee, Partha, and Matthias Finger. 1994. *The Earth Brokers: Power, Politics, and World Development.* London and New York: Routledge.

Chen, Ching-chih. 1984. "Police and Community Control Systems in the Empire." In Ramon H. Myers and Mark R. Peattie, eds. *The Japanese Colonial Empire, 1895–1945,* 213–39. Princeton: Princeton University Press.

Chen, Chun-kai. 1992. *A Study of Social Status of Taiwanese Doctor under Japanese Rules.* Taipei: Institute of History, National Taiwan Normal University. In Chinese.

Chou, Wan-yao. 1989. *Jih-chu-shih-tai ti T'ai-wan-i-hui-she-chih ch'ing-yuan-yun-tung.* Taipei: Tzu li pao hsi wen hua ch'u pan pu.

Chuchryk, Patricia M. 1989. "Feminist Anti-authoritarian Politics: The Role of Women's Organizations in the Chilean Transition to Democracy." In Jane Jaquette, ed., *The Women's Movement in Latin America: Feminism and the Transition to Democracy.* Boston: Unwin Hyman.

Clarke, Susan E., and Gary L. Gail. 1997. "Globalization and the Changing U.S. City." *The Annals of the American Academy of Political and Social Science* 551 (May):28–43.

Clemens, Elizabeth C. 1996. "Organizational Form as Frame: Collective Identity and Political Strategy in the American Labor Movement." In Doug McAdam, John D. McCarthy, and Mayer N. Zald, eds., *Comparative Perspectives on Social Movements,* 205–26. Cambridge: Cambridge University Press.

Clifford, James. 1994. "Diasporas." *Cultural Anthropology* 9 (3):302–36.

Collard, D. 1978. *Altruism and Economy: A Study in Non-selfish Economics.* Oxford: Oxford University Press.

Collier, Ruth Berins, and David Collier. 1991. *Shaping the Political Arena: Critical Junctures, the Labor Movement, and Regime Dynamics in Latin America.* Princeton: Princeton University Press.

Conovan, Margaret. 1981. *Populism.* London: Junction.

Conway, Martin. 1990. *Autobiographical Memory.* Philadelphia: Open University Press.

Cooke, Miriam, and Angela Woollacott. 1993. Introduction to Miriam Cooke and Angela Woollacott, eds., *Gendering War Talk.* Princeton: Princeton University Press.

Cooper, A. H. 1995. *Paradoxes of Peace: German Peace Movements since 1945.* Ann Arbor: University of Michigan Press.

Cooper, Frederick, and Ann Stoler, eds. 1997. *Tensions of Empire: Colonial Cultures in a Bourgeois World.* Berkeley: University of California Press.

Copper, John F. 1993. *Historical Dictionary of Taiwan.* Metuchen, NJ: Scarecrow.

Costa, Heloisa Lara Campos da, José Maria de Castro Santana, Edila Arnaud Ferreira Moura, Eleonora Arnaud Pereira Ferreira, and Maria Lucia Sá Maia. 1993. *Políticas Públicas, Desigualdades Sociais e Crianças no Amazonas.* Belém: UNAMAZ, FUA, UFPA.

Cott, Nancy F. 1994. "Early-Twentieth Century Feminism in Political Context: A Comparative Look at Germany and the United States." In Caroline Daley and Melanie Nolan, eds., *Suffrage and Beyond: International Feminist Perspectives.* New York: New York University Press.

Craton, Michael. 1974. *Sinews of Empire: A Short History of British Slavery.* Garden City, NY: Anchor.

Crowley, Stephen. 1994. "Barriers to Collective Action: Steelworkers and Mutual Dependence in the Former Soviet Union." *World Politics* 46 (July):589–615.

Crystal, Jill. 1994. "The Human Rights Movement in the Arab World." *Human Rights Quarterly* 16:435–54.

Culverson, D. R. 1996. "The Politics of the Anti-apartheid Movement in the United States, 1969–1986." *Political Science Quarterly* 111 (1):127–49.

Curtis, M., and J. Neyer, C. Waxman, and A. Pollack, eds. 1975. *The Palestinians: People, History, and Politics.* New Brunswick: Transaction.

Das, Veena. 1995. *Critical Events.* Delhi: Oxford University Press.

Davis, David Brion. 1987. "AHR Forum: Reflections on Abolitionism and Ideological Hegemony." *American Historical Review* 92 (October):797–812.

"Declaration of Principles on Palestinian Women's Rights." *Journal of Palestinian Studies* 24(1):137–38.

Deker, Nikolai K. 1958. "The Meaning of Genocide." In *Genocide in the USSR: Studies in Group Destruction,* 1–5. New York: Scarecrow.

della Porta, D., H. Kriesi, and D. Rucht, eds. 1999. *Social Movements in a Globalizing World.* London: Macmillan.

Derluguian, Georgi, and Scott Greer, eds. 2000. *The Uncertain Globalization: Political Projects and the Changing Geopolitics of the World-System.* Westport, CT: Greenwood.

Deutsch, Karl. 1961. "Social Mobilization and Political Development." *American Political Science Review* 55 (September):493–514.

Diamond, Larry, Juan Linz, and Seymour Martin Lipset, eds. 1989. *Democracy in Developing Countries.* Vol. 4: *Latin America.* Boulder: Lynne Reinner.

DIEESE (Departamento Intersindical de Estatística e Estudos Sócio-Econômicos). 1991. "A Necessidade de uma Política Salarial no Brazil." Special issue of *Pesquisa DIEESE,* August.

———. 1993. "Salário Mínimo: A Necessidade de uma Política para sua Recuperação." *Boletim DIEESE,* no. 146 (May):7–12.

Dimenstein, Gilberto. 1990. *A Guerra dos Meninos.* São Paulo: Brasiliense.

———. 1992. *Meninas da Noite: A Prostituição de Meninas-Escravas no Brasil.* São Paulo: Editora Ática.

———. 1993. *O Cidadão de Papel: A Infância, a Adolescência e os Direitos Humanos no Brasil.* São Paulo: Editora Ática.

Diniz, Ana. 1994. *Correndo Atrás da Vida.* Belém: CEJUP.

Dirks, Nicholas. 1994. "Ritual and Resistance: Subversion as a Social Fact." In Nicholas B. Dirks, Geoff Eley, and Sherry B. Ortner, eds., *Culture/Power/History: A Reader in Contemporary Social Theory,* 483–503. Princeton: Princeton University Press.

Dirks, Nicholas B., Geoff Eley, and Sherry B. Ortner, eds. 1994. *Culture/Power/History: A Reader in Contemporary Social Theory.* Princeton: Princeton University Press.

Donnelly, Jack. 1986. "International Human Rights: A Regime Analysis." *International Organization* 40 (3):599–642.

———. 1989. *Universal Human Rights in Theory and Practice.* Ithaca: Cornell University Press.

Donnelly, Peter. 1988. "Sport as a Site for 'Popular' Resistance." In Richard B. Gruneau, ed., *Popular Cultures and Political Practices.* Toronto: Garamond.

Douglas, M. 1989. "Il n'y a pas de don gratuit." *Revue du Mauss* 4:99–115.

Dubois, Ellen Carol. 1994. "Woman Suffrage around the World: Three Phases of Suffragist Internationalism." In Caroline Daley and Melanie Nolan, eds., *Suffrage and Beyond: International Feminist Perspectives.* New York: New York University Press.

Dunn, Fred L. 1976. "Traditional Asian Medicine and Cosmopolitan Medicine as Adaptive Systems." In Charles Leslie, ed., *Asian Medical System: A Comparative Study,* 133–58. Berkeley: University of California Press.

Dusenbury, Verne. 1995. "A Sikh Diaspora? Contested Identities and Constructed Realities." In Peter van der Veer, ed., *Nation and Migration,* 17–43. Philadelphia: University of Pennsylvania Press.

Dworkin, Ronald. 1977. *Taking Rights Seriously.* Cambridge: Harvard University Press.

Eckstein, Susan, ed. 1989. *Power and Popular Protest: Latin American Social Movements.* Berkeley: University of California Press.

Ekiert, Grzegorz. 1996. *The State against Society: Political Crises and Their Aftermath in East Central Europe.* Princeton: Princeton University Press.

Ekiert, Grzegorz, and Jan Kubik. 1998a. "Contentious Politics in New Democracies: East Germany, Hungary, Poland, and Slovakia, 1989–93." *World Politics* 50 (July):547–81.

———. 1998b. "Collective Protest in Postcommunist Poland, 1989–1993." *Communist and Post-Communist Studies* 31 (2):91–117.

———. 1999. *Rebellious Civil Society: Popular Protest and Democratic Consolidation in Poland, 1989–1993.* Ann Arbor: University of Michigan Press.

Ekins, P. 1992. *A New World Order: Grassroots Movements for Global Change.* London and New York: Routledge.

Elshtain, Jean Bethke. 1987. *Women and War.* New York: Basic Books.

Envio Editorial Board. 1991. "Women in Nicaragua: The Revolution on Hold." *Envio* 10, (June):34.

Esbenshade, Richard S. 1995. "Remembering to Forget: Memory, History, National Identity in Postwar East-Central Europe." *Representations* 49 (winter):72–95.

Escobar, Arturo. 1991. "Imaginando un futuro: pensamiento crítico, desarrollo y movimientos sociales." In Margarita Maya, ed., *Desarrollo y Democracia.* Caracas: Editorial Nueva Sociedad.

———. 1995. *Encountering Development: The Making and Unmaking of the Third World.* Princeton: Princeton University Press.

Escobar, Arturo, and Sonia E. Alvarez, eds. 1992. *The Making of Social Movements in Latin America.* Boulder: Westview.

Esser, H. 1991. *Alltagshandeln und Verstehen: Zum Verhältnis von erklärender und verstehender Soziologie am Beispiel von Alfred Schütz und "rational choice."* Tübingen: Mohr.

Etzioni, A. 1988. *The Moral Dimension: Toward a New Economics.* New York: Free Press.

Fan, Yen-ch'iu. 1993. "Jih-chih shih-ch'i T'ai-wan tsung tu fu I-lan i-yüan ch'u-t'an." *I-lan wen-hsien tsa-chih* 7:3–38.

Fanon, Frantz. 1963. *The Wretched of the Earth.* New York: Grove.

Faure, Jean-Michel. 1996. "Forging a French Fighting Spirit: The Nation, Sport, Violence, and War." In J. A. Mangan, ed., *Tribal Identities: Nationalism, Europe, Sport,* 75–93. London: Frank Cass.

Felman, Shoshana, and Dori Laub. 1992. *Testimony: Crises of Witnessing in Literature, Psychoanalysis and History.* New York and London: Routledge.

Fentress, James, and Chris Wickham. 1992. *Social Memory.* Oxford and Cambridge: Blackwell.

Ferrer, Ada. 1991. "Social Aspects of Cuban Nationalism: Race, Slavery, and the Guerra Chiquita, 1879–1880." *Cuban Studies* 21:37–56.

Fireman, B., and W. Gamson. 1979. "Utilitarian Logic in the Resource Mobilization Perspective." In J. McCarthy and M. Zald, eds., *The Dynamics of Social Movements,* 8–54. Cambridge, MA: Winthrop.

Fisher, Alan. 1978. *The Crimean Tatars.* Stanford: Hoover Institution Press, Stanford University.

Fisher, Jo. 1989. *Mothers of the Disappeared.* Boston: South End.

Fisher, Julie. 1993. *The Road from Rio: Sustainable Development and the Nongovernmental Movement in the Third World.* Westport, CT, and London: Praeger.

Fladeland, Betty. 1972. *Men and Brothers: Anglo-American Antislavery Cooperation.* Urbana: University of Illinois Press.

Fogel, Robert William. 1989. *Without Consent or Contract: The Rise and Fall of American Slavery.* New York: Norton.

Foner, Eric. 1980. *Politics and Ideology in the Age of the Civil War.* Oxford: Oxford University Press.

Forced Migration Projects of the Open Society Institute. 1996. *Crimean Tatars: Repatriation and Conflict Prevention.* New York: Open Society Institute.

Forsythe, D. 1991. *The Internationalization of Human Rights.* Lexington: Lexington Books.

Foucault, Michel. 1977a. "Truth and Power." In *Power and Knowledge,* 109–33. New York: Pantheon.

———. 1977b. "Nietzsche, Genealogy, History." In *Language, Counter Memory, Practice,* 139–64. Ithaca: Cornell University Press.

———. 1979. *Discipline and Punish: The Birth of the Prison.* New York: Vintage.

———. 1984. "Nietzsche, Genealogy, History." In *The Foucault Reader,* 76–100. New York: Pantheon.

Fox, Richard. 1985. *Lions of the Punjab.* Berkeley: University of California Press.

Frankel, Francine, and M. S. A. Rao. 1990. *Dominance and State Power in Modern India.* 2 vols. Delhi: Oxford University Press.

Fredrickson, George. 1995. *Black Liberation: A Comparative History of Black Ideologies in the United States and South Africa.* Oxford: Oxford University Press.

Freeman, Michael. 1994. "The Philosophical Foundations of Human Rights." *Human Rights Quarterly* 16:491–514.

Freidson, E. 1970. *Profession of Medicine: A Study of the Sociology of Applied Knowledge.* New York: Harper and Row.

———. 1986. *Professional Powers.* Chicago: University of Chicago Press.

———. 1994. *Professionalism Reborn: Theory, Prophecy, and Policy.* Chicago: University of Chicago Press.

Frohlich, N., and J. A. Oppenheimer. 1974. "The Carrot and the Stick: Optimal Program Mixes for Entrepreneurial Political Leaders." *Public Choice* 19:43–63.

Früling, Hugo E. 1993. "Human Rights in Constitutional Order and Political Practice in Latin America." In Douglas Greenberg, Stanley N. Katz, Melanie Beth Oliviero, and Steven C. Wheatly, eds., *Constitutionalism and Democracy,* 85–104. New York: Oxford University Press.

FSLN. 1986. "The Historic Program of the FSLN." In Peter Rosset and John Vandermeer, eds., *Nicaragua: Unfinished Revolution.* New York: Grove. First published in *Sandinistas Speak,* trans. Will Reissner. New York: Pathfinder, 1982.

Galanter, Marc. 1984. *Competing Equalities.* Berkeley: University of California Press.

Galt, Anthony. 1982. "The Evil Eye as Synthetic Image and Its Meaning on the Island of Pantelleria, Italy." *American Ethnologist* 9(4):664–81.

Gamson, William A. 1988. "Political Discourse and Collective Action." In Bert Klandermans, Hanspeter Kriesi, and Sidney Tarrow, eds., *International Social Movement Research.* Vol. 1: *From Structure to Action: Comparing Social Movement Research across Cultures,* 219–44. Greenwich, CT: JAI Press.

———. 1992. *Talking Politics.* New York: Cambridge University Press.

Gates, Henry Louis, Jr. 1994. "Authority, (White) Power, and the (Black) Critic: It's All Greek to Me." In Nicholas B. Dirks, Geoff Eley, and Sherry B. Ortner, eds., *Culture/Power/History, A Reader in Contemporaty Social Theory,* 247–68. Princeton: Princeton University Press.

Gay, Robert. 1994. *Popular Organization and Democracy in Rio de Janeiro.* Philadelphia: Temple University Press.

Gellner, Ernest. 1984. *Nations and Nationalism.* Oxford: Blackwell.

Gerhards, J. 1993. *Neue Konfliktlinien in der Mobilisierung öffentlicher Meinung. Eine Fallanalyse.* Opladen: Westdeutscher Verlag.

Gerhards, J., and D. Rucht. 1992. "Mesomobilization: Organizing and Framing in Two Protest Campaigns in West Germany." *American Journal of Sociology* 98 (3):555–95.

Giddens, Anthony. 1990. *The Consequences of Modernity.* Stanford: Stanford University Press.

———. 1994. *Beyond Left and Right: The Future of Radical Politics.* Cambridge: Polity Press.

Gilligan, Carol. 1982. *In a Different Voice: Psychological Theory and Women's Development.* Cambridge: Harvard University Press.

Gluck, Sherna Berger. 1995. "Palestinian Women: Gender Politics and Nationalism." *Journal of Palestine Studies* 24 (3):5–15.

Goldfarb, Jeffrey C. 1989. *Beyond Glasnost: The Post-totalitarian Mind.* Chicago: University of Chicago Press.

Gordon, Linda. 1983. *Cossack Rebellions: Social Turmoil in the Sixteenth-Century Ukraine.* Albany: State University of New York Press.

Gray, Spalding. 1992. *Monster in a Box.* Compact sound disk. Mill Valley, CA: Gang of Seven, Inc., disk 1.

Green, D. P., and I. Shapiro. 1994. *Pathologies of Rational Choice Theory: A Critique of Applications in Political Science.* New Haven and London: Yale University Press.

Greenspan, Henry. 1992. "Lives as Texts: Symptoms as Modes of Recounting in the Life History of Holocaust Survivors." In George C. Rosenwald and Richard L. Ochberg, eds., *Storied Lives,* 145–64. New Haven and London: Yale University Press.

Greskovits, Bela. 1998. *The Political Economy of Protest and Patience: East European and Latin American Transformations Compared.* Budapest: Central European University Press.

Greven, M. T., and U. Willems. 1994. "Moral Demands and Rational Moralists in a World of Special Interests." Paper presented at the Sixteenth World Congress of the International Political Science Association, Berlin, August 21–25.

Griffith, Elisabeth. 1984. *In Her Own Right: The Life of Elizabeth Cady Stanton.* New York: Oxford University Press.

Grimshaw, Patricia. 1994."Women's Suffrage in New Zealand Revisited: Writing from the Margins." In Caroline Daley and Melanie Nolan, eds., *Suffrage and Beyond: International Feminist Perspectives.* New York: New York University Press.

Guha, Ranjit, ed. 1982. *Subaltern Studies.* Vol. 1. New Delhi: Cambridge University Press.

———, ed. 1983. *Subaltern Studies.* Vol. 2. New Delhi: Cambridge University Press.

———, ed. 1984. *Subaltern Studies.* Vol. 3. New Delhi: Cambridge University Press.

———. 1994. "The Prose of Counter-insurgency." In Nicholas B. Dirks, Geoff Eley, and Sherry B. Ortner, eds., *Culture/Power/History: A Reader in Contemporary Social Theory,* 336–71. Princeton: Princeton University Press.

Gupta, Dipak K., Albert J. Jongman, and Alex P. Schmid. 1993. "Creating a Composite Index for Assessing Country Performance in the Field of Human Rights: Proposal for a New Methodology." *Human Rights Quarterly* 15:131–62.

Habermas, Jurgen. [1962] 1989. *The Structural Transformation of the Public Sphere: An Inquiry into a Category of Bourgeois Society,* trans. Thomas Burger with Frederick Lawrence. Cambridge: MIT Press.

———. 1992. "Further Reflections on the Public Sphere." In Craig Calhoun, ed., *Habermas and the Public Sphere,* 424–61. Cambridge: MIT Press.
Hacking, Ian. 1995. *Rewriting the Soul: Multiple Personality and the Sciences of Memory.* Princeton: Princeton University Press.
Halbwachs, Maurice. 1935. *Les Cadres Sociaux de la Memoire.* Paris: Alcan.
———. [1941] 1992. *On Collective Memory.* Chicago and London: University of Chicago Press.
Hall, Stuart. 1993. "Culture, Community, Nation." *Cultural Studies* 7 (3):349–63.
Hammami, Rema. 1990. "Women, the Hijab, and the Intifada." *Middle East Report* 164–65:24–28.
Han, Shih-ch'üan. 1966. *Liu-shih hui-i.* Tainan: Han shih-ch'üan hsien sheng shih shih san chou nien chi nien chuan chi pien yin wie yüan hui.
Handelman, Stephen. 1995. *Comrade Criminal.* New Haven: Yale University Press.
Haraway, Donna. 1988. "Situated Knowledges." *Feminist Studies* 14:575–99.
Hardin, R. 1982. *Collective Action.* Baltimore: Johns Hopkins University Press.
Harding, Susan. 1991. "Representing Fundamentalism: The Problem of the Repugnant Other." *Social Research* 58 (2):373–93.
Hartman, Geoffrey, ed. 1994. *Holocaust Remembrance: The Shapes of Memory.* Oxford and Cambridge, MA: Blackwell.
Harvey, David. 1989. *The Condition of Post Modernity: An Inquiry into the Origins of Cultural Change.* Cambridge: Blackwell.
Haskell, Thomas L. 1985. "Capitalism and the Origins of the Humanitarian Sensibility." Pts. 1–2. *American Historical Review* 90 (2–3):339–61, 547–66.
———. 1987. "Convention and Hegemonic Interest in the Debate over Antislavery: A Reply to Davis and Ashworth." *American Historical Review* 92 (October):829–78.
Hechter, M. 1988. *Principles of Group Solidarity.* Berkeley and Los Angeles: University of California Press.
———. 1990. The Emergence of Cooperative Social Institutions. In M. Hechter, K.-D. Opp, and R. Wippler, eds., *Social Institutions: Their Emergence, Maintenance, and Effects,* 13–33. Berlin and New York: Walter de Gruyter.
Heclo, Hugh. 1978. "Issue Networks and the Executive Establishment." In Anthony King, ed., *The New American Political System.* Washington, DC: American Enterprise Institute.
Helleiner, Eric. 1994. *States and the Reemergence of Global Finance: From Bretton Woods to the 1990s.* Ithaca: Cornell University Press.
Henkin, Louis. 1990. *The Age of Rights.* New York: Columbia University Press.
———. 1994. *International Law: Politics and Values.* Dordrecht, Neth.: Martinus Nijhoff.
Hernández Castillo, Rosalva Aída, and Ronald Nigh. 1998. "Global Processes and Local Identity among Mayan Coffee Growers in Chiapas, Mexico." *American Anthropologist* 100 (1):136–47.
Hill, Fiona. 1995. *Russia's Tinderbox: Conflict in the Northern Caucasus and Its Implications for the Future of the Russian Federation.* Cambridge: Harvard University, Strengthening Democratic Institutions Project.
Hirsch, E. L. 1990. "Sacrifice for the Cause: Group Processes, Recruitment, and Commitment in a Student Social Movement." *American Sociological Review.* 55:243–54.
Hirsch, Marianne. 1994. "Pictures of a Displaced Girlhood." In Angelika Bammer, ed., *Displacements: Cultural Identities in Question,* 71–89. Bloomington and Indianapolis: Indiana University Press.
Hirschman, A. O. 1982. *Shifting Involvements: Private Interests and Public Action.* Princeton: Princeton University Press.

Hirschmann, Nancy J. 1992. *Rethinking Obligation: A Feminist Method for Political Theory.* Ithaca: Cornell University Press.
Hirst, Paul, and Grahame Thomson. 1996. *Globalization in Question: The International Economy and the Possibilities of Governance.* Oxford: Blackwell.
Ho, Samuel Pao-San. 1984. "Colonialism and Development: Korea, Taiwan, and Kwantung." In Ramon H. Myers and Mark R. Peattie, eds., *The Japanese Colonial Empire, 1895–1945,* 347–98. Princeton: Princeton University Press.
Hobsbawn, Eric. 1990. *Nations and Nationalism since 1780: Programme, Myth, Reality.* Cambridge: Cambridge University Press.
Hobsbawm, Eric, and Terence Ranger. 1983. Introduction to *The Invention of Tradition,* 1–14. Cambridge: Cambridge University Press.
Hochschild, Adam. 1998. *King Leopold's Ghost.* Boston: Houghton Mifflin.
Hoffman, Lily M. 1989. *The Politics of Knowledge: Activist Movements in Medicine and Planning.* New York: State University of New York Press.
Holt, Richard. 1996. "Contrasting Nationalisms: Sport, Militarism, and the Unitary State in Britain and France before 1914." In J. A. Mangan, ed., *Tribal Identities: Nationalism, Europe, Sport,* 39–54. London: Frank Cass.
Holton, Sandra Stanley. 1996. *Suffrage Days: Stories from the Women's Suffrage Movement.* London: Routledge.
Howard, Rhoda, and Jack Donnelly. 1986. "Human Dignity, Human Rights, and Political Regimes." *American Political Science Review* 80 (September):801–17.
Hroch, Miroslav. 1993. "From National Movement to the Fully-Formed Nation." *New Left Review* 198 (March/April):3–20.
Hsieh, Chen-jung. 1989. "Jih-pen chih-min-chu-i hsia T'ai-wan wei-sheng cheng-ts'e chih yen-chiu." Master's thesis, Chung-kuo wen-hua ta-hsüeh jih-pen yen-chiu so.
Hunter, Janet. 1984. *Concise Dictionary of Modern Japanese History.* Berkeley: University of California Press.
Huntington, Samuel P. 1991. *The Third Wave: Democratization in the Late Twentieth Century.* Norman: University of Oklahoma Press.
———. 1996. *The Clash of Civilizations and the Remaking of World Order.* New York: Simon and Schuster.
Hutton, Patrick. 1993. *History as an Art of Memory.* Hanover and London: University of Vermont Press.
IBGE (Instituto Brasileiro de Geografia e Estatística). 1989. *Pesquisa Nacional por Amostra de Domicílios.* Rio de Janeiro: IBGE.
———. 1992a. *Censo Demográfico, 1991: Resultados Preliminares.* Rio de Janeiro: IBGE.
———. 1992b. *Crianças e Adolescentes.* Vol. 4: *Indicadores Sociais.* Rio de Janeiro: IBGE.
Ide, Kiwata. [1937] 1988. *Taiwan chisekishi.* Tokyo: Hastsubaimoto Godo Shuppan.
Inglehart, Ronald. 1977. *The Silent Revolution.* Princeton: Princeton University Press.
Jackowski, Jan Maria. 1993. *Bitwa o Polske.* Warsaw: Inicjatywa Wydawnicza "Ad Astra."
James, C. L. R. [1963] 1993. *Beyond a Boundary.* Durham: Duke University Press.
Jansen, Marius B. 1984. "Japanese Imperialism: Late Meiji Perspectives." In Ramon H. Myers and Mark R. Peattie, eds., *The Japanese Colonial Empire, 1895–1945,* 61–79. Princeton: Princeton University Press.
Jaquette, Jane, ed. 1989. *The Women's Movement in Latin America: Feminism and the Transition to Democracy.* Boulder: Westview.
Jasiewicz, Krzysztof. 1998. "Parliamentary Elections in Poland: How Much of a Deja Vu." *ACE: Analysis of Current Events* 10 (January):6–9.

Jatene, Simão Robison, Rosyan de Caldas Britto, Edila Arnaud Ferreira Moura, Elisa Vianna Sá, and Ana Diniz. 1993a. *A Meia-Vida da Criança na Amazônia.* Belém: UNAMAZ, UFPA.

Jatene, Simão Robison, Rosyan de Caldas Britto, Zildomar José Alves, Maria Adelina Braglia and Paulo Elcídio Nogueira. 1993b. *Crianças no Pará: A Explosão da Pobreza.* Belém: UNAMAZ, UFPA.

Jawlowska, Aldona. 1994, "Cultural Changes in Poland in the 1990s." In Aldona Jawlowska and Marian Kempny, eds., *Cultural Dilemmas of Post-communist Societies,* 284–99. Warsaw: IFiS.

Jeffrey, Paul. 1995. "Targeted for Death: Brazil's Street Children." In K. Danaher and M. Shellenberger, eds., *Fighting for the Soul of Brazil,* 154–62. New York: Monthly Review Press.

Jemilev, Reshat. 1986. *Human Torch.* New York: Crimea Foundation.

Jenkins, Brian. 1974. *Britain and the War for the Union.* 2 vols. Montreal: McGill-Queen's University Press.

Johnson, Terry. 1995. "Governmentality and the Institutionalization of Expertise." In Terry Johnson, Gerry Larkin, and Mike Saks, eds., *Health Professions and the State in Europe,* 7–24. New York: Routledge.

Johnston, Hank, and Bert Klandermans, eds. 1995. *Social Movements and Culture.* Minneapolis: University of Minnesota Press.

Jones, Adam. 1992. "Beyond the Barricades: The Sandinista Press and Political Transition in Nicaragua." *New Political Science* 23 (fall).

Jones, Howard. 1992. *Union in Peril: The Crisis over British Intervention in the Civil War.* Chapel Hill: University of North Carolina Press.

Jones, Stephen. 1994. "Old Ghosts and New Chains." In Rubie Watson, ed., *Memory, History, and Opposition,* 149–67. Santa Fe: School of American Research Press.

Jowitt, Ken. 1990. "Survey of Opinion on the East European Revolution." *East European Politics and Society* 4 (2):193–97.

Katznelson, Ira. 1986. "Working-Class Formation: Constructing Cases and Comparisons." In Ira Katznelson and Aristide R. Zolberg, eds., *Working-Class Formation,* 3–44. Princeton: Princeton University Press.

Keane, John. 1996. *Reflections on Violence.* London: Verso.

Keck, Margaret. 1992. *The Workers' Party and Democratization in Brazil.* New Haven: Yale University Press.

Keck, Margaret, and Kathryn Sikkink. 1998. *Activists beyond Borders: Advocacy Networks in International Politics.* Ithaca: Cornell University Press.

Kelly, John. 1991. *The Politics of Virtue.* Chicago: University of Chicago Press.

Kennedy, Michael D. 1990. "The Constitution of Critical Intellectuals: Polish Physicians, Peace Activists, and Democratic Civil Society." *Studies in Comparative Communism* 23:281–303.

———. 1991. *Professionals, Power, and Solidarity in Poland: A Critical Sociology of Soviet-Type Society.* Cambridge: Cambridge University Press.

———. 1994. "An Introduction to East European Ideology and Identity in Transformation." In Michael Kennedy, ed., *Envisioning Eastern Europe: Postcommunist Cultural Studies,* 1–45. Ann Arbor: University of Michigan Press.

Kennedy, Michael, and Daina Stukuls. 1998. "The Narrative of Civil Society in Communism's Collapse and Postcommunism's Alternatives: Emancipation, Polish Protest, and Baltic Nationalisms." *Constellations: An International Journal of Critical and Democratic Theory* 5 (4):541–71.

Khalidi, Rashid. 1997. *The Origins of Palestinian National Identity.* New York: Columbia University Press.

Khodarkovsky, Michael. 1995. "The Stepan Razin Uprising: Was It a 'Peasant War'?" *Jahrbücher für Geschichte Osteuropas* 42:1–19.

Killian, L. M., 1984. "Organization, Rationality, and Spontaneity in the Civil Rights Movement." *American Sociological Review* 49:770–83.

Kirsch, George B. 1989. *The Creation of American Team Sports: Baseball and Cricket, 1838–72.* Urbana: University of Illinois Press.

Klandermans, Bert. 1992. "The Social Construction of Protest and Multi-Organizational Fields." In Aldon D. Morris and Carol Mueller, eds., *Frontiers in Social Movement Theory.* New Haven: Yale University Press.

Klandermans, Bert, Hanspeter Kriesi, and Sidney Tarrow, eds. 1988. *From Structure to Action: Comparing Social Movement Research across Cultures.* Greenwich: JAI Press.

Klausen, Jytte. 1995. "Social Rights Advocacy and State-Building: T. H. Marshall in the Hands of Social Reformers." *World Politics* 47 (2):244–67.

Klein, Alan M. 1991. *Sugarball: The American Game, the Dominican Dream.* New Haven: Yale University Press.

Klosinska, Krystyna. 1992. "Mniejszosci narodowe w Polsce." In Miroslawa Grabowska, ed., *Barometr Kultury,* 53–63. Warsaw: Instytut Kultury.

Knight, Franklin W. 1990. *The Caribbean: The Genesis of a Fragmented Nationalism.* Oxford: Oxford University Press.

Knox, Paul L. 1997. "Globalization and Urban Economic Change." *Annals of the American Academy of Political and Social Science* 551 (May):17–27.

Kohli, Atul, ed. 1988. *India's Democracy.* Princeton: Princeton University Press.

———. 1990. *Democracy and Discontent.* Princeton: Princeton University Press.

Kolarska-Bobinska, Lena. 1992. "Konflikty w nowej Polsce." *Gazeta Wyborcza,* November 28–29, 11.

———. 1994. *Aspirations, Values, and Interests: Poland, 1989–1994.* Warsaw: IFiS.

Koopmans, R. 1995. *Democracy from Below: New Social Movements and the Political System in West Germany.* Boulder: Westview.

Korey, William. 1993. *The Promises We Keep: Human Rights, the Helsinki Process, and American Foreign Policy.* New York: St. Martin's.

Kornblatt, Judith Deutsch. 1992. *The Cossack Hero in Russian Literature: A Study in Cultural Mythology.* Madison: University of Wisconsin Press.

Korneva, K., and Izumov, A. 1995. "Pomogi Sebe Sam." *Express Khronika* 16 (402):4–11.

Korobovaya, Tatyana. 1995. "Shto Proizoshlo v Krimu." *Literaturnaya Gazeta* 5: (VII) 95 No. 27 (5558):11.

Kothari, Rajni. 1991. "State and Statelessness in Our Time." *Economic and Political Weekly,* annual issue (March):552–54.

Krasnodarskii krai nakanune vyborov–95. 1995. Krasnodar: Kraevaya administratsia.

Krich, John. 1989. *El Beisbol: Travels through the Pan-American Pastime.* New York: Atlantic Monthly Press.

Kriesi, H., R. Koopmans, J. W. Duyvendak, and M. G. Guigni. 1995. *New Social Movements in Western Europe: A Comparative Analysis.* Minneapolis: University of Minnesota Press.

Krüger, Arnd. 1996. " 'Buying Victories is Positively Degrading': European Origins of Government Pursuit of National Prestige through Sport." In J. A. Mangan, ed., *Tribal Identities: Nationalism, Europe, Sport,* 183–200. London: Frank Cass.

Kubik, Jan. 1994a. *The Power of Symbols against the Symbol of Power: The Rise of Soli-*

darity and the Fall of State Socialism in Poland. University Park: Pennsylvania State University Press.

———. 1994b. "Who Done It: Workers, Intellectuals, or Someone Else? Controversy over Solidarity's Origins and Social Composition." *Theory and Society* 23:441–66.

———. 1998. "Institutionalization of Protest during Democratic Consolidation in Central Europe." In David Meyer and Sidney Tarrow, eds., *The Social Movement Society: Contentious Politics for a New Century,* 131–52. Lanham, MD: Rowman and Littlefield.

Kundera, Milan. 1981. *The Book of Laughter and Forgetting,* trans. Michael Henry Heim. New York: Knopf.

Laba, Roman. 1991. *The Roots of Solidarity.* Princeton: Princeton University Press.

Ladokha, G. 1924. *Ocherki grazhdanskoi borby na Kubani.* Krasnodar: Burevestnik.

Langer, Lawrence. 1991. *Holocaust Testimonies: The Ruins of Memory.* New Haven and London: Yale University Press.

Lass, Andrew. 1994. "From Memory to History: The Events of November 17 Dis/membered." In Ruby Watson, ed., *Memory, Opposition, History,* 87–105. Santa Fe: School of American Research Press.

Le Goff, Jacques. 1992. *History and Memory.* New York: Columbia University Press.

Lee, Ben. 1998. "Peoples and Publics." *Public Culture* 10(2):371–93.

Lèna, Philippe, and Isolda Maciel da Silveira. 1993. *Uruará: O Futuro das Crianças numa Área de Colonização.* Belém: UNAMAZ, UFPA.

Leslie, Charles. 1976. Introduction to *Asian Medical Systems: A Comparative Study,* 1–17. Berkeley: University of California Press.

Letz, M. 1994. "Im Osten nichts Neues? Ostdeutsche Solidaritätsgruppen vor und nach der Wende." *Forschungsjournal Neue Soziale Bewegungen* 7 (3):49–62.

Levine, Daniel H., ed. 1986. *Religion and Political Conflict in Latin America.* Chapel Hill: University of North Carolina Press.

———. 1992. *Popular Voices in Latin American Catholicism.* Princeton: Princeton University Press.

Lewis, Gordon K. 1968. *The Growth of the Modern West Indies.* New York: Monthly Review Press.

Li, T'eng-yueh. 1952. *T'ai-wan-shen t'ung-chih-kao, cheng-shih-chih wei-sheng-p'ien.* Vol. 1. Taipei: Tai-wan sheng wen hsien wei yuan hui.

———. 1953. *T'ai-wan-shen t'ung-chih-kao, cheng-shih-chih wei-sheng-p'ien.* Vol. 2. Taipei: Tai-wan sheng wen hsien wei yuan hui.

Likhnitsky, N. T. 1931. *Klassovaia borba i kulachestvo na Kubani.* Rostov-na-Donu: Severny Kavkaz.

Lin, Po-wei. 1993. *Tai-wan wen hua hsieh hui tsang sang.* Taipei: Tai yuan i shu wen hua chi chin hui.

Lin, Yü-shu. 1935. "Hajimete hondōjin ishi to nirite." In Kagi [Chia-i] shiyakusho, ed., *Kagi [Chia-i] shih sei goshūnen kinenshi.* Kagi [Chia-i]: Kagi [Chia-i] shiyakusho.

Lipset, Seymour Martin. 1993. "The Significance of the 1992 Election." *PS* 26:7–16.

Lipski, Jan Jozef. 1985. *KOR: Workers' Defense Committee in Poland.* Berkeley: University of California Press.

Lo, Ming-cheng M. 1996. "From National Physicians to Medical Modernists: Taiwanese Doctors under Japanese Rule." Ph.D. diss., University of Michigan.

Long, Susan. 1980. "Fame, Fortune, and Friends: Constraints and Strategies in the Careers of Japanese Physicians." Ph.D. diss., University of Illinois, Urbana-Champaign.

Lowden, Pamela. 1996. *Moral Opposition to Authoritarian Rule in Chile, 1973–90.* Oxford: St. Anthony's.

Lüdtke, Alf, ed. 1995. *The History of Everyday Life: Reconstructing Historical Experiences and Ways of Life.* Princeton: Princeton University Press.
Mahmood, Cynthia Keppley. 1996. *Beyond Violence; Faith, Nation, and Meaning in Sikh Militancy.* Philadelphia: University of Pennsylvania Press.
Mahmood, Saba. 1996. "Cultural Studies and Ethnic Amsolutism." *Cultural Studies* 10(1):1–11.
Mainwaring, Scott. 1989. "Grassroots Popular Movements and the Struggle for Democracy: Nova Iguaçu." In A. Stepan, ed., *Democratizing Brazil: Problems of Transition and Consolidation,* 168–204. New York and Oxford: Oxford University Press.
Malkki, Liisa. 1992. "National Geographic: The Rooting of Peoples and the Territorialization of National Identity among Scholars and Refugees." *Cultural Anthropology* 7 (1):24–44.
———. 1994. "Citizens of Humanity: Internationalism and the Imagined Community of Nations." *Diaspora* 3 (1):41–68.
———. 1995. *Purity and Exile: Violence, Memory, and National Cosmology among Hutu Refugees in Tanzania.* Chicago and London: University of Chicago Press.
Mandela, Nelson. 1994. *Long Walk to Freedom: The Autobiography of Nelson Mandela.* London: Little, Brown.
Mangan, J. A., ed. 1992. *The Cultural Bond: Sport, Empire, Society.* London: Frank Caas.
———. 1996. *Tribal Identities: Nationalism, Europe, Sport.* London: Frank Caas.
March, J. G. 1978. "Bounded Rationality, Ambiguity, and the Engineering of Social Choice." *The Bell Journal of Economics* 9:587–608.
Margolis, H. 1982. *Selfishness, Altruism, and Rationality.* Cambridge: Cambridge University Press.
Markowski, Radoslaw. 1992. "Milczaca wiekszosc—o biernosci politycznej spoleczenstwa polskiego." In Stanislaw Gebethner and Jacek Raciborski, eds., *Wybory '91 a polska scena polityczna,* 81–107. Warsaw: "Polska w Europie."
———. 1998. "Polish Party System: Institutionalization, Re-shaping, and Democratic Consolidation." Paper presented at the conference Democratic Consolidation: The International Dimension, Hungary, Poland, and Spain, September 24–26, 1998, Vienna.
Marques, João Benedito de Azevedo. 1976. *Marginalização: Menor e Criminalidade.* São Paulo: McGraw Hill do Brasil.
Marshall, T. H. [1950] 1992. "Citizenship and Social Class." In T. H. Marshall and Tom Bottomore, *Citizenship and Social Class,* 1–51. London: Pluto.
Marty, Martin, and Scott Appleby. 1991–96. *The Fundamentalism Project.* (6 vols.). Chicago: University of Chicago Press.
Mason, Tony. 1995. *Passion of the People? Football in South America.* London: Verso.
Massey, Doreen. 1993. "Power-Geometry and a Progressive Sense of Place." In Bird et al., eds., *Mapping the Futures,* 59–69. London and New York: Routledge.
McAdam, Doug. 1988. *Freedom Summer.* New York: Oxford University Press.
———. 1996. "Conceptual Origins, Current Problems, Future Directions." In D. McAdam, J. McCarthy, and M. Zald, eds., *Comparative Perspectives on Social Movements: Political Opportunities, Mobilizing Structures, and Cultural Framings,* 23–40. Cambridge: Cambridge University Press.
McAdam, Doug, John D. McCarthy, and Mayer N. Zald, eds. 1996. *Comparative Perspectives on Social Movements: Political Opportunities, Mobilizing Structures, and Cultural Framings.* Cambridge: Cambridge University Press.
McCarthy, John. 1997. "The Globalization of Social Movement Theory." In J. Smith, C.

Chatfield, and R. Pagnucco, eds., *Transnational Social Movements and Global Politics: Solidarity beyond the State,* 243–59. Syracuse, NY: Syracuse University Press.

McCarthy, John D., and Mayer N. Zald. 1977. "Resource Mobilization and Social Movements: A Partial Theory." *American Journal of Sociology* 82:1212–41.

———, eds. 1979. *The Dynamics of Social Movements: Resource Mobilization, Social Control, and Tactics.* Cambridge, MA.: Winthrop.

McFarland, A. S. 1992. "Interest Groups and the Policymaking Process: Sources of Countervailing Power in America." In M. P. Petracca, ed., *The Politics of Interests: Interest Groups Transformed,* 58–79. Boulder: Westview.

McMichael, Philip. 1990. "Incorporating Comparison within a World-Historical Perspective." *American Sociological Review* 55 (3):385–97.

———. 1996. *Development and Social Change: A Global Perspective.* Thousand Oaks, CA: Pine Forge.

McNeal, Robert. 1987. *Tsar and Cossack, 1855–1914.* New York: St. Martin's.

Meehl, P. 1977. "The Selfish Voter Paradox and the Thrown-Away Vote Argument." *American Political Science Review* 71:11–30.

Melucci, Alberto. 1980. "The New Social Movements: A Theoretical Approach." *Social Science Information* 19:199–226.

———. 1981. "Ten Hypotheses for the Analysis of Social Movements." In D. Pinto, ed., *Contemporary Italian Sociology,* 173–94. New York: Cambridge University Press.

———. 1984. "An End to Social Movements? Introductory Paper to the Sessions on 'New Social Movements and Change in Organizational Forms.'" *Social Science Information* 24 (4–5):813–35.

———. 1989. *Nomads of the Present: Social Movements and Individual Needs in Contemporary Society.* Philadelphia: Temple University Press.

Meyer, David, and Suzanne Staggenborg. 1996. "Movements, Countermovements, and the Structure of Political Opportunity." *American Journal of Sociology* 101 (6):1628–60.

Meyer, John W., John Boli, George M. Thomas, and Francisco O. Ramirez. 1997. "World Society and the Nation-State." *American Journal of Sociology* 103 (1):144–81.

Migdal, Joel S., Atul Kohli, and Vivienne Shue, eds. 1994. *State Power and Social Forces.* Cambridge: Cambridge University Press.

Miller, William Lee. 1996. *Arguing about Slavery: The Great Battle in the United States Congress.* New York: Knopf.

Miranda, Henrique. 1992. *"Não é só os Humanos . . ." Percepções sobre a Criança Marginalizada na Amazônia.* Belém: UNAMAZ, UFPA.

Mische, Ann. 1995. "Projecting Democracy: The Formation of Citizenship across Youth Networks in Brazil." *International Review of Social History* 40 (suppl. 3):131–59.

Misztal, Bronislaw, and Barbara A. Misztal. 1988. "Democratization Process as an Objective of New Social Movements." In Louis Kriesberg and Bronislaw Misztal, eds., *Social Movements as a Factor of Change in the Contemporary World.* Research in Social Movements, Conflicts, and Change. Vol. 10. Greenwich, CT: JAI Press.

Moe, T. M. 1980. *The Organization of Interests: Incentives and the Internal Dynamics of Political Interest Groups.* Chicago: University of Chicago Press.

Molyneux, Maxine. 1985. "Mobilization without Emancipation? Women's Interests, the State, and Revolution in Nicaragua." *Feminist Studies* 11 (summer):227–54.

Moore, Barrington, Jr. 1966. *Social Origins of Dictatorship and Democracy.* Boston: Beacon.

———. 1978. *Injustice: The Social Bases of Obedience and Revolt.* White Plains, NY: M. E. Sharpe.

Morris, Aldon. 1984. *The Origins of the Civil Rights Movement.* New York: Free Press.

Morris, Aldon, and Carol Mueller, eds. 1992. *Frontiers in Social Movement Theory.* New Haven: Yale University Press.

Moura, Edila Arnaud Ferreira, Eleonora Arnaud Pereira Ferreira, Maria Lúcia Sá Maia, Heliosa Lara Campos da Costa, and José Maria de Castro Santana. 1993. *Zona Franca de Manaus: Os Filhos da Era Eletroeletrônica.* Belém: UNAMAZ, UFPA.

Movimento Nacional de Meninos e Meninas de Rua. N.d. "Cidadão Criança, Cidadão Adolescente: Contribuições para Definição de uma Política para Infância e Juventude no Brasil." Mimeo.

Movimento Nacional de Meninos e Meninos de Rua, Instituto Brasileiro de Análises Sociais e Econômicas, and Núcleo de Estudos da Violência da Universidade de São Paulo. 1991. *Vidas em Risco: Assassinatos de Crianças e Adolescentes no Brasil.* Rio de Janeiro: MNMMR, IBASE, NEV-USP.

Mukōyama, Hirō. 1987. *Nihon tochika ni okeru Taiwan minzoku undōshi.* Tokyo: Chuo Keizai Kenkyujo.

Murphy, Walter F. 1993. "Constitutions, Constitutionalism, and Democracy." In Douglas Greenberg, Stanley N. Katz, Melanie Beth Oliviero, and Steven C. Wheatley, eds., *Constitutionalism and Democracy,* 3–25. New York: Oxford University Press.

Muslih, Muhammad. 1988. *The Origins of Palestinian Nationalism.* New York: Columbia University Press.

Myers, Ramon H., and Mark R. Peattie, eds. 1984. *The Japanese Colonial Empire, 1895–1945.* Princeton: Princeton University Press.

Nadelmann, Ethan A. 1990. "Global Prohibition Regimes: The Evolution of Norms in International Society." *International Organization* 44 (4):479–526.

Nadinskii, Pavel Naumovich. 1951. *Ocherki po istorii kryma.* Simferopol: Tavrika.

Narr, W.-D. 1995. "Notizen zur Geschichte der Bürgerrechtsgruppen im Nachkriegsdeutschland." *Bürgerrechte und Polizei* 1:6–16.

Navarro, Marysa. 1989. "The Personal is Political: Las Madres de Plaza de Mayo." In Susan Eckstein, ed., *Power and Popular Protest: Latin American Social Movements,* 241–58. Berkeley: University of California Press.

Nekrich, Aleksandr M. 1978. *The Punished Peoples: The Deportation and Fate of Soviet Minorities at the End of the Second World War.* New York: Norton.

Nelson, Joan. 1970. "The Urban Poor: Disruption or Political Integration in Third World Cities?" *World Politics* 22 (3):393–414.

Ng, Yuzin Chiautong. 1989. *T'ai-wan tsung tu fu,* trans. Huang Ying-che (from Japanese to Chinese). Taipei: Tzu yu shih tai chòu pan she. Originally published as *Taiwan sōtokufu.* Tokyo: Kyoikusha, 1981.

Nickel, James W. 1987. *Making Sense of Human Rights: Philosophical Reflections on the Universal Declaration of Human Rights.* Berkeley: University of California Press.

Nolan, Melanie, and Caroline Daley. 1994. "International Feminist Perspective on Suffrage: An Introduction." In Caroline Daley and Melanie Nolan, eds., *Suffrage and Beyond: International Feminist Perspectives.* New York: New York University Press.

Nora, Pierre. 1989. "Memory, History." In Y. Afanasev and M. Ferro, eds., *50/50: Opyt slovaria novogo myshleniia,* 439–41. Moscow: Progress.

Oberoi, Harjot. 1987. "From Punjab to 'Khalistan': Territoriality and Metacommentary." *Pacific Affairs* 60 (1):26–41.

Oberschall, Anthony. 1996. "Opportunities and Framing in the Eastern European Revolts of 1989." In D. McAdam, J. McCarthy, and M. Zald, eds., *Comparative Perspectives on Social Movements,* 93–121. Cambridge: Cambridge University Press.

"Obrashenie k Delegatam III Kuraltai Krimskotatarskovo Naroda" (An Appeal to the Delegates of the III Kuraltai of the Crimean Tatar People). 1997. *Golos Krima* no. 47 (210), Nov. 28.

Oda, Toshirō. 1974. *Taiwan igaku 50 nen shi.* Tokyo: Kabushiki kaisha igaku shoin.

O'Donnell, Guillermo. 1993. "On the State, Democratization, and Some Conceptual Problems: A Latin American View with Glances at Some Post-communist Countries." *World Development* 21 (8):1355–69.

O'Donnell, Guillermo, Phillipe Schmitter, and Laurence Whitehead. 1986. *Transitions from Authoritarian Rule: Prospects for Democracy.* 4 vols. Baltimore: Johns Hopkins University Press.

Office of the Chief of Naval Operations. 1944. *Taiwan (Formosa): Civil Affairs Handbook, Opnav 50E-12.* [Washington, DC]: Office of the Chief of the Naval Operations, Naval Department.

Okrent, Daniel, and Harris Lewine, eds. 1991. *The Ultimate Baseball Book.* Boston: Houghton Mifflin.

Olejniczak, C. 1997. *Die Dritte-Welt-Bewegung in Deutschland.* Ph.D. thesis, University of Bochum, Social Sciences Faculty.

Oleksak, Michael, and Mary Adams Oleksak. 1991. *Béisbol: Latin Americans and the Grand Old Game.* Grand Rapids, MI: Masters Press.

Oliner, S., and P. M. Oliner. 1988. *The Altruistic Personality: Rescuers of Jews in Nazi Europe.* New York: Free Press.

Olson, Alison Gilbert. 1992. *Making the Empire Work: London and American Interest Groups, 1690–1790.* Cambridge: Harvard University Press.

Olson, M., Jr. 1965. *The Logic of Collective Action.* Cambridge: Harvard University Press.

———. 1982. *The Rise and Decline of Nations: Economic Growth, Stagflation, and Social Rigidities.* New Haven and London: Yale University Press.

Opp, K.-D. 1986. "Soft Incentives and Collective Action: Participation in the Anti-Nuclear Movement." *British Journal of Political Science* 16:87–112.

———. 1989. *The Rationality of Political Protest: A Comparative Analysis of Rational Choice Theory.* Boulder: Westview.

Ordem dos Advogados do Brasil, Comissão de Direitos Humanos. 1993. *Execuções Sumárias de Menores em São Paulo.* São Paulo: Departamento Editorial, OAB-São Paulo.

Ortner, Sherry. 1992. "Resistance: Some Theoretical Problems in Anthropological History and Historical Anthropology." In Terrence J. McDonald, ed., *The Historic Turn in the Human Sciences,* 281–304. Ann Arbor: University of Michigan Press.

———. 1995. "Resistance and the Problem of Ethnographic Refusal." *Comparative Studies in Society and History* 37 (1):172–93.

Ost, David. 1990. *Solidarity and the Politics of Anti-politics.* Philadelphia: Temple University Press.

Owen, John M. 1994. "How Liberalism Produces Democratic Peace." *International Security* 19 (fall):87–125.

Pagnucco, R. 1997. "The Transnational Strategies of the Service for Peace and Justice in Latin America." In J. Smith, C. Chatfield, and R. Pagnucco, eds., *Transnational Social Movements and Global Politics: Solidarity beyond the State,* 123–38. Syracuse, NY: Syracuse University Press.

Parelli, Carina. 1994. "Memoria de Sangre." In Jonathan Boyarin, ed., *Remapping Memory: The Politics of TimeSpace,* 39–67. Minneapolis: University of Minnesota Press.

Parks, Robert. [1937] 1961. Introduction to E. Stonequist, *The Marginal Man.* New York: Russell and Russell.

Passerini, Luisa. 1987. *Facism in Popular Memory: The Cultural Experience of the Turin Working Class,* trans. Robert Lumley and Jude Bloomfield. Cambridge: Cambridge University Press.

———. 1992. "A Memory for Women's History: Problems of Method and Interpretation." *Social Science History* 16 (4):669–78.

Passy, F. 1998. *L'action atruiste. Contraintes et opportunités de l'engagement dans les mouvement sociaux.* Geneva: Droz.

Pathak, Zakia, and Rajeswari Sunder Rajan. 1989. "Shahbano." *Signs* 12 (3):558–82.

Patterson, Orlando. 1995. "The Ritual of Cricket." In Hilary M. Beckles and Brian Stoddart, eds., *Liberation Cricket: West Indies Cricket Culture,* 141–47. Manchester and New York: Manchester University Press.

Peattie, Mark R. 1984. "Japanese Attitudes toward Colonialism, 1895–1945." In Ramon H. Myers and Mark R. Peattie, eds., *The Japanese Colonial Empire, 1895–1945,* 80–127. Princeton: Princeton University Press.

Pérez, Jr., Louis A. 1985. "Vagrants, Beggars, and Bandits: Social Origins of Cuban Separatism, 1878–1895." *American Historical Review* 90:1092–1121.

———. 1988. *Cuba: Between Reform and Revolution.* New York: Oxford University Press.

———. 1994. "Between Baseball and Bullfighting: The Quest for Nationality in Cuba, 1868–1898." *Journal of American History* (September):493–517.

Perlman, Janice. 1976. *The Myth of Marginality.* Berkeley: University of California Press.

Peteet, Julie. 1991. *Gender in Crisis: Women and the Palestinian Resistance Movement.* New York: Columbia University Press.

———. 1995a. "Transforming Trust: Dispossession and Empowerment among Palestinian Refugees." In E. Valentine Daniel and J. Knudsen, eds., *Mistrusting Refugees,* 168–86. Berkeley: University of California Press.

———. 1995b. "'They Took Our Blood and Milk': Palestinian Women and War." *Cultural Survival* 19 (1):50–53.

———. 1996. "The Writing on the Walls: The Graffiti of the *Intifada.*" *Cultural Anthropology* 11 (2):1–21.

———. 1997. "Icon and Militants: Mothering in the Danger Zone." *Signs: Journal of Women and Culture* 23 (1):103–29.

Pichardo, Nelson. 1997. "New Social Movements: A Critical Review." *Annual Review of Sociology* 23:411–30

Poe, Steven C., and C. Neal Tate. 1994. "Repression of Human Rights to Personal Integrity in the 1980s: A Global Analysis." *American Political Science Review* 88 (4):853–72.

Pontes, Felício, Jr. 1993. *Conselho de Direitos da Criança e do Adolescente.* São Paulo: Malheiros Editores.

Poyo, Gerald. 1989. *"With All, and for the Good of All": The Emergence of Popular Nationalism in the Cuban Communities of the United States, 1848–1898.* Durham: Duke University Press.

Prakash, Gyan, ed. 1995. *After Colonialism: Imperial Histories and Postcolonial Displacements.* Princeton: Princeton University Press.

Princen, T., and M. Finger. 1994. *Environmental NGOs in World Politics: Linking the Local and the Global.* Padstow: T. J. Press.

Putnam, Robert. 1971. "Studying Elite Political Culture: The Case of 'Ideology.'" *American Political Science Review* 65:651–81.

Ramirez, Francisco, Yasemin Soysal, and Suzanne Shanahan. 1997. "The Changing Logic of Political Citizenship: Cross-National Acquisition of Women's Suffrage Rights, 1890–1990." *American Sociological Review* 62:735–45.

Randall, Margaret. 1992. *Gathering Rage: The Failure of Twentieth Century Revolutions to Develop a Feminist Agenda.* New York: Monthly Review.

———. 1994. *Sandino's Daughters Revisited.* New Brunswick, NJ: Rutgers University.

Ray, James Lee. 1989. "The Abolition of Slavery and the End of International War." *International Organization* 43 (3):405–39.

Reddaway, Peter. 1988. "The Crimean Tatar Drive for Repatriation: Some Comparisons of Dissent in the USSR." In Edward Allworth, ed., *Tatars of the Crimea,* 194–201. Durham: Duke University Press.

Reis, Nancy. 1996. " 'Honest' Bandits and 'Warped People': Russian Narratives about Money, Corruption and Moral Decay." Paper delivered at the symposium Cultural Studies of Eastern Europe and Eurasia, University of Michigan, Ann Arbor, April 19,1996.

Riesebrodt, Martin. 1993. *Pious Passion: The Emergence of Modern Fundamentalism in the United States and Iran.* Berkeley: University of California Press.

Riker, W., and P. C. Ordeshook. 1973. *An Introduction to Positive Political Theory.* Englewood Cliffs, NJ: Prentice Hall.

Risse-Kappen, Thomas, ed. 1995. *Bringing Transnational Relations Back In: Non-State Actors, Domestic Structures, and International Institutions.* New York: Cambridge University Press.

Robertson, Jennifer. 1995. "Mon Japon: The Revue Theater as a Technology of Japanese Imperialism." *American Ethnologist* 22:1–27.

Robertson, Roland. 1992. *Globalization: Social Theory and Global Culture.* Thousand Oaks, CA: Sage.

Rodrigues, Leôncio Martins. 1995. "As Eleições de 1994: Uma Apreciação Geral." *Dados: Revista de Ciências Sociais* 38 (1):71–91.

Rogers, Mark. 1996. "Beyond Authenticity: Conservation, Tourism, and the Politics of Representation in the Ecuadorian Amazon." *Identities* 3 (1–2):73–125.

Rosaldo, Renato. 1980. *Ilongot Headhunting.* Stanford: Stanford University Press.

Rothman, Frank, and Pam Oliver. 1998. "From Local to Global: The Evolution of the Movement of People Affected by Dams in Southern Brazil, 1979–1992." Paper presented at the American Sociological Association meetings, San Francisco.

Rucht, D. 1996. "German Unification, Democratization, and the Role of Social Movements: A Missed Opportunity." *Mobilization* 1 (1):36–62.

———. 1998. "Komplexe Phänomene—komplexe Erklärungen: Die politischen Gelegenheitsstrukturen der neuen sozialen Bewegungen in der Bundesrepublik." In K.-U. Hellmann and R. Koopmans, eds., *Paradigmen der Bewegungsforschung* 109–27. Opladen: Westdeutscher Verlag.

———. 1999. "The Transnationalization of Social Movements: Trends, Causes, Problems." In D. della Porta, H. Kriesi, and D. Rucht, eds., *Social Movements in a Globalizing World,* 206–22. London: Macmillan.

Rucht, D., P. Hocke, and D. Oremus. 1995. "Quantitative Inhaltsanalayse: Wo, wie und warum wurde in der Bundesrepublik protestiert?" In U. von Alemann, ed., *Methoden der Politikwissenschaft,* 261–91. Opladen: Westdeutscher Verlag.

Rucht, D., and F. Neidhardt. 1998. "Methodological Issues in Collecting Protest Event Data: Units of Analysis, Sources and Sampling, Coding Problems." In D. Rucht, R. Koopmans, and F. Neidhardt, eds., *Acts of Dissent: New Developments in the Study of Protest,* 65–89. Berlin: Sigma.

Rucht, D., and T. Ohlemacher. 1992. "Protest Event Data: Uses, Problems, and Perspectives." In R. Eyerman and M. Diani, eds., *Issues in Contemporary Social Movement Research,* 76–102. Beverly Hills: Sage.

Ruddick, Sara. 1989. *Maternal Thinking: Toward a Politics of Peace.* New York: Ballantine.

Ryū, Mei-shū [Liu, Ming-hsiu]. 1983. *Taiwan tōchi to ahen mondai.* Tokyo: Yamakawa Shuppansha.

Sabatier, P. 1992. "Interest Group Membership and Organization: Multiple Theories." In M. P. Petracca, ed., *The Politics of Interests: Interest Groups Transformed,* 99–129. Boulder: Westview Press.

Safran, William. 1981. "Civil Liberties in Democracies: Constitutional Norms, Practices, and Problems of Comparison." In Ved P. Nanda, James R. Scarritt, and George W. Shepherd Jr., eds., *Global Human Rights,* 195–210. Boulder: Westview.

Sahlins, Marshall. 1994. "Cosmologies of Capitalism: The Trans-Pacific Sector of the World System." In N. Dirks, G. Eley, and S. Ortner, eds., *Culture/Power/History: A Reader in Contemporary Social Theory,* 412–56. Princeton: Princeton University Press.

Sahlins, Peter. 1989. *Boundaries: The Making of France and Spain in the Pyrenees.* Berkeley: University of California Press.

Said, Edward. 1986. *After the Last Sky: Palestinian Lives.* New York: Pantheon.

Salisbury, R. H. 1969. "An Exchange Theory of Interest Groups." *Midwest Journal of Political Science* 13:1–31.

Sassen, Saskia. 1991. *The Global City: New York, London, Tokyo.* Princeton: Princeton University Press.

———. 1996. *Losing Control? Sovereignty in an Age of Globalization.* New York: Columbia University Press.

———. 1998. *Globalization and Its Discontents: Essays on the New Mobility of People and Money.* New York: New Press.

Scheper-Hughes, Nancy. 1992. *Death without Weeping: The Violence of Everyday Life in Brazil.* Berkeley: University of California Press.

Scheper-Hughes, Nancy, and Daniel Hoffman. 1995. "Kids Out of Place." In K. Danaher and M. Shellenberger, eds., *Fighting for the Soul of Brazil,* 139–51. New York: Monthly Review.

Schlozman, K. L., S. Verba, and H. E. Brady. 1995. "Participation's Not a Paradox: The View from American Activists." *British Journal of Political Science* 25:1–36.

Scholch, A. 1993. *Palestine in Transformation.* Washington, D.C.: Institute for Palestine Studies.

Schwartz, Rosalie. 1989. *Lawless Liberators: Political Banditry and Cuban Independence.* Durham: Duke University Press.

Schwartz, Vera. 1994. "Chinese History and Jewish Memory." In Geoffrey Hartman ed., *Holocaust Remembered: The Shapes of Memory.* Oxford and Cambridge, MA: Blackwell.

Scoble, Harry M., and Laurie S. Wiseberg. 1981a. *Freedom of Association for Human Rights Organizations.* Washington, DC: Human Rights Internet.

———. 1981b. "Problems of Comparative Research on Human Rights." In Ved P. Nanda, James R. Scarritt, and George W. Shepherd Jr., eds., *Global Human Rights,* 147–72. Boulder: Westview.

Scott, James C. 1976. *The Moral Economy of the Peasant: Rebellion and Subsistence in Southeast Asia.* New Haven: Yale University Press.

———. 1990. *Domination and the Arts of Resistance: Hidden Transcripts.* New Haven: Yale University Press.

Scott, Rebecca. 1985. "Class Relations in Sugar and Political Mobilization in Cuba, 1868–1899." *Cuban Studies* 15 (1):15–28.

Sêda, Edson. 1992. *ABC do Conselho Tutelar.* São Paulo: Centro Brasileiro da Infância e Adolescência.

Seidman, Gay. 1994. *Manufacturing Militance: Workers' Movements in Brazil and South Africa, 1970–1985.* Berkeley: University of California Press.

Senmon gakkō kōyūkai. 1924. *Taiwan isengō seiritsu nijūgo shūnen, Horiuchi Tsukio Hakashi zaishoku nijūgo nen, jukuga kinengo.* Taiwan sōtokufu igaku senmon gakkō kōyūkai zasshi, no. 53. Taipei: Senmon gakkō kōyūkai.

Serbín Andrés. 1989. "La dinámica etnia-nación en el Caribe y sus consecuencias regionales." *El Caribe Contemporáneo* 19:38–44.

Shelly, L. 1989. "Human Rights as an International Issue." *Annals of the American Academy of Political and Social Science* 506:42–55.

Sheth, D. L. 1995. "Democracy and Globalization in India: Post–Cold War Discourse." *The Annals of the American Academy of Political and Social Science* 540 (July): 24–39.

Shriver, A. 1993. "Die westlichen Menschenrechtsorganisationen können vom Süden lernen: Zu den Perspektiven der Wiener Menschenrechtskonferenz." *Gewerkschaftliche Monatshefte* 9:521–31.

Simon, R. 1957. *Models of Man.* New York: John Wiley and Sons.

Singh, Khushwant. 1966. *A History of the Sikhs.* 2 vols. Princeton: Princeton University Press.

Singh, Nikhil Pal. 1998. "Culture/Wars: Recoding Empire in an Age of Democracy." *American Quarterly* 50 (3):471–522

Skocpol, Theda. 1979. *States and Social Revolution.* Cambridge: Cambridge University Press.

Skolnik, Richard. 1994. *Baseball and the Pursuit of Innocence: A Fresh Look at the Old Ball Game.* College Station: Texas A&M University Press.

Skotnicka-Illasiewicz, Elzbieta, and Wlodzimierz Wesolowski. 1995. "The Significance of Perceptions: Europe of Civil Societies and Europe of Nationalities." In Sukumar Periwal, ed., *Notions of Nationalism,* 208–27. Budapest: Central University Press.

Smith, Jackie, Charles Chatfield, and Ron Pagnucco, eds. 1997. *Transnational Social Movements and Global Politics: Solidarity beyond the State.* Syracuse, NY: Syracuse University Press.

Smith, Jackie, Kathryn Sikkink, and Margaret Keck. 1995. "The Emergence of a Transnational Social Movement Sector, 1953–1993." Mimeo.

Snow, David A., and Robert D. Benford. 1988. "Ideology, Frame Resonance, and Participant Mobilization." In Bert Klandermans, Hanspeter Kriesi, and Sidney Tarrow, eds., *International Social Movement Research.* Vol. 1: *From Structure to Action: Comparing Social Movement Research across Cultures,* 197–217. Greenwich, CT: JAI Press.

———. 1992. "Master Frames and Cycles of Protest." In Aldon D. Morris and Carol McClurg Mueller, eds., *Frontiers in Social Movement Theory,* 133–55. New Haven: Yale University Press.

Snow, David A., E. Burke Rochford Jr., Steven K. Worden, and Robert D. Benford. 1986. "Frame Alignment Processes, Micromobilization, and Movement Participation." *American Sociological Review* 51 (August):464–81.

Soares, Maria Clara Couto. 1995. "Who Benefits and Who Bears the Damage under World Bank/IMF-Led Policies." In K. Danaher and M. Shellenberger, eds., *Fighting for the Soul of Brazil,* 8–16. New York: Monthly Review Press.

Sohn, Louis B. 1995. "The Human Rights Movement: From Roosevelt's Four Freedoms to

Interdependence of Peace, Development, and Human Rights." Edward A. Smith Lecture, Harvard Law School, Human Rights Program, March 5.

Somers, Margaret. 1992. "Narrativity, Narrative Identity, and Social Action: Rethinking English Working-Class Formation." *Social Science History* 16 (3):591–630.

———. 1993. "Citizenship and the Place of the Public Sphere: Law, Community, and Political Culture in the Transition to Democracy." *American Sociological Review* 58(5):587–620.

———. 1994. "The Narrative Constitution of Identity: A Relational and Network Approach." *Theory and Society* 23:605–49.

Spiro, P. J. 1994. "New Global Communities: Nongovernmental Organizations in International Decision-Making Institutions." *Washington Quarterly* 18 (1):45–56.

Stange, Douglas Charles. 1984. *British Unitarians against American Slavery, 1833–65.* Canbury, NJ: Associated University Presses.

Stanislavskii, A. L. 1990. *Grazhdanskaia voina v Rossii XVII veka.* Moscow: Nauka.

Staniszkis, Jadwiga. 1986. *Poland's Self-Limiting Revolution.* Princeton: Princeton University Press.

———. 1991. *The Dynamics of Breakthrough in Eastern Europe: The Case of Poland.* Berkeley: University of California Press.

Stanton, T., and H. S. Blatch. 1922. *Elizabeth Cady Stanton as Revealed in Her Letters, Diary, and Reminiscences.* New York: Harper Brothers.

Statistisches Bundesamt, ed. 1971. *Statistisches Jahrbuch für die Bundesrepublik Deuschland.* Stuttgart: Kohlhammer.

Stattbuch. 1995. *Stattbuch Berlin 5.* Berlin: Stattbuch Verlag.

Steedman, Carolyn. 1994. *Landscape for a Good Woman.* New Brunswick, NJ: Rutgers University Press.

Steinmetz, George. 1992. "Reflections on the Role of Social Narratives in Working-Class Formation: Narrative Theory in the Social Sciences." *Social Science History* 16 (3):488–516.

Stepan, Alfred. 1988. *Rethinking Military Politics: Brazil and the Southern Cone.* Princeton: Princeton University Press.

Sterling, Dorothy. 1991. *Ahead of Her Time: Abby Kelly and the Politics of Antislavery.* New York: Norton.

Stevenson, Nick. 1997. "Globalization, National Cultures, and Cultural Citizenship." *Sociological Quarterly* 38 (1):41–66.

Stoddart, Brian. 1995. "Cricket, Social Formation, and Cultural Continuity in Barbados: A Preliminary Ethnohistory." In Hilary M. Beckles and Brian Stoddart, eds., *Liberation Cricket: West Indies Cricket Culture,* 61–88. Manchester and New York: Manchester University Press.

Stokes, Susan. 1995. *Cultures in Conflict: Social Movements and the State in Peru.* Berkeley: University of California Press.

St. Pierre, Maurice. 1995. "West Indian Cricket—Part II: An Aspect of Creolisation." In Hilary M. Beckles and Brian Stoddart, eds., *Liberation Cricket: West Indies Cricket Culture,* 125–40. Manchester and New York: Manchester University Press.

Stukuls, Daina. 1997. "Imagining the Nation: Campaign Posters of the First Postcommunist Electionis in Latvia." *East European Politics and Societies* 11 (1):131–54.

———. 1998. "Transformation, Normalization, and Representation in Postcommunism: The Case of Latvia." Ph.D. diss., University of Michigan.

Suny, Ronald Grigor. 1993. *The Revenge of the Past: Nationalism, Revolution, and the Collapse of the Soviet Union.* Stanford: Stanford University Press.

Swedenburg, Ted. 1995. *Memories of Revolt: The 1936–1939 Rebellion and the Palestinian National Past.* Minneapolis: University of Minnesota Press.

Swidler, Ann. 1986. "Culture in Action: Symbols and Strategies." *American Sociological Review* 51 (April):273–86.

Szporluk, Roman. 1990. "In Search of the Drama of History, or, National Roads to Modernity." *East European Politics and Societies* 1 (winter):134–50.

Taiwan kyōikukai, ed. 1939. *Taiwan kyōiku enkaku shi.* Taipei: Taiwan kyōikukai.

T'ai-wan she-hui yün-tung shi. 1988. 4 vols. Translated from Japanese to Chinese by Wang Nai-hsin et al. Taipei: Ch'uang-tsao ch'u pan she. Originally published as *Taiwan sōtokufu keisatsu enkaku shi.* Taipei: Taiwan sōtokufu, 1933–1941.

Taiwan sōtokufu jimu seiseki teiyō. 1919–41. Taipei: Taiwan sōtokufu.

Taiwan sōtokufu minsei jimu seiseki teiyō. 1896–1918. Taipei: Taiwan sōtokufu.

Tanaka, Stefan. 1993. *Japan's Orient: Rendering Pasts into History.* Berkeley: University of California Press.

Tarkowska, Elzbieta. 1993. "Temporalny wymiar przemian zachodzacych w Polsce." In Aldona Jawlowska, Marian Kempny, and Elzbieta Tarkowska, eds., *Kulturowy wymiar przemian spolecznych,* 87–100. Warsaw: Polska Akademia Nauk.

Tarrow, Sidney. 1992. "Mentalities, Political Cultures, and Collective Action Frames: Constructing Meaning through Action." In Aldon D. Morris and Carol McClurg Mueller, eds., *Frontiers in Social Movement Theory,* 174–202. New Haven: Yale University Press.

———. 1994. *Power in Movement: Social Movements, Collective Action, and Politics.* New York: Cambridge University Press.

———. 1995a. "Fishnets, Internets, and Catnets." Working paper, International Institute, University of Michigan, Ann Arbor.

———. 1995b. "Fishnets, Internets, and Catnets: Globalization and Social Movements," Paper prepared for the conference Structure, Identity, and Power: The Past and Future of Collective Action," Amsterdam, June 2–4, 1995.

———. 1997. *Power in Movement: Social Movements, Collective Action, and Politics,* 2d ed. Cambridge: Cambridge University Press.

Taylor, M., ed. 1988. *Rationality and Revolution.* Cambridge: Cambridge University Press.

Ter-Sarkisiants, A. E. 1994. *Mezhnatsional'nye otnoshenia v Krasnodarskom krae.* Issledovania po prikladnoi i neotlozhnoi etnologii, no. 55. Moskow: Institut etnologii i antropologii.

Thomas, Dorothy Q. 1993. "Holding Governments Accountable by Public Pressure." In Joanna Kerr, ed., *Ours by Right: Women's Rights as Human Rights.* London: Zed.

Thompson, E. P. 1971. "The Moral Economy of the English Crowd in the Eighteenth Century." *Past and Present* (50):76–136.

Thompson, L. O'Brien. 1995. "How Cricket is West Indian Cricket? Class, Racial, and Color Conflict." In Hilary M. Beckles and Brian Stoddart, eds., *Liberation Cricket: West Indies Cricket Culture,* 165–78. Manchester and New York: Manchester University Press.

Tilly, Charles. 1978. *From Mobilization to Revolution.* Reading, MA: Addison-Wesley.

———. 1979. "Repertoires of Contention in America and Britain, 1750–1830." In Mayer N. Zald and John McCarthy, eds., *The Dynamics of Social Movements,* 126–55. Cambridge, MA: Winthrop.

Tilly, Charles, Louise Tilly, and Richard Tilly. 1975. *The Rebellious Century: 1830–1930.* Cambridge: Harvard University Press.

Tismaneanu, Vladimir. 1992. *Reinventing Politics: Eastern Europe from Stalin to Havel.* New York: Free Press.

Touraine, Alain. 1971. *The May Movement: Revolt and Reform.* New York: Random House.

———. 1977. *The Self-Production of Society.* Chicago: University of Chicago Press.

———. 1981. *The Voice and the Eye: An Analysis of Social Movements.* Cambridge: Cambridge University Press.

———. 1988. *The Return of the Actor.* Minneapolis: University of Minnesota Press.

Touraine, Alaine, with F. Dubet, M. Wieviorka, and J. Strzelecki. 1983. *Solidarity: The Analysis of a Social Movement, Poland, 1980–81.* Cambridge: Cambridge University Press.

Tsai, Pei-huo, Feng-yüan Chen, Po-shou Lin, San-lien Wu, and Jung-chung Yeh. 1983. *T'ai-wan min tsu yun tung shih.* 3d ed. Taipei: Tzu li wan pao she.

Tseng, I-piao. 1995. "Huai-nien T'ai-pei i-chuan Chueh-nei [Horiuchi] hsiao-chang." In Kuo-li T'ai-wan ta-hsüeh i-hsüeh-yüan fu-she i-yüan, eds., *Centennial of National Taiwan University Hospital,* 269. Taipei: Kuo-li T'ai-wan ta-hsüeh i-hsüeh-yuan fu-she i-yüan. In Chinese.

Tsurumi, Patricia. 1977. *Japanese Colonial Education in Taiwan, 1895–1945.* Cambridge, MA: Harvard University Press.

Tu, Tsung-ming. 1989. *Tu Tsung-ming hui-i-lu.* Taipei: Lung-wen ch'u pan she.

Tukey, John W. 1977. *Exploratory Data Analysis.* New York: Addison-Wesley.

Tully, Mark, and Satish Jacob. 1991. *Amritsar: Mrs. Gandhi's Last Battle.* Columbia, MO: South Asia Books.

Turner, Bryan, ed. 1993. *Citizenship and Social Theory.* London: Sage.

UNICEF. 1992. *The State of the World's Children, 1992.* Oxford: Oxford University Press.

UNIPOP. N.d. *Estatuto da Criança e Adolescente: Coisa de Gente Grande.* Belém: Instituto Universidade Popular.

Urban, Michael, with Vyacheslav Igrunov and Sergei Mitrokhin. 1997. *The Rebirth of Politics in Russia.* Cambridge: Cambridge University Press.

Valdivia, Angharad N. 1991. "The U.S. Intervention in Nicaraguan and Other Latin American Media." In Thomas W. Walker, ed., *Revolution and Counterrevolution in Nicaragua.* Boulder: Westview.

van der Veer, Peter. 1988. *Gods on Earth.* London: Athlone.

———. 1994. *Religious Nationalism: Hindus and Muslims in India.* Berkeley: University of California Press.

Verdery, Katherine. 1995. "Notes toward an Ethnography of a Transforming State: Romania, 1991." In Jane Schneider and Rayna Rapp, eds., *Articulating Hidden Histories: Exploring the Influence of Eric R. Wolf,* 228–42. Berkeley: University of California Press.

———. 1996. *What Was Socialism and What Comes Next?* Princeton: Princeton University Press.

von Eschen, Penny. 1997. *Race against Empire: Black Americans and Anticolonialism, 1937–1957.* Ithaca: Cornell University Press.

von Mettenheim, Kurt. 1995. *The Brazilian Voter: Mass Politics in Democratic Transition, 1974–1986.* Pittsburgh: University of Pittsburgh Press.

Wakabayashi, Masahiro. 1983. *T'ai-wan Konichi undoshi kenkyu.* Tokyo: Kenbun Shuppan.

Wallace, Paul. 1990. "Religious and Ethnic Politics: Political Mobilization in Punjab." In F. Frankel and M. S. A. Rao, eds. *Dominance and State Power in Modern India,* 416–482. Delhi: Oxford University Press.

Wallerstein, Immanuel. 1995. *After Liberalism.* New York: New Press.

———. 1998. *Utopistics, or, Historical Choices of the Twenty-First Century.* New York: New Press.

Wallerstein, Immanuel, et al. 1996. *The Age of Transition: Trajectory of the World-System, 1945–2025.* London: Zed.

Walls, D. 1993. *The Activist's Almanach: The Concerned Citizen's Guide to the Leading Advocacy Organizations in America.* New York: Fireside.

Walton, John. 1989. "Debt, Protest, and the State in Latin America." In Susan Eckstein, ed., *Power and Popular Protest in Latin American Social Movements,* 299–328. Berkeley: University of California Press.

Walton John, and Charles Ragin. 1990. "Global and National Sources of Political Protest: Third World Responses to the Debt Crisis." *American Sociological Review* 55 (December):876–90.

Walton, John, and D. Seddon. 1994. *Free Markets and Food Riots: The Politics of Global Adjustment.* Oxford: Blackwell.

Waltz, Susan E. 1995. *Human Rights and Reform: Changing the Face of North African Politics.* Berkeley: University of California Press.

Wapner, P. 1996. *Environmental Activism and World Civic Politics.* Albany: SUNY Press.

Wary, Harry, and Hilary Conroy, eds. 1983. *Japan Examined: Perspectives on Modern Japanese History.* Honolulu: University of Hawaii Press.

Wasilewski, Jacek. 1995. "The Crystallization of the Post-Communist and Post-Solidarity Political Elite." In Edmund Wnuk-Lipinski, ed., *After Communism: A Multidisciplinary Approach to Radical Social Change,* 117–33. Warsaw: ISP PAN.

Watkins, Kevin. 1995. *The Oxfam Poverty Report.* Oxford: Oxfam.

Watson, Rubie. 1994. "Memory, History, and Opposition under State Socialism." In Rubie Watson, ed., *Memory, History and Opposition,* 1–21. Santa Fe: School of American Research.

Weedon, Chris. 1987. *Feminist Practice and Poststructuralist Theory.* New York: Blackwell.

Welch, Claude E. 1995. *Protecting Human Rights in Africa: Strategies and Roles of Nongovernmental Organizations.* Philadelphia: University of Pennsylvania Press.

Whittick, Arnold. 1979. *Woman into Citizen.* London: Atheneum.

Williams, Raymond. 1994. "Selections from Marxism and Literature." In Nicholas Dirks, Geoff Eley, and Sherry Ortner, eds., *Culture/Power/History: A Reader in Contemporary Social Theory,* 585–608. Princeton: Princeton University Press.

Wilson, J. C. 1973. *Political Organizations.* New York: Basic Books.

Wilson, Richard. 1991. "Political Pathology and Moral Orientations." *Comparative Political Studies* 24 (2):211–230.

Wiseberg, L. 1992. "Human Rights Nongovernmental Organizations." In R. P. Claude and B. Weston, eds., *Human Rights in the World Community: Issues and Action,* 372–83. 2d ed. Philadelphia: University of Pennsylvania Press.

Wnuk-Lipinski, Edmund. 1994. "Fundamentalizm a Pragmatyzm: Dwa Typy Reakcji na Radykalna Zmiane Spoleczna." *Kultura i Spoleczenstwo* 37 (1):1–12.

Women in a Changing World: The Dynamic Story of the International Council of Women since 1888. 1966. London: Routledge and Kegan Paul.

Wood, Charles H., and José A. M. de Carvalho. 1988. *The Demography of Inequality in Brazil.* London: Cambridge University Press.

Woolf, Virginia. [1924] 1950. "Mr. Bennett and Mrs. Brown." In *The Captain's Death Bed and Other Essays,* 96–97. New York: Harcourt, Brace.

World Bank. 1994. "Social Indicators of Development." Washington, DC: International Bank for Reconstruction and Development. Machine readable file.

Wu, Wen-hsing. 1983. *Jih-chü shih-ch'i T'ai-wan shih-fan chiao-yü chih yen-chiu.* Taipei: Institute of History, National Taiwan Normal University.

———. 1992. *Jih chu shih ch'i T'ai-wan she hui ling tao chieh ts'eng chih yen chiu.* Taipai: Cheng chung shu chu.

Yanagisako, Sylvia, ed. 1995. *Naturalizing Power: Essays in Feminist Cultural Analysis.* New York: Routledge.

Yanaihara, Tadao. 1929. *Teikoku shugi ka no Taiwan.* Tokyo: Iwanami shoten.

Yoneyama, Lisa. 1994. "Taming the Memory Scape: Hiroshima's Urban Renewal." In Jonathan Boyarin, ed., *Remapping Memory: The Politics of TimeSpace,* 99–137. Minneapolis: University of Minnesota Press.

Young, D. R. 1991. "The Structural Imperatives of International Advocacy Associations." *Human Relations* 44 (9):921–41.

Zald, Mayer N. 1996. "Cultures, Ideology, and Strategic Framing." In Doug McAdam, John McCarthy, and Mayer Zald, eds., *Comparative Perspectives on Social Movements: Political Opportunities, Mobilizing Structures, and Cultural Framings,* 23–40. Cambridge: Cambridge University Press.

Zald, Mayer, Doug McAdam, and John McCarthy. 1996. "Introduction: Political Opportunities, Mobilizing Structures, and Framing Process." In Doug McAdam, John McCarthy, and Mayer Zald, eds., *Comparative Perspectives on Social Movements: Political Opportunities, Mobilizing Structures, and Cultural Framings,* 1–22. Cambridge: Cambridge University Press.

Zald, Mayer N., and John D. McCarthy. 1987. *Social Movements in an Organizational Society.* New Brunswick, NJ: Transaction.

Zald, Mayer N., and Bert Useem. 1987. "Movement and Countermovement Interaction: Mobilization, Tactics, and State Involvement." In Mayer N. Zald and John D. McCarthy, eds., *Social Movements in an Organizational Society,* 273–92. New Brunswick, NJ: Transaction.

Zaluar, Alba. 1994. *Condomínio do Diabo.* Rio de Janeiro: Revan, Universidade Federal do Rio de Janeiro.

Ziolkowski, Marek. 1993. "Two Orientations in the Post-monocentric Order in Poland." *Sysyphus,* 2 (9):35–43. Warsaw: IPS Publishers.

Contributors

Patrick Ball is Deputy Director of the Science and Human Rights Program at the American Association for the Advancement of Science in Washington, D.C.

Lorraine Bayard de Volo is Assistant Professor of Political Science and Women's Studies at the University of Kansas in Lawrence.

Georgi M. Derluguian is Assistant Professor of Sociology at Northwestern University in Evanston, Illinois.

John A. Guidry is Assistant Professor of Political Science at Augustana College in Rock Island, Illinois.

Margaret Keck is Associate Professor of Political Science at The Johns Hopkins University in Baltimore, Maryland.

Michael D. Kennedy is Vice Provost for International Affairs, Director of the International Institute, and Associate Professor of Sociology at the University of Michigan, Ann Arbor.

Jan Kubik is Director of the Center for Russian, Central, and East European Studies and Associate Professor of Political Science at Rutgers University in New Brunswick, New Jersey.

Ming-cheng M. Lo is Assistant Professor of Sociology at the University of California, Davis.

José Raul Perales is a doctoral candidate in Political Science at the University of Michigan, Ann Arbor.

Julie Peteet is Associate Professor of Anthropology at the University of Louisville in Kentucky.

Dieter Rucht is Professor of Sociology at the University of Kent at Canterbury, England.

Gay W. Seidman is Associate Professor of Sociology at the University of Wisconsin, Madison.

Kathryn Sikkink is Associate Professor of Political Science at the University of Minnesota in Minneapolis.

Greta Uehling is a doctoral candidate in History at the University of Michigan, Ann Arbor.

Peter van der Veer is Professor of Comparative Religion and Director of the Research Center for Religion and Society at the University of Amsterdam, The Netherlands.

Mayer N. Zald is Professor of Sociology, Social Work, and Business at the University of Michigan, Ann Arbor.

Index